HISTORY
OF RUSSIA

Sergei Mikhailovich Soloviev

The
Academic International Press
Edition
of
Sergei M. Soloviev
History of Russia From Earliest Times

G. EDWARD ORCHARD
General Editor

Contributing Editors
HUGH F. GRAHAM
JOHN D. WINDHAUSEN
ALEXANDER V. MULLER
K.A. PAPMEHL
RICHARD HANTULA
WALTER J. GLEASON, JR.
WILLIAM H. HILL
G. EDWARD ORCHARD
LINDSEY A.J. HUGHES
NICKOLAS LUPININ
GEORGE E. MUNRO
DANIEL L. SCHLAFLY, JR.
ANTHONY L.H. RHINELANDER
PATRICK J. O'MEARA
PETER C. STUPPLES
T. ALLAN SMITH
MARTHA L. LAHANA
ANTHONY V. KNOWLES
HELEN Y. PROCHAZKA

SERGEI M. SOLOVIEV

History of Russia

Volume 3

The Shift Northward

Kievan Rus, 1154–1228

Edited

By

G. Edward Orchard

Preliminary Translation
by Leo J. Sobel

Academic International Press

2000

The Academic International Press Edition of S.M. Soloviev's
History of Russia From Earliest Times in fifty volumes.

Volume 3. *The Shift Northward. Kievan Rus, 1154–1228.*
Unabridged translation of the text of Volume 2, Chapter 6 and
Volume 3, Chapter 1 as contained in Volume I of S.M. Soloviev's
Istoria Rossii's drevneishikh vremen published in Moscow in
1959-1966, with added annotation by G. Edward Orchard.

Maps from John Fennell, *The Crisis of Medieval Russia, 1200–
1304,* courtesy of the publishers, Addison Wesley Longman.

ISBN: 0-87569-223-0

Composition by Llano F. McCowen

Printed in the United States of America

A list of Academic International Press publications is found at
the end of this volume.

ACADEMIC INTERNATIONAL PRESS
Box 1111 • Gulf Breeze FL 32562-1111 • USA
www.ai-press.com

CONTENTS

Weights and Measures   ix

Preface   x

Introduction   xiii

I NORTH AND SOUTH OF RUS LANDS   1

Andrei Bogoliubsky Remains in the North—Andrei's Charac-
ter and Conduct in the North—Vladimir-on-the-Kliazma—
Andrei's Brother Gleb Rules in Kiev—Gleb's War with
Mstislav Iziaslavich—Death of the Adversaries—Bogoliubsky
Gives Kiev to Roman Rostislavich of Smolensk—Quarrel of
the Sons of Rostislav with Andrei—Mstislav Rostislavich the
Brave—Andrei Fails Against the Sons of Rostislav—Yaroslav
Iziaslavich Rules in Kiev—Yaroslav's Struggle Against
Sviatoslav of Chernigov—Murder of Andrei Bogoliubsky—
Aftermath of Andrei's Death—Rivalry of Rostov and Vla-
dimir—Victory for Mikhail Yurievich and Vladimir—Renewal
of Struggle after Mikhail's Death—Final Fall of Rostov—War
in the South Between the Descendants of Monomakh and
Oleg—Sviatoslav Vsevolodovich of Chernigov Against Vse-
volod—Sviatoslav Gains a Foothold in Kiev—Weakness of the
Kievan Prince in Relation to Suzdal

II THE PRINCIPALITY OF GALICH   40

Struggle of Yaroslav of Galich with the Boyars—Death of
Yaroslav of Galich—Boyars Expel Vladimir and Invite Roman
Mstislavich—Hungarian King's Interference in Galich Af-
fairs—Roman's Struggle for Galich—Death of Rostislav, Son
of Berladnik—Hungarian Violence in Galich—Vladimir
Yaroslavich Consolidates His Rule in Galich—Riurik
Rostislavich's Rule in Kiev—Vsevolod of Suzdal Embroils
Riurik with Roman of Volhynia—Roman's Participation in
Polish Civil Wars—War between the Descendants of Mono-
makh and Oleg—Roman of Volhynia Confirmed in Galich—
Roman Expels Riurik Rostislavich from Kiev—Riurik Again

Occupies Kiev—Roman Forces Riurik to Take Monastic Vows—Roman Dies in Battle Against the Poles—Roman's Minor Sons Surrounded by Enemies—Sons of Roman Expelled from Galich—Galich Boyars Invite the Sons of Igor from Severia—Miserable Fate of Roman's Sons—Hungarians Occupy Galich—Sons of Igor Expel the Hungarians but Alienate the Boyars—Boyars Enthrone Daniel Romanovich in Galich—Daniel Leaves Galich—Boyar Vladislav Takes Power in Galich—The Hungarians and Poles Divide Galich

III VSEVOLOD III'S LAST YEARS   70

Continuation of Internecine War—Descendants of Monomakh in Chernigov—Consolidation of Vsevolod III's Power in the North—Relations with Riazan, Smolensk and Great Novgorod—Mstislav the Brave in the North—Mstislav's Death—Changes in Novgorod the Great—Mstislav Mstislavich Delivers Novgorod from Vsevolod—Vsevolod III's Death

IV INTERNECINE WARS IN SUZDAL LAND AND MSTI-
SLAV'S RISE   89

War between Vsevolod's Sons—Mstislav of Toropets Intervenes—Victory on the Lipitsa Strengthens Konstantin—Yury Again Grand Prince of Vladimir—Events in Riazan and Novgorod—Mstislav of Toropets in Galich—Changes in Kiev, Chernigov and Pereiaslavl—The Retinue

V RUS AND ITS ENEMIES   118

The Germans in Livonia—Novgorod and Pskov War Against the Chud—Unrest in Novgorod and Pskov—Novgorod Expeditions Beyond the Portage—Struggle of the Suzdal Princes Against the Bulgars—Foundation of Nizhny Novgorod—Wars With Lithuania and the Yatviags—The Struggle with the Polovetsians—The Tale of Igor's Campaign—Later Campaigns Against the Polovetsians—Tatar Invasion—Considerations

Addendum: Response to Critics of Volume II   165

VI GOVERNMENT AND PRINCELY POWER   183

Significance of the Prince—Princely Titles —The Prince's Enthronement—The Prince's Activities—Princely Revenue— The Princes' Way of Life—The Retinue—Senior and Junior Retinues—The Levy—Types of Service and Military Equipment—Military Tactics—Size of Military Forces—Hero-Warriors—Urban and Rural Population—Senior Cities and Junior Towns—Novgorod and Pskov—The Assembly—Special Character of Novgorod Life—View of a Town—Fires—Population —Local Government—Nomads—Size and Number of Towns—Obstacles to Population Growth—Trade—Monetary System—Art—Daily Life

VII RELIGION AND LAW   233

The Struggle between Paganism and Christianity—Missionary Work—Church Organization—Revenues of the Rus Church— Activities of the Clergy—Holy Orders—Legislation—Customary Law—Piety—Duality of Faith—Family Morality—General State of Morality

VIII LITERARY AND HISTORICAL WORKS   259

Literacy—Literary Monuments—St. Feodosy—Metropolitan Nikifor's Epistle—Epistle of Bishop Simon—Metropolitan John's Epistle—Kirik's Questions—Political and General Teachings—Cyril of Turov's Sermons—Other Sermons— Vladimir Monomakh's Instruction—Pilgrimage Literature— Epistle of Daniel the Exile—Poetry—The Tale of Igor's Campaign—Songs—Chronicles—The Nature of Historiography—Local Characteristics of Chronicles

Table

Genealogy of Rus Rulers, 862-1124   316

Maps

Russia in the Thirteenth Century   317

Suzdalia in the Thirteenth Century   318

Kiev, Chernigov, Pereiaslavl, Turov-Pinsk in the
  Thirteenth Century   319

Illustrations

Helmet of Yaroslav Vsevolodovich   100

Collecting Tribute from the Chud   128

Battle Between Rus and Polovetsians   142

St. George in Armor   199

Novgorod Silver Grivna   224

Notes   320

Index   362

WEIGHTS AND MEASURES

Linear and Surface Measure

Arshin: 16 vershoks, 28 in. (diuims) 72.12 cm
Chetvert (quarter): 1/4 arshin, 1/2 desiatina, 1.35 acres (sometimes 1.5 desiatinas or c. 4.1 acres)
Desiatina: 2,400 square sazhens, 2.7 acres, 1.025 hectares
Diuim: 1 inch, 2.54 cm
Fut: 12 diuims, 1 foot, 30.48 cm

Obza (areal): c. 10 chetverts, 13–15 acres
Osmina: 1/4 desiatina, 600 sq. sazhens, .256 hectare
Sazhen: 3 arshins, 7 feet, 2.133 m
Vershok: 1.75 in., 4.445 cm, 1/16 arshin
Verst: 500 sazhens, 1,166 yards and 2 feet, .663 miles, 1.0668 km
Voloka (plowland): 19 desiatinas, 20 hectares, 49 acres

Liquid Measure

Bochka (barrel): 40 vedros, 121 gallons, 492 liters
Chetvert (quarter): 1.4 bochkas, 32.5 gallons
Korchago (wine): Rus, unknown

Kufa: 30 stofy
Stof: Kruzhka (cup), 1/10 vedro, c. 1.3 quarts, 1.23 liters
Vedro (pail): 3.25 gallons, 12.3 liters, 10 stofy

Weights

Berkovets: 361 lbs., 10 puds
Bezmen: c. 1 kg, 2.2 lbs.
Chetverik (grain measure dating from 16th century): 1/8 chetvert, 15.8 lbs.
Chetvert (grain measure): 1/4 rad, 3.5 puds, 126.39 lbs., c. 8 bushels
Funt: 96 zolotniks, .903 lbs., 14.4 oz., 408.24 kg
Grivenka: 205 grams
Kad: 4 chetverts, 14 puds, 505.56 lbs.
Kadka malenkaia: 12th-century, small measure

Kamen (stone): 32 funt
Korob (basket): 7 puds, 252 lbs.
Osmina (eighth): 2 osmina to a chetvert (dry measure)
Polbezmen: c. 500 g, 1 lb.
Polosmina (sixteenth): 1/2 osmina
Pud: 40 funts, 36.113 lbs. (US), 40 lbs. (Russian), 16.38 kg
Rad: 14 puds, 505.58 lbs.
Zolotnik: 1/96 lbs., 4.26 grams

Money

Altyn: 6 Muscovite dengas, 3 copecks
Bel: Rus, pure silver coin
Chervonets (chervonnyi): gold coin of first half of 18th century worth c. 3 rubles
Chetvertak: silver coin equal to 25 copecks or 1/4 ruble (18–19th centuries)
Copeck: two Muscovite dengas
Denga: 1/2 copeck
Grivna: 20 Muscovite dengas, 100 grivnas equals 1 ruble, 10 copecks
Grosh: 10 peniaz
Grosh litovsky (Lithuanian grosh): 5 silver copecks
Kopa grosh: 60 groshas, one Muscovite poltina, 1/2 ruble
Kuna: 12th-century Rus coin comparable to Westerns denarii or Eastern dirhems. Varied in value by region. Replaced late 14th century by the denga or serebro (silver). Also a marten skin.
Moskovka: 1/2 copeck
Muscovite denga: 200 equals 1 ruble
Novgorod denga: 100 equals 1 ruble
Novgorodka: 1 copeck

Peniaz: 10 equals one grosh (Lithuania)
Poltina (poltinnik): 50 copecks, 100 dengas, 1 ruble
Poltora: 1 1/2 rubles
Polupoltina (-nik): 25 copecks, 50 dengas
Rezan: 12th century Rus coin. 50 rezan equals one grivna kuna
Ruble: 100 copecks, 200 dengas
Shiroky grosh (large silver coin): 20 Muscovite copecks
Veksa: 12th-century Rus small coin equal to one squirrel pelt (belka)

Foreign Denominations
Chervonnyi: c. 3 rubles
Ducat: c. 3 rubles
Dutch efimok: "lion dollar" or levok, 1 thaler, 2.5 guilders
Efimok: foreign currency, 1 thaler, .75-1 ruble, 1 chervonets or chervonnyi
Levok: Dutch silver lion dollar
Thaler (Joachimsthaler): c. 1 ruble, 1/3 chervonets or chervonnyi

Note: Weights and measures often changed values over time and sometimes held more than one value at the same time. For details consult Sergei G. Pushkarev, *Dictionary of Russian Historical Terms from the Eleventh Century to 1917* (Yale, 1970).

PREFACE

This book is an unabridged translation of Volume II, Chapter VI and Volume III, Chapter I of Soloviev's *Istoriia Rossii s drevneishikh vremen* (History of Russia from Earliest Times, 29 volumes, St. Petersburg, 1851-1879), corresponding to Book I, pp. 528-688 and Book II, pp. 7-123 of the Soviet edition (Moscow, 1960). For the sake of convenience I have divided Soloviev's text into eight chapters. Chapter I of the translation corresponds to Book I, pp. 528-563, Chapter II to pp. 563-589, Chapter III to pp. 589-606, Chapter IV to pp. 606-630 and Chapter V to pp. 630-670. The Addendum (pp. 671-688), which constitutes Soloviev's reply to his critics as printed in the 1879 and subsequent editions of his History, is appropriately reproduced at this point, where Soloviev's second volume ended.

The opening chapter of Soloviev's Volume III is divided in the translation into three chapters, Chapter VI corresponding to pp. 7-50, Chapter VII to pp. 50-73 and Chapter VIII to pp. 73-123 in Book II of the "gray" Soviet edition. The uneven length of the chapters in the translation reflects the space devoted by Soloviev to a given theme.

The present translation endeavors to render the text and Soloviev's thought as accurately as possible. No attempt has been made to reproduce his style and text word for word for this would have yielded a bizarre Russianized text. The main consideration is to make his history as readable as possible consistent with accuracy, while retaining at least something of the flavor of the language of the era. An effort has been made to find English-language equivalents for all technical terms Soloviev employs (ranks, offices, titles, legal, administrative and so forth) in the belief that English is no less rich in such terms than other languages. This is intended to smooth the flow of the narrative for the reader and to avoid marring the pages with annoying untranslated words. The exception involves Russian words which have become common in English—boyar, tsar, cossack. In all of this the translator remains painfully aware of the inevitable shortcomings that may remain.

Soloviev's pages are featureless and interminable, one long and complex sentence marching after the last. To make the text easier to follow for today's readers, long paragraphs and sentences have been broken into shorter ones. Most of the subtitles are based on the descriptive topic headings clustered at the beginning of the Russian original chapters. These headings have been moved into the body of the text as subtitles to mark and ease for the reader the transition from one subject to another. In some cases the topic headings have been used as chapter headings in the translation. New subtitles have been created to show topics not listed by Soloviev. Soloviev's arrangement of the material has been followed strictly.

Brief explanatory or interpretive materials have been inserted into the text enclosed in brackets, or added as footnotes to each chapter at the end of the book. All material enclosed in brackets has been added by the present editor and all materials in parentheses are the author's. Emphasized words or phrases in italics are the author's.

In some places Soloviev's rendition of passages from literary works, chronicle entries and legislative statutes of this period is extremely garbled. Where necessary I have taken the liberty of adapting the text from standard English translations, in which spelling is modified to conform with the usage of the main body of the text. Wherever I have done so, this borrowing has been acknowledged in my notes.

The general policy followed in annotating has been to identify prominent personalities at first mention, and to give explanations and elucidations of less common or obscure terms and passages, assuming the typical reader to have relatively little familiarity with Russian history. These appear as numbered footnotes at the back of the book by chapters. With a few exceptions, Soloviev's own notes are not included because of their highly specialized archival, documentary and bibliographic nature. In addition, most of the notes added by the editors of the edition published in the Soviet Union which are also technical in nature—fuller bibliographic citations than those in Soloviev's notes—have not been included. When the author's notes and those of the Soviet editors are included, they are so designated. All other notes are those of the present editor.

Russian personal names are preserved in their Russian form with a few exceptions: Alexander, Alexis, Nicholas, Jonas, Joseph, Peter, Sergius and others. The names of many important ecclesiastical figures have been recast into their Latin or Greek equivalents. This applies to prominent individuals; Russian forms usually are used for the less prominent. Certain other names and terms have been anglicized for the sake of clarity and because they are used widely—Casimir, Sophia, boyar, versts, Dnieper river, and others.

The editors of the edition published in the USSR frequently added patronymics and other names, and these have been retained without brackets. Patronymics appearing in the original edition have been included. Plural forms for names and terms which might be confusing have been anglicized—the Miloslavskys and not the Miloslavskie, and so forth. Most Slavic surnames show gender, and this has been preserved. Since an "a" at the end of a name usually signifies a female, Lvov would have a wife or daughter Lvova. The final "iia" in feminine personal names has been shortened to "ia" — "Maria" instead of "Mariia."

Non-Russian names, locations, terms, ranks and so on are spelled according to the language native to the person or particular to the city, region or culture when this can be determined. Confusion arises at times because the text is not clear about nationalities. Individuals whose names were once non-Russian but were in Russian service for generations are given in the original spelling of the family name. Turkish, Tatar, Persian and other names and terms are spelled in the original according to accepted forms in scholarly books. In some instances, if not otherwise ascertainable, they are translated from the Russian as given by Soloviev. The names of geographical locations conform to commonly accepted English usage—Podolia, Moscow, Copenhagen, and so forth.

Finally, with respect to transliteration, this translation follows a modified Library of Congress system omitting diacritical marks and ligatures, and rendering initial "Ia-" and "Iu-" as "Ya-" and "Yu-" ("Yaroslav" and "Yury"), the suffixes "-ii", "-skii", "-skaia" and "-skoe" ("Yury Dolgoruky" instead of "Yurii Dolgorukii"), and the form "-oi" has been replaced by "-oy" ("Svinoy" not "Svinoi"). Except for final "-ei" in "Andrei" and "Sergei", "-ei" has been rendered "-ey." In some cases "-i-" has been inserted in place of hard and soft signs, or apostrophes indicating these signs. Hence Soloviev, not Solov'ev. The soft sign is not indicated by an apostrophe, as it is some transliteration systems, but is dropped completely.

I am indebted to Leo J. Sobel for an early draft of this volume. Unfortunately he was unable through pressure of other commitments to complete the work of re-editing the text and updating the annotation. Much of his original material remains, and his sturdy effort in breaking the ground for this volume must be acknowledged.

G. Edward Orchard

INTRODUCTION

The preceding volume of this series broke off in the middle of Andrei Bogoliubsky's reign, with the sack of Kiev by forces allied to him, though he himself did not take direct part in the campaign. Bogoliubsky's reign is seen by many as a transition from one system of rulership to another. Soloviev himself stressed how the increasingly autocratic ruler began to view his fellow-princes not as relatives but as underlings. In his magistral thesis Soloviev emphasized the "theory of the new towns," how by moving their capital the princes sought to exercise their jurisdiction untrammeled by the real or notional rights of urban assemblies or princes' "natural advisers," the boyars and senior retinue. Further studies only served to reinforce Soloviev's original views.

Bogoliubsky's reign also is perceived as the point at which Russian and Ukrainian history part company. "The Volodimir [Vladimir]-Moscow State was neither the successor nor the inheritor of the Kievan State. It grew out of its own roots and the relation of the Kievan State toward it may more accurately be compared to the relations that existed between Rome and the Gaul provinces than described as two successive periods in the political and cultural life of France. The Kievan Government transplanted onto Great Russian soil the forms of a socio-political organization, its laws and culture—all nurtured in the course of its own historical process; but this does not mean that the Kievan State should be included in the history of the Great Russian nationality. The ethnographic and historical proximity of the two nationalities, the Ukrainian-Ruś and the Great Russian, should not give cause for confusing the two. Each lived its own life above and beyond their historical meetings and encounters.

"By attaching the Kievan State to the beginnings of the governmental and cultural life of the Great Russian people, the history of the Great Russians remains in reality without a beginning. The history of the formation of the Great Russian nation remains unexplained to this day simply because it has been customary to trace it from the middle of the 12th century. Even with the history of the Kievan State attached, this native beginning does not appear quite clear to those who have studied 'Russian history.' The process of the reception and modification of the Kiev sociopolitical forms, laws and culture on Great Russian soil is not being studied thoroughly. Instead they are incorporated into the inventory of the Great Russian people, the 'Russian State,' in the form in which they existed in Kiev, in Ukraine. The fiction of the 'Kievan Period' does not offer the opportunity to present suitably the history of the Great Russian nationality."[1]

Apart from the fact that Soloviev rejected the whole concept of periodization, maintaining that "one era flows into another," and the illogicality of a history "without a beginning," it is to be suspected that Hrushevsky was as guilty as his opponents of *a priori* reasoning. It may well be that we know little about the history of the origins of Northeastern Rus, but that is very different from asserting that such a history did not exist. The autochthonous inhabitants of what became Northeastern Rus were Finnic tribesmen, the Merians (in Russian Meria), probably akin to the Cheremissians, whose self-designation, Mari, is cognate to Meria. There were also related tribes, the Muroma and the Ves. According to archeological evidence Slavic colonists began to appear among these Finnic tribes beginning in the tenth century. There is even literary evidence, though not conclusive, of a pre-Kievan "Norman-Slav kaganate" on the upper Volga.[2]

The scale of this migration is difficult to estimate. According to M.P. Pogodin the "Great Russian race" lived in Kiev from very ancient times, or at least the Polianians who settled Kiev and its environs were Great Russians who later migrated north into the land of Suzdal under Yury Dolgoruky and Andrei Bogoliubsky. "The real Great Russian race moved outward into this land, where it grew and multiplied."[3] The picture Pogodin gives of the descendants of the Polianians pulling up stakes and marching in orderly columns from the middle Dnieper to Suzdalia, there to put down instant roots, seems at best an oversimplification. Slav migration took place over two or three centuries, and not necessarily from the Kievan land, although the flow from the south may well have intensified from about the middle of the twelfth century. Be that as it may, by the end of the century the Merians were completely slavicized, though Finnic traces remain in the place names, especially the hydronyms, of the Volga-Oka "Mesopotamia."[4]

Sometimes it is the task of the historian, in the absence of hard evidence, to hazard a reasonable guess. Naturally we have no statistical data as to the numbers of Slavic settlers involved. The normal pattern is for newcomers to be assimilated. Thus the Scandinavians who established their dominion on the banks of the Seine or the Dnieper within a couple of generations spoke the language of the indigenous population, as did the Bulgars who ruled their Slav subjects in the Balkans. That the reverse process took place between the Volga and the Oka suggests a combination of the following explanations.

First, the Slavic colonization was peaceful "since neither in our written annals nor in our popular traditions is there to be found any general or prolonged struggle between them."[5] Second, the Slavic migration took place overland, as opposed to overseas, so the settlers very probably brought their womenfolk and families. Third, upon the establishment of Christianity the language of the Slavs was also the hieratic language and that of literacy even if the chronicles hint that pagan revivals in the Northeast may have been racially motivated. As Arabic displaced numerous local dialects in the Islamic world, so Slavonic became the *lingua franca* of large parts of Orthodox Christendom. As the Finns were Christianized, so also were they slavicized.

That the coming together of Slav and Finn in the Northeast created a new Great Russian stock, radically differing from that of the "Ruś-Ukrainian" is indisputable. Yet, situated as they are athwart the steppe, that highroad of innumerable *Völkerwänderungen*, with the most porous frontiers imaginable, can it be imagined that the Ukrainians themselves retained their pristine Polianian racial purity?[6]

Kliuchevsky, while giving us the classic exposition of the origins of the Great Russians,[7] does not accord equal courtesy to the Ukrainians. "Treatment of the Ukrainians was summary: he simply considered them Russians. He did not use the word *Ukrainian* and rarely referred to them as Little Russians. In his judgement, the term *Little Russian* appeared first in a 1347 reference to Russians who lived on the right or west bank of the Dnieper. Muscovite Russia so dominated his view that his M.A. thesis on the lives of old Russian saints utterly neglected the noted saints of Kiev."[8]

Elsewhere Kliuchevsky's biographer summarizes the Soloviev-Kliuchevsky version of Great Russia's "manifest destiny" in which Andrei Bogoliubsky played a major part. "In the thirteenth and fourteenth centuries, social disintegration of the slave-owning Kievan society and raids from the steppes broke up Kiev and dispersed the population. In Kliuchevskii's view, the groups who separated them and their descendants remained forever Russian. One aggregate remained on the right or west bank of the Dnieper River, spread westward into Galicia, and by the fourteenth century was called Little Russian. The second group migrated northeastward to the region of the Oka and the upper Volga, a move he ascribed to internal divisions before the Mongols appeared. By the sixteenth century, it had absorbed the Finns in that area and formed the Great Russians. These migrant settlers proved their Kievan origins by bringing with them the epic poems and names of the villages they had left behind, much as seventeenth-century English settlers carried their values and village names to North America.

"As early as the twelfth century, Andrei Bogoliubskii in the remote northeast proclaimed the unity of all Russian land. Between the twelfth and sixteenth centuries, national priorities gradually became greater than local ones. The Great Russians in the northeast established a new order of princely rule and a spirit of national self-confidence. From this foundation, they slowly began accumulating strength and gathering all Russians."[9]

Other historians, to their mind viewing the larger picture, assert that the decline of Kiev was due less to deliberate sabotage by the Northeastern princes than to drastic changes in the international situation. "Another essentially economic explanation of the fall of Kievan Russia stresses trade, or rather the destruction of trade. In its crude form it argues that the Kievan state arose on the great commercial route 'from the Varangians to the Greeks,' lived by it, and perished when it was cut. In a more limited and generally accepted version, the worsening of the Kievan position in international trade has been presented as one major factor in the decline of Kiev. The city on the Dnieper suffered from the change in trade routes which began in the eleventh century and resulted, largely through the activities of Italian merchants in the Mediterranean, in the establishment of closer connections between western and central Europe on the one hand and Byzantium and Asia Minor on the other, and a bypassing of Kiev. It was adversely affected by the Crusades, and in particular by the sacking of Constantinople by the Crusaders in 1204, as well as by the decline of the Caliphate of Bagdad. The fact that certain towns and areas, such as Smolensk and especially Novgorod, profited by the rearrangement of the commercial map of Europe and the rise of Italian and German cities only tended to make Kievan control over them less secure. Finally, Kiev experienced tremei.dous difficulty, and ultimately failed, in protecting from the steppe peoples the commercial line across the southern steppe to the Black Sea."[10]

Did Bogoliubsky consciously try to create a new system? In some historical writings, from which those of Soloviev cannot be excepted, Andrei appears almost as a fully-fledged theorist of the nineteenth-century Historical-Juridical School. For instance, "Andrey established a new political system in his state: absolutism. Circumstances were favorable to it. While in Rostov, as in Suzdalia, there was a *veche* [assembly] like those of the other Russian cities, the new cities founded by princes ignored the traditions of the *veche* and lacked a powerful merchant class disposed to curb the princely authority. The scarcity of commercial centers, the preponderance of agricultural labor, and the belated colonization of the country contributed to create between the prince and the population very different relations from those existing in the Dnieper regions: the inhabitants, most of whom had arrived with the prince or even after his installation and had established themselves as farmers in the country or artisans in the city, regarded him not as a servitor of the commercial city, a protector of existing trade routes, but as the master and sovereign of the country to which they had emigrated. This was also Andrei's notion. Having become the suzerain of the whole Suzdalia region and then Grand Prince of Kiev, he preferred Vladimir to the older cities, and he enlarged and beautified it with devotion. He flaunted his contempt for the old cities, their customs and the *veche*; rejecting the bond that elsewhere linked the prince and the elders of his guard, he refused to take counsel with the old boyars and brutally drove some of them away. Finally, the victim of his own despotic nature, he was assassinated...by his servants."[11]

Bogoliubsky's most recent biographer is probably nearest the truth. "Andrei Bogoliubsky was a transitional figure in the history of Kievan Rus and the emergence of the so-called appanage period. He participated in the evolution of the principality of Rostov from a minor province at the northeastern border to one of the strongest principalities of Rus. The Rostov land survived the incessant wars, the economic dislocation, and the constant hostilities of pagan neighbors which threatened to undermine all of post-Kievan Rus. Andrei must have experienced acute disillusion in the later part of his reign, for he was neither master of his own house nor the legislator of all-Russian politics. Yet his remarkable energies, combined with what must have been enormous administrative talent, contributed to making Vladimir-on-the-Kliazma one of the most powerful cities of his day and one of the successor cities to Kiev, upon whose model the newer city was developed... he tried, harder than most, to fulfill the quest for *samovlastie* [autocratic power]. His stubborn, willful staying power, despite overwhelming obstacles, forced the issue: the only way to check his determination was to kill him.

"It seems tragic that Prince Andrei acquired the coveted grand princely title only after his death. To be sure, the meaning of the title *velikii kniaz'* [grand prince] had been weakened by a century of internecine struggle. The grand prince of the mid-twelfth century was fortunate if he controlled his own patrimony and at the same time ruled tentatively in Kiev either personally or through a dependent prince or *podruchnik* [personal agent, lieutenant]. Yet Prince Andrei sought to give the title a renewed meaning.

"It was the fascination for Kiev more than any other factor which impeded Andrei's quest for *samovlastie*. Chosen prince of his native principality, Andrei stubbornly persisted in his efforts to hold on to the south, a policy which strained the pockets of the boyars of Rostov and Suzdal who appointed him. He lost his most crucial supporters and paid with his life for eroding their fortunes in the pursuit of the traditions of Monomakh and Dolgoruky. Ironically, Andrei's decision to remain in Vladimir after his allies took Kiev in 1168 may have been a blunder. Had he abandoned his patrimony and ruled in Kiev he might not have been murdered. But he had learned a valuable lesson from Yury's failure: Kiev was a fading town. He sought to neutralize the old *stol'nyi gorod* [capitol city]—rather than to rule it—and to replace it with Vladimir."[12]

Further Hurwitz states "Vladimir grew to pre-eminence in a period of intense internecine struggle and political disintegration, when many doubted their commitment to autocratic rule. In his quest for *samovlastie* Prince Andrei fought against overwhelming odds with disarming determination. For an entire decade he ruled the Rus land. Yet his ambitions for Vladimir were thwarted by opponents from Kiev, Constantinople and Rostov, antagonistic to the city of the new and still more to the Prince who created it. Their resentment of the ambitious ruler yielded one of the bloodiest murders to cross the pages of the chronicles of Rus.

"The murdered Prince was a true hero in the history of Russia. Within two centuries the tsars of Moscow would assume those same prerogatives of translation which Andrei had utilized so boldly and so tragically in his own time. Yet when the Muscovite mythmakers seized upon Andrei's creative role in the formation of their tsardom, they went too far. Andrei tried—desperately—to replace Kiev with Vladimir, but he only partially succeeded. We must recognize him as an enormously creative and ambitious appanage prince—not as Russia's first tsar."[13]

Bogoliubsky is taken to task for turning his back on Kiev, yet his downfall was at least in part due to the fact that he did *not* shun Kiev, but continued to intervene in its affairs, as witness the disastrous campaign of 1173. By this time the Land of Rus, strictly speaking, consisted of no more than the environs of the city of Kiev, with the addition of the towns along the Ros river. Moreover it had been ravaged repeatedly by interprincely civil wars and nomadic raids. In short, it was a status elevator rather than an economic asset. A prince could not hope to hold Kiev without either independent means or powerful alliances.

In any case, was the Northeast such a backwater? Soloviev gives us the impression of Bogoliubsky as a brooding presence lurking in the gloomy forests of the North. Perhaps, rather, the mid-twelfth century was a period when the vital forces of Rus migrated from the center to the periphery, to Galich-Volhynia, Smolensk, Novgorod-Pskov and not least to Vladimir-on-the-Kliazma. Dolgoruky, Bogoliubsky and Big Nest all engaged in an ambitious building program. They founded numerous towns, some of them on the site of previous Merian fortifications. Bogoliubsky built the Dormition cathedral in Vladimir (1158-1160), and a cathedral with the same dedication at Rostov. At Vladimir he also built the Holy Savior cathedral, and a cathedral and palace at his favorite residence of Bogoliubovo.

The most famous church founded by Bogoliubsky, probably the best known Russian church after St. Basil's on Red Square in Moscow since it adorns numerous Intourist travel-agency posters and textbook covers, is that of the Intercession on the Nerl. The dedication reflected a new cult which Andrei instituted on his own initiative. "Built in the mid 1160s after Andrei's victory over the Volga Bulgars, the *pokrov* [Intercession] church was given an unusual location. It did not have to jostle for attention in the citadel, or in the market, or in the palace. It stood alone, on a bend in the river about a kilometer outside Bogoliubovo, as if guarding the way to the prince. Andrei's *pokrov* church now tends to be seen as a little gem of harmonious simplicity, modest yet elegant, in quiet sympathy with its rustic setting. The impression is anachronistic. It was a huge project for which nature was demonstratively transformed. The area of the building was originally much larger, for it has lost its ambulatory; and the grassy bank on which it stands, apparently so felicitous, was in fact a massive artificial construction built up to withstand the floodwaters and itself faced with limestone. This was no reticent rural shrine but a monumental statement of divinely protected princely power. A carved figure of the crowned King David stares out from every wall."[14]

What financed such a spectacular and sustained building program? "By itself this ecclesiastical architecture is sufficient cause to reject the notion that northeastern Russia in the twelfth century was a dark and primitive country where the general level of culture, wealth, and urban life stood far below that of Kiev in the south."[15] Whether the work was done by native or imported craftsmen, it would not have been possible unless the cities controlled a relatively rich agricultural hinterland. There is circumstantial evidence of agricultural surplus, since Novgorod and Pskov were dependent upon imports of food from the "Lower Lands." Withholding of food supplies was a potent weapon used by the rulers of Vladimir-Suzdal against refractory townsmen who inhabited what was in effect a food deficit area. The cities of the Northwest acted as entrepôts for luxury goods from the German cities and elsewhere. While suspension of trade constituted temporary inconvenience for the princes and boyars of Vladimir-Suzdal, for Novgorod and Pskov it meant famine.

An important contribution to the mystique of Vladimir-on-the-Kliazma, seized upon by the "Muscovite bookmen" of the fifteenth and sixteenth centuries, was Bogoliubsky's attempt to inject a sacral element into the grand-princely dignity. We have alluded to his institution of the Feast of the Intercession (October 1), though it is unclear by what authority he acted.[16] He attempted to establish a breakaway metropolitanate in his capital.[17] He brought the greatly revered icon of the Theotokos from Vyshgorod to Vladimir, later pressed into miraculous service against Tamerlane in 1395.[18] He promoted the local cult of St. Leonty of Rostov.[19]

Even within his lifetime his prayers performed miracles. "The pious Prince Andrei built the Golden Gates in time for the holiday of the Holy Virgin, saying to his boyars: 'When the people come down for the holiday they will see the gates.' And the holiday came to pass and the people approached the gates. But the mortar in the gates had not yet set, and all of a sudden the gates separated from the walls and fell on the people, covering twelve men. When Prince Andrei heard this, he prayed with a sigh to the Icon of the Holy Virgin and Mother of God. 'If You do not save these people, I, a sinner, will be responsible for their death.' And he sent his boyar to prepare all things for the dead. And the boyar came and they lifted away the gates and beheld all those who had been under the gates alive and well. When Andrei heard this he rejoiced. The people saw this miracle and marvelled."[20]

His death, by all accounts purely politically motivated, was accorded the aura of martyrdom. Inevitably he was mentioned in the same breath as Boris and Gleb, whereas unlike them he did not meet his doom unresisting. As Soloviev narrates, he put up a very stiff single-handed fight. Nevertheless, having as a prince died *in* the faith, somehow he was regarded as having died *for* the faith.[21]

All this provided powerful ammunition in the propaganda wars of the Muscovite bookmen. If not the Third Rome, Vladimir-on-the-Kliazma was at least the second Kiev, complete with its Golden gates, churches, palaces and greatly revered icon. This combination had a mesmerizing effect. As Miliukov so aptly put it, "In the last [nineteenth] century [he was writing prior to his involvement in parliamentary politics], when Russian historical scholarship began gradually to uncover its sources, these sources came into the hands of historians with their own ready-made view evolved over the centuries. It is not surprising that ready-made ideology presented in sources led the student of history along well-worn paths, ordering historical facts for him as they were seen and understood by contemporary writers. The student imagined that he was discovering and giving meaning to history when in reality he was riding on the shoulders of fifteenth and sixteenth-century philosophers."[22]

For the Historical-Juridical School, exemplified by Soloviev, Kavelin and Chicherin, the nation-state was the supreme achievement of human endeavor.[23] Ukrainian nationhood was ignored since a nation without a state was an absurdity. In his *Course of Russian History* Kliuchevsky almost completely ignores Galich-Volhynia. Soloviev admittedly devoted some space to the Southwest (Chapters II and V of the present volume) but nevertheless regards it as a historical cul-de-sac.[24] What is real is rational and what is rational is real, so history proceeded majestically northeastward along the path dictated by the Hegelian *Zeitgeist*. Also how could anyone who heard Kliuchevsky's fascinating lecture on the subject, or read its printed version,[25] possibly doubt that it *had* to be the Muscovite land and its rulers that were destined reassemble the *disjecta membra* of the Russian nation and create its all-embracing state? The brilliance of his exposition temporarily blinds us to the *post hoc ergo propter hoc* nature of his argument, for instance not allowing us to consider why, when it was at least as well endowed by nature and history, Tver failed where Moscow succeeded.[26] "The domination of theoretical concepts in our historical scholarship has led to a one-sided selection of data, involving the omission from the theories developed of everything that does not serve to illustrate or confirm the premises of an established theme."[27] As Kliuchevsky himself admitted on one occasion, "Theory does not explain," or on another, "History must be itself. It must not attempt to become philosophy."

Whereas Bogoliubsky, while promoting his northeastern principality, still looked over his shoulder at Kiev, his half-brother and near-successor unhesitatingly continued his work in the Northeast and also encouraged the chronicle tradition glorifying his deeds. Vsevolod had a Greek mother and also spent seven years (1162-1169) in honorific exile at Constantinople. He was if anything an even more indefatigable builder than his brother, and indubitably imported foreign craftsmen, mostly German, to achieve a felicitous blend between native and Western designs. In Vladimir he restored the cathedral of the Dormition, and dedicated another cathedral to St. Dmitry, his nameday saint.[28] He ordered the refortification of Suzdal and Pereiaslavl-Zalessk. Clearly Vsevolod and his descendants were there to stay. "[Vsevolod III] had participated in the disastrous campaign of 1173, and he learned from his brother's failure. From time to time he pulled levers and exerted influence and even issued threats, but in general he showed little inclination to become directly involved in southern affairs. After 1173 the competition for 'the Rus land' was left to the princes of Smolensk, Chernigov, Vladimir-in-Volynia and eventually Galich. For the northeastern family the more critical competition was over Novgorod."[29]

Vsevolod also by his final testament flew in the face of tradition by punishing his eldest son Konstantin for disobedience,[30] promoting his second son Yury over his head. Thereby he demonstrated that the grand principality was *his* property, not that of the family as a whole, of which he could dispose at will. The inevitable result was armed conflict between the two eldest brothers, culminating in the battle on the Lipitsa and the succession treaty of 1217. This represented a compromise between the old and the new. Succession was restricted to the sons of Konstantin and Yury, although on Konstantin's death his sons were passed over in favor of their uncle. Yury Vsevolodovich found an able propagandist for his reign (1212-1238) in the continuator of the Laurentian Chronicle.[31]

The fifth chapter of this volume is devoted to the external relations of late Kievan Rus. The history of Galich-Volhynia with its involvement in the affairs of Central Europe and even the Holy Roman empire is ably discussed. The achievements of Yaroslav Osmomysl, the two Mstislavs (Rostislavich and Mstislavich) and the kingdom of Daniel are described in glowing colors. Contemporary chroniclers could scarcely be blamed for thinking that the system in the Northeast was an aberration and that the future belonged to the Southwest. They could hardly have foreseen that the dark night of Mongol conquest would descend and that the Poles and Lithuanians, the latter at this time of no greater significance than the various other pagan tribes of the Baltic coast, thereafter were left to pick up the pieces. To the south, Kievan relations with the Polovetsians and other steppe tribes continued on the old pattern, which partially explains why the Mongols, making their first armed reconnaissance in 1227, were not appreciated as a major threat.

In the Northwest and increasingly in Vladimir-Suzdal the pattern of warfare was characterized by what amounted to merely raids and counter-raids. "The apparent inconclusiveness of Northern wars was partly owing to the limited aims of the men who fought them. Rulers were content with a show of submission and the payment of tribute; if that was not obtained, they would burn and loot and withdraw, and their poets would assure them that they had obtained a great victory. They were not trying to change political geography.

"In addition, techniques of warfare were limited by natural obstacles which made large-scale campaigning and annexation virtually impossible. All over the North, it was accepted that there were two kinds of campaign. One was the summer raid, which went out either before or after the harvest, usually within the periods May-June and August-September. Since land communications were at their worst in March-April and October-November, with melting snow and autumn rains, it was essential not to exceed these limits, and the preferred method of fighting a summer campaign was always by sea, when this was feasible. Winter campaigns usually went overland, taking advantage of frozen bogs and rivers, and went out and back either before or after the Christmas or Midwinter feast; cold spells and shortage of foodstuffs usually made them either small or short affairs. . . large armies could not survive a whole winter in enemy territory, or prefer the long-term gains of lordship and annexation of land to the quick advantage of a blackmail payment, loot and a safe journey home."[32] An exception to this rule were the German knights and colonists, who built an impressive infrastructure of castles, towns, cathedrals and priories, indicating that they were there to stay. Northeastern Rus too was changing the political geography by its vigorous town building, culminating in 1221 by Yury Vsevolodovich founding the town of Nizhny Novgorod at the confluence of the Volga and Oka. Although in an exposed position, it also served as an advance post for attacks on the Volga Bulgars and eventually the Kazan khanate.

With the fifth chapter of this volume the political chronicle breaks off for a while. Space is devoted in the Addendum to rebuttal of the critics of Soloviev's second volume. Particularly acerbic is his treatment of his former mentor Pogodin, for whom he developed a pronounced dislike.[33] Pogodin was doubtless patronizing towards his young former student, who was all of thirty-two years old, setting himself up in competition with Tatishchev, Shcherbatov and Karamzin. It must be remembered that this was only the second volume of Soloviev's *magnum opus*, which many doubted would ever see completion, which in fact it did not. The criticisms of Kavelin and Sergeevich are of much later provenance, and the Addendum as a whole was included only in the reissue of 1879, the last year of the author's life.[34]

The present volume continues with Chapters VI-VIII, corresponding to the opening chapter of Soloviev's third volume. First appearing in 1853, during Soloviev's lifetime it reappeared in 1857, 1862 and 1870, and posthumously in 1880 and 1890, as well as in the *Obshchestvannaia Pol'za* (Popular Use) editions of 1893, 1895 and 1911. The "gray" (because of the color of its binding) edition published in the Soviet Union is based on the 1870 version, the last during Soloviev's lifetime. The chapter in question deals with the domestic situation of society in Russia from the death of Yaroslav the Wise to that of Mstislav of Toropets (1054-1228).

The first of these three last chapters in our translation deals with the nature and evolution of princely power, as well as the military organization of the principality. Next we have a glimpse of life in the towns, with special attention given to the northwestern towns of Novgorod and Pskov, whose history is especially rich in documentation.

The next chapter is devoted to religion and law, the two powerful checks on violent and arbitrary behavior. Although Soloviev paints a dim picture of the state of law and morality, he does point out the vigorous missionary effort which continued particularly in Northern Rus, where paganism fought a stiff rearguard action. This was also a turbulent time in the history of the Rus church which found itself restive under the tutelage of Byzantium, especially when the church of Constantinople was forced as a result of the Fourth Crusade to spend the next six decades in exile at Nicaea. Attempts, if unsuccessful, to assert independence from patriarchal authority as exemplified by the Klim Smoliatich and Feodorets incidents, demonstrated that the eventual triumph of autocephaly was merely a matter of time. As far as law is concerned, there were a number of codes in existence and rules of evidence were evolving. Nevertheless it was deemed better to settle disputes without recourse to legal action. "Wherever there is law, there is also much injury" is the maxim uttered several times in the course of this volume.

The final chapter, dealing with literary and historical works broadly speaking deals with several types of writing. Since the clergy were the only literate class, despite evidence of princes and urban elites having acquired the love of books, much of the literature is homiletic in nature. In that category we might also include Vladimir Monomakh's *Instruction*. Pilgrimage literature was widely read at this time, despite the strictures of the clergy that charity and good works begin at home. Less easy to categorize is the *Epistle of Daniel the Exile,* according to Soloviev addressed to Prince Yury Dolgoruky, but now more commonly thought to have been addressed to Prince Yaroslav Vsevolodovich of Pereiaslavl (reigned 1238-1246).[35] Soloviev then discusses poetry, inevitably turning to the *Tale of Igor's Campaign,* the greatest epic of medieval Rus, although some have disputed its authenticity.[36]

The final literary genre discussed here by Soloviev is the chronicle. By the time of Soloviev's writing a number of important primary sources found their way into print, not until the turn of the century were they subjected by A.A. Shakhmatov (1864-1920) to scholarly scrutiny.[37] Considering that Soloviev was without benefit of this scholarship, his analysis of the chronicles is quite impressive.

Soloviev drew on the chronicles extensively, especially since during the time of writing and revisions to previously published volumes the *Complete Collection of Russian Chronicles* (PSRL) was appearing. The chronicles basic to the early period of Rus history are the Laurentian and the Hypatian.[38] He also used an old edition of the Nikonian Chronicle, though a new scholarly edition became available during his lifetime.[39]

The Novgorod and Pskov Chronicles were contained in the third, fourth and fifth volumes of PSRL.[40] Soloviev also referred to an early edition of the Resurrection (Voskresensk) Chronicle.[41] An important source concerning the history of Northeastern Rus was the *Chronicle of Pereiaslavl-Suzdal*.[42] Another rather primitive chronicle compilation used by Soloviev was the *Chronicle Containing Russian History from 852 to 1598*.[43] Soloviev also had invaluable genealogical resources at his disposal, not all of them in print, particularly the *Book of Degrees*.[44]

Soloviev acknowledged his debt to his predecessors in the writing of a comprehensive Russian history, notably those of Tatishchev, Karamzin and Artsybashev,[45] as well as Ewers's tentative probing of early Russian history.[46] Also for all of his derisory remarks about Pogodin, Soloviev extensively quarried his works.[47] Pogodin never achieved much of monographic dimensions, but the fruits of his labors descended like volcanic dust on the available learned journals.

Details of social history are gleaned from the essay of A. Danilovich on ancient Slav towns[48] and I. Krasov's study of ancient Novgorod.[49] Information also is presented regarding the clothing and equipment of ancient Rus warriors.[50] Soloviev further cited recently discovered numismatic evidence.[51] Light is also cast on early systems of excise.[52] The development of civil and commercial law is traced by Soloviev through the work of K.A. Nevolin, I. Ewers and E.S. Tobien.[53]

Foreign primary sources used include Henry of Livonia,[54] the papal legate Giovanni Plano di Carpini[55] and the Sephardic voyager Benjamin of Tudela.[56] For Georgian affairs, Soloviev relied upon the general history translated from Georgian into French by M. Brosset,[57] as well as a specialized account of dynastic relations between Rus and Georgia.[58] Documentation on the affairs of the Hanseatic League also was utilized.[59] Information on Poland is largely drawn from the chronicle of Maciej Stryjkowski.[60]

For church history, Soloviev's main authority was the *History of the Russian Church* by Metropolitan Makary (Mikhail Petrovich Bulgakov, 1816-1882).[61] Its is true that this history was in print only for Soloviev's third and subsequent editions, but the two men contemporaneously pursued academic careers before Makary joined the ranks of the episcopacy in 1857. He became metropolitan of Moscow in 1879, the year of Soloviev's death. The other nineteenth-century standard Russian church history, that of Evgeny Evstigneevich Golubinsky (1834-1912), began to appear after Soloviev's time.[62] Yet since Soloviev's scholarly career overlapped with those of Makary and Golubinsky it is very probable that there was informal consultation between them. For information on the liturgy of the early Rus church, Soloviev was indebted to another leading prelate, Metropolitan Filaret.[63] On the thorny relations between the Rus church and the patriarchal authorities, Soloviev drew upon the study by A. Zernin.[64] Hagiographical sources utilized by Soloviev include the *Patericon of the Kiev Caves Monastery*,[65] the *Life of St. Avraamy of Rostov*,[66] and the *Historical Dictionary of Saints*.[67]

While Soloviev was writing his history Russia was rediscovering much of its ancient literary heritage. Tribute is paid to the pioneering folklorist Kirsha Danilov,[68] and several other contributions towards the study of ancient Russian literature are acknowledged.[69]

The English-language literature available for this period of Rus history is mentioned either in the text of or the annotation to this Introduction, so it would be pointless to repeat it here.

HISTORY OF RUSSIA

Volume 3

The Shift Northward

Kievan Rus, 1154–1228

I

NORTH AND SOUTH OF RUS LANDS

ANDREI BOGOLIUBSKY REMAINS IN THE NORTH

It seemed that following the death of Rostislav Mstislavich[1] events in Rus would follow exactly the same course as previously, after the death of Vsevolod Olgovich,[2] in that Kiev, the senior seat, was occupied by Mstislav Iziaslavich[3] despite the rights of his uncle Andrei of Suzdal. Similarly Mstislav's father Iziaslav occupied Kiev disregarding the rights of Andrei's father Yury,[4] who fought his nephew and several times expelled him from Kiev. So now also Andrei fought Mstislav, expelled him and took over the seniority. The struggle might well be expected to continue, in which as before luck favored one side or the other, depending whether Andrei's alliance with eleven other princes held, whether he satisfied their wishes.

These expectations are quite mistaken. Andrei himself did not lead his troops against Kiev, neither did he come later to the ancestral capital. He handed the devastated city over to his younger brother[5] while he himself remained in the North, in his familiar surroundings at Vladimir-on-the-Kliazma. Andrei's step was an event of the greatest significance, a *turning point* at which history took a new direction. A new system took hold in Rus.

It was not a transfer of the capital from one location to another. There was no single sovereign in Rus, which was ruled by a large princely clan[6] whose unity was supported by the fact that no single line held a leading position, nor did any subjugate others in the sense of their position in the land. Every member of that clan in turn, as a result of biological seniority, had the right to be the senior, the grand prince, to have Kiev, the chief seat in the best city of Rus. This explains the absence of individual territories,[7] patrimonies, among the equal princely-clan members.[8] Each regarded the whole Land of Rus as his patrimony. This explains the community of interests for all the princes, the notion of common duty, equally binding on all the princes, to defend the Land of Rus, to stake their lives in its defense. Thus during the whole preceding period, despite the interprincely wars, no territory or principality expanded, at least not to any significant degree, at the expense of others. No benefit accrued to the prince from enlarging a territory he ruled only temporarily. For example, Iziaslav Mstislavich[9] during his lifetime ruled six different territories. Why should he take the trouble to extend the borders, to strengthen any one of these territories? The dominant care of his life was the struggle against his uncles for the right of seniority, the opportunity to be senior prince and rule in Kiev. Why should the prince of Novgorod-Seversk take care of his territory when he knew that after the death of his uncle, the prince of Chernigov, he would rule in Chernigov and must yield his previous territory of Severia to his cousin, son of the previous prince of Chernigov? He knew also that he would not stay long in Chernigov. He would end as prince of Kiev and his son would be left in Turov, Volhynia or Great Novgorod. It follows that the main aim of these domestic wars was to support the right to seniority, the position in the clan hierarchy, determining who ruled over this or that district.

The supreme wish, the main cherished goal of each prince-clansman was to achieve supremacy over the whole clan. This degree of seniority necessarily was linked with ruling Kiev, the foremost city of Rus, the mother of all Rus cities. Therefore the enormous significance of this city for the princes easily may be understood. The strongest foundation of princely clan unity was the absence of separate sovereign lands, the absence of separate property for the clan members, the common right to the main seat. The most ardent wishes of the princes were directed towards Kiev, on which centered their main activity. Kiev represented unity of the princely clan and that of the land, ultimately also ecclesiastical unity, for it was the seat of the supreme pastor of the Rus church. Kiev, in the words of the princes themselves, was the *senior* city in the whole of the land. Iziaslav Davydovich did not want to depart from Kiev "because," as the chronicler[10] says, "he had taken a great liking to ruling the grand principality of Kiev. Who would not like to rule in Kiev? After all here was all the honor, glory and grandeur, Kiev was the head of all the Russian lands. To Kiev come people and merchants from faraway kingdoms, all sorts of riches from all countries are gathered there."

There came a prince who did not care to rule in Kiev. He preferred a northern city, Vladimir-on-the-Kliazma, poor and only recently founded, over the famous and rich Kiev. It is easy to understand the consequences of the upheaval caused by Bogoliubsky. Had the change of abode of the senior prince been agreed upon by all the prince-clansmen; had Kiev lost completely its previous importance for them all, passing to Vladimir-on-the-Kliazma; had all princes, both Northern and Southern, descendants of Monomakh and descendants of Oleg, begun now to fight for Vladimir as earlier they had fought for Kiev, great changes would have taken place in interprincely relationships. The consequences of such a transfer of the main stage of events to a new area with its own characteristics would have been very great.

This did not happen, and could not have happened. For all the Southern princes, descendants of Monomakh and of Oleg, Kiev had not lost its previous significance. None of these princes preferred the remote and poor land of Suzdal to that blessed land which commonly was called the Land of Rus. Kiev remained as before the senior city of the Land of Rus, yet the most senior and the most powerful prince did not live there. He stayed in the remote North, disposing of Kiev by giving it to the prince next in seniority. In this way the Northern prince of Suzdal, despite the fact that like past grand princes he was acknowledged only as senior of the clan, appeared as an outside force hanging over Southern Rus, a separate, independent force. In the past there were several separate districts such as the lands of Galich, Polotsk, Riazan, Gorodets and Turov, which districts became separated because their princes were excluded from the main line of succession.[11] These princes were relatively so weak that they could not have any decisive influence on the affairs of Rus.

The Northern regions, those of Rostov and Suzdal, did not grow apart because their princes were excluded. Their prince was acknowledged as the first, the senior in the entire clan, besides being the richest. Hence in effect he was endowed with double influence. His awareness of this and his independence and power prompted him to change his way of dealing with the weakest, the junior princes, demanding from them complete obedience. The princes were not accustomed to this because of the indeterminate, exclusively clan-like relationships between seniors and juniors.

In this way a blow was struck at clan relationships for the first time. For the first time a different type of relationship was encountered. For the first time there arose the possibility that clan relationship might be transformed into a governing relationship. If the Northern princes maintained permanently their dominant position in relation to them, naturally the fate of the Southern princes quickly would fall to the arbitrary rule of the Northern, which inevitably would cause a change of the entire way of life in Southern Rus, in its relationships with the North. If the Northern princes temporarily lost their power, and hence their influence on the fate of Southern Rus, the final separation of the two parts of Rus, each with its own center, its own separate sphere of influence, inevitably must follow.

It is easy to understand that the separation of Northern from Southern Rus meant much more than, for instance, the separation of small districts like Galich, Polotsk or Riazan. Now a large region went its own way, a region with a distinctive natural environment and population, with different aspirations and different civic relationships. Did Bogoliubsky's refusal to transfer to Kiev, his insistence on remaining in the North to create there an independent and powerful position, become the cause of separation between Southern and Northern Rus? Could he change previously accepted relationship patterns between the senior prince and the junior princes? Were such a change realized, would it be repeated? Would the senior princes imitate Bogoliubsky, each staying in his territory? Would each expand and strengthen his own territory, creating there an independent and powerful position? Exercising this power, could he change clan relationships towards the junior or weaker princes into governing relations? Where in Rus, in the South or in the North, would Bogoliubsky's example bear fruit? Where would it be emulated?

In the Southern half of Rus he found no imitators. There was failure and unwillingness to understand the importance of this development. There Bogoliubsky could not be emulated. The most valiant princes put up the most desperate resistance to him. There the old traditions were entrenched too strongly. No single prince held enough strength to create for himself an independent and powerful position in his territory. During the struggles of various branches[12] (lines) of Yaroslav's heirs for seniority this status and the Kievan throne usually fell to the senior of the victorious branch. The grand prince was strong not because of the number of his territories but because of the sum total of power possessed by the entire clan line of which this prince was the elder. His strength was not in his aggregate, hence he distributed the towns situated near to Kiev to his sons, brothers and nephews. This was all the same for him, or even more advantageous, than giving these towns to his burgraves[13] who were more likely to go over to another prince than a prince would betray his branch and its senior member. Finally, the establishment of a new order in the South was hindered by various other relationships based, or at least developing and strengthening, because of clan-like interprincely relationships. We have in mind attitudes towards the retinue, the towns, the army consisting of barbarian tribesmen from the borderlands known as Karakalpaks,[14] and so on.

In the North things were different. Here the soil was new and virginal. The new order could take root more easily. It could and did take root, as we shall see later. There were no deeply rooted traditions pertaining to the unity of the princely clan. The North began its historical life with this step by the prince towards the new order. Vsevolod III inherited his brother's aspirations. All Northern princes were descendants of Vsevolod III. Hence among them there was a new tradition of princely relationships, the clan tradition, the tradition of their father and grandfather. The most important circumstance here was that for the new ambitions of the princes in the North a free field of action opened. They encountered no obstacles in other relations, in dealings with the local population.

It has been observed what significance the cities and towns had in clan reckonings and civil wars between the princes, the influence they wielded on the outcome of these wars, and on changes in those reckonings, what significance Kiev had when the rights of Sviatoslav's descendants were infringed for the benefit of Monomakh and his sons.[15] Following the death of Vsevolod Olgovich the people of Kiev declared that they did not wish to pass to his brother as if they were a *legacy.*

Consequently by calling Monomakh to Kiev, giving its throne to his sons despite the claims of the princes of Chernigov, the people of Kiev refused to establish the rights of inheritance in one particular branch of the clan. They were against heredity in general. In Polotsk there was similar opposition. Later the pattern was repeated in Smolensk. Therefore if in the South some prince wished to introduce a new system of allocating territories he would face strong opposition in the towns, which together with the opposition of the numerous princely clan members would frustrate his aim.

Did such an obstacle exist in the North? Did such indeterminate relationships exist between princes and citizens as existed in the old towns, the old communities which recalled the former tribal relationships of the population with their elders, supported by clan relationships, by constant shifting and wars among the Riurikid princes? In the North, a large land bordering regions belonging to the line of banished descendants of Sviatoslav, adjacent to the lands of Novgorod the Great, in this severe and sparsely populated land there was only one ancient city mentioned by the chronicler even before the arrival of the Varangians. This was Rostov the Great, from which the whole surrounding area received its name "the Land of Rostov." Soon new towns started to appear around it. Monomakh's son Yury[16] in particular won fame as a relentless builder.

The status of new towns was that of junior to senior, to older towns or cities, becoming their bytowns[17] and necessarily dependent on them. New towns or bytowns lacked independent existence. They were entirely dependent on decisions taken by the older towns, which in order to administer these new towns sent their burgraves or reeves.[18] This dependence is expressed by the chronicle when it states "what the senior [towns] decide, the bytowns do." Clearly if in these junior towns lacking independence and accustomed to obeying the decisions of the older town's assembly[19] a prince established his seat, his power would develop much more freely. Let us not forget that towns in the Land of Rostov were built and populated by the princes. Since the prince brought these towns into existence, naturally they were considered his property.

Thus in the North, in the Land of Rostov, around old assembly seats, around the solitary Rostov, the prince established for himself a special world of towns where he was absolute ruler, an omnipotent lord. He considered these towns his property, of which he might dispose at will. No wonder that here appeared the first prince to whom the chronicler ascribes aspirations towards monarchical rule. No wonder that here, for the first time, ideas appeared about individual princely property, which Bogoliubsky hastened to isolate from the general clan property of the descendants of Yaroslav. He thus left an example for his descendants to follow without hindrance. Consider the evidence of the chronicle concerning the difference between the old and the new cities and towns, the triumph of the new over the only old town in the North. Consider this contrast and the hostility later developing between the towns of Northeastern and Western Rus. Consider the way of life of the Western Rus cities and towns during the period of Lithuanian rule, bearing clear traces of olden times, differing greatly from the way of life in the Northeastern towns. We cannot help ascribing to this difference an important influence on the life of Northeast and later on the life of the whole of Russia in general. Were we to be shown at the beginning the same developments in the Northeast as are evident in the West and the South, why then were these institutions not replicated? Why despite their favorable beginnings did they disappear without a trace? Clearly the ground was unsuitable.

Finally the difference in character between the populations of Northern and Southern Rus must not be forgotten. This difference inevitably contributed also to the establishment of the new order in the North, to the significance of the Suzdal territory in the North for the other parts of Rus.

ANDREI'S CHARACTER AND CONDUCT IN THE NORTH

During his father's struggle for seniority, for Kiev, against Yury's cousin Iziaslav Mstislavich, Yury's second son Andrei distinguished himself by unusual valor. He began battle at the head of the regiments, carried away on his fiery horse into the midst of the foe, scorning danger. Yet it was noticeable that he had no liking for the South, for Rus proper, only for the North. This sharply distinguished him from his father and his other brothers, who shared their love for Kiev with all the other descendants of Yaroslav. When Yury's cause was lost in the South, he still refused to abandon it. He procrastinated in complying with the demands of his brother and nephew who declared they could not tolerate him. Andrei by contrast hurried to the North ahead of his father, claiming that there was nothing for him to do in the South. Later when Yury, after the death of his older brother and nephew, finally strengthened his position in Kiev and placed him nearby in Vyshgorod, Andrei failed to stay even one year in his Southern district. Without his father's consent he left for the North, never to return.

By way of explanation it should be pointed out that Andrei, who undoubtedly was born in the North, spent there most of his life, especially the formative years which make the greatest and most indelible impression on the human soul. Yury lived not in Vladimir but Suzdal, a relatively new and dependent city. Andrei apparently received from his father the district of Vladimir-on-the-Kliazma. He therefore grew up and matured in a new environment, that which prevailed in the new towns or bytowns of Rostov. Only in 1149, when he was over thirty years old, did Andrei come to the South, to Rus, with his father's hosts. He was accustomed to the North and the system prevailing there. It is hardly surprising that he did not take to the South, where life seemed to him foreign, incomprehensible and hostile. In the South all princes from their youth were used to living in their common clan circle, seeing each other at the head of the hosts and during peaceful councils, living in close vicinity and maintaining constant relations. From early childhood they participated actively in all clan clashes and absorbed all the clan reckonings and quarrels. This was their main interest in life.

Andrei by now had spent over thirty years in the North, alone with his family, remote from the other princely lines. Seldom did he meet them. He had little personal knowledge of his other princely relatives, whether near or distant. News of events in their alien world came to him only from afar. Because of prolonged absence Andrei's link with his clan relations inevitably weakened. This cleared the way for him to act as a senior prince who dealt with other princes as subordinates rather than as relatives. Not only remoteness and hostility but even hatred separated Andrei from his Southern relatives. Even the closest, his first cousins the sons of Mstislav, whom he tended to see as his sworn enemies, had tried to rob his father and all of Yury's family of the status that was their due. His alienation and estrangement from all clan members, his hostility towards the sons of Mstislav and alienation from the South in general, could not change when Andrei appeared in Rus where his father and his entire family had failed to win the favor of the populace. Consequently there was little hope of capturing the senior seat in the near or even remote future, still less of holding it.

VLADIMIR-ON-THE-KLIAZMA

No wonder Andrei moved from Vyshgorod to the North where he confirmed his position in his previous territory, Vladimir-on-the-Kliazma. For the rest of his father's life he was not the prince of the main Northern lands, neither Rostov nor Suzdal, which Yury wished to leave to his younger sons, placing the older sons in the South, in Rus proper. It seems that during Yury's lifetime the towns had no desire directly to rebel against his wishes. When Yury died the people of Rostov and Suzdal, consulting among themselves, accepted Andrei as their prince and put him on his father's throne. From this chronicle entry it is evident that the inhabitants of Rostov and other old towns believed it their duty to fulfill the will of the dead prince, who left these districts to his younger sons. They thought they had the right to choose whom they liked as their prince. Andrei accepted the thrones of Rostov and Suzdal yet also strengthened his presence in his former district of Vladimir. He mainly beautified this town and wanted even to establish a separate metropolitan see for Northern Rus to gain independence from the South in ecclesiastical matters as well.[20] He realized that Kiev would keep its advantage if the supreme shepherd of the Rus church continued to reside there. Such conduct on Andrei's part could not find favor with the people of Rostov. For some reason his conduct apparently displeased the senior boyars, probably because Andrei failed to maintain comradely relations with them, not sharing with them his innermost thoughts, as was the custom in old Rus.

Those dissatisfied with his rule could easily find an excuse for rebellion. Andrei took over the district against his father's will. Yury's younger sons, to whom his father had bequeathed the land of Suzdal, continued to live there, and malcontents might act on their behalf. Andrei expelled from the North his younger brothers Mstislav, Vasilko and Vsevolod, his dangerous rivals, who were exiled to Greece.

Two other sons of Yury held districts in the South. Gleb ruled in Pereiaslavl, Mikhail probably in Torchesk. Soon Vsevolod Yurievich with his nephews, the sons of Rostislav, returned from Greece. According to some accounts they ruled in Gorodets Ostersk. Together with his brothers Andrei expelled also his nephews, sons of his older brother Rostislav. Finally he expelled his father's old boyars, his father's men, men of primary importance, as the chronicler puts it. He did so, continued the chronicler, because he wished to be the sole ruler of all the land of Suzdal.

The people of Rostov and Suzdal were dissatisfied. Men of primary importance were not content, nor were the princely brothers. The question therefore is how Andrei became sole ruler, despite the dissatisfaction of Rostov and Suzdal to expulsion of his brothers and the boyars. It must be assumed that his power was based on the loyalty of the least, the new towns or bytowns. Andrei apparently understood well the basis of his power. He did not abandon these new towns when his troops took Kiev, the oldest and the richest of Rus cities.

ANDREI'S BROTHER GLEB RULES IN KIEV

Gleb Yurievich,[21] placed by his brother in Kiev, could not rule there in peace while the expelled Mstislav Iziaslavich still lived. Mstislav fought his nearest neighbor, Vladimir Andreevich of Dorogobuzh,[22] who was Yury's ally during his banishment. Together with his brother Yaroslav and the men of Galich he approached the town of Dorogobuzh and fought around it. Despite the illness of Vladimir Andreevich, who could not command his forces personally, and that Gleb of Kiev despite his promises gave Vladimir Andreevich no help, Mstislav failed to take Dorogobuzh. He had to be satisfied with pillaging the smaller, less fortified towns belonging to Vladimir, and returned home.

Vladimir Andreevich soon passed away, probably without issue. The landless prince Vladimir Mstislavich was waiting for Vladimir Andreevich's district. He came from the Northeast and lived in the town of Polonny in Volhynia, belonging to the Kievan church of the Tithes. When he learned of the death of Vladimir Andreevich he appeared before Dorogobuzh. The late prince's retinue would not admit him, so he sent to tell them "I swear to you and your princess kissing the cross, that I will do no evil to you or to her." He kissed the cross, entered the town, immediately forgetting his oath because, the chronicler says, he was frivolous in dealings with his brothers. He grabbed the property, flocks, herds and villages of the deceased Vladimir Andreevich and sent the widowed princess from the town. She took her husband's body to Vyshgorod, whence she wanted to travel to Kiev, but Prince Davyd Rostislavich would not give her leave. "How can I let you go?" he said. "During the night I received information that Mstislav is in Vasiliev. Let somebody from the retinue accompany the body." "Prince!" the Dorogobuzh retinue answered him, "you know yourself what we have done to the people of Kiev. We cannot go there, for they will kill us." "Prince!" said Abbot Polikarp to Davyd, "his retinue will not go with him. Let somebody from your retinue go, that someone may lead the horse and carry the banner." Davyd refused to send his retinue at this dangerous moment, answering Polikarp "His banner and honor passed away with his soul. Take the priests of the Boris and Gleb church and go alone." Polikarp set out and together with the people of Kiev buried Vladimir in the St. Andrew monastery.

GLEB'S WAR WITH MSTISLAV IZIASLAVICH

Meanwhile Mstislav with a great force, with his brother Yaroslav, with the Galich, Turov and Gorodets regiments went to the Karakalpaks, then continued to Tripolie. From there they advanced to Kiev, which they entered without hindrance because at this time Gleb was in Pereiaslavl to deal with Polovetsian[23] affairs. The first thing Mstislav did after occupying Kiev was to reach an agreement with the allies who helped him recapture the senior seat. He immediately came to an agreement with Vladimir Mstislavich. As can be seen from the events that followed Vladimir refused to seek Kiev not only against Mstislav, but also against his brother Yaroslav and his sons, which is why his nephews allowed him to stay in Dorogobuzh.

The content of the pacts with the other allies is not known. Agreements were made with the people of Kiev and with the Karakalpaks who, as was their custom, only deceived the princes. Having concluded these agreements, Mstislav marched on Vyshgorod and fought its defenders.

The besieged did not yield because their prince Davyd had many of his large retinue. His brothers also sent him some help. Prince Gleb sent to him his chiliarch[24] with a military detachment. Otherwise he had some Wild Polovetsians and his own Berendey,[25] while Mstislav's allies started to disperse. The first to leave was the commander[26] of Galich, Konstantin,[27] with his regiments. He sent a message to Mstislav, saying "Prince Yaroslav ordered me to besiege Vyshgorod for five days only, and then go home." "My brother Yaroslav," answered Mstislav, "told me to keep my regiments until you settle affairs with your brothers." Konstantin wrote a forged document, wherein supposedly Prince Yaroslav ordered him to return. He then left with the men of Galich. According to some very plausible information Konstantin was bribed by Davyd of Vyshgorod, otherwise it is difficult to explain his conduct.

After the men of Galich departed Mstislav retreated towards Kiev and stood in front of the Golden gate, in the orchards. The Polovetsians and Berendey came out of Vyshgorod and inflicted great losses on his regiments. Mstislav saw that his allies were dispersing, exhausted by uninterrupted battle. Hearing that Gleb and the Polovetsians were crossing the Dnieper, that help had arrived to join Davyd, he called his brothers for a conference. "Our troops are dispersing," they said, "and the other side is receiving fresh troops. The Karakalpaks are deceiving us. Therefore we can stay here no longer. Better for us to return to our districts. After a while we will come back."

Mstislav understood that the princes spoke the truth and he left for Volhynia, surviving a short battle with the Polovetsians sent by Davyd to pursue him. Though the Polovetsians could not cause much damage to Mstislav, they considerably devastated the countryside through which they passed. Mstislav's nephew Vasilko Yaropolchich, who ruled in Mikhailov, one of the Ros river towns, tried to mount a surprise attack against him. He only succeeded in losing his retinue, barely escaping to his town. Soon afterwards he was besieged by Gleb, accompanied by three sons of Rostislav, namely Riurik, Davyd and Mstislav. The allies burned Mikhailov, filled in the moat and let Vasilko go to Chernigov.

DEATH OF THE ADVERSARIES

Mstislav promised that after a short rest he would return to Kiev. He could not meet his promise. In August 1170 he fell seriously ill and sent for his brother Yaroslav to make arrangements for his children. Yaroslav had sworn an oath not to take their districts. Soon afterwards Mstislav died before, like his father, gaining seniority over his uncles. It is not known what forced Yaroslav to abandon Vladimir to his nephews and remain in his previous district of Lutsk, even though seniority in his branch of the clan was his. Later it was evident that he had at his disposal all the forces of Volhynia and was the representative of his branch of the clan, preserving his right to Kiev. We have seen examples of how the significance of districts changed occasionally, depending on circumstances, such as when the prince of Kiev placed his older son in Vyshgorod or Belgorod, the younger son in Pereiaslavl. Yet Mstislav had conquered Vladimir by force and defended it from Yury and his allies. Consequently he had full right to demand from his brother not to take the districts from his nephews, which their father had conquered *at peril of his life.*

Gleb Yurievich of Kiev did not survive his enemy for long. He died the next year, 1171, leaving the reputation of one who loved his brothers, a man who kept his oath. His successor in Kiev, Vladimir Mstislavich, was a prince whose qualities were quite different. Three sons of Rostislav, with seats around Kiev, sent for him to take the senior seat, as he was their uncle. All the sons of Rostislav, following their father's example, respected seniority. Still, they lacked Mstislav's advantage over Vladimir, namely seniority of age. Finally they found it more convenient to see Vladimir in Kiev rather than a descendant of Iziaslav, towards whom their hostility was open and undisguised.

Vladimir, landless for so long and expelled from everywhere, suddenly thanks to circumstances had the opportunity to gain the throne of Kiev. In secret from the other Volhynian princes, Yaroslav and his nephews, to whom he earlier had sworn not to seek seniority, Vladimir departed for Kiev, leaving Dorogobuzh to his son Mstislav. His luck did not last long, for Kiev already was dependent on the Northern prince Andrei Bogoliubsky, who according to the chronicler did not relish the fact that Vladimir ruled in Kiev. He told him to leave Kiev, ordering Roman Rostislavich of Smolensk to go there in his place. Perhaps he also was angry with Vladimir for allying himself with the Volhynian descendants of Iziaslav, occupying the throne in Kiev without his permission. He disliked his younger blood brothers for well-known reasons. He was favorably disposed only towards the sons of Rostislav, who recognized his seniority and until now supported him strongly. "You called me father," he told them, "so I wish you well. I give to your brother Roman the city of Kiev."

Very soon the consequences became apparent, consequences which inevitably overtook Southern Rus as a result of the strengthening of Northern Rus. The absolute ruler of Northern Rus violated all the clan rules through his arbitrariness, thus confusing all earlier clan reckonings. According to clan rules Kiev first of all belonged to Vladimir Mstislavich, then to the younger brothers of Andrei if he himself refused to have his seat there, finally to Yaroslav Iziaslavich of Lutsk. Andrei passed over all these princes, giving Kiev to one of Rostislav's sons. Death saved Vladimir from banishment. He died in Kiev after only four months as senior prince. "He suffered many troubles," says the chronicler, "he fled from Mstislav to Galich, then to Hungary, then to Riazan, then to the Polovetsians. All this was his own fault, for he was unfaithful to his oath."

BOGOLIUBSKY GIVES KIEV TO ROMAN ROSTISLAVICH OF SMOLENSK

Although Roman on Andrei's order arrived in Kiev and was accepted joyfully by all the people, this joy was short-lived. We have noted the autocratic manner with which Andrei treated the junior, Southern, princes. He expelled one from Kiev, sending another to replace him, without examining their rights. The sons of Rostislav were silent when this autocratic behavior favored them. Soon they realized they must choose between implicit compliance with Andrei's wishes and entering a desperate struggle for the old clan rights. In this struggle of the sons of Rostislav against the descendants of Yury the opposite characters and aspirations of the Northern and Southern princes grew fully apparent. Hitherto struggles resulted either from expulsion, when disinherited princes lacking their own patrimonial rights lost their districts which they then were compelled to seize by force, or from struggle for seniority among various branches, or within one branch between uncles and nephews.

The struggle for seniority in the Monomakh branch, during which we cannot help notice also the struggle between Northern and Southern Rus, ended in fact with the capture of Kiev by Bogoliubsky's forces, the triumph of Northern over Southern Rus. From this time onwards the offspring of Iziaslav, the older son of Mstislav the Great, left the stage where the struggle for seniority unfolded, where heretofore they played the leading role. They removed themselves to the West, where they played a different and no less brilliant role.

In their place the struggle with the Northern princes or the sons of Yury was assumed by the heirs of Rostislav,[28] second son of Mstislav the

Great, but this third struggle of our princes was completely new in character. Now the struggle was conducted not by landless princes, exiles trying to gain districts. Neither was the struggle for seniority. It was the Southern princes, descendants of Rostislav, who fought for the old order, for the old Rus, for clan-type relationships, which the descendants of Yury wished to oust. In this very ambivalent struggle both warring branches or, to put it more correctly, both Northern and Southern Rus, put into the fray two princes each. Old Rus, the descendants of Rostislav, entered the two Mstislavs, father and son. The new, Northern Rus was represented by two sons of Yury, Andrei Bogoliubsky and Vsevolod III.

QUARREL OF THE SONS OF ROSTISLAV WITH ANDREI

Andrei learned that his brother Gleb had died a violent death in Kiev. The murderers were pointed out to him, namely Grigory Khotovich, who was Gleb's chiliarch, somebody called Stepanets, and Oleksa Sviatoslavich. Andrei easily could have believed this slander, knowing how hated Yury's sons were in the South. For that reason he sent word to the descendants of Rostislav saying "Hand over to me Grigory Khotovich, Stepanets and Oleksa Sviatoslavich, for they are our enemies. They murdered my brother Gleb." The descendants of Rostislav, apparently considering the denunciation against the boyars groundless, did not heed Andrei, handing over only Grigory Khotovich. Then Andrei sent to Roman, saying "You and your brothers refuse to obey me, now leave Kiev. Davyd must leave Vyshgorod and Mstislav must leave Belgorod. All of you go to Smolensk and divide it as you wish."[29]

The descendants of Rostislav took terrible offense that Andrei expelled them from the Land of Rus, giving Kiev to his brother Mikhail. The older brother Roman hesitated to oppose him and withdrew to Smolensk, but the others did not leave their districts. It seems Mikhail feared them and did not depart Torchesk to Kiev, instead sending his younger brother Vsevolod with his nephew Yaropolk Rostislavich. Vsevolod was five weeks in Kiev when Riurik, Davyd and Mstislav, sons of Rostislav, told Andrei "Brother! We called you our father, we swore an oath to you by kissing the cross and we keep our oath. We wish you well, yet you expelled from Kiev our brother Roman, while us you expel from the Land of Rus through no fault of ours. Let God and the power of the Cross be our judge."

When no answer came the descendants of Rostislav plotted together, entered Kiev at night, captured Vsevolod Yurievich, his nephew Yaropolk and all their boyars, and installed their brother Riurik in Kiev. Then they set out towards Torchesk to attack Mikhail, who defended himself for six days. On the seventh he made peace with the descendants of Rostislav, promising to join them against Andrei and Sviatoslav of Chernigov. For that offer the descendants of Rostislav promised to capture for him not only Torchesk, but also Pereiaslavl, where his younger nephew Vladimir, son of the deceased Gleb, was ruling. Mikhail's brother Vsevolod was freed from captivity but his nephew Yaropolk was not, while his brother Mstislav was expelled from his district in Trepolie.

MSTISLAV ROSTISLAVICH THE BRAVE

Andrei, when he learned of the events in the South, grew very angry, which delighted the descendants of Oleg of Chernigov. They sent someone to Andrei to stir him against the sons of Rostislav. "Your enemy," they told him, "is our enemy. We are ready to go with you." Andrei, as the chronicler put it, took their advice. Full of foolhardiness he waxed very angry. Placing his hope in the power of the flesh he surrounded himself with numerous troops. Inflamed with wrath, he called his swordbearer Mikhno, saying "Go to the sons of Rostislav and tell them 'You refuse to act according to my will. Then you, Riurik, go to Smolensk, to your brother, to your patrimony.' Say to Davyd 'Go to Bîrlad,[30] I forbid you to reside in Rus.' Tell Mstislav 'You are the instigator of all this and I banish you from Rus.'"

Mstislav, according to the words of the chronicler, from his youth feared no one but God. He ordered the head and the beard of Andrei's envoy shaven in his presence[31] and returned him to his master with the words "Go to your prince and tell him from us 'Until now we respected you like our father, lovingly, but when you sent us such words, not like to a prince but like to an underling[32] or an ordinary man, then do what you must, and God will be our judge.'" The fatal word "underling," as opposed to prince, was uttered. The Southern princes understood the change in the treatment meted out to them by the Northern autocrat. They understood that he wanted to change the former clan relationship between senior and junior, substituting the new relationship between master and underling. No longer was he satisfied merely that the juniors accepted him as a father, in the spirit of love, rather wished them to obey his orders without question, as subjects would rulers.

ANDREI FAILS AGAINST THE SONS OF ROSTISLAV

Andrei's face fell when Mikhno told him Mstislav's reply. He ordered his troops gathered immediately. The troops came from Rostov, Suzdal, Vladimir, Pereiaslavl, Beloozero, Murom, Novgorod and Riazan. Andrei counted them and found there were fifty thousand men. He sent his son Yury and the commander Boris Zhidislavich with them. "Expel Riurik and Davyd from my patrimony," he ordered, "and apprehend Mstislav, but do him no harm. Bring him to me." "Prince Andrei," says the chronicler, "was wise in all matters and valiant, but he lost his sense because of impatience. While inflamed by anger he uttered such insolent words."

When Andrei's host passed by Smolensk the local prince Roman was forced to send his regiments and his son to join Andrei to fight against his brothers because he was in Andrei's hands. All the princes of Polotsk, Turov, Pinsk and Gorodets were ordered to go as well. In the Land of Chernigov the descendants of Oleg joined Andrei's host, then Yury's sons Mikhail and Vsevolod, their nephews Mstislav and Yaropolk Rostislavich, Vladimir Glebovich from Pereiaslavl, the Berendey and the men from the Ros river region. Altogether there were more than twenty princes. They crossed the Dnieper and entered Kiev unopposed because the sons of Rostislav chose not to defend themselves in the city but dispersed to their previous districts. Riurik shut himself up in Belgorod, Mstislav with Davyd's regiment was besieged in Vyshgorod, while Davyd himself went to Galich to seek help from Prince Yaroslav.

Senior in years and position in the clan among the allied princes was Sviatoslav Vsevolodovich of Chernigov. Because of his position he was given supreme command of all the troops. First he sent Vsevolod Yurievich with Igor Sviatoslavich of Severia and other junior princes to Vyshgorod. When they approached the town Mstislav Rostislavich deployed his regiments and rode against the enemy. Both sides were eager for battle, the archers already having let fly their arrows. Andrei's host was arranged in three sections. On one side stood the troops of Novgorod, on the other those from Rostov. In the middle stood Vsevolod Yurievich with his regiment. Mstislav, seeing his archers engage the enemy warriors, followed behind calling to his retinue "Brothers! Let's strike with the help of God and the holy martyrs Boris and Gleb!" They crushed Vsevolod's middle regiment and engaged the enemy, who surrounded this small force on all sides. A terrible disarray followed, says the chronicler, moans could be heard, shouts, some sort of strange voices, the crash of spears, the sound of swords. In the thick dust a rider could not be distinguished from a foot soldier. In the end, after fierce hand-to-hand fighting, the forces separated. Many were wounded, though only a few were killed. After this battle of the junior princes the remaining elders with their regiments approached Vyshgorod. Daily they renewed their attacks. Mstislav lost many of his best soldiers killed and wounded, but did not think about surrender. Thus the princes besieged Vyshgorod for nine weeks, when Yaroslav Iziaslavich of Lutsk with all forces of the Land of Volhynia appeared. He came to gain the seniority for himself, yet the descendants of Oleg refused to yield Kiev to him. Then he started negotiations with the sons of Rostislav. They ceded Kiev to him and he proceeded to Riurik in Belgorod.

Andrei's allies grew frightened, saying that the sons of Rostislav undoubtedly would join with the troops from Galich and the Karakalpaks to attack them. Among the troops a terrible confusion set in. Without waiting for dawn everybody rushed to cross the Dnieper, where many drowned. Mstislav, seeing the general flight, sallied from Vyshgorod with his retinue and attacked the enemy camp, taking many prisoners. "Thus did the whole force of Prince Andrei, and of Suzdal, return," says the chronicler. "He gathered all the lands, his army was countless. They marched with a haughty attitude and returned home humbled."

The reason for such unexpected success by the descendants of Rostislav is clear from the chronicle story. An enormous host marched in the hope of certain success. When first they realized that this success demanded great efforts, the high spirits of the besiegers were deflated. It is known from subsequent events that the population of the North was not distinguished by warlike spirit. The Smolensk regiments fought reluctantly, moreover it is highly unlikely that the men of Novgorod fought with great fervor. Neither did the princes of Polotsk, Turov, Pinsk and Gorodets, who were completely indifferent as to who won, Andrei or the descendants of Rostislav. Yury's sons scarcely could have fought zealously for their brother, with whom their relations were hardly friendly, especially when they saw that two princes, those of Chernigov and Volhynia, were arguing as to whom Kiev should fall.

It may be assumed that Andrei promised Kiev to Sviatoslav of Chernigov, for if he promised no one anything, no prince knew who would benefit from the victory of the prince of Suzdal over the sons of Rostislav, or upon whom the Northern tyrant would look favorably. It is clear how such uncertainty weakened the princes' resolve. They saw the princes of

Volhynia changing sides and throwing their support behind Rostislav's clan. This enabled the besieging troops to be attacked by Riurik from one side, from Belgorod, while Mstislav could do the same from Vyshgorod. Davyd might then arrive, bringing help from Galich. The Karakalpaks could cross over to the sons of Rostislav. It is not surprising that terror befell Andrei's combined host, which hastily recrossed the Dnieper.

YAROSLAV IZIASLAVICH RULES IN KIEV

After the victory Rostislav's sons fulfilled their promise. They handed seniority to Yaroslav and with it Kiev. He did not linger there for long in peace, for Sviatoslav Vsevolodovich of Chernigov sent him word saying "Remember our earlier agreement, to which you swore by kissing the cross. 'If I gain Kiev,' you told me, 'I will give you something. If you gain Kiev you will give me something.' Now you have gained Kiev by hook or by crook, give me something." "Why," replied Yaroslav, "do you need our patrimony? You do not need this land." "I am not a Hungarian or a Pole," retorted Sviatoslav. "We are the grandchildren of the same grandfather, and you are as removed from him as I am (in other words, we have the same level of seniority in the family hierarchy). If you refuse to keep our old agreement, let that be your say."

At a time when the descendants of Mstislav were fighting the new ambitions arising in the North, defending clan relationships between the senior prince and juniors, they faced a struggle against a prince in relation to whom they were in the position of innovators, violating the old order. This prince not only was defending the old clan relations between the senior and junior princes. He also called to mind the unity of all the descendants of Yaroslav. His struggle was for communal rule over the whole of the Land of Rus, whereas the sons of Mstislav merely wanted to keep Kiev forever.

YAROSLAV'S STRUGGLE AGAINST SVIATOSLAV OF CHERNIGOV

When the prince of Chernigov saw that Yaroslav refused to observe old agreements he decided, following the example of his father and uncle, to try to seize Kiev by force. The time was favorable. Andrei's influence over the South was lost. Rostislav's descendants, if by force of circumstance compelled to acknowledge Yaroslav's seniority, were indifferent to him, as were Yury's sons. Thus Sviatoslav united his forces with those of his brothers, appearing suddenly near Kiev. Yaroslav, loath to shut himself up alone in the city, escaped to Lutsk. The prince of Chernigov entered Kiev, captured Yaroslav's property, his wife and son as well as his retinue, sending them to Chernigov. He himself could not linger in Kiev because his cousin Oleg Sviatoslavich attacked the district of Chernigov, apparently wishing to succeed Sviatoslav, who conquered Kiev by chance (by foray) with no hope of staying there. Yaroslav feared the fate of Iziaslav Davydovich would befall him, hence he refused to abandon to his cousin his previous territory. He advanced against Oleg, burned his district and, as was his custom, caused much damage.

In the meantime Yaroslav, learning that Kiev had no prince, marched there again and in his anger wanted to seize from the people of Kiev what Sviatoslav had taken away from him. "You brought Sviatoslav against me," he said, "now find the means to ransom my princess and my son." When the people of Kiev did not know how to respond he ordered all of Kiev pillaged, the abbots, priests, monks, nuns, foreigners, merchants and even the hermits' cells. He had no cause to fear Sviatoslav who, preparing to attack Oleg, had made peace with Yaroslav to be free to defend his faithful territory.

At that time the descendants of Rostislav renewed their relations with Andrei. They knew, or at least should have guessed, how unfavorably he viewed the fall of Kiev to the hostile descendants of Iziaslav who refused to acknowledge his seniority. They decided to send requesting him to help their brother Roman, against whom he could feel no hostility, regain Kiev. "Wait awhile," Andrei replied, "I have sent to my brothers in Rus. When I have news from them I will give you an answer." These words make it clear that Andrei did not intend to leave the South in peace. He communicated with his brothers, probably planning new changes there. The sons of Rostislav took care that any changes were to their advantage. News from his brothers never came.

MURDER OF ANDREI BOGOLIUBSKY

Andrei expelled from his district his father's old boyars and surrounded himself with new. The commanding tone of voice he used even with the princes has been noted. It can be concluded that he was imperious and strict with those who surrounded him. Thus he sentenced to death one of his nearest relatives on his wife's side, a man called Kuchkovich. The brother of the executed man, Yakim, with his brother-in-law Peter and several other of the prince's servants then decided to free themselves from this strict master by an evil deed.

It also is known that the Rus princes accepted into their service men from other countries and nations. In this respect Andrei followed the example of other princes, willingly employing newcomers from Christian and non-Christian countries, Latins and Orthodox. He liked to show them his splendid church of the Mother of God in Vladimir, that infidels might see true Christianity and convert, which indeed many of them did.

Among these new converts was one man, a Yas[33] by nationality, called Anbal. He came to Andrei in a very sorry state, was taken into service as a steward and obtained great influence in the household. Among those close to Andrei there was a man called Yefrem Moizich, whose patronymic Moizich or Moiseevich points to his Jewish origin. These two oriental slaves are mentioned by the chronicler, together with Kuchkovich and his son-in-law, as ringleaders. Altogether there were twenty conspirators. "Today he executed Kuchkovich," said they, "tomorrow he will put us to death. Let us do something about this prince!" Apart from anger and fear for their own fate the conspirators might have been driven by envy of Andrei's favorite, a certain Prokopy. On Friday, June 28, 1174, at dinner time in the village of Bogoliubovo, where Andrei usually lived, the conspirators gathered in the house of Peter, Kuchkov's son-in-law. They decided to murder the prince the next day, during the night of the twenty-ninth.

At the appointed hour they armed themselves and entered Andrei's bedchamber, then grew frightened and fled from the antechamber to the cellar. There they got drunk. Their courage thus revived, they returned to the antechamber. They approached the door of the bedchamber and one of them called out to the prince "Sire! Sire!" to learn if Andrei was there. Andrei on hearing the voice shouted "Who is there?" and was answered, "Prokopy." "Boy!" said Andrei to the servitor[34] who slept in his room, "It's not Prokopy, is it?" The murderers heard Andrei's voice, battered on the door and broke it down. Andrei jumped up, tried to grab the sword he always kept close (it once belonged to St. Boris) but it was not there. Anbal the steward had stolen it during the day from the bedchamber. While Andrei sought his sword two murderers entered the bedchamber and attacked him. Andrei was a strong man and had brought one of them down when the rest ran in. Unable to distinguish who was who in the darkness, they wounded their own man who was lying on the floor. Then they attacked Andrei. He defended himself a long time, though they hacked him with swords, sabres and spears from every direction. "Villains," he shouted, "why do you want to do what Goriaser (the murderer of St. Gleb) did? What evil did I do to you? If you spill my blood on the ground, God will take revenge on you for the bread I have given you."

In the end Andrei succumbed to their blows. The murderers thought the deed was done, took their wounded man and left the bedroom trembling. As soon as they left Andrei stood up and staggered to the antechamber groaning loudly. The murderers heard these moans and returned. One of them said "I myself saw the prince leaving the antechamber." "So let's go and look for him," answered the others. They entered the bedchamber. Seeing he was not there, they said "We are lost! Let's look for him quickly." They lit some candles and found the prince by the trail of blood he left. Andrei was sitting behind the staircase pillar. Now the struggle could not last very long because he was weak from the wounds inflicted on him. Peter cut off his hand, others finished him off.

After murdering the prince the conspirators sought and killed his favorite, Prokopy. Then they proceeded to the antechamber and took the gold, precious stones, pearls, cloth and other property, loaded the horses and before dawn sent the spoil to their homes. They themselves took the prince's weapons and rallied the retinue around them, fearing that the people of Vladimir would attack them. To avoid this they planned to cause violence in the city, to sow discord and hostility among the citizens. With this aim they sent to tell them "Are you getting ready to attack us? We are ready to receive you and finish you off. We were not alone in killing the prince. Among you we have supporters." "If anyone is of the same mind as you," answered the men of Vladimir, "let him stay with you. We do not need him."

The murderers had no cause to be afraid. The men of Vladimir did not move against them. Without a prince and unsure of their future, unaccustomed to acting independently, they could take no decisive action. They waited to see what the senior cities would do. Meanwhile inaction incited unrest and looting everywhere. We know the murderers looted the prince's treasury. They were followed by the people of Bogoliubovo and other courtiers, who looted anything the conspirators left. Then they pillaged the church and palace builders whom Andrei had invited to Bogoliubovo, and robbed them. Plunder and killings engulfed the district. Burgraves and reeves, younger servants[35] and swordbearers[36] were robbed and beaten. The prospect of booty also made the villagers rise. They came to town and joined in the looting, which started also in Vladimir, then halted when the priests with the icon of the Mother of God passed in procession around the city. The chronicler wrote that the people beat and robbed burgraves and reeves, not understanding that where there is law there is also much injury.[37] This demonstrates that under Bogoliubsky's rule there was much injustice in the North.[38]

AFTERMATH OF ANDREI'S DEATH

As these disturbances continued the body of the murdered prince remained unburied. On the first day following the murder a devoted servitor of the prince, Kuzma of Kiev, went to the court. Seeing that the body was not where the prince was killed, he asked "Where is the prince?" He was given the answer "He is there in the orchard. Do not even dare to take him. Everybody wants to throw him to the dogs. If somebody wants to bury him, he is our enemy. We will kill him." Kuzma approached the body. "My lord! my lord!" he cried. "Why did you not sense that you had foul and dishonorable enemies, when they attacked you? Why couldn't you defeat them? Earlier you knew how to defeat the host of the pagan Bulgars."[39] As Kuzma was crying over the dead body, the steward Anbal approached him. Kuzma looked at him and said "Anbal, you are a son of the devil! Give at least a carpet or something else to put under and cover our lord." "Go away," answered Anbal, "we want to cast him to the dogs." "You heretic," answered Kuzma, "you want to throw him to the dogs? Don't you remember, you Yid,[40] in what clothes you arrived here? Now you are dressed in velvet while the prince lies naked. I ask you on my honor, give me something." He touched the conscience of Anbal, who gave him a carpet and a coat.

Kuzma wrapped the body and took it to the church. He begged that the church be opened, but he was told "Throw him in the vestibule, don't you have anything else to do but to carry on," for they were all drunk by now. "Sire," again cried Kuzma, "your slaves no longer want to know you. Merchants once visited from Byzantium or another country, from Rus or Latin lands. Whether Christian or pagan you ordered them taken to the church, to the vestry, to see true Christianity and convert. This indeed happened, for many were baptized. Bulgars, Jews and other pagans, when seeing God's glory and the church ornaments, cried for you terribly, yet these men will not let you lie in the church." Having wept awhile, Kuzma laid the body in the church vestibule, covered it with a coat and there it lay for two whole days. On the third day Abbot Arseny of the St. Cosmas and St. Damian monastery arrived. "How long," he said, "are we to wait for the senior abbots to act, how long is the prince to lie there? Open the church. I will pray over the prince and we will bury him. When this time of strife ends he will be taken to Vladimir."

The choir monks of Bogoliubovo arrived, carried the body into the church, placed it in a stone coffin and said prayers with Arseny. On the sixth day, when the riots in Vladimir subsided, citizens said to Abbot Feodul and Luke, precentor[41] of the church of the Mother of God, "Arrange for bearers. Let us take Andrei, our prince and lord." "Gather all your priests," they said to Archpriest Mikulitsa, "put on your vestments and come outside the Silver gate with the icon of the Holy Mother of God, and there wait for the prince." Feodul complied with their wishes. With the choir monks from the church and some people from Vladimir they travelled to Bogoliubovo, took the body and transported it to Vladimir with great honors and much wailing. When they recognized from afar the princely banner carried before the coffin the people of Vladimir waiting at the Silver gate could not hide their tears and said "It is not to Kiev that you are going, lord, into that church at the Golden gate, which you ordered built at the great court of Yaroslav. 'I want to build a church just like it,' you said, 'at the Golden gate of Vladimir, and this will be in memory of my father's line.'" Andrei was buried in the church of the Mother of God, which he himself had built (1174).[42]

RIVALRY OF ROSTOV AND VLADIMIR

As soon as the news of Andrei's death spread through his district the people of Rostov, Suzdal, Pereiaslavl and his retinue, the young and the old, came to Vladimir saying "There is nothing we can do. What is done is done. Our prince was killed, he has no children here, his young son is in Novgorod, his brothers are in Rus. Which prince should we send for? Our neighbors are the princes of Murom and Riazan. We must beware lest they attack us suddenly. Let us send to the prince of Riazan, Gleb (Rostislavich), and say to him, 'Our Prince was taken away by God, so we want Rostislav's sons Mstislav and Yaropolk, your brothers-in-law' (sons of the older son of Yury)." They forgot, says the chronicler, that they had kissed the cross to Yury to grant their throne to his younger sons Mikhail and Vsevolod. They breached their sacred promise and put Andrei on the throne. His younger brothers were expelled. Now, after Andrei's death, they did not recall their former oath. Everybody listened to Dedilets and Boris, envoys from Riazan. What was decided was done. They kissed the icon of the Mother of God and sent to Gleb to tell him

"Your brothers-in-law will be our princes. Send your envoys and ours together to Rus."

Gleb was overjoyed by this honor, that his brothers-in-law were chosen to be princes. He sent his envoys to Chernigov, where they resided at that time. "Your father was good when he lived in our land," said the envoys from the Northern retinue to Rostislav's sons, "come to be princes in our land. We do not want any others." The "others" were Yury's younger sons Mikhail and Vsevolod, who at that time also lived in Chernigov. It seems all four, uncles and nephews, moved there together with Sviatoslav after the siege of Vyshgorod, not daring to return to their former districts on the Ros river. "Let God help the retinue," replied the descendants of Rostislav to the envoys, "which has not forgotten the love of our father. Although only the sons were asked to go, they refused to leave without their uncles, the sons of Yury. 'We're all in this together for good or ill,' they said. 'All four of us will go, the two sons of Yury and the two sons of Rostislav.'"

The first two to depart were Mikhail Yurievich and Yaropolk Rostislavich. Mikhail was given seniority, yet all kissed the cross held by the bishop of Chernigov. When the princes arrived in Moscow the people of Rostov grew angry on hearing that Yury's sons arrived together with those of Rostislav. They sent to Yaropolk and told him "Come here," and to Mikhail "Tarry awhile in Moscow." Yaropolk without telling his uncle moved to Pereiaslavl, where the retinue sent to meet the princes was at that time. Mikhail, when he learned that Yaropolk Rostislavich travelled on the Rostov road, withdrew to Vladimir and locked himself in the city alone with the citizens because the Vladimir retinue which numbered fifteen hundred also had gone to Pereiaslavl on orders from Rostov. There the entire retinue swore an oath on the cross to Yaropolk and set out with him to Vladimir to expel Mikhail from the city. The regiments from Murom and Riazan joined forces with all the forces of the Land of Rostov. The surrounding areas were burned, the city was besieged.

What inspired the people of Vladimir, unaccustomed to independent action, to oppose the decision of senior cities, take a separate prince and defend him against the combined forces of the Rostov and Riazan lands? They were forced to this because of the openly expressed hostility of the old city of Rostov, which looked with hatred at its bytown, populated mostly by simple people, artisans who made their living from Prince Andrei's building enterprises. Moreover, it deprived the older city the honor of having the princely seat. "Let us burn Vladimir," the people of

Rostov and Suzdal used to say, "or send our burgrave there. They are our slaves,[43] stonemasons." It should be noticed that these words conveyed chiefly the opinion of the higher strata of the inhabitants of Rostov, the boyars and the retinue in general, who apparently particularly disliked Andrei because of his innovations. Be that as it may, the important thing was the beginning of the struggle between the old and the new cities. This struggle was to resolve the question of the permanent location of the princely throne, in old Rostov or in new Vladimir. On this all development of the history of the North depended. Other new towns, as was to be expected, joined Vladimir. The people of Pereiaslavl also wanted Yury's sons, for their subjection to the sons of Rostislav was against their will.

For seven weeks the people of Vladimir defended themselves against the besieging troops. In the end hunger forced them to say to Mikhail "Seek peace or take care of yourself." "You are right," answered Mikhail, "you are not to die for me." He left the city and departed to Rus. The chronicler says that the people of Vladimir saw him off with great sorrow. After his departure they made an agreement with Rostislav's descendants, who had sworn to cause no harm to the city. The people of Vladimir opened their gates and met the princes, carrying crosses. The final agreement was concluded in the church of the Mother of God. Rostislav's younger son Yaropolk stayed as prince in Vladimir, while the older Mstislav went to Rostov.

Thus thanks to the courage of the people of Vladimir, Rostov gained only a partial victory. It is true that the seat of the older brother was established in their city, yet the hateful bytown gained its own prince, not a burgrave from Rostov. The people of Rostov, in particular the boyars who were forced to yield to the demands of the people of Vladimir, continued to be hostile, challenging them to renew the struggle so important to the fate of the North.

The Southern districts quite often suffered inconvenience when princes moved, bringing their retinue and servitors whom they appointed to various positions. These men sought riches as quickly as possible at the expense of the citizens because they knew they would not stay long. Now the North in turn experienced this harassment. The sons of Rostislav came to the Land of Rostov with their retinue recruited in the South, appointing its members as burgraves. These Rus (meaning Southerners), young servants, as the chronicler calls them, soon became a heavy burden on the people because of the court fines they imposed and the bribes they took.

It was not only from the young Rus servants that the people of Vladimir suffered. The princes, says the chronicler, were young and listened to the boyars, who taught them to take as much as possible. Thus, for example, they took gold and silver from the church of the Mother of God in Vladimir. On the very first day they took the keys from the vestry, confiscating the towns and the entire tax money Prince Andrei had granted to this church.

It is clear that, apart from greed, hatred of Andrei's memory also played a part, hatred of everything he had done. They wanted to loot the cathedral in Vladimir, a splendid monument to himself left by Andrei. The princes and their retinues looted churches only in conquered towns. It is easy to understand how the people of Vladimir felt after their cathedral, their best ornament, the pride of their city, was looted. They gathered and said to each other "We accepted the princes in good faith. They kissed the cross, swearing not to cause any evil to our city. Now they behave as if they don't govern their own district, as if they don't wish to stay here for long. They are looting not only the district, yet even the churches. Let's do something, brothers." These words suggest that the people of Vladimir were offended not just that the princes treated their district as a conquered country. They also feared that Yaropolk, having looted the district, might leave altogether and Rostov would send a burgrave to rule them. "The prince behaves as though he had no wish to rule here," they kept saying.

Acting according to ancient custom the people of Vladimir turned to the older cities, Rostov and Suzdal, to complain. Rostov and Suzdal supported them in word only, having no intention of intervening on their behalf. The boyars firmly supported descendants of Rostislav, adds the chronicler, thus informing us that it was mainly the boyars who wanted to run things differently than in Andrei's time. When Vladimir saw the open malevolence of the senior cities and the boyars they decided to act independently together with Pereiaslavl and sent to Mikhail in Chernigov, saying "You are the senior among the brothers. Come to us in Vladimir. Should the people of Rostov and Suzdal conspire against us because of you, we will deal with them as God and the Mother of God will." Accompanied by his brother Vsevolod and Vladimir Sviatoslavich, son of the prince of Chernigov, Mikhail proceeded to the North. He barely covered eleven versts[44] after leaving Chernigov before he fell ill and was still sick when he arrived in Moscow. There a detachment of Vladimir troops with the young prince Yury Andreevich, son of Bogoliubsky, who lived among them after being expelled from Novgorod, was waiting for him.

VICTORY FOR MIKHAIL YURIEVICH AND VLADIMIR

In the meantime the sons of Rostislav, having learned of Mikhail's approach, took counsel in Suzdal with their retinue. They decided to send Yaropolk with his troops against Yury's sons in Moscow, to engage them and not let them through to Vladimir. Mikhail just had sat down to dine when the news arrived that his nephew Yaropolk was coming to fight against him. Yury's sons gathered their troops and took the Vladimir trail to meet the enemy, but missed Yaropolk in the forests. Then the Muscovites, learning that Yaropolk had bypassed their forces and was continuing towards Moscow, turned back to defend their homes, leaving Mikhail. Yaropolk, realizing he had missed Mikhail, set off from Moscow in pursuit. Meanwhile he sent a message to his brother Mstislav in Suzdal. "Mikhalko is ill," he said, "he is being carried on a stretcher and his retinue is small. I am following him, capturing his rearguard units. You, my brother, advance on him as soon as possible, to prevent him entering Vladimir." Mstislav relayed this news to his retinue and the following morning left Suzdal very early. He hurried as though hunting hares, causing the retinue difficulty keeping up with him. Five versts before Vladimir he met the sons of Yury. Mstislav's host, ready for battle, fully armed with their banner raised, suddenly moved from the village of Zagorie.

Mikhail hastily arranged his troops, while the enemy advanced shouting loudly as if they wanted to devour his retinue, as the chronicler put it. This courage was short-lived. When the battle started and the bowmen loosed arrows from both sides, Mstislav's retainers, without engaging with the enemy even once, dropped their banner and fled. Yury's sons took many prisoners and could have taken many more because the victors had difficulty in distinguishing friend from foe. Mstislav escaped to Novgorod while Yaropolk, hearing about Mstislav's rout, escaped to Riazan. Their mother and wives were taken prisoner by the people of Vladimir. Mikhail entered Vladimir with honor and glory, his retinue and the citizens who took part in the battle leading the prisoners.

The first thing Yury's sons did was to return to their owner the towns confiscated by Yaropolk from the church of the Mother of God. There was, says the chronicler, great rejoicing in Vladimir when again they witnessed the grand prince of all the Land of Rostov in their city. "Let us marvel," continued the chronicler, "at the new great and famous miracle of the Mother of God, how she defended her city from great trouble and strengthened its citizens. God did not make them fearful, they were unafraid of the two princes and their boyars, heeding not their threats. They lived without their prince for seven weeks, placing all their hope in the Holy Mother of God and their own righteousness.

"The people of Novgorod, Smolensk, Kiev and Polotsk and all the authorities came to the town assembly like to a council, and what the senior towns decided the bytowns followed. Yet in the senior cities, Rostov and Suzdal, the boyars wanted to establish their own rule, not following God's. 'We will do what we like,' said they. 'Vladimir is our bytown.' They came out against God, the Mother of God and God's truth, they listened to evil men, sowers of dissension who did not wish us well because they were envious. The people of Rostov and Suzdal did not know how to observe the truth of God, thinking that because they were the senior towns they might do what they wanted. The new people, the poor people of Vladimir, understood where truth resided, and held to it. 'Either we have Mikhail as our prince,' they said, 'or we will sacrifice our lives for the Holy Mother of God and for Prince Mikhail.' God and the Holy Mother of God consoled them. The people of Vladimir became famous in the land for their righteousness."

Soon envoys from Suzdal appeared in Vladimir to see Mikhail. "We, prince," they said, "did not fight against you with Mstislav, only our boyars were with him. Do not be angry with us, come to us." Mikhail went to Suzdal and from there to Rostov. He arranged an agreement with the people, confirmed it by kissing the cross, and accepted many gifts from Rostov. Placing his brother Vsevolod in Pereiaslavl, he returned to Vladimir. Thus the last bytown settled by "slave-stonemasons" once more was the capital of the entire Land of Rostov. Once more the prince freed himself of the influence of cities accustomed to deciding matters in the assembly, whose decisions were observed by the lesser towns. Moreover Mikhail's younger brother Vsevolod went to rule in the new town of Pereiaslavl-Zalessk, not in Rostov. Was this move an expression of open preference shown by the princes for the new towns over the old, or did he want to reward the zeal of the people of Pereiaslavl, who had joined the people of Vladimir? Whatever the case, this development was very important as evidence of the complete victory of the bytowns and total defeat of a custom capable of opposing the new order.

Mikhail's priority after his entry into Vladimir was to return to the cathedral the towns confiscated by the sons of Rostislav. Next, after establishing himself in all the Land of Rostov, he had to attack Prince Gleb of Riazan, who held many treasures looted from this church, among them the actual icon of the Mother of God brought by Andrei from Vyshgorod, as well as books. Mikhail set off with his regiments against Riazan. On the way he met Gleb's envoys, who were instructed to tell him "Prince Gleb bows to you and says 'I am guilty, so now I return everything I took from my brothers-in-law, the sons of Rostislav, to the last penny.'" This he did. Mikhail made peace with him, returning to Vladimir where, according to some fairly reliable information, he executed the murderers of Andrei. Then for some reason he visited Gorodets on the Volga, where he fell ill and died (1176).

RENEWAL OF STRUGGLE AFTER MIKHAIL'S DEATH

The people of Rostov without even waiting for confirmation of Mikhail's death sent a message to Novgorod, to their previous prince, Mstislav Rostislavich. "Come, prince, to us," they said. "Mikhalko was taken by God on the Volga at Gorodets. We want you and nobody else." Mstislav responded to this call, gathered the people of Rostov, then set off against Vladimir. There was already a prince in the city, for immediately after Mikhail's death the people of Vladimir gathered before the Golden gate and, remembering the old oath given to Yury Dolgoruky, swore an oath by kissing the cross to Vsevolod Yurievich and to his children. This was a curious development in that the people of Vladimir not only swore an oath to Vsevolod, but also to his children. It meant that they were unafraid, as were the people of Kiev, to pass an inheritance from father to son, having no second thought about their right to choose a prince. Vsevolod, learning of the arrival of a son of Rostislav in Rostov, gathered the men of Vladimir, his retinue, the boyars who stayed with him (the majority of the boyars, it seems, went over to the prince of Rostov) and set off against the enemy. He sent his nephew Yaroslav Mstislavich to gather and bring to him the men of Pereiaslavl.

It was not in his character to trust his future entirely to fortune in battle. He did not want trial by combat to decide between him and his nephew, the way the Southern princes liked to solve their disputes. First he sent a message to Mstislav Rostislavich. "O brother!" said he. "If you were brought by the senior retinue, go to Rostov and we will make peace there. You were brought here by the people of Rostov and the boyars. My brother and I were brought here by God and by the people of Vladimir and Pereiaslavl. Let the people of Suzdal choose which of us they want."

The men of Rostov and the boyars would not let their prince make peace. Their anger at Vladimir and Yury's sons only grew thanks to the recent humiliation. "If you want to make peace with him," they said to Mstislav Rostislavich, "we refuse." The boyars Dobrynia Dolgy, Mateiash Butovich and others did all in their power to incite to war. Vsevolod after this rebuff proceeded to Yuriev, where he waited for the men of Pereiaslavl. He announced to them that Rostov rejected peace. "You wanted to favor Mstislav," the men of Pereiaslavl answered, "yet he seeks your life. Therefore, O prince, advance to attack him, and we will not spare our lives for your cause. God forbid that any of us turn back. If there is no help from God, let them step over our dead bodies and take our wives and children. It is only nine days since your brother died, yet already they want to spill blood." On the field of Yuriev, on the other bank of the Kza river, the battle took place. The men of Vladimir with their prince again were victorious and their losses were very small. On the enemy side a number of boyars were killed, others were taken prisoner. Mstislav himself escaped first to Rostov and from there to Novgorod. The victors took the boyars' villages, horses and cattle. For the second and now last time the old city was defeated by the new. Thereafter it ceased to advance any more claims.

FINAL FALL OF ROSTOV

Victory on the field of Yuriev did not end the struggle between Vsevolod and his nephews. When Mstislav Rostislavich arrived in Novgorod, the inhabitants rebuffed him. "When the people of Rostov called you," they said, "you turned your back on Novgorod, going against your uncle Mikhail. He died, and in your quarrel with his brother Vsevolod God judged you. Why then have you come to us now?"

Mstislav, rejected by the people of Novgorod, went to his brother-in-law Gleb of Riazan, there inciting him to war against Vsevolod. That very autumn Gleb attacked Moscow and burned the city. Vsevolod advanced to confront him but when he passed Pereiaslavl people from Novgorod arrived. "O prince!" they said. "Do not go without men of Novgorod, wait for them." Vsevolod was always careful, seeking to act without taking risks. Therefore he agreed to wait for the Novgorod contingent in order to have twice the force to attack his enemies. He withdrew, but waited in vain for the Novgorod levies. Instead two princes of Chernigov, Oleg and Vladimir Sviatoslavich, came to his help, as well as Vladimir Glebovich, the prince of Southern or Rus Pereiaslavl.[45] Vsevolod advanced with them to Kolomna where he received information that Gleb, with Polovetsians, had taken another route to Vladimir, looted the cathedral of St. Andrew and burned other churches and boyars' villages, giving the wives and children and other goods to the pagans as spoils of war. Vsevolod immediately returned to his district, encountering Gleb on the Kolaksha river.

For a month the enemies stood on opposite river banks without attempting any action. Finally the battle started, and Vsevolod prevailed once more. Mstislav Rostislavich was the first to flee. He was followed by Gleb, then their enemies caught up. They took both prisoner, also Gleb's son Roman and the entire Riazan retinue. Among other prisoners was Boris Zhidislavich, Bogoliubsky's infamous governor who apparently had gone to Riazan, either directly or together with the sons of Rostislav, not wishing to serve Yury's sons. Also taken was Dedilets who, following the death of Bogoliubsky, strongly supported bringing Rostislav's sons to Rostov. There was great joy in Vladimir, says the chronicler, adding immediately that there was judgment without mercy for those who had shown no mercy themselves.

These words are evidence of the feelings of the people of Vladimir, whose hatred of Gleb and the sons of Rostislav reached its highest pitch following the newest calamity they had suffered. Two days they waited for Vsevolod to dispense judgement without mercy to the nephews. On the third day they mutinied. "O prince," the boyars and the merchants said to him, "we wish you well and we would sacrifice our lives for you, yet you let your enemies alone, your enemies and ours, the men of Suzdal and Rostov. Either execute or blind them, or give them to us." Vsevolod refused this demand. To pacify the rebellion, he merely ordered the prisoners of war confined, then sent word to Riazan, saying "Give me our enemy (Yaropolk Rostislavich) or I will come to you." They decided to obey him. "Our prince and our brothers," they said, "died for the sake of a prince who was a stranger." They went to Voronezh where they captured Yaropolk, brought him to Vladimir, where Vsevolod also ordered him imprisoned.

In the meantime Gleb of Riazan's brother-in-law, the famous Mstislav Rostislavich of Smolensk, sent a message to Sviatoslav of Chernigov to intercede with Vsevolod for the descendants of Rostislav. The princess of Riazan, Gleb's wife, sent the same plea, asking for her husband and son. Sviatoslav dispatched to Vladimir his emissaries, Bishop Porfiry of Chernigov and Abbot Efrem, to negotiate the fate of the prisoners of war. He proposed that after being freed Gleb renounce his claims to Riazan and live in Rus. Gleb refused. "I'd rather die in prison," he said, "than go as an exile to Rus." This matter dragged on for two years. In the interval Gleb died and his son Roman was set free and allowed to go to Riazan on condition of full subordination to the prince of Vladimir.

The fate of Rostislav's sons was decided differently. The men of Vladimir, having learned that negotiations were in progress about the release of the prisoners, refused to let them go without extracting revenge for their offenses. A large crowd gathered and marched to see Vsevolod at his court, saying to him "Why do you still keep them? We want to blind them." Vsevolod did not much like this demand, but nothing could be done. His men blinded Rostislav's sons, or at least pretended they did so, and sent them to Smolensk.[46]

Thus the struggle in the North ended with the victory of the last of Yury's sons, who now was as strong as his brother Andrei and immediately followed in his brother's footsteps. After bending the princes of Riazan to his will he desired also to become autocrat in the land of Suzdal, the sole beneficiary of all of his father's inheritance. He therefore exiled from his district his nephew Yury Andreevich, who was forced to seek his fortune in Georgia. His second nephew, Yaroslav Mstislavich, also failed to receive a district in the land of Rostov. Had Vsevolod fully followed the example of Andrei in the North we might expect that in relation to Southern, old Rus and Novgorod the Great he would have acquired the same stature.

WAR IN THE SOUTH BETWEEN THE DESCENDANTS OF MONOMAKH AND OLEG

In the South Andrei's death allowed the previous struggle between the descendants of Monomakh and those of Oleg to flare up again. This struggle was intensified both by the hostile relationships within Oleg's branch of the family, and the hostility between descendants of Rostislav and Iziaslav within Monomakh's branch. Sviatoslav Vsevolodovich of Chernigov was forced to abandon his plans concerning Kiev in order more freely to defend his district of Chernigov against his cousin Oleg of Severia. Taking his revenge on Oleg for the devastation he had caused, he returned to Chernigov. Oleg did not think to leave matters at that. He entered into alliance with his brothers-in-law the sons of Rostislav, as well as with Yaroslav of Kiev.

The allies decided to attack Sviatoslav from two directions. Rostislav's sons and Yaroslav, having burned Chernigov towns, made peace with Sviatoslav, leaving Oleg to his own devices. He and his brothers proceeded to Starodub. They failed to take the town, then from the surrounding area captured cattle, which they drove to Novgorod Seversk. There Sviatoslav soon arrived with the army of Chernigov and approached the town. Oleg came to meet them but his retinue hardly loosed an arrow before turning their backs on the enemy and fleeing. The prince barely escaped into the town. Half of his retinue was captured, the other half killed, and the stockade burned.

The following day Oleg asked for peace. His request was granted, but the conditions remain unknown. In the meantime there was a change on the other side of the Dnieper. The eldest son of Rostislav, Roman of Smolensk, came to the rescue. Thus did Yaroslav Iziaslavich realize the intent of the sons of Rostislav to oust him from Kiev. "You have brought your brother Roman," he protested, "you are giving him Kiev." He abandoned the city of his own accord for his previous district of Lutsk.

The descendants of Rostislav had besought Andrei even earlier to give Kiev to Roman. Yaroslav hence had the right to suspect them of hostile intentions. His prompt cession to his cousins might be explained by the fact that he could not count on the support of Kiev after his latest act there, namely his looting of the entire city. Rostislav's sons sent for him to return to Kiev. He refused, therefore Roman took his place. Whether the sons of Rostislav indeed refused to oust him or merely pretended, it is difficult to say.

Roman was not left to rule in Kiev for long. The Polovetsians attacked Rus, took six Berendey towns and dealt a considerable blow to Rostislav's sons. Davyd Rostislavich was to blame, for the quarrel he started with his brothers prevented a completely successful defense. Sviatoslav of Chernigov hastened to exploit the difficulties of Rostislav's family, for which an excuse was needed. He sent the following message to Roman. "O brother! I do not seek anything against you, but it is customary that if a prince is guilty he pays with his district. If a boyar is guilty he pays with his head. Davyd is guilty, take his district from him." Since Roman paid no heed, Sviatoslav's brothers Yaroslav and Oleg crossed the Dnieper, conveying a message to his own son-in-law Mstislav Vladimirovich, son of the deceased Vladimir Mstislavich, to join them. Mstislav heeded their plea and surrendered Tripolie to them.

Meanwhile Sviatoslav himself stood with his regiments near Vitichi, where the Karakalpaks and the men of Kiev arrived to tell him that Roman had departed for Belgorod. Sviatoslav advanced to Kiev and ruled there, but again not for long. The famous Mstislav of Smolensk came to help his brothers. The sons of Rostislav announced that next day they would do battle with Sviatoslav.

Sviatoslav took fright and escaped across the Dnieper because the Polovetsians for whom he had sent had not arrived. He dared not move against Mstislav with only his own retinue. Rostislav's sons then decided that it would be better to let Sviatoslav keep Kiev. Roman apparently was not a very bellicose prince. He knew he must rule Kiev in constant fear of Sviatoslav, who had expelled him once already and, of course, would not abandon attempts to conquer Kiev. Permanent internecine wars would ensue. Sviatoslav's Polovetsian allies already were in Torchesk and had captured many people. The sons of Rostislav, according to the words of the chronicler, not wishing to bring disasters to the Land of Rus and spill Christian blood, considered every avenue. Ultimately they gave Kiev to Sviatoslav, while Roman returned to Smolensk. It seems that Chernigov fell to Oleg Sviatoslavich, but he soon died and Yaroslav Vsevolodovich, brother of the Kievan prince, went to rule there. Oleg's brother Igor went to rule in Novgorod Seversk. This arrangement was according to clan order.

SVIATOSLAV VSEVOLODOVICH OF CHERNIGOV AGAINST VSEVOLOD

Hitherto Sviatoslav Vsevolodovich lived in friendship with Vsevolod of Suzdal. He actively helped him in his struggle with his nephews, this alliance strengthened by a family bond. Vsevolod summoned Sviatoslav's son Vladimir and married him to his own niece, a daughter of Mikhail Yurievich. Soon this friendship turned into hostility because of developments in Riazan. Roman Glebovich and his brothers had sworn to submit to Vsevolod's will, but Roman was Sviatoslav's son-in-law who, because of this family connection, considered he had the right to interfere in Riazan affairs. His influence also clashed with that of Vsevolod. Sviatoslav may have thought that Vsevolod, grateful for earlier favors, would surrender his influence in Riazan. He was deceived cruelly in his expectations.

In 1180 the younger brothers of Roman of Riazan, Vsevolod and Vladimir Glebovich, sent to tell Vsevolod Yurievich of Vladimir "You are our lord and father. Our older brother Roman takes our districts because he listens to his father-in-law, yet he swore an oath to you by kissing the cross, then broke his oath." Vsevolod immediately set out on campaign. When he approached Kolomna the two sons of Gleb greeted him bowing, although Sviatoslav's son Gleb remained in Kolomna where he was sent by his father to help Roman of Riazan. Vsevolod asked Gleb to come to him. At first Gleb hesitated. When he realized resistance was futile, he obeyed. Vsevolod ordered him arrested and sent him in irons to Vladimir, where he was kept under guard. His retinue suffered the same fate.

Meanwhile the vanguard of Roman's host, having crossed the Oka river, suffered defeat from the forward units of Vsevolod's forces. Part of the host was taken prisoner, part drowned in the river. Roman, hearing of the disaster, escaped past Riazan to the steppe, entrusting the defense of the city to his two brothers Igor and Sviatoslav, who did not even consider opposing Vsevolod when he appeared before Riazan. They made peace on his terms. The prince of Vladimir made arrangements between the brothers, distributing the districts according to seniority before returning home.

It is easy to understand Sviatoslav's anger when he learned of Vsevolod's actions against his son. The less he expected this, the greater his anger. He was furious. According to the chronicler he said "I would take revenge on Vsevolod, but it is impossible. Rostislav's sons are near me, they cause me annoyance in the Land of Rus in every possible way, but it is all the same to me. Whoever is nearest me from the Vladimir branch is mine."

From these words it is clear that Sviatoslav did not like very much the close proximity of the descendants of Rostislav, who surrounded him. Meanwhile Davyd Rostislavich was hunting with boats on the Dnieper, and Sviatoslav hunted opposite him on the Chernigov side. This opportunity seemed to the prince of Kiev favorable to execute his plan. He took counsel only with the princess and his favorite Kochkar. Without saying a word to his senior boyars, he crossed the Dnieper and attacked Davyd's camp, thinking "I will capture Davyd, expel Riurik, and rule the entire Land of Rus with my brothers, then take revenge on Vsevolod for his offense."

The plan failed. Davyd and his wife got into a boat and sailed away. Enemy arrows caused him no harm. Sviatoslav captured only Davyd's retinue and camp and proceeded to Vyshgorod. After spending the night near that town, he looked for Davyd everywhere. After a prolonged but unsuccessful search he crossed to the eastern side of the Dnieper, saying to his followers "Now that I have declared war upon the sons of Rostislav, I can stay no longer in Kiev."

Reaching Chernigov he called all his sons and younger brothers, gathered all the forces of Chernigov, all his retinue and told them "Where should we go? To Smolensk or to Kiev?" His first cousin Igor of Seversk answered him "Little father! It would have been better had we made peace. As it did not turn out that way, God grant you health." "I am older than Yaroslav," Sviatoslav then said, "and you, Igor, are older than Vsevolod. So now I am in place of a father to you and I order you, Igor, to stay with Yaroslav here, to defend all the district, while I will go with Vsevolod to Suzdal to rescue my son Gleb. Let God judge between me and Vsevolod Yurievich."

Sviatoslav also divided the Polovetsians into two detachments. He took one with him, the other he left with his brothers. Thereupon he set off taking with him Yaropolk Rostislavich. Near the mouth of the Tvertsa river he was joined by his son Vladimir and the host from Novgorod (because Vladimir at that time ruled in Novgorod). In the chronicler's words, he devastated everything along the Volga, burned all the towns and at a distance of forty versts from Pereiaslavl Zalessk, on the Vlena river, then met with Vsevolod, who came out against him with the hosts from Suzdal, Riazan and Murom.

In earlier times the princes preferred to be at the head of their troops, wanted to move first into the enemy formations, hastened to decide the matter by combat, which they regarded as God's judgment. Vsevolod was guided by different considerations. He had chosen a convenient position, surrounded by hills and gullies. He disregarded the pleas of his retinue and refused decisive battle with the Southern forces, who distinguished themselves by their dashing attacks, whereas the Northerners were quite the opposite. They were weak in open field but invincible defending fortified places. Vsevolod sent forth only the princes of Riazan, who broke through to Sviatoslav's baggage train and initially seemed successful, then later were chased away with great losses. They stood thus for two weeks opposing each other, exchanging arrows across the river.

Finally Sviatoslav grew restive and sent his priests to tell Vsevolod "Brother and son! I did much good to you. I did not expect to receive from you such ingratitude. If you wish me harm and want to capture my son, you haven't got far to look for me. Move away from this river, let me move to the other side, and God will judge between us. If you refuse to let me move to the other side, I will let you cross the river and let God decide." Instead of sending an answer, Vsevolod kept the envoys, sent them to Vladimir and stayed put as before. Sviatoslav stood there for some time. Then, fearing the thaw, he retreated, travelling lightly. He abandoned his baggage trains, which were captured by Vsevolod's forces. Following their prince's orders they dared not chase the retreating Sviatoslav who, having sent Vsevolod's brother, Oleg's son, and Yaropolk Rostislavich to Rus, proceeded with his son Vladimir to Novgorod the Great.

SVIATOSLAV GAINS A FOOTHOLD IN KIEV

Davyd Rostislavich meanwhile, having escaped capture by Sviatoslav, arrived in Belgorod to join his brother Riurik who, hearing that Kiev was abandoned by Sviatoslav, hastened there and sat on his father's and grandfather's throne. Because he expected a difficult struggle, he began to recruit allies. He sent for the princes of Lutsk, Vsevolod and Ingvar the sons of Yaroslav, and brought them to his side. He sought help from Yaroslav, prince of Galich, who arrived with his boyar Tudor, and he sent his brother Davyd to help their older brother Roman. On the way Davyd met a messenger with the news of Roman's death. Davyd continued on his way with tears in his eyes. When he entered Smolensk he was met by clergy with crosses and by the townsmen, and occupied his brother's throne. According to the chronicler, all Smolensk mourned Roman, remembering his kindness, and his princess stood by his coffin. "My good tsar," she wailed, "good, gentle, humble and true! Truly the name Roman suited you, you were similar in kindness to St. Roman (meaning St. Boris).[47] You were annoyed many times by the people of Smolensk, yet I never saw you render evil for evil." The chronicler repeats that this prince was unusually kind and true.

Davyd, after his brother's funeral, had to think first of the defense of his district because the princes in Chernigov, Yaroslav and Igor, seeing no attacks on their district, decided to march on the Land of Smolensk. First they moved with Polovetsians against Drutsk, the seat of Gleb Rogvolodovich, an ally of the Rostislav's sons. Although one of the princes of Polotsk supported the sons of Rostislav, the majority of his clan was against them. This was a quarrel among three branches or lines, the descendants of Boris, Gleb and Vasilko. At the same time the descendants of Rostislav of Smolensk actively supported the heirs of Boris and Vasilko. Now, as a result of family ties with the Northern branch of Rostislav's clan, the sons of Vasilko were in alliance with the princes of

Chernigov against the Smolensk branch of Rostislav's descendants. Near Drutsk the Chernigov regiments were joined by Vseslav Vasilkovich of Polotsk, his brother Briachislav of Vitebsk and some other clan members with a crowd of Livs[48] and Lithuanians.

The alliance of the princes of Chernigov with the princes of Polotsk placed the Polovetsians in the same camp with the Livs and Lithuanians, the Black Sea barbarians with the Baltic barbarians. Davyd of Smolensk arrived with all the regiments in Drutsk, where Gleb had been, wishing to battle the Chernigov forces before Sviatoslav arrived from Novgorod, but Yaroslav and Igor dared not start the battle without Sviatoslav. They chose a convenient position on the bank of the Drucha river and stood there for a week, exchanging arrows with the enemy over the river. On Sviastoslav's arrival they built a pontoon bridge over the Drucha to cross and attack Davyd, who refused to fight and fled to Smolensk. Sviatoslav approached Drutsk, burned the fortifications, but did not tarry there. Having sent the Novgorod troops away, he marched to Rogachev, whence he sailed on the Dnieper to Kiev. All that time Igor with the Polovetsians awaited him opposite Vyshgorod.

When Riurik learned of Sviatoslav's approach he moved from Kiev to Belgorod, sending his troops against the Polovetsians, who with Igor of Seversk were camped near the Dolobsk lake. The troops were headed by Prince Mstislav Vladimirovich, accompanied by Riurik's chiliarch Lazar with the junior retinue. The forces included Boris Zakharich, the favorite commander of Mstislav the Brave, the followers of the young Prince Vladimir, whom his father on his deathbed asked the commander to protect, and Sdeslav Zhiroslavich, a commander of Mstislav Vladimirovich, with the regiments from Tripolie.

The number of Polovetsians was considerable. They camped without precautions, without posting guards, trusting in their strength and in Igor's host. The Karakalpaks, not heeding the orders of the Rus commanders, attacked the Polovetsians, cutting into their camp, then were thrown back and in fleeing were entangled with Mstislav's retinue, who also turned to flight followed by the prince. The best men, namely Boris Zakharich and Sdeslav Zhiroslavich, stood fast. Without hesitation they attacked the Polovetsians and trampled them. Many barbarians drowned in the Chartoryia river, others were killed or taken prisoner. Prince Igor took a boat and crossed to the eastern bank. Riurik used this victory only to obtain an advantageous peace settlement with Sviatoslav, from whom he did not hope to wrest the seniority. Sviatoslav also did not wish to leave Kiev once more. He was pleased by the proposal of Riurik, who yielded him seniority and Kiev, allowing for himself all the Land of Rus, namely all the remaining towns of the Kiev district.

A peace agreement with Vsevolod of Suzdal followed. Vsevolod returned to Sviatoslav his son Gleb. Peace between the descendants of Monomakh and the descendants of Oleg was confirmed by a double family alliance. One of Sviatoslav's sons, Gleb, married a princess from Riurik's family, the other, Mstislav, married Vsevolod's sister-in-law (1182).

WEAKNESS OF THE KIEVAN PRINCE IN RELATION TO SUZDAL

Thus the son of Vsevolod Olgovich finally succeeded in affirming his seniority in Kiev, a seniority of significance only in the South. The senior prince in Monomakh's clan did not struggle with Sviatoslav for Kiev which had lost for him the significance it once had for his father Yury. Vsevolod inherited all the sway of that prince, who granted Kiev to whom he wished. How much Kiev had lost of its previous material importance after the devastation inflicted on it by Bogoliubsky's army is clear from the events described. During the changes of princes and interprincely wars nothing is heard about the participation of the people of Kiev, about the strong Kievan host which once decided the fate of Rus, the fate of princes during the struggle of Yury Dolgoruky with his nephew. Now the populace of Kiev passively submitted to every change without showing any signs of life. The strength of the Northern prince Vsevolod and the comparative weakness of Sviatoslav, the senior prince of Southern Rus, is illustrated by the following event.

In 1194 Sviatoslav gathered his kinsmen, his brother Yaroslav and his cousins Igor and Vsevolod. He took counsel with them on how to attack the princes of Riazan, with whom the princes of Chernigov were long in dispute concerning some border areas. The descendants of Oleg dared not launch a direct military campaign, so sent first to Vsevolod of Suzdal to ask permission. Vsevolod refused and Sviatoslav was forced to postpone his campaign. Sviatoslav lived in peace with the descendants of Rostislav, also probably because he was afraid of Vsevolod. In 1190 there was the threat of a quarrel between them, about the reasons for which the chronicle is very vague. Apparently Sviatoslav had a dispute with Riurik, Davyd and the Land of Smolensk, therefore he crossed the Dnieper to talk to his brothers to avoid losing his advantages. Riurik also took steps in that he communicated with Vsevolod and with his brother Davyd of

Smolensk. The three sent to tell Sviatoslav "You, brother, kissed the cross for your agreement with Roman when our brother Roman ruled in Kiev. If you still honor this agreement, you are our brother. If you want to awaken the old disputes from the times of Rostislav you have broken the agreement and we will not stand for that. We are sending back the charters of this agreement." At first Sviatoslav argued much with the envoys and almost sent them away carrying his message of refusal. Then he thought better of it, recalled them on their way back, and kissed the cross according to the wishes of the descendants of Monomakh.

II

THE PRINCIPALITY OF GALICH

STRUGGLE OF YAROSLAV OF GALICH WITH THE BOYARS

The powerful influence of Vsevolod of Suzdal also affected the fate of remote Galich. During the 1170s in this borderland Rus principality a development not found in any other Rus area appeared. This very important factor was that in Galich the boyars overshadowed the prince. Frequent reference has been made to the willful action of the Galich boyar Konstantin Seroslavich, who despite the wish of his prince, Yaroslav, led his regiments away, abandoning Mstislav Iziaslavich.[1] This Konstantin played an important role in the domestic troubles of his principality. The might of Yaroslav Vladimirovich of Galich, the only ruler of a rich and flourishing principality, may have seemed great in other countries. This is how it is described in the *Tale of Igor's Campaign.* "O prince of Galich, Yaroslav Osmomysl! High are you seated upon your throne wrought of gold, upbearing the Hungarian mountains with your iron hosts, barring the way to the king, closing the gates of the Danube, hurling weights through the clouds, executing justice as far as the Danube. Your thunder hurtles over the lands, you open the gates of Kiev, from your father's golden throne you hurl bolts at sultans beyond your lands."[2] This powerful prince was surrounded by men mightier than he. They could subjugate his power to their will. Yaroslav's marriage with Olga, sister of Yury Dolguruky's sons the princes of Suzdal, was not happy. He had as a mistress some woman called Nastasia. In 1173 Olga with her son

Vladimir, the boyar Konstantin Seroslavich and many other boyars fled Galich for Poland.

After eight months in Poland, Vladimir and his mother went to Volhynia, where he planned to settle for a while. On his journey he met an envoy sent by the boyars from Galich. "Go home," they sent to tell him, "we have arrested your father and killed his friends. Your enemy Nastasia is in our hands." The people of Galich burned the wretched woman at the stake, her son was imprisoned, and Yaroslav swore an oath to live with the princess properly.

DEATH OF YAROSLAV OF GALICH

In 1187 Yaroslav died. According to the chronicler he was a wise, eloquent, pious and honest prince in all the lands, famous for his hosts. When somebody offended him he did not go himself with his troops, instead he sent his commanders. When he felt the approach of death he called the boyars, lay clergy, monks and the poor. He spoke with tears in his eyes. "O fathers, brothers and sons," he said, "I am leaving this vain world. I go to meet my maker. I am the greatest sinner. O fathers and brothers, please forgive me."

For three days he wept before all the people, ordering his property distributed to monasteries and to the poor. The property was distributed throughout all Galich for three whole days, and still some remained. In his appeal to the boyars the dying prince said "I have devoted my whole wretched life to the Land of Galich. Now I give my place to Oleg, my younger son. To the older, Vladimir, I give Peremyshl."

This Oleg was born of Nastasia[3]. For that reason he was much loved by Yaroslav, says the chronicler, yet Vladimir disregarded his wishes. He had left his father and accompanied his mother, returning as a result of the triumph of Nastasia's enemies. Vladimir, with all the boyars, had to swear to his father not to deprive Oleg of the Galich throne. Was it reasonable to rely on such an oath? Could the killers of Nastasia quietly look on while her son occupied the senior throne?

When Yaroslav died a great rebellion erupted in the Land of Galich. Vladimir and the boyars violated their oath and expelled Oleg, who was forced to flee to Riurik at Ovruch while Vladimir sat on his father's and grandfather's throne. The boyars soon regretted their choice. Vladimir, in the words of the chronicler, was only interested in drinking. He did not care to deliberate with the boyars. He took away a priest's wife and cohabited with her, fathering two sons. When he fancied somebody's wife or daughter he took her by force.

BOYARS EXPEL VLADIMIR AND INVITE ROMAN MSTISLAVICH

At that time the nearest neighbor to the prince of Galich was Prince Roman Mstislavich,[4] who ruled in Vladimir-in-Volhynia. He inherited from his father and grandfather an unusually active temperament, enterprise and indefatigability. He did not like to abandon his plans, nor was he squeamish over means of achieving them. Roman was a close relative of Vladimir of Galich. His daughter was married to Vladimir's elder son. Disregarding this fact, when he learned that relations between the boyars of Galich and their prince were strained, Roman entered into communication with them, incited them to expel Vladimir, and proposed himself as their prince in Vladimir's place. Many of the boyars willingly agreed to his proposal, gathered their troops, bound themselves by oaths, yet dared not rebel openly against Vladimir, capture or kill him, because not all boyars opposed the prince, who had friends amongst them. The conspirators then devised a different way of banishing Vladimir. They sent word to him. "O prince," they declared, "we did not rebel against you, but we refuse to bow to a priest's wife. We want to kill her, and you may marry whom you wish." They hoped he would not think of letting her go, and thus threatened her so as to be rid of him as soon as possible. They were not mistaken. Vladimir, fearing his mistress would suffer the same fate as Nastasia, took much gold and silver, his wife, his two sons and his retinue, and fled to Hungary.

HUNGARIAN KING'S INTERFERENCE IN GALICH AFFAIRS

We left this country under the rule of King Géza II,[5] brother-in-law and ally of Iziaslav. Géza's most dangerous enemy was the famous Greek emperor Manuel Comnenos, the last of the great emperors occupying the Byzantine throne.[6] Géza's interference in Serbian affairs gave Manuel cause to attack the Hungarians and extend the borders of the empire at their expense. At first he supported Boris, previously mentioned, against Géza. He was the son of Monomakh's daughter. Later, when Boris was killed in battle, he supported Géza's brothers Stephen and Ladislas, who found refuge at the Byzantine court.

Géza died in 1161, leaving his throne to his twelve-year-old son Stephen III. The king's minority gave Manuel good opportunity to realize his ambitious plans in relation to Hungary. He immediately moved with a large army and both princes, Stephen and Ladislas, towards the Hungarian borders. He sent to the magnates to tell them that by ancient tradition the throne passed not to the son but to the brother of the deceased king, therefore they must pass the throne to Géza's brother Stephen. In answer the Hungarians stated that such a custom was unknown in their country, where from time immemorial the crown passed to the eldest son, not to the brother of the deceased king. Therefore they could not accept Prince Stephen the Elder as their king. They also refused him because they refused to have the emperor's underling as king.

Despite this brave reply Manuel's money and promises had some influence. Many of the aristocrats left young Stephen, who was forced to vacate the throne for his uncle, though it was the younger, Ladislas, not Stephen. Ladislas died after six months and his brother Stephen occupied the throne but not for very long. When it was clear in Hungary that he promised Manuel to cede Sirmium as a reward for his assistance, nearly everyone went over to his nephew, who as a result finally strengthened his hold over the country.

When Manuel realized the general dislike of the Hungarians for Stephen the uncle, he acknowledged the nephew as king. Moreover, because he did not have sons, he married his daughter to Béla, the younger brother of Stephen III, appointing him successor on condition that he be educated in Constantinople and keep Sirmium as the land given to him by his father. The king and magnates agreed to this proposal and young Béla went to Constantinople, where he was given the [baptismal] name Alexis. He was betrothed to the emperor's daughter and declared heir to the throne. Suddenly circumstances completely changed the course of events.

Manuel's second wife gave birth to a son. The overjoyed emperor ordered the immediate coronation of the child and deprived Béla not only of all hope to succeed him, but even took away his fiancée, his daughter, and betrothed to him his sister-in-law. At the same time Béla's brother, the twenty-four-year-old King Stephen III of Hungary died, according to rumors poisoned by his brother (1173). Béla hastened to Hungary where he encountered three parties, one of which wanted him to be king. The second party, composed mainly of the upper clergy, feared that Béla, educated in Constantinople, would be influenced by the emperor and be hostile to Catholicism. They wanted to wait for Stephen's wife, who was pregnant at the time, to give birth. The third party supported Béla's younger brother. It was headed by the old dowager-queen Evfrosinia Mstislavovna, the wife of Géza II, who wanted to see her favorite, younger, son on the throne. Béla III waged a long struggle aided by two hostile parties, eventually gaining the upper hand.

For more than ten years Béla ruled Hungary peacefully. Then Vladimir, fleeing Galich, arrived with a request for help. Domestic and external peace gave Béla ample opportunity to interfere in the affairs of Galich. He led all his troops to that land. Roman, who occupied the throne of Galich, could see no way of opposing Béla's army. He took the remnants of the princely treasury and returned to Volhynia, yet neither did Vladimir receive his father's throne. Béla, having arranged the domestic affairs of Galich, considered it more useful, both for him and for Galich, to appoint as prince his own son Andrew. By force Vladimir was returned to Hungary, stripped of his possessions and imprisoned in a tower. The king took also with him to Hungary the sons or brothers of the most important boyars to ensure their compliance.

ROMAN'S STRUGGLE FOR GALICH

In the meantime Roman, with the boyars of Galich who summoned him to the throne, wandered in various lands looking for a place to rule. When he left to rule in Galich he gave Vladimir to his brother Vsevolod, telling him "I do not need this city any more." Now escaping from the Hungarians in Galich he tried to return to Vladimir, but was halted by his brother. He went to Poland to look for help, sending his wife to her father Riurik Rostislavich in Ovruch. Failing to obtain assistance from the Polish princes he went to his father-in-law Riurik, together with his faithful boyars from Galich. There he asked his father-in-law to help him regain Galich. "The people of Galich call me to return to rule there," he told him. "Let your son Rostislav go with me."

Riurik agreed and Roman sent his advance detachment to capture Plesnesk, one of the border towns. This force was rebuffed by Hungarians and the men of Galich. When Roman heard about this disaster he sent his brother-in-law home and journeyed again to Poland. This time he had greater fortune. He received some assistance and moved against his brother Vsevolod in Vladimir. For a second time Vsevolod barred his entry. Roman went again to his father-in-law, who gave him the district of Torchesk to rule temporarily. At the same time he sent envoys to threaten Vsevolod. This action produced some effect. Roman received Vladimir, while Vsevolod moved to Bełz, his previous district.

Roman was summoned again to Galich. Apparently some there were dissatisfied with the Hungarian prince. Still Béla could not imagine that the Rus princes would accept calmly a foreign ruler in an ancient Rus district. Thus he hastened to persuade Sviatoslav of Kiev to support him. In 1189 he sent word, saying "Brother! Send your son to me. I wish to fulfill the promise I made when I kissed the cross to you." Then Sviatoslav, without Riurik's knowledge, sent his son to the king, thinking that Béla would give him Galich. Riurik, when he learned about this, sent to tell Sviatoslav "You have sent your son to the king without consulting me. Thus you have broken our agreement."

Strong arguments flared up among the princes, yet did not become a quarrel. Sviatoslav sent to tell Riurik "Brother and kinsman! I have sent my son not to incite the king against you, but in my interest. If you want to march against Galich I am ready to march with you." The metropolitan was particularly instrumental in settling the argument. He did not like the fact that a Catholic ruled in Galich. "Foreigners took away your fatherland," said he to Sviatoslav and Riurik. "It would be fitting to return it to our rule."

The princes listened to him and marched together to recapture Galich, Sviatoslav with his sons, and Riurik with his brothers. Even before they reconquered this district they started to discuss its future and quarrelled again. Sviatoslav wanted to give Galich to Riurik and take all the Land of Rus around Kiev for himself, but Riurik refused to give up his patrimony, exchanging something old and certain for something new and uncertain. He wanted to share Galich with Sviatopolk, who refused. In this way the two kinsmen parted, returning home without any profit.

DEATH OF ROSTISLAV, SON OF BERLADNIK

Having lost all hope of assistance from the more powerful Rus princes the people of Galich, unhappy with the rule of the [Hungarian] prince, turned to the scion of their native princes, the descendants of Rostislav. This was Rostislav Ivanovich, son of the famous Berladnik. Rostislav, like his father a prince without land, lived at that time at the court of Prince Davyd Rostislavich of Smolensk. When the invitation reached him he immediately set off to the borders of Galich, captured two frontier towns and proceeded to Galich itself. Not all the local boyars favored him. Some strongly supported the prince because their sons and brothers were at the court of Béla, who sent troops to help his son, fearing hostile moves by the Rus princes.

The Hungarian prince and his commanders, learning of Rostislav's attack at the invitation of some of the boyars of Galich, assembled all of the boyars and made them swear on the cross to be loyal. The boyars not part of the conspiracy swore the oath willingly. The guilty swore for fear of the Hungarians.

Meanwhile Rostislav and his small retinue approached the Galich troops, hoping that as promised they would join his cause when they saw his host. Indeed several of the Galich boyars crossed over to him, then left when it became apparent that the rest would not follow. Then his retinue told Rostislav "You can see that they have deceived you. Go away!" "No, brothers!" answered Rostislav. "You know what they have sworn to me. If now they seek to kill me, let God and this cross they kissed be their judge. I have had enough of wandering in foreign lands. I want to die in my patrimony." Saying these words, he threw himself into the thick of the Galich and Hungarian regiments. He was surrounded on all sides and thrown from his horse. Half dead from his wounds, he was taken to Galich. In the city there was a commotion. There was talk of rescuing Rostislav from the hands of the Hungarians and establishing him as their prince. Then the Hungarians found a way to end this affair. They applied poison to Rostislav's wounds and the wish of the son of Berladnik was fulfilled. He was buried in his fatherland, among his ancestors.

HUNGARIAN VIOLENCE IN GALICH

Witnessing from this event that the people of Galich wished to have a Rus prince, the Hungarians sought revenge through acts of violence. They took the inhabitants' wives and daughters as concubines. They stabled their horses in Orthodox churches and living quarters. Galich grieved and felt great remorse for having removed Vladimir as their prince. A rumor circulated[7] that Vladimir had escaped from his Hungarian prison (1190). On the tower where he was imprisoned there was a tent. He cut the material and made a rope to let himself to the ground. Two of his guards who were bribed led him to the German border, to the land of Emperor Frederick Barbarossa[8] who, when he learned that Vladimir was a blood relative on his mother's side of Prince Vsevolod of Suzdal, received him with love and great honor. When Vladimir promised him to pay annually two thousand silver grivnas, Frederick sent him with his own envoy to the Polish prince Casimir,[9] ordering the Pole to help him regain the throne of Galich.

VLADIMIR YAROSLAVICH CONSOLIDATES HIS RULE IN GALICH

Casimir complied, sending his governor Nicholas to Galich with Vladimir. When the people of Galich heard about their *rightful heir* approaching accompanied by Polish troops, they came out to meet him with joy and acclaimed him their prince. The Hungarian king's son was expelled from the land. Vladimir did not consider himself secure from neighboring princes, Rus or foreign, until such time as his uncle, the powerful prince of Suzdal, lent him support. He sent him a message, saying "Father and lord! Keep Galich under my rule, and I am God's servant and yours, with the whole of Galich at your disposal forever." Vsevolod dispatched his envoys to all Rus princes and to Poland, compelling all to swear not to seek to deprive his nephew of Galich. From this time, says the chronicler, Vladimir was established in Galich, and no one went to war against him.

RIURIK ROSTISLAVICH'S RULE IN KIEV

The influence of the Northern prince on the affairs of Southern Rus grew even more marked after the death of Sviatoslav Vsevolodovich (1194),[10] who is remembered in the chronicles as a wise prince. His successor in Kiev was Riurik Rostislavich, whom everybody in Rus, the people of Kiev, Christians as well as pagans, accepted with great joy because, as the chronicler says, he received everybody with love. Christian or pagan, he rejected nobody. When he settled in Kiev he sent word to his brother Davyd of Smolensk, saying "O brother! We are now the most senior in the Land of Rus. Come to me in Kiev. We will see each other and deliberate about the Land of Rus, about our brothers, about the clan of Vladimir, and we will settle all our affairs."

This prince, though he considered himself the senior in the Land of Rus, in fact obtained his seniority from another prince, the most senior and powerful prince, that of Suzdal. Vsevolod, the Northern chronicler says, sent his men to Kiev and they established Riurik Rostislavich there. Davyd of Smolensk agreed to his brother's proposal and sailed towards him down the Dnieper. The brothers met in Vyshgorod and started feasting. First Riurik invited Davyd to dine. The princes enjoyed themselves, presented gifts to each other and parted with great affection.

Later Davyd was invited by his nephew Rostislav Riurikovich to Belgorod, where there was also a great deal of feasting. Davyd reciprocated with a feast and gifts. First he invited his brother Riurik and nephews to dine, then he invited brethren from the monasteries, giving them and the poor many charitable gifts. Finally he invited the Karakalpaks, and gave them plenty to drink and gifts. The people of Kiev, on their part, invited Davyd to dine and presented him with gifts. Davyd reciprocated with a joyous feast. While enjoying themselves the brothers also engaged in business, making all agreements relating to the Land of Rus, to their brothers, and to the clan of Vladimir. After that Davyd returned to Smolensk.

VSEVOLOD OF SUZDAL EMBROILS RIURIK WITH ROMAN OF VOLHYNIA

The sons of Rostislav soon realized that they could not uphold their agreements concerning the Land of Rus without the participation of the prince of Suzdal. Envoys from the city of Vladimir arrived in Kiev and told Riurik on behalf of their prince "You called me the senior in the whole of Vladimir's branch. Now that you rule in Kiev, you have not yielded me any part in the Land of Rus, yet you have given it to others, the junior brothers. If I have no part in it, do as you like. Whoever has a part in it, you guard [Rus] with him, because it no longer is any concern of mine."

According to the words of the envoys from Vladimir it would seem that their prince was cross with Riurik for having granted the best district to his son-in-law Roman of Volhynia, namely the five towns of Torchesk, Trepolie, Korsun, Boguslav and Kanev. These were situated on the Ros river, on the border with the steppe, in the area populated by Karakalpaks, who played such an important role in the interprincely wars.

Riurik consulted with his boyars about how to settle this matter. He did not wish to remove this district from Roman because he had sworn not to give it to anybody else. He offered Vsevolod other towns, but he wanted the Ros river district only, threatening war if he did not get his way. In this difficult situation Riurik turned to Metropolitan Nikifor,[11] telling him he had sworn to Roman by kissing the cross not to withdraw from him the Ros river region. He did not wish to break his word, which would cause the war with Vsevolod which was about to erupt.

"Prince," replied the metropolitan, "we were put by God in the Land of Rus to hold you from bloodletting. If Christian blood is shed because you have given the district to a junior prince, omitting the senior, and sealed the oath by kissing the cross, I absolve you from the oath and take it upon myself. Listen to me. Take the district from your son-in-law and give it to the senior prince, giving Roman some other district." Riurik sent word to Roman, saying "Vsevolod wants your district and complains about me because of you." "My father," Roman replied, "there is no reason to quarrel with your kinsman. You can give me another district instead, or compensate me with money." After consultation with his brothers and boyars, Riurik sent to tell Vsevolod "You have complained about me, my brother, because of a district. Here, you can have the district you wanted."

There is no need to assume that it was merely the inherited dislike of Vsevolod for the descendants of Iziaslav that pushed him to single out the district given to Roman. Yury may have hated Roman's grandfather, Iziaslav, because he took away his seniority.[12] Andrei Bogoliubsky perhaps disliked Roman's father Mstislav, who likewise did not acknowledge his seniority, wishing to rule in Kiev as the senior and independent prince. But there was no reason for Vsevolod to be angry with Roman. He had no claims against Vsevolod, who was acknowledged by all as the most powerful and strongest prince. Perhaps he wanted this district in order to strengthen his influence in Rus, but why did he demand particularly the towns on the Ros river? Perhaps he considered this border district and the Karakalpaks who lived there as particularly important, but he paid little attention to it when Riurik recaptured it.

Vsevolod could have been against strengthening Roman, who demonstrated in Galich his enterprising spirit and ambition. In any case Riurik would have given him another district, equal in importance, or money to hire Polovetsians or lure the Karakalpaks. Finally Vsevolod may have taken offense that Riurik, distributing territories, dishonored him by giving him none. Yet such claim would have been strange coming from Vsevolod, who was acknowledged as senior. Kiev belonged to him. He could go to that city and take charge of all the surrounding districts yet he, like his brother before him, scorned Kiev. He granted it to a junior prince and then took offense that this junior did not give him a district! Although these considerations perhaps influenced Vsevolod's behavior, the wish to stir quarrels among the Southern descendants of Monomakh, a closely-knit union, should be regarded as the main reason. Unless it were undermined, such a union would weaken the influence of the Northern prince in the South.

Obtaining from Riurik the district he requested, Vsevolod immediately gave its best town, Torchesk, to Riurik's son and his own son-in-law

Rostislav, sending his commanders to the other four towns. His calculation was correct, for when Roman learned that Torchesk was removed from him, and through Vsevolod's decision transferred to Riurik's son, he complained to his father-in-law. He was certain that he was in collusion with Vsevolod, having taken back the district with the sole purpose of giving it to his son. "I gave you this district as first of all," replied Riurik, "then Vsevolod suddenly sent a complaint that he was not given precedence. After all, I have informed you about all his messages, and you gave up this district out of your own goodwill. You yourself know that we could not have acted against his will. We cannot do without him. All brothers acknowledged him as senior in Vladimir's clan. You are like my son. Accept another district of equal value."

Roman could not have been pacified at this stage, or assured that there was no conspiracy against him. He consulted his boyars on how to avenge this offense. They decided to send to Yaroslav Vsevolodovich in Chernigov, to give him seniority and invite him to Kiev against Riurik. Yaroslav, glad of this opportunity, accepted their proposal.

Then Riurik sent word to Vsevolod about the plans of Roman and the descendants of Oleg. "You, brother," he said, "are the most senior in the whole clan of Vladimir, so think and ponder on the Land of Rus, about your share and ours." To his son-in-law Roman he sent his boyars to expose him and throw in his face the oath charters. Roman was alarmed when he saw that his father-in-law knew of the conspiracy with the descendants of Oleg. Since he was not yet prepared to start war, he went to Poland to seek help.

ROMAN'S PARTICIPATION IN POLISH CIVIL WARS

In Poland after the expulsion of Władysław seniority passed to his brother Bolesław IV the Curly[13] (1142). The exiled Władysław,[14] after unsuccessful attempts to recapture the seniority, died in Germany. His three sons Bolesław, Mieszko and Konrad, most likely with the emperor's support, returned to their fatherland and regained Silesia. After the death of Bolesław IV the Curly, seniority passed to his brother, Bolesław's third son Mieszko III.[15] Soon he alienated the magnates, who expelled him and proclaimed as prince the last of Bolesław's heirs, Casimir the Just[16] (Henryk, Bolesław's fourth son, died earlier). Casimir and his famous Palatine Nicholas played an important part in restoring Vladimir Yaroslavich to the throne of Galich.[17] After the death of Casimir (1194) the question arose as to who should become senior in the clan of

Bolesław because one of Bolesław III's sons, Mieszko the Old, denied seniority earlier, was still alive. Mieszko had no hope of occupying the senior throne of Cracow for a second time. Dissatisfaction with him lingered among the magnates. It was more beneficial for them to have as prince a minor nephew rather than an old uncle. Prelates and magnates who assembled in Cracow decided to give the senior throne to a son of Casimir the Just, Leszek, who was a minor. Mieszko, refusing to relinquish his rights, prepared for war against his nephews.

At the same time Roman of Volhynia arrived in Cracow requesting help against his father-in-law Riurik. Reasonably he could expect help because Casimir's widow Elena was his niece by his brother Vsevolod Mstislavich of Bełz. "We would like to help you," Casimir's sons answered Roman, "but our uncle Mieszko offends us, tries to take away our lands. First you help us, and when all we Poles are behind one shield, let us go to avenge your injury!" Roman agreed to this proposal and went to fight against Mieszko on the side of Casimir's sons. Mieszko did not want to fight against Roman, whom he sought as an intermediary in his dispute with his nephews. Roman heeded neither him nor his boyars and joined the battle, in which he suffered a crushing defeat. Wounded, he escaped with Casimir's sons to Cracow, whence his retinue carried him to Vladimir-in-Volhynia.

Realizing how dire his situation was, he sent an envoy to his father-in-law Riurik begging his forgiveness, also a message to Metropolitan Nikifor to intercede for him with Riurik. The metropolitan fulfilled his request and Riurik, after listening to him, answered "If Roman pleads and begs forgiveness, I will receive him, accept his oath, and give him a district. If he holds his oath, he will indeed have in me a father. If he wishes me well, I will treat him like a son, as I did before, wishing him well." Indeed Riurik sent a message to Roman saying that he was no longer angry with him. He accepted his oath and gave him some lands.

WAR BETWEEN THE DESCENDANTS OF MONOMAKH AND OLEG

Roman was humbled but it could not be forgotten that he had offered the seniority and Kiev to Yaroslav of Chernigov, who accepted his offer. This is why, after exchanging messages with his relative Vsevolod and his brother Davyd, he sent to tell Yaroslav and the descendants of Oleg on behalf of those of Monomakh "Give us your pledge by kissing the cross with all your brothers that you will not seek our patrimony, Kiev and Smolensk, or to deprive us or our children or all our clan of Vladimir. Our grandfather Yaroslav divided us up to the Dnieper, thus you do not need Kiev." The sons of Oleg took offense at such a proposal and sent word to Vsevolod, saying "We have an agreement not to seek Kiev from you and your relative Riurik, and we are keeping our agreement. Why do you instruct us to renounce Kiev forever? We are not Poles or Hungarians, but grandchildren of one grandfather. We do not seek Kiev while you are alive. After you, God will decide to whom it goes."

There were many feuds between them and long speeches still they reached no agreement, says the chronicler. Vsevolod wanted during that winter to march against Chernigov. The sons of Oleg took fright and sent an abbot with a humble message, promising to accede to his wishes. He believed them and put away plans for the campaign. Meanwhile messengers from Chernigov visited Riurik with a message from their princes. "O brother," they pleaded, "we never had a quarrel. We could not make a final agreement either with Vsevolod or with you, or your brother Davyd. Since you are nearest to us, pledge by kissing the cross not to attack us until we finish our negotiations with Vsevolod and Davyd."

Riurik, after deliberating with his boyars, accepted Yaroslav's offer, sent his envoy to Chernigov, and made efforts to reconcile Vsevolod and Davyd with the sons of Oleg. At the same time Riurik promised Yaroslav to let him have Vitebsk. He sent an envoy to his brother Davyd to announce this concession. Afterwards, hoping for peace, he dismissed his retinue, his brothers, his sons and the Polovetsians, having presented them with rich gifts, while he himself went to Ovruch to see to his own affairs.

Yaroslav did not await the end of negotiations concerning Vitebsk before sending his nephew Oleg Sviatoslavich to capture this city, where one of the Polovetsian princes, a brother-in-law of Davyd of Smolensk, resided. Davyd was unaware of the arrangements between Riurik and Yaroslav. When he heard that some of the followers of the sons of Oleg before reaching Vitebsk had looted the Smolensk district he sent against Oleg a force commanded by his nephew Mstislav Romanovich, who attacked Oleg, trampled his banners and killed his son.

While Mstislav was successful in one place, the Smolensk chiliarch Mikhalko suffered defeat from the men of Polotsk, allies of the prince of Chernigov. Mstislav, returning from pursuing the defeated Oleg, met the victorious men of Polotsk. Thinking that they were his own troops, he went among their ranks and was taken prisoner. Oleg Sviatoslavich, overjoyed, sent word to his uncle in Chernigov, claiming the victory as his. "I took Mstislav prisoner and defeated his host, as well as the

Smolensk host of Davyd. The prisoners from Smolensk tell me that their brothers have bad relations with Davyd. There will be no time like the present, my little father, so collect your forces and we shall hurry to claim our honor."

Yaroslav and all the sons of Oleg were delighted and hurried to Smolensk but were intercepted on their way by Riurik's envoy with a message from his prince to Yaroslav. "If you intend to use this opportunity to kill my brother," he said, "you are in breach of our agreement sealed by kissing the cross. Here are your oath charters. If you go to Smolensk, I will go to Chernigov. God and the true cross be our judges."

Yaroslav took fright, returned to Chernigov and sent his messenger to Riurik to justify his actions. He put the blame on Davyd for helping his son-in-law. "I gave you Vitebsk," replied Riurik, "and sent an envoy to my brother Davyd to let him know about this concession. Without awaiting the outcome of the matter you sent your nephews to Vitebsk, and on their way they ravaged the Smolensk district. Davyd then sent against them his nephew Mstislav." They had a lengthy dispute, which they failed to settle.

In 1196 Riurik sent word to his kinsman Vsevolod of Suzdal, saying "We agreed to go on campaign after Christmas and to meet in Chernigov. I was ready with my brothers, retinue and the Wild Polovetsians, sitting ready and waiting, but that winter you did not mount your horse. You believed the sons of Oleg when they said they agreed to our conditions. When I heard that you were not going I dismissed my brothers and the Wild Polovetsians and kissed the cross with Yaroslav of Chernigov not to fight before trying to reach a settlement. Now my brother, your son, and my son Mstislav are prisoners of the sons of Oleg. Mount your horse without further delay, and let us meet to avenge your injury and shame. We must rescue our nephew and learn the truth."

Vsevolod did not reply for a long time. "You go ahead," he finally replied, "and I will be ready." Riurik gathered his brothers and Wild Polovetsians and fought against the sons of Oleg. Yaroslav then sent word to him. "Why, brother," said he, "do you fight against my district and fill pagans' hands? Why are we quarrelling? Do I want to deprive you of Kiev? Because Davyd sent Mstislav against my nephews God adjudged this matter, still I release Mstislav to you without ransom, out of love. Please let us kiss the cross and negotiate peace between me and Davyd. If Vsevolod wishes to settle with us, we will settle. This is neither your business nor that of your brother Davyd."

"If you really want peace," Riurik answered, "let me pass through your lands. I will send a messenger to Vsevolod and Davyd. After negotiations among us we will settle our differences with you." Riurik, according to the chronicler, in fact wanted to send messengers only with the aim of arranging a general peace, but Yaroslav did not trust Riurik's words. He thought that the descendants of Monomakh wanted to conspire against him, hence he did not let Riurik's messengers through his district. The sons of Oleg blockaded all the roads. All summer until autumn the war continued in the form of raids. In the autumn the sons of Oleg acquired an ally in Roman of Volhynia who, encountering troubles, was forced to seek his father-in-law's favors. He now had recovered and wished to use this opportunity to take revenge for earlier humiliations. Sending a detachment to the border town of Polonny, he ordered it to devastate the territory of Kiev by raids.

When he learned of this new enemy, Riurik turned to a prince whom he could regard as his natural ally against Roman, namely Prince Vladimir Yaroslavich of Galich, sending to him his nephew Mstislav Mstislavich, son of the famous Mstislav Rostislavich, Andrei's rival. "My son-in-law," Mstislav was to tell Vladimir on Riurik's behalf, "has broken an agreement and attacked my territory. So you, brother, with my nephew from Galich, attack his district. I myself wanted to go against Vladimir-in-Volhynia, then received news that my kinsman Vsevolod mounted his horse, joined my brother Davyd, and together they burn the territory of the sons of Oleg. They took and burned the towns of the Viatichians.[18] I have everything ready, waiting for reliable news." Vladimir went with Mstislav, attacking and burning Roman's district which also was raided and burned by Rostislav Riurikovich with the sons of Vladimir Mstislavich and the Karakalpaks. They took many prisoners and much cattle.

The intelligence received by Riurik on the movement of Vsevolod and Davyd was accurate. They actually entered the lands of the sons of Oleg and burned them. When Yaroslav learned of this he gathered his brothers, put two descendants of Sviatoslav, Oleg and Gleb, in Chernigov, and strengthened other towns in anticipation of attacks by Riurik. He personally with the rest of the clan and the Polovetsians marched against Vsevolod and Davyd. He stood near his forests, surrounded by field fortifications, ordering bridges over the rivers dismantled. Prepared in this manner he sent a message to Vsevolod, saying "Brother and kinsman! You have taken our fatherland and our bread. If you want peace with us and to live in friendship, we do not turn our backs on friendship, and agree to all your demands. If you have other intentions, we do not run away from you, let God and the Holy Savior judge between us."

Vsevolod disliked fighting decisive battles, which the Southern princes considered to be God's judgments. Moreover the sons of Oleg promised to satisfy his demands without battle. He started consultations with Davyd, the princes of Riazan and the boyars about conditions for peace with the sons of Oleg. Davyd did not want peace and continued to demand that Vsevolod go to Chernigov, repeatedly saying to him "You have an agreement with my brother Riurik and with me to meet in Chernigov, there to arrange peace on our terms. You have not informed Riurik about your movements. He fights against them, he burned his district for you, while we want to make peace without his counsel and knowledge. You do as you like, but I can tell you that such a peace will not be to my brother's liking."

Vsevolod did not like the words of Davyd and the princes of Riazan. He began negotiations with the sons of Oleg, demanding (1) that they renounce any right to Kiev and Smolensk, (2) that they free Mstislav Romanovich, (3) that they banish his old enemy Yaropolk Rostislavich, who lived at that time in Chernigov, and (4) that they break off relations with Roman of Volhynia.

Yaroslav agreed to the first three demands, but refused to abandon Roman, who did him a great favor in attacking his father-in-law and halting him from marching against Chernigov. Vsevolod did not insist on this condition. This confirmed the suspicion that he was interested in continuing to stir trouble in the South, for he did not wish the descendants of Rostislav to strengthen definitively their position there. After concluding peace with Yaroslav he sent word to Riurik. "I have come to terms with Yaroslav," he said. "He kissed the cross that he would not try to take Kiev from you, or Smolensk from your brother."

Riurik grew very angry. "Kinsman!" he retorted. "You have sworn that my enemies are your enemies. When you asked me for a share in the Land of Rus I gave you the best territory, not because I had too much, for I took it from my brothers and my son-in-law Roman. Following this Roman became my enemy, not because of somebody else but because of you. You promised to mount your horse and help me, but you wasted all summer and winter. Now that you have mounted your horse, how have you helped me? You yourself made peace as well as an agreement that suited you. My quarrel with Roman you have left to the will of Yaroslav.

Is it conceivable that Yaroslav would seek reconciliation between me and him? For whose sake was this whole affair started? Why did I ask you to mount your horse? What sort of grievances had I against the descendants of Oleg? They did not want to take Kiev from me. For your sake I quarrelled with them, attacked them, and they burned my lands. You kept none of the promises we agreed upon, promises sealed by kissing the cross." Being angry, Riurik took back from Vsevolod all the towns he gave him earlier, again installing his brothers there.

It seems that Vsevolod paid no more heed to the matter, but it is clear that thereafter he did not wish Riurik well. Vsevolod lost territory on the west bank of the Dnieper. On the eastern side he continued to hold in his clan Southern or Rus Pereiaslavl.[19] After the death of Vladimir Glebovich another nephew of Vsevolod, Yaroslav Mstislavich, ruled there and obeyed his uncle's wishes. This is proven by the fact that Pereiaslavl, even in church matters, depended on Vsevolod. In 1197 he sent a bishop there. The following year, 1198, Yaroslav Mstislavich died. In his place Vsevolod sent to Pereiaslavl his son Yaroslav (1201). Vsevolod also sent instructions to rebuild his father's small fortress on the Oster (1194), destroyed by Iziaslav Mstislavich.

ROMAN OF VOLHYNIA CONFIRMED IN GALICH

Riurik had good reason to be anxious about his relations with the prince of Volhynia, whose power had doubled, because after Vladimir Yaroslavich's death, once again with Polish help, he occupied the throne of Galich. This time it was for good (1198). The chronicle does not mention why three years later (1201) Riurik prepared to attack Roman. Very likely the prince of Kiev was displeased with Roman's takeover in Galich, but why did he tarry so long before attacking his son-in-law? Under the year 1197 the chronicle mentions the death of Roman's brother Davyd of Smolensk, who according to custom bequeathed the throne to his nephew by an older brother, Mstislav Romanovich, entrusting his son Konstantin to the care of his older brother Riurik.

In 1198 Prince Yaroslav of Chernigov died and his throne was occupied, according to the same custom, by his cousin Igor Sviatoslavich of Novgorod Seversk, the famous hero of the *Tale of Igor's Campaign,* but he died soon afterwards (1202) leaving the Chernigov throne to his eldest nephew Vsevolod Sviatoslavich the Red, grandson of Vsevolod Olgovich. All these changes, in particular the lack of trust of the descendants of Oleg, could have hindered Riurik's war plans against Roman.

Then in 1202 he convinced Vsevolod the Red, prince of Chernigov, to cooperate with him against the prince of Galich-Volhynia. The sons of Oleg appeared in Kiev as allies of the local prince who was a descendant of Monomakh. Such an alliance had not occurred for a long time, but Roman forestalled his enemies. He gathered his Galich and Vladimir contingents, and attacked the Land of Rus.

ROMAN EXPELS RIURIK ROSTISLAVICH FROM KIEV

An interesting development then occurred, reminiscent of what happened during the war waged by Roman's grandfather Iziaslav against his uncle Yury. Either Riurik could not win the support of the population, or the memory of and devotion to Roman's grandfather and father was still alive. Perhaps Roman finally with promises lured the Karakalpaks to his side. Perhaps all these reasons were at work. Rus (the Kiev district) rebelled against Riurik, and everybody went over to Roman. First to abandon Riurik were the sons of Vladimir Mstislavich who, like their father, apparently possessed no land. They were followed by the Karakalpaks, and finally groups from all Kiev's towns appeared. Roman, when he became aware of the general movement in his favor, moved with all his forces towards Kiev. The citizens opened the Podolian gate to let him in, and he occupied Podol.

Riurik and the sons of Oleg were in the upper part of the city (on the Hill). When they saw that everything was against them, they no longer could hold out in Kiev. They started negotiations with Roman. Riurik renounced his right to Kiev and withdrew to Ovruch. The sons of Oleg crossed the Dnieper and proceeded to Chernigov, while Kiev was given by Grand Prince Vsevolod and Roman to Roman's first cousin Ingvar Yaroslavich of Lutsk.

This was remarkable, the necessary consequence of domination by a stronger Northern prince who was at the same time the clan's senior member, yet ceased to reside in Kiev. Vsevolod, hostile to Riurik, refused to support him against Roman. Subject to an agreement with Roman, he gave Kiev to youngest of the sons of Mstislav, who had no right whatsoever, neither in relation to Roman, nor in relation to Riurik. Roman himself could not be placed in Kiev. Very likely Vsevolod refused to allow this, dreading the concentration of the Kiev, Vladimir-in-Volhynia and Galich territories in the hands of any one prince, least of all such a prince as Roman. On the other hand the honor of ruling in Kiev was not sought by Roman himself, whose presence was necessary in newly-acquired Galich.

RIURIK AGAIN OCCUPIES KIEV

Riurik refused to suffer calmly his banishment and see his nephew rule Kiev. The following year (1203) he again united his forces with the sons of Oleg, hired many Polovetsians and with them captured Kiev. It seems the allies had no money to pay the barbarians, instead they promised to let them plunder Kiev. Riurik had no reason to feel sorry for the people of Kiev, who had opened their gates to Roman. Thus the Polovetsians scattered all over the city. They burned not only Podol, but also the Hill. They plundered the Holy Wisdom cathedral, the Tithe church and all the monasteries. Monks and nuns, priests and their wives, the old and disabled were killed. The young and healthy were taken into slavery, as were the rest of Kiev's inhabitants. Only the foreign merchants who took refuge in churches were spared. The Polovetsians confiscated half their property, but set them free.

After this terrible devastation Riurik did not want to rule in Kiev. Either he refused to rule in a burned-out, plundered and empty city, waiting for it to recover, or he was fearful that Roman might attack again. In any case he returned to Ovruch, where soon he was besieged by Roman who arrived, in the words of the chronicler, to separate him from the sons of Oleg and the Polovetsians.

ROMAN FORCES RIURIK TO TAKE MONASTIC VOWS

Riurik was forced to kiss the cross to Grand Prince Vsevolod *and his children*, which meant abandoning his seniority in the clan, and promised, after Vsevolod's death, to obey the prince of Suzdal and his children. "You kissed the cross," Roman afterwards told him, "now send a messenger to your kinsman, and I will send my boyar to my father and lord, Grand Prince Vsevolod. Ask, and I will ask, that he give you Kiev again." Vsevolod agreed, and Riurik again ruled in Kiev. Vsevolod made peace with the sons of Oleg as well, also thanks to Roman's request.

From all this it seems clear that Roman truly wanted peace in Rus, probably to gain more freedom of action to manage affairs in Galich and to act against foreign enemies. His wishes were in vain. Returning in 1203 from war against the Polovetsians, Princes Roman and Riurik with their sons stopped in Tripolie to discuss the division of districts. A quarrel erupted, which ended with Roman capturing Riurik, whom he sent to Kiev. There he was tonsured, together with his wife and daughter and Roman's own wife, from whom he was divorced. Roman took Riurik's sons Rostislav and Vladimir with him to Galich. The chronicle does not mention whom he left to rule in Kiev. Vsevolod of Suzdal could not take this calmly. He sent his representatives to Roman, who was forced to let Riurik's sons go. To the elder, Rostislav, who was Vsevolod's son-in-law, he was forced to give Kiev. Riurik did not stay in the monastery for long.

ROMAN DIES IN BATTLE AGAINST THE POLES

Roman had close relations with the Polish princes Casimir the Just and his sons, whom he helped against their uncle Mieszko. They in turn helped him conquer Galich after the death of Vladimir Yaroslavich. Even though he defeated Roman, Mieszko did not become ruler in Cracow. Unsuccessful in achieving his purpose by force, he resorted to negotiations and persuasion. Finally he induced Casimir's widow and her son Leszek to yield the seniority to him. It seemed to them more beneficial to renounce temporarily their rights to Cracow, later to obtain them by right of princely succession, rather than rule through the favor of the magnates and be dependent upon them. For the second time Mieszko obtained the seniority and Cracow, and was banished for the second time. Once again he flattered Casimir's widow and her son with promises. So for the third time he occupied Cracow and held the city until his death in 1202.

The death of Mieszko the Old marked the end of the first generation of Bolesław's sons. Again the Cracow aristocracy, passing over older first cousins, sent messengers to Leszek, son of Casimir, to call him to the senior throne on condition that he remove Hoverk, palatine of Sandomir, who had a strong influence on his master. The Cracow magnates, it seems, wished to eliminate the kind of inconvenience suffered by Rus boyars through princely peregrinations from one territory to another, with the consequent displacement of old by new boyars.

Here we see beginnings of terms being presented by Polish aristocrats to their princes. Still it is easy to understand that, because the aristocracy was so important, clan reckonings of the princes could not continue in Poland. Leszek, who earlier resigned the seniority to his uncle to be free of aristocratic influence, in particular the influence of the most powerful of them, Palatine Nicholas of Cracow, now refused to agree to terms proposed by the magnates in order to rule in Cracow. He answered the messengers that the magnates must elect another as their prince, one who could agree to their terms.

The aristocrats then turned to a prince who had more rights to seniority than Leszek, namely Władysław Spindleshanks,[20] son of Mieszko, whom they proclaimed as grand prince. Then Władysław soon turned the prelates against him. Together with the magnates they banished him from Cracow and called in his place Leszek, son of Casimir, this time it seems without preconditions, probably because by then Palatine Nicholas was dead.

Leszek received his seniority mainly thanks to the prelates. He probably looked for supporters among the clergy to offset the influence of the magnates. Therefore immediately after gaining the throne in Cracow he transferred all his lands to the protection of St. Peter and promised to pay Rome an annual tax. The clergy soon repaid the favor granted by their benefactor. For a long time they had been hostile to interprincely clan relations and interprincely reckonings. After the death of Casimir the Just, Bishop Fulkon of Cracow defended the principle of father-son inheritance against the order of inheritance based on clan seniority, and kept Cracow for Casimir's son. When Leszek placed himself and his heirs under the protection of St. Peter, the Roman church solemnly confirmed his hereditary title to Cracow, as well as the right to bequeath the throne to his eldest son. Thus two powerful principles opposed interprincely clan relationships in Poland, the power of magnates and the power of clergy, against which such relationships lost the struggle.

Roman of Volhynia, a constant ally of Leszek, continued his hostility to Mieszko and his son Władysław Spindleshanks, but when Leszek strengthened his position in Cracow Roman demanded from him some land as a reward for erstwhile friendship. Leszek refused and, in the words of the chronicler, Władysław Spindleshanks was very active in deepening the rift between Leszek and Roman. Consequently, the prince of Galich besieged Lublin. When he learned that Leszek and his brother Konrad were marching against him, Roman abandoned the siege and set out to intercept them. Crossing the Vistula he camped near the town of Zawichost where messengers from Leszek reached him, and negotiations began. They agreed to halt hostilities while talks were in progress. Roman, trusting this arrangement, left the camp with a small retinue to hunt. A Polish detachment lay in wait for him. Roman was ambushed and after heroic resistance was killed with his retinue (1205).

Thus perished the famous grandson of Iziaslav Mstislavich. In his enterprising spirit and boldness he very much resembled his father and grandfather. He acquired Galich and an extensive material base for his activity. He was also in constant touch with his foreign neighbors, among whom at that time interprincely clan relationships were superseded by crown relationships. Roman therefore necessarily was influenced by customs prevalent in the nearest Western countries, and possibly was a conduit for such new ideas in Southern Rus, contributing to the change of clan into monarchical relationships. Like his father and grandfather he could enter the struggle against the Northern princes, but this struggle had to have had a new character.

Roman should have striven to achieve sole rule in the South, as did the sons of Yury in the North. Yet the similarity between Roman's situation and that of the Northern princes is illusory. Conditions in Southwestern Rus, in particular in the principality of Galich, lacked the prerequisites for strong monarchy which existed in the North and were exploited by the Northern princes to unite the Rus lands, there to establish unity and order. The boyars of Galich were powerful, dwarfing the importance of the prince. It is easy to understand how a prince like Roman soon would clash with this power. "Without squashing the bees you cannot eat honey," he used to say. The best boyars perished because of him, it is said, in terrible torment, while others fled. Roman lured them to return, promising all sorts of favors yet, using various pretexts, he forced on them the same fate.

Leaving such a bloody memory of Galich in the rest of Rus, Roman nevertheless was remembered as a dangerous scourge of the barbarians, whether Polovetsians, Lithuanians or Yatviags.[21] He labored with dedication for the good of the Land of Rus, a worthy heir of his great-grandfather Monomakh. "He fought the pagans like a lion," says the poetic folk legend. "He was angry like a lynx, he exterminated them like a crocodile, flew over their lands like an eagle and he was as brave as a tiger, the equal of his grandfather Monomakh."

One of the main spheres of the princes' activity was construction of towns, and populating empty lands. Roman forced the vanquished Lithuanians to clear forests for cultivation. Yet his contemporaries considered that his attempts to teach the savages not to plunder but to work peacefully on the land bore no fruit. There is a folk saying "O Roman! Roman! You live in poverty, you yoke Lithuanians to the plough."[22]

ROMAN'S MINOR SONS SURROUNDED BY ENEMIES

Clearly Roman did not squash all the bees. It was a long time before his children could enjoy the honey in peace. He had two sons by his second wife, the four-year-old Daniel and the two-year-old Vasilko. Apart from the boyars of Galich he left his sons other enemies. Riurik, learning of Roman's death, left the monastery and proclaimed himself prince of Kiev in place of his son. He wanted his wife to leave the nunnery but she refused and took solemn vows.[23] Oleg's sons also took up arms, appearing with their troops by the Dnieper. Riurik met them, and they agreed to march together to Galich to deprive Roman's sons of their inheritance.

The allies met the troops from Galich and Volhynia near the Seret river. The battle continued for a whole day. The allies forced their enemies to retreat to Galich but could not take this city, and returned home empty-handed. The reason for this failure was the presence in Galich of a strong Hungarian garrison. The people of Galich did not dare submit to the enemies of Roman's sons because they feared the Hungarians.

At that time Andrew II, son of Béla III, ruled in Hungary, for a time having ruled Galich. After his father's death he waged constant struggle with his brother King Emerich and later with his son, the young Ladislas III, whose death opened his way to the throne. As can be learned from the chronicle, Andrew during this struggle not only abandoned his claims to Galich, but was closely allied with Roman. Both swore that the survivor must care for the deceased's family. Andrew was crowned the same year as Roman's death, and was obliged to fulfil his duties towards Roman's family. In Sanok he met with Roman's widow. He received Daniel as his dear son, in the words of the chronicle, and sent five commanders with a strong force to save Galich from Riurik and his allies.

SONS OF ROMAN EXPELLED FROM GALICH

Nevertheless dangers and troubles were only beginning for Roman's sons. The following year, 1206, all the descendants of Oleg gathered in Chernigov for an assembly. Vsevolod Sviatoslavich the Red with his brothers, and Vladimir Igorevich of Seversk with his brothers, were joined by Prince Mstislav Romanovich of Smolensk with his nephews. Many Polovetsians were present, and they all moved to the other side of Dnieper. In Kiev they were joined by Riurik with his two sons Rostislav and Vladimir, who brought his nephews and the Berendey. They marched on Galich, while the Polish prince Leszek marched on Galich from the other direction. The Galich princess and her followers, when they heard at night a strong force approaching from all sides, grew frightened and sent to the king of Hungary to ask for help. Andrew moved with all his troops, but Roman's widow and children could not bide until the king's arrival. A powerful rebellion started around her, forcing them to escape to Roman's old patrimony, Vladimir-in-Volhynia.

GALICH BOYARS INVITE THE SONS OF IGOR FROM SEVERIA

The people of Galich were left without a prince. In the meantime the king crossed the Carpathian mountains. Rus princes and the Poles approached from two directions, then both halted on hearing of the king's arrival. Andrew also halted, fearing a sudden encounter with two enemy forces. Domestic troubles caused by the conduct of Queen Gertrud and her brothers forced Andrew to return home. He hurriedly started negotiations with the Pole, Leszek. He agreed with Galich to accept Prince Yaroslav of Pereiaslavl, son of Grand Prince Vsevolod of Suzdal, as its ruler. Then he departed for Hungary.

The Rus princes returned even earlier. Then the men of Galich waited two weeks for Yaroslav. Fearing that the sons of Oleg might learn about the king's retreat and come back to Galich, they decided to send secretly to Vladimir Igorevich of Severia, inviting him to be their prince. This decision was supported strongly by two boyars who, after being banished by Roman, stayed in the Severian district and returned at that time singing the praises of the sons of Igor. Vladimir Igorevich with his brother Roman, receiving the invitation, slipped away to Galich at night, keeping their departure secret from the other princes. Vladimir took his seat in Galich, and Roman in Zvenigorod. Yaroslav Vsevolodovich was also on his way to Galich. He was three days late. When he learned that Galich accepted the sons of Igor, he returned to Pereiaslavl.

MISERABLE FATE OF ROMAN'S SONS

Neither the descendants of Igor nor the boyars of Galich who incited the rebellion against Roman's sons remained easy while Roman's sons were alive and free in their fatherland, Vladimir-in-Volhynia. A messenger-priest sent by the prince of Galich arrived and delivered to the people of Vladimir the prince's message, saying "Your city will be razed to the ground if you do not hand Roman's sons over to me and accept my brother Sviatoslav as your prince." The people of Vladimir, angered by this speech, wanted to kill the priest, but three men persuaded them not to kill the messenger. These three acted in this way not because of respect for the calling of the messenger, but because they favored the prince of Galich.

When the following day the princess learned that a messenger from Galich was visiting the city, and that there were in Vladimir those who supported the sons of Igor, she consulted her son's tutor Miroslav, who said that there was nothing they could do save escape from the city. At night, through a breach in the city wall, the wife of Roman the Great with four other persons left the city. Her son's tutor the priest Miroslav and a wet nurse carried the little princes Daniel and Vasilko. The refugees knew not where to go, for there were enemies on every side!

They decided to escape to Leszek in Poland although they could not expect a very warm welcome from him. After all, Roman was killed in a war against him, and peace was not yet concluded. Fortunately in Leszek's heart pity overwhelmed hostility. He received the refugees with honor, saying "I do not know how it could have happened. It was the devil himself who incited me and Roman to quarrel." He sent the little Daniel and his messenger to Hungary to tell the king "I have forgotten my quarrel with Roman, who was your friend. You swore to each other that the survivor would look to the family of the deceased. Now Roman's sons have been expelled from every refuge. Let us go and return their fatherland to them."

It seems that at the beginning Andrew took to heart Leszek's proposal. Later, when the prince of Galich sent expensive gifts to both of them, his support for Roman's family cooled. When the sons of Igor quarrelled among themselves one of them, Roman, travelled to Hungary and persuaded Andrew to give him some troops. These forces helped him expel from Galich his brother Vladimir, who was forced to flee to his old district of Putivl. The following year (1207) the Polish prince Leszek and his brother Konrad finally marched on Vladimir where after the escape of Roman's sons Sviatoslav, Igor's third son, ruled.

Leszek did not march on Vladimir to return it to Roman's sons. He intended to place there his maternal uncle, Roman's nephew Alexander Vsevolodovich of Bełsk. The people of Vladimir opened the gates of the city to Alexander. "This is Roman's nephew," they said. Alexander's Polish allies, although they entered the city without opposition, looted Vladimir. They were about to pull down the gates of the cathedral of the Mother of God when, at Alexander's request, Leszek and his brother arrived and chased them away. The people of Vladimir complained bitterly against the Poles. "We trusted their oath," they said. "Were not Alexander with them, we would not have let them cross the Bug."

Sviatoslav Igorevich was taken prisoner and sent to Poland. In his place the Polish princes first selected Alexander, then later changed their minds. The oldest descendant of Iziaslav Mstislavich was Ingvar Yaroslavich of Lutsk, whom we have seen in Kiev. He later was placed in Vladimir, there also only to spend a short time. The boyars did not favor him, and with Leszek's permission Alexander again was invited to rule in Vladimir, while Ingvar returned home to Lutsk. His younger brother, Mstislav, nicknamed "the Mute," ruled in Peresopnitsa, and the minor Vasilko Romanovich was given Brest by Leszek at the request of the townsmen, happy to receive the little prince for in him they saw a reincarnation of Roman.

Later Vasilko's mother sent to Leszek a new request. "Alexander," she said, "holds all our land and fatherland, and my son rules only in Brest." Leszek ordered Alexander to hand over Bełz to Roman's son, and Alexander's brother Vsevolod ruled in Cherven. In this way the death of powerful Roman gave the Polish prince the opportunity to dispose of Volhynian territories.

HUNGARIANS OCCUPY GALICH

Meanwhile disturbances in Galich continued. The Kievan prince Riurik, reaching an agreement with the Hungarian king, sent his son Rostislav to Galich. The people received him with honors and expelled Roman, then soon banished Rostislav and accepted Roman once more. This development convinced King Andrew to put an end to Galich and annex it to his own lands. He sent his palatine Benedict Bora against Roman Igorevich. The palatine arrested Roman while he was in the bathhouse, and in the name of the king took power in Galich. He ruled in such a way that people called him Antichrist. He tortured boyars as well as common citizens. His voluptuousness knew no bounds, he dishonored married women, nuns and priests' wives.

The oppressed people of Galich sent for Mstislav Yaroslavich, prince of Peresopnitsa, to help them. He arrived, then found the people of Galich unready for rebellion or, more likely, the retinue he brought in their opinion was too weak to help mount an uprising against the Hungarians. One of the chief boyars, Ilia Shchepanovich, brought Mstislav to the grave of a man of Galich and said to him with a sneer "Prince! You have sat on a Galich grave, it is as if you have ruled in Galich." Thus ridiculed, Mstislav returned to Peresopnitsa.

SONS OF IGOR EXPEL THE HUNGARIANS BUT ALIENATE THE BOYARS

Then the people of Galich turned to the sons of Igor who ruled in Novgorod Seversk and sent word to Vladimir and Roman, who had escaped from the Hungarian king. "We are guilty before you," they pleaded. "Save us from the torturer Benedict." Igor's sons answered this call, appeared with strong force, forced Benedict to flee to Hungary, and again assumed the principality of Galich. Vladimir ruled in Galich proper, Roman in Zvenigorod, Sviatoslav in Peremyshl. Vladimir gave his son Iziaslav the town of Terebovl and sent his other son Vsevolod to Hungary with gifts to the king that he leave them in peace to rule beyond the Carpathian mountains.

The Hungarian king could be bought off with gifts. Besides, he had many problems in his own country. The issue remained of how Igor's sons could deal with the Galich boyars who continually disturbed them with their sedition? They decided to follow Roman's example, that is, squash the bees to enjoy the honey. Using the first opportunity, they began to kill the Galich retinue. Five hundred were killed, including the two most powerful boyars, Yury Vitanovich and Ilia Shchepanovich, and others fled, including Vladislav [Kormilchich], to whom the descendants of Igor were particularly indebted for obtaining Galich. Two others, Sudislav and Filipp, fled to Hungary. "Give us our lawful heir Daniel," they begged King Andrew, "and we will go with him to take Galich from the sons of Igor."

BOYARS ENTHRONE DANIEL ROMANOVICH IN GALICH

The king agreed, sending the banished boyars with the young Daniel to Galich, accompanied by a strong military force under eight commanders. Vladislav went first to Peremyshl. "Brothers!" said he to the people there. "Why do you hesitate? Didn't the sons of Igor kill your fathers and brothers, loot your property, marry your daughters to your slaves? Your inheritance was taken by foreigners! Surely you do not want to lay down your lives for them!"

These words swayed the inhabitants of Peremyshl. They arrested their prince Sviatoslav Igorevich and surrendered their town to Daniel. The boyars and the Hungarians then proceeded to Zvenigorod where the people were strong supporters of Igor's sons. They warded off the besiegers even though reinforced by regiments sent by Vasilko Romanovich from Bełz and by Leszek from Poland. The princes of Volhynia also joined them, Mstislav the Mute from Peresopnitsa, and Alexander with his brother from Vladimir. Prince Ingvar of Lutsk sent his regiments too. Only the Polovetsians brought by his nephew Iziaslav Vladimirovich came to help Roman Igorevich of Zvenigorod. Despite the success of the Polovetsians and the people of Zvenigorod in the battle against the Hungarians, Roman realized that he could not hold the town for long, and escaped.

On the way he was captured and brought to Daniel's camp. The Hungarian commanders sent to Zvenigorod to tell the inhabitants "Surrender, for your prince has been captured." The men of Zvenigorod did not believe this news at first, but when they learned that Roman was indeed captured they surrendered their town. From Zvenigorod Daniel and his allies marched to Galich. Vladimir Igorevich and his son did not wait for the arrival of their enemies, fleeing instead. Daniel easily entered Galich, where the boyars of Galich and Vladimir seated him on his father's throne in the cathedral church of the Mother of God.

DANIEL LEAVES GALICH

The boyars were not happy with this triumph, and sought revenge. The Hungarians imprisoned those of Igor's sons who fell into in their hands. The commanders wanted to take them to the king but the boyars of Galich distributed gifts to the commanders, took the sons of Igor and hanged them.

It is easy to understand that the boyars seated Daniel on the throne with no intention of obeying a young prince. His mother, who came to Galich soon after learning of his success, wanted to rule in his name. The boyars immediately banished her. Little Daniel did not want to part with his mother and wept. When Alexander, the steward of Shumavin, wanted to pull his horse by force Daniel drew his sword to strike Alexander. He missed him, only wounding his horse. His mother pulled the sword from his hands, persuading him to be calm and remain in Galich. She herself went again to Vasilko at Bełz, and from there to the king of Hungary.

Andrew championed her cause, summoned the boyars of Vladimir and Prince Ingvar of Lutsk, and marched on Galich where, since the expulsion of the princess, Boyar Vladislav governed in all things with two of his companions, Sudislav and Filipp. The king ordered these three arrested and imprisoned under a harsh regime. Sudislav bought his freedom with money, but Vladislav was forced to accompany the king to Hungary. He did not remain there for long. His two brothers, Yavold and

Yaropolk, escaped to Peresopnitsa where they persuaded the local prince, Mstislav the Mute, to march with them for a second time on Galich.

When the boyars heard of Mstislav's attack on their land they went over to him. Daniel with his mother were forced to flee again to Hungary. His brother Vasilko lost Belz, taken away from him by the Polish Leszek to grant it once more to Alexander Vsevolodovich of Vladimir. Vasilko was forced to flee to Kamenets. While Vladislav's brothers successfully looked after Peresopnitsa and Galich, Vladislav himself was active at the court of King Andrew.

BOYAR VLADISLAV TAKES POWER IN GALICH

It seems from the following story as related by the chronicler that Vladislav persuaded Andrew not to give Galich to any Rus prince but to keep it for himself, and promised to prepare everything in Galich for the new order. Otherwise it would be difficult to explain the information that the king prepared to go to Galich and sent Vladislav ahead. The king could not follow Vladislav, being held up by terrible events in Hungary. These we will examine because of their similarity to what happened in Galich, which the Carpathian mountains could not shield from Hungarian influences.

The conduct of the boyars in Galich can be explained by that of the Hungarian magnates. During the period of civil war preceding Andrew's accession the importance of the magnates increased so much that Andrew, when he took the throne, was the first monarch to confirm by oath the rights and privileges of the upper class. We are aware by now that the conduct of Queen Gertrud and her brothers constantly aroused the dissatisfaction of the magnates, and in the end caused open rebellion when one of the queen's brothers, Ekbert, with his sister's knowledge and even in her rooms, dishonored the wife of the Antichrist of Galich, Palatine Benedict Bora. The latter, despite the fact that he was wont to commit similar felonies in Galich, burned with vengeance against those who caused this shame and, together with other magnates, organized a plot. Taking advantage of Andrew's absence on campaign in Galich the plotters entered the palace, looted it and hacked the queen to pieces. The king was forced to abandon his expedition to deal with rebellion at home. After Mstislav of Peresopnitsa escaped the city, Vladislav used the same opportunity to enter Galich in triumph. He *became the prince and sat on the throne*, in the words of the chronicler, although it seems he acknowledged the suzerainty of the king of Hungary.

THE HUNGARIANS AND POLES DIVIDE GALICH

In the meantime Daniel, witnessing the terrible rebellion in Hungary, left first for Poland. When Leszek gave him nothing save an honorable welcome he went to his brother Vasilko in Kamenets. This time war was launched by Mstislav the Mute of Peresopnitsa. He spurred Leszek to take part in the expedition to Galich. Leszek took with him Daniel from Kamenets, Alexander from Vladimir and his brother Vsevolod from Bełz. He marched against the new boyar-prince of Galich.

Vladislav left his brothers to defend Galich and proceeded with his troops recruited among the Hungarians and Czechs (apparently mercenaries) to meet the enemy on the Bobrok river. The allies defeated Vladislav yet failed to capture Galich. They had to be satisfied with plundering the district, then left. Later Leszek ordered Prince Alexander of Vladimir to transfer two towns, Tikhoml and Peremyshl, to Roman's sons. In these towns, says the chronicler, Daniel and Vasilko ruled with their mother, and when they gazed at Vladimir said "Sooner or later Vladimir will be ours."

Meanwhile King Andrew, after settling some of his domestic problems, set off against Leszek to punish him for plundering the district of Galich he considered his own. Leszek did not wish to stand against the king, and sent his governor Pakosław with a proposal. "It is not seemly," he urged, "that a boyar rules in Galich. Better to let my daughter be married to your son Kálmán, and we will place him there." Andrew agreed, and after a personal meeting with Leszek they arranged a wedding, and young Kálmán began to rule in Galich. The boyar Vladislav was captured and died in prison, causing much misery for his children and his clan because no prince was willing to shelter the sons of a boyar who dared usurp a princely title.

Apart from a profitable marriage arrangement for his daughter, Leszek obtained from the king the towns of Peremyshl and Liubachev from the district of Galich. Liubachev was given to the governor Pakosław, who arranged this profitable alliance. Pakosław was friendly to Roman's young sons and their mother. On his advice Leszek sent word to Alexander Vsevolodovich. "Return Vladimir to the sons of Roman," he urged. "If you do not agree to return it, I will march with them against you." Alexander refused to surrender it willingly, but later was forced to yield.

III

VSEVOLOD III'S LAST YEARS

CONTINUATION OF INTERNECINE WAR

Thus scions of other branches[1] divided the patrimony of the sons of Rostislav. One after another the Rus princes were forced to abandon Galich or die a shameful death. Though other Rus princes were very angry with the people of Galich for the dishonor brought on their clan by the hanging of Igor's sons, they were powerless to take revenge because the descendants of Monomakh and Oleg continued their customary struggle. In 1206, after returning from the second expedition against Galich, the sons of Oleg were quite content that they had seized it for their branch members, the descendants of Igor, and decided to take the seniority and Kiev away from those of Monomakh.

Vsevolod Sviatoslavich the Red occupied Kiev and "confident of his own power," as the chronicler says, sent his burgraves[2] to Kievan towns. Riurik, realizing his powerlessness, or in the words of the chronicler, *misfortune*, returned to his previous district, Ovruch. His son Rostislav fled to Vyshgorod, his nephew Mstislav Romanovich to Belgorod.

Having taken Kiev from the descendants of Monomakh, the sons of Oleg wanted also to seize Pereiaslavl from them. Moreover the prince of Pereiaslavl, Yaroslav Vsevolodovich, was the rival of the descendants of Igor for the Galich throne. Thus Vsevolod the Red sent word to Yaroslav. "Leave Pereiaslavl," he said, "and go to your father in Suzdal. Do not contend with my brothers over Galich. If you do not go willingly, I will attack you." Yaroslav had no hope of assistance from any quarter. He sent to Vsevolod to ask free passage to the North by way of the Chernigov lands. His request was granted. He swore to the sons of Oleg by kissing the cross to follow their will. The son of the Red took his place in Pereiaslavl.

The Red did not stay in Kiev long. That same year Riurik came together with his sons and nephews, chased Oleg's descendants from Kiev and Pereiaslavl, took Kiev for himself and sent his son Vladimir to Pereiaslavl. In winter the Red arrived with his brother and Polovetsians to retake Kiev. He besieged the city for three weeks. He failed to capture it, returning empty-handed. He had better luck the following year, 1207. The enemies of the descendants of Monomakh came from three directions. From Chernigov came the Red with his brothers, from Turov Prince Sviatopolk, and Vladimir Igorevich from Galich.

Riurik, when he heard that an innumerable force was converging upon him from all directions, and that no help was on the way, fled from Kiev to Ovruch. Tripolie, Belgorod and Torchesk were taken from the descendants of Monomakh who because of hunger could not withstand long sieges. Vsevolod took the Kievan throne once again, causing much damage to the Land of Rus by using the Polovetsians as allies.

Vsevolod of Suzdal moved against him. Hearing that the descendants of Oleg were allied with the pagans in attacking the Land of Rus, he took pity on it. "Is the Land of Rus their patrimony only," he asked, "and not ours as well? God's will be done. I will go to Chernigov." Vsevolod collected a strong force, then problems with Riazan interfered with his campaign against Chernigov. When the princes of Riazan were captured Riurik was overjoyed by Vsevolod's success in the campaign against the allies of the sons of Oleg. He appeared suddenly near Kiev and removed the Red, who unsuccessfully tried to regain the city by force. He regained it only as a result of negotiations with Vsevolod of Suzdal.

DESCENDANTS OF MONOMAKH IN CHERNIGOV

In 1210 the Red and all the sons of Oleg sent Metropolitan Matthias to Suzdal asking for peace, in all matters submitting to Vsevolod. A short time earlier one of the descendants of Rostislav, Mstislav Mstislavich the Daring,[3] caused Vsevolod many problems in Novgorod. Vsevolod was not well disposed towards this princely branch. He agreed that Vsevolod the Red, as the oldest among fifth cousins in Yaroslav's clan, be awarded Kiev. To Riurik he gave Chernigov.

Thus whereas the trend towards a new order became clearly visible in the North, in the South of Rus, following a lengthy struggle, ancient ideas of the unity of Yaroslav's clan and non-hereditary succession in districts of one branch of the family triumphed. Not only did a descendant of Oleg receive Kiev, the next senior descendant of Monomakh became prince of Chernigov. The ancient procedure of migration of princes among districts was renewed. This order was violated during Monomakh's time by excluding Oleg's sons from seniority. The peace concluded between them and the prince of Suzdal was strengthened by the marriage of Vsevolod's son Yury to the Red's daughter.

CONSOLIDATION OF VSEVOLOD III'S POWER IN THE NORTH

At a time when the lands of South Rus remained faithful to the old traditions which deprived them of the strength to regain their lost significance and prime position, the Northern prince grew ever more powerful. Since 1179 the princes of Riazan, Gleb's sons, were in Vsevolod's thrall. In 1186 a quarrel arose between them. The older brothers, Roman, Igor and Vladimir, armed themselves against the younger, Vsevolod and Sviatoslav, who ruled in Pronsk. To deal with them more easily they issued an invitation to a meeting, intending to capture them there and then. The younger brothers found out about this plan. Instead of going to the meeting, they fortified their town, expecting an attack. They did not have to wait long. The older brothers appeared with a large force and pillaged the environs of the town. Then Vsevolod of Suzdal sent a message to them. "Brothers," he asked, "what are you doing? Is it surprising that the pagans attack us, while you seek to kill your own brothers."

These princes did not listen. Instead they grew angry with Vsevolod for his interference, and hatred of their brothers grew even stronger. Gleb's younger sons then asked Vsevolod for help. He sent them three hundred men from the Vladimir retinue, who entered Pronsk and defended it together with the besieged. Later he sent another force, joined by the princes of Murom.

When they learned of the approach of forces from Vladimir, Gleb's older sons lifted the siege of Pronsk and rushed home to Riazan. Vsevolod Glebovich came to meet the regiments of Vsevolod *the Great.* The men of Vladimir learned that the siege of Pronsk was lifted. There being no longer any need to go there, they returned to Vladimir. Gleb's younger sons also went with them to ask Vsevolod's advice about how to deal with their older brothers.

Meanwhile the princes of Riazan, hearing that the army from Vladimir had withdrawn, and only Sviatoslav was in Pronsk, besieged that town. They cut off the water from the inhabitants and sent to their brother Sviatoslav. "Do not starve yourself, your retinue and your people," they urged. "Come over to us. You are our brother, we will not devour you. Only do not ally yourself with your brother Vsevolod." Sviatoslav told this to his boyars. "Your brother went to Vladimir and betrayed you," they responded. "Why should you wait for him?" Sviatoslav took their advice and opened the town gates. His brothers returned Pronsk to him but took Vsevolod Glebovich's wife, children and retinue with them to Riazan.

Together with Vsevolod Glebovich's retinue they also imprisoned those of Vsevolod the Great's retinue who participated in the defense of Pronsk. When Vsevolod Glebovich heard that his family and retinue were arrested, first he grieved, then later occupied Kolomna. From there he pillaged his brothers' territory. They repaid him in kind, and hatred between them intensified.

Vsevolod the Great also was very angry with Sviatoslav for allowing his brothers to imprison Vladimir retainers. "Give me back my retainers without violence," he demanded, "the way you took them from me. If you want to make peace with your brothers, do so, but why did you let my men be captured? I sent them to you at your request, you begged me to send them, bowing low to me. When you were under arms, they were under arms, so when you make peace, they also are at peace." The sons of Gleb, when they heard that Vsevolod the Great was about to march against them, sent word to him. "You are our father, lord and brother," they said. "If there is any offense against you, we will be the first to sacrifice our lives for you. Do not be angry with us. If we went to war with our brother, it was because he did not heed us. We bow to you and set your retinue free." Vsevolod did not want peace, which meant that war was more advantageous and success assured.

The following year (1187) Bishop Porfiry of Chernigov arrived in Vladimir to intercede for Gleb's sons because Riazan belonged to his diocese. He convinced Bishop Luka of Vladimir to act together with him. They both interceded with Vsevolod on behalf of Gleb's sons. Vsevolod listened to their arguments and sent Porfiry to Riazan with peace proposals. Together with the bishop went also Vsevolod's envoys and those of the princes of Chernigov, bringing with them the Riazan prisoners freed by Vsevolod as a token of his desire for peace. Yet Porfiry, when he arrived in Riazan, did not conduct the negotiations the way Vsevolod wished, bargaining instead behind the envoys' backs. Vsevolod grew angry and apparently wished to send his men to pursue Porfiry, but he soon changed his mind. Yet while he decided to let Porfiry be, he did not want to leave Gleb's sons in peace. That same year he marched against them, taking along the prince of Murom and Vsevolod Glebovich from Kolomna. He crossed the Oka river and ravaged the Riazan land. This expedition apparently achieved his aim because later, during the war with the descendants of Oleg, the princes of Riazan served in his army. At the same time Pronsk was returned to Vsevolod Glebovich, who died there soon after.

RELATIONS WITH RIAZAN, SMOLENSK AND GREAT NOVGOROD

When in 1207 Vsevolod the Great decided to march against the descendants of Oleg in Chernigov, he met in Moscow with his son Prince Konstantin of Novgorod, and awaited the princes of Riazan. Suddenly he learned they were deceiving him, being in collusion with Oleg's descendants to join him in order later to betray him to his enemies. All the princes of Riazan appeared with their retinues. There were eight princes: Roman and Sviatoslav Glebovich, accompanied by two of Sviatoslav's sons, and their nephews; the sons of the deceased Igor and Vladimir and two sons of Igor, Ingvar and Yury, together with Gleb and Oleg, two sons of Vladimir. Vsevolod received them all cordially and invited them for dinner, which was served in two tents. In one feasted six Riazan princes, in the other Grand Prince Vsevolod and two other Riazan princes, Gleb and Oleg, who told Vsevolod "Do not believe our brothers. They are in collusion with the princes of Chernigov against you." Vsevolod sent Prince Davyd of Murom and his boyar Mikhail Borisovich to expose the Riazan princes. The accused swore that they had no such intention.

Prince Davyd and his boyar Mikhail shuttled between the two tents for a long time when finally, in the Riazan tent, two members of their clan, Gleb and Oleg, appeared and exposed them. When Vsevolod heard that truth was established, he ordered the discovered princes arrested together with their advisors, and sent them to Vladimir.

The following day he crossed the Oka and marched on Pronsk, ruled by Mikhail, son of the deceased Vsevolod Glebovich. When this prince heard that his uncle was seized, and Vsevolod with his forces was approaching his town, he took fright and escaped to his father-in-law in Chernigov. This was a clear sign that he was in league with the arrested princes and the prince of Chernigov, his father-in-law. Otherwise there was no reason for him to fear Vsevolod, who always was well disposed towards his father.

The people of Pronsk invited Vladimir's third son Iziaslav, who apparently was not in league with his brothers, to rule there, and they closed the town gates. Vsevolod sent to them the boyar Mikhail Borisovich with peace proposals, to which they refused to listen. The chronicler calls their answer "a turbulent speech." Then Vsevolod ordered the town besieged from every direction, and the water supply cut off. The people did not lose heart and made valiant sorties, stealing water by night. Vsevolod ordered guards mounted day and night, and his regiments deployed at all the gates. His older son Konstantin with the men of Novgorod and

Beloozero were deployed on the hill at one gate, Yaroslav with men from Pereiaslavl at the second, Davyd and troops from Murom at the third gate, while he himself with his sons Yury and Vladimir, and Vladimir's two sons, stayed on the other side of the river from the direction of the Polovetsian steppe.

The men of Pronsk did not surrender and made frequent sorties, not to fight with the besieging troops, but to get water because they were dying of thirst. Meanwhile the besieging troops began to suffer food shortages. Vsevolod sent a detachment under the command of Oleg Vladimirovich to the Oka, where his boats laden with grain were moored. On the way Oleg learned that his cousin Roman, Igor's third son, left by his uncles in Riazan, had quit the city with his troops and was attacking Vladimir's boatmen moored by Olgovo. At this news [Oleg] Vladimirovich went forth to help the boatmen. The Riazan force left off attacking the boatmen and turned against the newly arrived troops, then were defeated because they were positioned between two adversaries, Oleg's regiment and the boatmen. Oleg returned to the host victorious, bringing the grain.

After a three-week siege Pronsk was forced to surrender. Vsevolod gave them as their prince Oleg Vladimirovich. He himself marched to Riazan, placing in all towns his own burgraves, thereby showing his intention of controlling them. He was only twenty versts from Old Riazan, near the village of Dobry Sot, planning to cross the Pronia river, when envoys appeared from Riazan, bowing before him and entreating him not to enter their city. Bishop Arseny of Riazan repeatedly petitioned him. "O grand prince," he said, "do not disrespect shrines, do not burn holy churches in which sacrifice is offered to God and prayers are said for you, and we will fulfil all your wishes." Vsevolod listened to their pleas and returned to Vladimir by way of Kolomna. Vsevolod demanded that Riazan hand over all the remaining princes with their princesses. Riazan complied. The following year, 1208, Vsevolod's son Yaroslav came to rule there.

The men of Riazan swore allegiance to him, but planned treason. They arrested his followers and put them in chains. Some were buried alive in pits. Then Vsevolod marched against Riazan, and again near the city met with his son Yaroslav. The men of Riazan came to the Oka *for a council*, which meant for an accord between them and their prince Yaroslav. Instead of justifying themselves they sent a turbulent speech expressing their customary disobedience, says the chronicler. Vsevolod ordered his troops to arrest and send them to the city, seizing their wives and children. The city was burned and the inhabitants dispersed to various towns.

He did likewise in Belgorod. He then returned to Vladimir with some men from Riazan and their bishop Arseny. The previous prince of Pronsk, Mikhail Vsevolodovich, with his cousin Iziaslav Vladimirovich (apparently freed after the capitulation of Pronsk) marched the same year to attack Vsevolod's territory near Moscow. They were defeated by the grand prince's son Yury, and saved their lives by fleeing, abandoning all their followers.

This is the story repeated in the majority of the chronicles known to us, but in the *Chronicle of Pereiaslavl-Suzdal*[4] we read that Vsevolod, after taking Pronsk, entrusted it to Prince Davyd of Murom. The following year Oleg, Gleb and Iziaslav Vladimirovich, and Prince Mikhail Vsevolodovich of Riazan, marched on Pronsk against Davyd, asking "Is Pronsk his patrimony or ours?" "Brothers," replied Davyd, "I myself never would have fought for Pronsk. I was placed here by Vsevolod. Now the town is yours. I will go to my own land." Lord Mikhail[5] ruled Pronsk. Oleg Vladimirovich died the same year in Belgorod.

This account is more credible because it is difficult to assume that the expedition of the princes of Riazan against Pronsk to fight Davyd was invented with all the details. For the same year, 1208, the Pereiaslavl chronicler has the further curious information that Vsevolod III sent his commander Stepan Zdilovich to Serensk, and this town was burned. This expedition seems very likely, being Vsevolod's revenge against the princes of Chernigov for expelling his son Yaroslav from Southern Pereiaslavl.

Vsevolod was also a menace for other neighbors, the princes of Smolensk. For the year 1206 the chronicle states that Bishop Michael of Smolensk, together with the abbot of the Otroch monastery, came to Vladimir to beseech Vsevolod to forgive their prince Mstislav Romanovich for his alliance with the sons of Oleg.

Novgorod the Great also was threatened in the time of Vsevolod with change of its old ways. We left the discussion of Novgorod at the time when, despite the wishes of Bogoliubsky and the sons of Rostislav, its inhabitants accepted as their prince the son of Mstislav Iziaslavich, the famous Roman Mstislavich.[6] In consequence they had to prepare for a dangerous struggle with the powerful prince of Suzdal. In 1169 Danislav Lazutinich, the same who brought Roman to Novgorod, went to the Northern Dvina with a retinue of four hundred to collect tribute. Andrei sent a force of seven thousand to intercept him, but Danislav forced the Suzdal troops to flee. He killed thirteen hundred of them, losing only fifteen of his own troops. Afterwards Lazutinich turned back, evidently afraid to go any further. Nevertheless after some time he moved on and exacted the tribute, thus imposing double taxation on the subjects of Suzdal.

Andrei did not suffer Novgorod's triumph for long. Having expelled the father from Kiev, he sent a strong force to chase the son out of Novgorod. This took place in the winter of 1169. The army was led by Andrei's son Mstislav and his commander Boris Zhiroslavich. It included the retinue and all the regiments from Rostov and Suzdal. They were joined by the princes of Smolensk, Roman and Mstislav Rostislavich, as well as the princes of Riazan and Murom. This army, according to the chronicles, was innumerable. After terrible devastation of the Novgorod district it approached the city. The inhabitants with their young prince closed the gates, while the burgrave Yakun struggled valiantly. Four attacks failed, then during the last, which continued the whole day, Prince Mstislav entered the city through the gate and killed several defenders. Nevertheless he was forced to retreat. The men of Novgorod, together with Roman, celebrated their victory. Meanwhile a pestilence arose among the besieging regiments. Men and horses began to die. Andrei's host was forced to withdraw without results. This retreat through a ravaged countryside was their undoing. Some died on the way, others reached their homes on foot, many were taken prisoner by the men of Novgorod, who were selling a man for two small coins.[7]

The ravages inflicted by Andrei's host had serious consequences for Novgorod as well. There was great famine since grain was available only from the East, from Andrei's territories. In addition Mstislav Iziaslavich died. There was no further justification for keeping his son, so they expelled Roman.[8] They initiated peace negotiations with Andrei, asking him for a prince.

Riurik Rostislavich was sent to rule there. It is not known how Yakun lost his position as burgrave. Very likely the peace between Andrei and the sons of Rostislav was concluded on condition that the burgrave who was the mainstay of Novgorod opposition to the prince of Suzdal be replaced. Yakun's successor was Zhiroslav, but Riurik withdrew his position of burgrave and gave it to Ivan, son of the previous burgrave Zakhary, who was killed for his support of Riurik's brother Sviatoslav. Riurik, not content with stripping Zhiroslav of his position, banished him from the city. He took refuge with Andrei in Suzdal.

That same year Riurik left Novgorod. His brother Roman took the throne of Kiev and gave him a district in Rus. Delegates from Novgorod appeared before Andrei to request another prince. Andrei sent Zhiroslav to be their burgrave, accompanied by some of his boyars. The following year he sent his son Yury. Apparently Zhiroslav was unpopular in Novgorod. Archbishop Elias visited Andrei in Vladimir to settle all issues once and for all. As a result of this journey Ivan Zakharievich was restored to the office of burgrave.

Bogoliubsky's death brought changes in Novgorod. His son Yury was supposed to leave in his place the son of Mstislav Rostislavich, invited by the people of Rostov. Then the same year Mstislav himself, defeated by his uncle Mikhail and expelled from Rostov, took his son's place in Novgorod. Also the same year, 1175, the burgrave Ivan Zakharievich died and his place was taken by Zhiroslav. Later this year he again lost this position, and Zavid Nerevinich took it. He was the son of the boyar Nerevin who was killed alongside Zakharia. Mstislav Rostislavich only had time to get married in Novgorod to the daughter of Yakun Miroslavich when he was called again by the people of Rostov. Again he was defeated and chased away by his uncle Vsevolod. He journeyed to Novgorod where he was expelled together with his son, who apparently had been left for the second time in his place.

Novgorod then accepted a prince from the victor Vsevolod, who sent to Novgorod his nephew Yaroslav Mstislavich. In all probability Mstislav Rostislavich left behind in Novgorod a strong faction under the leadership of his father-in-law Yakun. The following year, 1177, he appeared in Novgorod and assumed the rulership. His brother Yaropolk received Torzhok and the previous prince Yaroslav received Volokolamsk. This was a sign that he had forsaken Vsevolod and joined his enemies, the sons of Rostislav.

It is easy to understand that Vsevolod could not accept calmly the descendants of Rostislav as princes in the neighboring Novgorod districts. Nor could he forgive the people of Novgorod for violating their promise to acknowledge his suzerainty, as well as their undertaking to assist him in his war against Prince Gleb of Riazan. In 1178, when Mstislav Rostislavich died and Novgorod invited his brother Yaropolk to be its prince, Vsevolod ordered the arrest of all Novgorod merchants in his territories. Novgorod took fright and expelled Yaropolk. The honor of sending princes to an ancient city did not satisfy the prince of the new towns. Seeking a more tangible benefit, he marched against Torzhok, whose inhabitants promised to pay him tribute.

When Vsevolod approached the town at first he refrained from storming it, waiting for the inhabitants to fulfill their promise. His retinue complained, urging him to storm the town. "We did not come to kiss them," they said, "they lie to God and to you." The army attacked the town and captured it. The people were taken prisoner and the town was burned because of Novgorod's perfidy, "because," as the chronicler added, "the men of Novgorod kiss the cross and then break their promise the same day." After sending the prisoners from Novy Torzhok to Vladimir, Vsevolod moved against Volokolamsk, whose inhabitants escaped. Their prince Yaroslav Mstislavich was captured and the town was burned. In the meantime Novgorod sent for the nearest prince, Roman Rostislavich of Smolensk, who indeed came. Vsevolod, satisfied with rich booty and apparently unwilling to struggle against the Southern branch of Rostislav's clan, returned to Vladimir.

MSTISLAV THE BRAVE IN THE NORTH

Roman did not stay long in Novgorod. The following year, 1179, he returned to Smolensk. Novgorod sent an invitation to his cousin Mstislav Rostislavich,[9] famous for his struggle against Bogoliubsky.[10] This marks the beginning of Novgorod's relationship with the two Mstislavs [Rostislavich and Mstislavich], father and son, the most illustrious representatives of the old Southwestern Rus, fighting against the new Northeastern Rus. This alliance was necessary because of identical aspirations. Novgorod, like the Mstislavs, wanted to support the old order against the new, to support clan relationships among princes and, at the same time, the ancient customs of the old towns. At first Mstislav seemed reluctant to go to Novgorod because of the general attachment of his branch to the South, to its own Rus, and because of the danger the descendants of Oleg posed for those of Monomakh. "I cannot leave my patrimony and part from my brothers," said Mstislav. He tried very hard to advance his patrimony, says the chronicler. He always strove to perform great deeds, took counsel with his men, and wished to be faithful to his origins and his princely importance (wishing to "fulfill his patrimony").[11] Nevertheless his brothers and his retinue persuaded him to go to Novgorod. "If this is an honest invitation," they urged him, "then go. Is it not also our fatherland?" Mstislav went, but made a vow. "If God grants me health," he said, "I cannot forget the Land of Rus." The character of this Mstislav, the representative of our ancient princes, how he understood the duties of his calling, *fulfillment of his patrimony*, is seen in the fact that the moment he arrived in Novgorod he immediately contemplated where to fight.

A short time before, in 1176, the Chud[12] came to the Land of Pskov and fought a violent battle with the men of Pskov, many being killed on both sides. Mstislav therefore decided to attack the Chud. He gathered the men of Novgorod. "Brothers," he told them, "pagans offend us. Should we not ask God and His Holy Mother for help, to take revenge and free the Novgorod land from pagans?" His speech pleased the men of Novgorod. "O prince," they answered, "if it is to God's liking and yours, we are ready." Mstislav gathered the Novgorod troops. After counting them he found he had twenty thousand men. With this powerful force he entered the land of the Chud, burned it, took many prisoners and cattle, in the words of the chronicler returning home with victory, fame and great honor. On his way from the land of the Chud he visted Pskov, where he arrested the hundredmen who refused to accept his nephew Boris Romanovich. Consolidating his position there, he returned to Novgorod for the winter.

In spring he again took counsel with his retinue where else to fight. He conjured the idea of attacking his son-in-law Vseslav, prince of Polotsk. About a hundred years earlier Vseslav's grandfather attacked Novgorod, took church plate, and one Novgorod trading settlement[13] was turned over to Polotsk. Mstislav decided to recover the district for Novgorod and avenge this offense. He stood with his troops at Velikie Luki when an envoy appeared, sent by his older brother Roman in Smolensk. "Vseslav did not cause you any offense," Roman told Mstislav. "If you attack him without reason, you have to attack me first." Faithful to the old traditions, Mstislav forbore to offend his older brother, especially as he had dispatched his son to help Vseslav, which meant that the men of Novgorod must fight the men of Smolensk instead of those of Polotsk.

MSTISLAV'S DEATH

Returning to Novgorod, Mstislav fell dangerously ill, lost all his strength and could hardly speak. When he felt death near he looked first at his retinue, then at his princess, sighed deeply and burst into tears. "I entrust my child Vladimir to Boris Zakharievich," he said, "and both of them I entrust to my brothers Riurik and Davyd, with their territory. God will take care of me." With these arrangements made Mstislav raised his hands to heaven, sighed again, burst into tears and died.

The people of Novgorod buried him in the same tomb as the first prince who died among them, Vladimir Yaroslavich, founder of the cathedral of the Holy Wisdom.[14] All the Land of Novgorod wept for

Mstislav, says the chronicler. The best men in the land especially wept most bitterly. "Now we cannot go fight against foreign lands," they said during the funeral, "to bring pagans as slaves to the Land of Novgorod. You planned many expeditions against the pagan lands. We would be better off dying with you! You gave us great freedom from the pagans, just like your grandfather Mstislav freed us from all impositions. You were his equal and followed in his footsteps. Now that we will not see you any more our sun has set, we are defenseless, now anybody can offend us with impunity."

Mstislav, according to the chronicler, was of medium height, handsome, and adorned with every virtue. He was well mannered, loved everybody, was very generous to the poor, endowed monasteries, fed the monks and received them with love. Parish churches were richly endowed by him, and he bestowed great honors on the clergy. He was brave in war, not sparing himself fighting for the Land of Rus and for Christianity. When he saw Christians taken to slavery by pagans he said to his retinue "Brothers! Doubt not that if now we die for Christianity we will be cleansed of sins and God will make our blood that of martyrs. If God spares us, praise God! If die we must, it is all the same, for we have to die some time or another." With such words he encouraged his retinue, which fought most ardently for their patrimony.

He loved his retinue, not sparing his wealth for them, gathering for himself neither gold nor silver, instead distributing it to the retinue, to the churches or to the poor for the salvation of his soul. There was no corner in Rus where he was not desired or loved. His brothers grieved when they heard of his death. All the Land of Rus wept for him, his valor could not be forgotten, neither could the Karakalpaks forget his *tender care* (1180).

CHANGES IN NOVGOROD THE GREAT

After Mstislav's death Novgorod faced a choice whence to summon a prince. From Vsevolod III of Suzdal, prince of the new Northern Rus, or from the hands of Sviatoslav Vsevolodovich, who ruled in Kiev, and therefore was considered the senior in the old Southern Rus? Novgorod acted according to ancient traditions and received from Sviatoslav his son Vladimir, for Vsevolod recently demonstrated by his hostility towards Novgorod that truly he was Bogoliubsky's brother.

After taking Vladimir as prince Novgorod participated in the war his father Sviatoslav waged with Vsevolod and, of course, according to his wishes again in Torzhok he placed Vsevolod's nephew and enemy Yaropolk Rostislavich. This inevitably led to a clash with the prince of Suzdal. As the men of Novgorod sent their regiments to Drutsk to aid Sviatoslav, Vsevolod reappeared near Torzhok and besieged Yaropolk. The siege lasted five weeks, during which the people of Torzhok suffered terrible hunger. When their prince Yaropolk was wounded in a skirmish they surrendered to Vsevolod, who placed Yaropolk in irons and spirited him away. Expelling all the men of Torzhok with their wives and children, he burned the town. When the citizens of Novgorod realized that danger was near and ominous, and hope of help from Chernigov rather remote, they expelled Vladimir Sviatoslavich and requested Vsevolod to send a prince. Vsevolod sent his relative Yaroslav Vladimirovich, a landless son of a landless father, Vladimir Mstislavich. Yaroslav did not stay long in Novgorod. He aroused strong opposition, causing Vsevolod to remove him. Novgorod, apparently not without his knowledge and consent, invited Mstislav Davydovich from Smolensk. Burgrave Zavid Nerevinich was replaced immediately after Vladimir Sviatoslavich arrived in Novgorod. This was a sign that he did not support this descendant of Oleg. His position went to Mikhail Stepanovich.

The expulsion of this descendant of Oleg inevitably brought about a change in burgraves. Mikhail Stepanovich was replaced and his position once again went to Zavid, then in 1186 Zavid was ousted and went to Davyd in Smolensk. His place once again was assumed by Mikhail Stepanovich. Zavid's relatives and friends did not cease their activity, but were defeated by the other party. Zavid's brother Gavrilo Nerevinich was thrown off a bridge, together with one Ivach Svenevich.

It is interesting to note that at the same time the citizens of Smolensk also rebelled against Prince Davyd. As the chronicler puts it, many of the best people lost their heads. Possibly these events in Novgorod and Smolensk were somehow connected. There is no doubt that the disturbances in Novgorod, the struggle between the factions of Zavid and Mikhail, were connected with the changes of princes. Zavid, who was burgrave during the time of Mstislav the Brave, supported the descendants of Rostislav. This is indicated by his replacement when a descendant of Oleg came to rule, and his departure to Davyd in Smolensk after he lost his position for the second time. Mikhail Stepanovich's faction was at the same time the party which supported Prince Yaroslav. No wonder therefore that when they triumphed over their enemies the following year, 1187, Mstislav Davydovich was expelled and Novgorod sent to Vsevolod in Vladimir to petition once more for Yaroslav Vladimirovich. This suggests that he was expelled earlier, not as a result of general indignation, rather because of the opposition of one faction only. The burgrave was not replaced, but the following year the other faction gained the upper hand. Mikhail Stepanovich lost his position and Miroshka Nezdinich became burgrave. His father Nezda was killed for his connection to the Smolensk branch of the Rostislavich clan. Therefore it may be supposed that Miroshka inherited this connection and supported Mstislav Davydovich against Yaroslav.

This supposition is confirmed by information that in 1195 Miroshka, together with Boris Zhiroslavich and the hundredmen Nikifor, Ivanko and Foma, visited Vsevolod to beseech the prince to replace Yaroslav and send his son instead. What did Vsevolod do? To ensure peace for Yaroslav in Novgorod, he arrested Miroshka and his companions as heads of the anti-Yaroslav faction. Later he freed Boris and Nikifor but kept Mirosha, Ivanko and Foma, notwithstanding pleas from Novgorod to send them back. Finally he freed Foma, but kept Miroshka and Ivanko. This angered the citizens of Novgorod, namely the anti-Yaroslav faction. Yaroslav was expelled and an envoy journeyed to Chernigov to request the son of the local prince. The fact that just one faction acted there is borne out by the words of the chronicler, who says that good people regretted Yaroslav, while bad people rejoiced that he was expelled.

The times were past when princes expelled from Novgorod left without thinking about revenge. Remember how Sviatoslav Rostislavich, hoping to receive help from Bogoliubsky, refused to leave the borders of the Novgorod district peacefully. Yaroslav Vladimirovich followed his example. He went to Torzhok, where the inhabitants received him respectfully, and he collected tribute from the upper country along the Msta river and even beyond the portage. Vsevolod at the same time intercepted men of Novgorod everywhere, not letting them leave Vladimir, though they were not imprisoned.

Meanwhile Prince Yaropolk Yaroslavich arrived from Chernigov. He stayed in Novgorod just six months. The hostility between the Vladimir prince and Yaroslav, who was in Torzhok and collected the tribute, could not be very convenient for Novgorod. Taking advantage of this situation, Yaroslav's faction gained the upper hand, expelled Yaropolk in 1197 and sent to Torzhok for Yaroslav, who nevertheless did not go directly to Novgorod. First he went to Vladimir to visit Vsevolod, who apparently denied Novgorod the right to quarrel and make peace with princes without reference to him. The best (most important) men and the hundredmen had to travel from Novgorod to Vladimir, there to receive Yaroslav from Vsevolod's hand with all truth and honor, as the chronicler put it. When, as the same chronicler writes, Yaroslav arrived in Novgorod he made peace with people and there was reconciliation. The burgrave Miroshka also returned safe and sound after two years' detention in Vladimir for Novgorod's sake, and everybody in Novgorod was happy, from the greatest to the least. Iziaslav, son of Yaroslav, went to rule in Velikie Luki, acting as Novgorod's defense against the Lithuanians.

As the circumstances demonstrate it is very likely that Novgorod accepted Yaroslav on terms dictated by Vsevolod, who from that time disposed of Novgorod as Monomakh or his son Mstislav once did. Peace between Yaroslav and Miroshka and his faction was short-lived. After one year (1199), the best people from Novgorod arrived in Vladimir, the relatives and friends of Miroshka, who bowed low to the prince and presented Novgorod's request. "You are lord," they said, "you are Yury, you are Vladimir! We plead you to send your son to rule in Novgorod because Novgorod is your father's and grandfather's land." Vsevolod agreed, ordering Yaroslav to leave Novgorod and come to Vladimir. The archbishop, the burgrave Miroshka and the best men were instructed to present themselves in Vladimir, there to receive as their prince his ten-year-old son Sviatoslav, as this was the will of the grand prince.

During the journey Archbishop Martiry died. Vsevolod, despite the ancient Novgorod custom of electing the archbishop at the city assembly, discussing the matter only with the burgrave, chose and sent to Novgorod Archbishop Mitrofan.[15] Later this cleric was sent to the metropolitan to arrange reconciliation between the Novgorod dignitaries and those of Vsevolod.[16] In 1203 Burgrave Miroshka died and his place was taken by his opponent, the former burgrave Mikhail Stepanovich. A year later Vsevolod sent word to the citizens of Novgorod. "Your land is being attacked," he said, "and your prince, my son Sviatoslav, is still small, now I give you my older son Konstantin." There is no information about attacks during the three preceding years, and the possibility that this exchange was dictated by domestic disorders in Novgorod is proven by the fact that the change of princes was followed closely by a change of burgraves. More likely, after the change of the Vladimir boyars who governed the estate of the minor Sviatoslav, the office of burgrave was stripped from Mikhail Stepanovich and given to Dmitry, son of the late

Miroshka. The fact that the minor Sviatoslav and the burgrave Mikhail were changed because of Novgorod's complaints is suggested by the words of the chronicler when he writes that after Konstantin's arrival the entire city was satisfied that its wish was fulfilled. The Vladimir chronicler says that when Vsevolod sent Konstantin to Novgorod he said to him "My son Konstantin! God gave you seniority among all your brothers, and Novgorod the Great is the senior seat in all the Land of Rus. Your name gives you such honor. Not only has God given you seniority among your brothers, I also grant you seniority in all the Rus lands. Go to your city."

The new burgrave, son of Miroshka, as well as his brothers and friends, with the support of the Suzdal prince wanted to enrich himself at the expense of the inhabitants, and acted in a manner which turned the entire city against him. Among the dissatisfied citizens apparently was one Alexis Sbyslavich. The burgrave's brother Boris Miroshkinich travelled to Vsevolod in Vladimir and returned with Lazar, a boyar of the prince of Vladimir, who brought with him an order to kill Alexis Sbyslavich. This order was carried out. Alexis was killed in the Court of Yaroslav.[17] He was innocent of any crime, noted the chronicler, because the usual agreement with the prince not to sentence anybody to death without announcing his crime no longer existed. Vsevolod reigned in Novgorod like an absolute ruler.

Following this event Vsevolod marched against Chernigov and ordered Konstantin with the Novgorod forces to follow him. Konstantin joined his father in Moscow, whence instead of going to Chernigov they marched against Riazan. It seems that during this expedition Novgorod informed the grand prince of the deeds of the burgrave and his followers. When after the expedition Vsevolod released the Novgorod contingent home from Kolomna, he gave them generous gifts and, as the chronicler says, confirmed the privileges and charters granted by princes of old as they requested. "Love those who are good for you," he told them, "but the wicked you may sentence to death." He kept with him his son Konstantin, the burgrave Dmitry who was seriously wounded near Pronsk, and seven of the best people. This first and the last circumstance may indicate that these new instructions from Vsevolod were a result of Novgorod's complaints. These caused the prince's dissatisfaction with the burgrave and his friends, and with his own son who allowed them to commit violent deeds.

Whatever the cause, when the Novgorod troops arrived home they immediately summoned the city assembly against the burgrave Dmitry and his brothers, accusing them of levying additional taxes from Novgorod and the districts. They extracted wild bloodwite[18] from the merchants and ordered them to supply transport services. They committed many other breaches of law and all manner of wickedness, as the chronicler wrote. During the assembly it was decided to pillage the houses of those accused of robbery. The homes of Miroshka and Dmitry were set on fire, their property seized, their villages and slaves sold, the money divided among the inhabitants of the city, and the debt records left to the prince. During all this some took things in secret, as only God knows, adds the chronicler. It is known only that after the pillage of the Miroshkinich estate some became rich.

Popular outrage against the former burgrave reached such proportions that when the body of Dmitry, who died in Vladimir, was brought home the people of Novgorod wanted to throw it from the bridge into the river. Archbishop Mitrofan[19] prevented this. Sviatoslav Vsevolodovich became prince of Novgorod, where he ruled once before. Tverdislav Mikhailovich was elected burgrave. Most likely he was the son of the deceased Mikhail Stepanovich, the opponent of Miroshka, hatred towards whose family was behind this election. Novgorod kissed the cross that they wanted to maintain neither the children of Dmitry nor his brothers, nor his friends. The new prince, Sviatoslav, sent them as prisoners to his father. Others paid large sums of money to avoid such treatment.

MSTISLAV MSTISLAVICH DELIVERS NOVGOROD FROM VSEVOLOD

The change of princes, as a matter of fact, did not bring about change in Novgorod, neither did it satisfy all the factions. Vsevolod's son, no matter what he was called, Konstantin or Sviatoslav, could not treat the people of Novgorod the same way as did the former princes of Southwestern Rus. According to some very reliable sources, the dissatisfied souls sent to Toropets for Prince Mstislav, son of the famous Mstislav the Brave, with the request to save Novgorod from Suzdal's oppression. Mstislav agreed to undertake this hereditary task to fight for Old Rus, for the old against the new order introduced by the sons of Yury in the North. Since he was unsure whether the whole city of Novgorod wanted him, he first captured Torzhok, arrested Sviatoslav's servitors and burgraves, whose property was robbed by whoever had the chance. Afterwards he sent word to Novgorod. "I bow to the Holy Wisdom," he said, "the tomb of my father and to all the people of Novgorod. I came to you when I heard about the violence you suffered from the princes. I took pity upon my patrimony." "Come and rule here, O prince!" the inhabitants of Novgorod replied. They confined Sviatoslav Vsevolodovich with his retinue under house arrest in the archbishop's palace until accounts were settled with his father.

Mstislav journeyed to Novgorod, being received with great joy. Immediately he marched to Torzhok because Vsevolod had arrested Novgorod merchants in his lands. He sent his sons with a force to the Novgorod borders, but there was no battle. Vsevolod was careful not to get involved in decisive battles with princes of Old Rus. Moreover his son was a prisoner in Novgorod. Vsevolod, according to the chronicler, sent Mstislav an explicit message. *"You are my son and I am a father to you.* Free Sviatoslav and his retinue and return everything you have seized, and I will free the merchants and their goods."

As is seen from his subsequent conduct, Burgrave Tverdislav, a strong supporter of the old order, could not support Yury's descendants. Most likely he was no less satisfied and assisted the changes. Therefore he could not be replaced as a result of these changes. Dmitry Yakunovich, son of the old burgrave Yakun Miroslavich, arrived from the South, from Rus, soon after Mstislav established himself in Novgorod. Yakun was closely allied with the Northern branch of Rostislav's descendants, the enemies of Vsevolod. His daughter was married to Mstislav Rostislavich. After Vsevolod established his power over Novgorod, Yakun's son Dmitry was forced seek refuge in Rus. Now he returned to Novgorod when there was nothing to fear from the prince of Suzdal. Tverdislav voluntarily stepped down and gave him the post of burgrave as to a senior. Whereas Tverdislav could not be suspected of being Vsevolod's friend, Archbishop Mitrofan easily could, because his appointment to the Novgorod see came from Vsevolod in violation of the old customs. Mstislav and the people of Novgorod removed Mitrofan and banished him to Toropets (1211).[20]

VSEVOLOD III'S DEATH

Thus at the end of his life Vsevolod the Great suffered failure in his endeavors, as had his brother Andrei, thanks to the efforts of the princes of Old Rus. Andrei's forces fled ignominiously from Mstislav the father, Vsevolod was forced to relinquish Novgorod to Mstislav the son. He was forced to speak with him in his own language. In 1212 Vsevolod grew ill. He wanted while still alive to arrange the affairs of his sons. He had six sons: Konstantin, Yury, Yaroslav, Sviatoslav, Vladimir and Ivan. He sent for the oldest, Konstantin, who ruled in Rostov, wishing to give him Vladimir to rule after his death, sending to Rostov his second son Yury. Konstantin refused to agree to such an arrangement, wanting to receive both Rostov and Vladimir. The seniority of these two cities was at the time, it seems, still a disputed matter, consequently Konstantin feared to relinquish either to a younger brother. He still feared the old claims of Rostov, which could be used by Yury. "Father," he answered, "if you wish to make me the senior, give me the principal city of Rostov, with Vladimir in addition, or if it is more convenient, give me Vladimir with Rostov in addition." Vsevolod grew angry, called the boyars and held lengthy deliberations with them. He then sent for Bishop John.[21] After consultation with him, he decided to give the seniority to his younger son Yury, bypassing the older, who disobeyed his father's will. This was an important development! It was not enough that in the North seniority was taken from a senior city and given to a junior town, a bytown. Now a father deprived seniority from an older to give to a younger son. The traditional custom violated, the younger princes in the North would not fail to follow this example. It is interesting to note that the boyars dared not advise this course of action, whereas a bishop did.

On April 14 Vsevolod died. He was sixty-four years old, having ruled in the Land of Suzdal for thirty-seven years. He was adorned by all fair traits, according to the opinions of the Northern chronicler, who did not miss an opportunity to justify the order introduced by the descendants of Yury and praise them for it. According to him, Vsevolod sentenced to death evildoers and loved well-intentioned men because a prince carried not his sword save to punish the wicked and reward the good. His name sufficed to cause other lands to tremble with fear. His fame spread all over the world, and his enemies (wicked men) God vanquished by Vsevolod's hand. Always fearing God in his heart, he gave charity to the needy. He was a just and unbiased judge despite his powerful boyars, who were unjust to simple people.

Northern Rus lost its Vsevolod. On his deathbed he placed a sword among his sons. The wicked struggle among them threatened to destroy the work of Andrei and Vsevolod, the expression of historical forces, not merely that of forceful personalities. The old Southwestern Rus was straining free of the influence of the North which loomed over it. The last remaining link between the two, seniority and the power of Yury's sons, was falling apart. For long each would go its own way, leading separate lives until such time as once again in the North autocratic rulers appeared, unifiers of the Russian land. Then once more the word was heard that the South of Rus could not exist without the North, and the final union of the two was consummated.

Yet after Vsevolod's death it seemed that Southern Rus not only had freed itself from the influence of the North, now it would submit the North to its own influence. Whereas Northern Rus lost Vsevolod, and his sons dissipated their energies in internecine wars, in the South was Mstislav, whose brilliance by that time was clearly evident. Neither in Rus nor in neighboring lands was there a prince more valiant. Wherever he went, he brought victory. He would not wait until the Northern princes sent large forces to the South before he repulsed them. He repulsed them like his father vanquished Andrei's forces. He himself marched deep into that fearful, severe, gripping North and defeated its princes who relied on their large levies.

At the same time he destroyed the legacy of Vsevolod. In the Rus by the Dnieper he did not permit the descendants of Oleg to offend those of Monomakh. In the end he liberated Galich from the clutch of usurping princely branches.[22] It seemed that a splendid future awaited Southwestern Rus under Mstislav, that his activity would have vital, far-reaching effects, were the future of Southwestern Rus to depend solely on his personality.

IV

INTERNECINE WARS IN SUZDAL AND MSTISLAV'S RISE

WAR BETWEEN VSEVOLOD'S SONS

When in 1212 Vsevolod the Great died his sons already were fighting amongst themselves. Konstantin could not be reconciled to his loss of seniority. According to the chronicler, he was inflamed by anger. His wrath was directed against his brother Yury and every one who advised the old Vsevolod to deny him seniority. At the same time serious disturbances erupted in the Suzdal land. A mass migration began from one end of the land to the other. Prince Sviatoslav Vsevolodovich also grew angry for some reason with his brother Yury. He left him and during this period fled to the older brother Konstantin in Rostov. Vsevolod's other son, Prince Vladimir of Yuriev, was also against the prince of Vladimir.

Seeing all this, Yury hurried to forge a strong alliance at least with Prince Yaroslav Vsevolodovich of Pereiaslavl. "My brother Yaroslav!" he told him. "If Konstantin or Vladimir march against me, be with me as one. If they march against you, I will come to your aid." Yaroslav agreed, kissed the cross with Yury and returned to his town of Pereiaslavl, where he called the inhabitants to the Holy Savior church. "Brothers of Pereiaslavl!" he told them. "When my father went to dwell with God he entrusted you to me and me to you. Tell me, brothers, do you wish to have me as your prince and risk your lives for me?" The people of Pereiaslavl answered with one voice "We do! You are our lord, you are Vsevolod!" After that they kissed the cross.

While these events took place in Pereiaslavl, Konstantin in Rostov was still angry with Yury. "Can it be," he said, "that a junior prince occupies a father's throne while I, the senior, do not?" He made ready with his brother Sviatoslav to attack Vladimir. Yury was afraid of war and sent word saying "Brother Konstantin! If you want to come and rule here in Vladimir, give me Rostov." This Konstantin did not want. He wanted to place his son Vasilko in Rostov and himself rule in Vladimir. He answered Yury "You take your seat in Suzdal." Yury refused, informing his brother Yaroslav "My brother Konstantin is marching against me. You go to Rostov and there it will be as God wills. Either we make peace or open war."

Yaroslav marched with the men of Pereiaslavl, Yury with the men of Vladimir and Suzdal. They came near Rostov on the other side of the Ishnia river. Konstantin placed his regiments near the fords and began the battle for the river. The river was very muddy, which was why Yury and Yaroslav could not approach the city. They burned the surrounding villages, took the cattle and destroyed the crops. Afterwards they stood facing each other for four weeks before making peace and returning to their respective cities.

The conflict was far from over. Yury, knowing that the peace he made was unreliable, took his own measures. Apparently he had difficulties holding his father's gains, the territories of Riazan, whose princes and retinues were imprisoned in Vladimir. He freed them, gave the princes and the retinue gifts of gold, silver and horses, concluded an alliance by kissing the cross, and sent them to Riazan.

Internecine war soon flared up again, ignited by Vladimir Vsevolodovich. He left his city of Yuriev and first attacked Volok. From there went
to Moscow and took up residence after taking this city from Yury. Later
Konstantin also opened his campaign. He took Sol Galitskaia from Yury,
burned Kostroma and took Nerekhta from Yaroslav.

The offended brothers gathered their forces and marched against
Rostov together with Prince Davyd of Murom. They stopped in the previous place beyond the Ishnia river and ordered the troops to burn villages. Meanwhile Vladimir with the Muscovites and his retinue marched
to Dmitrov, one of Yaroslav's towns. The people of Dmitrov themselves
burned the [outside] town quarters, closed the town and repulsed all attacks. Vladimir, frightened by news of Yaroslav's approach, withdrew to
Moscow. He lost the rearguard detachment of his retinue, killed by the
men of Dmitrov pursuing the stragglers.

Yury and Yaroslav stood near Rostov. According to the Northern custom they did not initiate battle. Once again they came to terms, having
persuaded Konstantin to promise not only not to help Vladimir, but also
to send troops to regain Moscow from him. When they approached
Moscow Yury sent to Vladimir, saying "Come to me, do not fear. I will not
devour you, you are my brother." Vladimir came out without fear and the
brothers agreed that Vladimir would give Moscow back to Yury and he
himself would rule in Pereiaslavl.[1]

MSTISLAV OF TOROPETS INTERVENES

So it was that Yury, the younger son of Vsevolod, twice gained victory
over his older brother Konstantin, who surely after suffering two defeats
should have given up his attempts to conquer Vladimir. Then suddenly
Northern Rus clashed with Southern Rus, which gained a brilliant victory.
Consequently the old ways were resurrected for a time. The clash occurred in Great Novgorod. Mstislav ruled there for three years, pursued
the Chud as far as the coast and took from them tribute, of which he gave
two thirds to the people of Novgorod and one third to his retinue. The
men of Novgorod were delighted with such a prince. Everything was
peaceful when suddenly, in 1214, Mstislav received news from his brothers in Rus that the descendants of Oleg there were offending those of
Monomakh. Riurik Rostislavich apparently died at the same time as his
relative Vsevolod the Great. Vsevolod the Red quickly used this opportunity to drive the descendants of Monomakh from Rus. Events in Galich,

namely the hanging of Igor's sons by the boyars, served as pretext for this war.

Because the place of Oleg's sons in Galich was taken by Daniel, a descendant of Monomakh, the Red told the members of that clan closest to him "You hanged two of my princely brothers like criminals in Galich and reproached everyone. Now you have no part in the Land of Rus!" The grandsons of Rostislav thereupon sent to Novgorod to tell Mstislav "Vsevolod Sviatoslavich refuses to give us a part in the Land of Rus. Come, we will seek our patrimony." Mstislav called an assembly in the Court of Yaroslav and called on Novgorod to go to Kiev against Vsevolod the Red. "Wherever, O prince, you cast your eyes," the people of Novgorod answered him, "we will risk our lives for you."

Mstislav marched south with them when in Smolensk the Novgorod troops picked a quarrel with local inhabitants, killed one of them and refused to march further. According to some very probable evidence, the Novgorod levies refused to let the troops of Smolensk led by Mstislav Romanovich, the oldest among the grandsons of Rostislav, take first place. Mstislav Mstislavich called the Novgorod contingent to the assembly, but they failed to appear. Then, embracing all, he bowed to the assembly and went with a retinue drawn from the Smolensk host. The Novgorod levies reflected on their position, gathered at an assembly and deliberated what to do. "Even as our grandfathers and fathers strove for the Land of Rus," Burgrave Tverdislav told them, "so shall we, brothers. Let us follow our prince." The men of Novgorod heeded their burgrave, caught up with Mstislav and launched a joint attack on the Chernigov territories along the Dnieper, *plundering*[2] Rechitsa and many other towns. Near Vyshgorod they encountered the Red and a battle ensued. Mstislav and his brothers were victorious. Two descendants of Oleg were taken prisoner. The people of Vyshgorod opened their gates and Vsevolod fled to the other side of the Dnieper, to the Land of Chernigov. After seating Mstislav Romanovich on the throne of Kiev, Mstislav of Novgorod laid siege to Chernigov, belabored it for twelve days then made peace with the Red, who died soon afterwards.

Mstislav Mstislavich returned to Novgorod, but stayed there only briefly. Given the constant struggle between the parties with all their inherited hatreds and aspirations, no single prince could please all equally. Each must favor one party or another, which in turn would support him. The party supporting the princes of Suzdal was forced to give way to the hostile majority emerging because of Vsevolod's conduct, even though Vsevolod himself was no more. Meantime Mstislav and his party oppressed the opposition party, a fact well illustrated by the information on the fate of Bishop Mitrofan.[3] Yakunich came from Rus and obtained the office of burgrave. Each important house had its supporters and its enemies. The enemies of the boyars who supported Mstislav were also the enemies of Mstislav, who sought an opportunity to be rid of him. Mstislav learned that the enemy party was calling secret assemblies with the purpose of expelling him. Perhaps they used his absence to strengthen themselves. The burgrave was neither Dmitry Yakunich nor Tverdislav, but Yury Ivanovich.

Mstislav did not wait to be expelled. He called an assembly to Court of Yaroslav and told Novgorod "I have business to settle in Rus. You are free in your choice of prince." After bidding farewell to Mstislav the citizens of Novgorod deliberated for a long time. In the end they sent Burgrave Yury Ivanovich, Chiliarch Yakun and ten senior merchants for Prince Yaroslav Vsevolodovich of Pereiaslavl.

It was a clear sign that the Suzdal party had gained the upper hand. Another sign was the fact that after his arrival in Novgorod Yaroslav arrested two boyars and sent them in chains to his nearest town, Tver. He also arrested the chiliarch Yakun Namnezhich. Prince Yaroslav summoned an assembly. From there people rushed to the court of Yakun, ransacked his house, and captured his wife. Yakun himself came with the burgrave to the prince, who ordered his son Khristofor arrested.

Disturbances caused by struggles of hostile parties did not end there. The inhabitants of Prus street killed the boyar Ovstrat and his son, casting their bodies into the moat. Such lawlessness was not to Yaroslav's liking. He refused to stay any longer in Novgorod. He departed for Torzhok to rule there, sending his vicegerent to Novgorod. In this instance he followed the example of his grandfather, uncle and father, who left the ancient town of Rostov to take their seats in a new town.[4]

Soon there arose an opportune development to teach Novgorod a lesson and to subjugate it finally to Yaroslav's will. Early frost in autumn destroyed the entire harvest in the Novgorod territories. Only in Torzhok was it saved. Yaroslav forbade even one wagon with grain passage from the Lower Lands.[5] In these circumstances Novgorod sent to him three boyars with an invitation to come once again. The prince arrested the envoys.

All the while hunger grew worse. A measure[6] of rye sold for ten grivnas, oats for three grivnas, a wagon load of turnips two grivnas. Poor people ate pine barks, linden leaves and moss, selling their children into permanent slavery. A new cemetery was opened and it was so filled with corpses that there was no more room left. Corpses were dragged out into the marketplace, the streets and fields. The dogs could not devour all the corpses. Most of the simple folk died of hunger, the rest migrated to other lands. "Thus our territory and our city was deserted," says the chronicler.

The surviving population of Novgorod sent Burgrave Yury Ivanovich, Stepan Tverdislavich and other important men to Yaroslav to invite him back to the city. Yaroslav ordered the envoys arrested. Instead of an answer he sent to Novgorod two of his boyars to bring back his wife, the daughter of Mstislav Mstislavich. Then the citizens of Novgorod sent to him Manuil Yagolchevich with their latest appeal. "Come to your patrimony, the Holy Wisdom," he urged. "If you will not come, say so openly." Yaroslav arrested Yagolchevich and all Novgorod merchants. There was great sorrow and lament in Novgorod, says the chronicler.

Yaroslav's calculation was correct. The old traditions of Novgorod were not impervious in such conditions, yet Old Rus remained powerful because of Mstislav. When he learned of the evil perpetrated in Novgorod Mstislav marched there (February 11, 1216), arrested Yaroslav's vicegerent Khot Grigorevich, put his servitors in chains, entered the Court of Yaroslav and kissed the cross to the men of Novgorod not to part from them, whether in life or in death. "Either I will free the men of Novgorod and regain its territories or yield my life for Novgorod," said Mstislav.

Yaroslav, when he learned the news from Novgorod, prepared his defense. He ordered barriers erected on the Novgorod road and the Tvertsa river. He sent to Novgorod a hundred citizens thought devoted to him. They were to raise the party hostile to Mstislav and force him to leave the city. Instead these hundred men, immediately on arriving in the city, declared for Mstislav, as did all the others. Mstislav sent a priest to Torzhok to tell Yaroslav "Son! I bow to you. Free the men and the merchants, leave Torzhok and take my love with you."

Yaroslav did not like this proposal. He dismissed the priest without making peace. Then he called together all the men of Novgorod kept in Torzhok, of whom there were over two thousand, in a field outside the town, ordered their arrest, put them in chains and distributed them to his various towns. Their property and horses were divided among his retinue.

News of these developments caused great sorrow to the people in Novgorod. There were very few left, for the best people were imprisoned by Yaroslav, the lesser people either had fled or died of hunger. Mstislav did not lose heart. He called an assembly in the Court of Yaroslav. "Let us go and seek out our brothers and territories," said he, "so that Torzhok does not become Novgorod and Novgorod Torzhok, because where the Holy Wisdom is, there is Novgorod. God is powerful and will aid our just cause though we be few!" The men of Novgorod decided to follow him.

On March 1, 1216, the first day of the New Year[7] according to the old calendar, Mstislav and the men of Novgorod set out against his son-in-law Yaroslav. The following day it became clear how strong were the divisions and hatred between the parties in Novgorod. Although everybody in Novgorod kissed the cross and to a man supported Mstislav, four men with their wives and children fled to Yaroslav. Mstislav went by Lake Seliger and after entering his territory, Toropets, told the men of Novgorod "Take supplies, but imprison no one." The troops seized food and fodder for the horses. When they approached the upper reaches of the Volga they learned that Yaroslav's brother Sviatoslav Vsevolodovich with a force of ten thousand men was besieging Mstislav's town of Rzhevka, where Burgrave Yakun defended himself with a hundred men.

Mstislav and his brother Vladimir of Pskov had a host of only five hundred men. Nevertheless they moved to relieve Rzhevka. Sviatoslav fled without waiting for the Novgorod forces. Mstislav went on to take Yaroslav's town of Zubtsov. On the Vazuza river his first cousin Vladimir Riurikovich of Smolensk with his regiments caught up with him. Despite this help Mstislav refused to go further. While camping on the Kholokholna river he sent to Torzhok to propose peace to Yaroslav, who answered "I do not want peace. If you come, advance. For each of your men I have a hundred." When the sons of Rostislav received this answer, they said to each other "You, O Yaroslav, have your carnal passions but we have the true cross," and deliberated where to go next.

The men of Novgorod, who primarily wanted to liberate their own territory, pressed the princes to march against Torzhok. "If we go to Torzhok," the latter answered, "we will ravage Novgorod territory. Better we go to Pereiaslavl, where we have a third ally." The sons of Rostislav were sure that Konstantin of Rostov would join them against his younger brothers. They marched to Tver, capturing and burning villages, not knowing whether Yaroslav was in Torzhok or in Tver. When Mstislav heard that the sons of Rostislav were attacking villages around Tver he left Torzhok for Tver, taking with him the senior boyars and the men of Novgorod, selecting the younger, and all the people of Novy Torzhok. From among them he sent a hundred men with a group of picked men to form a screen. On March 25, at a distance of fifteen versts from the city, the commander Mstislav Yarun with the junior retinue attacked them. Thirty-three were taken prisoner, seventy were killed, and the rest escaped to Tver.

Following their first success, enabling troops to collect supplies without hindrance, the sons of Rostislav sent the Smolensk boyar Yavolod to Prince Konstantin Vsevolodovich in Rostov with an invitation to form an alliance against his brothers. The envoy was accompanied by Vladimir of Pskov with troops from Pskov and Smolensk. The princes allied to Novgorod continued to burn villages on the Shosha and Dubna rivers. At the same time Vladimir of Pskov captured the town Konstantinov (Ksniatin) at the mouth of the Great Merla, and burned the whole of the [upper] Volga region.

Konstantin of Rostov did not delay his reply. He sent his commander Yeremey to the sons of Rostislav. "Prince Konstantin bows to you," he said. "He was glad to hear of your arrival and sends five hundred troops to help you. As for the remainder of the agreement, send to him his brother-in-law Vsevolod (son of Mstislav Romanovich of Kiev)." The sons of Rostislav sent Vsevolod with a strong contingent, and they went down along the Volga. Later, to end their expedition as soon as possible, they abandoned their wagons and on horseback hurried to Pereiaslavl. On April 9, Easter day, the sons of Rostislav, camping on the Sara river, were joined by Konstantin of Rostov with his forces. He feared to leave his city without defense, so to Rostov the sons of Rostislav sent Vladimir of Pskov with his retinue. They, accompanied by Konstantin, marched to Pereiaslavl and encamped near the town during the octave of the feast of St. Thomas [October 6].

There, near the town wall, they captured a man from whom they learned that Yaroslav was not in the town. He had marched to his brother Yury with his regiments, the men of Novgorod and those of Novy Torzhok. Prince Yury and his brothers Sviatoslav and Vladimir also abandoned their town. The younger sons of Vsevolod gathered a strong host consisting of men from Murom, Brody, Gorodets and all the towns of the Suzdal land. They took all the men from the villages. Those who had no horse marched on foot. "It was a terrible thing, brothers," says the chronicler, "because sons went against fathers, fathers against sons, brother against brother, slaves against masters and masters against slaves."

VICTORY ON THE LIPITSA STRENGTHENS KONSTANTIN

Yaroslav and Yury and the brothers stood on the Kza river. Mstislav and Vladimir with the men of Novgorod deployed their regiments near Yuriev. Konstantin of Rostov was positioned with his troops on the Lipitsa river.[8] When the sons of Rostislav caught sight of the regiments of Yaroslav and Yury they sent the hundredman Larion to tell Yury "We bow to you, we have no quarrel with you. Our quarrel is with Yaroslav." "I and my brother Yaroslav are one," Yury answered. Then they sent to tell him "Free the men of Novgorod and those of Novy Torzhok, return the territory of Novgorod captured by you, namely Volok. Make peace with us and kiss the cross, do not spill blood." "I do not want peace," Yaropolk replied. "The men of Novgorod and Novy Torzhok I will keep with me. You have come a long way and are like fish on dry land."

When Larion repeated all this to the sons of Rostislav they despatched their ultimatum to the brothers. "We did not come, brothers Yury and Yaroslav, to spill blood. God forbid we see any blood, it is better to settle our differences. We are all of one clan, let us give seniority to Prince Konstantin and place him in Vladimir, and you will receive the whole of the Land of Suzdal." "Tell my brothers, Princes Mstislav and Vladimir," replied Yury, "they have marched, now let them do what they will. Tell my brother Prince Konstantin that if he defeats us the whole land will be his."

Vsevolod's younger sons, encouraged by the peaceful propositions of their enemies, seeing in them a sign of their weakness and desperate situation, began to feast with their boyars. During the feast one old boyar, Andrei Stanislavich, told the young princes "Make peace, Princes Yury and Yaroslav! The younger brothers are under your sway. In my opinion, it is better to make peace and to give seniority to Prince Konstantin. You should not be misled by the fact that against you are ranged only a few of Rostislav's clan. They are wise princes, experienced and brave. Their troops from Novgorod and Smolensk are courageous in battle. As for Mstislav Mstislavich, you know yourselves that, of all your family, God gave him more courage than to all the others put together. Think about it, my lords!"

This speech was not to their liking and one of Yury's boyars said "Princes Yury and Yaroslav! It never happened in your great-grandfather's, nor in your grandfather's, nor in your father's times that someone invaded the mighty Land of Suzdal with impunity. Even if the whole

Land of Rus gathered, the lands of Galich, Kiev, Smolensk, Chernigov, Novgorod and Riazan banded together, in no way could they withstand our might. As for their regiments, we will cover them with our saddles."

The princes liked his speech. They called their boyars and told them "When we capture the enemy camp you will have horses, armor and clothing. Whosoever tries to take a man alive will be killed himself. Even if clad in gold, they must be killed. We will not leave a single man alive. If anyone escapes from their host and is captured, hang him or stretch him alive and we will think later what to do with the princes."

After dismissing their followers the princes entered the tent and started to divide the territories. "My brother Yaroslav," said Prince Yury, "I will take the land of Vladimir, you will have Novgorod. Smolensk will go to our brother Sviatoslav. Kiev we will give to the princes of Chernigov, and we shall keep Galich." The younger brothers agreed, kissed the cross and wrote out documents. The most interesting point here is the contempt of the Northern princes for Kiev, which for their ancestors and for all the Southern princes meant seniority and higher honor, whereas Vsevolod's sons reserved for themselves the rich Galich land.

After dividing the Rus towns, Yury and Yaroslav challenged the enemy to do battle. The sons of Rostislav on their part called Konstantin and consulted with him for a long time. They made him swear an oath not to join his brothers and moved at night to the Rostov camp on the Lipitsa river. In all the regiments cries were heard. Konstantin's troops sounded trumpets and this frightened Yury and Yaroslav. They backed over the thickets and mustered their regiments on the Avdova hill.

At daybreak the sons of Rostislav arrived at the Lipitsa. When they saw that the enemy had withdrawn to the Avdova hill they deployed their forces opposite the Yuriev hill. Once again he despatched three men with a peace proposal to the sons of Vsevolod. "If you do not want peace," they told the envoys to say, "retreat further to flat ground and we will go to your side, or we will withdraw to the Lipitsa and you can cross over to our side." "Neither will I agree to peace nor to the withdrawal," answered Yury. "You have crossed our entire land, can you not cross a mere thicket?"

Vsevolod's sons relied on their field fortifications, surrounding their camp with a palisade bristling with stakes, in fear the enemy might attack them at night. After receiving their answer the sons of Rostislav sent their young men to fight against Yaroslav's regiments. The fighting continued all day until nightfall, although not very fierce because there was a storm and it was very cold.

The following morning, Thursday, April 21, during the second week after Easter, the sons of Rostislav decided to march directly to Vladimir without clashing with the enemy. Their regiments prepared to leave their positions. Noticing this movement, Yury's regiments descended from the hill thinking the enemy was running away, but they were stopped and repulsed. Simultaneously Prince Vladimir of Pskov arrived from Rostov and Rostislav's sons deliberated their next step. "Brothers, Princes Mstislav and Vladimir!" Konstantin told them. "If we go past their forces they will attack our rear and my men are not keen for battle. If they see us do this, they will disperse to their towns." "Princes Vladimir and Konstantin," answered Mstislav, "the hill will not help us, nor will the hill defeat us. Let us ask for help from the true cross and go against them relying on the justice of our cause."

They all agreed and arranged the regiments. Vladimir Riurikovich of Smolensk placed his troops on the flank. Next to him were Mstislav and Vsevolod with the Novgorod contingent, and Vladimir of Pskov with the men of Pskov. Next to him was Prince Konstantin with the men of Rostov. Opposite stood Yaroslav with his regiments from Pereiaslavl, Tver, Murom, Gorodets and Brodniki against Vladimir and the Smolensk regiments. Yury stood opposite Mstislav and the Novgorod levies with all the Suzdal land, and the younger brothers faced Konstantin.

Mstislav and Vladimir encouraged their forces from Novgorod and Smolensk. "Brothers," they said, "we have entered a mighty land. Now putting our trust in God let us stand fast. There is no looking back. If you run away, you will not escape. Brothers! Forget our homes, wives and children. You must die some day! Advance the way you wish, either on foot or on horseback." "We do not wish to die on horseback," the men of Novgorod answered. "We want to fight on foot like our fathers in the battle of Kolaksha."[9] Mstislav was heartened to hear this. The men of Novgorod dismounted, pulled off their hose and boots and attacked barefoot, followed by the men of Smolensk who also attacked on foot. After the men of Smolensk, Prince Vladimir sent Ivor Mikhailovich with his host, while the senior princes and all the commanders rode behind.

When Ivor's host entered the thicket his horse stumbled and he had to stop. The infantry attacked Yaroslav's foot regiments without waiting for Ivor, and with a cry threw their clubs and axes. The men of Suzdal could not bear it and started to run. The troops from Novgorod and Smolensk attacked them, cut down Yaroslav's banner, and when Ivor arrived they made way for another banner. When Mstislav noticed this he said to Vladimir Riurikovich "God forbid we should let good men down!"

Helmet of Yaroslav Vsevolodovich
Moscow Kremlin Armory

All the princes together struck at the enemy with their foot soldiers. Three times Mstislav cut through the enemy regiments. In his hand he held an axe with a rope, hacking with it. Prince Vladimir kept up with him and after a fierce battle they plunged into the camp of Vsevolod's sons who, seeing the sons of Rostislav mowing down their regiments as with a scythe, scattered away together with the princes of Murom. "Brothers, men of Novgorod!" Prince Mstislav called out to his troops. "Do not stop to loot. First finish fighting the battle or the enemy may turn back and finish you off."

The men of Novgorod, says the chronicler, did not enter the camp and fought on, although the men of Smolensk started pillaging, stripped the dead and did not think about the battle. "Great was God's work, brothers," the same chronicler says, "on this terrible battlefield. Only five men of Novgorod were killed, and one of Smolensk. All were protected by the power of the true cross and the justice of their cause." On the other side many were killed, sixty taken prisoner from all the camps. Had Princes Yury and Yaroslav guessed the outcome they would have made peace, for they lost their fame and honor, and strong regiments were annihilated. Prince Yury had thirteen banners, sixty trumpets and drums. It was said about Yaroslav that he had sixteen banners and forty trumpets and drums. Most of all, people complained about Yaroslav saying "We have suffered from you such a calamity. They say about your false oath 'Come, O fowls of the air, drink human blood, you beasts of the field eat human flesh!'" Not just ten were killed, not a hundred, but altogether 9,233 men. The screams and shouts of the wounded were heard in Yuriev and in its vicinity. There were not enough to bury the dead. Many drowned in the river while escaping, other wounded reached empty places and died without help. The survivors fled either to Vladimir, or to Pereiaslavl, some to Yuriev.

Yury rode to Vladimir on his fourth horse, having exhausted three others. He arrived only in his undershirt, for he had thrown away his chain mail. He arrived about midday, and the battle had taken place at dinner time the previous day. In Vladimir there were only unarmed people, priests, monks, wives and children. When they noticed someone approaching on horseback at a distance they were overjoyed because they thought it was the messenger from the prince, bringing news of victory. "Our side is winning," they said. Suddenly only Prince Yury appeared, riding round the city and shouting "Fortify the walls!" Everybody grew somber. Instead of crying for joy they started weeping. Towards evening and during the night the rank-and-file began to appear. Some were wounded, others naked.

The following morning Yury gathered the people and said "Brothers of Vladimir! Let us close the city, we will defend ourselves from the enemy." "Prince Yury!" they answered him. "With whom should we close the city? Our brothers are killed, others are prisoners, the rest have returned without weapons. With whom do we defend the city?" "I know all that myself," said Yury, "just do not deliver me to Konstantin and the sons of Rostislav, let me leave the city." This the citizens of Vladimir promised.

Yaroslav likewise arrived in Pereiaslavl on his fifth horse, leaving four exhausted on the way, and shut himself in the city. The previous evil was not enough for him, says the chronicler, he had not yet drunk enough human blood. It was not enough for him that he killed many in Novgorod, Torzhok and Volok. When he entered Pereiaslavl he ordered the arrest of all men of Novgorod and Smolensk who came to trade there. Some he ordered put in cellars, others locked in crowded quarters where they all died. There were a hundred and fifty altogether. He was less angry with the men from Smolensk, and fifteen of them who were locked up separately survived.

This was not the way of the merciful princes of Rostislav's clan. They halted for the rest of the day on the battlefield. Had they pursued the enemy princes, Yury and Yaroslav could not have escaped, and Vladimir would have been taken by storm. The sons of Rostislav quietly approached Vladimir, surrounded the city and deliberated from which direction to take it. When at night a fire started in the princely court and the men of Novgorod wanted to use this opportunity to attack, Mstislav halted them. The next day another fire started in the city and burned until morning. The men of Smolensk also urged an attack on the city, but Prince Vladimir forbade them.

Then Prince Yury sent to do obeisance to the besieging princes. "Do not attack me today," he pleaded, "tomorrow I will leave the town." Indeed the following morning he left the city, bowed to Princes Mstislav and Vladimir Riurikovich and said "Brothers! I pay you my homage. You can give me my life and feed me with bread, for I am at the mercy of my brother Konstantin." He gave them gifts, and they found peace with him. They also made peace between him and his brother Konstantin who had taken Vladimir. Yury had to be satisfied with Radilov Gorodets on the Volga. The bishop, the princess and all his court sailed down the Kliazma river. Before his departure Prince Yury visited the cathedral, fell to his knees before his father's tomb and, with tears in his eyes, said "O Lord, judge my brother Yaroslav who brought me to this misfortune."

YURY AGAIN GRAND PRINCE OF VLADIMIR

After bidding farewell to Yury the people of Vladimir, clergy and laymen, went to greet their new prince Konstantin, who that day presented splendid gifts to the princes and the boyars, making the people swear an oath of loyalty to him. Yaroslav remained angry. Refusing to submit, he blockaded himself in Pereiaslavl, thinking to remain there. When Rostislav's sons and Konstantin marched on him he took fright and relayed messages asking for peace. In the end he appeared before his brother Konstantin, did obeisance to him bowing to the ground. "Lord! I am in your power," said he, "do not deliver me to my father-in-law Mstislav, nor to Vladimir Riurikovich, rather give me your bread." Konstantin arranged peace between him and Mstislav, who was still on the way. When the princes arrived in Pereiaslavl, to them and the commanders Yaroslav gave splendid gifts. Mstislav accepted the gifts, sent to the town for his daughter, Yaroslav's wife, and for the survivors of Yaroslav's Novgorod regiments. Yaroslav asked several times for his wife to be sent back, but Mstislav refused.

Thus Mstislav destroyed Vsevolod III's testament, apparently re-establishing old customs in the North, although Konstantin's victory actually opened the way to victory for the new order. This was because the older brother became much more powerful than the younger after receiving Rostov and Vladimir, which was what he wanted in the first place. It was Konstantin's branch of the family that was supposed to grow in strength at the expense of other sons of Vsevolod. Fate decreed otherwise, and the task of gathering Northern Rus was accomplished by the family of the third son of Vsevolod, the same Yaroslav who was the main culprit in these events.

Konstantin's health was weak and he ruled in Vladimir only for a short time. Sensing his approaching death, he realized his sons were still minors and hastened to make peace with his brother Yury, lest he be a dangerous enemy to his children. The following year, 1217, he summoned Yury and gave him Suzdal, promising that Vladimir would be his after his death. He gave him many gifts, and pressed him to kiss the cross to be a father to his nephews. In 1218 Konstantin sent his older son Vasilko to rule in Rostov, and Vsevolod to Yaroslavl. According to the chronicler he told them, "My dear sons! Love each other, fear God with all your soul, keep His commandments. Follow my customs and habits. Do not despise the poor and the widows. Do not separate from the church, love bishops and monks. Listen to teachings in the books and to your elders who instruct you in good things, because you both are still young. I feel, my children, that my end is near and I entrust you to God, to His Immaculate Mother, to my brother and to Lord Yury who will be like a father to you in my place."

Konstantin died on February 2, 1218. The chronicler praised him for his gentleness, charity, and his care for the churches and the clergy. He told that Konstantin often read books with devotion, following what was written there. After his death he was called Konstantin *the Good*. Konstantin's brother Yury returned to rule in Vladimir as before.

EVENTS IN RIAZAN AND NOVGOROD

The Suzdal principality was closely associated, because of its physical setting, with the principalities of Riazan and Murom. Prince Davyd of Murom as a rule followed the wishes of Vsevolod the Great, helping him defeat the princes of Riazan. During the battle on the Lipitsa the princes of Murom were in the army of Vsevolod's younger sons. Yury freed the princes of Riazan from prison and allowed them to return to their territories, where they lived in peace only for a short time. The same Gleb Vladimirovich, who with his brother Oleg previously denigrated his other brothers in Vsevolod III's presence, with another brother Konstantin planned to free himself of his entire family. The two then would rule the whole of the Riazan lands together.

The division of the land into small territories was the reason for strong hostility among the sons of Yaroslav of Riazan. The fratricidal plans of the sons of Vladimir (this is almost a unique example among the Rus princes after Yaroslav) were rooted in the rough and wild customs prevailing in Riazan, this isolated and remote Slavonic-Rus colony in the Finnish East.

Whatever the reason, in 1217 during a family meeting of Riazan princes the sons of Vladimir invited the other six princes to a feast in their tent. The guests went with their boyars and servants, suspecting nothing. Then, when they started to drink and make merry, Gleb and his brother unsheathed their swords and attacked them with their servants and Polovetsians hidden near the tent. All the guests were murdered. Only

Ingvar Igorevich, absent from this meeting, survived to keep Riazan for himself. In 1219 Gleb came with Polovetsians to attack him, but was defeated and barely escaped.

Mstislav returned victorious to Novgorod, but stayed there only a short while. The following year, 1217, he visited Kiev, leaving his wife and Vasily his son in Novgorod. He took with him three boyars, including the old burgrave Yury Ivankovich. It seems that they were his hostages, to ensure the safety of his wife and son. So strong was factional strife in Novgorod, and fear that the Suzdal party might gain the upper hand! Apparently Mstislav returned to Novgorod the same year, arrested Stanimir Dernovich and his son Nezdiloy, put them in chains and confiscated their wealthy estate. This is indicative of the scale of the opposition to Mstislav. In 1218 he went to Torzhok, arrested there Borislav Nekurishinich, and took his extensive lands. Later these captives were released.

The same year Mstislav called an assembly in the Court of Yaroslav and told the men of Novgorod "I bow to the Holy Wisdom, the tomb of my father and to you. I desire to conquer Galich, but I will not forget you. God grant my wish to be buried near my father in the Holy Wisdom." The men of Novgorod tried to dissuade him. "Do not go, O prince," they said, but could not restrain him.

After bidding Mstislav farewell Novgorod sent to Smolensk for his nephew Sviatoslav, son of Mstislav Romanovich. That same year, 1218, great trouble arose. A certain Matey Dushilchevich tied up an official, Moiseich, and ran away. He was captured and taken to Gorodishche. Suddenly a false rumor spread in the city that Burgrave Tverdislav had delivered Matey to the prince. An uprising occurred as the people of Zarechie (Onipolovtsy)[10] rang the bells of St. Nicholas church all through the night. The people of Nerev district started to ring the bells of the church of the Forty Saints and gathered forces to go against Tverdislav.

When the prince learned of the rebellion he freed Matey, although by now the people could not be pacified. The Onipolovtsy were armed as if for battle, as were the inhabitants of the Nerev district. Those living outside the town did not join any party, waiting to see what would happen. Then Tverdislav, facing the Holy Wisdom cathedral, said "If I am guilty, let me die. If I am in the right, defend me, O Lord!" and went into battle with the inhabitants of Liudin district and Prus street.

This struggle took place near the city gate. The Onipolovtsy and the inhabitants of Nerev district fled after losing Ivan Dushilchevich, Matey's brother. Nerev lost Konstantin Prokopich and six others. The Liudin district and Prus street gained a victory, having lost one man each, but there were many wounded on both sides.

For a whole week after this battle there were assemblies in the city. In the end all the brothers of the city joined and kissed the cross to a man. Prince Sviatoslav immediately sent his chiliarch to the assembly. "I cannot have Tverdislav as burgrave," said the prince, "I strip him of this office." "What is his fault?" asked the citizens of Novgorod. "He is not guilty of anything," the prince replied. Then Tverdislav said "I am glad there is no fault of mine. You, brothers, may choose your burgraves and your princes freely." "O prince," the men of Novgorod replied, "Tverdislav is not guilty, and you have promised not to strip anyone of his office without cause. We bow to you, yet he is our burgrave and we will not let you strip him of his office when he is guilty of no offence." Sviatoslav did not insist, and peace returned to the city.

The following year Prince Mstislav Romanovich of Kiev sent his son Vsevolod to Novgorod. "Accept Vsevolod, and send the older Sviatoslav to me," he asked of Novgorod, which complied with his wish. That winter Semiun Emin with a detachment of four hundred men marched on the Finnish tribe of Toimokary but the princes of Suzdal, Yury and Yaroslav, refused them passage through their lands, and they were forced to return to Novgorod. When Semiun and his comrades were encamped in the field a rumor spread in the city that Burgrave Tverdislav and Chiliarch Yakun had sent envoys to Yury asking him not to let the troops through. This rumor caused unrest in the city. Tverdislav and Yakun lost office. The office of burgrave passed to Semeon Borisovich, probably the grandson of the famous Miroshka, and the office of chiliarch went to Semiun Emin. They remained in their respective offices less than a year, for in the same year, 1219, the office of burgrave reverted to Tverdislav and that of chiliarch to Yakun.

Even the archbishops were involved in the troubles and party struggles. Remember how Mstislav and his supporters removed Mitrofan from the bishop's office as he was Vsevolod's appointee. After Mstislav left Novgorod in 1218 Mitrofan returned from Vladimir and went to live in the Annunciation monastery. In 1219, when his successor Anton left for Torzhok, Novgorod restored Mitrofan as archbishop and sent word to Anton, saying "Go where you wish." He went to live in the monastery of the Savior on the Nereda. In the end Prince Vsevolod and the men of Novgorod told both bishops "Go to the metropolitan in Kiev. He who is confirmed by him will be our archbishop." In 1220 Archbishop Mitrofan returned, supported by God and the Holy Wisdom, in the words of the chronicler. The metropolitan kept Anton honorably with him and gave him the Peremyshl see.

Vsevolod Mstislavich inherited the hatred of his brother Sviatoslav towards Burgrave Tverdislav. In 1220 he proceeded to Smolensk to settle his affairs. From there he continued to Torzhok and when he returned to Novgorod he incited half of the inhabitants against Tverdislav. He wanted to kill Tverdislav, who was ill at the time. Vsevolod marched from Goro-dishche,[11] where he lived with his court, clad in armor as if for war. He came to the Court of Yaroslav. There he was met by armed men of Nov-gorod, who camped like a host in the princely court. The sick Tverdislav was taken in a sledge to the church of St. Boris and St. Gleb, where he was joined by inhabitants of Prus street and the Liudin district, as well as men who lived outside the town who came to defend him, surround-ing him with five regiments. The prince, seeing them ready to fight to the death, as the chronicler says, did not attack. He sent Archbishop Mitrofan with kind speeches. The prelate negotiated a peace between the parties.

Tverdislav resigned his office. Knowing his illness was worse, in se-cret from his wife, his children and entire family he retired to the St. Arcadius monastery and was tonsured. Ivanko Dmitrievich was chosen as his successor. Probably he was the son of Dmitry Yakunich.

All the while the peace between the prince and Tverdislav's party was fragile. The following year, 1221, Novgorod sent Vsevolod away.[12] "We do not want you, go where you wish," they told him. The inevitable re-sult of Vsevolod Mstislavich's expulsion was an approach to the sons of Prince Yury of Suzdal. Archbishop Mitrofan, Burgrave Ivanko and lead-ing citizens travelled to Yury Vsevolodovich in Vladimir to beseech him to give his son, and he gave them Vsevolod Yurievich according to their wishes.

After the battle on the Lipitsa the princes of Suzdal could not treat Nov-gorod as before. Yury apparently was very pleased that Novgorod turned to his branch of the family. He gave splendid gifts to the archbishop and other envoys, and sent his brother Sviatoslav with an army to help Nov-gorod fight against the Chud.

Yury's son did not like Novgorod, therefore he departed the city with all his court the same year. The citizens of Novgorod were unhappy and again sent their senior men to tell Yury "If you do not wish to hold Novgorod through your son, send us your brother." Yury gave them his brother Yaroslav, the same who earlier starved them. Novgorod was pleased with Yaroslav, says the chronicler, and when in 1223 he left them for his own territory of Pereiaslavl-Zalessk they bowed to him and tried to dissuade him, saying "Do not go, O prince." He ignored their pleas. Once again Novgorod requested Yury to send a prince, and once again he gave them his son Vsevolod. In 1224 Vsevolod came for the second time to Novgorod, and again left the city at night. This time the matter did not end there. Vsevolod, following his uncle's example, occupied Torzhok, whither came his father accompanied by his regiments, his uncle Yaroslav, his cousin Vasilko Konstantinovich with the men of Rostov, and Yury's brother-in-law Mikhail with the men of Chernigov.

Novgorod sent word to Yury saying "Prince! Send us your son and leave Torzhok." "Deliver to me Yakim Ivanovich," replied Yury, "together with Nikifor Tudorovich, Ivanko Timoshkinich, Sdil Savinich, Viachko, Ivats and Radek. If you do not surrender them, even as I watered my horses from the Tvertsa river, so also I will water them from the Volkhov."[13]

Novgorod summoned the entire land, built a fortification around the city and relayed word to Yury. "O prince," they said, "we bow to you, although we will not surrender our brothers. Do not spill blood, but as you wish. It is your sword, and our heads." Meanwhile Novgorod posted guards on the roads, erected barriers and decided to die defending the Holy Wisdom. Yury dared not try to water his horses from the Volkhov. He sent word to Novgorod, saying "Take as your prince my brother-in-law Mikhail of Chernigov." Novgorod agreed and sent for Mikhail. Yury left Torzhok, but not empty-handed, for Novgorod had to pay him seven thousand.[14] For the first time Novgorod was forced to buy off a Northern prince. Yury's successors followed this example.

A Southern prince from Old Rus was to Novgorod's liking. Their land enjoyed an easy time under his rule, although like all the princes Mikhail was not to stay long. First he went to Vladimir to ask Yury to return the Novgorod goods captured in Torzhok and in his territory. When he returned with the goods to Novgorod he stayed in the Court of Yaroslav and said to Novgorod "I do not want to rule here. I go to Chernigov. Send me your merchants, let your land be like my land." Novgorod begged him to stay, but could not persuade him.

After honorably bidding farewell to Mikhail, Novgorod once again must turn to Yaroslav in Pereiaslavl. He came to Novgorod, this time staying for almost three years. When he left for Pereiaslavl his two sons Fedor and Alexander remained in Novgorod with the boyar Fedor

Danilovich and the reeve Yakim. The rule of Yaroslav and his sons was not as easy for Novgorod as that of Mikhail of Chernigov. New duties and new rules appeared which were not part of the old charters of Yaroslav.[15] On the other hand the young princes, or rather their uncle Fedor Danilovich, could not be pleased with life in Novgorod since constant unrest and assembly arbitrariness were unknown in the Lower Lands.

In the autumn of 1228 torrential rains continued day and night. From the feast of the Dormition [August 15] until the feast of St. Nicholas [December 6] there was no sun, hay was not gathered, the fields were not ploughed. Then the devil, as the chronicler says, envious of the Christian deeds of Archbishop Arseny, incited the rabble against him. The assembly was summoned in the Court of Yaroslav and marched on the archbishop's palace shouting "It is Arseny's fault that the weather has been bad for so long. He banished the previous archbishop Anton to Khutyn, and took office himself by bribing the prince." They pushed him out of the gates like a criminal, and nearly killed him. He locked himself in the church of the Holy Wisdom, thence went to the Khutyn monastery.[16] The earlier archbishop was appointed in his place, but this was not the end of the matter. The entire city grew excited, people took up arms and marched from the assembly against the chiliarch Viacheslav, whose house was pillaged, as were those of his brother Boguslav, Andrenich the archbishop's table attendant, and others. They marched to pillage the house of Dushilets, the elder of Lipitsa. They wanted to hang him, but he escaped to Yaroslav. They took his wife and said "These men made the prince do evil."

After taking the office of chiliarch from Viacheslav and giving it to Boris Negochevich, Novgorod sent word to Yaroslav. "Come to us, do not levy new duties, do not send judges to the lands, be our prince on our conditions and according to Yaroslav's charters, or you do as you please, and we will do the same." Instead of replying, Fedor Danilovich and the reeve Yakim took the two princes and fled Novgorod. "Why did they run away?" asked the inhabitants of Novgorod. "Did they offend the Holy Wisdom? We did not expel them, we punished only our own people, and did no harm to the prince. We will rely upon God and the true cross, and will find our own prince." They kissed the icon of the Mother of God to preserve unity and sent to Chernigov for Mikhail. At Yaroslav's instigation the envoys were intercepted at Smolensk by the local prince. This was because it seemed likely that the descendants of Rostislav could not wish Novgorod well after Vsevolod's expulsion.

Nevertheless Mikhail learned somehow of the events in Novgorod and that the envoys sent for him were arrested in Smolensk. He rode to Torzhok and from there in 1229 to Novgorod, to the greatest joy of the people. He kissed the cross to agree to their will and to observe Yaroslav's charters. The peasants received tax exemption for five years. The fine for decamping to a foreign land remained as ordered by previous princes. Having received the prince they wanted, Mikhail's party turned against their enemies, those who supported Yaroslav, mainly the people of Gorodishche. They did not pillage their houses, instead they took a sizable money contribution to construct the main bridge. They took the post of burgrave from Ivan Dmitrievich and gave it to Vnezd Vodovik. Ivanko received Torzhok, but the men of Torzhok refused to accept him, so he went to Yaroslav.

This time also Mikhail did not tarry long in Novgorod. The same year, 1229, he left there his son Rostislav. He took with him several important citizens of Novgorod and went to his brothers in Chernigov. They sent to Yaroslav, saying "Withdraw from Volok and all Novgorod possessions you have taken by force, and kiss the cross." "I do not withdraw from anywhere," answered Yaroslav, "nor do I kiss the cross. You do what you must, as I will." He held the envoys throughout the summer.

The next year Mikhail appeared in Novgorod, celebrated his son Rostislav's first hair clipping,[17] placed him on the throne and returned to Chernigov. For Novgorod to have a minor prince amounted to not having a prince at all. Once again fierce disturbances erupted. The new burgrave Vodovik quarrelled with Stepan Tverdislavich, son of the old burgrave, who was supported by Ivanko Timoshkinich. The burgrave's servants attacked Timoshkinich, who the following day summoned an assembly at the Court of Yaroslav. Consequently the burgrave's home was pillaged but Vodovik, together with Semeon Borisovich, an old burgrave and an opponent of Tverdislav and his son, aroused the whole city against Ivanko and his friends, marched from the assembly and pillaged many houses. Volos Bludkinich was killed at the assembly when Vodovik said to him "You wanted to burn down my house." Later Vodovik also killed Timoshkinich by throwing him into the Volkhov.

During the winter when the burgrave, together with the little prince Rostislav, went to Torzhok, Semeon Borisovich was killed by his enemies. His house and villages were sacked and his wife was taken. The house and the villages of Vodovik, his brothers and his friends and that of the chiliarch Boris were pillaged as well. When Vodovik and his brothers, the chiliarch Boris and the boyars of Torzhok heard about this, they fled to Mikhail in Chernigov.

In Novgorod the office of burgrave went to Stepan Tverdislavich, that of chiliarch to Nikita Petrilovich, and the property of Semeon and Vodovik was divided among the hundreds.[18] Prince Rostislav was banished from Torzhok and told "Your father promised to mount his horse (go to war) beginning at the Exaltation [September 14], and now it is St. Nicholas Day [December 6]. The promise kissed on the cross is broken, now go away. We will chose another prince."

They summoned Yaroslav entirely on their own terms. He returned at once, swore to observe the charters of Yaroslav the Wise, and as before did not stay permanently in Novgorod. His place was taken by his sons Fedor and Alexander. According to some information new tax privileges granted by Mikhail were abolished.

Thus Mstislav's victory on the Lipitsa had no lasting consequences for the North. Yury, as before, ruled in Vladimir, and Novgorod after many disturbances once again had to accept Yaroslav, who despite all his failures did not change his conduct. Nor did he abandon his intentions to constrain the ancient way of life in Novgorod, whereas the Southern prince of Chernigov granted new privileges to the old city ruled by its assembly.

MSTISLAV OF TOROPETS IN GALICH

Now we turn our attention to Mstislav's activity in the Southwest. The kinsmen Andrew of Hungary and Leszek of Poland quarrelled very soon. The king took away Peremyshl and Liubachev from Leszek, who was not powerful enough to avenge this dishonor and occupy Galich. He sent word to Mstislav, saying "You are my brother, come and take Galich."

Mstislav must have been pleased to receive this invitation because at that time (1215) his affairs in Novgorod were not going well. When he appeared in Galich the Hungarians left hastily and Mstislav established himself on Roman's throne, having married his daughter Anna to Roman's son Daniel, now grown, who everybody soon saw would be like his famous father. Using the opportunity created in Volhynia after the death of Roman and during the minority of his sons, the Poles occupied the borderlands. Daniel now decided to reconquer these borderlands, then visited his father-in-law Mstislav to say "My father! The Poles have taken my patrimony!" "My son," replied Mstislav, "because of our previous good relations I cannot attack Leszek. Look for other allies."

Daniel had one constant ally all his life, his brother Vasilko. They marched together against the Poles and reconquered the Volhynian borderlands. Leszek was very angry with Roman's sons and sent a host against them, but his troops came back defeated. Although Mstislav refused to help his son-in-law against Leszek, he could not allay suspicion that the war began on his advice, and Leszek was angered. He allied with the Hungarian king and invited him once more to seize Galich for his son and Leszek's son-in-law. Prince Kálmán[19] arrived with a strong force, which Mstislav [who had entered the fray] could not oppose with his retinue alone, as the boyars did not support him. He left the country, saying to young Daniel, who displayed exceptional courage during the retreat from Galich, "Prince! Go to Vladimir, and I will go to the Polovetsians. We will avenge our shame."

Mstislav did not visit the Polovetsians, instead went north and liberated Novgorod from Yaroslav Vsevolodovich, won the battle on the Lipitsa, and only in 1218 reappeared in the South. He hired Polovetsians and the following year marched on Galich. The forces of Kálmán were under the command of Filia, whom the chronicler nicknames "the Proud." Filia spoke about the Rus regiments with contempt, saying "One stone will break many pots." "A sharp sword and a swift steed," he also said, "is all we need to defeat a host of Rus." Yet in a hard-fought battle with Mstislav neither a sharp sword nor a swift steed nor Polish help saved him, for he was defeated and taken prisoner.

After this victory Mstislav besieged Galich. The Hungarians locked themselves in a strong tower built by Filia over the church of the Mother of God and defended themselves, loosing arrows and hurling stones at the population. The chronicler saw the conversion of a church into a fortress as profanation of a holy place, reproached Filia and said that the Mother of God, unable to countenance the offense against her house, delivered the fortress and its defenders into Mstislav's hands. The Hungarians, suffering from thirst, surrendered. There was a great joy, related the chronicler, for God saved the people from foreigners. The Hungarians and the Poles either were slain, taken prisoner or drowned in the rivers. Some were killed by the villagers, none escaped with his life.

Among the prisoners was a famous boyar named Sudislav. When brought to Mstislav he fell at his feet and swore to serve him faithfully. Mstislav trusted him, gave him great honor and sent him to administer Zvenigorod. When during Mstislav's absence Roman's sons had to fight against the dangerous Hungarians and Poles no one came to their assistance save God. Even one of their kinsman, their cousin Alexander Vsevolodovich of Bełsk, was against them. After Mstislav defeated the Hungarians, Leszek hurried to make peace with the sons of Roman, who hastened to take revenge on Alexander and ravage his land. Thanks only to Mstislav's intervention could the prince of Bełsk keep his land.

Clearly this did nothing to lessen Alexander's hatred of his cousins. Soon an opportunity arose to take revenge, for Daniel's good relations with his father-in-law did not last very long. There could not but be many causes for mutual dislike, given the clash over their rights to Galich. Whereas Mstislav conquered Galich by the sword from foreigners, Daniel did not forget that it had been his father's territory. All the while there were many troublemakers, for the boyars were in rebellion, and Alexander of Bełsk aggravated the situation.

When he saw that Mstislav's relations with his son-in-law were strained, Alexander was gleeful. He urged Mstislav to attack the descendants of Rostislav. Thus began a quarrel between two among the most distinguished Russian princes, one of the old and one of the new generation. Daniel allied himself with the Poles, Mstislav brought Polovetsians and incited Vladimir Riurikovich, prince of Kiev. The greatest losses in this struggle were sustained by the main culprit, Alexander of Bełsk. Mstislav acted sluggishly on his behalf, allowing his Bełsk territories to be ravaged fearfully by Roman's sons. The enraged Alexander incited Mstislav against Daniel even more. "Your son-in-law wants to kill you," he claimed.

In the end Mstislav the Brave opened his eyes. He realized that Daniel was slandered, and found peace with his son-in-law. Even then quiet was not restored. The boyar Zhiroslav stirred a sedition, persuading other boyars that Mstislav visited the steppe to his father-in-law the Polovetsian khan Kotian in order to kill them all. The boyars took fright and fled to the region of Peremyshl in the Carpathian mountains. Thence they sent to Mstislav to tell him why they fled, pointing directly to Zhiroslav. Mstislav, who according to the chronicler planned nothing against the boyars, sent his priest Timofey to reassure them. Timofey fulfilled his mission and brought back the boyars. Zhiroslav was banished by Mstislav.

Although Zhiroslav was banished his friends remained, and one sedition followed another. The boyars persuaded Mstislav to betroth his younger daughter to the Hungarian prince Andrew and grant his future son-in-law Peremyshl. Andrew lived there in peace only a very short time. He listened to the boyar Semeon the Red, fled to his father in Hungary and persuaded him to attack his father-in-law Mstislav. The Hungarians were joined by the Poles. The king with strong troops captured the towns of Galich land. Then near Zvenigorod he suffered a great defeat at the hands of Mstislav, and hurriedly retreated to his own land.

The sons of Roman who came to Mstislav's help tried to persuade him to pursue the king, but the king had supporters among the boyars. One of the most distinguished, Sudislav, and also Gleb Zeremeevich, not only dissuaded him from pursuing the king. They persuaded him to marry his daughter to the prince to whom she was betrothed and give him not only Peremyshl, but the whole of the Galich principality. "Prince," they said to Mstislav, "you cannot keep Galich yourself, for the boyars do not want you. If you give Galich to the prince of Hungary you can reclaim it from him when you want. If you pass it to Daniel, Galich will never be yours because the people love Daniel very much."

Mstislav complied with the boyars' wishes and granted Galich to Prince Andrew. For himself he took the Lower Lands.[20] Later he regretted this action and sent to Daniel. "My son!" said he. "I committed a sin in not giving you Galich, by handing it over to a foreigner on the advice of the sycophant Sudislav. He flattered me, but if it is the will of God this matter can be amended. Let us go against them. I will take the Polovetsians and you take your troops. If God helps us, you will take Galich and I will take the Lower Lands." Mstislav the Brave had no time to correct his mistakes because he could not escape the lifelong influence of Gleb Zeremeevich, who prevented him from seeing Daniel before his death, in order to entrust to him his house and his children.

Mstislav died in 1228. He was famous for his glorious deeds, yet they were not put to good use. This suggests the failure of Old Southern Rus, its unsuitability as a basis for further development of a unified Rus. In the North Mstislav liberated Novgorod from Vsevolod and later from Vsevolod's son. Finally the battle on the Lipitsa destroyed Vsevolod's testament. We know that results of this victory did not last very long. In the South Mstislav captured Galich, seizing it from the Hungarians, later freely returning it to them. Only just before his death did he display vain remorse for his lack of character. In the South everything remained as it was before, as if there were no Mstislav. Southern Rus continued to live out its days in endless quarrels among the descendants of Monomakh, Oleg, Rostislav and Iziaslav.

CHANGES IN KIEV, CHERNIGOV AND PEREIASLAVL

In 1214 Mstislav the Brave, expelling Vsevolod the Red from Kiev, sent in his place the oldest among the descendants of Rostislav, his grandson Mstislav Romanovich, who stayed on the senior throne until 1224. After his death the Kievan throne descended in turn to the next most senior nephew, Vladimir Riurikovich.

After the death of Vsevolod the Red his brother Mstislav ruled in Chernigov. After his death in 1224 his nephew who had experienced the strife of Novgorod, namely Mikhail the son of Vsevolod the Red, ruled there. It is difficult to decide whether he occupied Chernigov immediately after the death of Mstislav because it seems strange that in 1224 he decided to change his seat from Chernigov to Novgorod. One thing is certain, Mikhail could not make his position in Chernigov secure without a struggle with his uncle Oleg of Kursk. It is not known how this struggle would have ended were it not for the help of a strong ally, Mikhail's father-in-law Prince Yury of Suzdal with two of his nephews, the sons of Konstantin (1226). It is clear that Oleg of Kursk could not withstand the united forces of Yury of Suzdal and Mikhail of Chernigov, and was forced to relinquish his rights to his nephew. The chronicle says Oleg made peace, using the good offices of Metropolitan Cyril.

Thus the Northern prince broke with the old ways also in the South, even while Mstislav the Brave still lived. The descendants of Oleg were numerous. The chronicler mentions the princes of Kozelsk, Trubech, Putivl and Rylsk. The older sons of Yury of Suzdal handed over Kiev to the descendants of Mstislav, the branch following in clan seniority. They retained Pereiaslavl for Yury's younger sons, equal in seniority to the descendants of Mstislav who occupied the Kievan throne. Vsevolod's son Yaroslav was expelled from Pereiaslavl by Vsevolod the Red in 1207. Afterwards Pereiaslavl was occupied for a time by the descendants of Rostislav. In 1213 the sons of Vsevolod III sent their brother Vladimir there. He been in Moscow and was taken prisoner by the Polovetsians in 1215. In 1218 he was set free and went north with his brother, received Starodub and some other territories, and died in 1227.

The same year Yury Vsevolodovich sent to Pereiaslavl his nephew Vsevolod Konstantinovich. It is not known who ruled there during Vladimir's imprisonment and stay in the North, but Vsevolod Konstantinovich spent less than a year in Pereiaslavl. In his place Yury sent his brother Sviatoslav.

On the western bank of the Dnieper we watched the fate of the older line of Iziaslav Mstislavich ruling in Vladimir-in-Volhynia. As far as the younger line of the princes of Lutsk is concerned, after the death of Yaroslav Iziaslavich his son Ingvar ruled in Lutsk. He was at one time in Kiev. After Ingvar's death Lutsk was ruled by Mstislav the Mute who on his death entrusted his patrimony and his son Ivan to Daniel Romanovich. Ivan soon died and Lutsk was occupied by his cousin Yaroslav Ingvarevich. Chartoriysk was occupied by Prince Rostislav of Pinsk, then Daniel took both Lutsk and Chartoriysk and passed Lutsk and Peresopnitsa to his brother Vasilko, who ruled also in Brest and Peremyshl. Mezhibozh he gave to Yaroslav.

The prince of Pinsk has been mentioned. After Sviatopolk's grandson Yury Yaroslavich established himself in Turov territory that land began to divide between two princely lines initiated by his sons Sviatopolk and Gleb. In the main the Turov territory was divided into two principalities, Turov and Pinsk. There were other lesser principalities as well. Sviatopolk Yurievich, Riurik Rostislavich's brother-in-law, died in 1195. Among the various lines of the princes of Polotsk, as before, there were internecine wars of no particular import.

THE RETINUE

In discussion of Rus princes during the period between the capture of Kiev by Bogoliubsky's troops and the death of Mstislav the Brave mention has been made of boyars and servitors. In the North, in the Suzdal lands, there was Bogoliubsky's famous commander Boris Zhidislavich who after Andrei's death, together with some of his friends, supported the victorious cause of the descendants of Rostislav against the sons of Yury. After this victory Boris went to serve their enemy Prince Gleb of Riazan, together with whom he was taken prisoner by Vsevolod III in the battle of Pruskova mountain. On Boris's side there were also Dobrynia Dolgy, Ivanko Stepanovich and Mateiash Butovich. The first two died in the struggle between Vsevolod III and Mstislav of Rostov. Apparently at the same time Butovich was taken prisoner.

Apart from personalities present at Andrei's court who took part in the conspiracy against him there was Mikhna, his envoy to the Southern branch of Rostislav's clan. Those around Vsevolod III include the executor of his instructions, one Mikhail Borisovich (maybe the son of Boris Zhidislavich), who administered the oath to the descendants of Oleg in 1207 and participated in affairs of Riazan and Novgorod. Others were

Lazar, who acted on behalf of his prince in Novgorod; the steward Giuria whom Vsevolod sent to the South to rebuild Gorodets Ostersk in 1195; the swordbearer Kuzma Ratyshich, who took Tepra in 1210; Foma Lazkovich and Dorozhaia, participants in the Bulgar expedition in 1182; and the boyar Yakov, nephew of Grand Prince Vsevolod through his sister.

Mentioned among boyars of Vsevolod's sons are Ivan Rodislavich, killed in the battle of Rostov; Andrei Stanislavich, who tried to persuade the younger sons of Vsevolod to make peace with Mstislav the Brave before the battle on the Lipitsa; Yeremey Glebovich who first served Konstantin and later Yury; Voislav Dobrynich, commander of Rostov, who served Konstantin's sons.

Among boyars with princes of Southern Rus in 1171 Pauk, the governor of Shum, is mentioned. He was the guardian of Prince Vladimir Andreevich of Dorogobuzh. Gleb Yurievich appointed one Grigory as chiliarch in Kiev. It is not known whether he was one of the Kievan boyars, or whether he came with Gleb from Pereiaslavl.

The expatriate Pole Vladislav Vratislavich, after Mstislav was expelled from Kiev, went over to his enemies. He was sent by Davyd Rostislavich of Vyshgorod to pursue Mstislav in 1127, during the war of Yury's sons Gleb and Mikhail with the Polovetsians (1172). Vladislav, "Jan's brother," possibly the same Pole or somebody else, was the commander of their troops. It is possible that the fact that he was Jan's brother was stressed to distinguish him from another well-known Pole who after Gleb's death stayed in Kiev. He sided with Bogoliubsky against the sons of Rostislav, who captured him there together with Vsevolod Yurievich in 1174.

The cause of the famous war between Bogoliubsky and the sons of Rostislav was the indictment of three Kievan boyars, Grigory Khotovich, Stepanitsa and Alexis Sviatoslavich, for poisoning Prince Gleb. Grigory Khotovich was probably identical with the chiliarch Grigory, brother of Konstantin Khotovich, who was taken prisoner by the Polovetsians.

From among the boyars of Sviatoslav Vsevolodovich in Kiev his favorite Kochkar is mentioned. In all probability he was brought by the prince from Chernigov. The chronicler relates that the prince revealed his secret plans only to Kochkar, and nobody else. The Chernigov boyars Olstin Oleksich and Roman Nezdilovich are known from the expeditions against the Polovetsians (1184, 1185 and 1187). With Riurik Rostislavich of Belgorod and later of Kiev are mentioned the commander Lazar, Sdeslav Zhiroslavich, Boris Zakharich, guardian of Vladimir, son of

Mstislav the Brave. Sdeslav Zhiroslavich also is mentioned later among the boyars of Mstislav the Brave. Later with Riurik in Belgorod the commander Slavin Borisovich is encountered, who later was chiliarch in Kiev. Also in Kiev, during the rule of Riurik, the boyar Churynia is mentioned, who in 1187 was sent together with Slavin to fetch the daughter of Vsevolod III.

Riurik's son Rostislav had a boyar named Rogvolod, who in 1192 was sent to his father Riurik to discuss the expedition against the Polovetsians. The chiliarch of Smolensk during the reign of Davyd Rostislavich was Mikhalko. During the battle on the Lipitsa the boyar Yavolod is found with Vladimir Riurikovich and later Ivor Mikhailovich, possibly the son of Mikhalko. Among the boyars of prince Gleb of Riazan, Boris and Dedilets are found. They contributed much to remove the sons of Yury for the benefit of the Rostislavich princes after Bogoliubsky's death. Dedilets, together with another Riazan boyar Olstin, was captured by Vsevolod III in 1177. Later during the war of Sviatoslav of Chernigov against Vsevolod III, Ivan Miroslavich is noted as one of the Riazan boyars.

V

RUS AND ITS ENEMIES

THE GERMANS IN LIVONIA

After discussing Rus domestic matters, let us turn to external affairs, which in the latter part of the period under consideration began to acquire a specific and very important character. We know that ancient Russian possessions in the Baltic territories were divided into two parts. The northern element depended more or less on Novgorod, the southern on Polotsk. In 1158 a ship belonging to some Bremen merchants, driven by a storm, arrived on the shores of this part of Rus possessions, near the mouth of the Dvina river. They met a hostile reception from the natives. After a clash in which the Germans gained the upper hand the Livs grew more receptive, allowing the strangers to trade. The advantage offered by this trade caused the Bremen merchants to return several times to the mouth of Dvina. Then they persuaded the natives to establish a permanent trading post there. They chose a place near the Dvina, on a hill where they constructed a large building and a small fortress called Uexküll. Soon afterwards another trading post was built, called Dalen.

News of the settlements established by the Germans at the mouth of the Dvina among the pagan population attracted the attention of the archbishop of Bremen, who could not miss such an opportunity to extend the confines of his diocese.[1] He informed Pope Alexander III,[2] who instructed the archbishop to send there an experienced missionary. The archbishop sent Meinhard,[3] a monk of the Augustinian order, who persuaded the prince of Polotsk to allow him to spread the gospel among the pagans under his rule. He built a church in Uexküll and converted several natives.

Soon Lithuanians attacked the neighborhood of Uexküll. Meinhard with the inhabitants hid in the forests, where a battle with the enemy took place. After the Lithuanians departed Meinhard chastised the Livs for living badly and having no fortified places. He undertook to build strong castles for them if they promised to convert to Christianity. The Livs agreed. The following summer builders and masons arrived from Gotland. Before the construction of Uexküll castle part of the nation converted, the rest promised to do so after the castle was finished.

The castle was built, Meinhard was consecrated bishop, yet nobody wanted to convert. On the basis of the same promise a second castle was built at Holm, and once again nobody was prepared to convert. Moreover the pagans started to display clearly hostile intentions towards the bishop, robbed his property and attacked his servants. Most of all, Meinhard was saddened that the native Christians immersed themselves in the Dvina in order, as they put it, to wash away the baptism and send it back to Germany.

Meinhard had a fellow-preacher, Brother Theodorich of the Cistercian order.[4] The Livs determined to sacrifice Theodorich to their gods to ensure a better harvest and prevent rains from spoiling their crops. People gathered, placed the spear on the ground, brought the sacral horse and watched which leg it used to cross the spear. If it crossed with the right leg it meant death, with the left, life. The horse chose life. Then the pagan priest objected, claiming that this was the sorcery of the hostile religion. Once again they brought the horse, and the same thing happened. Theodorich was saved. Another time the same Theodorich was in Estonia when on the day of St. John the Baptist [June 24] a solar eclipse occurred. The unfortunate monk was again in danger from the pagans, who blamed him for the eclipse, claiming that he ate the sun.

When Meinhard realized the difficulty of spreading Christianity among the Livs by peaceful means, he sent an envoy to the Pope to tell him of the sorry state of the new church. The Pope ordered a crusade preached against the pagan Livs. Meinhard did not live to see the crusaders begin, as he died in 1196. That same year the Danish king Canute VI[5] landed on the Estonian coast, established himself there and converted the natives to Christianity by force.

The Livonian Christians meanwhile delegated envoys to the archbishop of Bremen requesting a replacement for Meinhard. The new bishop, Berthold,[6] arrived without troops, invited local leaders and tried to sway them through hospitality and gifts, to no avail. At the first opportunity they plotted against the new bishop, whether to burn him in his church, or kill him or drown him in the Dvina. In secret Berthold boarded his ship and sailed first to Gotland and then to Germany. There he sent a letter describing the sorry state of affairs to the Pope, who promised an indulgence to all who joined a crusade against the Livonians. Thereupon a sizable unit of crusaders gathered around Berthold, who returned with them to Livonia.

The natives armed themselves and sent to ask the bishop why he had brought an army. When Berthold explained that the troops came to punish apostates, the Livonians told him "Send the army home and go to your see peacefully. Whoever has converted, you may force to remain Christian. The others you should convert through words, not by force." This lesson had no effect on Berthold, who took part in a battle between the crusaders and the natives. When the natives fled, a fast horse brought the bishop into the middle of the withdrawing pagans, who killed him.

The Germans used their victory to plunder the area without mercy. The natives were forced to submit and convert, to accept priests and donate for their upkeep a set amount of food per plough. Yet the moment the crusaders boarded their ships the Livonians jumped into the Dvina to wash away their baptism, robbed the priests and forced them from their land. They wanted to do the same to the merchants, but the elders were bribed and the merchants were allowed to stay.

The priests soon returned. A new bishop, Albert,[7] came with them, accompanied by a contingent of crusaders on twenty-three ships. Albert was one of those historical personalities destined to change the life of old societies, to lay a firm basis for the new. When he came to Livonia he immediately understood the situation, found the right way to ensure victory for Christianity and for his nation over paganism and the natives. He pursued his aim with a particular single-mindedness and achieved it.

The natives met the new bishop with hostility. He had to endure the siege they laid to Holm. The newly arrived crusaders freed him, but Albert understood that it was impossible to become established in Livonia with the help only of these temporary guests. The natives did not know how to fight skilled German troops. When they were defeated and saw their homes and fields destroyed, they surrendered and promised to embrace Christianity. Again, when the crusaders boarded their ships, the natives hurried to return to their old religion, remaining hostile to the newcomers.

The struggle therefore had to be conducted not by sporadic and temporary expeditions but by standing firm in the new place, by creating a strong German colony, by building a town where the church could find permanent protection. With this aim in mind Albert established in 1200 the city of Riga at the mouth of the Dvina.

It was not enough to establish a town. It needed population, and Albert himself went to Germany to recruit colonists and bring them to Riga. One town with German population also was not enough. The population could not devote its efforts to peaceful occupations because it must wage permanent war with the natives. It needed a military estate to undertake the constant fighting and defense of the new colony.

At the outset Albert issued a call for knights from Germany, granting them castles as fiefs with this aim in mind. This method could bring the desired effect only very slowly. Soon he conceived a new and a better idea. He organized an order of military brethren based on the example of the military orders in Palestine.[8] Pope Innocent III[9] approved Albert's plan and in 1202 the Order of the Sword Brothers[10] was established and granted a charter modeled on that of the Templars. The new knights wore white coats with a red sword and cross, later replaced by a star. The first master of the order was Veno von Rohrbach.[11]

In this manner the Germans established themselves firmly at the mouth of the Dvina. What did the princes of Polotsk think about this? They were accustomed to leading expeditions against the Chud to take tribute if it was not paid voluntarily. They wanted to treat the Germans in the same manner. In 1203 the prince of Polotsk suddenly appeared at Uexküll and laid siege to the city. The inhabitants, who were unprepared, offered tribute to him. This he accepted and went to besiege the other castle, Holm, to which the bishop sent a garrison. The Rus lost many horses to the arrows of the defenders and withdrew from the castle.

In Livonia on the banks of the Dvina two territories belonged to the princes of Polotsk, Kukenoys (Kokenhausen) and Gerzika. The prince of

Gerzika with Lithuanians (who served the princes of Polotsk just as the Polovetsians served other Rus princes) plundered the neighborhood of Riga, although such raids barely harmed the colonists. Then, in 1206, the relationship between the colonists and the princes of Polotsk grew more serious. Albert, wishing to establish himself without hindrance in the area of the lower Dvina, decided to allay the suspicions of the prince of Polotsk and sent Abbot Theodorich to him with gifts and friendly proposals.

After his arrival in Polotsk Theodorich learned that envoys from the Livonian elders were present. They came to complain to the prince about German violence, petitioning him to expel the hated newcomers. In the presence of the Livonians the prince asked Theodorich why he visited him. When he replied that he had come for peace and friendship, the Livonians exclaimed that Germans neither could nor would preserve the peace. The prince dismissed the bishop's envoys, ordering them to await his reply in their lodging. He did not want to send them back to Riga immediately lest anyone learn of his hostile intentions. The abbot bribed one of the boyars, who told him that the Rus, together with the natives, were preparing to attack the newcomers.

When the abbot learned this, he lost no time. He found in the town a pauper from Holm and hired him to carry a letter to the bishop in Riga informing him of all he had seen and heard. The bishop prepared the city for defense. When the prince learned that his plans were no longer secret, instead of troops he sent his envoys to Riga with instructions to hear out both parties, the bishop and the Livonians, and decide whom to favor. When the envoys arrived in Kukenoys they invited Deacon Stefan to visit the bishop in Riga to invite him to a meeting with the Livonian elders to decide their quarrel, then went to the countryside to invite the natives. Albert was offended by Stefan's proposal and replied that the envoys, according to the custom of all lands, must visit the ruler to whom they were sent, not ask him to come forward to meet them.

In the meantime the Livonians, who assembled at the appointed time and place, seeing the Germans fail to come to the meeting, decided to capture Holm castle, and thence advance upon Riga. Their plan did not have the desired outcome. They suffered defeat and lost their leaders, some killed in battle, others taken in chains to Riga. Once more they were forced to submit to the newcomers. Among the dead was Ako, whom the chronicler names as the chief culprit. He persuaded the prince of Polotsk to march against Riga and called the Letts and all of Livonia against the Christians. The bishop was in church after mass when a knight brought Ako's bloody head as a trophy.

When the matter calmed for the time being the irrepressible Albert again left for Germany to recruit new crusaders, foreseeing a fresh and prolonged struggle. His absence allowed the natives once again to send envoys to the prince of Polotsk with a request to liberate them from their oppressors. The prince sailed down the Dvina and besieged Holm. In response to his appeal the entire local population rebelled, yet this helped him very little during the siege. The Holm garrison, despite its small numbers, caused the Rus much damage by using catapults unknown to the Polotsk army. Although the Rus constructed a small machine based on the German design, their first attempt to use it was unsuccessful, causing casualties among the Rus. The citizens of Holm and Riga were in a position to defend themselves only briefly because they had to deal with an enemy inside their walls. The natives were constantly in touch with the Rus.

Suddenly German ships appeared at sea. The prince, who sustained heavy casualties from the catapult during the siege of Holm, refused to enter into battle against fresh enemy forces, and sailed back to Polotsk. This failure was a terrible blow for the natives. Their leaders sent to Riga, asking for baptism and priests. The Germans complied, but first took from the elders their sons as hostages. The triumph of the newcomers is understandable. They were headed by a man with a unique gift for thought and action, with powerful instruments, a knightly Order and crowds of temporary crusaders who came to help the Riga church, opposed only by a mob of unarmed natives.

As far as relations with Rus were concerned, the bishop and the Order had dealings only with the principality of Polotsk which, as a result of the separation of Rogvolod's grandchildren from the main branch of Yaroslav's descendants,[12] must rely only on its own resources, which were very insignificant. The princes of various Polotsk lands warred among themselves, fought their own subjects, and faced in the Lithuanians dangerous enemies. How could they act effectively against the Germans as well? A prime example of the discord reigning among them and their resulting weakness is the death of Prince Viacheslav of Kukenoys. When unable to fight the Lithuanians with his own resources and those of his clan he appeared in 1207 at Riga and offered the bishop half of his land and town were the bishop to defend him from the barbarians. The bishop joyfully agreed to such a proposal. Although the chronicler does not indicate that he used this help immediately, it is likely that Viacheslav only agreed to accept a German garrison in the event of Lithuanian aggression.

Whatever the agreement, the Rus prince soon learned from experience that instead of defenders the knights were his enemies, more dangerous than the Lithuanians. Between the prince and the knight Daniel von Lenevarden there arose a personal quarrel. Lenevarden suddenly attacked Kukenoys at night and took it without opposition, imprisoned the inhabitants, confiscated their property and put the prince in chains. When the bishop learned about this he ordered Daniel to free the prince, and immediately return the town and the property. Later he invited Viacheslav, received him with honor, gave him rich gifts of horses and clothes and settled his dispute with Daniel. At the same time he reminded him of the previous promise to give the Germans half of his fortresses, and sent soldiers to Kukenoys to occupy and fortify the town in case of a Lithuanian attack.

The prince left Riga outwardly satisfied but in his heart he harbored thoughts of revenge. Seeing that in Riga everything was prepared for the departure of the bishop and many of the crusaders for Germany, he decided to seize this opportunity to liberate the town from its uninvited guests. When he thought that the bishop and crusaders were out to sea he consulted with his retinue, and when the Germans went down the shafts to quarry stone for town construction and left their swords and other equipment above ground, the prince's servants and men stole to the shafts, seized the weapons and killed their owners. Three Germans managed to save themselves, escaped and reached Riga. They told the people what happened to them and their comrades in Kukenoys.

Viacheslav thought this was a good beginning. He sent the enemy's horses and arms to the prince of Polotsk and requested him to march as soon as possible against Riga. It would be an easy conquest because the best men were killed in Kukenoys, while the others had left with the bishop for Germany. The prince of Polotsk was convinced and started to gather troops. Viacheslav was very much deceived in his hopes. Contrary winds halted Albert at the mouth of the Dvina. When news of what happened in Kukenoys reached Riga he returned immediately and rallied his companions once again to work for the holy cause. The Germans, dispersed all over Livonia, gathered in Riga.

When the Rus saw that they could not fight the combined forces of the Order they collected their property, set fire to Kukenoys and pressed further east. The neighboring natives sought salvation in their deep and dense forests from the avenging newcomers, but not everyone escaped. The Germans chased them in forests and marshes. On those whom they captured they inflicted a terrible death.

The fall of Kukenoys soon brought about the conquest of another Rus principality in Livonia, namely Gerzika. In 1209 the bishop, says the chronicler, constantly concerned for the defense of the Livonian church, took counsel with the wisest men on how to safeguard the young church from Lithuania and Rus. They decided upon an expedition against the enemies of Christianity. The chronicler adds that the prince of Gerzika, Vsevolod, was a terrible enemy of Christianity, *in particular of the Latins.* He was married to the daughter of a Lithuanian prince, and was in constant alliance with the Lithuanians, often acting as leader of their armies. He had prepared safe crossings of the Dvina as well as supplies.

Lithuanians, continues the chronicler, at that time were the dread of neighboring peoples. Few Letts dared live in villages. Most looked for safety in deep forests to escape the Lithuanians, who sought them out there, killed some, took others as prisoners and seized all their property. The Rus fled to escape the Lithuanians, the many fleeing the few like hares from hunters. Both Livs and Letts fell to the Lithuanians like sheep without a shepherd fall to the wolf.

God sent them a good and faithful shepherd, namely Bishop Albert. This good and faithful shepherd unexpectedly attacked Gerzika with a large force and captured it. Prince Vsevolod escaped by boat to the other side of the Dvina, but his wife and members of his household were taken prisoner. The Germans spent a day in the town and took much booty from all corners, including clothes, silver, church bells, icons and other ornaments. The following day, having restored order, they marched out and burned the town. When Prince Vsevolod viewed the flames from across the Dvina, he wept bitterly. "Gerzika my beloved town," he cried, "my dear patrimony! It has come to this, that I see my town burning and my people lost!"

The bishop and his forces divided the loot between themselves, including the princess and other prisoners, and returned to Riga. Thence they summoned Prince Vsevolod to appear if he desired peace and to see his people set free. The prince arrived in Riga, called the bishop his father and the Latins his brothers, asking them to free his wife and the other Rus. He was given the following condition, "to grant in perpetuity his principality as a gift to the church of the Virgin and then accept it back from the bishop. When he agreed, he would receive the princess and other prisoners." Vsevolod agreed, promising to reveal to the bishop and the Order the plans of the Rus and the Lithuanians. When he returned home with his wife and his retinue he forgot this promise and again plotted with the Lithuanians, inciting the pagans against the Germans in Kukenoys.

NOVGOROD AND PSKOV WAR AGAINST THE CHUD

While the Germans established themselves by seizing the lower [Western] Dvina lands from Polotsk, Novgorod and Pskov continued their struggle with the Chud living to the south and north of the Gulf of Finland. In 1176 the entire Chud land, as the chronicler says, came to Pskov, where they were repulsed with great losses. Mstislav the Brave exacted revenge on the Chud for these injuries.[13] Usually Novgorod's warfare against the Chud occurred during periods of harmony in Novgorod between prince and citizens. Such periods of stability were very rare. For this reason Novgorod was unable to establish itself in Estonia and compete successfully with the Germans for mastery of this land.

In 1190 the Chud once again attacked Pskov, using boats to cross the lake, and this time the Pskov forces made sure no one returned alive. Yuriev once again was captured by the Chud and recaptured by the men of Novgorod and Pskov in 1191. As was customary, the land of the Chud was burned and many prisoners were taken. The following year Pskov again attacked the Chud and captured Odenpe.[14] Nothing more is heard about expeditions against Estonia until 1212.

That year according to the calculations of our chronicler, and two years earlier according to a German chronicler, Mstislav the Brave with his brother Vladimir attacked the land of Chud-Tormy, the present district of Dorpat. As was customary, he took numerous prisoners and cattle and brought them home. Later that winter Mstislav and the men of Novgorod went against the Chud town of Odenpe, destroyed the villages around it and besieged the town itself. The Chud submitted and paid tribute, and the men of Novgorod returned home without losses.

The German chronicler[15] describes this expedition in greater detail. The prince of Novgorod with the prince of Pskov and accompanied by the Rus troops arrived in great force in Ungannia and besieged the fortress of Odenpe. The Chud defended it for eight days. Finally lack of food forced them to ask for peace. The Rus agreed, baptized some of the natives, took four hundred marks of nogats[16] and returned home. They promised to send [Orthodox] priests yet did not because they feared the Germans, adds the chronicler. It may be assumed that it was not so much fear of the Germans as lack of interest in Estonian matters. Thus the men of Novgorod, as long as Mstislav lived among them, penetrated the Chud land to the seashore, burned villages, captured fortifications and forced the people pay homage and tribute. When Mstislav soon departed for the South, and Novgorod began its quarrels with the Northern princes of Suzdal, the Chud once again were forgotten. Meanwhile the Germans acted with united forces, constantly in one direction and with a single aim.

To conquer the Ests, the Letts and other natives, and make Riga rich through trade with lands on the upper reaches of the Dvina and the Dnieper, the Germans decided to seek peace with the prince of Polotsk. The bishop undertook to pay an annual tribute for the Livs, who were in servitude to the Riga church and the Order.

Just as the prince of Polotsk, satisfied with the tribute, found peace with the dangerous newcomers, Pskov for the first time discovered a strong hostility towards them. This was to become a feature of its history thereafter. In 1213 Pskov expelled Prince Vladimir for marrying his daughter to Bishop Albert's brother. The exiled prince first went to Polotsk and, as the welcome there was not very cordial, he visited his son-in-law in Riga, where he was received with all honors, according to the German chronicler. Vladimir soon found opportunity to repay the bishop for such hospitality. The prince of Polotsk, realizing that the Order was using peace with the Rus merely to enslave the natives further and compel them to accept Christianity, arranged a meeting with Albert in Gerzika. The bishop arrived at the meeting with Prince Vladimir, knights, Liv and Lett nobles and a crowd of merchants, all of them well armed. The prince at first spoke to Albert affectionately, then turned to threats to force him to stop the violent conversion of the natives, his subjects. The bishop replied that he would not abandon his mission and neglect the duty imposed on him by the supreme pontiff of Rome.

Apart from forceful conversions, it is clear from the chronicle that the bishop failed to observe the main clause of the agreement, payment of the tribute. His excuse was the natives' reluctance to work for two masters, the Germans and the Rus. They begged him to liberate them from the yoke of the Rus. The prince, continues the chronicler, refused to accept these fair explanations, threatened to burn Riga and all German castles, and ordered his men to leave the encampment and gird for battle. The bishop's escort did the same.

Then Johann, provost[17] of the Riga church of the Virgin, and the Pskov exile Prince Vladimir, approached the Polotsk prince, wishing to persuade

Collecting Tribute from the Chud
Miniature for 1130 in the Fifteenth-Century
Königsberg or Radziwill Manuscript

him not to war with Christians. They suggested the difficulty of fighting the Germans' brave soldiers, skilled in battle and burning with desire to measure themselves against the Rus. The prince seemingly admired their courage and ordered his troops back to the encampment. He himself went to the bishop and called him his spiritual father. The bishop for his part accepted him as his son. Peace negotiations began and the prince, as if by divine inspiration, granted all Livonia exemption from paying tribute, on condition of an alliance against Lithuania and free navigation of the Dvina.

No matter how implausible this story of the German chronicler, a historian may accept as reliable that the bishop stopped paying tribute to the prince of Polotsk, who lacked means of enforcing such payment. Vladimir of Pskov received his reward for services rendered, being appointed to the office of advocate[18] of one of the Livonian provinces. There when he was judging the natives he reaped much where he had not sown, in the chronicler's words. His judgments were not to the liking of the bishop of Ratzenburg and all others. He was forced to go to Russia[19] as many wished, writes the chronicler. Soon thereafter he returned with his wife, sons and entire family to resume his office, which did not cheer his subordinates, adds the same chronicler. Once again complaints arose, and he had to listen to the reproaches of German clerics. Annoyed by all this, in the end he returned to Russia, where again he was received by the inhabitants of Pskov.

After driving Vladimir away the Germans plotted the same for the other Rus prince remaining in Livonia, namely Prince Vsevolod of Gerzika, despite the fact that he was the bishop's vassal. The knights of Kokenhausen (Kukenoys) accused him of failing to attend the court of the bishop, his father and lord, also of being in communication with Lithuania and giving it constant aid. Several times they demanded his presence that they might hear his explanation, but Vsevolod never appeared. Then the knights, with the bishop's consent, approached the town secretly, seized it by deceit, robbed the inhabitants and withdrew. This happened in 1214.

The following year, 1215, the Germans again gathered their forces, captured Gerzika and plundered it a second time. Vsevolod sent for the Lithuanians to come to his help. They arrived and forced the Germans to leave the town, inflicting upon them a heavy defeat.

This is the story as related by the most ancient Livonian chronicler, although in an even older chronicle[20] we read another version, namely that Prince Vsevolod was killed during the second German attack on his town, when it was finally sacked. There is nothing in the chronicle about Lithuanian help. The oldest chronicle for the year 1225 mentions once more Prince Vsevolod of Gerzika visiting Riga to meet the papal legate. Be that as it may, it is clear that Gerzika sooner or later fell under German rule.

Meanwhile Vladimir of Pskov avenged his injury. In 1217 he went with the men of Novgorod and Pskov against Odenpe, that constant goal of Rus expeditions, besieging the town. The Chud, as was customary, sent homage, but this time they deceived the Rus and sent to the Germans for help. The citizens of Novgorod called an assembly away from the encampment and took counsel with Pskov on the Chud proposals. The night guards had left their posts and the day guards had not yet arrived. Suddenly the Germans appeared and broke into the deserted tents. The men of Novgorod broke from the assembly, ran to the encampment, took up arms and repulsed the Germans, who escaped in the direction of the town, having lost three commanders. The Novgorod troops took seven hundred horses and returned home without loss.

The German chronicler adds that the Rus made an agreement according to which the Germans were to leave Odenpe. Vladimir captured his son-in-law Theodorich, brother of the bishop, and took him to Pskov. Vladimir's successful expedition probably encouraged the Ests and they decided to remove the yoke of the newcomers. With this purpose they sent envoys to Novgorod to ask assistance. Novgorod promised to march to their land with a large force. This they failed to do because from 1218 until 1224 the princes changed five times, constant disturbances erupted, as did quarrels between the princes and the famous burgrave Tverdislav.[21] The Ests, relying on Novgorod promises, rose up but could not withstand the Germans and were forced to submit once again.

In 1219 the Novgorod forces with their prince Vsevolod came late to Livonia. They were successful in a battle with the Germans, then wasted their time for two weeks near Wenden and returned safely home. Two other Novgorod expeditions, in 1222 to Wenden and in 1223 to Reval, came to nothing. The chronicler tells us, using the customary phrases, that they attacked the whole of the Chud land, brought countless prisoners and much gold, failed to capture any towns and all returned safely home.

In the same place in the chronicle it can be learned why these expeditions, apart from plundering the countryside, had no other consequences. After the first expedition, in 1223, Prince Vsevolod with all his court left Novgorod in secret, much saddening the citizens. After the second expedition Prince Yaroslav also left for his permanent seat, Perei-aslavl-Zalessk, even though Novgorod begged him to stay.

Meantime the Germans acted and in the fateful year 1224, when Southern Rus for the first time had a taste of the Tatars, in the North the strongest Russian settlement in the land of the Chud, namely Yuriev or Dorpat, was taken by the Germans. Prince Viacheslav or Viachko[22] ruled there at that time. He was forced by the Germans to abandon his patrimony Kukenoys. Viachko well remembered the injury and was an unrelenting enemy of his persecutors. He collected tribute from the surrounding lands, says the German chronicler, and sent forces to plunder the lands of those who refused, causing the Germans as much loss as he could.[23] All natives who rebelled against the newcomers found support in him.

This in particular angered the Germans against Viachko. Finally they decided to muster all their forces to conquer the hateful den where, according to their chronicler, all the evil people, traitors and murderers, all the enemies of the Livonian church, were gathered under this prince, who from the very beginning was the root of all evil for Livonia. When they arrived at Yuriev the knights of the Order, servants of the church of Rome, crusaders from foreign lands, merchants, Riga citizens, and baptized Livs and Letts, besieged the town on August 15, the day of the Dormition.

The Germans prepared many siege engines, built a tower from very large trees to the height of the town walls. Under its protection they started sapping operations. Day and night half of the force worked, one half digging, the other half carrying away the earth. The following day the larger part of the underground gallery collapsed and the engine had to be brought nearer to town. Despite this the besieging forces attempted again to negotiate with Viachko. They sent to him several clergy and knights, offering free passage from the fortress with all his retinue, horses and property if he agreed to leave behind the native apostates. Viachko, expecting the arrival of the Novgorod forces, refused all terms.

The siege resumed with renewed vigor and continued for many days without success, the skill and bravery of both sides matching. Neither besiegers nor besieged rested day or night. By day they fought, by night they played and sang. Finally the Germans called a council. Two leaders of the visiting crusaders, Friedrich and Fredehelm, expressed their opinion. "We must attack," they said, "and after capture of the town punish the inhabitants very severely as an example to others. Until now in all captured fortresses we left the citizens alive and free. This aroused no fear in others. Now let us announce that the first among our army to climb the wall will be given honors. He will get the best horses and the most distinguished prisoner except for the treacherous prince, whom we will elevate higher than all others by hanging him on the tallest tree." This proposal was approved.

The following morning the besiegers opened the attack, but were repulsed. The besieged made a large hole in the wall and from there threw burning wheels to ignite the tower which had caused so many losses to the fort. The besieging forces had to concentrate all their efforts on extinguishing the fire and saving their tower. Meantime the bishop's brother Johann von Appeldern, weapon in hand, was the first to climb over the rampart, followed by his servant Peter Oge. They reached the wall without difficulty. When the other soldiers saw this, they followed him. Each hurried to be the first into the fortress, but it was not known who was first. Some helped each other climb the wall, others entered through the breach made by the besieged to roll the burning wheels. The Germans were followed by the Letts and Livs, and carnage began. No quarter was given. For a long time the Rus defended themselves inside the walls, but in the end they were exterminated. The Germans surrounded the fortress on all sides and let none save themselves by flight. Of all the men in town, one survived, a servant of the prince of Suzdal. He was given a horse and sent to Novgorod to relate the fate of Yuriev. "That summer Prince Viachko was killed by the Germans in Yuriev," noted the Novgorod chronicler, "and they took the town."[24]

UNREST IN NOVGOROD AND PSKOV

What did the men of Novgorod do? Did they take calmly the destruction of Rus possessions in the land of the Chud? This account from the chronicle shows clearly whether Novgorod was capable of decisive action. In 1228 the prince of Pereiaslavl-Zalessk, Yaroslav Vsevolodovich, was invited to rule in Novgorod, and went with the burgrave and the chiliarch to Pskov. When Pskov learned that the prince was coming they locked themselves in the city and did not admit him. There was a rumor that Yaroslav was bringing with him chains, intending to arrest their leading men. Yaroslav returned to Novgorod, summoned an assembly in the archbishop's palace and announced to the citizens that he had no evil intentions towards Pskov. "I did not bring them any chains," said he, "but gifts in cases, cloth and fruit, yet they treated me dishonorably."

He complained much to the people of Novgorod. Soon afterwards he brought his regiments from Pereiaslavl to march against Riga.

The citizens of Pskov, when they learned of this, made a separate peace with the Germans, giving them forty hostages to ensure they would help them in case of war with Novgorod. The people of Novgorod also became suspicious of Yaroslav. "The prince calls on us to go against Riga," they said, "but he himself wants to march against Pskov." "Join me in my expedition," Yaroslav once more urged Pskov. "I have nothing against you. Hand over those who spread evil rumors about me."

"We bow to you, O prince, and to your Novgorod brothers," Pskov answered him, "but we will not go with you, nor will we hand over our brothers. We have peace with Riga. You went against Kolyvan (Reval), took silver and returned without achieving anything. You did not capture the town, nor did you capture Kes (Wenden) or Bear's Head (Odenpe). For this our brothers were killed by the Germans on the lake, and others taken prisoner. You only annoyed the Germans, then went away, and we had to pay the price. Why do you think we would now advance with you? So with all due respect, and with the aid of the Mother of God, we are against you. Better that, rather than the pagans, you kill us and take our wives and children as slaves. On these conditions we will bow to you." "With all due respect, O prince," said the citizens of Novgorod, "we will not go against Riga without our brothers of Pskov." Yaroslav tried hard to convince them but, failing, sent his regiments back to Pereiaslavl. Was it possible in such circumstances to fight effectively against the Germans?

Novgorod conducted wars to the north of the Gulf of Finland against another Chud tribe, the Häme.[25] The nature of these expeditions was similar to those against the Ests. Thus in 1188 Novgorod's young men went against the Häme with someone called Vyshata Vasilievich, and returned home safely with captives. In 1191 the men of Novgorod went with Karelians[26] against the Häme, brought war to their land, burned it and killed cattle. In 1227 Prince Yaroslav Vsevolodovich went with the men Novgorod against the Häme, attacked their land, and took innumerable slaves. The following year the Häme sought revenge for the plunder of their lands. They came by boats on Lake Ladoga and looted Novgorod possessions.

The citizens of Novgorod, when they heard this news, took to their boats and sailed down the Volkhov to Ladoga. The men of Ladoga and their burgrave Vladislav did not wait for them, instead chased the Häme in their boats, caught up with them and started a battle which stopped only at nightfall. In the night the Häme sued for peace, which the men of Ladoga refused. Then the Finns killed their prisoners and abandoned the boats to escape into the forests, where most of them were slain by the Karelians. What did the men of Novgorod do? They halted on the Neva, summoned an assembly and wanted to kill one of their own men, some-one called Sudimir, whom the prince hid in his boat. They returned home without achieving anything.

NOVGOROD EXPEDITIONS BEYOND THE PORTAGE

There were also clashes between Novgorod and the Finnish tribes beyond the portage, in the area of the Northern Dvina and further to the east. For 1187 there is information that Novgorod tribute[27] collectors were killed in Pechora and beyond the portage. About a hundred were killed. Rebellion apparently broke out simultaneously in many places.

In 1193 the men of Novgorod commanded by Yadrey set out on an expedition beyond the Urals to Yugra. When they arrived in Yugra they captured one town, besieged another and remained there for five weeks. The besieged sent to them in deceit, saying "We are collecting silver, sables and other goods. Why do you want to lose your peasants and your tribute?" Instead of silver they gathered armed men and acted with a Novgorod traitor, one Savka, who was in league with the prince of Yugra.

When their forces were ready the besieged sent to tell the Novgorod leader to visit the town with twelve of his best men to receive the tribute. The commander, suspecting nothing, complied and was killed with his companions. Later another thirty were lured into town and still later a further fifty. "If you do not kill Yakov Prokopich, O prince, but let him return to Novgorod alive," said the traitor Savka, "the army will return and ravage your land. Order his death." Yakov was killed, but before his death he said to Savka "Brother! God and the Holy Wisdom will be your judge for what you have contrived against your brothers. You will stand with us before God, and will answer for our blood." In the end the besieged, after killing the best men of Novgorod, attacked the rest who were half starved, and killed a large number. Only eighty escaped to reach Novgorod in a sorry state. Understandably their arrival caused great commotion when it was learned that their failure was due to treachery. The survivors killed three citizens, considering them guilty of evil intent. Others who were accused paid fines. The chronicler relates that only God knows who was guilty and who was innocent.

From this very rare information in the chronicle can be formed a picture of Novgorod's relations with its possessions beyond the portage and their Finnish population. Groups of tribute *collectors*[28] visited to gather silver and furs. Occasionally they encountered resistance, and were killed in various places. It is not known whether Yadrey's expedition was to collect fur tribute from the tribes who hitherto had not paid it, or from old tributaries who now refused to pay. "We are collecting silver...," said one lesser prince. "Why do you want to kill your own peasants?" This suggests the latter possibility. If Novgorod tribute collectors were not always successful beyond the portage, Novgorod exiles who for various reasons left their land settled in the last quarter of the twelfth century in the Kama region, on the banks of the Viatka river. There they created an independent community which sheltered exiles in the Northeast, similar to Bîrlad and Tmutorokan in the South.[29]

STRUGGLE OF THE SUZDAL PRINCES AGAINST THE BULGARS

Novgorod fought the Finnish tribes beyond the portage, in present-day Finland and Estonia. In the former it was to collect rich tribute in silver and furs, in the latter partly to loot, partly to protect its possessions against ravaging by savages. The Northern princes of Suzdal, following the geographical imperative, extended their possessions down the Volga, forced to fight constantly against the Bulgars, Mordvinians and other non-Rus nations.

In the winter of 1172 Andrei Bogoliubsky sent his son Mstislav against the Bulgars. He was supposed to join the sons of the princes of Murom and Riazan. This expedition, says the chronicler, was not to everybody's liking. Winter was not the time to fight the Bulgars, for the armies moved very slowly and reluctantly. At the mouth of the Oka river the princes waited for two weeks for various reinforcements, then decided to proceed just with the vanguard retinue of which Boris Zhidislavich was in sole charge. The Rus forces entered the pagan land by surprise, took six villages and a town. They killed the men, taking the women and children prisoners. When the Bulgars heard that the princes were accompanied by only a small retinue, they gathered six thousand troops and went against the Rus. Before they came within twenty versts they turned back. "Our men," says the chronicler, "praised God for that, because it is clear that the Mother of God and Christian prayers saved them from an unavoidable disaster."

In 1184 Vsevolod III undertook a campaign against the Bulgars, requesting help from Prince Sviatoslav Vsevolodovich of Kiev, who sent his son Vladimir with word to the Northern prince. "God grant, my brother and son," said he, "to fight the pagans in our times." Vsevolod proceeded by the Oka to the Volga in the company of eight princes. When they landed the grand prince left the Beloozero regiment to guard the boats under two commanders, Foma Liaskovich and Dorozhay, then moved with the rest to the capital city of the Silver Bulgars.[30] A screen detachment sent ahead saw an army in the field and thought they were Bulgars, but they turned out to be Polovetsians. Five of them approached Vsevolod, bowed low to him, saying "Prince! The Polovetsians of the Yamiak bow to you. We also have come to fight the Bulgars." Vsevolod, after deliberations with the princes and the retinue, made the Polovetsians swear an oath according to their custom, and marched together with them to the Bulgar capital.[31] When they approached he consulted with his retinue. Meantime his nephew Iziaslav Glebovich took the spear and galloped with his retinue to the town, where Bulgar foot soldiers had erected fortifications. Iziaslav dislodged them, reached the city gate but broke his spear there, and was wounded when an arrow pierced his armor near the heart. He was brought almost dead to the encampment.

The Beloozero contingent, left to guard the boats, came under Bulgar attack. The Bulgars came by the Volga from various towns and numbered five thousand. They were routed, and more than a thousand were drowned. Vsevolod besieged the Bulgar capital another ten days then, when he saw that his nephew was mortally wounded and the Bulgars requested peace, he returned to the boats, where Iziaslav died. The grand prince returned to Vladimir and sent his horsemen against the Mordvinians.

In 1186 Vsevolod sent five commanders with men of Gorodets against the Bulgars. The Rus captured many villages and returned with captives. After that date there is no information about expeditions against the Bulgars during Vsevolod's reign. After his death the internecine wars for a long time prevented the Rus from paying attention to their neighbors. Using this opportunity, the Bulgars began to raid, capturing Ustiug in 1217. Only in 1220 could Grand Prince Yury Vsevolodovich organize a strong force against the Bulgars. He sent his brother Prince Sviatoslav of Yuriev and his own regiments commanded by Yeremey Glebovich. Yaroslav Vsevolodovich of Pereiaslavl also sent his regiments. The grand prince ordered his nephew Vasilko Konstantinovich to send the Rostov and Ustiug regiments up the Kama. The Murom prince Davyd sent his son Sviatoslav, Yury sent Oleg, and they all came together at the mouth of the Oka, sailed down the Volga and landed opposite the town of Oshel.

Sviatoslav arranged the troops. The Rostov contingent was deployed on the right, the Pereiaslavl on the left, while Sviatoslav with the prince of Murom took the central position. In this order he moved towards the forest, leaving one contingent to guard the boats.

Having crossed the forest the Rus entered the open field before the town. The Bulgar horsemen met them there. Standing there for a short while, they loosed some arrows at the Rus force and galloped back to town. Sviatoslav pursued them and besieged Oshel. A stockade surrounded the town with a strong oak paling, behind which were two further fortifications with a rampart between them. The besieged came up on this rampart and fought with the Rus. Prince Sviatoslav approached the town, sending before him men with fire and axes. These were followed by bowmen and spearmen. The Rus cut down the palisade, destroyed two other fortifications and set fire to them, later setting fire to the town itself. Suddenly a wind started to blow in the opposite direction and wreaths of smoke were blown towards the Rus regiments, making it impossible to distinguish friend from foe. Heat and especially thirst forced the besieging troops to withdraw.

After they rested, Sviatoslav said "Let us go now to the upwind side of the town." The regiments moved near the town gate, where the prince addressed them. "Brothers and retinue," said he, "today either good or evil may befall us, so let us go as quickly as we can!" The prince himself rode in front to the town and the remaining troops followed. They cut down the paling and bulwarks and set them on fire. They then set alight the whole town from all sides. At this moment a fierce storm started, the spectacle was terrible to behold, and loud weeping arose in town. The Bulgar prince escaped on horseback accompanied by a small retinue. Other Bulgars who escaped on foot were killed by the Rus. Women and children were taken prisoner. Some Bulgars burned to death in the town, yet others killed their wives and children and then themselves. A few Rus troops dared enter the town to seek booty. Some barely escaped the flames, while others burned to death. After burning the town Sviatoslav returned to his boats. When he reached them a severe rainstorm started, and the boats scarcely kept their moorings. Later the storm abated and Sviatoslav, after staying the night and dining the next day, sailed back up the Volga.

In the interval the Bulgars from the capital and other towns, learning of the fall of Oshel, gathered with their princes and arrived on the bank.

Sviatoslav learned of the enemy's approach and ordered his troops to gird for battle. They marched, one contingent after another, beating their drums, sounding their trumpets, struggling for breath, with the prince in the rear. The Bulgars approached the shore and saw among the Rus their own people held as prisoners. One saw his father, another his sons and daughters, yet others their brothers and sisters. They wept, hung their heads and shut their eyes but dared not attack the Rus, allowing Sviatoslav to reach safely the mouth of the Kama river. Here he joined the forces from Rostov and Ustiug commanded by Voislav Dobrynich. The men of Rostov and Ustiug came with much loot after fighting their way down the Kama and capturing many towns and villages. From the mouth of the Kama together they advanced to Gorodets, landed there and continued to Vladimir on horseback. Prince Yury met his brother by Bogoliubovo and held for him and the whole army a great banquet. They feasted for three days. Sviatoslav and the army received rich gifts.

As a result of Sviatoslav's expedition, that same winter Bulgar envoys appeared before the grand prince and sued for peace. Yury initially refused, sending to gather troops. He wanted personally to take part in a campaign, and indeed travelled to Gorodets. On the way he encountered new Bulgar envoys who paid him homage. Still he would not hear of it. In the end, when he was in Gorodets, other envoys met him with gifts and offered good terms, to which the grand prince finally agreed. They concluded peace as in the old times, as in the reign of Yury's father and uncle.

FOUNDATION OF NIZHNY NOVGOROD

After the successful expedition against the Bulgars Yury decided to strengthen the Rus frontier at that important point where the Oka joins the Volga, where Suzdal and Murom forces customarily met. In this place Nizhny [Lower] Novgorod was founded in 1221. It was built in the lands of the Mordvinians, with whom consequently a struggle ensued. In 1226 the grand prince sent his brothers Sviatoslav and Ivan against the Mordvinians, whom they defeated, capturing several villages. In September 1228 Yury sent against the Mordvinians his nephew Vasilko Konstantinovich of Rostov with his commander, the famous Yeremey Glebovich They soon returned because of torrential rains which poured day and night. He himself campaigned in January with his brother Yaroslav, his nephews the sons of Konstantin, and Prince Yury of Murom.

The Rus expedition entered the land of the Mordvinian prince Purgas, burned and trampled the crops, killed livestock and sent home prisoners.

The Mordvinians hid in the forests and strongholds, Those who failed to hide were killed by Yury's younger retinue. When the success of Yury's retinue was learned, the following day the younger retinues of Yaroslav and Konstantin's sons in secret entered a dense forest to look for Mordvinians, who allowed them deep into the forest then ambushed them. Some were killed outright and others were dragged to the Mordvinian fortifications and killed there. Meanwhile a Bulgar prince attacked Puresh, the vassal princeling of Yuriev, then when he heard that the grand prince was burning Mordvinian villages he hastened back by night. Yury with his brothers and all his regiments returned safely home.

In general, despite the slowness and lack of coordination in the Rus offensive against them, the Finnish tribes could not oppose the Rus successfully. Despite all the difficulties of unifying the land the Rus advanced down this road whereas the Finnish tribes fell behind. At this time they remained at the stage of development of the Slavic tribes of the Dregovichians, Severians and Viatichians[32] of the mid-ninth century. They lived as separate and therefore powerless tribes, divided and hostile to each other. Local legend very faithfully illuminates the reasons why the Finnish tribes were subject to the Rus. It tells that on the site of the future Nizhny Novgorod there lived a Mordvinian called Skvorets, friend of Nightingale the Robber.[33] He had eighteen wives and seventy sons. The sorcerer Diatel prophesied that if his children lived in peace they would receive their father's inheritance. If they quarrelled, they would be conquered by the Rus. The descendants of Skvorets lived in hostility among themselves, and Andrei Bogoliubsky expelled them from the Oka estuary.

WARS WITH LITHUANIA AND THE YATVIAGS

The relations of Rus with its savage Western neighbors, the Lithuanians, were different. Rus attacks grew more fierce and coordinated. In 1190 Riurik Rostislavich, while still prince of Belgorod, undertook a campaign against Lithuania. This was because of his kinship with the prince of Pinsk, who suffered particularly from Lithuania. He failed to reach the Lithuanian lands because the weather suddenly grew warm and the snow melted. In these marshy lands it was possible to fight only during very cold weather. His son-in-law, the famous Roman of Volhynia, had more luck. His behavior towards the captive Lithuanians and the Yatviags was mentioned earlier. In 1196, according to the chronicle, Roman marched to their land to *take revenge* for an attack on his territories. When Roman entered their land they could not withstand his might and escaped to their forts. Roman burned their lands, *took revenge* and returned home.

The internecine wars which flared in Volhynia after Roman the Great's death gave the Yatviags and Lithuanians the opportunity to plunder that land. For the year 1205 the chronicle states that Lithuanians and Yatviags attacked the lands from Turiisk to Cherven. They reached the gates of Cherven. There was trouble in the land of Vladimir because of Lithuanian and Yatviag raids, says the chronicler. In 1215 twenty-one Lithuanian princes agreed to peace with Roman's widow, who immediately turned them against the Poles. In 1227 Yatviags came to plunder the area around Brest, but were defeated by Daniel Romanovich.

The northwestern borders of Rus were not safe from Lithuanian attacks. In 1183 Pskov fought with the Lithuanians and suffered much evil from them. In 1200 the Lithuanians plundered the banks of the Lovat. The men of Novgorod gave chase and turned them to flight, killed eighty men and recaptured the loot. The same year the commander of Velikie Luki, Nezdila Pekhchinich, went with a small retinue against Letgolia.[34] He surprised the enemy while they slept, killed forty men and took captive their wives and children. In 1210 once again a Lithuanian assault against Novgorod territory is mentioned. In 1213 Lithuanians burned Pskov, in 1217 they again raided along the Shelon river, in 1225 they fought near Toropets and in 1224 reached Rusa. The burgrave Fedor rode to repulse the Lithuanians, then was defeated. In 1225 seven hundred Lithuanians terribly plundered the villages near Torzhok and came within three versts of the town, killed many merchants and took numerous prisoners throughout the Toropets land. Prince Yaroslav Vsevolodovich caught up with them near Usviat, killed two thousand and recovered their loot. In this battle Prince Davyd of Toropets, son of Mstislav the Brave, was killed.

THE STRUGGLE WITH THE POLOVETSIANS

In the South and the Southeast the struggle with the peoples of the steppe or the Polovetsians continued. When Andrei Bogoliubsky established his brother Gleb in Kiev many Polovetsians appeared in the Land of Rus. Half appeared in the Pereiaslavl, the rest in the Kiev principality. Both groups sent Gleb a message, saying "God and Prince Andrei put you in your patrimony in Kiev and we want to come to terms with you. Later we will swear to you, and you will swear to us, that you do not fear us, nor do we fear you." "I am ready," replied Gleb, "to come to a meeting with you." He consulted with his retinue as to which group of Polovetsians to visit first. They decided that it would be better to go first towards Pereia-slavl, as the local prince Vladimir Glebovich was a minor, only twelve years of age. Gleb came to meet with the Polovetsians of Pereiaslavl and sent to tell the others in Rus (meaning those around Kiev) "Wait for me here, for now I am going to Pereiaslavl. When I have made peace with these Polovetsians I will come and make peace with you." The Polo-vetsians near Kiev, when they heard that Gleb had gone to the other side of the Dnieper, said "Gleb went to the other side of Dnieper, to the other Polovetsians, and he will be there a long time. He did not come to us, so we will attack Kiev, capture the villages and go home with the loot."

Indeed they went to attack the Kievan territories and inhabitants who, not expecting this raid, could not escape. All were taken prisoner and together with their flocks were driven into the steppe. Gleb was return-ing from Pereiaslavl and intended to go to Korsun, where the Polovetsians were staying earlier, when he was informed that the barbarians, without waiting for the meeting, had plundered and were still fighting. Gleb wanted to give chase at once, but a Berendey took the bridle of his horse. "Prince do not go!" he said. "Your position demands that you to go only in command of a large host, when all the brothers have come together. For now send some other prince, and also some of us, the Berendey."

Gleb listened to them and sent his brother Mikhail with a hundred Pereiaslavl men and fifteen hundred Berendey. Mikhail intercepted the Polovetsians on their way, attacking their unprepared guards numbering three hundred, killing some and taking others prisoner. When he interro-gated them to learn how many of their men were further back, and they answered that there were many, about seven thousand men, the Rus thought "There are many Polovetsians further on, and only a few of us. If we leave the prisoners alive they will be our first enemies during the battle." So they killed all the prisoners. Then they marched against the rest of the Polovetsians, crushed them, took away their loot and once again asked the prisoners "Are there many of your men following?" "Now the main force is approaching," they answered. The Rus waited for this force and attacked it. The pagans had nine hundred horses, the Rus only ninety. The men of Pereiaslavl wanted to ride ahead with Prince Mikhail, but the Berendey once again held Mikhail's horse by its bridle and said "You must not ride first, because you are our *defense*.[35] We, the archers, should go first." The battle was fierce, and Prince Mikhail was wounded three times. Finally the Polovetsians fled, and fifteen hundred were taken prisoner by our troops.

Battle Between Rus and Polovetsians

Miniature for 1185 in the Fifteenth-Century

Königsberg or Radziwill Manuscript

In the winter of 1174 the Polovetsians once again appeared in the Kiev land and captured many villages. Gleb was ill and sent against them Torks and Berendey under the command of his brothers Mikhail and Vsevolod, who reached the Polovetsians and crushed them beyond the Bug river. Four hundred Rus captives were freed.

After Gleb's death, during the reign of Roman Rostislavich in Kiev, the chronicle mentions Polovetsian raids on the Ros river borderlands. On the left side of the Dnieper the struggle with the barbarians was more interesting. There the prince of Severia, Igor Sviatoslavich, marched against the Polovetsians past the Vorskla river. He learned on his way that two khans, Kobiak and Konchak, planned to plunder the Pereiaslavl lands. Igor gave chase, forced them to flee and seized their loot. Thus the struggle against the Polovetsians started by Igor Sviatoslavich was successful. He was to became famous because of his later unfortunate expedition against them.[36]

In 1179 Konchak caused much injury to the Christians in the Pereiaslavl land. In 1184 the chronicle mentions another attack by Konchak. Until then the civil war between the descendants of Monomakh and Oleg in the South prevented the princes from retaliating against the Polovetsians by expeditions into the steppe. Then, upon the final establishment of Sviatoslav Vsevolodovich in Kiev, internecine strife ceased and a series of campaigns into the steppe began. As early as 1184, following Konchak's raid, Prince Sviatoslav after deliberating with his relative Riurik marched against the Polovetsians and stood by Olzhich waiting for Yaroslav Vsevolodovich from Chernigov. Yaroslav arrived and told him "Brother do not go now. Better let us fix a date and we will go, God willing, in summer." The senior princes listened and returned, sending the junior into the steppe instead. Sviatoslav sent Igor Sviatoslavich of Severia, and Riurik sent Vladimir Glebovich of Pereiaslavl. The junior princes, Vladimir the descendant of Monomakh and Igor the descendant of Oleg, immediately argued about seniority and fell out. Vladimir asked Igor to ride ahead, but Igor refused. Then Vladimir grew angry and instead of attacking the Polovetsians attacked towns of Severia, taking large booty. Igor, alone with his allies from among the descendants of Oleg, went against the Polovetsians and forced them to flee, but could not harry them because of rivers swollen with the rains.

The senior princes Sviatoslav and Riurik observed their promise. In summer they announced an expedition against the Polovetsians. They gathered the princes of Pereiaslavl, Volhynia, Smolensk and Turov, with an auxiliary unit from Galich, and marched down the Dnieper. The men of Chernigov refused to accompany them and sent word to Sviatoslav Vsevolodovich, saying "We must go a long way down the Dnieper. We cannot leave our lands open to attack. If you go against Pereiaslavl, we will meet you on the Sula river."

Sviatoslav did not like this unruliness among junior princes. He continued without them down the Dnieper and landed on the eastern bank near Inzhir ford. He sent the junior princes with 2,100 Berendey to look for the Polovetsians. Vladimir Glebovich of Pereiaslavl convinced Sviatoslav to let him precede the rest. "My territory is empty because of the Polovetsians," he said, "so, O my father Sviatoslav, let me lead with the screen detachment!" When the Polovetsians observed Vladimir's host advancing they withdrew. The Rus vanguard could not catch up with them, returning to the Erela river. The Polovetsians halted as well and Khan Kobiak, thinking that the Rus army consisted only of Vladimir's forces, approached and loosed arrows at them across the river. When Sviatoslav and Riurik learned this, they sent sizable regiments to help the screen detachment and they moved as well. The Polovetsians, when they saw the first regiments sent to help the screen detachment, mistook them for Sviatoslav and Riurik, and turned away. The Rus pursued them, slaying the enemy. They took seven thousand prisoners, including Kobiak, two of his sons and many other princes. Sviatoslav and Riurik, as the chronicler puts it, returned with great honor and glory.

In the meantime Igor Sviatoslavich of Severia, hearing that Sviatoslav of Kiev marched against the Polovetsians, summoned Vsevolod's brother, the nephew of Sviatoslav Olgovich, Vladimir's son and his retinue. "The Polovetsians," said he, "now have turned against the Rus princes, so we will attack their tents while they are away." The princes mounted their steeds. On their way, beyond the Merl river, they encountered a Polovetsian force numbering four hundred men intending to invade the Land of Rus. Igor attacked them and chased them away.

The next year, 1185, the cursed, godless and damned Konchak with many Polovetsians marched to capture Rus towns and burn them. He found a certain infidel[37] who could shoot live fire.[38] The Polovetsians also had huge arbalests which fifty men hardly could drag. The Polovetsians first encamped on the Khorol river. Konchak, wanting to deceive Yaroslav Vsevolodovich of Chernigov, sent to him as if to ask for peace. Yaroslav, suspecting nothing, sent his boyar to negotiate, whereupon Sviatoslav of Kiev sent a message to Yaroslav. "Brother, do not believe them," he said, "do not send any boyars. I am going to attack them." He marched against the Polovetsians together with Riurik Rostislavich and all his men, sending ahead the junior princes Vladimir Glebovich and Mstislav Romanovich. On the way merchants returning from Polovetsian lands pointed out Konchak's camp. Vladimir and Mstislav attacked him and forced him to flee. The infidel who could shoot live fire was taken prisoner. This clever fellow was taken to Sviatoslav with his apparatus.

Yaroslav of Chernigov did not go with his brother against the Polovetsians. "I have sent my boyar to them," he pleaded, "so I cannot endanger my own man." Igor Sviatoslavich of Severia disagreed. "God forbid," said he, "that we refuse to go against the pagans, who are our common enemy." Yaroslav then took counsel with his retinue where to catch up with Sviatoslav. "Prince! You cannot fly like a bird," the retinue told him. "The boyar came from Sviatoslav on Thursday, he himself left Kiev on Sunday. How can you catch up with him?" Igor disliked this answer and wanted to ride through the steppe, along the Sula river. Suddenly there was a thaw which blocked all movement. Sviatoslav returned to Kiev and in spring sent his boyar Roman Nezdilovich with the Berendey against the Polovetsians. On Easter Sunday (April 21) Roman took the Polovetsian camp, capturing many prisoners and horses.

THE TALE OF IGOR'S CAMPAIGN

Meanwhile Igor Sviatoslavich refused to abandon his intention of going against the Polovetsians. The princes of Severia were constantly bothered that they had not participated in the number of successful battles with the Polovetsians launched from the other side of the Dnieper. "Are we not princes," they said, "let us gain such glory for ourselves." Thus on April 23 Igor departed Novgorod Seversk and ordered his brother Vsevolod of Trubchevsk, his nephew Sviatoslav Olgovich of Rylsk, and his son Vladimir of Putivl to march with him. Yaroslav of Chernigov was persuaded to send his boyar Olstin Oleksich with the Koui[39] of Chernigov.

The princes of Severia marched slowly while building their retinue because their horses were very fat. When they reached the Donets it was nearly evening. Igor looked at the sky and saw that the sun was like the moon. "Look," he asked his boyars and retinue, "what does it mean?" They looked and hung their heads. "O prince," they said, "it is not a good sign." "Brothers and retinue!" Igor replied. "Nobody knows the secrets of God, who is the creator of everything, even portents. We will see what God has in store for us, good or evil." Thereupon Igor crossed the Donets river and arrived at Oskol. There for two days he awaited his brother Vse-volod, who took a different route from Kursk. From Oskol they advanced together to the Salnitsa river, where they were met by scouts sent to capture prisoners for interrogation. "We have seen the enemy," they told the princes. "Your enemies are ready, either advance quickly or return home, now is not our time." "If we return without giving battle," replied Igor and the other princes, "our shame will be worse than death. We will advance in hope of God's grace."

They marched all night and at morning encountered the Polovetsian regiments. The pagans gathered, young and old, and stood on the opposite bank of the Siuiurlia river. The Rus princes were deployed in six regiments. Igor's regiment was in the middle. On the right was his brother Vsevolod's regiment, on the left his nephew Sviatoslav's, and in front his son Vladimir's with the Chernigov Koui. Before these formations were archers sent by all the regiments.

"Brothers," Igor exhorted, "this is what we have sought, let us go." They advanced. The Polovetsian archers rode to the front, loosed arrows at the Rus and retreated. The Rus had not crossed the river when the rest of the Polovetsians started to flee. The vanguard Rus regiment pursued the enemy, killing and taking prisoners. The senior princes Igor and Vse-volod progressed slowly, not committing their regiments. As the Polovet-sians ran past their tents, the Rus captured many of them. The Severian regiments stood fast and rejoiced, saying "Our brothers went with Grand Prince Sviatoslav against the Polovetsians and fought with them looking over their shoulders at Pereiaslavl. They dared not enter the Polovetsian land, but now we are in the Polovetsian land, we have killed the pagans, taking their wives and children prisoner. Now we will go beyond the Don and destroy them completely. If we gain victory there, we will go to Luko-morie[40] where even our grandfathers never reached. We will take glory and honor."

When the vanguard returned from the chase, Igor said to his brothers and boyars "God gave us victory, honor and glory. We have seen the Polovetsian regiments and they were numerous. Were they all gathered here? Let us travel through the night and the others will follow in the morning." "I have been chasing the Polovetsians a long way," Sviatoslav Olgovich answered his uncles, "and my horses are exhausted. If I go now, I am sure I will have to stop on the way." His uncle Vsevolod took his side and they decided to stay the night there. Then, at dawn the follow-ing morning suddenly, one after another, Polovetsian regiments began to appear. The Rus princes were surprised. "We have gathered all the land against us," said Igor, and the princes consulted on what to do. "If we flee," they said, "we will save ourselves but leave behind all our men. It would be a sin in the eyes of God to leave them defenseless. Better we live or die together."

This being their decision, they dismounted and went to battle although weakened because they had no water to drink. They fought bravely all day until evening. In the Rus regiments many were wounded or killed. They continued to fight in the evening and through the night. Early the following morning the Koui broke ranks and ran away. Igor was wounded in his hand at the beginning of the battle, so he was on horseback. When he saw the Koui fleeing, he rode to stop them. There he was taken prisoner. He was surrounded by the Polovetsians who held him. He saw his brother Vsevolod repulsing the enemy and asked for death rather than see his brother slain. Vsevolod did not die, but also was taken prisoner.

From among the numerous Severian regiments only a very few survived, fifteen Rus and even less of the Koui, surrounded by Polovetsian regiments like strong walls. When he was led into captivity, Igor remembered his sin. Once when he plundered the town of Glebov near Pereiaslavl, he did not spare Christian blood. "I am not worthy to stay alive," he said. "Now I see the retribution of my God. Where is my beloved brother, my nephew, where is my son, where are my boyars and councillors, where are my brave *fighters* and ranks of my regiments? Where are my horses and precious weapons? I lost them all, and God has sent me in chains into the hands of the pagans!"

At this time Sviatoslav of Kiev was in Korachev gathering an army in the Upper Lands.[41] He intended to march against the Polovetsians towards the Don for the whole summer. Returning from Korachev, near Novgorod Seversk, he learned that Igor and his brothers, without telling him, mounted against the Polovetsians. Sviatoslav was angry at this insubordination. From Novgorod Seversk he went by the Desna river to Chernigov, where he was informed of the disaster which befell the princes of Severia. Sviatoslav burst into tears. "O my beloved brothers," he said, "sons and boyars of the Land of Rus! God would have granted my wish to defeat the pagans but you could not restrain your youth. Now you have opened the gates to the Land of Rus. God's will be done. As I was angry once with Igor, so now I grieve for him."

Sviatoslav lost no time in vain complaints. He sent his sons Oleg and Vladimir to the lands along the Seim river. There was great sorrow in towns along the Seim, in Novgorod Seversk and all of the Chernigov land that the prince was taken prisoner, that some of the retinue were killed and others taken prisoner. According to the chronicler the people were in despair, caring not for their own souls in their grief for the princes. Sviatoslav took other measures as well. He sent to tell Davyd of Smolensk "We agreed to march against the Polovetsians and spend the summer on the Don, but now the Polovetsians have defeated Igor and his brothers. So come, brother, to guard the Land of Rus." Davyd travelled by the Dnieper, and other forces came to help as well. They stood guard at Tripolie while Yaroslav gathered his regiments and stood ready in Chernigov.

The Polovetsians, having defeated Igor and his brothers, grew haughty and gathered all their nation to march against the Land of Rus. When they deliberated how to proceed, a quarrel flared among the khans. "Let us go against the Kievan lands," said Konchak, "where our brothers and our grand prince Boniak were killed." Another khan, Kza, said "Let us go to the Seim, where only women and children remain. There are many prisoners along the Seim for the taking, and we will seize the town without difficulty."

They divided the forces into two parts. Konchak marched against Pereiaslavl, besieged the city and fought all day. In Pereiaslavl ruled the famous Vladimir Glebovich who was valiant and strong in battle. In the words of the chronicler he rode out of the city and fell upon the Polovetsians with a very small retinue because the rest dared not join his sortie. Vladimir was surrounded by a multitude of Polovetsians and received three spear wounds when the rest of the retinue, seeing their prince in danger, poured out of the city and saved him. Prince Vladimir, seriously wounded, rode into the city and sweated blood for his beloved fatherland. He sent notice to Sviatoslav, Riurik and Davyd, saying "The Polovetsians have attacked me, come and help me!" Sviatoslav sent for Davyd, who did not move because the people of Smolensk called together an assembly and said "We would go to Kiev if there were any forces there, and we would do battle. Now it is useless to look for another fight. We are already exhausted." Davyd was forced to turn back with them to Smolensk.

Sviatoslav and Riurik, on the other hand, took to their boats and sailed down the Dnieper against the Polovetsians who, when they heard about this, left Pereiaslavl, on their way besieging the town of Rimov. The people of Rimov locked the gates and manned the walls to defend the town. Suddenly part of the *stone fortifications* collapsed, and some men fell straight into the hands of the Polovetsians. The rest of the inhabitants were terrified and the town was taken. The only people saved in Rimov were the troops who left the town to fight the enemy in the marshes. Thus the Polovetsians, taking advantage of the slowness of the princes waiting in vain for Davyd of Smolensk, captured Rimov and safely returned with the loot to their steppes. The princes did not pursue them there, instead with sadness dispersed to their own territories. The other group of Polovetsians with Khan Kza marched against Putivl, burned the surrounding villages and nearby fort, returning with their loot.

Igor Sviatoslavich lived as prisoner of the Polovetsians who, as if shamed by his bravery, according to the chronicler, did not oppress him in any way. They assigned him twenty guards and allowed him to hunt where he liked and to take his own servants, five or six men. The guards obeyed him and showed him every respect. Anyone whom he sent on an errand complied without demur. Igor also invited a priest to stay with him and celebrate services, thinking he would stay a prisoner for a long time, but God, as the chronicler says, saved him thanks to Christian prayers, since many wept for him.

Among the Polovetsians one man called Lavor came forward. A good thought came to him, and he said to Igor "I will go with you to Rus." Igor at first did not trust him. Because of his youth he was proud, and planned to capture Lavor and escape with him to Rus. "For my fame," he said, "I did not escape during the battle and leave my retinue. So also now I will not take the road of shame." With Igor was his chiliarch's son and master of the horse. They both encouraged the prince to accept Lavor's proposal, saying "Go, prince, to the Land of Rus, if God wants to save you." Still Igor could not decide. When the Polovetsians returned from Pereiaslavl his advisers once again said "You are proud, O prince! You do not please God. You still await an opportunity to capture Lavor and escape with him. Do you not consider the rumor that the Polovetsians want to kill all princes and all Rus? In that case there will be no fame or life for you."

This time Igor heeded them. He feared the Polovetsians' coming to Rus, and looked for an opportunity to escape. He could not escape either by day or by night because the guards were very watchful. Escape was possible only at sunset. Igor sent his master of the horse to tell Lavor to come to his side of the river with a bridled horse. When the appointed time arrived and darkness fell, the Polovetsians drank kumis.[42] The master of the horse arrived and told Igor that Lavor was waiting. Igor arose with fear and trepidation, bowed to the icon of the Savior and the true Cross and said "Lord, unto whom all hearts be open, save me, unworthy as I am." He put on the cross and the icon, lifted the flap of the tent and slipped out. The guards were busy playing and enjoying themselves, thinking that Igor was asleep, but he crossed the river and sped through the steppe. In eleven days he reached the town of Donets, whence he proceeded to his Novgorod Seversk. From Novgorod he went to his brother Yaroslav in Chernigov and later to Sviatoslav in Kiev to seek help against the Polovetsians. The princes were overjoyed at his return and promised to help him.

LATER CAMPAIGNS AGAINST THE POLOVETSIANS

It was only one year later (1187) that Sviatoslav with his relative Riurik gathered forces to march against the Polovetsians. They intended a surprise attack when they received information that the Polovetsians were near Tatinets at the Dnieper ford. Vladimir Glebovich arrived with his retinue from Pereiaslavl and sought to march in the vanguard with the Karakalpaks. It appears that Sviatoslav did not want Vladimir to take precedence over his sons. Yet Riurik and others favored this because the prince of Pereiaslavl was brave and strong in battle, always aspiring to valiant deeds.

The Karakalpaks informed their kinsmen, the Polovetsians, that Rus princes were marching against them, causing them to withdraw. The princes could not pursue because the Dnieper ice was breaking and spring was approaching. Returning from this expedition the distinguished defender of the borderlands from the Polovetsians, Prince Vladimir Glebovich of Pereiaslavl, fell ill and died. The chronicler says that all the Orthodox wept for him, because he loved his retinue and distributed his possessions among his retainers rather than amassing gold. He was a fair prince, strong in valor and replete with good deeds. The borderlands grieved for him and not without cause, because the Polovetsians immediately attacked these lands.

In winter Sviatoslav exchanged messages with Riurik, calling on him to march against the Polovetsians. "You, brother," replied Riurik, "go to Chernigov, gather your brothers there and I will gather my brothers here." The princes gathered and proceeded along the Dnieper. There was no alternative because the snow lay very deep. Near the Snoporod river they captured some Polovetsian pickets who related that the Polovetsian camp and flocks were near the Blue Forest. Yaroslav of Chernigov refused to go any further. "I cannot go any further from the Dnieper," he said to his brother Sviatoslav. "My land is distant and my retinue is tired." Riurik sent word to Sviatoslav, encouraging him to continue the expedition. "Brother and relative," he said, "what we ought to have implored God has come to pass. The Polovetsians are only half a day away. Let those of changed mind who do not want to continue see that we paid attention to nobody, but did as God wished."

Sviatoslav himself desired to continue the expedition. "I am ready, my brother," he answered Riurik, "but send to my brother Yaroslav urging that we all march together." Riurik sent to tell Yaroslav "Brother! You must not destroy our cause. We have reliable information that the Polovetsian camp is but half a day away. Is that too far to ride? I ask you, O brother, do it for me and march for half a day, and I will go with you for ten days." Yaroslav refused. "I cannot go alone," said he, "my regiment is on foot. You did not tell me at home that the distance was so great." A quarrel flared among the princes. Riurik encouraged the sons of Vsevolod to march forward. Sviatoslav wanted to push on, but not without his brother. When the brother refused, they all returned home empty-handed.

At the end of that year, in winter, Sviatoslav and Riurik sent the Karakalpaks with the commander Roman Nezdilovich against the Polovetsians across the Dnieper. Roman took their camp and returned with great fame because the Polovetsians were not there, instead they were on the Danube. For 1190 the chronicle states that Sviatoslav and Riurik made the Land of Rus tranquil and came to peace with the Polovetsians on their own terms. Afterwards they went hunting in boats down the Dnieper towards the mouth of the Tiasmina, killed many animals and enjoyed themselves.

Peace with the Polovetsians did not last for very long. In the autumn of that year Sviatoslav, thanks to information he received, caught Konduvdey, the prince of the Torks.[43] Riurik interceded on his behalf because he was brave and popular in Rus, according to the chronicle. Sviatoslav listened to Riurik, made Konduvdey swear an oath and set him free, but the Tork wanted to avenge his disgrace. He therefore went to the Polovetsians who, delighted, deliberated with him where to attack Rus. They decided to march against Churnaev (the town of Prince Churnay), captured the outer fortifications, set fire to the princely court, took the prince's property, his two wives and many slaves. Later, after resting their horses, they marched against another town, Borivoy. When they learned that Rostislav Riurikovich was in Torchesk they returned to their main camp. From there, together with Konduvdey, they mounted frequent attacks against places along the Ros river.

Sviatoslav did not stay that autumn in Kiev, he crossed the Dnieper to confer with his brothers. Riurik also went to Ovruch to arrange his affairs, leaving his son Rostislav in Torchesk to watch. He knew that Konduvdey would attack Rus to avenge Sviatoslav's offense. With this in mind he sent word to Sviatoslav, saying "We do what we must, we will not leave the Land of Rus defenseless. I have left my son with troops, you also leave your son." Sviatoslav promised to send his son Gleb, then failed to keep his word. He quarreled with the descendants of Monomakh. Luckily the princes quickly made peace. During winter the best men among the Karakalpaks came to Torchesk to Rostislav Riurikovich. "The Polovetsians are raiding us often this winter," they told him. "We do not know whether we should move to the Danube. Your father is far away and there is no point in asking help from Sviatoslav, for he is angry with us because of Konduvdey." Afterwards Rostislav sent Rostislav Vladimirovich, son of Vladimir Mstislavich, saying "Brother! I wish to attack the Polovetsian encampments. Our fathers are far away. There are no other senior princes, so we will be as seniors. Come quickly."

After joining the Karakalpaks Rostislav Riurikovich suddenly attacked the Polovetsian encampment, captured their wives, children and many cattle. When the Polovetsians learned that their camp was captured they chased after Rostislav and caught him. Rostislav Riurikovich, undeterred by the large number of Polovetsians, ordered his young archers to start battle. The Polovetsians started to shoot back. Then, when they saw Rostislav's personal standards, they fled. The Rus archers and the Karakalpaks took six hundred prisoners. The Karakalpaks captured among others the Polovetsian khan Koban, but did not take him to the main regiment because they feared Prince Rostislav. Secretly making an agreement with the khan for ransom, they let him go free.

That same winter the Polovetsians with two khans entered Rus by Rostislav's Road.[44] When they learned that Sviatoslav of Kiev was prepared for war they turned to flight, having cast to the ground their banners and spears. Afterwards Sviatoslav proceeded to Kiev, leaving his son Gleb in Kanev. The Polovetsians, knowing Sviatoslav had gone home, returned with Konduvdey but, challenged by Gleb, they withdrew, and on the Ros disaster struck them. Many were intercepted and killed, many were drowned, but Konduvdey escaped.

The following year, 1191, Igor of Severia once more marched against the Polovetsians. This time he was successful. The sons of Oleg went for the second time in winter to the steppe, where the Polovetsians were prepared to meet them. The Rus, deciding not to fight, withdrew by night. In 1192 Sviatoslav and Riurik and all their brothers camped the entire summer near Kanev, defended their land from the pagans, then dispersed to their homes. Later Sviatoslav and Rostislav Vladimirovich with the Karakalpaks intended to march against the Polovetsians, but the Karakalpaks refused to cross the Dnieper because their kinsmen were there. After a quarrel with the princes they turned back. In the end Riurik lured Konduvdey to desert the Polovetsians, settled him in his territory and gave him one of the Ros towns called Dreven.

After making peace with Konduvdey the princes wanted to come to terms with his old allies the Polovetsians. In 1193 Sviatoslav sent to Riurik, saying "You have come to terms with the Lukomorian Polovetsians, now let us call the rest, the Burchevichi."[45] Riurik sent to Lukomoria for two of their khans, while Sviatoslav summoned two Burchevichi khans. In autumn Sviatoslav and Riurik met in Kanev, where the Lukomorian khans met them. The Burchevichi stopped on the other bank of the Dnieper, and told the princes "If you want agreement with us, cross the river to our side." The princes after deliberation answered "Neither our grandfathers nor our fathers went to you. If you wish come to us, do so. If not, do as you wish." The Burchevichi refused and went away. Sviatoslav refused to make peace with the Lukomorians. "There is no purpose," he said to Riurik, "in making peace only with one half." The princes returned home empty-handed.

Afterwards Riurik, having deliberated with his boyars, sent to tell Sviatoslav "My brother! You did not want peace, now we must be prepared. We have to think about our land. Do we march in winter, as you declared earlier? I shall order my brothers and retinue to prepare. If you intend only to guard your own land, send us word." "Brother, we cannot march," responded Sviatoslav. "Our grain harvest has failed. May God help us defend our own land." "Brother and kinsman," answered Riurik, "if we do not march against the Polovetsians, I will march against the Lithuanians in my own interests." "Brother and kinsman," Sviatoslav angrily answered him, "if you abandon the patrimony for your own interests, and I cross the Dnieper to pursue my own, who will stay in the Land of Rus?"

This speech prevented Riurik from an expedition against Lithuanians. In winter the best men from among the Karakalpaks came to Rostislav

Riurikovich, calling him against the Polovetsians. "Prince," they said, "come with us to attack the Polovetsians' camp. It is the best time. We wanted earlier to ask your father to let you go, we heard that he is preparing to march against the Lithuanians and thus will not let you go. We will have to wait a long time for such a good opportunity." Rostislav agreed and went to Torchesk straight from a hunting expedition, without informing his father. He sent word to his retinue, saying "Now is the time. Let us march against the Polovetsians. As for my father's expedition against the Lithuanians, we will return before he sets off."

It took the retinue three days to gather. Rostislav sent to Tripolie for his cousin Mstislav Mstislavich (the Daring). He arrived immediately with his boyar Sdeslav Zhiroslavich and caught up with Rostislav beyond the Ros. When they joined the Karakalpaks the princes captured Polovetsian pickets who told them that the Polovetsians were encamped with their flocks on the western or Rus bank of the Dnieper, a day's march away. Acting on this information, the Rus princes set off at night. At sunrise they attacked the Polovetsians, taking countless loot.

When Sviatoslav heard this news, he sent word to Riurik saying "Your son has attacked the Polovetsians and started war. Yet you want to go to another country and abandon your own land. Better you go to Rus to guard your land." Riurik listened to him. Postponing his expedition against the Lithuanians, he proceeded with all his forces to Rus. Sviatoslav and Riurik stood a long time near Vasilievo guarding their land, but the Polovetsians made no appearance. Just as Sviatoslav crossed the Dnieper to go to Korachev and Riurik had returned to his territory, the pagans struck the borderlands.

Even during peaceful times Sviatoslav and Riurik were not powerful enough for offensives against the Polovetsians. When they marched into the steppe they looked over their shoulders at Pereiaslavl. The brave princes of Severia decided to go further, although they paid a high price for their bravery. The might which enabled Monomakh and his son Mstislav to push the pagans across the Don, towards the sea, was now in the North. For the year 1198 the chronicle states that Vsevolod the Great with his son Konstantin marched against the Polovetsians by an unknown route. Learning of this, the Polovetsians fled with their camps to the sea. The grand prince went round their winter pastures along the Don and returned.

Soon afterwards in the South appeared another powerful prince, one who perhaps reminded the Polovetsians of Monomakh's times. This prince was Roman of Volhynia and Galich. In 1202 he moved against the Polovetsians, captured their camp and took many prisoners. He also freed many Christians, bringing great joy to the Land of Rus.

This joy turned to grief when in the following year Riurik and the descendants of Oleg, together with all the Polovetsians, took and then looted Kiev. Its inhabitants were taken prisoner and led to the enemy camp. Later, for a time, Vsevolod and Roman made peace among the princes. During the hard winter of 1208 the Southern princes marched against the Polovetsians. The pagans grieved and the Christians of the Land of Rus rejoiced, the chronicler says. At the same time the princes of Riazan raided the Polovetsians and captured their camp.

Soon new troubles erupted among the princes. The famous Roman died and the Polovetsians had no one to fear in the South. In 1210 they ravaged the countryside around Pereiaslavl. In 1215 once again they appeared at Pereiaslavl. The local prince Vladimir Vsevolodovich went to meet them with his regiments, but was defeated and taken prisoner.

TATAR INVASION

While Rus, the European borderland, was conducting this endless and monotonous struggle with the steppe peoples, the Polovetsians, in the remote eastern steppes of Asia an event took place which changed the course of this struggle. From time immemorial Chinese chronicles recorded information about two nomad nations called Mongkul and Tata in the steppes to the northwest of their own country. The way of life of these two peoples was identical with that of their brethren in earlier history, namely the Scythians, Huns and Polovetsians. In the first quarter of the thirteenth century a strong movement was detected among them. One of the Mongol khans, Temuchin, better known as Genghis Khan, assaulted other khans and subjugated them. Various hordes joined under a single rule to bring together a large warlike mass of people, now awakened from prolonged slumber to bloody activity. Unconsciously driven by this impetus, they attacked neighboring nations towards the east, south and west, destroying everything in their path. In 1224 two military leaders of Genghis Khan, Jebe and Subetey, passed the customary nomads' gateway between the Caspian and the Urals, enslaved the Yas and Obezy, and entered the lands of the Polovetsians.

The Polovetsians went to meet them under the command of their strongest khan, Yury son of Konchak, were defeated and forced to retreat to the Rus borders on the Dnieper. Their khan Kotian, Mstislav of Galich's father-in-law, begged his son-in-law and other Rus princes for help. He did not skimp on gifts, gave away many horses, camels, buffaloes and slave girls, saying to the princes "We lost our lands to the Tatars, tomorrow they will take yours. Defend us, for if you do not and we are killed now, you will be killed tomorrow."

The princes came to Kiev for a conference. Three senior princes were present, Mstislav Romanovich of Kiev, Mstislav Sviatoslavich of Chernigov and Mstislav Mstislavich of Galich. From among the junior princes were Daniel Romanovich of Volhynia, Vsevolod Mstislavich, son of the prince of Kiev, and Mikhail Vsevolodovich, nephew of the prince of Chernigov. Mstislav of Galich tried to convince the princes to help the Polovetsians. "If we brothers do not help them," said he, "they will surrender to the Tatars, who will be even stronger." After many deliberations the princes in the end agreed to march against the Tatars, saying "Better to fight them on foreign soil than on our own."

When the Tatars heard of the expedition of the Rus princes, they sent to tell them "We have heard that you are marching against us, that you have listened to the Polovetsians. We have not occupied your land, your towns or villages, nor have we attacked you. We came as God's punishment on our slaves and horse handlers, the pagan Polovetsians, but we have no quarrel with you. If the Polovetsians run to you, chase them away and take their property for yourselves. We have heard that they caused you much trouble. This is why we fight them from here."

In reply the Rus princes ordered the Tatar envoys killed, and marched on. When they stopped on the Dnieper before reaching Oleshie, new Tatar envoys arrived and said "You have listened to the Polovetsians, killed our envoys and continue marching against us, come and let God judge between us. We have not laid a hand on you." This time the princes let the envoys return alive.

When the Rus and Polovetsian regiments were gathered Mstislav the Daring with a thousand men crossed the Dnieper, attacked the Tatar pickets and turned them to flight. The Tatars sought to hide in a Polovetsian burial mound but even there they were not safe, nor could they conceal their commander Gemiabek. The Rus found him and gave him to the Polovetsians, who killed him. When the Rus princes learned of the defeat of the enemy pickets they crossed the Dnieper and found that the Tatars had come to look at their boats. Daniel Romanovich, other princes and commanders mounted their horses and rode to look at their new enemies. Everybody had his own opinion about them. One said that they were good archers, another that they were not as good as the Polovetsians. The Galich commander, Yury Domamerich, claimed that the Tatars were good warriors.

Daniel and his comrades returned with this information about the Tatars. "There is no sense standing here," said the junior to the senior princes, "let us go against them." The senior princes listened and all the Rus regiments crossed the Dnieper. The Rus archers met the Tatars on Polovetsian ground, defeated them, chased them far into the steppe, seized their herds and returned with them to their own regiments. Then the army marched for eight days to the Kalka river where a new battle with Tatar pickets took place. The Tatars rode away and Mstislav of Galich allowed Daniel Romanovich with some regiments to cross the river. They were followed by the rest of the army, made camp and posted as guards Yarun with the Polovetsians. Mstislav the Daring left the camp to reconnoitre the Tatars. When he returned he ordered his troops to arm quickly, whereas the other two Mstislavs stayed in their camp and did nothing. Mstislav the Brave told them nothing because of envy, so the chronicler says, for there was a great quarrel between them.

The battle started on June 16. Daniel Romanovich rode ahead and was the first man against the Tatars. He was wounded in his chest but felt nothing because of his youth and zeal. He was eighteen years of age, very strong, brave and bold and without a fault from head to toe. When his uncle Mstislav the Mute of Lutsk saw that Daniel was in danger, he dashed to help. The Tatars turned their tails from Daniel on one side and from Oleg of Kursk on the other. Then the Polovetsians, as usual, fled from the enemy and trampled the units of the Rus princes who, because of Mstislav the Daring's neglect, were not yet ready for battle. This decided the struggle for the Tatars. Daniel, realizing that the Tatars were winning, turned his horse, rode to the river to drink. Only then did he feel his wound. The Rus suffered a terrible defeat everywhere. Such disaster was unknown since the beginnings of the Land of Rus.[46]

Mstislav of Kiev, his son-in-law Andrei and Alexander of Dubrovitsk,[47] seeing the disaster, stayed put, standing on a hill overlooking the Kalka river. This place was stony. The Rus surrounded it with a ring and for three days defended themselves in this fortification against two Tatar forces under the command of Chegirikan and Tashukan. The other Tatars pursued the remaining Rus princes across the Dnieper. While the Polovetsians gave the victory to the Tatars, other assorted barbarians finished their work by killing Mstislav of Kiev. The Tatars were accompanied by

Brodniks[48] with their commander Plotskinia. He kissed the cross to Mstislav and other princes that if they surrendered the Tatars would ransom, not kill them. The princes trusted their promise, surrendered and were crushed to death under planks on which the Tatars spread their feast. Six other princes were killed while fleeing, Mstislav of Chernigov with his son among them. Apart from the princes a famous epic hero, Alexander Popovich, with seventy men of his family also perished.

Vasilko of Rostov, sent by his uncle Yury to help the Southern princes, heard in Chernigov about the battle on the Kalka and turned home. Mstislav of Galich with the rest of the princes crossed the Dnieper and ordered the boats burned or destroyed, cast off from the shore lest the Tatars pursue. The Tatars, having reached Novgorod Sviatopolchsk, then turned east. The inhabitants of Rus towns and villages on their way met them with crosses but all were killed. Many perished, says the chronicle, wailing and cries were heard in all the towns and countryside. We do not know, continues the chronicle, whence came these wicked Tatars or whither they disappeared. Some speculated that these were the unclean nations whom Gideon once expelled into the desert,[49] destined to appear before doomsday to conquer all lands.

CONSIDERATIONS

Having reviewed the events characterizing the 174-year period from the death of Yaroslav I until the death of Mstislav Mstislavich of Toropets, let us say a few general words on the course of these events. The sons of Yaroslav originally ruled the Land of Rus as a whole family, without divisions, acknowledging the right of the senior in the family to occupy the senior throne and to be called father by all the relatives. Yet even under the first princes troubles and internecine wars began as a result of communal family rule and absence of separate territories ruled by each prince and inherited by his sons. Disinherited princes[50] appeared, orphan-princes deprived by the early death of their fathers of the right to seniority and orderly promotion through the rungs of the family ladder. They depended on the charity of senior members of the family, condemned to the difficult fate of orphans. Naturally they strove to find a way out of their predicament and acquire a territory in the Land of Rus. They had at hand all the necessary means, for in the steppes they could recruit large forces ready to attack Rus in the hope of loot under any convenient banner.

There were other reasons for the troubles. The relationship between the town population and the princes was ephemeral and undefined.

Iziaslav, the older son of Yaroslav, was forced to leave Kiev, where the prince of Polotsk occupied his place contrary to all family rights and reckonings. The Polotsk prince did not stay long on the senior throne of Rus. Iziaslav returned to his father's throne, but soon was chased away by his own brothers. He returned once more after the death of his brother Sviatoslav, which brought about renewed troubles because Iziaslav added the sons of Sviatoslav to the number of disinherited princes. Iziaslav was killed in a battle with his disinherited nephews.

The rule of his brother Vsevolod was equally troublesome. During the reign of the first senior prince of Yaroslav's grandsons strife caused by disinherited princes ceased on both the eastern and the western bank of the Dnieper. This was achieved at two interprincely congresses. The sons of Sviatoslav regained all the rights of their father and received their father's territory, the principality of Chernigov. In the West, as a result of a settlement with the disinherited princes, apart from the long-separated territory of Polotsk another distinct land, Galich, emerged with princes enjoying no right to move to seniority or to other thrones. The small separate territory of Gorodets likewise was created for the descendants of Davyd Igorevich.

It seemed that, following princely clan agreements made during the life of Iziaslav's son, troubles should have ceased. This was not the case. After Sviatopolk's death Kiev acclaimed Monomakh as its prince, disregarding the rights of his cousins the sons of Sviatoslav. Thanks to Monomakh's material and moral strength, both he and his older son Mstislav ruled Kiev peacefully. The family's collective rule was shared among the three lines of Yaroslav's descendants and thus their strongest bond was certain to fail. The princes of Chernigov, descendants of Sviatoslav, were forever limited to the eastern side of the Dnieper, their territory forever separate, similar to Polotsk and Galich in the West. Even among Sviatoslav's descendants the uncle lost seniority to his nephews. He and his descendants were limited solely to the Murom land, which consequently was separated from other Chernigov territories. The senior line of Iziaslav also lost seniority and its territory, owing to lack of respect of Sviatopolk's son Yaroslav for his uncle and father-in-law. Later the territory of Turov became a separate principality.

After the death of Mstislav the Great, among the descendants of Monomakh internecine conflicts erupted between the nephews of the older brother and the young uncles. This allowed Oleg's descendants in Chernigov to gain seniority in Kiev and thus restore the joint rule of two lines of Yaroslav's descendants which earlier was broken. After the death of Vsevolod Olgovich, thanks to widespread popular dislike of Oleg's descendants on the western bank of the Dnieper, they lost their seniority, which passed to the son of Mstislav the Great, omitting the senior uncles.

These developments could have had numerous consequences had Iziaslav Mstislavich succeeded in holding the seniority in his hands. Because the descendants of Oleg were excluded from the seniority and common possession of lands, as was Monomakh's young son Yury, the main central possessions of the Riurikids divided into three separate parts: Kievan Rus, Chernigov Rus, and Rostov or Suzdal Rus. Yet while the strong clan feeling and other important features of its ancient existence still existed in the South, in Old Rus, the changing nature of relations between the urban population and the borderland's barbarians prevented the division and breach of common clan possessions existing among the princes. When the uncle Yury appeared in the South his nephew heard from many quarters "Bow to your uncle and make peace. We will not go against Monomakh's son." Iziaslav, despite his valor and popularity, must repent his sins and acknowledge the seniority of his uncle Viacheslav, to enter into a father-son relationship with him.

Iziaslav died before his uncle. His brother was not equal to his position and thus the notion of the seniority of all uncles over nephews won the day, and with it the notion of clan rule. Yury died in the senior seat of Kiev. Thereafter this throne was occupied by a descendant of Davyd of Chernigov. He in turn was ousted by Mstislav, son of the famous Iziaslav Mstislavich. Mstislav invited his uncle Rostislav to Kiev from Smolensk. After Rostislav's death he himself reigned on the senior throne, but was forced out by his uncle Andrei Bogoliubsky.

Andrei changed the course of events. He did not go to Kiev, instead giving it to his younger brother, himself remaining in the North where a new world of interrelations emerged. Here the old urban centers gave way to new, whose relationships with the prince were better defined, where alongside towns governed by old type of relationships there were no Karakalpaks, unused to anything resembling defined rule. Because of Andrei's decision the South, Old Rus, clearly fell under the influence of the North where both economic and moral leadership were concentrated. Here ruled the senior princes descended from Monomakh. All these relationships existed under Andrei's rule and during the times of his brother Vsevolod III. Thus the generation of Yury, the younger son of Monomakh, thanks to the fact that he settled in the North, was strengthened in comparison with other generations of Yaroslav's descendants. This invigoration suggested the possibility of abolition of clan relationships between princes and the possibility of unification of Rus as a whole appeared.

Yet what was the fate awaiting the illustrious descendants of Monomakh's eldest son, Mstislav the Great? Iziaslav Mstislavich and his son Mstislav suffered defeat in their struggle against the accepted idea of uncles' seniority over their nephews. Mstislav Iziaslavich, after his removal from Kiev by Bogoliubsky's troops, had to be satisfied with Volhynia only. There he and his descendants displayed hereditary aspirations and hereditary talents because circumstances were favorable. Volhynia was a borderland Rus territory, having uninterrupted relations with Western countries, where at that time because of various conditions and clashes, clan-like relationships were breaking up. The clergy of its nearest neighbor, Poland, were discussing the advantages of hereditary rule within one line over common clan rule. In Hungary it was long since anybody wanted to know about the rights of uncles over nephews, sons of the older brother.

All this seemed in perfect agreement with the hereditary aspirations of Iziaslav Mstislavich's descendants. Perhaps at first they did not realize this but, forced by circumstances, these aspirations later proved justified and were accepted. Perhaps it was not in vain that Vladimir, the senior seat in Volhynia, after the death of Mstislav was inherited by his son Roman, in disregard of his brother. It was no accident, it was said, that Roman admonished the Rus princes to change the existing order, to move to a new way as was the custom in other countries. The princes of Old Rus turned a deaf ear to Roman. Only compulsion could persuade them to accept a new order, and Roman attempted to gain such means. He won the principality of Galich, becoming the most powerful prince in the South.

This opened for the South the possibility of unified rule. Everything depended on whether the descendants of the senior son of Monomakh in the Southwest enjoyed the same favorable conditions and circumstances as those enjoyed by the descendants of the younger son of Monomakh in the North. Could Southwestern Rus accept the new ways to the same degree as did Northeastern Rus? History immediately provided a negative answer, showing clearly after the death of Roman the nature of relations in Galich, as well as conditions of life in Southwestern Rus. In the meantime Vsevolod III passed away. Northern Rus for a time was in turmoil and lost its influence in the South where new opportunities occurred for strengthening itself at the expense of the North, thanks to the merits of the famous representative of this region, Mstislav the Daring.

Yet the deeds of this archetypal representative of Old Rus demonstrated fully its inability to create a new and firm order of rule. Mstislav appeared merely as a knight errant, a savior of the oppressed. He had no understanding of governing, no ambitions for ordered rule. He recaptured Galich from a foreign power only to hand it over later, voluntarily, to another foreigner!

Northern Rus followed its own path. Its princes spread their rule further and further eastwards and incessantly exerted pressure on Novgorod, which sooner or later must fall prey to their hands. They extended their strong influence over the nearest areas of Southern Rus and established a nephew on the Chernigov throne, bypassing an uncle.

Thus we observe at the beginning the unity of the Russian land was supported by the unity of the princely clan, by common rule. Despite the independence, from the point of view of overall rule, of each prince in his territory, the princes represented a series of provisional regional rulers. They changed, if not by the will of the chief prince, then at least subject to an agreement with him in line with common clan reckonings and accords. The fate of each territory was not determined internally. Rather, it was permanently dependent on events in the main arena of Rus proper, in Kiev, around the senior throne. Severia, Smolensk, Novgorod and Volhynia changed princes because of events in Kiev, whether Oleg's descendant sat there instead of Monomakh's, Mstislav's instead of Oleg's or conversely. This necessarily contributed to common interest, to awareness of the unity of the land.

Soon it will be apparent that some areas became individual principalities, severing their ties with the common unity. This was particularly the case in the far West and East, whose special character also was determined earlier by physical and historical circumstances. A number of regions separated, such as the Western Dvina and Polotsk, which from the very early stages of history became the possession of a separate princely clan. The territory of Galich also grew apart. It was always a border area and disputed territory between Poland and Rus. In the East remote Murom and Riazan separated, the very distant Tmutorokan ceased to be a Rus territory. The separation of those areas could not have failed to influence events in the chief central territories. In the southern, Dnieper half, the changes in the existing situation may be observed. The separation of main territories happened not because physical, tribal or political circumstances demanded it. As soon as one branch of the princely clan became established in the Northern, Volga-centered half of Rus, as soon as its princes obtained clan seniority, the separation of Northern Rus followed immediately, with far-reaching consequences. The separation occurred, not as a result of specific princely clan relations, but because of special conditions, historical and physical. The breakdown of common clan rule and transition from clan-princely relations to ordered rule were conditioned by the difference of two main parts of Ancient Rus and the ensuing separatist trends.

Thanks to conditions in the neighboring states and nations, all these domestic movements and changes in Rus took place unhindered. In Sweden at that time there was domestic struggle, hence Swedish clashes with Rus during periods of domestic peace were insignificant. Poland, apart from domestic troubles and wars, was preoccupied by the struggle with dangerous external enemies, namely the Germans, Czechs and Prus.[51] Hungary was in similar straits, although both neighboring states from time to time participated actively in the events of Southwestern Rus. One example was the Hungarian participation in the struggle of Iziaslav Mstislavich with his uncle Yury. Such intervention was never decisive and could not have influenced events determined by domestic causes. The influence of Poland and Hungary on the life of Rus was palpable in Galich, was noticeable in neighboring Volhynia, but did not extend further. Poland and Hungary could not pass West European influence on to Rus. It may even be said they kept such influence at arm's length because they themselves, apart from religious links, had little in common with Western Europe as far as their domestic life was concerned.

Even less could Rus share such life, lacking as it did links with the Western church. It belonged to the Eastern church and consequently lived under the spiritual influence of Constantinople. Byzantine education, we will observe, penetrated into Rus, and trade with Greece made it rich. Yet the main events moved to the Northeast, far from the great waterway linking Northwestern with Southeastern Europe. Rus withdrew more and more to the Northeast. In this solitude, far from outside influences, it developed a strong foundation. Novgorod could not convey foreign influences because of hostility based on the differences between its life and that of other Northern territories. Whereas Rus at this time was separated from Western Europe by Poland, Hungary and Lithuania, no peoples separated it from the East, with which it was obliged to conduct a permanent struggle.

Southern Rus proper was a borderland, the European fringe of the steppe. It was a low fringe, unprotected in any way by nature, therefore open to frequent overflow of nomadic hordes. Artificial barriers, towns which began to be constructed by our first princes, were insufficient to defend Rus from this influx. Not only did the nomads attack Rus, they cut it off from the Black Sea coast, making communication with Byzantium difficult. Rus princes with large retinues had to go to meet Greek merchants and escort them to Kiev, shielding them from the steppe robbers. Barbarian Asia strove to deny Rus all routes and ways by which it communicated with educated Europe. Southern Rus, the borderlands, the European fringe of the steppe, were infested from all sides by steppe peoples. Along the borders of the Kiev, Pereiaslavl and Chernigov territories barbaric crowds settled, "our" pagans as they were called to differentiate them from the "wild," or independent steppe peoples or Polovetsians.

These barbaric peoples of the borderlands were semi-dependent on Rus princes yet lacked civic links to the princes' new European fatherland. Their numbers and warlike nature influenced vitally the course of events in Southern Rus. Together with the Wild Polovetsians they increased pillage and disorder. They were powerful stimulants to internecine wars, offering themselves to the eternally squabbling princes as retinues ready to devastate any countryside. Exactly as the Cherkass in later times,[52] the borderland barbarians at this time ostensibly served princely rule, defended it against the steppe people while maintaining close family ties with them, looking after their interests, betraying the princes to them. Indifferent to the future of Rus, to the triumph of this or that prince, they fought for nothing but loot. The wild Polovetsians, "our pagans," or the Karakalpaks, were first to betray and usually the first to flee. Southern Rus must deal continually with such people. Meanwhile its historical life was ebbing to the North. It therefore lost its material might, which was transferred to the Volga region, and its political significance and prosperity. Kiev, its glory and pride, the senior capital city of all Rus, was scorned and abandoned by the most senior and powerful princes, and looted several times.

ADDENDUM

RESPONSE TO CRITICS OF VOLUME II[1]
The viewpoints concerning interprincely strife we have set forth in my second volume met with criticism on all sides when first they appeared in my book *History of Relations Between the Rus Princes of the House of Riurik.*[2] For the present we consider it useful to summarize these criticisms.

Kavelin[3] in his review printed in the 1847 issue of *The Contemporary* offered these criticisms. "Soloviev talks of clan relations and then of princely relations which conflicted with and finally changed them. What relationship they had to each other, whence princely relations emerged in our evolution in succession to clan relations he does not explain, or at least offers an unsatisfactory explanation. In the first place he does not show the natural continuity of judicial life after the clan period. Secondly, his viewpoint is not fully separated from the exaggerations with which he colors Ancient Rus in such a way as to make it unrecognizable. True, his viewpoint is incomparably simpler and more natural, but we must go a step further in order entirely to free the history of Ancient Rus from concepts inappropriate to it. This Soloviev has not done. This explains why the author is compelled to have recourse to the ingenious though false hypothesis of distinguishing between the new and princely towns, and the old towns governed by the civic assembly to explain the new order arising in Northeastern Rus.

"Viewing the dimensions of Vladimir and Muscovite Rus larger than life, Soloviev sees in them what they did not in any way represent, or did not represent in the light which the author seeks to throw on them. Why according to Soloviev was there in the period before and after the thirteenth century a chasm which can be filled with something extraneous, outside the organic development of our most ancient way of life? This extraneous circumstance was according to the author the system of new towns. To deduce this system from clan principles, filling with its development the political history of Russia until the time of Ivan III, is clearly impossible.

"Let us explain. We have asserted that the political element alone concentrates within itself the interest and all the life of Ancient Rus. If this element was expressed in clan and patriarchal forms, clearly at the time they were the highest and only possible form of existence for Ancient Rus. No powerful revolutions occurred in the domestic composition of our country. Thus we may conclude *a priori* that all changes which proceeded gradually in the political existence of Russia developed organically from the very patriarchal clan mode of existence. At the same time we see that the history of our princes shows a completely natural transition from consanguinity to juridical and civic ties. At first the princes comprised the whole clan ruling the whole of the Land of Rus in common. There were no property relations, neither could there be, because there were no permanent habitations. Princes incessantly moved from place to place, from one domain to another, calculating among themselves only according to kinship and seniority. Subsequently they began to settle in various places. As soon as this happened the princely clan separated into its branches, each of which began to rule its own separate portion of land, the district or principality.

"This was the first step towards private property. True, in each individual territory the old order persisted, namely common ownership, unity of the princely stem which ruled it and movement of the princes, but let us not forget that these territories were incomparably smaller and the princely branches fewer. Now began, now much more easily could arise, the idea that the principality was no more and no less than the princely patrimony, hereditary property, the ruler of which could dispose of it unconditionally. When this idea, albeit unconsciously, finally took strength and grew, territorial and proprietary interests inevitably triumphed over the personal, meaning at that time blood and clan interests ... Brothers settled interests of seniority among themselves so that when the father died they constituted a whole, defined by permanent laws, but the children of each had much closer relations with their own fathers, with only a secondary and indirect allegiance to the clan. For them the interests of their own immediate family were first and foremost. The clan was considerably more remote and could not claim their attention and affection in as lively and complete a manner. Besides, even for their father the interests of the family were closer at heart and often came into conflict with the interests of the clan and even outweighed them. As long as the clan was small and the lineages had not diverged very far, it still could hold together. What happened when after the patriarch three or four generations had come along, when each princely line already had its own family and clan traditions, and the interests of the clan as a whole were relegated to third or fourth place? Naturally now everyone must grow cool towards the clan, which had become a phantom. Why? Because the patrimonial and familial principle caused its descendants to break the clan into parts or branches independent of one another. This process was repeated several times. From branches arose new clans which in turn split up because of the family principle, and so on, until the clan principle no longer could endure."

Let us now explain our own point of view. "At first the princes comprise a whole clan," says Kavelin, "ruling all the Land of Rus in common. The princes incessantly move from place to place. Subsequently they become settled in one place. This is the first step towards private property." Why, we ask, did they begin to settle in one place? What compelled them to do so? The solution of this problem, the search for the cause, is the historian's principal task. The princes could settle down only when they accepted the principle of separate property, but in Kavelin's opinion the process was the other way around. Effect is mistaken for cause, how this basic phenomenon occurred is unexplained. "True," he says, "in each individual territory the old system still persisted, namely common ownership, unity of the princely stem which ruled it and movement of the princes, but let us not forget that these territories were incomparably smaller and the princely branches fewer. Now began, now much more easily could arise, the idea that the principality was no more and no less than the princely patrimony, hereditary property." Let us not forget that, the smaller the territory and the princely stem, the more it is possible to develop through clan relations, for the concept of common ownership to take root, because extensive territory and multiplicity of the princely branches are conducive most of all to the breakup of the clan and rupture of the clan bond. Thus here Kavelin proposes as cause what must have had the opposite effect.

We do not need to contradict Kavelin, since he contradicts himself. "As long as the clan was small and the lineages had not diverged very far, it still could hold together. What happened when after the patriarch three or four generations had come along, when each princely line already had its own family and clan traditions, and the interests of the clan as a whole were relegated to third or fourth place? Naturally now everyone must grow cool towards the clan which had become a phantom. Why? Because the patrimonial and familial principle caused its descendants to break up the clan into parts or branches independent of one another."

Is there not a contradiction here? At first he says that the clan link is broken when the princely branches become fewer, and then asserts that the clan principle weakened because of the diversification of the clan! The clan scatters because of its proliferation, and so everyone grows cold towards the clan. Kavelin asks what caused this, and replies "because the patrimonial and familial principle caused its descendants to break the clan into parts or branches." Now that the great clan has broken up into smaller clans or families, what prevented them from again developing into clans or larger families? Perhaps the paucity of branches, as Kavelin previously suggested? No, nothing prevented it. "This process was repeated several times. From branches arose new clans which in turn split up because of the family principle, and so on, until the clan principle no longer could endure."

Thus first it is stated that the clan principle weakened as a result of the paucity of princely branches, then that it weakened because of the diversification of the clan and the multiplicity of its members. Finally it is demonstrated to us that neither the one nor the other could have destroyed clan relations, because when the clan dispersed into several discrete princely lineages these lineages once again tried to develop into clans. Consequently the paucity of princely branches posed no hindrance. What then destroyed clan relations? Nothing. The clan began to disappear of itself! Can anything, either in history or in nature, be destroyed or disappear by itself without any outside agency?

Need we point out whether Kavelin's foregoing opinion corresponds to reality or facts? On the contrary, he arrived at his opinion by ignoring facts, any live historical chain of events, any real historical interaction, among which we must consider first of all historical personalities, the soil and conditions in which they functioned.

The first blow against clan-princely relations was struck when Northeastern Rus separated from the Southwest, on which it received the opportunity to act thanks to the deeds of Andrei Bogoliubsky. How his character was developed, his outlook and activity, how he despised the South, why he initiated the new system, and why this new order was accepted and took root in the North and not in the South, can only be explained by examining the soil of the North and the South, not by dry abstract pondering on how the family displaced the clan principle, though not until the clan principle had faded away completely.

At first the senior princes looked, and they could only look, upon the younger princes as relatives equal in rights, for apart from deeply rooted conceptions the former had no physical power. They were dependent on their younger relatives. Then appeared a prince who, having achieved independence from his clansmen, having won physical power, demanded from the younger that they be subject to him unconditionally. They understood clearly that he wanted to replace the old with new, political, relationships. He wanted to deal with them not as kinsmen equal in rights, but as subjects, commoners. There began a prolonged struggle in which the younger were forced to acknowledge the new relationships, were compelled to submit to the senior as subjects to a sovereign.

The historian regards this struggle as the conflict between clan and sovereign relationships beginning in the twelfth century and ending with the complete triumph of sovereign relationships in the sixteenth century, though others would argue that we should not speak of state relations until the time of Peter the Great. It was from the time of Andrei Bogoliubsky that there originated the family principle which undermined and displaced clan relationships, but to state relations there was a long way to go.

Did Andrei Bogoliubsky in fact transform his clan relations with Rostislav's sons into family relations? Did the new subject relations such as those which Rostislav's sons refused to recognize in fact emerge as family as opposed to clan relations? What could be simpler and more natural than a direct transition from the role of the grand prince as eldest in the clan, dependent only on his clansmen, to that of a sovereign when he gained independence from his clansmen and an independent base of power? Yet Kavelin says that between these two elements there is a chasm which we have left empty, which in his opinion is filled with the dominance of the family principle.

Kavelin explains the disappearance of the clan principle as it being undermined by the family principle, decaying without cause, without any outside agency. He does this to repudiate our explanation about the old and new towns. Yet (p. 194) he himself acknowledges the influence of the towns in eroding the clan way of life, and reproaches us for not having advanced this as a moving principle. This even though we specifically advanced the relation between the towns as a moving force, and the relationship between the new towns and the princes as the principal condition in creation of the new system. On the other hand we pointed out that the old towns supported the old order because the old communes did not understand hereditary succession, and therefore tried to prevent the princes from settling in one or another district, or from regarding these districts as their personal property. These old communes sometimes tampered with princely genealogical calculations, thus giving rise to conflicts. Still they could not lead to the displacement of the clan principle because the preferred lineage once again developed into a clan with its previous genealogical calculations and relations. Princes could not rely on their relations with the old communes because of their instability, and the imprecision of these relations.

Previously Kavelin asserted that the clan principle disappeared of its own accord as a consequence of repeated erosion by the family principle, without any participation of outside agencies, which according to him were entirely lacking in Rus. Later, alongside the family or patrimonial principle he places the influence of the communes on the decay of the clan mode of life.

We see here an inconsistency, a contradiction. All the same we rejoice that the author finally recognizes the possibility of outside influences. Yet if he has recognized the influence of the towns, why does he take such strong issue with us for having presented this influence but not having accepted his explanation, according to which the clan principle disappeared without any reason, without any extraneous influence? We accept the influence of urban relations, and now he also accepts this influence. Therefore the problem boils down to whether we need introduce it. Why does Kavelin say that our hypothesis concerning the influence of urban relations is not necessary to scholarship?

Kavelin insists that alongside clan and blood interests among our ancient princes there also developed other, proprietary interests which subsequently and gradually displaced all others. "We have permitted ourselves," he says, "to go even further and express our opposition to Soloviev's opinion, namely that these interests already occupied the foreground, concealed only by the forms of clan relations which, so to speak, restrained them. The struggle for seniority which the author characterizes as constituting the interprincely relations of this epoch were in fact nothing but expressions of these proprietary aspirations, which the princes tried to legalize through the then existing clan right."

Our answer is that the historian is not concerned with proprietary interests, taking these for granted. His sole concern is to ascertain how these proprietary interests were expressed, how the princes ruled, what gave them the opportunity to rule over this or that land, how they defined these opportunities themselves, and how contemporary society defined them. It is only these aspirations which characterize the given century or given society. It is this characteristic which the historian needs to learn more than anything else. Furthermore this opinion concerning the predominance of proprietary interests was developed further by Pogodin,[4] who in his article concerning civil wars expresses himself as follows.

"'Where there is law there is injury,' says the Russian proverb.[5] So with us the law of succession consisted of family custom which of old transferred from the fathers to the sons, from clan to clan without any definite form, least of all the juridical. Extending according to the very nature of things only to the closest progeny and depending in many relationships on the authority of the protagonists, it easily gave cause for misunderstandings, quarrels and consequently wars on every kind of *new* occasion resulting inevitably from the multiplication of princely clans. Add to this situation the belligerent spirit of the ruling lineage, the redundancy of physical force, the indomitability of spontaneous passions and thirst for action which nowhere more than in the changing circumstances of that time found scope, and it is understandable how internecine struggles occupied the most prominent position in our history from the death of Yaroslav to the Mongol domination, from 1054 to 1240. Besides, they were not at all like they have been and continue to be presented to us without closer scrutiny. Let us subject them to a rigorous and detailed chemical analysis or dissection, investigating why, how, where and by what means these wars were waged, and what influence they might have had on the protagonists, on all the land and its fate. Let us try and conduct our investigation in a rigorous and *mathematical* manner."

We see that Pogodin begins his investigation, as he should, with the principal cause of the phenomenon under study. He refers to the principal source, family custom. Yet while ascertaining the principal cause, the chief source of internecine strife, in family custom we must, following a *rigorous path*, first try to learn the nature of this family custom, how it gave rise to quarrels, what new instances occurred leading to war. To do so we must examine all the warfare from year to year according to the chronicles and, knowing that the source of every war lay in family law, we must explain which war was waged on account of what genealogical reckonings and calculations. By what right, according to the dominant concepts of the time, did a prince consider himself wronged, causing him to declare war. Was a war started because a junior received more territory than a senior prince, or because a senior prince offended a junior, or because perhaps a junior prince did not respect the rights of the senior?

This is how we must conduct research into the internecine wars if we wish to pursue a rigorous mathematical path.

Is this in fact how Pogodin proceeds? Having demonstrated at the beginning of his article the chief cause of family strife as being rooted in family custom, he then poses the question as to what was the object of the princes' contention. "The principal cause," he replies, "the source, the goal of all these internecine wars was *territory*, that is, possessions. Examine all the conflicts and you will find that from the very beginning to the very end there is no other cause. He then begins to itemize. Rostislav took Tmutorokan from Gleb Sviatoslavich, Vseslav of Polotsk took Novgorod, Iziaslav recaptured Kiev and took Polotsk away from Vseslav, and so on.

Before offering any counter-arguments let us try to survey exactly in the same way events of world history and argue accordingly. The main cause, the source and goal of all wars between nations in ancient, medieval and modern history is territory, that is, possessions.

Examine all wars from beginning to end and you will discover no other cause. For example the Persians fought the Greeks, took Athens and other cities, and the Greeks reconquered these cities from the Persians. The Spartans fought the Athenians and took Athens, and the Athenians reconquered their city from the Spartans. Philip of Macedon defeated the Greeks and Alexander of Macedon conquered Persia. The Romans took Carthage, the crusaders took Jerusalem, the Spaniards took Granada, and so on.

Until now we thought that the historian was obliged to present events in sequence, to explain the causes of events and not to break the link between them. If one prince came and took a town and another came and deprived him of his booty, that would signify merely that the princes were contesting specifically for ownership of that town. Consequently, the war waged by Yury Dolgoruky against his nephew Iziaslav Mstislavich was completely analogous to the war of the Carthaginians against the Romans because in each case they were fighting over territory. Wars are characterized by causes and not by the form, which is the same everywhere and always. Pogodin called his article "Civil Wars," yet from the body of that article it is impossible to guess that the wars under discussion were civil wars. From the chronicle extracts the reader does not derive a specific understanding of the relations between the contending princes, whether they were independent rulers of completely separate realms, or whether there was some link between them. Apparently they were related to each other, but it is not apparent what relationships motivated them, or the significance of the towns of which they sought to deprive one another.

On the five printed pages there are citations of chronicle entries. At the end of the article we are informed that these princes who took towns from each other were guided by ancient custom, and that is all. Let us look at these extracts. "In 1064 Rostislav took Tmutorokan away from Gleb Sviatoslavich." What was the cause of this event? We do not know, or rather Pogodin does not explain it to us. He states elsewhere that Rostislav took Tmutorokan without any pretext. Who or what was Rostislav? He was the son of Prince Vladimir of Novgorod, the eldest son of Yaroslav. Then was Rostislav also prince of Novgorod? No, but how did this come about? Not only did the son of Yaroslav's eldest son not receive the throne of Kiev, he was even deprived of his father's throne of Novgorod and was forced to obtain a throne by means of the sword.

This development is explained by family custom whereby Rostislav was considered a dispossessed prince. Thus the cause of the capture of Tmutorokan from Gleb by Rostislav was family custom, which even Pogodin at the beginning of his article posited as the main cause of interprincely strife. As a consequence of the same family custom there occurred other dissensions within the territories of Chernigov and Volhynia. Lands were distributed as a result of clan relations, as a result of clan custom (which Pogodin insists on calling "family custom," fearing to give it its proper name, as though it could be reduced to a question of semantics), on the basis of seniority. The senior received more, the junior less. *Injury* resulted when he who considered himself senior received less than he whom he considered junior or equal to himself. The injured party resorted to arms, and civil strife ensued. From what did it proceed? What was its main cause, its source? It was the clan reckoning and not the territory, which itself was governed by seniority. *Strife proceeded from the injury,* which consisted of, in the opinion of the wronged, an unjust reckoning, an incorrect assessment of his seniority. "I am wronged because I was given too little." Why did he think he was given too little? This was the principal cause, only this could he advance in vindication of his right. On the death of Grand Prince Vsevolod his son Vladimir said "If I sit on my father's throne I will have war with Sviatopolk, because previously this throne belonged to his father." "There will be civil strife," said Monomakh, "*because* (this being the principal and only cause of civil strife!) Sviatopolk is senior to me. He is the eldest son of Yaroslav, who before my father occupied the senior throne."

On this occasion Monomakh did not violate the rule of seniority, so there was no civil strife. With elimination of the cause came elimination of the consequences. When Sviatopolk died Monomakh was compelled to break the rule of seniority, injuring the descendants of Sviatoslav of Chernigov, whence originated the feud between the progeny of Monomakh and that of Oleg.

Let us listen again to the protagonists, the princes themselves. Vsevolod Olgovich reasserted his authority by conquering Kiev. As death approached he said "Monomakh violated our rule of seniority. He was enthroned in Kiev despite the rights of our father Oleg. He bequeathed the throne to his son Mstislav, who in turn enthroned his son Yaropolk. I will do likewise and bequeath Kiev to my brother Igor."

Violation of the seniority rights of Sviatoslav's lineage by Monomakh and his descendants compelled those of Oleg to do likewise. Monomakh's progeny had to resist this tendency, whereupon civil strife arose. Once again we hear the cause Monomakh's grandson Iziaslav attributed to this civil strife, namely clan reckonings, clan custom. "I tolerated Vsevolod on the throne of Kiev," said Iziaslav, *"because he was the eldest brother. My* cousin and my son-in-law were senior to me in place of my father, but with these (Vsevolod's brothers) I will settle accounts as God gives me strength."

In extracting entries from the chronicle where territories are mentioned we are asked to believe that these were the matter at issue. This obscures the causes entirely, the entire chain of events. Once the events are scattered and the link between them lost, you can prove whatever you like. Thus the clan strife among the descendants of Monomakh, between the uncle Yury and the nephew Iziaslav, the cause of which was clan reckonings concerning a dispute over seniority, in Pogodin's version is represented merely as a territorial dispute. Let us read the chronicle extract. "Yury said 'I will expel Iziaslav and take his district.' Iziaslav regained Kiev, and Yury tried to capture Pereiaslavl. Yury took away Kiev." But the most significant passages are omitted from the prince's speeches. Yury said to Iziaslav "Give me Pereiaslavl and I will place my son there, and you will rule in Kiev." Yet in the original the speech begins "Your brother came against me and conquered my land *and took the seniority from me."* Omitted also is Viacheslav's speech to his cousin Yury, in which the direct cause of the war is spelled out. "You (Yury) told me (Viacheslav) *'I cannot do obeisance to someone junior to me* (meaning his nephew Iziaslav),' but now he has obtained Kiev and he has done obeisance to me and called me father, and I am enthroned in Kiev. If previously you had said 'I will not do obeisance to someone junior to me,' now I am senior to you and not junior."

Tell someone totally unacquainted with Russian history that internecine wars in Ancient Rus were clan quarrels between princes who ruled over their own principalities according to seniority, anyone will understand you. The ancient character of our history will be clear to anyone in contrast to the history of other nations. To say that the cause and source of our ancient civil wars was struggle over territories and possessions is to say nothing. What understanding of ancient Russian history can be gained from such a definition? How else can we differentiate the ancient period of our history from the feudal period in the history of Western nations? In both were there not internecine wars over possessions? But in Rus seniority?

That is why in the preface to our *History of Relations Between the Rus Princes of the House of Riurik* we considered it necessary to take issue with the customary expressions such as "the division of Rus into appanages," "appanage princes," "the appanage period," "the appanage system," for these expressions lead to a false impression concerning our ancient history. They bring into the foreground the division of possessions and districts, relations between the possessors and the manner in which they ruled their possessions.

"We cannot agree with the author," says Kavelin, "that the princes were fighting for seniority, still less with his assertion that Sviatoslav's descendants did not want Kiev for its own sake, but for the sake of seniority. On the contrary, we maintain that the princes wanted to obtain better and if possible larger possessions, citing seniority as their justification."

First of all we must ask Kavelin what gave a prince the opportunity to acquire a better territory. The right of seniority? "Iziaslav could not maintain himself in Kiev by his own merits," Kavelin himself says, "having to recognize as Kievan prince and as his father his insignificant uncle Viacheslav, because he was senior. This recognition was an empty form. Viacheslav did not interfere in anything and had no children, while all power in fact belonged to Iziaslav." Here the historian sees not the meaningless form which compelled the brilliant Iziaslav to make way for his weak uncle. Viacheslav was incapable of doing anything for himself. It was only the right of seniority which gave him everything, completely depriving his brilliant nephew. If Viacheslav yielded the reins of power to Iziaslav, it was of his own volition.

"For the same reason," says Kavelin, "namely because they needed some pretexts, the indisputably junior princes in the Kievan clan did not seek the throne of Kiev." Yet this very fact is important for the historian, that they needed pretexts, for such pretexts characterized the time. At the very beginning the junior prince could not seek the senior throne without some kind of pretext, then later could do so without any pretext. The historian [Kavelin] similarly differentiates between these two periods. In one he shows the dominance of clan relations, in the other he demonstrates the dominance of proprietary interests and scorn of clan reckonings.

Secondly Kavelin states that the princes sought to obtain richer and if possible larger possessions. Yet in fact during this period princely power was based not on the number and quality of districts, but on the power of the lineage. To avail himself of this strength he must be the senior member of his lineage. The first right and duty of the eldest when he ascended the senior throne was to distribute territories to the lineage, retaining only Kiev. He had no physical might at his disposal, only moral superiority based on his seniority. The lineage called Rostislav Mstislavich to the senior throne of Kiev. If he had in mind only receiving a better territory, naturally he would have come unconditionally. Had Kiev given him any physical power, he would not have sought any other significance. Yet Rostislav wanted to come to Kiev only on condition that the other members of the lineage recognize him as their senior and father, and obey him. That was what Rostislav wanted, not a richer territory. As soon as Viacheslav heard that his nephew called him father and heaped him with honor, he was content and renounced further active participation in ruling. Sviatoslav Vsevolodovich, angry with Vsevolod III, said "I shall seize Davyd and drive Riurik from the land, and seize power in Rus *together with my brothers,* and then take revenge on Vsevolod for all the wrong he has done me."

Thirdly, Kavelin knows very well to what measures our boyars were driven through fear of disparaging clan honor in precedence disputes. Does he seriously argue that the ancient princes, finding themselves in identical circumstances, thought only of territories? In 1195 one of Oleg's descendants, seeing an opportunity to overcome those of Monomakh, wrote to his senior in Chernigov "Now, little father, there is a good opportunity. Come quickly, gathering together with our brothers, and let us take *our honor.*" He did not say "take territories, obtain Kiev."

In 1867 Sergeevich's book *The Popular Assembly and the Prince*[6] appeared. "Despite the incompleteness of our chronicle sources," said the author, "they nevertheless indicate the existence of a popular assembly in all the principal towns, but in many they were relegated to a secondary or even tertiary position." Then the author begins to itemize all information about the popular assemblies. Such an incautious method does not lead to the desired goal. We know that in our sources the word "assembly" is used in its broadest and most imprecise sense, meaning any gathering of several persons or any meeting of the populace. Consequently we must pay attention to the circumstances under which these assemblies met and what they resolved. Most of all we must look at this problem in a historical manner, following the development of the popular assembly, and the conditions which led to its strengthening or weakening. We should not simply collect from various epochs information about their appearance and assume that they existed everywhere.

The first extract concerning the popular assembly quoted by Sergeevich relates to the year 997. "The inhabitants of Belgorod had to endure a prolonged siege by the Pechenegs. When all supplies were exhausted and no help from the prince could be expected, they called an assembly and decided to surrender." A town in grave danger was temporarily abandoned without help and left to its own devices. Therefore its inhabitants gathered together and decided to surrender. Let us ask in what town, in what country, and at what time, under identical circumstances, would we not observe the same thing? Should the principal of a school in a moment of danger abandon his charges, would they not straight away gather together to discuss what to do?

Let us now proceed by the historical path. The first instance cited by Sergeevich relates to the year 997, the second to 1097. In other words the author could find no trace of a popular assembly for over a hundred years! For the historian this must have great significance.

From the end of the eleventh century we begin to encounter more frequent mention of popular assemblies. What does this mean? It means that favorable circumstances emerged for development of the popular assembly. To be more specific, these were the princes' clan reckonings and the subsequent civil wars. As the princes fought each other, they tried to arouse the populations of various towns against their princes and win them to their side. The populace either remained deaf to these promptings or were swayed by them, something common to all times and all peoples.

Therefore from this we cannot conclude that the development of the popular assembly was universal. Napoleon I at the time of his attack on Russia also tried to stir up our populace in a similar manner. Does that mean that in 1812 he was inspired by the example of the medieval popular assembly? This is what our scholars are doing when they deduce from information about stirring urban populations by the warring princes that the popular assembly was developing in these towns.

The historian notes that frequently when a town population had the opportunity to decide its own destiny this developed naturally into a way of life governed by a popular assembly, and that these assemblies became the general custom. The historian may not assume that this development occurred everywhere, for if some town or other happened to share the resolution of its fate, this isolated incident did not establish a new custom or destroy the old.

What constituted old custom is indicated by the famous line in the chronicle saying that the principal and oldest towns were accustomed to the popular assembly, whereas the junior towns and bytowns were accustomed to abide by the decisions of the older towns. "Whatever the older towns decide, the bytowns will follow." So long as this chronicle entry exists it serves as a foundation for explaining the origin of the new order in the North, the relationship between the older and the newer towns.

Sergeevich in his attempt to attribute the popular assembly system to the newer towns cites items concerning unrest in Moscow, one relating to the fourteenth century, the other to the fifteenth. In both instances the inhabitants rose in revolt after being abandoned by their rulers. We turn once again to our analogy and assert that even schoolchildren would do likewise when abandoned by their supervisor.

Yet why did not Sergeevich go further and cite the example of the inhabitants of Moscow during the reign of Alexis Mikhailovich, and then in the eighteenth century at the time of the plague? These happenings are completely analogous! Perhaps because by now the word "popular assembly" had gone out of usage? Yet he indicates instances of this type where the word "popular assembly" is not used. He refers to the popular assembly in connection with the rising of the Northern towns against the Tatars. Yet by the same token the rising of the Bashkirs and other natives ought to indicate the strong development of the popular assembly way of life among them.

The famous passage in the chronicle concerning relations between the ancient towns and their bytowns began to undergo in our literature the same tortuous scholarly examination as earlier did the chronicle entry concerning the summoning of the princes, with its clear indication of their Scandinavian provenance. It is very reassuring that the question of the origins of the Varangian-Rus has given place to a problem concerning domestic relations. Less reassuring is the fact that, in attempting somehow to discard inconvenient testimony, previous examples and distortions are employed. "What the ancient towns decide, the bytowns follow," said the chronicler. Thus in accordance with these relations Vladimir, a bytown in relation to Rostov being oppressed by the princes, addressed a complaint to Rostov. It did so in the custom of subservience to senior towns, a custom which cannot have weakened so quickly, even though this was accentuated by a specific circumstance, namely the rise in Vladimir's status through establishment there of the grand-princely throne by Andrei Bogoliubsky. Rostov verbally supported Vladimir but in fact brushed off its complaint, causing Vladimir to summon other princes.

Sergeevich ventures the opinion that "the chronicler does not state that the inhabitants of Vladimir, being discontented with their prince, could not speak out against him and therefore raise the question of his replacement." He takes as fact their wish to expel the sons of Rostislav, neither does he blame them for it. Rostov and Suzdal in their reply did not say that recognition of the prince was their exclusive right, therefore Vladimir must remain loyal to the lineage of Rostislav as long as it was convenient to them. On the contrary they *verbally* supported Vladimir, thereby showing that they had as much of a say as themselves in the recognition of the prince."

Yet what right did the chronicler have to say what never really happened? Remote as we are from the exaggerated representation about the high degree of development and of freedom in Ancient Rus, we certainly cannot suppose that relations were such that the injured had no right to speak out and complain against his oppressor. The inhabitants of Vladimir complained to their seniors, at that time Rostov, about the princes who wronged them, whom Rostov had given them, or rather imposed upon them. Rostov also did not need to say that calling princes was their exclusive right, for the simple reason that it was never questioned. The men of Vladimir were merely plaintiffs. It was for Rostov to decide whether this complaint was justified, not to discuss its own rights on which nobody was infringing. Conversely Vladimir solemnly recognized these rights and addressed their complaint to the senior city.

Best of all is Sergeevich's following conclusion. "They (the men of Rostov) were verbally in favor of Vladimir, thereby showing [Vladimir] they had as much part as themselves in the calling of princes." A town complains to the king about a governor, the king declares the complaint justified, *therefore* the king thereby declares that the citizens have as much say in the appointment of governors as the king himself! The chronicler championed the men of Vladimir as the underdogs whom God nevertheless helped. The chronicler championed them for two reasons. First the inhabitants of Vladimir were wronged, were denied justice, and thus naturally enlisted the sympathy of everyone in whom the desire for justice was not totally extinguished. Second, the men of Vladimir were in the right because they turned to their lawful princes, lawful both by reason of seniority and through the disposition of Yury Dolgoruky, whereas Rostov ignored this legality. Consequently there was a conflict of relationships [of Vladimir] between that with the senior city and that with the prince. These loyalties clashed in the present instance, and the historian's task is to devote equal attention to both, and learn which prevailed and under what circumstances.

Concerning relations between the princes themselves, Sergeevich follows Pogodin's lead. The princes were at war, seized territories from one another as owners having no relationship to one another. Reading Sergeevich's book we enter some kind of jungle inhabited by wild beasts, not human beings constantly having to justify their actions. Discounting clan relations between the princes, Sergeevich naturally tries also to deny the dominance of these relations in society. Of course he passes over in silence information concerning clan unity in the sixteenth and seventeenth centuries. He cites the clause in *Rus Justice* concerning inheritance where it states that the property of the commoner who left no sons escheated to the prince. It must be understood here that the *Rus Justice* dealt with the case of a commoner without a clan. In common clan ownership the question of inheritance simply did not arise, nor were there any problems about individual property.

It is interesting that Sergeevich, seeking in *Rus Justice* evidence against the existence of the clan, ignored the first article, that concerning clan vengeance. Sergeevich also has great difficulty with the famous passage in the chronicle which clearly described the clan way of life among the Slavs ("each lived in his own clan and in his separate locality," and so on). In his study of the *popular assembly* he must conceal the fact that the word has also a broad significance and origin, meaning "the populace," which is also what we should understand by the word "clan." Seeing this, Sergeevich resorts to a desperate measure when he says "Every member of the Polianians could have had his own clan *separately*, meaning his own family."

Yet where is the proof? There is none. Perhaps we are to accept as proof the words of the author. "Common ownership by brothers and other clan members can be found also in the most ancient times. There are even grounds for thinking that at that time it was encountered more frequently. In the absence of developed governmental authority, for self-preservation the private individual had to enter some form of private association, and the most natural association was with clan members." The idea appears clear, namely that circumstances of the time were such as to give rise inevitably to the tendency towards clan association, to its perpetuation. Every Polianian could have had his own clan *separately,* in the form of the family.

The implacable chronicler continues to pursue us with his clan. Speaking of the domestic strife among the Slavs after they expelled the Varangians, he states that clan rose up against clan, "and they began to fight one another." How does Sergeevich deal with this? "They rose up," says he, "not as one clan against another, but as members of one and the same clan (that is to say, origin), children against parents and brother against brother. This is merely a literary device borrowed from the gospel of St. Mark, which was well known at the time [of the chronicler]. "Brother will deliver up brother to death, and the father his child, and children will rise against their parents and have them put to death."[7]

Sergeevich forgets that the chronicler in no way could have had in mind the words of the evangelist, for he knew very well what prompted the fearful internecine strife which the gospel recounts. He knew at the same time that the cause of contention among the Slavs was the absence of law, which could cause children to rise up against parents and kill them. The absence of law specifically led separate clans in their clashes to take the law into their own hands and decide matters by the sword.

There are other interesting examples of Sergeevich's treatment of the sources. About Andrei Bogoliubsky the chronicler said "Andrei expelled Bishop Leon from Suzdal and expelled his brothers Mstislav and Vasilko and the sons of the two Rostislavich princes, and also the men devoted to his father. He acted as though he were an autocratic ruler." "The words 'autocratic ruler' were used here," says Sergeevich, "in relation to the other princes, the grandsons and younger sons of Yury. The word more properly means 'monarch' in contrast to the division of territory among several princes, and does not contain any reference to the character of his authority."

Of course if we omit the words "men devoted to his father" as Sergeevich does, we might agree with him, but if these words remain it emerges that the prince, having expelled the influential boyars, strove not towards monarchy but towards autocracy. Therefore, as Sergeevich knows very well, evidence of Andrei Bogoliubsky's autocracy was not confined to one isolated chronicle entry. Contemporary princes also bore witness to his character when they complained that Andrei treated them not as kinsmen but as subjects. Finally, Andrei's character is revealed most of all by the manner of his death. What motivated his murderers to commit a deed unprecedented in all of Rus?

For the year 1174 the chronicler says, "Having summoned the descendants of Rostislav against Prince Andrei, they asked Roman Rostislavich to rule in Kiev." "We can consider," writes Sergeevich, "that Andrei had a *right* to distribute the Rus territories. From the foregoing we have seen that Prince Andrei, as a powerful prince of the Vladimir territory, in conjunction with other princes could seize Kiev and plunder it, but only when he had more allies than did the Kievan prince. He did not have a superior right. When they approached him the sons of Rostislav did no more than offer him an alliance, one of the aims of which was to gain the Kievan throne for Roman. We find a similar expression under the entry for 1202. "I shall send to my kinsman Grand Prince Vsevolod," said Roman Mstislavich to his father-in-law Riurik, "I shall send to him and implore him to restore Kiev to you." In other words, he meant to give it to him because of the overwhelming force at the disposal of the grand prince of Vladimir, and not by virtue of any supreme right."

We have no evidence that there were any proposals for alliance as a result of pleas for granting anything, but that is not the issue. Sergeevich seeks to prove that in Ancient Rus only the right of the strong was recognized, and no other *superior* right. With this aim in mind he sedulously excludes all evidence that princes recognized a superior right. He omits to mention that Rostislav regarded Andrei as having more than the right of the strongest on his side. Those who took up arms against Andrei also claimed the right of the strongest. Yet they recognized that Andrei had another right, according to which they reckoned him their father and addressed to him the words "We called you father, and hitherto we have respected you as a father, out of love." This same right was held by Grand Prince Vsevolod who claimed it in saying to the descendants of Rostislav "You called me the eldest in your own lineage of Vladimir."

That the princes occupied their thrones not by right of conquest but through clan seniority is indisputably established by the words of Grand Prince Yaroslav I to his son Vsevolod, inserted into the chronicle. "If God grants that you receive the authority of my throne, act towards your brothers *with justice* and not by violence. This you will swear on my grave."

How does Sergeevich deal with that chronicle entry? He hides it in a long footnote dealing with the testaments of the Muscovite grand princes. "Since this passage," writes Sergeevich, "is found in a eulogy to Vsevolod, written by a very partial hand, we are forced to conclude that it was written by the chronicler to justify events after the fact." Such ingenious arguments do not help. Even if we suppose that for some reason the chronicler put words into Yaroslav's mouth, this testimony still does not lose its force, for it reflected contemporary reality.

VI

GOVERNMENT AND PRINCELY POWER

SIGNIFICANCE OF THE PRINCE

In the review of the first period of our history it was noted how the tribes became united under the rule of one overall leader or prince invited by the Northern tribes from an alien clan. The honor of the princes of Rus remained solely within this clan. In the tenth century Novgorod said to Sviatoslav that if he did not give them a prince from among his sons they would choose a prince from another family. Later such words no longer were heard. The title of prince belonged solely to the members of the house of Riurik. It belonged to them all, based on the right of origin. No one from this house might be denied this title. The title of prince was acquired only by being born into the house of Riurik. It was inalienable, not dependent on any other conditions. It made all descendants of Riurik equal.

First of all they were brothers. The special significance connected with the princely dynasty is expressed clearly in the chronicle. In 1151 the people of Kiev could not prevent the enemy from crossing the Dnieper over the Zarub ford because, as the chronicler puts it, the prince was absent and not everybody would obey a boyar. "The retinue and the Polovetsians do not fight very hard when we are not with them," said the princes in 1125. When the Galich boyar Vladislav stole the princely honor the chronicle says that for the sake of power he caused evil to his clan and his children because no prince would hold any regard for his children thanks to their father's presumption. According to an interprincely agreement a prince could not be sentenced to death for his crimes like a boyar. His only punishment was deprivation of his territory. Oleg Sviatoslavich[1] refused to allow himself to be judged by a bishop, abbots and peasants or commoners.[2] His brothers invited him to Kiev. "Come," they said, "we will deliberate about the Land of Rus before the bishop and abbots, before the men of our fathers and the people of the city." "It is not seemly," Oleg responded, "that a bishop or an abbot or commoners sit in judgment on me."

These words indicate that the population (apart from the clergy) were called "commoners," not excluding the retinue and boyars, because Oleg refers to his father's men and the city people by this general term, the meaning of which is interchangeable with the term "black" people.[3] Thus the princes of Severia during the famous expedition against the Polovetsians said "If we run away, we will save ourselves but leave behind all our men.[4] It would be a sin in the eyes of God to leave them defenseless."

PRINCELY TITLES

"Prince" was the general, inalienable name for all the members of the house of Riurik. The senior prince in the clan was called "grand prince." At the beginning this title was found very rarely in the chronicles alongside the name of the senior prince. Usually it was used only for the most important rulers and only in descriptions of their death, where the chronicler's language is customarily very florid in praise of the prince. Yaroslav I is called a Rus grand prince. Here the word "Rus" is identical to "all Rus," or the prince of all Rus, because Yaroslav[5] after the death of his brother Mstislav[6] ruled all Rus lands apart from Polotsk. After Yaroslav the title of grand prince was attached to his son Vsevolod,[7] his grandson Monomakh,[8] his great-grandson Mstislav and his sons and grandsons, but only in descriptions of their death. Riurik Rostislavich[9] was called grand prince during his lifetime, and also prior to becoming the most senior of all princes in Rus, before ascending the Kievan throne. It may be concluded therefore that the title "grand prince" was used sometimes simply out of courtesy, because of the writer's esteem for the famous prince, but had no fixed, determined meaning.

While in the Southern chronicle we encounter the title "grand prince" very rarely, in Northern Rus it was attached permanently to the name of

Vsevolod III[10] and his sons who held seniority. There this title was used even without the proper name to signify Vsevolod III. Monomakh is called grand prince of all Russia in the description of his death. It was used for Yury Dolgoruky[11] in the description of Vsevolod III's death. Monomakh had sufficient right to this title, while Dolgoruky probably received this title because of the particular zeal the Northern chronicler felt towards his princes. In one place the chronicle, where praising Monomakh and his son Mstislav, the word "great" is found after their proper names and placed after the name of Vsevolod III several times, once clearly to distinguish him from the other Vsevolod, prince of Riazan.[12]

The relationship between the senior and the junior princes has been observed. When a senior prince was a titular, not the real, father of the junior princes he instructed them usually with their consent and subject to agreement. Hence it is clear that when a prince rid himself of clan members and became sole ruler this made him an autocrat in the land. For that reason the word "autocrat" in the chronicle is used in the meaning of "sole ruler." It is said of Yaroslav I that he became sole ruler in the Land of Rus after the death of his brother Mstislav. To indicate the higher power as well as to show courtesy and zeal towards their princes, the words "tsar" and "tsar-like" were used. Thus Yury Dolgoruky said to his nephew Iziaslav[13] "Allow me to put my son in Pereiaslavl, and you sit and rule like a tsar in Kiev." This meant "rule Kiev in peace, independently, safely, not fearing anybody and not receiving orders from anybody." When speaking about Bishop Fedor[14] the chronicler adds that God saved his people using the strong, mighty and pious hand of the true tsar, the pious Prince Andrei. When after the battle on the Ruta river[15] Iziaslav's soldiers on finding their prince alive expressed their great joy, the chronicler says that they called Iziaslav "tsar." Daniel the Exile[16] wrote to Yury Dolgoruky "Have pity on me, O son of the great tsar Vladimir." The wife of Roman of Smolensk lamented over his grave, "My kind, gentle and humble tsar!" The expression "autocrat" and the Greek word for "lord"[17] were used. In oral address the word "lord" or more often simply "prince," or sometimes both, were used together.

THE PRINCE'S ENTHRONEMENT

In the event of dispute over rights or uncertainty about relationships a new senior prince sometimes needed the recognition of his clan members, of the inhabitants of the city as well as of the barbarian population of the borderlands. They all sent envoys inviting him to ascend the throne. The first sign that a prince was recognized as ruler in a given territory was his enthronement. This rite was considered indispensable. Without it the prince was not fully a prince, and therefore to the expression "became a prince" the words "and sat on the throne" were added. The enthronement took place in the main church, in Kiev or Novgorod in the Holy Wisdom church.

To demonstrate that the prince was placed on the throne by right of legal succession, that he belonged to the princely house and was not an outcast, the expression "and sat on the throne of his father and grandfather" was customary. Recognition of the prince was accompanied by an oath and kissing of the cross, when the people taking the oath said "You are our prince!" When the family rights of the prince were in doubt or when his recognition was preceded by some unusual circumstance deemed necessary to change or to support, an agreement or contract was made. Thus there was an agreement concerning reeves with Oleg's sons Igor and Sviatoslav after the death of their older brother Vsevolod. Following the death of Iziaslav Mstislavich his brother Rostislav ascended the Kievan throne with the proviso that he honor his uncle Viacheslav as his father.[18] The agreement and the kissing of the cross was called *confirmation*. Agreements according to these relationships were threefold, with brothers, with the retinue and with the townsmen.

THE PRINCE'S ACTIVITIES

The prince in this period, as earlier, mainly was concerned with ruling the land, questions of war and legislation. He conducted relations with foreign rulers, sent and received envoys, waged wars and concluded peace. Sometimes the prince himself announced a campaign to the people during assemblies. During the internecine war between Iziaslav Mstislavich and his uncle Yury the people of Kiev at first dared not raise their hand against Monomakh's son, the senior in the clan. Iziaslav had to be satisfied with volunteers, men who were devoted to him.

In Novgorod similar developments occurred. In general the population was most reluctant to take part in interprincely wars. Usually the princes themselves commanded the troops. Only on rare occasions was the host sent with commanders. Apart from personal bravery and inclination to fight, another reason is noticeable. In the absence of princes regiments lacked fighting spirit. Not everybody would obey any boyar because the importance of the commander was closely connected with the standing of the prince. For a senior and mighty prince to command a small unit was considered unseemly. Thus once the Berendey[19] took the rein of the horse of the Kievan prince Gleb Yurievich and told him "Do not go, prince. It is seemly for you to go with a large host when you gather forces with your brothers. For now send somebody else from among the brothers." For junior princes to march with the forward regiment was considered an honor because particular courage was needed. The right to draw up the regiments before battle belonged to the senior prince in the host. There was a tradition that the good prince opened battle. In days of yore young Sviatoslav was required to throw his spear first in the battle against the Drevlianians. Now Iziaslav Mstislavich and Andrei Bogoliubsky were the first to go into the enemy ranks.

The prince had the right to issue legislative acts. After Yaroslav, his sons Iziaslav, Sviatoslav and Vsevolod with five boyars (chiliarchs) gathered to introduce certain amendments to their father's legislation. Vladimir Monomakh with his boyars legislated in the matter of interest rates. Here the difference is perceptible in interprincely relations, when the senior prince was the older brother, and when he was a father to the other princes. To introduce amendments to the legislation, Iziaslav met with his brothers. Monomakh had no need to summon his sons, who in any case were obliged to accept their father's statute. With him we see only Ivanko Chudinovich, a boyar of Chernigov (Oleg's man). Perhaps he was sent as his prince's representative. As before, the prince held the right to judge and punish. When Vsevolod was old and ill, princely justice became unavailable. Monomakh among other princely activities mentions *meting justice* to the people. Praising Davyd of Smolensk, the chronicler says that the prince punished the wrongdoers the way tsars should do. To dispense justice, hold court and issue sentences, the prince travelled around his territory. This was called "going among the people."[20] The prince appointed to various functions those close to him and his servants as burgraves, reeves and so on. He also imposed taxes.

PRINCELY REVENUE

The revenue of the princely treasury consisted as before of tribute. We noted that tribute was imposed on conquered tribes, partly paid in pelts from a hearth[21] or an inhabited household, partly by collecting a shilling[22] per plough. We come across information that during the time of this chronicler the subjugated population paid tribute and provided transport services to the princes, who sent their servants to collect tribute in the provinces. Thus Yan Vyshatich was sent by Prince Sviatoslav to Beloozero to collect tribute. Oleg Sviatoslavich, after conquering the Murom and Rostov lands, appointed governors for the towns and collected tribute. In the charter Rostislav of Smolensk granted to the Smolensk see (1150) it is said that everybody in the trading settlements[23] must pay his tribute and measures fee. The poor[24] were to pay according to their ability. The Smolensk principality collected a tribute of more than three thousand grivnas. Apart from the tribute, Rostislav's charter mentions circuit tax and town tax.[25] It is known further that the Kievan prince received tribute from Novgorod. Other sources of princely revenue were market dues, court dues, gifts to a senior from junior princes, and revenues from private properties of the prince. This private property probably came to him as a result of primary occupation and colonization of empty land belonging to nobody. Later acquisitions were through purchase. For the year 1158 the chronicle specifically mentions princely acquisition of villages. Another source was confiscation of land from boyars and others convicted of crime. When, for example, one prince expelled another from a territory he took the property of that prince's boyars.

Together with common clan ownership the princes understandably had personal property scattered in various territories. A father granted to his sons villages without relation to the thrones they were to occupy. Moreover, these thrones were not permanent. It may be assumed that at this time, given common clan ownership, the princes were not in the habit of making agreements, as they did later, not to acquire land by purchase in another's territories. On lands belonging to princes as private property they might build towns and grant them to their children as private property. It is thought that Vladimir Monomakh, who built Gorodets Ostersk on his own land, gave it as private property to his younger son Yury, who ruled there when he was prince of Suzdal. Similarly Rostislav Mstislavich, prince of Smolensk, obtained from his father or grandfather as private property lands or revenues from the region of Suzdal. Yaropolk Iziaslavich, who ruled in Turov and Volhynia, owned various private lands near Kiev and granted all of them while still alive to the Caves monastery.

Lands in private princely ownership were populated by household slaves. On these lands princes built residences where every variety of goods accumulated. In the Putivl residence of Sviatoslav Olgovich there were seven hundred slaves, pastures, and storage cellars where five hundred vats of mead and eighty tuns of wine were kept.[26] In a village owned by Igor Olgovich a stout enclosure held large amounts of mead, wine and various types of bulky goods such as iron and copper. In the barn there were nine hundred stooks of hay. A main source of wealth for princes was in their large herds. Near Novgorod Seversk the enemy took from Oleg's sons three thousand mares and one thousand stallions. The significance of the lands, residences and stores for the princes is demonstrated by the term used for it, "life."[27] "Brothers," said Sviatoslav Olgovich to Davyd's sons, "you attacked my lands, you took my herds and those of my brother, you burned rye and destroyed all *life*!" Iziaslav Mstislavich said to his retinue about the princes of Chernigov "We have burned their villages and all their *life* and they have not come against us, so let us go towards Liubech where all their *life* is."

THE PRINCES' WAY OF LIFE

Let us now look how a Rus prince lived in this era, from birth unto death. When a baby prince was born he received a Slavonic or a Varangian name which was called the *princely* name. When he was christened he was given a second name, after a Greek saint. The first name was used mainly, and both names were given in honor of some senior ancestor, alive or deceased. This custom applied to infants of both sexes. Apparently at birth a prince received a territory or a town, although is impossible to decide whether from the private property of the prince-father or whether the newborn was considered a prince of this territory or town and later exchanged it according to the general tribal and clan order. Godparents at the font were the prince's clan members.

When the child was two, three or four years old, there was the ceremony of *haircutting* for male children.[28] For the first time the hair was cut, with an accompanying church blessing. The young child was put on a horse, and there were feasts in his father's house. Sometimes the haircutting ceremony was arranged to coincide with the child's nameday.[29] Sometimes two princes had a joint haircutting ceremony.

The rearing of young princes was entrusted to wet nurses. The chronicle under 1198 provides us with information on the education of princesses. "A daughter was born to Rostislav Riurikovich and she was called Evfrosinia, nicknamed Izmoragd, meaning "precious stone."[30] Mstislav Mstislavich (the Daring) and her aunt Predslava took her to see her grandfather and grandmother and she was brought up in Kiev, on the hills."

Very early in life the princes participated in campaigns and visited their territories. Sometimes this happened at the age of five or seven. Generally the princes married off their sons at a very early age, sometimes when they were eleven, the daughters sometimes at the age of eight. There is a description of the wedding of Vsevolod III's daughter Verkhuslava, who married Rostislav Riurikovich, ruler of Belgorod. "Prince Riurik sent to Suzdal his brother-in-law Prince Gleb of Turov with his wife, the chiliarch Slavin with his wife, Churinia with his wife and many other boyars with their wives, to the great Vsevolod Yurievich to bespeak his daughter Verkhuslava for [Riurik's] son Vsevolod. On St. Boris's day [May 2] Grand Prince Vsevolod gave his daughter Verkhuslava in marriage. Her dowry contained a countless quantity of gold and silver. The matchmakers received rich gifts, and were sent back with great honor. He went with his beloved daughter as far as three post stations, and both father and mother wept because they loved her and she was very young, only eight years of age. The grand prince sent with her the son of his sister, Yakov, with his wife, and other boyars with their wives. Prince Riurik, for his part, gained for his son Rostislav a rich match such as never was seen before in Rus. Over twenty princes feasted at the wedding. Prince Riurik gave his daughter-in-law many gifts and the town of Briagin. He sent the matchmaker Yakov and the boyars back to Vsevolod in Suzdal with great honor, giving them many gifts."

From this information as well as many instances elsewhere we may deduce that marriages were arranged by the parents of the bride and groom. Those acting in negotiations and sent by the father of the groom to bring the bride, as well as those accompanying the bride, appointed by her father, were called *matchmakers*.[31] The bride's father gave her gold and silver, *gave for her* or *with her,* which clearly points to the dowry, while the father-in-law also gave the bride gifts and a town as a dower for her upkeep. The fact that princesses had towns is borne out by other information in the chronicle. In some poor territories the princesses are mentioned as having only villages. The princesses who did not marry, who stayed in the territories of their brothers or fathers, also had villages.

Princes married mainly within their own clan removed seven or six degrees in the father's family, or six or five degrees by marriage. They also married members of other ruling houses including the Scandinavian, Anglo-Saxon, Polish, Bohemian, Hungarian and Byzantine, and very often into families of Polovetsian khans. Sometimes they took wives from the Caucasian Yas,[32] and married daughters of Novgorod boyars or even married their daughters to Novgorod boyars. Princes Sviatopolk Iziaslavich and Yaroslav of Galich had illegitimate sons whom the fathers treated no differently from the legitimate. If princes married early for the first time, a second marriage sometimes took place very late. For example Vsevolod married for the second time when he was over sixty. Mention is made of princely divorces owing to their wives' illness or desire to take the veil.

The occupations of an adult prince after his enthronement can be ascertained from the words of Monomakh to his sons. "Do not be lazy in doing every good. First to all, do not be lazy about attending church. The sun should not find you in your bed. My father and all good men have lived thus. On return from church it is advisable to sit and deliberate with your retinue or to *dispense justice* to people (to sit in court and pass sentences), or go hunting or travel somewhere or sleep. The time decreed by God for sleeping is noon."

Hunting was the favorite princely pastime. Monomakh tells that they caught wild horses in the forest, hunted aurochs,[33] deer, elk, wild boar, bears, wolves (wild animals). They also hunted hare, using snares. Monomakh said that he kept a full company of hunters, while he personally saw to his falcons and hawks. Princes hunted for long periods, taking along their wives and retinues. They hunted from boats along the Dnieper, travelling from Kiev down to the mouth of the Tiasmin (on the border of Kiev and Kherson provinces). Igor Sviatoslavich, when he was prisoner of the Polovetsians, spent his time hunting with falcons. In the Nikon compilation of chronicles it is said that Vsevolod of Novgorod liked to play and enjoy himself, but did not rule his people. He gathered his hawks and dogs, but did not dispense justice to his people.

From the chronicles it is learned that princes sat at table three times a day. They had breakfast, dinner and supper. The time of either breakfast, dinner or supper cannot be determined. Perhaps dinner was before noon. This is understandable if we take into account that people arose before sunrise and breakfasted soon afterwards. The description of the Lipitsa battle contains information that Prince Yury came to Vladimir around noon, and the battle started during the dinner hour. At midday people napped. As in earlier times, the princes liked to feast with their retinue. Apart from the retinue they sometimes invited priests. The chronicle relates that Prince Boris Yurievich gave a feast for his retinue and clergy in Belgorod, in the outbuildings. During Lent every Saturday and Sunday Rostislav Mstislavich invited for dinner twelve monks and the abbot made the thirteenth. On Lazarus Saturday[34] he invited all the monks from the Kiev monastery of the Caves and other monasteries. During the rest of the year he invited the monks of the Caves monastery for fast days, Wednesdays and Fridays. The chronicle calls these occasions "consolation feasts."

For especially solemn occasions such as christening, haircutting ceremonies, saints' days, weddings or visits by other rulers, princes arranged great feasts. The guests and hosts exchanged invitations and gifts on the occasion of an enthronement. In the Nikon compilation Vsevolod Olgovich, when he came to rule in Kiev, arranged a great feast. Beer, wine, cheap ale,[35] all sorts of foods and vegetables were distributed in the streets. Princes sometimes invited for dinner all citizens, who in turn invited the princes to their banquets. Princes also attended feasts given by private citizens. Thus Yury Dolgoruky before his death went to drink at Petrila the taxgatherer's house. Large feasts were organized by princes to celebrate religious ceremonies, for consecration of churches. Sviatoslav Vsevolodovich, after the consecration of St. Basil's church situated in the Great Court in Kiev, invited for a religious feast the metropolitan, the bishops, the abbots, all the church dignitaries and the people of Kiev. During princely feasts music usually was played.

Princes were buried immediately upon death unless there were unusual circumstances. Yury Dolgoruky died May 15, on Wednesday night, and was buried next day, Thursday. Members of his family, the boyars and the servants of the deceased, dressed in black robes and black hats. When the body was driven for burial a horse was led, the prince's banner was carried before the coffin, alongside which a spear was placed. After a prince's funeral members of his family distributed rich alms to the clergy and the poor. Rostislav Mstislavich after the death of his uncle Viacheslav distributed all his movables and kept for himself only a cross with which to be blessed. Yaroslav of Galich before his death gave away his property to monasteries and the poor. Members of the family, boyars and servants wept over the princely coffin, with lamentations pronouncing an eulogy over the deceased. Praise of a good prince as phrased by a chronicler noted that he was brave in war. He honored, supported and consoled the clergy, gave plentiful alms to the poor, loved and honored his retinue and begrudged no largesse. Particular merit was attached to fidelity to his oath, observance of chastity, dispensing justice, severity towards the wicked, fearlessness in facing a stronger man who offended and injured the weak.

An illustration appended to the well-known *Sviatoslav's Collection*[36] gives us an idea of how princes dressed. Sviatoslav and his sons Gleb and Yaroslav are depicted wearing long caftans, reaching below their knees.

Sviatoslav's caftan is green and he wears a blue coat with red lining on top. On his left shoulder there is a red clasp with a golden ornament. His sons wear raspberry-colored caftans and gold belts with four ends. The collars and sleeves of the young princes' dress and the edge of Yaroslav's coat are laced with gold, the hems of the caftans of Yaroslav and Gleb are red. Little Yaroslav has a golden lacing with three horizontal gold strips hanging from his neck and reaching to his belt. Sviatoslav's shoes are green, Yaroslav's red, all are pointed. The young princes have tall blue hats with red earflaps and a green lining (unless this lining is a separate skullcap). Sviatoslav's hat is not very tall, yellow with blue earflaps and dark red trimming. Little Yaroslav has a blue hat, not very tall. Sviatoslav and Roman have mustaches but no beards. The headdress of the princess is tied under her chin. Her outer garment is red with wide sleeves and a wide yellow strip at the hem. She wears a golden belt, and the sleeves of the inner dress are visible, adorned with golden cuffs. On her feet she wears golden shoes.

THE RETINUE

The relationship between the prince and his retinue remained mainly as it was in the past. During the time of Yaroslav new recruitment for the retinue took place. During the reign of his sons internecine wars already raged, accompanied by the movement of princes from one territory to another. It is easy to understand how this affected the situation of the retinue, whose members were obliged to move together with the princes from one territory to another. If they remained in the old territory, they had to join the service of the new prince and accept the fact that the old retinue of the new prince, arriving with him from his previous territory, must take precedence.

During the reign of Vsevolod Yaroslavich and his nephew Sviatopolk we find clear indications by the chronicler that such relationships between the old and the new retinue existed when there was a change of princes. If the retinue suffered even when the change was peaceful, what was it like during strife or internecine wars when one prince drove out another by force from his territory? In such a case the retinue of the defeated prince had to depart with him to a new town, leaving the field to the victor's retinue. Because of princes' movements the retinue could not settle permanently either. From 1051 until 1228 the chronicles tell of one hundred and fifty names of retainers, of whom no more than fifteen are found whose patronymics denote them as sons of men previously well known. In such cases scholars are guided mainly by assumptions. It is likely that some Lazarevich was the son of the previously famous Lazar. Of this number we find only six examples of a retainer serving in succession to his father. On the other hand there are no more than six examples of retainers remaining in the same territory continually. Finally, there are just two examples of the post of chiliarch passing in succession in the same family.

Clearly such mobility made it difficult for retainers during this era to establish stable and direct relationships with a territory, to gain important roles there as permanent, rich landowners or as holders of hereditary office. The boyars as before remained boyars of the prince, not of the principalities. They acted to gain personal advantage associated closely with that of the prince, rather than advantages related to their estate.

The activity of the retinue always was significant and was influential when its interests coincided with those of the town or the land. This was the case in Kiev when Vsevolod Olgovich died, or in the Land of Rostov after the death of Bogoliubsky. In the second instance the boyars acted against Yury's younger sons to the advantage of Rostislav's sons, in agreement with the people of Rostov. The situation developed unfavorably for them because of the special relationships of new towns. Here it should be remembered that from the very beginning in Rus, because the members of the princely family were numerous, the government of territories or towns of any significance passed to the princes who were clan members, not to boyars, who for that reason could not gain influential positions as regional governors. This important role remained with the princes.

The boyars of Galich were the sole exception. The Galich principality became a special domain of Rostislav's descendants, princes excluded from the seniority order of the Yaroslav branch. For this reason princes did not change, allowing the principality to avoid division into small territories within Rostislav's branch because Vladimir succeeded in ridding himself of all the other clan members, becoming the single ruler in Galich. His only son Yaroslav continued as sole ruler. Thus the Galich boyars became established in this area, gaining influence in the region as rich landowners and regional governors. For that reason the influence of the retinue on the affairs of Galich was of such exceptional importance. Strong participation of towns in the events after the death of Roman the Great is not noticeable, although the people as a whole were attached to the young Daniel. The influence of the neighbors of Galich, namely Poland and Hungary, must be mentioned as well.

If the peregrinations of the retinue from one territory and prince to another were both frequent and necessary it is easy to understand that its relationship with the prince cannot be determined precisely. A retainer enjoyed full freedom to transfer his services from one prince to another. A prince gladly received him because he needed brave warriors. Movement was easy for the retainer in all other respects because the Land of Rus retained its unity. Like the princely clan the retainer, moving from one prince to another, in no sense betrayed the Land of Rus, nor did he betray the princely clan which ruled it indivisibly. The princes could not agree to forbid such transfers because it was very rarely that all of them lived in peace among themselves. The first internecine war enabled retainers to cross from one hostile prince to another.

Circumstances made the custom of transferring service a right. Later compacts among princes contained clauses where the princes undertook not to hinder movements of retainers. "To the boyars among us and to free servitors, freedom." Because texts of interprincely compacts have not survived, it is difficult to decide whether such clauses were included in the interprincely agreements of this era, or whether they were implied as a natural and necessary provision, appearing in subsequent agreements, when clan bonds grew weaker and separate principalities appeared. We know only that such charters then existed.

A good prince, according to the notions of the time, joined his assets to those of his retinue, begrudged it nothing, and put nothing aside for himself. He lived with his retinue as in a brotherhood, in a group of like-minded comrades, hiding from them neither property nor his thoughts and plans. "Prince," said the retinue to Mstislav Iziaslavich, "do not plan or do anything without us. We know your real love for the brotherhood." "You have planned this on your own," the retinue said to Vladimir Mstislavich, "we knew nothing about it, now we won't go with you." The tone of the chronicle leaves no doubt that it was frowned upon if a prince had a favorite to whom he disclosed his thoughts, concealing them from the rest of the retinue. Thus in the story about the crime committed by Sviatoslav Vsevolodovich against the sons of Rostislav the chronicler says "Sviatoslav took counsel with the princess and his favorite Kochkar, but did not tell his thoughts to the other men."

A prince spent almost all his time with the retinue. He deliberated with them, hunted and feasted with them. In the *Life of St. Feodosy* when Prince Iziaslav wanted to visit the holy man he sent the boyars home and appeared at the monastery with a young servant.[37] This is described as an exception to custom. Given such close relations between the prince and the boyars, naturally their advice and suggestions were not without consequence in the interprincely strife and internecine wars. In the case of Vasilko's blinding the chronicler specifically accuses Davyd's boyars. More than once the prince behaved wickedly because he listened to bad advisers. If a retainer left one prince because he was unhappy in his service and went to serve another, this of course did not enhance their friendship. Mstislav Iziaslavich allowed two boyars, the two sons of Borislav, to leave him, *being angry*, as the chronicler puts it, that their slaves stole horses from his herd. Borislav's sons went to Davyd Rostislavich and stirred up a quarrel between him and Mstislav. The chronicle states that as a result of such relations, when interprincely agreements were concluded the boyars kissed the cross, promising to wish good between the princes, guard their honor and not stir quarrels among them.

SENIOR AND JUNIOR RETINUES

Differentiation between senior and junior retinues was unchanged. When Sviatoslav Olgovich was informed of the death of his brother Igor it was said that he called his *senior* retinue together and told them about it. Vsevolod III sent word to his nephew Mstislav Rostislavich, saying "Brother! Your senior retinue brought you, now go to Rostov." The senior retinue in the same story is translated as *boyars*.

In contrast to the "senior retinue" we encounter the term "junior retinue." Thus Iziaslav Mstislavich told his brother Vladimir "Go to Belgorod and we will send our *junior* retinue with you." The junior retinue also is referred to simply as "youth," "the young," "young men,"[38] and continued to be called "the bodyguard."[39] Members of the senior retinue, the boyars, were mainly princely advisors, counsellors, but there is information that sometimes the princes called to the council the boyars and all their retinue. Part of the retinue consisted of personal servants of the prince, living permanently with him in his house, his court. There were so-called "young servitors," "children" and "stepsons," who were divided into senior and junior or younger groups.[40] Thus the retinue was composed of three parts, namely the boyars, the bodyguard and "stepsons." The chronicle tells that Mstislav Rostislavich on his arrival in Rostov called together the boyars, bodyguard, "stepsons" and all his retinue. The other component of the retinue, the household or the princely servants who lived in the prince's house, began in the North to be called "the court," "courtiers."[41] It was only natural that in contrast to the town regiments the entire retinue, all the prince's own forces, were called "courtiers."

Boyars' houses were in the prince's capital. They also possessed villages but it is not known what sort of villages they were, apart from patrimonies. Whether retainers received from princes any service tenures[42] is not known. Apart from the capital city, the retinue (mainly, in our opinion, the junior) lived also in other towns, where its units constituted the guard or garrisons. They also lived in their villages. After every expedition the retinue was sent home. Princely servants lived at court, but they could be rotated, having their own homes. During expeditions the boyars had their own households and their own young servants.

The chiliarchs were appointed by the prince from among the boyars. As for the governors, they could be nominated from among the junior retinue. The reeves of the princes and the boyars had not lost their importance. Among the service ranks in the household and the princely court the post of steward[43] is encountered. A description of his duties is found in the story that after Rostislav Mstislavich buried his uncle Viacheslav he summoned Viacheslav's boyars, reeves and stewards and ordered them to lay out all the possessions of the deceased prince. The office of chamber boy[44] seems to correspond to the later post of the gentleman of the bedchamber.[45] The offices of the master of the horse, table attendant and swordbearer[46] are self-explanatory. We also find young servants,[47] which might signify a general type of servant in the prince's host. There were saddle grooms, whose appellation describes their position. Both young servants and saddle grooms accompanied the host during expeditions. Saddle grooms lived together in settlements, in known places. In the Novgorod Chronicle for 1181 the name "yeomen"[48] denotes the best warriors. This name is rendered in some compilations as "men of substance."[49] Monomakh said that he took prisoner five Polovetsian princes and their fifteen young yeomen.

THE LEVY

As earlier there are clear indications in the chronicles of the difference between the retinue and the regiments[50] called up from the town and the rural population. The retinue was different from the "regiment" or "host." Viacheslav Vladimirovich said to his nephew Iziaslav "We will share my retinue and my host." Yaroslav of Galich said to the boyars of Kiev about his father "His host and retinue are with me." It is clear that the word "host" preserved the general meaning of a military force, just like the retinue, whereas "host" or "regiment" might denote a particular military unit. In the story of the battle between Iziaslav Mstislavich and his uncle Yury which took place near Kiev, Kievan regiments are clearly differentiated from princely retinues. "Viacheslav and Iziaslav did not enter the city, but pitched their camp before the Golden gate. Iziaslav Davydovich stood between the Golden and the Jewry gates and Rostislav with his son Roman in front of the Jewry gate. Boris of Gorodets stood near the Polish gate and between the princes stood the people of Kiev, on horseback or on foot." The same story mentions that Viacheslav and his nephews listened to the retinue, the men of Kiev and the Karakalpaks.

The chronicle contains direct information about the participation of the rural population in military expeditions, namely in the story of Monomakh's and Sviatopolk's forces concentrating against the Polovetsians. The retinue said that spring was a bad time for an expedition because villagers (peasants) and horses were needed, and must be taken away from field work. "It is strange," replied Monomakh, "that you are sorry for the peasants and their horses, yet consider how when the peasants begin field work with their horses the Polovetsians will appear and shoot the peasants with arrows and take their horses."

TYPES OF SERVICE AND MILITARY EQUIPMENT

Were someone to ask how the population participated in expeditions, for what purpose they and their horses were used, it would be difficult to answer because of lack of evidence. We may cite only one item of information, namely that during their war against Mstislav of Toropets the younger sons of Vsevolod III rode to war "from villages," as the chronicle puts it. Yet in the chronicle it is stated that Iziaslav Mstislavich, in Kiev and in Novgorod, announced expeditions in the assembly. It is not known whether this was an accepted custom. How the citizens went to war becomes clear from the words of Iziaslav's boyars, who called the people of Kiev to make war on behalf of the prince. "Now, brothers of Kiev," they urged, "follow us to Chernigov against the sons of Oleg. Gather all of you, from the least to the greatest. Whoever has a horse shall ride. Those without horses shall follow by boat." From this entry and many other writings it appears that the levy was composed of cavalry (spearmen) and infantry (archers). We encounter the term *bridled* horses, meaning mounts, and *working* horses for camp needs as well as pack horses.

St. George in Armor with a Shield Bearing the
Coat of Arms of the Princes of Vladimir

Relief, Cathedral of St. George in Yuriev Polsky, c. 1234

Archers usually began battle before the main military force, the spearmen, entered the fray. When the host was on the march the weapons were transported on carts and included armor, helmets, shields, swords, spears, sabres, arrows, clubs, lances, poignards, bear spears, javelins and axes. Axes sometimes had cords attached. In the *Tale of Igor's Campaign* shields were called red, helmets had pointed tops and iron visors or covers in the form of half masks. To protect neck and cheeks an iron chain mail netting was attached, fastened by a clasp under the chin.

Banners or standards were present, as were trumpets and drums. Carts transported arms and equipment as well as warriors. Apart from carts with arms the army probably was accompanied by wagon trains with food supplies. At any rate there is information that food stores sometimes were transported by river boats, while there were occasions when princes on entering enemy land ordered food collected. This activity was called *foraging* and those sent to collect food were called *foragers*.

MILITARY TACTICS

Before battle warriors donned their armor. Yet Mstislav the Brave, before the battle on the Lipitsa, gave the men of Novgorod a choice between fighting on horseback or on foot. They answered that they did not wish to die on horseback but wanted to fight on foot, like their fathers at Koloksha,[51] who after taking off their outer garments and boots, charged barefoot against the enemy.

The princes arranged the troops and made speeches. As in the past the army was arranged in three units, the main regiment or the head, and two wings. During this period the vanguard regiment or *front* is mentioned also. The forward regiment, which acted as a screen to inform the main force of the whereabouts of the enemy and his movements, is also mentioned. When the enemy retreated the victorious troops rushed to their camp and stripped the dead. There is one description of the division of spoils. Mstislav the Brave after collecting tribute from the Chud gave two parts to the men of Novgorod and the third to members of his court.

There is also information about fortified camps. Before the battle on the Lipitsa Vsevolod's younger sons surrounded their camp with a wattle fence laced with thorns. It was customary to surround the camp with obstacles. It was told about Yaroslav Vsevolodovich of Chernigov that he made a camp with obstacles near his forest to defend it from the enemy.

In the camps there were *marquees* and *tents*. In the story of the capture of the princes of Riazan by Vsevolod III we are told that the grand prince, after exchanging greetings, asked them to sit in a marquee while he himself entered a tent. In the story of the murder of the Riazan princes by their relatives Gleb the murderer hid armed servants and Polovetsians in a tent near the marquee where his victims were supposed to be feasting.

During this period troops sometimes moved by boats on rivers. For 1185 we read that Sviatoslav Vsevolodovich sailed on the Desna river from Novgorod Seversk to Chernigov. There is even mention of a river battle on the Dnieper between the forces of Iziaslav Mstislavich and his uncle Yury, where Iziaslav *captured the boats by wonderful cunning*, as the chronicler puts it. Only the oars were visible, not the oarsmen, because the boats were decked. The warriors stood on these decks in their armor and shot arrows. There were two helmsmen, one at the bow and another astern, allowing movement in any direction without having to put about.

Expeditions took place mainly in winter. This is understandable when we consider that the country contained numerous rivers and marshes which in winter were covered by natural ice bridges and facilitated movement. Princes usually hurried to end expeditions before the snow started to thaw and rivers began flooding. Apart from difficult roads there were other arguments against expeditions other than in winter. Monomakh's retinue opposed a spring expedition against the Polovetsians because it would draw field laborers from their work.

Distances were calculated by days of travel. For the year 1187 it is mentioned that Riurik Rostislavich said to Yaroslav of Chernigov "We have good information that the Polovetsian camp is half a day away. For me that is a half day's march, but for you it is ten days." In the entry for 1159 we read "Following him (Iziaslav Davydovich) beyond the Desna, both Sviatoslavs and Riurik went for a day's distance and lost him." In 1147 the Novgorod levies went to meet Iziaslav Mstislavich "some three days, and some one day away from Novgorod."

There are mentions of taking towns *by spear* (by storm) or taking them *on the shield* (burning, pillaging, capturing and killing the inhabitants). There is no reason to think that when capture "on the shield" was mentioned, storming the town necessarily preceded it. In descriptions of sieges almost never are siege engines, catapults or mining mentioned. Usually we are told that the town was surrounded and the attackers fought the besieged by the gates. There is one story in the Pskov Chronicle that Vseslav of Polotsk came close to Pskov, labored very hard and *used battering rams*. The Pskov Chronicle is of late compilation and this expression is used purely formally. Sieges lasted from two days to ten weeks. There is no mention of longer sieges. From over a hundred descriptions of attacks against towns only once is there mention of a town being taken "by spear," twenty times "on the shield" with pillage, forty times by surrender and simply occupying the town. The expression that a town was taken suddenly by *riding in* is used seven times. Seven times the besieged had to accept the conditions of the besiegers, five times peace followed a siege, and twenty-five times sieges were abandoned.

SIZE OF MILITARY FORCES

Undoubtedly it is very important to know the numbers of troops during campaigns and sieges. Unfortunately the chronicles provide very limited information. For 1172 we read about a battle fought between the Rus and the Polovetsians where the pagans numbered nine hundred spears and the Rus ninety. The number of spears is not equal to the overall number of troops because later in the account it is said that after the victory over the Polovetsians (nine hundred spears), the Rus took fifteen hundred prisoners, killed some others, while some escaped. From this story certain conclusions may be drawn. Earlier in the account it is mentioned that when the Rus captured the Polovetsian guards they asked "How many men do you have in your forces left behind?" They were told that there were seven thousand. The Rus advanced against the seven thousand, crushed them, and when they asked the same question again, the answer was "Now the great regiment is coming." In this great regiment there were nine hundred spears. Consequently, a force of nine hundred spears had an overall number of troops much larger than seven thousand, since its ratio to a seven-thousand strong unit was as to a great regiment. The Rus regiment, consisting of ninety spears, was considered a small force. Thus it was considered that the senior prince ought not to command it.

When Grand Prince Sviatoslav Iziaslavich announced to the boyars of Kiev in 1093 that he had eight hundred young servitors of his own who could be used against the Polovetsians, the boyars replied "Even if you had eight thousand it would not go amiss, because our land has fallen into decline." This information about the eight hundred (in some compilations five hundred) young servitors may indicate the numbers in the princes' own service household, which should be treated separately from other constituent parts of the retinue, namely the boyars and bodyguard. When Monomakh left Chernigov for Pereiaslavl, escaping from Oleg, he had less than a hundred in retinue, but this was after an unsuccessful battle with the Polovetsians in which Monomakh lost many of his troops. In Galich the sons of Igor killed five hundred boyars. Novgorod the Great in the second half of the twelfth century could field an army twenty thousand strong. North Rus, the territories of Novgorod, Rostov with Beloozero, Murom and Riazan could field fifty thousand. During the battle on the Lipitsa the losses of Vsevolod's younger sons amounted to 9,233, not including the sixty taken prisoner and those who drowned in the rivers during the escape.

It must be remembered that wars were fought by the combined forces of several principalities, or two princes fought using their own forces. If South Rus could field about fifty thousand troops, this number should divided by the six territories of Chernigov, Pereiaslavl, Smolensk, Turov, Volhynia and Kiev. When war was fought by princes singly, for example between the princes of Chernigov and Severia, it may be assumed that any one prince might field more than five thousand troops. On the other hand it should be noted that, in almost every war, groups of Wild Polovetsians and friendly Karakalpaks took part. In 1127 seven thousand Polovetsians came to assist Vsevolod Olgovich, and twenty thousand came to the assistance of Iziaslav Davydovich. Finally in the Nikon Compilation[52] it is stated that in 1135 Vsevolod Mstislavich of Novgorod had Germans in his army. Under 1149 Germans also are mentioned in the Rus army of the South.

HERO-WARRIORS

During this era we encounter information about hero-warriors. Thanks to his physical ability a man could stand out, achieve a special status and bring victory to a prince. It seems that the hero-warriors earned special respect, being called *God's men*. The chronicle for the year 1148 tells the story of a hero-warrior called Demian Kudenevich, who lived in Southern Pereiaslavl at the court of Prince Mstislav Iziaslavich at the time Yury Dolgoruky's son Gleb suddenly tried to attack Pereiaslavl. When Prince Mstislav learned about Gleb's approach he immediately sent for Demian. "God's man," he urged him, "now is the time for God and His Immaculate Mother to help, and for your valor and strength." Demian, with his servant Taras and five young lads, for the rest had dispersed nobody knew where, immediately mounted his horse. The hero left the town, met Prince Gleb Yurievich in a field by the town quarter and attacked his troops with fury, mercilessly slaying many warriors. Prince Gleb took fright, turned back and sent to tell Demian Kudenevich "I came for love and peace, not to fight." Yet soon afterwards Gleb returned to Pereiaslavl with Polo-vetsians. Once again Demian rode out without armor, killed many en-emies but was wounded in many places by Polovetsian arrows and returned to the town exhausted. Prince Mstislav visited him, brought many gifts and promised him a territory to rule, to which the hero re-sponded "O human vanity! Who wishes for futile gifts and fleeting power when he is about to die?" Thereupon he fell into his eternal sleep and there was great lamentation in the town. In the story of the Lipitsa battle hero-warriors also are mentioned as fighting on the side of Mstislav of Toropets. In the story of the Kalka battle eighty brave men or hero-war-riors were killed.

URBAN AND RURAL POPULATION

Let us now turn to the population of the countryside and the towns. The Rus land in the broad sense of the word, signifying all Rus possessions, was divided into several lands or territories. There were the Land of Rus (in the narrow sense, the Land of Kiev), Volhynia, Smolensk, Suzdal and so on. The word "territory" signified princely rule (authority) and prin-cipality (possession, district). Between the word "territory" and the word "land" there is a difference. "Land" was of purely geographical signifi-cance, whereas "territory" always denoted a certain piece of land depen-dent on a prince or a capital city. In this sense the surrounding land bore the name of a territory as opposed to a town, as did the rural inhabitants as opposed to town dwellers. Thus the Land of Novgorod is "Novgoro-dia," the land inhabited by the people of Novgorod, in the same way as the Polish land is Poland, the Czech land Bohemia.[53] Novgorod territory means lands under the administration and control of Novgorod the Great.

The change in the word "rule" from the meaning of the ruler to the meaning of the ruled was very easy.[54] The prince and the senior city were the powers ruling the surrounding populated settlements. Here resided their power, these places were in their power, and they were their author-ity. At the beginning, before the calling of Riurik, the chronicler tells about independent tribes. It is clear from his words that each tribe had its *own* homeland. At the beginning there were also toponyms based on tribal names, for example the Land of Derevsk. Therefore it might be assumed that in the beginning borders between lands corresponded to intertribal borders. From the time of the Riurikid princes this correspon-dence of borders was upset. In the subsequent division of lands or terri-tories between princes the previously existing basis no longer can be found. Thus the Land of Novgorod included the lands of Slovenians and Krivichians, the Land of Polotsk the lands of the Krivichians and Dregovichians, Smolensk the Krivichians and Radimichians, Chernigov the Severians and Viatichians.[55] The change of names alone, the disappearance of tribal names and their substitution by names derived from main cities, shows that the basis of division differed from previous tribal divisions.

SENIOR CITIES AND JUNIOR TOWNS

Despite the appearance of this new strong authority, princely rule, under the influence of which the transformation of the tribal into a regional way of life undoubtedly took place, the importance of main cities in earlier times for neighboring populations remained unchanged. This was due primarily to the initially indeterminate nature of relations between town dwellers and the prince. Relations depended mainly on interprincely clan relations, on frequent moves of princes to another district. Because inheritance rights of princes were contestable, in times of internecine wars or absence of princes territories were compelled to look to main, senior cities and conform to their decisions. This is why the ancient senior cities preserved in relation to the territory, to junior towns or bytowns, the powers of authority, and were called *authorities.* "The people of Novgorod from the very beginning," says the chronicler, "and the people of Smolensk, Kiev and Polotsk and all the authorities came to the assembly as to a council, and the bytowns followed what the main city decided."

Such chronicle passages as may serve as sources of information regarding the relationship between junior and senior towns are few and far between. In the story of the chronicler for the year 1175 it is clear that the men of Rostov considered they had the right to send a burgrave to their bytown of Vladimir. Later the men of Vladimir, oppressed by the sons of Rostislav, appealed for help to the inhabitants of the senior cities, Rostov and Suzdal.

NOVGOROD AND PSKOV

The Novgorod Chronicle provides but scanty information on the relations between Novgorod and its bytowns, mainly Pskov and Ladoga. It is impossible to look in the pre-Riurik era for the initial relationship between the main city and the bytown. Pskov was the town of a completely different tribe, the Krivichians. It is not known how Pskov became the main center of the neighboring area instead of Izborsk or Slovensk (as it is called in the Pskov chronicle) which was Truvor's capital.[56] Be that as it may, the dependence of the Izborsk Krivichians on the Novgorod Slovenes at the time of the princes' invitation should not be assumed, nor that the later dependence of Pskov on Novgorod resulted from any previous dependence. The White Lake settlements, like the Izborsk Krivichians, participated in the calling of the princes. Sineus, Riurik's second brother, became their ruler, but later Beloozero left the Novgorod land to join another principality.

Therefore it is reasonably certain that Pskov's dependence on Novgorod dates back to the times of the Varangian princes, and was the result of princely relationships. Riurik's brothers, according to the chronicler, soon passed away, and Riurik came to rule their territory. Consequently the country of the Izborsk Krivichians, together with Pskov, following Truvor's death became dependent on Riurik, who had established his throne in Novgorod. For that reason Novgorod became a main city, a government center for the whole area acknowledging Riurik as its prince. This is where the beginning of Pskov's dependence on Novgorod must be sought or, to put it better, on the authority present in Novgorod. The prince of Novgorod was simultaneously the prince of Pskov, and he appointed his burgrave to rule in Pskov. This is the origin of the custom whereby Pskov always accepted a burgrave from Novgorod. In 1132 as a result of considerable disturbances following the departure of Prince Vsevolod Mstislavich to Southern Pereiaslavl, the men of Pskov and Ladoga came to Novgorod to receive burgraves. In 1136 Novgorod decided to go over to Oleg's sons and summoned the men of Pskov and Ladoga to come to their city. This account shows that senior cities sometimes did not take important decisions without the knowledge of the bytowns. The word "sometimes" is used because, given the indeterminate nature of the relationship at the time, it would not be justified on the basis of one or two instances to conclude that it was necessarily always so. Under the year 1148 it is said that Grand Prince Iziaslav Mstislavich on his arrival in Novgorod called an assembly where the men of Novgorod and Pskov gathered. It cannot be decided whether the men of Pskov came expressly to meet the grand prince, or whether the assembly was attended merely by citizens of Pskov coming to Novgorod on their own business. The indeterminate nature of these relationships is demonstrated further by the fact that sometimes men of Pskov and Ladoga attended the assembly, sometimes only those of Pskov, while there is no mention at all of the inhabitants of other bytowns.

The same indeterminate relations between the senior cities and the junior towns existed in the Land of Rostov. After Bogoliubsky's death[57] the men of Rostov, Suzdal, Pereiaslavl and the *whole retinue,* from the most junior to the senior, gathered for a meeting at Vladimir and decided to call the princes. The Vladimir retinue, instructed by the citizens of Rostov, also joined the retinues of the other cities. The rest of the inhabitants of Vladimir were against it because they refused to submit to those of Rostov who threatened to treat Vladimir as their bytown. Later Vladimir, oppressed by the sons of Rostislav, turned to Rostov and Suzdal together, not solely to the men of Rostov. The meeting was attended only by representatives of Rostov, Suzdal, Pereiaslavl and Vladimir, other towns not even being mentioned.

The chronicler terms as "authorities" the inhabitants of the senior cities who came both for a council and for an assembly. Their decisions were accepted by the lesser towns or bytowns. The chronicler writes about delegates from Novgorod as well as about men of Kiev, Smolensk and Polotsk. Therefore at this time a sharp differentiation should be made between the Novgorod way of life and that of other large Rus cities.

THE ASSEMBLY

In Novgorod the assembly, as in other cities, was of indeterminate nature. Its forms were not clear cut. The word "assembly" meant any undefined meeting, any conversation or negotiation, not specifically a popular convention or a popular council. The princes themselves called assemblies when they had something to announce to the citizens. Usually assemblies were summoned by the princes to announce war or open a campaign. An assembly customarily was roused by ringing the bells, hence the expression "to ring for an assembly." The assembly gathered at familiar places suitable for many people, in Novgorod at the Court of Yaroslav, in Kiev on the square before the Holy Wisdom church. During the earliest period in Russian history the prince called to the council his boyars and city elders, representatives of the inhabitants. When the urban population grew and families fragmented, instead of just the elders there evolved the general popular meeting or assembly. Sometimes in the chronicle even the constituent parts of the assembly indicate that indeed it replaced the earlier council composed of the retinue and elders. Thus Grand Prince

Iziaslav called to an assembly the boyars, all his retinue and the people of Kiev. In one version of the chronicle it is stated that the people stood in assembly, in another that the people of Kiev *sat* close by the Holy Wisdom church. Both versions mention that a great multitude gathered, all Kievans from the greatest to the least. An assembly was rung on occasions important for a city, for example after the loss of a prince when the people were left to fend for themselves, as happened in Vladimir-in-Volhynia in 1097. Or an assembly met in cases of extreme danger, for example that same year when Rostislav's sons sent to Vladimir to surrender the wrongdoers who enticed Prince Davyd to blind Vasilko.[58]

Finally any gathering of dissatisfied citizens against a prince or anyone else was called an assembly. Later such gatherings were deemed conspiracies or rebellions, when in Northeast Russia relationships between the parties became better defined. In the eyes of the people of the Northeast the inhabitants of Novgorod became "assembly people," meaning "rebels." The word "assembly" came to mean rebellion or popular unrest, but during this period it was viewed differently. In 1209 Vsevolod III granted the citizens of Novgorod the right to deal with those who incurred their displeasure. The chronicler adds that the grand prince granted Novgorod its former privilege of loving the good and sentencing to death the wicked.

Whereas it is impossible to distinguish clearly between the way of life in Novgorod and other ancient cities, it is clear that in Novgorod conditions were more favorable for development of an assembly-based system than elsewhere. Here princes changed more often because of their own clan relations, and they more frequently called for popular participation in deciding the most important matters. Here people were more developed as a result of their extensive commerce. Wealth contributed to the emergence of strong families which strove for greater participation in political affairs, main arena of princely activity occurring far away in the South. Strong princes had neither inclination, time nor means to deal with Novgorod affairs. When more powerful princes appeared in the North they immediately began to encroach on Novgorod. In the beginning the Southern princes were still quite powerful, enabling Novgorod to find a defender there against the princes of the North. Novgorod had to deal only with junior princes whereas other cities must deal with those of greater seniority and more power. The direct consequence was that the assembly-based way of life developed more easily in Novgorod than in other cities.

SPECIAL CHARACTER OF NOVGOROD LIFE

On the basis of what we know about contemporary conditions we have explained from the historical point of view the assembly and the growth of its significance in some cities. Yet there is evidence that Novgorod enjoyed special rights granted by Yaroslav I. The question arises as to the nature of the charter. Given the terms which subsequent grand princes vowed to observe, a full picture can be formed of the rights granted to Novgorod. The main, basic right was that of equal footing of prince and burgrave. Let us try to determine if the grant of these rights can be related to the times of Yaroslav I.

The main duty of the prince in Novgorod, as elsewhere, was that of chief judge. In discharging this duty he observed the laws in force in the city. If the prince was born, was raised and lived permanently in Novgorod, he knew the customs and relationships in his homeland, and he knew how to change them in keeping with demands. Yet princes changed all the time. They came from remote places, from Kiev, Volhynia, Smolensk, Chernigov and Suzdal. Newly-arrived princes had no idea of Novgorod customs, just as Novgorod knew nothing of the customs of other Rus regions. Therefore in the princely court misunderstandings were the order of the day. To avoid this, Novgorod demanded that every new prince sit in judgement in the presence of an official elected by the citizens and familiar with the customs and relationships of the country. "Without the burgrave you, O prince, must not judge."

The other right of the prince in Novgorod, as elsewhere, was to appoint administrators in the territories. The inconvenience has been observed which the frequent movement of princes from one throne to another caused the inhabitants. Every prince brought his retinue whose members displaced the previous boyars and aroused dissatisfaction amongst the people. They treated their new fellow-citizens as strangers, trying to win riches at their expense. In Novgorod this inconvenience was even more acute because the change of princes happened more often. For this reason there arose the second and main condition, that the prince appoint Novgorod inhabitants, not his own men, as judges. Because princes changed frequently they could not know who in Novgorod was trustworthy, yet they could not appoint only their own supporters. Therefore the necessary condition was added of not granting any lands without the consent of the burgrave. "Without the burgrave you, O prince, shall not grant any lands." The third princely right was to grant charters, to issue laws known to all, and confirm them in his name. In this matter as well newly-arrived princes could not manage without the guidance of a local official. They were unaware of the customary limits of these rights, and might harm the common good in favor of private individuals who were their supporters. Hence the third, necessary, condition. "Without the burgrave, prince, you must not issue any charters."

Constant change of princes, usually hostile to each other, resulted in other troubles. Every new prince was hostile to his predecessor and so viewed everything this predecessor had done. Officials appointed by a descendant of Oleg naturally failed to please a descendant of Monomakh. A charter issued by Mstislav's descendant was considered illegal by Yury's. Thus every change of prince brought a change of officials and loss of previously granted rights. To prevent this every new prince undertook, first, not to dismiss anybody without a trial, without cause; second, not to amend charters issued by his predecessors. "Without cause you, prince, may not deprive any man of his landed property, nor may you amend charters." The burgrave was an indispensable official at every trial and retrial.

Because the different roles of prince and burgrave was the main characteristic of the Novgorod way of life, and of the main law of Novgorod, and because this right was granted by Yaroslav I, the burgrave perforce became a popular official, one who limited princely power. Yet events demonstrate that a burgrave of such authority appeared in Novgorod only much later. Monomakh and his son Mstislav sent burgraves from Kiev to Novgorod, from which it could be concluded that originally the burgrave was the same as the later vicegerent, a boyar sent by the grand prince from Tver or Moscow to represent him. It is difficult to determine the role of the burgrave as compared to the prince when in Novgorod lacking a burgrave there already was a prince, namely Vsevolod, son of Mstislav. What was the role of the burgrave alongside the prince, as his official, and not as a local man? Naturally he was the prince's helper, assisting him in dispensing justice and executing his orders. Mainly he exercised authority during the prince's absence. The possibility of the burgrave's coexistence with the prince is clear from the example of Polotsk.

Only one question remains, namely how and when the burgrave became a mayor, transformed from a princely into a municipal official? If the main duty of the burgrave was to act on behalf of the prince during his absence from the city, a burgrave was most needed in the city from which the prince absented himself most frequently. Certainly changes of princes were most frequent in Novgorod. If a change of prince was the result of dissatisfaction a burgrave was needed to execute princely functions until the arrival of a new prince. Might an official appointed by a banished prince remain in office? A change of prince necessarily meant replacement of his burgrave. Who would act in the prince's place until a new prince arrived? The city must elect the burgrave. Even later, when the prince resided in the city, appointment of the burgrave was not completely removed from the town's influence. The prince chose the burgrave together with the citizens. If at first the burgrave was appointed by the prince, his term of office naturally depended on the prince.

Subsequently, when the burgrave became a mayor, a municipal official, his term depended on the city. It has been shown that burgraves always changed in the wake of change of princes, following the victory of this or that party. At the same time former burgraves sometimes assumed the position of the current or acting burgrave. There is only one mention that, during burgrave elections, and all other things being equal, age was taken into account. Thus in 1211 Tverdislav surrendered the office of burgrave to Dmitry Yakunich, who was older. Sometimes a burgrave removed from office in Novgorod became a burgrave in a bytown. The people of the bytown might reject him, perhaps because of some connection with city factions. Nonetheless it is clear that burgraves usually were elected from the same circle of boyar families.

Everything noted above about the transformation of a princely into an urban official becomes clear from the example of the office of chiliarch. Everywhere the chiliarch was at the prince's side as his official. The chronicle tells that this or that prince gave the office to someone from his entourage. In Novgorod this office, together with that of burgrave, became subject to local elections.

It appears, then, that the right of the burgrave to have equal footing with the prince was not granted to Novgorod by Yaroslav I, but took place later. If this is so, obviously neither can other conditions mentioned in treaties which Novgorod concluded with grand princes be related to the era of Yaroslav I. For example, "From the land of Suzdal you must neither govern Novgorod, nor dispose of its territories," or "You must not judge men of Novgorod while in the Lower Towns."[59] It is known that Monomakh governed Novgorod, judged men of Novgorod and granted territories while in Kiev. It should be added that Novgorod, when demanding oaths from the grand princes to comply with these conditions, and citing examples of previous princes swearing similar oaths, never mentioned Yaroslav I.

This fact is even more significant because in other instances Novgorod referred to Yaroslav's charters. The content of these charters can be surmised according to circumstances surrounding their mention. In 1228 Novgorod quarrelled with its prince Yaroslav Vsevolodovich because he violated Yaroslav's charters by imposing new duties and dispatching judges to the territories. The following year Prince Mikhail arrived in Novgorod and kissed the cross, confirming all of Yaroslav's charters. At the same time he freed the peasants from paying tax for five years. In 1230 this same Yaroslav again was invited to Novgorod, conceded Novgorod's demands and kissed the cross to confirm all Yaroslav's charters. In 1339 when Grand Prince Ivan Danilovich[60] sent to Novgorod to collect money to fulfill the khan's demands, he was told "Such as this has not happened here since the creation of the world. For you, prince, kissed the cross to collect only the customary duties, and to uphold Yaroslav's charters."

All these are instances when Novgorod cited Yaroslav's charters. Inasmuch as all of these instances treated financial matters, it may be concluded that Yaroslav's charters touched only financial matters. This is indeed so. In the chronicle it is stated that Novgorod received a similar charter from Yaroslav I. Only in the *Book of Degrees*[61] is it written that Yaroslav I allowed Novgorod to receive as prince whichever member of his clan it wished.

Yet, first, Novgorod never mentioned this right as emanating from Yaroslav I when, for example, they refused Sviatopolk's son in place of their favorite Mstislav. Surely they would have cited this right first of all, yet never mentioned it, finding other reasons, namely that Sviatopolk had left them, and the instructions of Grand Prince Vsevolod. Secondly, it is written in the chronicles that Novgorod was granted civic freedoms by the previous princes, great-grandfathers of the current princes, and not by Yaroslav, and this is confirmed by the same *Book of Degrees*. In view of these circumstances it may be assumed with certainty that the special character of Novgorod life evolved slowly, as a result of familiar historical conditions, not as a result of Yaroslav's grant, which is not mentioned in any chronicle except for the *Book of Degrees*.

VIEW OF A TOWN

As far as the internal appearance of a Rus town is concerned, during this period it consisted of several parts. There was the town proper, a space surrounded by walls. Later new settlements grew up around the town, which in turn were walled. This is why a town had double fortifications, the inner and outer town. The inner town also was called a citadel,[62] the outer a fortress.[63] The settlements positioned around the main town or the citadel were called *suburbs*.[64] Walls were made either of stone or (mainly) of timber, with parts made of planks. Towers and gates were named according to location, for example the Eastern gates, or because of their ornaments, for example the Golden or Silver gates, or to the part of the town to which they were close, or because of their inhabitants. In Kiev there were the Jewry or Polish gates. Names could derive from churches, icons or other factors, for example Watergate in the Novgorod citadel, facing the river. Two ramparts are mentioned, the space between them being called the grassed area. A suburb was divided into "ends" [quarters], and "ends" into streets.[65]

Town buildings at that time were made solely of timber. Churches were constructed both of stone and timber. With respect to churches, in Novgorod from 1054 until 1229 there were sixty-nine, of which fifteen probably were built of timber, because either this was directly mentioned, or it was said that they were built of logs.[66] As for the rest, nothing is said. The sixty-nine included monastery churches. It is difficult to think that there were many churches in Novgorod before 1054. This number of churches in almost the richest city of Rus, second only to Kiev, may suggest the number of churches in Kiev.

Among urban structures chronicles mention timber bridges, which could be dismantled. The Novgorod Chronicle notes construction of bridges over the Volkhov river. In Kiev in 1115 Vladimir Monomakh built a bridge over the Dnieper. The sources mention other communal buildings, for example prisons or dungeons. We know they had windows (small openings). Iziaslav's retinue advised him to call the imprisoned Vseslav of Polotsk to the window and kill him. When the freeing of Igor Olgovich from prison is described the chronicler says that Grand Prince Iziaslav gave orders "to break the dungeon over him, and they took him from the dungeon when he was very ill and put him in a cell." In the *Book of Degrees,* when the miracles of St. Boris and St. Gleb are described, it is mentioned that Grand Prince Sviatopolk Iziaslavich put two men in prison without investigating their guilt, on the basis of slanderous accusation, and forgot about them. They prayed to St. Boris and St. Gleb and one night "they were locked behind doors, but found a way out, thanks to a ladder." One of the prisoners was freed miraculously from his fetters, came to church and told everybody what had happened. They went to the prison and "saw the keys and lock intact, and the ladder to go up and down lying outside." Every town had a marketplace, market and fairs. It is known from the chronicle that markets took place on Fridays.

FIRES

Because structures were built almost exclusively of wood, fires must have been devastating. In Novgorod between 1054 and 1228 there were eleven large fires. In 1097 the Zarechie[67] and the citadel burned down. In 1102 the residences from the stream near the Slavno as far as the church of St. Elias were destroyed. In 1113 one half of the city and the town of Kromny were consumed. In 1139 the market area as well as ten churches perished in the flames. In 1144 the buildings on the hill burned down. In 1152 all the market with eight churches and a ninth, the Varangian, or Latin church,[68] were destroyed. In 1175 three churches were lost. In 1177 the Nerev quarter with five churches were incinerated. Two churches and many residential courts burned in 1181. In 1194 during the summer, in All Saints week,[69] one residence in Yaryshev street caught fire and a great conflagration began in which three churches burned. The flames spread to St. Luke street and the next day another ten churches were lost.

At the end of the week a new fire broke out. Seven churches and some large houses were consumed. People were driven from the houses and had to move into the fields. Later the Gorodishche and Liudin quarters succumbed. Fires raged from All Saints Day [May 31] until the Dormition [August 15].[70] The same year fires raged in Ladoga and Rusa. In Novgorod in 1211 fifteen churches and 4,300 houses burned down. The entire Zarechie area was destroyed in 1217. Those who took refuge with their possessions in stone churches also perished with all their property. In the Varangian church all the wares of the German merchants were lost. Fifteen wooden churches burned down, together with the spires and vestibules of the stone churches. Among other towns in 1183 a great fire in Vladimir-on-the-Kliazma is mentioned. Nearly the whole town was destroyed, including thirty-two churches. Half the town was destroyed in 1192, including fourteen churches. In 1198 a serious fire in the same town is mentioned. Sixteen churches and almost half of the houses burned. Almost all of Rostov perished in 1211, including fifteen churches. In 1221 all of Yaroslavl, including seventeen churches, burned. Once again fire destroyed Vladimir in 1227, including twenty-seven churches. The following year there was another fire in the princely mansions, and two churches burned. Almost all of Kiev burned in 1124, and about six hundred churches (??)[71] were lost. In 1183 all of Goroden was destroyed, set on fire by lightning.

POPULATION

Knowing the outward appearance of the Rus town at that time, it is time to deal with its population. The retinue and its various elements lived in towns, where the population clearly differed from the retinue. The retinue of Kievan princes differed from the people in Kiev, the retinue in Vladimir from the people of Vladimir. In the assembly the people of Kiev are set apart from the retinue. Who made up the population and how was it divided?

Contemporary sources mention traders and craftsmen, people occupied in industries of various types. There is no need to cite information about merchants, for they are mentioned very often. Rostov called the people of Vladimir stonemasons. In Novgorod the silversmith-weighmaster is mentioned. In Vyshgorod gardeners with their elders[72] are mentioned. It is likely that during this as in later periods, people engaged in the same occupation lived together in particular quarters and had their own wardens or elders. The names of the Novgorod "ends" [quarters] such as the Carpenters' or Potters'[73] point to that possibility. There is information about peasants in towns. Probably what is meant is simple folk, commoners,[74] or perhaps even the entire population as opposed to the retinue.

Thus for the year 1152 it is stated that Ivan Berladnik besieged the Galich town of Ushitsa, where Prince Yaroslav's garrison was. They fought very bravely although the peasants rushed through a breach in the walls to join Ivan. Three hundred went over to him. In this instance the peasants are the inhabitants of Ushitsa, contrasted with the soldiers of the garrison, the princely retinue which fought hard against Berladnik, whereas peasants joined him. Then, as later, the urban population was divided into hundreds. Direct evidence of the names of hundredmen of special status are found in the sources. The close relationship of the chiliarch and townsmen during both peace and war is clear.

The men of authority in a capital city were the prince and his reeve. In a non-capital town there was the burgrave, who also probably had his own reeve. There were chiliarchs, hundredmen, tenmen,[75] quarter and street elders, or elders for particular trades. Among officials in the courts and administration were constables, criers and court heralds.[76] In Novgorod

wardens and constables were dispatched by Prince Iziaslav Mstislavich to
call the people into the streets or invite them to banquets given by the prince.

It seems that there were no special officers to uphold law and order
in the towns. Under 1115 in the chronicle there is a description of the
translation of the relics of St. Boris and St. Gleb. The chronicler writes
that Monomakh, seeing the crowds pushing from all sides and disturb-
ing the proceedings, ordered money thrown among the people to make
them move back. Apart from the native population in some trading towns
or cities, in particular Kiev and Novgorod, there were foreigners living
on a permanent or temporary basis (settlers). In Novgorod there were
German merchants who had their own church (the Varangian). In Kiev
permanently, or at least at this time, were Jews who lived in their own
quarter or street, after which one of the gates was called Jewry. The
Polish gate in Kiev points to the existence of a Polish quarter or street.
Latins are mentioned among the people of Kiev for the year 1174.

LOCAL GOVERNMENT

Concerning subdivisions of local government, mention has been made of
rural settlements[77] and also of staging posts.[78] Thus it is said of Vsevolod
III that he accompanied his daughter as far as the third staging post.[79] It
is not known whether at that time a staging post was also an administrative center. Also it is uncertain whether the rural settlements and staging
posts were synonymous. Both evolved from being a place for a temporary halt by the ruler to being a permanent administrative center.

Apart from towns, some populated places dotted around the countryside were called free settlements.[80] This designation was applied to a
newly founded habitation enjoying special privileges such as tax exemp-
tions[81] or freedom from certain imposts. From contemporary sources it
is evident that free settlements, like villages, could be privately owned or
obtained by purchase.

The rural as opposed to the town population generally was referred to
as "peasants." This population consisted of the free as well as the unfree,
private property of the prince, boyars and others. There is information
about villages with household and ordinary slaves.[82] What is written about
hired hands and bondsmen[83] in the period before the death of Yaroslav I
is also relevant for this era. It should be noted that only in the Novgorod
Chronicle is the expression "full bondsman" equivalent to an earlier term
so used.[84]

NOMADS

In addition to the population described in the Southeastern areas of Rus possessions, on the borders of the Kiev, Pereiaslavl and Chernigov principalities there was a foreign population known under the general term Karakalpaks, and specifically Torks, Berendey, Koui and Turpei. Their importance and participation in the events of this era have been mentioned. The chronicle makes clear that they were ruled by their various petty princes such as the famous Konduvdey. Their life clearly was semi-nomadic and semi-settled. Most probably in summer they migrated to the borderland steppe with their camps and flocks. Thus in 1151 they obtained leave from Iziaslav to go to their camps, flocks and families. In winter they lived in towns to shelter their families from enemy attacks. "If you give us each a better town," they told Mstislav Iziaslavich, "we will come over to your side." Sviatoslav Olgovich complained that his towns were empty, that only kennelmen and Polovetsians lived in them. It may be assumed that the Polovetsians were not hostile but rather his "own" pagans, the Karakalpaks. Churnay, prince of the Torks, lived in his own town. The long-used term "pagans" makes clear that the Karakalpaks were not Christians. Polygamy is another indication of their paganism, for it is related that Churnay had two wives, although perhaps some of the Karakalpaks converted to Christianity. Apart from Karakalpaks, both in the South and the North "wanderers"[85] are mentioned, probably groups or roving bands similar to the cossacks of later periods.

SIZE AND NUMBER OF TOWNS

There is no indication in the sources of population numbers in Rus towns and territories during this era. We may form an idea of the number of towns in various principalities by collating the place names from the chronicle, dividing them approximately by the principalities. First, it cannot be assumed that all place names found their way into the chronicles. This is particularly true for principalities remote from main centers such as Polotsk, Smolensk, Riazan, Novgorod or Suzdal.

The second difficulty is that it is impossible to determine whether a given place name represents a town or a village. In the principality of Kiev, on the basis of the chronicle, up to forty towns may be counted. In Volhynia there is a similar number. In Galich there are about forty, in the Turov principality over ten. In the Chernigov principality, together with Severia and Kursk and the land of the Viatichians, there are about seventy towns. In Riazan principality there are about fifteen towns, in Pereiaslavl about forty, Suzdal about twenty, Smolensk about eight, Polotsk about sixteen, and Novgorod about fifteen. In all of the Rus territories more than three hundred towns are mentioned.

It is known that princes experienced difficulties because of sparse population in their territories and endeavored to people them by attracting settlers from all quarters. One of the main methods of settling new people was to bring in prisoners of war and slaves bought in the market. Prince Yaropolk transferred the population of a whole town (Drutsk) from an enemy territory to his own. In princely villages lived a population consisting of household slaves and bondsmen.

OBSTACLES TO POPULATION GROWTH

The endeavors of the princes to increase the population encountered obstacles. These included political obstacles such as internecine and foreign wars, and natural obstacles such as famine and pestilence. Internecine wars in the period from 1055 to 1228, calculated as years of domestic warfare as opposed to peaceful years, numbered eighty years of conflict and ninety-three without, just thirteen years' difference. Roughly speaking, almost every other year there was war, some continuing for twelve to seventeen years without interruption. This sad impression is somewhat softened when the size of the Rus domains is considered, and that internecine wars did not rage everywhere simultaneously. Thus the Kiev principality witnessed internecine war during this era no more than twenty-three times, the Chernigov principality no more than twenty, Volhynia fifteen, Galich until Roman's death no more than six, Turov four, Polotsk eighteen, Smolensk six, Riazan seven, Suzdal eleven and Novgorod twelve times.

Damage sustained by Rus territories from internecine wars may seem considerably less because of the above factors. Still, we need not go to the other extreme and declare this damage negligible. Thus some students of history[86] have noted that "usually there were few troops. Inhabitants along the road, indeed, had to supply them with food which everywhere was plentiful. There was nothing else that could be taken from them. People who lived away from the roads along which they passed might live in peace."

While Rus forces were not numerous, it should not be forgotten that they were accompanied almost always by large groups of Polovetsians, infamous for their looting. Perhaps there was nothing apart from food the

Rus forces could seize from the inhabitants of the countryside. On the other hand, enemy forces took the people themselves as prisoners, their main loot. They beat old people and burned homes. The contemporary notion of warfare meant devastating, burning, looting and taking prisoners. Mstislav Mstislavich, by sending the Novgorod levies in 1216 *to forage* in his territory of Toropets, ordered "Go forage, but do not take captives." If troops must be threatened to prevent them taking prisoners in the lands of allies, it is easy to guess what they did in enemy territory.

It is wrong to assume that princes fought only each other and not the civilian population, that they wanted to rule the towns they attacked, and consequently that it was contrary to their interests to destroy them. Princes fought each other whereas their troops, mainly the Polovetsians, fought the civilian population, unable to conceive any other way of waging war. Oleg Sviatoslavich fought for the territory of Chernigov, then when he conquered it he loosed his Polovetsian allies loot it. In 1160 the Polovetsians brought by Iziaslav Davydovich against Smolensk took there ten thousand prisoners apart from those they slew. Iziaslav Mstislavich's expedition against the Land of Rostov in 1149 cost that land seven thousand inhabitants.

Apart from constant participation in wars between the princes, the Polovetsians often assaulted the Rus lands on their own account. The chronicler records thirty-seven significant attacks by Polovetsians but it seems that there were others, recorded neither in detail nor in chronological order. The principalities of Chernigov and Pereiaslavl suffered terribly. Sviatoslav Olgovich said that his towns were empty, only kennelmen and Polovetsians remaining. Vladimir Glebovich of Pereiaslavl said that his territory was empty because of the Polovetsians. The principality of Kiev suffered from their attacks as well. The lands of Volhynia, Turov, Polotsk and Novgorod suffered much from the Lithuanians and Chud, particularly towards the end of this period. In the first twenty-eight years of the twelfth century Lithuanian raids are mentioned eight times. The Polotsk Chronicle has not survived and therefore the terrible ravages inflicted there can be studied only from information contained in the German chronicles and the *Tale of Igor's Campaign*. Perhaps the principalities of Riazan and Murom also suffered from Polovetsians and other barbarians living on their borders. The most peaceful, from the point of view of internecine wars and barbarian attacks, was the principality of Rostov or Suzdal, a fact which must claim our special attention. This circumstance contributed not only to the preservation of population in

Suzdal, it also possibly attracted people from other, more dangerous places. When from ninety-three peaceful years we subtract forty-five of the more significant Polovetsian and Lithuanian attacks, few years remain when some territory or other was not ravaged.

Besides political disasters, natural calamities also are mentioned, such as famine and pestilence. As far as the South is concerned, the grain-rich Little Russia,[87] no frequent complaints about bad harvests appear in the chronicle. Such descriptions are found only in passing. In 1193 Prince Sviatoslav of Kiev said that it was impossible to march against the Polovetsians because the grain crop had failed. Obviously famine might follow when an enemy attack or princely wars halted work in the fields. Still, this could decrease the number of consumers because the enemy killed the inhabitants or took them prisoner. As for the Rostov land, the chronicle mentions crop failure in 1070.

The Novgorod territory suffered famine more frequently. For the year 1127 it is written that snow did not melt until St. James's Day [July 25]. The autumn frost damaged the grain crops and there was famine in winter. An eighth measure[88] of grain cost half a grivna. The following year also was famine too, and times were hard. An eighth measure of grain was one grivna. People ate linden leaves and birch bark, insects, straw, moss and horseflesh. They died of hunger. Dead bodies lay in the streets, in the market place and on the roads everywhere. Workers were hired to remove corpses from the city. Since the stench made it impossible to leave the houses, disaster struck everyone. Fathers and mothers sent their children away on boats, or gave them away to merchants. Some died and others dispersed to foreign lands. In 1137, for the whole summer, a large measure of grain was sold for up to seven rezans.[89] Such a high price was because there was no food from surrounding lands such as Suzdal, Smolensk or Polotsk, clear evidence that Novgorod was not self-sufficient in food.

In 1161 there were clear skies all through summer, and the rye crop was scorched. In autumn frost destroyed the summer crops. The winter was warm and rainy. As a result a small measure[90] of grain went up to seven kunas,[91] and the chronicle says great grief prevailed among the people and great poverty. Four chetverts of rye in 1170 sold in Novgorod for four grivnas, bread for two nogats and honey for ten kunas a pud. It seems that these high prices resulted from Bogoliubsky's plundering army and cessation of trade with the Suzdal lands. In 1188 bread was two nogats, and a four chetverts of rye six grivnas. Finally, in 1215, terrible famine and pestilence spread thanks to early autumn frosts and Prince Yaroslav's embargo on grain imports coming through Torzhok. Between 1054 and 1228 the chronicle mentions famine and high prices just seven times. High mortality is mentioned by the chronicle in 1092 in the South. In Polotsk people suddenly fell to some kind of plague, which contemporaries blamed on the dead riding through the air.[92] The plague started in Drutsk. The weather in summer was clear and there were numerous fires in the forests and marshes. In the South many died of various illnesses. Undertakers (probably in Kiev) between St. Philip's Day [May 3] and Shrovetide sold seven thousand coffins.

The Novgorod Chronicle mentions great pestilence and a cattle plague occurring in the city in 1158. Many people, horses and cattle died. The stench was so bad that it was impossible to cross the city to the markets either by the moat or through the fields. In 1203 a plague struck horses in Novgorod and the surrounding villages. The Suzdal Chronicle mentions for the year 1187 that not a single residence was without someone sick. There were homes where nobody could go to draw water.

There was no medication given in such cases, although it is known that there were physicians in Rus. The Rus Justice[93] mentions physician's fees. Thus in the *Life* of St. Agapit of the Caves monastery it is said that in his time there was a famous Armenian physician in Kiev who needed to look just once at the patient to tell the day and time of his death. St. Agapit treated people with herbs from which he prepared food for himself. The Armenian, when he looked at them, said they were Alexandrian herbs, and the saint laughed at his ignorance. Prince Sviatoslav (Sviatosha) Davydovich of Chernigov had a skillful physician called Peter, who was from Syria. Vladimirko of Galich, affected by paralysis, was placed in dill, but it is not clear whether it was a herb called thus, or a hot bath, which also is signified by the same term.[94]

So it was that the population grew or diminished on the great Northeastern plain which, in relation to its size, was very sparsely populated. Following the death of Yaroslav I the borders of the Rus possessions did not extend to the west, south or southeast. Internecine wars prevented the Rus from making conquests of Hungarian, Polish or Lithuanian territories. On the contrary, Rus was forced to abandon to the Germans its possessions on the Baltic. In the South and Southeast princely warfare and the Polovetsians halted expansion. There were losses here as well, because Tmutorokan[95] no longer belonged to Rus.

There remained only one direction, namely the Northeast, where expansion might continue without hindrance. Internally divided, the wild Chud could not offer strong opposition. Suzdal, the Rus principality of the Northeast, for obvious reasons was more capable than any other land of offensives. On the other hand Novgorod was bound to the Northeast by advantageous local trade, and rich tribute in silver and furs. Thus Rus possessions were found along the Northern Dvina and Kama, while Novgorod expeditions reached the Ural mountains. Even so, it is best to speak with caution about Novgorod territory stretching from the Gulf of Finland to the Urals because of the story about attacks on tribute collectors in the area beyond the portage, and Yadrey's expedition against the Yugra,[96] demonstrate the uncertain character of relations there.

Novgorod was not alone in having possessions beyond the portage. Suzdal's peasants (subjects) were there as well. Ustiug belonged to the princes of Rostov. One thing is certain. The Novgorod colony of Viatka, although at first independent of the metropolis, was in the Kama territory. The princes of Suzdal, by constructing Nizhny Novgorod in the land of the Mordvinians, gained a strong foothold at the mouth of the Oka river. In summary, the borders of Rus domains at this time were characterized by losses in the West and South and new acquisitions in the North and East, indicating the main direction of historical development.

TRADE

The concentration of population in certain places was assisted by their convenient situation in relation to trade. The great trade route of the Northeastern plain was the waterway from the Baltic to the Black Sea. Therefore the most important cities of Rus were those situated at both ends of this route, Novgorod the entrepôt of Northern goods, and Kiev the entrepôt of goods in the South. Novgorod merchants engaged in foreign trade with countries of the Baltic Sea. The Swedes in 1142 attacked Rus merchants returning from overseas. This is confirmed by foreign sources. On the other hand foreign merchants lived permanently in Novgorod. There is extant an agreement between Novgorod and the Germans and Gotlanders concluded during the reign of Prince Yaroslav Vladimirovich about 1195. On the basis of this agreement and other foreign sources, a detailed picture of foreign trade in Novgorod emerges. German merchants coming to trade were divided into seafaring and overland merchant guilds. This arrangement also is supported by the Rus chronicle, saying that Varangians arrived overland in 1201. These and others were divided also into winter and summer merchants. The winter merchants arrived in autumn, probably at the end of the navigation season, staying in Novgorod until the spring, when they returned overseas and the summer merchants arrived.

According to this agreement, if a Novgorod envoy, hostage or priest were killed overseas, or a German in Novgorod, the fine was twenty grivnas of silver for each, for a merchant ten grivnas. If an innocent man was put in chains, the fine was twelve grivnas paid in old kunas for the dishonor he suffered. If a man was struck with a weapon or stick, the fine was six grivnas in old kunas. If the wife or daughter of a man were struck, the prince received forty grivnas in old kunas and the same amount was paid to the victim. If somebody removed the headdress of someone's wife or daughter and her hair could be seen, six old grivnas were paid for that dishonor. If a fight occurred, but without bloodletting, the witnesses, both Rus and German, assembled and cast lots to settle the matter, swearing on oath declaring who was in the right. If a Varangian claimed money from a Rus, or a Rus from a Varangian, and the debtor refused to pay, the plaintiff, accompanied by twelve witnesses, swore an oath and took what was his due. The Germans in Novgorod and the men of Novgorod in German lands could not be imprisoned. Instead reparation was sought from the guilty party. Anyone acting violently towards a female slave, without raping her, paid one grivna for her dishonor. If she was raped, she was given her freedom.[97]

Men of Novgorod received foreign merchants in their city, and went abroad to buy goods. They were interested in acquiring foreign silver while not paying their own silver for foreign goods. Therefore they aimed to buy abroad goods which they could resell to visiting merchants from other Baltic countries, and make a profit. It is clear why they pushed further and further to the Northeast, to the Ural mountain range, because there they received tribute in furs, which were very valuable for their foreign trade. Yet the Rus territories themselves also were rich in fur and other raw materials. In Kiev were Greek goods which Novgorod could buy and then sell with profit in Northwestern Europe. Consequently many from Novgorod resided in Kiev, where they had their own church or temple of St. Michael, apparently close to the marketplace. There were many Novgorod merchants also in the Suzdal territory. Prince Mikhail of Chernigov, on leaving Novgorod, asked the men of Novgorod to send merchants to Chernigov.

Nothing more need be said about the importance of the Greek trade centered on Kiev after what we have noted when discussing the first period of Russian history. A famous Jewish traveller, Benjamin of Tudela,[98] found Rus merchants in Constantinople and Alexandria. It is interesting that nowhere does the chronicler mention Greek merchants in Kiev, while clearly indicating Western or Latin merchants. It is very likely that Greeks rarely hazarded the dangerous route along the Dnieper, through the steppe, content instead to offer their goods to Rus merchants

Novgorod Silver Grivna (Grivna of New Martens)
Twelfth Century. Average weight 197 grams of silver

in Constantinople. Benjamin of Tudela says about the Byzantines that they liked their pleasures, eating and drinking while sitting under their own vines and fig trees. From the words of Kuzma of Kiev, weeping over the dead body of Andrei Bogoliubsky, it is known that merchants from Constantinople sometimes visited Vladimir-Zalessk, and Piano di Carpini[99] says that after the Mongol invasion merchants from Constantinople continued to visit Kiev. These merchants turned out to be Italians.[100] From foreign sources it is known that merchants from Regensburg, Ems and Vienna lived in Kiev.

It is difficult to imagine that in this period trade links with the East were cut. For the year 1184 the chronicle notes that the princes marching against the Polovetsians met merchants returning from the Polovetsian lands. It is unlikely that they were Rus merchants trading with the Polovetsians. They easily could have been foreign merchants from Eastern lands travelling to Kiev through Polovetsian lands. Finally, thirteenth-century travellers tell about cities on the shores of the Black and Azov seas serving as entrepôts for exchange between Rus and the Orient. Benedict, a monk who was a fellow traveller of Piano di Carpini, relates that in the olden days before Ornas was destroyed by the Tatars, Rus, Alan and Khazar[101] merchants visited. William of Rubruck[102] says that at Soldaia [Sudak], a town on the south shore of Taurida opposite Sinope, all merchants travelling from Turkey to the Northern countries stopped on their way. This was also a staging post for merchants travelling from Rus and Northern countries to Turkey.

Apart from Novgorod and Kiev merchants, the people of Smolensk, Polotsk and Vitebsk engaged in foreign trade. Information on their trade can be gleaned from the agreement concluded in 1229 by Prince Mstislav Davydovich of Smolensk with Riga and the Gotland coast. It is clear from the text that good relations between Smolensk and the Germans were violated for some reason. To prevent such a "loss of love" and allow Rus merchants in Riga and on the Gotland coast, and Germans in Smolensk, to live in peace and assure good relations for all time, a *law* (which means an agreement) was written. It was agreed that ten grivnas of silver be paid for killing a freeman, one grivna for a bondsman. For beating a bondsman, one grivna of kunas. For bodily damage, five grivnas in silver. For a broken tooth, three grivnas. For being hit with a wooden stick and drawing blood, one and a half grivnas. For being hit on the face, for hair-pulling or whipping, three quarters of a grivna of silver must be paid. For assault without drawing blood, one and a half silver grivnas. Priests and envoys received twice these amounts. The guilty party might be put in stocks, prison or in irons only if no bail were paid. Debts were to be paid in the first instance by foreigners. A foreigner could not produce as witnesses one or two of his compatriots. The plaintiff had no right to force the respondent to trial by iron or to challenge him to a duel. If somebody found a foreigner with his wife, he took for his dishonor ten grivnas of silver. The same amount was to be paid if a free women was violated who previously was not noted for debauchery.[103]

When the portage reeve[104] learned that a German merchant arrived at Volok (between the Dvina and the Dnieper), he ordered the portage workers to take the merchants across with their goods and assure their safety because the people of Smolensk had suffered much at the hands of the pagans (Lithuanians). The Germans had to cast lots who was to go first and when there was a Rus merchant among them, he was to go last. On arrival in the city the German merchants were to present the princess a bale of cloth, and the portage reeve must be given gloves from Gotland.

If goods were lost at the portage, the workers there were collectively responsible. Foreign merchants could trade without any hindrance and without any problems. They could go freely to another town with their merchandise. Goods taken outside the trading court could not be returned. A plaintiff might not force a defendant into any court save that of the prince of Smolensk. Guard could not be mounted over a foreigner without informing a senior official.

Should someone lodge claims for foreign goods he might not seize them by force, he must follow due process according to the laws of the country. For weighing goods the weighmaster[105] was to be paid one Smolensk kuna for each twenty-four puds. When buying precious metals Germans must pay the weighmaster one nogat for each grivna of gold, and for one grivna of silver two vekshas,[106] for a silver vessel one kuna per grivna, although when selling he paid nothing. When buying goods for silver he must pay for a grivna one Smolensk kuna.

To check the scales, one set of standards was to be kept in the church of the Mother of God on the Hill, and a second set in the German church of Our Lady. These standards must be used to verify the pud given by Germans to the portagers. Foreigners could trade without paying tolls. They were not obliged to go to war together with the locals, but might join them if they wished. When a foreigner caught a thief near his goods he might do with him as he wished. Foreigners paid no judicial court dues, either to the prince or to the reeve, or to a community court.

The bishop of Riga, the master of the Order and all local officials of the entire lands of Riga granted free navigation and passage rights on the Dvina, from the mouth to the upper reaches on water and on the banks, to every Riga or German merchant travelling up and down the river. In the event of difficulties he might land his goods on the bank, and if he hired men to help him they were not to take more than was agreed when they were hired.

Smolensk trade with other Rus lands is described in the chronicle for the year 1216 when Prince Yaroslav Vsevolodovich arrested fifteen Smolensk merchants coming to trade in his territory. From the words of Kuzma of Kiev, lamenting over the body of his prince, we learn of the visits of foreign and Rus merchants in Vladimir-Zalessk.

The geographical location of Rus between Europe and Asia contributed to the increase in Rus trade during this era. As there were no roundabout sea routes, Rus played an important part in trade. Other reasons included increased trading activity of the North German cities, which needed to develop close trade relations in the East. There was a decline in piracy in the Baltic because the Scandinavian nations abandoned their Viking ways. The waterways were more convenient for trade. The princes took care to develop profitable trade. The character of the population was peaceful. There was religious tolerance and respect for foreigners, and readiness to grant them various privileges.

Given these circumstances beneficial for trade development, the difficulties encountered by trade at this time also need mention. Quarrels with foreigners are cited, leading to cessation of trade relations. Thus in 1134 Novgorod merchants were imprisoned in Denmark. In 1188 the men of Novgorod suffered the same fate from Germans overseas, causing merchants to be banned from going abroad in the spring. The city refused to send an envoy to the Varangians [Germans], whose own envoys were sent home in disgrace. In 1201 the Varangian envoys again were sent home without peace being concluded. In autumn, when they came by land to parley, Novgorod made peace on its own terms. There are only three instances [recorded] of quarrels with foreigners, not counting the account of a Swedish attack on merchant ships sailing to Novgorod.

In may be concluded therefore that disputes presented few difficulties for trade. Considerably greater obstacles to foreign trade between Kievans and Greeks were created by the Polovetsians, who robbed merchant ships sailing on the Dnieper. Sometimes princes with a large retinue had to hasten to defend the Greeks. Mstislav Iziaslavich complained that Polovetsians cut off all Rus trade routes. Civil wars and interprincely conflicts offered yet another obstacle in the way of external and domestic trade development. During the two-day sack of Kiev by Bogoliubsky's troops, when according to the chronicler no one was spared, foreign merchants undoubtedly also sustained losses. Later, in 1174, Yaroslav Iziaslavich took much money from all Kievans, including Latins and merchants. In 1203 the Polovetsians and Riurik, after taking Kiev, plundered the city terribly, taking half the goods of the foreign merchants. In this case some allowances were made for them, but they could not easily forget their losses. Novgorod merchants suffered because their fellow-citizens quarreled with the various princes of Kiev and Suzdal.

In 1161, when Rostislav Mstislavich heard that his son was arrested in Novgorod, he ordered the arrest of Novgorod merchants in Kiev and threw them in the Peresechen dungeon, where in a single night fourteen died. Following this event Rosatislav ordered the rest to be freed and taken to other towns. Information on Novgorod merchants arrested in

Suzdal territories is encountered on seven occasions. In 1215 Yaroslav Vsevolodovich arrested in Torzhok more than two thousand Novgorod citizens and merchants. If these difficulties are taken into account, their numbers compared to the number of years in this period, it must be surmised that there were few obstacles to trade.

MONETARY SYSTEM

Problems of trade were associated closely with the question of the monetary system. The general name corresponding to the present word "money" was the word "marten" (kuna), which superseded the word encountered during the earliest period, namely "cattle."[107] The highest denomination was the grivna, a piece of metal in a familiar form, equal to a specific weight which also was called a grivna. That the grivna was a coin in circulation is clear from a somewhat (though not very much) later item of information. In 1288 the prince of Volhynia, Vladimir Vasilkovich, ordered silver vessels and silver and gold cups be broken before his eyes, and grivnas minted from them.

There was another coin, the "silver,"[108] whose existence is clearly indicated in the chronicle for the year 1115. "Vladimir ordered various kinds of cloth to be cut and distributed among the people, and silver pieces to be cast." There is clear evidence concerning the existence of leather money, both in foreign and Rus sources. One chronograph says directly "Kunas also are marten pelts." In support of the contrasting view, that these were actually figurative terms for metal coinage, a passage may be cited from the chronicle for the year 1066. "They plundered the princely court and took a countless amount of gold and silver and martens and white cloth."

Taking together these words, in their context, it may be concluded that *martens* and *squirrels* were necessary adjuncts and had a relationship to *gold* and *silver*. Nevertheless it is known (1) that the chronicler used a very free grammatical construction, thus allowing "martens and white cloth" to be understood as something quite different from "gold and silver." (2) The term means fur, the pelt of a specific animal or, as some think, a special cloth. For the year 1116 it is stated that Monomakh ordered cloth to be cut and thrown to the people, but here cloth is differentiated clearly from silver coins. (3) In the passage cited from the Hypatian compilation, instead of "cloth" it says "leather." Consequently it is justifiable to conclude that kuna (marten) meant money in general, and "squirrel" meant furs.

We have another piece of evidence from a somewhat later period. In 1257 Prince Daniel Romanovich of Galich ordered tribute taken from the Yatviags "in black martens and silver squirrels." It is clear that here the words "squirrel" and "silver" must be treated separately. The chronicler had no need to explain that "squirrel" meant silver but a later copyist, who did not understand this, put "silver squirrel" as something corresponding to black martens, as can be read in several compilations. As far as numbers are concerned, for the year 1160 it is mentioned in the chronicle that there are calculations based on thousands.[109] "Much wickedness was caused by the Polovetsians taking more than a thousand souls."

ART

Trade at this time was the main means of accumulating wealth in Rus. There is no more information about profitable [military] expeditions to Greece or to the East, or about pillage of wealthy cities and peoples. The increase in wealth resulting from contact with more enlightened nations is demonstrated by the desire to make life more beautiful through art, which first of all served religion. The chronicle frequently describes church construction in detail. At the end of the eleventh century Metropolitan Ephraim, who lived in Pereiaslavl where the metropolitan see was first located, was famous for his ambitious church-building plans. In Pereiaslavl he built St. Michael's church and decorated it "with all things beautiful," as the chronicler puts it. When this church was completed he built another over the city gate, dedicated to St. Theodore, and a third, dedicated to St. Andrew. Near the church, by the gate, there were public baths, something never before built in Rus. Around the city a stone wall rose. In a word, he embellished the city of Pereiaslavl by constructing churches and other buildings.

In 1115 the united princes built in Vyshgorod a stone church where the relics of St. Boris and St. Gleb were translated from a wooden church, and a silver shrine was constructed around the reliquary. Andrei Bogoliubsky was famous as the builder and beautifier of churches in the North. The main monument to this passion is the church of the Mother of God in Vladimir-Zalessk, built in 1158 all in white stone transported by river from the land of the Bulgars.[110] Latest research confirms that it was built by Western artists sent to Andrei by Emperor Frederick I.[111] In this church was the famous icon of the Virgin brought from Constantinople.[112] Onto it, according to the chronicle, Andrei encrusted thirty grivnas of gold, quite apart from silver, gems or pearls. In 1194, during the reign of

Vsevolod III, this church was rebuilt following a large fire. Also during
Vsevolod's reign St. Dmitry's cathedral was built and "wonderfully decorated with icons and paintings." In 1194 the church of the Mother of God
in Suzdal was renovated, which according to the words of the chronicler
was falling down because of great age and disrepair. A lead roof was
constructed, covering it from the top to the outside arches and vestibules.
"A wonderful thing!" says the chronicler.

Bishop John[113] did not seek master builders among the Germans, finding them instead among the servants of the church of the Mother of God
in Vladimir and among his own people. They knew how to pour lead, to
erect the roof and to whitewash, using lime. Here the chronicler specifically mentions that the bishop did not seek master builders among the
Germans. This suggests that other master builders (Greeks), apart from
Westerners (Germans), were unknown in the North, and that the previous buildings, Bogoliubsky's churches, were built by Germans. At least
one church newly renovated in this manner did not last long. In 1222
Prince Yury Vsevolodvich was forced to demolish it because of dilapi-
dation and the collapse of the upper part of the structure. It had been built
in the reign of Vladimir Monomakh.

This church of St. Michael in Pereiaslavl collapsed after less than fifty
years. Stone churches were built very quickly. In Novgorod in 1179 the
foundation of the Annunciation church was laid on May 21 and construction was completed by August 25. In 1196 St. Cyril's church was started
in April and finished on June 8. In 1198 in Rusa the Transfiguration
church was begun on May 21 and completed on July 31. In the same year
in Novgorod the church of the Transfiguration was begun on June 8 and
completed in September. In 1219 a small stone church of the Three Holy
Youths was finished in four days. Churches had lead roofs, and their
copulas were painted in gold. Inside they were decorated with icons,
murals and silver chandeliers. Icons were decorated in gold and enamel,
precious stones and pearls. Among Rus painters St. Alimpy of the Caves
monastery is mentioned. He learned his art from Greek masters who
decorated the Caves monastery. It seems he also was skillful in making
mosaics. For the year 1200 the construction of a stone wall under the
church of St. Michael by the Dnieper in Vydubichi is noted. The builder
was Miloneg Peter, whom Grand Prince Riurik selected from among his
friends, as the chronicler put it.

DAILY LIFE

Material well-being, which in the main cities of Rus depended chiefly on trade and encouraged construction of more or less well built and decorated buildings for the community, churches for the most part, should have influenced the comfort of everyday life of the Rus people during this time. Unfortunately information about this sphere of life is very scarce. It is known that there were very rich people and their houses held much to be plundered. Such were, for example, the Miroshkins in Novgorod, from whom in 1209 the people took countless treasures, the rest being equally divided among the population, three grivnas a head in the city. Some took things unnoticed and many became very rich. No matter what the interpretation of this passage, it is clearly stated that everyone in Novgorod received three grivnas. The creature comforts characterizing the wealth of Novgorod citizens and other rich men is unknown. They had villages, many household slaves, large herds. Obviously they had large houses, yet nothing is known of their design.

Public buildings and churches were not built solidly. Some collapsed by themselves, others had to be demolished and replaced. No wonder, that private buildings did not survive very long since they were built mainly, if not exclusively, of timber. There are no grounds to suppose that they differed from the buildings of the previous period. Simplicity of construction, cheapness of material, namely timber which was plentiful, simplicity and sparseness of what we call furniture helped people to survive disasters caused by domestic wars and enemy attacks. Money and the few precious possessions or expensive clothing were easy to hide or carry when seeking refuge in the nearest forest or fortified town during times of trouble. People returned after the enemy departed, and with ease rebuilt and settled down. Absence of solid housing, coupled with a simple way of life, enhanced the ease with which the populations of whole cities resettled. Entire towns fled the enemy and took refuge in other towns.

Sometimes princes transferred entire towns from one region to another. The people of Kiev told the sons of Yaroslav that they would set their city on fire and go live in Greece. The ancient wooden cities of Rus represented the transition from the nomadic camp of Polovetsians and Torks to the stone-built cities of Western Europe. The population of Ancient Rus, despite its settled existence, had no strong attachment to its ancient cities, which differed little from one another. Nature in the country was similar everywhere. There were open spaces everywhere, making it

equally convenient to settle anywhere. The princes, worried by the sparseness of population, were glad to receive settlers. Not only during this
period, but much later as well, the ease with which the Rus moved from
place to place usually was noted. It was easy for them under difficult
conditions to go elsewhere.

It has been remarked that concerning the design, construction and fur-
nishings of houses, nothing can be added to what has been said earlier, about
the most ancient period. The princes liked to sit and feast with their retinue
in the outer hall. The word "throne"[114] denoting a small bench or chair given
to guests is found in other sources. There is information on dresses, mantles,
coats or hats, which were removed neither indoors nor in church. In agreements with the Germans mention is made of the use of mittens with fingers,
meaning gloves bought probably by foreigners. From this information on
mittens, the use of simple Rus gloves may be inferred.

Among jewelry for men, gold chains are mentioned. Among women's
clothes, the headdress is noted, and among jewelry, necklaces and silver
earrings. Such fabrics as linen or homespun and velvet are mentioned.
Boyars' clothes are described as decorated with golden embroidery. For
the year 1183 the chronicler, describing the fire in Vladimir-Zalessk, adds
"Also destroyed was the cathedral church of the Mother of God with
golden cupolas, all five golden spires and all decorations inside and outside. There were silver chandeliers, countless silver and gold vessels,
vestments embroidered with gold and pearls, which during holidays hung
on two lines from the Golden gate to the church of the Mother of God,
and thence also on two lines to the outer hall of the bishop's house."

Here the vestments mentioned belonged to priests. According to other
information the princes hung their expensive garments in churches by way
of ostentation. It is very likely that these clothes were remodelled into
priests' vestments. Ornaments and luxuries in general were very noticeable.
A passage contained in some chronicles relates. "I pray you, Christ's flock,
with love open your ears wisely and listen how ancient princes and their men
lived, how they defended the Land of Rus and conquered foreign lands.
These princes accumulated little property, levied no unnecessary tribute and
taxes from their people. When they had to take taxes, they distributed the
money to the retinue for purchase of weapons. The retainers supported themselves from what they took in foreign lands, and when they fought they said
'Brother, let's strive harder for our prince and the Land of Rus.' They did
not say 'Two hundred grivnas is too little for me, O prince!' They did not
dress their wives in golden ornaments, for their wives wore silver."

VII

RELIGION AND LAW

THE STRUGGLE BETWEEN PAGANISM AND CHRISTIANITY

Earlier the material side of life in Rus society at this time was considered. Now we turn to its spiritual condition. It is obvious that the state of religion and the church require discussion. It is known that Christianity first was adopted in Kiev, in the South, where it was known long before the conversion. Slowly and with great difficulties it spread to the North and East. The first bishops of Rostov, Theodore and Hilarion, were forced to flee their see because of pagan ferocity. Their successor, St. Leonty, who did not abandon his flock of mainly children, among whom he hoped the new religion would take root more easily, was martyred by adult pagans. Paganism in the Finnish North did not merely wage a defensive war against Christianity. Sometimes it was aggressive through its magi.[1]

At one time in the Land of Rostov during a famine two magi appeared from Yaroslavl. Saying "We know who has grain," they travelled along the Volga and in every rural settlement they came to they pointed to the wealthiest women and said "These are hoarding grain, those honey, fish and fur." People brought to them their sisters, mothers and wives. The pagan priests cut their bodies open behind their shoulders and pretended to extract either grain or fish. In this way they killed many women and took their property. When they arrived in Beloozero they had three hundred followers.

At the same time it happened that Yan, son of Vyshata, arrived from Prince Sviatoslav to collect tribute. People of Beloozero told him that two magi killed many women along the Volga and Sheksna rivers and were in their city. He asked whose peasants these pagan priests were, and eventually learned that they belonged to Sviatoslav. "Hand the magi over to me," he commanded their followers, "because they are my prince's peasants," but they would not listen. Yan approached them, at first unarmed, but his young servitors told him "Do not go without weapons, they will humiliate you." Yan ordered the young servitors to take arms. Accompanied by twelve young servitors he went into the forest. Armed with an axe, he advanced straight towards the magi. From among the crowd surrounding them three men stepped forward. "You are going to your death," they said, "don't you go!" In response Yan ordered them killed and continued towards the others. They started attacking. One man swung his axe but missed, and Yan turned his axe round and struck him with the butt, ordering his young servitors to assail the rest, who turned and fled.

During the fight Yan's own priest was killed. Then Yan returned to the city. "If you do not catch these pagan priests," he told the people of Beloozero, "I will stay here the whole summer." The people of Beloozero caught the magi and brought them to Yan, who asked them "Why did you destroy so many souls?" "Because they were hoarding all sorts of goods," they answered. "If we finish them off, there will be plenty for everybody. See for yourself! We will get grain, fish or anything else." "All this is a lie," Yan responded. "God created man out of earth. Man is made of bones, veins and blood and there is nothing else in him. A man cannot know anything else about himself, only God knows."

The pagan priests saw the matter ending badly for them. "We want to answer before Sviatoslav," they said, "for you have no authority over us." In response Yan ordered them beaten and their beards torn out.[2] When this was done Yan asked them "What do your gods tell you?" "To stand before Sviatoslav," the magi answered. Then Yan ordered wooden gags placed in their mouths. They were tied to a boat and he sailed behind them down the Sheksna. When they arrived at the mouth of the river, Yan ordered the boat to halt and once again asked them "What do your gods tell you?" "Our gods tell us," they answered, "that we will perish because of you." "They tell you the truth," answered Yan. "If you let us go," the magi told him, "great good will come your way. If you kill us, you will suffer a great sorrow." "If I let you go," he responded, "God will punish me." Turning to the boatmen, he asked "Did they kill any of your relatives?" "They killed my mother," one told him. A second told him "They killed my sister," and a third told him "They killed my daughter." "So take revenge for your relatives," Yan told them. The boatmen took the magi and killed them, hanging them on an oak tree. Yan went home. The following night a bear climbed the tree and ate the magi's corpses. The chronicler adds an interesting item, that during his times pagan practices mainly were followed by women, who engaged in witchcraft, poison and other devilish practices.

How weakly Christianity was rooted in the North is best demonstrated by the following chronicle story. A magus appeared in Novgorod during Gleb Sviatoslavich's reign and preached to the people, presenting him-

Christian religion, claimed he knew everything and that he would cross the Volkhov river as if it were land, in view of everybody. There was unrest in the city. Everybody believed the magus and wanted to kill the bishop. The bishop donned his vestments, took the cross and stood his ground. "Whosoever wishes to believe the pagan priest," he said, "join him. Those who believe in Christ, approach the cross." The inhabitants divided into two groups. Prince Gleb and the retinue stood by the bishop while all the simple people went to the magus. There was great mutiny among them. Then Prince Gleb, secretly taking an axe, approached the magus. "Do you know," he asked, "what will happen tomorrow morning or evening?" "I know everything," he answered. "Do you know what will happen just now?" "Now," answered the magus, "I will perform great miracles." Whereupon Gleb took out his axe and killed the magus. The people, seeing him dead, dispersed. In 1091 a magus once again appeared in Rostov, but soon perished.

Such stories show that magi appeared and were successful mainly in the North, in lands inhabited by the Finns. Magi appeared in Yaroslavl, on territory inhabited by the Finnish tribe of Merians. In the land of the Chud, from ancient times famous for its magi, a man from Novgorod went to be told his fortune. In Rostov, St. Avraamy destroyed the last stone idol of Veles.[3] In Murom the destruction of paganism is ascribed to Prince Konstantin. Of the Slavonic tribes the last to convert were the Viatichians. They originally lived distant from the main routes and consequently were the last to fall under the sway of the Rus princes, the last to convert to Christianity. In the second half of the eleventh century St. Kuksha, a monk of the Caves monastery in Kiev who preached Christianity, died a martyr's death in their territory. In the twelfth century, according to the words of the chronicler, the Viatichians still preserved pagan customs, cremated their dead and so forth.

The fact that in the South, in Kiev, Christianity was better established than in the North is demonstrated by a story in the chronicles about a magus who visited Kiev but found much less success than with similar appearances in the North. This magus predicted that in five years the Dnieper would flow the other way and that countries would exchange places. The land of the Greeks would be where Rus was, and Rus where the Greek land was. Gullible people, said the chronicler, listened to him, but believers made fun of him. "The devil plays with you," they said, "in order to bring you to perdition." So it happened, for one night the magus disappeared without a trace. In what part of society the new religion was better established may be gleaned from the story of the magus in Novgorod. The prince and his retinue joined the bishop's side, the rest of the population, simple people, followed the magus.

MISSIONARY WORK

In spite of all obstacles Christianity spread continually in the lands controlled by Rus. If at the beginning of this period all lower classes in Novgorod went over to the magus, at the end, in 1227, four magi were burned at the stake in Novgorod. Despite the fact that in the Rostov lands Finnish paganism displayed strong resistance to Christianity, Christian missionaries went further and further north. In 1147 Brother Gerasim, a monk of Glushinsk monastery in Kiev, did missionary work in the area of present-day Vologda. Novgorod migrants took their faith with them to the Northern Dvina and Kama. We have observed the circumstances through which the Rus church failed to compete successfully with the Roman church in Livonia,[4] yet for the year 1227 it is mentioned that Prince Yaroslav Vsevolodovich baptized a multitude of Karelians.[5]

CHURCH ORGANIZATION

The Rus church, as before, was subordinate to the patriarch of Constantinople, who appointed all metropolitans and had the last word in church matters. There was no appeal from his judgment. Information about Rus metropolitans of this era is very scarce. This is explained by their foreign, Greek origin, a fact which hindered knowledge of their activity. Their foreign origin was probably one of the reasons why the metropolitans at first lived not in Kiev, but in Pereiaslavl. After all, Patriarch Jeremiah proposed that he be patriarch, but reside in Vladimir, because of his foreign origins.[6] Of the sixteen metropolitans during the period under discussion the more outstanding were (1) John II (1080-1089),[7] about whom the chronicler says that he was accomplished in books and learning, charitable to the poor and widows, kind to everybody, rich or poor, simple or noble. He was humble and meek, silent, yet eloquent when there was need to comfort with holy books those who were in misery. There was no one like him before in Rus nor would there be anyone like him again. Thus the chronicler concluded his eulogy. (2) Nikifor (1107-1121) was renowned for his letters to Vladimir Monomakh.[8] (3) Kliment Smoliatich [1147-1155] who was, according to the chronicler, a man of learning and a philosopher. There was no one like him before in the Land of Rus, said the chronicler.[9]

During the initial period of Russian history there were instances when metropolitans of Rus origin were appointed by Rus bishops independently of the patriarch of Constantinople. During this period, in 1147, Prince Iziaslav Mstislavich appointed as metropolitan Klim or Kliment from Smolensk who, as was mentioned, was renowned for his learning. The reason might have been the unrest which rocked the Byzantine patriarchal throne at that time[10] and the prince's dissatisfaction with Michael, the previous metropolitan, who left for Greece without authorization.[11]

Whatever the reason, among the bishops who gathered to consecrate Klim in Kiev there was strong resistance to the prince's wishes. They were not against appointment of a Rus metropolitan, only that Klim lacked the blessing of the patriarch in Constantinople. "There is nothing in the law," they told him, "that allows a bishop to become metropolitan without the patriarch. If the patriarch appoints another metropolitan, we will not bow to you, nor will we take service with you, because you have no blessing from the Holy Spirit and the patriarch. If you set matters right and receive the blessing of the patriarch, we will bow to you. We have written instructions from Metropolitan Michael that without a metropolitan we must not serve in the Holy Wisdom cathedral."[12]

Then Bishop Onufry of Chernigov proposed a way of reaching agreement with the bishops, namely to appoint the new metropolitan by the hand of St. Clement, following the Greek custom of appointment by the hand of St. John. The bishops agreed, and Klim was consecrated. Only Nifont of Novgorod[13] opposed it until the end, for which he was persecuted by Iziaslav whereas the patriarch sent him letters praising and comparing him to the saints. In the chronicle Nifont is called standard-bearer of all Rus. Generally in this matter the chronicler takes Nifont's side against Iziaslav's innovation. Perhaps other factors were involved in this matter. The chronicler says that Nifont was friendly with Sviatoslav Olgovich. Clearly in Novgorod the party supporting the sons of Mstislav was not well disposed towards Nifont. The chronicler indicates that many there spoke ill of him.

When following Iziaslav's death Yury Dolgoruky obtained the seniority, the party supporting the rights of the patriarch gained the upper hand. Klim was deposed, and Metropolitan Constantine I was sent from Constantinople to replace him. The first thing the new metropolitan did was to curse the memory of the deceased Prince Iziaslav, which was not without negative impact on the Rus church and Constantine himself. When following Dolgoruky's death Mstislav the son of Iziaslav gained the Kievan throne for his uncle Rostislav, he demanded the immediate removal of Constantine for cursing his father. His uncle Rostislav, on the other hand, refused to restore Klim, as he was not elected canonically. Finally, to end the dissension, the princes ordered both metropolitans removed, and asked the patriarch to send a third. The patriarch agreed and a new metropolitan arrived, a Greek called Theodore.[14]

Despite restoration of the patriarch's right to send appointees to Kiev as metropolitan, the grand princes did not renounce their right to accept only a metropolitan of whom they approved. In 1164 Grand Prince Rostislav Mstislavich rejected Metropolitan John,[15] appointed by the patriarch without his agreement. The emperor was to expend considerable efforts and dispatch many gifts to convince Rostislav to receive this cleric. "If the patriarch sends a metropolitan without our approval," apparently was the grand prince's answer to the imperial envoy, "not only will I reject him, we will decide henceforth to elect and appoint the metropolitan by Rus bishops with the permission of the grand prince."[16]

After the unsuccessful attempt to free the Rus metropolitan from the authority of the patriarch of Constantinople there was a fruitless effort to free Northern Rus from the authority of the Southern Rus church by making the Vladimir bishop independent of metropolitan of Kiev. The chronicle mentions that Andrei Bogoliubsky wished to have a metropolitan for Vladimir-Zalessk, and besought the patriarch of Constantinople to grant his wish, but to no avail. The prince accepted the patriarch's decision but not Bishop Theodore [Feodorets], who refused to submit to the metropolitan of Kiev, claiming that he was appointed in Constantinople by the patriarch himself. When Andrei wished to convince him to go to Kiev to be blessed by the metropolitan, Theodore closed the churches in Vladimir. Andrei forced him to visit Kiev, where Metropolitan Constantine II, a Greek, firmly resolved to stop attempts of Northern clergy to separate from Kiev. Theodore was accused of various crimes and punished severely.[17]

"In 1172 God and His Holy Mother," writes the chronicle, "worked a new miracle in the city of Vladimir by removing the evil, arrogant and proud flatterer Bishop Theodore from the gold-topped cathedral of the Mother of God and from all the Land of Rostov. This dishonest man refused to listen to the Christ-loving Prince Andrei, who commanded him to visit the metropolitan in Kiev. He refused, but it would better to say that God and His Mother did not desire him, because if God wants to punish someone He takes away his reason. The prince liked him and wished him well, yet not only did he refuse to attend the metropolitan, he also closed all churches in Vladimir, took the keys and there was no bell-ringing, no liturgical chant in the whole city. He even dared close the cathedral where the miracle-working icon of the Mother of God is found. He angered God and His Mother so much that he was expelled the very same day.

"People suffered much from him. Some lost villages, some weapons, some horses, others were enslaved, imprisoned and robbed, not only simple folk, but also monks, abbots and priests. He was a merciless torturer. People lost their heads and had their beards cut off, others lost eyes and tongues, still others were crucified on the walls and tortured without mercy because he wanted to obtain their property, for he was very avaricious. Prince Andrei sent him to Kiev, where Metropolitan Constantine accused him of these crimes, ordered him transported to Dogs' Island[18] where as a wicked heretic his tongue was cut out, his right hand was cut off and his eyes were gouged because he blasphemed against the Mother of God... Without repentance he suffered until his last breath.

"In this way do devils treat those who revere them. They incited, raised his thoughts sky high, made him a second Sataanill[19] and threw him down to hell... When God saw the suffering of the simple people in the Land of Rostov who perished because of the beastly Theodore, he took pity and saved them by His strong hand, and the pious ruling hand of the true prince Andrei. We have written this to prevent further attacks on the high holy orders, so that only those called to them by God may take their place there."[20]

This fragment quoted from the chronicle clearly demonstrates the basis of the accusations. The devils made Theodore's thoughts rise to the heavens and made him a second Sataanill. "We have written this," it is said in conclusion, "to prevent further attacks on high holy orders." It is difficult to decide now to what degree were Theodore's crimes exaggerated by those wishing to condemn him of every crime. For an historian this is of particular interest as an attempt of a North Rus bishop to renounce obedience to the Kiev metropolitan.[21]

This attempt failed. The Kiev metropolitan continued to appoint bishops to all the sees of the Rus church. There were fifteen sees at this time.[22] Just as the grand princes of Kiev barely suffered the patriarch of Constantinople to send metropolitans to their city, the princes of other lands refused to let the Kiev metropolitan decide the bishops of their cities. When in 1183 Metropolitan Nikifor appointed a Greek called Nicholas to Rostov, Vsevolod III refused him, and sent word the metropolitan. "He was not elected by the people of our land," he protested. "If you appoint him, keep him where you wish, but as far as I am concerned appoint Luka, the humble and gentle abbot of the Holy Savior monastery in Berestovo." The metropolitan at first refused to appoint Luka, yet later submitted to Vsevolod Sviatoslavich (the Kievan prince) by appointing Luka bishop of the Land of Suzdal. He sent his own candidate Nicholas the Greek to Polotsk.

Generally the attitude towards Greeks was not very positive, as is suggested by the chronicler's words about the Chernigov bishop Anthony. "He said this with his lips but in his heart he harbored deceit, for he was of Greek origin." Thus the election of a bishop was not exclusively the business of the metropolitan. How was election accomplished?

In Novgorod the participants in the proceedings leading to a bishop's selection were the prince, abbots, officials of the Holy Wisdom cathedral and the secular clergy. In case of disagreement lots were drawn. The successful candidate then was sent to the metropolitan for consecration. This is what the chronicle relates about the election of Bishop Martiry. "The Novgorod archbishop Gavrila died Novgorod with Prince Yaroslav and the abbots, together with the officials and priests of Holy Wisdom deliberated whom to elect in his place. Some wanted to elect Mitrofan, others Martiry, yet others a Greek. Arguments commenced and to settle them they placed in the church of Holy Wisdom, on the throne, three lots, and sent a blind man from the assembly to pick one. He drew Martiry, who was summoned at once from Rusa, inducted and placed in the court of the Holy Wisdom. Then word was sent to the metropolitan, telling him 'Install our bishop.' The metropolitan sent for him with great honor and Martiry went to Kiev with the most prominent men. He was received amiably by Prince Sviatoslav and the metropolitan, and was consecrated bishop."

In other territories selection depended mainly on the will of the prince. The chronicler writes that after the death of Belgorod's bishop Maxim, Grand Prince Riurik appointed his confessor, Abbot Adrian of the Vydubets monastery. The manner in which princes sometimes attempted to select bishops is suggested in a passage from a letter from Bishop Simon to Polikarp, a monk of the Caves monastery. "Princess Verkhuslava, Rostislav's wife, has written to me that she wishes you to be made bishop, either in Novgorod in place of Anthony, or in Smolensk in place of Lazar, or in Yuriev in place of Alexis. She writes that if necessary a thousand grivnas of silver may be distributed. She will not skimp on that."

In the same way as either the people or the prince influenced the election of a bishop, popular discontent or the displeasure of a prince could cause a bishop's removal and exile. An example is when the simple people of Novgorod expelled Bishop Arseny because the weather was unseasonably hot. There were accusations that Arseny displaced his predecessor, Bishop Anthony, and banished him to a monastery, obtaining office by passing rich gifts to the prince. This illustrates the strong influence of the prince in electing a bishop, even in Novgorod. On the other hand Vsevolod III refused to receive Bishop Nicholas because he was not elected by the people of the Suzdal land. Rostislav Mstislavich in his charter wrote that he brought a bishop to Smolensk, *having deliberated with his people.* In 1159 the people of Rostov and Suzdal expelled their bishop Leon. Other information suggests that the guilty party in this expulsion was Prince Andrei Bogoliubsky, who recalled the bishop only later to expel him again.

Apart from authority to consecrate bishops the metropolitan held the right to try and sentence them. In 1055 the Novgorod bishop Luka Zhidiata, following a false accusation, was sentenced by Metropolitan Ephraim and kept in Kiev for three years until acquitted. Bishop Nestor of Rostov, accused falsely by his own household, for a time was denied his see by Metropolitan Constantine. The conduct of the metropolitan towards Bishop Theodore of Vladimir has been discussed.

In important questions, for example the election of Klim Smoliatich to the metropolitan see, and in particular in questions of heresy and false doctrine, synods were convoked at Kiev. There is evidence of heresy during the period under discussion, that of the Paulicians or Bogomils.[23] Attempts to spread this heresy were undertaken by a monk called Adrian as early as 1004. Adrian, having been imprisoned, recanted. In 1123 his effort was repeated by a certain Dmitry, who soon was sent into solitary confinement. In 1149 a heretic called Martin arrived in Kiev from Constantinople and expounded his teachings in a book called *The Truth.* Martin preached in Kiev for seven years and converted many simple people as well as many clergy. Finally in 1157 the Kiev synod condemned his teachings. The synod in Constantinople having confirmed the verdict of the Kievan synod, the heretic was burned at the stake in Constantinople.

Earlier it was mentioned that Bishop Leon was expelled by Rostov and Suzdal. In the Northern chronicle for the year 1159 the reason given is that he caused losses to clergymen by multiplying the number of churches. For 1162 the same chronicle mentions the beginnings of the Leontinian heresy. According to this source Bishop Leon was elected unlawfully to the see of Suzdal because the previous bishop, Nestor, was still alive. Leon taught that it was wrong to eat meat on holy days such as Christmas or Epiphany if they fell on Wednesdays or Fridays. A disputation was held in the presence of Prince Andrei and all the people. Leon lost, and he went to Constantinople to seek decision in the matter. There Adrian, a Bulgarian bishop, won the disputation in the presence of Emperor Manuel. Leon spoke against the emperor himself, whose servants beat him about the shoulders. They also wanted to drown him in the river. All this was witnessed by envoys from Kiev, Suzdal, Pereiaslavl and Chernigov.

This story is told differently in the Southern chronicle for the year 1162. Prince Andrei Bogoliubsky expelled Bishop Leon together with his brothers and his father's boyars because he wished be sole ruler. Later the bishop was recalled and the prince repented of his sins. He returned the bishop to Rostov, not to Suzdal, keeping him four months in the diocese. Afterwards the prince asked the bishop's permission to eat meat on Wednesdays and Fridays from Easter Sunday until All Saints [May 13].[24] The bishop refused, and was banished a second time. He went to Chernigov, to Sviatoslav Olgovich, who supported him and sent him to Rostislav in Kiev.

This was not the end of the matter. Shortly before Kiev was captured by the forces of Andrei Bogoliubsky, Abbot Polikarp of the Caves monastery and his brethren ruled that during holy days falling on Wednesdays and Fridays only cheese, butter, eggs and milk might be eaten. This was agreed by Prince Sviatoslav of Chernigov and other princes and bishops, whereas the metropolitan disagreed. Many were the arguments concerning this matter. Eventually Grand Prince Mstislav Iziaslavich ordered a synod of all bishops, abbots, priests and learned monks. About a hundred and fifty took part.

At the synod different opinions were voiced. The metropolitan's chief supporters were two bishops, Anthony of Chernigov and Anthony of Pereiaslavl, while others supported Polikarp. The majority, not wishing to annoy either the metropolitan or the princes, found excuses, saying they were unprepared to decide this issue. The decision rested with the metropolitan, or the abbots within their monasteries. Some thought that the best solution was to refer the matter to the patriarch. Andrei Bogoliubsky wrote to Mstislav that it would be best to expel the metropolitan, that a new metropolitan be elected by the Rus bishops, who then might examine the matter calmly at a synod. He expressed the view that dependence on the patriarch of Constantinople was both burdensome and harmful for Rus. Mstislav, aware of the hostility of other princes towards him, feared to arouse the anger of the bishops and left the matter unresolved. When the bishops who disagreed with the metropolitan departed he, with both Anthonys, the bishops of Chernigov and Pereiaslavl, sentenced Polikarp to prison. Sviatoslav Vsevolodovich of Chernigov banished Bishop Anthony from his city. It is interesting that the Northern chronicle saw the capture and ransacking of Kiev by Bogoliubsky's forces as punishment for that city's sins, in particular for the metropolitan's crime in acting against Polikarp.

REVENUES OF THE RUS CHURCH

The sources for upkeep of the metropolitan and bishops were (1) tithes fixed by the princes from their revenues for major churches in their territories. St. Vladimir fixed for the Kievan church of the Mother of God a tenth part of his estates and revenues.[25] About Yaropolk Iziaslavich of Volhynia the chronicler relates that he offered tithes from all his estates to the Mother of God. Whether these tithes went to the Kievan church of that name is not stated. The term "Mother of God" might also mean the monastery of the Caves, mentioned later in the story about the generosity of the same Yaropolk. Andrei Bogoliubsky gave the church of the Mother of God in Vladimir tithes from his herds and a tenth of his market dues. (2) Another source was property. The Kievan Tithe church owned the town of Polonny. Andrei Bogoliubsky granted the church of the Virgin of Vladimir the town of Gorokhovets. He also granted settlements and villages, and Gorokhovets was not the only town. This is evident from the chronicle as well as from the letter of Bishop Simon of Vladimir to the monk Polikarp of the Kievan monastery of the Caves. "Who does not know," he wrote, "that I, sinful Bishop Simon, have a cathedral church in Vladimir, the ornament of the entire city, and another in Suzdal which I built myself? How many towns and villages do they have? Tithes are collected from this land and everything in the possession of our unworthiness." It is likely that these revenues went to the metropolitan and the bishops as well as for the support and embellishment of the churches, for the upkeep of the clergy, hospitals, almshouses and schools. (3) A further source consisted of fines by ecclesiastical courts. (4) Yet another was entry fees for the induction of incumbents and church servitors.

Concerning the upkeep of the lower clergy no information has survived. Apparently Yaroslav I while organizing the church everywhere made some provision for the maintenance of the clergy. Obviously princes and private individuals when endowing a church designated certain possessions or revenues for the maintenance of the vestry cloths and the clergy.

This is seen most clearly in the regulatory charter granted by the Novgorod prince Vsevolod Mstislavich to the church of St. John the Forerunner on the Opoki. In this document Vsevolod endowed the church with icons and diverse books and appointed priests and a parish clerk. For the church he assigned from his possessions the weighing fee for wax, retaining only part for himself. In Torzhok he donated the weighing fee for wax, half to the Savior church, half to St. John's. From these weighing fees the priests, the parish clerk, the deacon and the church warden received their annual stipend.

Around this church of St. John there developed a merchant guild, the governing body of which consisted of three elders from the more prosperous citizens, a representative for each thousand of the common people and two elders from the merchants. They maintained their own commercial court with which neither the boyars nor the burgrave might interfere. The entrance fee for a new member was fifty grivnas of silver, and a length of Ypres cloth for the chiliarch. Part of this payment was deposited in the church coffers. The scales for weighing wax were kept in the church vestibule, and only established guild brethren or men of good character might act as weighmasters. A sliding fee scale was applied, the merchants from the Lower Towns paying most, those from Polotsk and Smolensk less, those of Novy Torzhok less still, while Novgorod merchants paid least of all.[26]

Apart from the charter to St. John's, Vsevolod issued another applicable to all of Novgorod and the domain of the Holy Wisdom, similar to the Church Statute of St. Vladimir, with a few additions and amendments. The ten hundredmen were summoned, along with the elder Boleslav, the town crier Miroshka and Vasiata, an elder from St. John's. These took counsel with the bishop, Vsevolod's princess, his boyars, ten hundredmen and elders. The maintenance of standard weights and measures for wax, honey, cloth and salt was entrusted to the St. John's guild, which also had custody of the ruble grivna.[27] Half of the dues collected by the priest was designated for the support of the monastic clergy. Similarly duties paid by merchants from Rus proper were divided equally between the priest and his counterpart in the parish of St. Boris and St. Gleb. The church warden was assigned the stamp duty on Rus cloth and the ten percent duty on salt.

The archbishop together with the hundredmen was to manage the estates of the Holy Wisdom. The elders and merchants must supply the archbishop. Whoever of Vsevolod's kin might be prince in Novgorod must maintain the house of St. John. The bishop was responsible for maintaining honestly all weights and measures for goods, neither making them smaller nor bigger, and verify them every year. Should anyone tamper with them, he must be thrashed within an inch of his life and his property divided into three parts. One third was to be given to the Holy Wisdom, another to St. John's and the last to the hundredmen and Novgorod. Those considered church personnel were abbots, abbesses, priests, deacons and their children and those in the choir, the priest's wife, monk, nun, pilgrim, candle-attendant, watchman, blind person, cripple, widow, hermit, the mourner. Protection of the church was extended to the outcast, meaning an illiterate priest's son, a slave who bought himself from slavery or bankrupt merchant. A fourth type of outcast was added, the orphaned prince. Considered to be in a similar position to the orphan was the child of an uncanonical union, whom the law considered illegitimate. The statute stipulated that third and fourth wives[28] be identified, and the children provided for from the father's possessions. From a father who was prosperous the child received a portion sufficient for his maintenance. If the father was less well-to-do, the son received at least a horse and a suit of armor, that he might earn his living as a military servitor.

The charter of Prince Sviatoslav Olgovich to the Novgorod cathedral of the Holy Wisdom dates from 1137. At the beginning Prince Sviatoslav refers to his great-grandfathers and grandfathers who granted the right to the bishops to collect a tithe from the tribute, fines and sales of all revenue coming to the princely court. The charter of Prince Rostislav Mstislavich of Smolensk to Bishop Emmanuel of 1150 was granted to the Smolensk see. Because of the ancient unification of the Smolensk territory with that of Pereiaslavl under one prince, the Smolensk church was governed by the bishop of Pereiaslavl. In later times this unification proved very inconvenient simply because the Smolensk territory was distant from Pereiaslavl, separated by the invariably hostile territory of Chernigov. Monomakh's son Mstislav intended to establish in Smolensk a separate bishopric. Understandably his son Rostislav hastened to fulfill his father's wish. In the preamble to his charter Rostislav stated that he was establishing the bishopric in consultation with his followers in accordance with his sainted father's wishes. For the upkeep of the bishop and clergy he granted to the church of the Holy Mother of God income from honey, martens (kunas) and sales. He forbade anyone save the bishop to pass judgement on the clergy. He granted the church and bishop a tithe from all tribute received by Smolensk in the form of martens (kunas), apart from fines for crimes, fines for murder of a freeman, and the circuit tax.[29] In addition the prince granted several villages with new settlers and land. The church residential court was granted exclusively to the bishop. At the end of the charter Rostislav wrote that should anyone in envy wish to reunite the sees of Smolensk and Pereiaslavl the prince reserved the right to retrieve everything allocated for the upkeep of the bishop.

This charter of Rostislav Mstislavich contained no incongruity and therefore is above suspicion, serving as best proof for the validity of the church statutes of St. Vladimir and Yaroslav I. Like them it lists an enactment concerning church courts belonging to the bishop. Earlier it was mentioned that courts date from the conversion of Rus to Christianity. The first statues relating to them must pertain to the times of Vladimir and Yaroslav, although perhaps not in the form in which they were handed down. The recognition and application of these statutes during this period, namely from 1054 until 1228, appears beyond doubt. The *Nomocanon* used by the Greek church was accepted from the very beginning as a manual, as was the *Pilot Book* in the church court administration in our country. Most probably it was used at this time in the Greek original because the metropolitan and some of the bishops were of Greek origin. A Slavonic translation probably was used as well.[30] There is evidence from the sixteenth century of the existence of Slavonic copies of the *Pilot Book* on parchment written at the time of Yaroslav I and his son Iziaslav. As for the rights of the clergy as a social group, they were freed of secular jurisdiction and taxation.[31]

ACTIVITIES OF THE CLERGY

The importance of clergy during the first period after conversion, when bishops were indispensable counsellors to princes in all matters concerning government of the country, has been demonstrated. Subsequently their importance did not at all diminish. The clergy took an active part in events, reconciled princes, quelled popular uprisings. After the blinding of Vasilko the citizens of Kiev sent Metropolitan Nicholas to Monomakh. He persuaded the prince to make peace with Sviatopolk. Monomakh heeded the metropolitan because he respected his office, says the chronicler.

Abbot Gregory prevented war between Mstislav Vladimirovich and Vsevolod Olgovich of Chernigov. Viacheslav employed the metropolitan for negotiations with the same Vsevolod Olgovich. Bishop Fedor of Belgorod and Abbot Feodosy of the Caves monastery acted as intermediaries during peace negotiations between Grand Prince Iziaslav Mstislavich and the princes of Chernigov. When Yury Dolgoruky wanted to hand over his cousin Ivan Berladnik to Yaroslav of Galich to certain death, the metropolitan said to Yury "It will be your sin that after kissing the cross to Ivan you keep him in dire straits, and now you want to send him to his death." Yury heeded the metropolitan.

When the Hungarians conquered Galich the metropolitan encouraged the princes to retake this Rus territory from the foreigners. Metropolitan Nikifor, to avoid war between Riurik Rostislavich and Vsevolod III, absolved Riurik of the oath sworn to his son-in-law Roman of Volhynia. "Princes," he said, "we were appointed by God in the Land of Rus to keep you from spilling blood." The same metropolitan later made peace between Riurik and Roman. Timofey, confessor to Mstislav of Toropets, mediated the peace between the prince and his boyars. In Novgorod the archbishop repeatedly acted as pacifier of popular uprisings, as peacemaker between hostile parties and intermediary between prince and citizens. In an age when notions of popular rights were very weak and people did not hesitate to kill or arrest envoys if they did not like the message they brought, clergy usually acted as envoys because they were in less danger, for their status was universally respected.

HOLY ORDERS

It is easy to realize that people of that age had a special disposition for, and felt particular respect towards, the monastic order. The ancient Rus monks, in particular those of the monastery of the Caves in Kiev, earned this respect by reason of their heroic deeds. In the society of those times, still crude and semi-pagan, new and higher notions brought by Christianity encountered powerful resistance. The first monasteries represented a special, higher social order where the new dispensation, the new religion, was preached not only by word but through deeds. Outside the monastery base passions were quick to receive full rein. Within the walls of the monastery monks ate communion bread only every other day, wore hair shirts, never lay down to sleep, instead napping briefly sitting up, and never left the hermitage by day. Some fasted for weeks on end, wore chains and buried themselves to their armpits to kill carnal lust. Yet others placed in their cave a millstone and took grain from the bins to mill at night to extirpate in the soul all thought of avarice, and even succeeded in regarding gold and silver as nothing.

Passing through the gates of a monastery a layman entered a different world where everything was a marvel, where his imagination was excited by wondrous stories about the heroic deeds of monks, about miracles, visions, about supernatural help in the struggle against the powers of evil.

Little wonder then that monasteries attracted many of the best people. As the fame of Anthony's deeds in the cave quickly spread in Kiev, the hermit could not remain alone for long. Brethren gathered around him, boyars of the grand prince appeared, cast off their boyar raiment at the feet of the abbot, took vows of poverty and performed acts of spiritual heroism. Feodosy supported and enlarged the fame of the new monastery. Anthony in his time clashed with Grand Prince Iziaslav who, observing magnates leaving his court for Anthony's tiny cave, grew angry with the Caves monks and threatened to expel them from Kiev and fill in their caves. Because he was also angry with Anthony for his favorable attitude towards Vseslav of Polotsk, Anthony was forced to seek refuge with Prince Sviatoslav in Chernigov.

Despite such hostile relations between Iziaslav and the monastery Feodosy took his side against his brother Sviatoslav, when the prince of Chernigov seized the throne from his older brother. While everybody recognized the right of the stronger party, only the abbot of the Caves monastery denied this right, only in the Caves monastery in prayers for the ruler's health did Iziaslav continue to be commemorated as the ruling prince and senior in the clan. Sviatoslav suffered but listened with respect to Feodosy's admonitions. It was not only the exile Iziaslav who found a supporter in the abbot of the Caves monastery. People who suffered injustice in the courts went with their complaints to Feodosy, and judges reviewed their cases. In his cell Feodosy looked after a sick, weakened monk. At night, when everything was quiet, he went to the Jewish quarter of the city to engage in disputation with opponents of his religion.

Apart from Anthony and Feodosy, the Caves monastery yielded missionaries, bishops and chroniclers. St. Kuksha, St. Leonty and St. Isaiah were from this monastery. Another monk of this monastery, Nikon, escaping Iziaslav's wrath, visited Tmutorokan where every variety of exile, princes and monks, found shelter. Christianity was very weak in Tmutorokan. Monks were unknown there. The local savages were amazed when they viewed Nikon's heroic deeds. Crowds came to see this wondrous man, and quickly submitted to his influence. Soon afterwards Nikon became the leader of the people, a mediator in negotiations with the prince. It is not surprising therefore to read in twelfth-century sources that "the deeds of holy monks shine with miracles more than the worldly powers. Thanks to them, the lords of this world bow their heads before monks." "You can see," Bishop Simon wrote to Polikarp, a monk of the Caves monastery, "how you are respected by princes and boyars and all your friends."

Monasteries spread to other towns and cities. The monasteries in Turov, Pereiaslavl, Chernigov, Vladimir-in-Volhynia are mentioned, as are those in the principalities of Galich, Polotsk, Smolensk, Rostov and Novgorod the Great. Convents were established as well. In 1086 Grand Prince Vsevolod Yaroslavich built in Kiev the convent of St. Andrew, where his daughter Yanka took the veil. She gathered many nuns and they lived according to the monastic rule. Predslava, the daughter of Prince Georgy Vseslavich[32] of Polotsk, as a young girl entered a convent where her aunt, the wife of Roman Vseslavich, was a nun. She entered the religious life under the name of Evfrosinia. At first she begged the bishop's permission to dwell by the cathedral church of the Holy Wisdom in the columbarium, where she copied books, sold them and distributed the money to the poor. Later she established her own convent by the Holy Savior church where her sister, a cousin (a daughter of Boris Vseslavich) and two nieces took the veil. Her wish was to visit Jerusalem, and there she died, in the Rus monastery of the Mother of God.

Not only young and widowed princesses took the veil when in good health. There was a prince who of his own free will forsook his principality and made his profession in the monastery of the Caves in Kiev. This prince, namely Nikolay Davydovich of Chernigov, known already from the chronicle, was called Sviatosha or Sviatoslav. He spent three years in the monastic kitchen working for the brethren, chopping wood and carrying it to the monastery from the river on his own back. Later he served for three years as a doorkeeper, finally serving in the refectory. After finishing his novitiate he went to live in his own cell, where he had a garden. He was never seen idle. He always had something to do, and he ate only according to the monastic rule.

The monasteries possessed landed property for their maintenance. Prince Yaropolk Iziaslavich granted to the Kiev monastery of the Caves three estates. His daughter granted five villages with household slaves. Bishop Ephraim of Suzdal granted this monastery a property in Suzdal, together with the church of St. Dmitry and some villages. The charter of Prince Mstislav Vladimirovich (1128-1132) granted the St. George monastery in Novgorod an estate with tributes, fines for murder of freemen and amercements for crimes, and a specific portion of the princely revenue. The original document is still extant.

An original charter of Brother Varlaam, dating from the end of twelfth century, granting the Khutyn monastery lands, fisheries and fowling rights has come down to our time. It is likely that everyone entering the religious life who owned property gave some kind of endowment to the monastery in the form of chattels or immovable property. Other religious people offered gifts of money or other valuables.

It was the custom for the princes to distribute charity to the monasteries. Gleb Vseslavich of Polotsk gave the Kiev monastery of the Caves six hundred grivnas of silver and fifty of gold. After his death his wife donated one hundred grivnas of silver and fifty of gold. Some monks in monasteries continued to hold property, and for that reason there were rich and poor monks. The *Patericon*[33] tells us that when one monk called Afanasy died, none of his brethren wanted to bury him because he was poor.

There is another story about the monk Fedor who entered the monastery after distributing all his property to the poor. Later he regretted having done so. "If you wish to possess things," another monk called Vasily then told him, "take everything I have." A third monk, Arefa, had much property in his cell, and never gave anything to the poor.

With respect to administration, there is mention of the abbot (archimandrite), œconomus[34] and cellarer. The election of abbots depended on the brethren, though sometimes there were rebellions or forced changes of abbots. On occasion monks elected as abbots members of the secular clergy. For the year 1112 the chronicle relates that "The brethren of the Kiev monastery of the Caves who were left without an abbot assembled and elected Prokhor, a parish priest, as abbot. They informed the metropolitan and Prince Sviatopolk, who gladly allowed the metropolitan to

appoint Prokhor." Under the year 1182 the following story is told. "Polikarp the blessed abbot of the Caves monastery died, and after his death
there was unrest in the monastery. They could not agree whom to elect
as abbot. The brethren were much grieved because such a great house
should not be even one hour without a shepherd. On Tuesday the brethren rang the bells, gathered in the church, prayed to the Holy Mother of
God and a miracle happened. 'Let us send to Shchekovitsa,' all said in
one voice, 'for the priest Vasily to be abbot and governor of the monks
of the Caves monastery.' They came to Vasily and bowed to him, saying 'As brothers and monks we all bow to you and wish to have you as
our father abbot.' The priest was surprised, returned their bow and said
'Fathers and brothers! I have thought about taking the tonsure, but what
has possessed you to select me as your abbot?' They argued with him for
a long time and in the end he agreed, and the monks took him to the monastery."

In the relationship of the Kiev Caves monastery with the grand prince
of Kiev the words of St. Feodosy uttered before his death to Prince Sviatoslav are significant. "I am leaving this world and I entrust this monastery to your care, if there are disturbances. The office of abbot I entrust
to Stefan. Do not let anyone offend him." In some manuscripts of the
Patericon it is added "Let nobody own it, neither the archbishop nor
anybody from among the Holy Wisdom clerics, rather let the prince govern it, and after you your children, until the last in your line." Accordingly legend has it that Andrei Bogoliubsky confirmed the Caves
monastery's independence from the Kiev metropolitan, terming the monastery the lavra[35] and stauropigia[36] of the prince and patriarch.

LEGISLATION

In a discussion of the moral state of society we must examine the dominant legal concepts of the time. Among the statutes that undoubtedly
appeared in Rus during this era are amendments to the Rus Justice[37] introduced by the sons of Yaroslav I concerning revenge for homicide.
There it is said that three of Yaroslav's sons, Iziaslav, Sviatoslav and Vsevolod, assembled with their men (chiliarchs) and decided to end the blood
feud, agreeing that a killer compensate for the deed in marten pelts. In all
other respects they decided to uphold Yaroslav's laws. In this way clan
revenge and arbitrariness, the remnants of clan separateness, ceased to
exist as legal notions in Rus at the beginning of the second half of the
eleventh century. Manslaughter committed in personal relationships,

when one killed another by chance, in a quarrel, or brawl, or at a feast, or under the influence of alcohol, continued to be considered a private matter, not a criminal offense. In such instances the killer continued to be regarded as a full member of society. Only brigands, who were equally dangerous for everyone, were rejected by society and surrendered to the prince with their whole family for banishment.

Thus the first type of homicide (manslaughter) no longer involved personal or social revenge or punishment. The fact that manslaughter was frequent is witnessed by the custom of uniting for payment both the ordinary and the "dark" bloodwite.[38] A new element in comparison with earlier times is information on judicial combat employed as proof in court.

At this time there were limits imposed by Monomakh on interest rates, probably resulting from exorbitant practices by Jews during the reign of Sviatopolk. High interest rates usually stemmed from lack of security for debt repayment and the inadequate state of justice in the country, about which the chronicles and other sources contain loud complaints. The main reason was the frequent movements of princes from one territory to another.

Beginning during this era, the time of princely clan relationships, members of the retinue or junior members of the princely household customarily viewed appointment to a princely or judicial post as a source of income. Therefore they squeezed maximum profit from such a post, having no ties with a territory to which they were strangers. To understand better this type of relationship we should imagine a longtime retinue member dispensing justice in place of the prince as an old soldier posted somewhere. During the reign of Vsevolod Yaroslavich the chronicler complains about the devastation of the country thanks to the poor state of justice. Under Sviatopolk nothing better could be expected. For the year 1138 the chronicler writes that people living in the area along the Sula river suffered badly, partly from Polovetsians and partly from their own burgraves. Under Vsevolod Olgovich reeves ruined Kiev and Vyshgorod. During the reign of Rostislav's sons, governors in the North appointed from among the South Rus *junior boyars* ruined the territory of Vladimir.

The best evidence of poor administration of justice at that time is found in contemporary opinion about reeves. In the *Epistle of Daniel the Exile*[39] it says "Do not live near the princely court, do not own a village near the princely village because his *steward* is like fire and his *servants* are like sparks." An interesting item of information survives as to how the prince of Polotsk once asked a priest the fate awaiting a reeve in the next world. "A reeve," the priest answered, "is an unjust judge. He takes bribes, torments people and causes their suffering." The word *agent*[40] also acquired a negative meaning. Unable or unwilling to explain the poor administration of the law, the chronicler resorts to the saying "Where there is law there is also much injury."[41]

CUSTOMARY LAW

Ideas about popular law can serve as a measure of the morality of a society. To wage war meant causing enemy territory as much damage as possible by burning, looting, fighting and taking prisoners. If prisoners slowed troop movement or jeopardized engagements with the enemy, they were killed. Sometimes after a war princes agreed to return everything taken by both sides. On the other hand after a war one prince took the entire population of a captured city and resettled it on his own lands. Wars were fought the same way in Rus territories as other countries, whether Christian or pagan. While concluding peace agreements an oath was used, accompanied by kissing the cross and invoking the memory of father and grandfather, in the words of the princes. For that reason charters containing conditions of peace became known as "cross charters."[42]

There is frequent mention of broken oaths. Two princes in particular were notorious in this respect, Vladimir of Galich and Vladimir the younger son of Mstislav the Great. Monomakh was renowned for keeping his promises, yet even he once allowed himself to be persuaded to break an oath given to the Polovetsian khans, using as an excuse that pagans frequently violate their promises. Monomakh's son Mstislav, even with the permission of the clergy, all his life regretted breaking the oath he swore to Yaroslav of Chernigov. Among the later princes the chronicler praises Gleb Yurievich for keeping his word.

The return of "cross charters" to the parties constituted a declaration of war. It has been remarked that clergymen frequently acted as envoys because they were exposed to lesser danger. Yet Vsevolod III did not scruple to arrest the priests sent by Sviatoslav of Chernigov for negotiations. Mstislav the Brave ordered the head and beard of Bogoliubsky's envoy shaved.[43] Iziaslav's envoy Peter Borislavich received in Galich no transport or food, and he feared further oppression by Vladimirko. Yet it was accepted that envoys were not to be killed. When the people of Vladimir-in-Volhynia wanted to kill a priest sent by Igor's sons, the princes of Galich, their friends said that killing envoys was not acceptable.

Clearly the beneficial influence of Christianity may be seen. Igor of Severia admitted after taking the town of Glebov by force and failing to show mercy to the Christians he had committed a great sin for which God punished him with imprisonment in the land of the Polovetsians. Monomakh made peace with Gleb of Minsk, refusing to spill Christian blood during Lent. Towns were not assaulted on Sundays. Vsevolod Olgovich, "full of fear of God" as the chronicler put it, refused to take advantage of the fire to capture Pereiaslavl. Similar scruples were demonstrated by the sons of Rostislav during their war with those of Yury after the battle on the Lipitsa.

PIETY

Everywhere among the princes and the common people the struggle may be observed between the new and better Christian ideas and aspirations and the still scarcely restrained passion of the newborn society, with former pagan customs. In the lives of many princes a strong religious orientation may be observed. Monomakh was pious not only in words and in instructions to his children. In the words of the chronicler "he loved God with all his soul and proved it by deeds, obeying God's commandments, always having the fear of God in his heart. He had charity without bounds." The chronicler adds that his was such a gift from God that when he entered a church and heard singing he could not restrain his tears. The chronicle mentions the asceticism of Sviatoslav Davydovich of Chernigov, the religious leanings of Rostislav Mstislavich, the Christian death of Yaroslav of Galich.

Nevertheless for some piety was limited to outward devotions. When they lusted to satisfy their passions they paid little heed to the commandments of their religion and its servants. Monomakh's brother Rostislav killed the holy monk Gregory for having denounced him. Sviatopolk Iziaslavich was religious, he respected the Caves monastery in Kiev and its monks, but when it came to satisfying his avarice he made the monks suffer and expelled the abbot after his remonstrances. His son Mstislav killed St. Fedor and Vasily. Vladimirko of Galich, after mocking an oath, said "What can such a small cross do to me?" and entered church for vespers. They did not spare their treasures for construction and adornment of churches, yet considered it no sin to burn and rob churches in enemy territories. Alongside those who entered a monastery to combat their passions were those who sought to satisfy their passions but still went there.

In encyclicals of the twelfth century there are frequent reproaches directed at monks who pampered their bodies, changed their clothes, used the excuse of holy days for special meals with beer, and feasted at length. They sought to dominate their superiors and assembled not for the sake of God or to discuss something useful, rather for violent quarrels and shameless attacks against the œconomus and cellarer. Church pastors preached against feasts in monasteries attended by both men and women. The dispute preoccupying Rus society for so long, namely what to eat on certain days, was a further characteristic of this period.

DUALITY OF FAITH

The church, struggling against deviations from Christian morality, further had to combat the old pagan ideas and customs still very firmly established in Rus society, particularly its lower stratum. In Novgorod all the common people joined the magus. Only the prince and his retinue stood by the bishop. There is information that people continued to sacrifice to devils (meaning the earlier gods), to swamps and wells. There were men with two wives, nor did the common people seek the blessing of the church on their marriages, considering it a custom proper only for princes and boyars. The pagan custom of splashing was enough for them. Women took sick children to the magi. When they noticed a cooling in the affections of their husbands they washed their bodies with water, giving it to their husbands to drink.

It was particularly difficult to banish memories of the old religion from popular entertainments, songs, dances and games of pagan origin. Hence the church from the beginning fought fiercely against such entertainments. "Don't we live like pagans," says the chronicler "if we believe in such gatherings? If someone meets a monk on the road and turns away, isn't this acting like a pagan? Is it not the devil's teaching? Some even believe that sneezing makes the head healthy. With all these customs the devil drives us from God, leading us with pipes, minstrels, stringed instruments and celebrating the Rosalia.[44] At games there are crowds of people. When they start fighting people come running to watch this devilish amusement while the churches stand empty during services, for you will find very few in church." From these words it is clear that a favorite popular entertainment was wrestling or boxing.

FAMILY MORALITY

As far as family morality is concerned, the chronicles praise two princes who kept their bodies pure. It is said of Vsevolod Yaroslavich that he abstained from drunkenness and lust, about Sviatoslav Vsevolodovich that he kept his body pure. In versions of the chronicle preserved until our times it is said about Sviatopolk Iziaslavich that he had children by his mistress. In the Tatishchev compilation[45] of the chronicle there are similar examples. Respect for elders of the clan constantly was praised as a positive attitude and deviation was criticized severely, yet deviations were quite frequent. There are several examples of disobeying a father's will. Without his father's consent Andrei Bogoliubsky left the South to go north. Oleg Sviatoslavich of Chernigov without his father's knowledge sent to Iziaslav Davydovich. Konstantin Vsevolodovich refused to fulfill his father's will concerning distribution of territories.

On the important question of the position of women in Ancient Rus society there is very sparse information in the sources for this period. It is known that princesses had their own real estate, property and chattels, of which they might dispose at will. For example, the wife of Prince Gleb Vseslavich of Polotsk gave her money and landed property to the Kiev Caves monastery. The wife of Sviatopolk Iziaslavich on his death distributed great treasures among the monasteries, churches and the poor.

The respect shown by relatives to women is illustrated by Monomakh who listened to his stepmother's wishes. "He did as the princess asked," the chronicler writes, "because he respected her like a mother." The respect and love which princesses enjoyed in their families and among the people may be judged on the basis of the description of the death of Princess Maria, wife of Vsevolod III.[46] "The grand princess took the veil in the Mother of God convent which she herself had built, and was accompanied to the convent with tears by Grand Prince Vsevolod, his son Georgy and his daughter Verkhuslava, wife of Rostislav Riurikovich, who was visiting her father and mother at that time. Also Bishop John,[47] her confessor Abbot Simon, and other abbots, monks, boyars and their ladies, nuns from all convents and all the people escorted her to the convent weeping, because she was very good to everyone. The same month she died, the grand prince wept over her. His son Yury refused to be consoled, because he was her favorite."

The influence of princesses on events when acting as their husbands' advisers is evident in information for 1180 about Prince Sviatoslav

Vsevolodovich and Rostislav's sons. As the chronicle says, Sviatoslav attacked Davyd Rostislavich, consulting only with the princess and his favorite Kochkar, failing to share his thoughts with his best men. The chronicler hints that Sviatoslav's action caused general disapproval, for it was an exception to the accepted custom of consulting about everything with the retinue. The influence of the princesses may be gleaned also in the passage from the letter of Bishop Simon to the monk Polikarp. It is said there that Princess Verkhuslava attempted to obtain Polikarp a bishopric, sparing no expense.

Yet all this information yields no idea about the relations between the sexes and about life of women in society. Princesses and mothers in general then enjoyed exactly the same importance as in the later Muscovite state, except that women from higher classes lived secluded from men. In this respect the information cited above about feasts in monasteries with both men and women is important, as is the question put by the monk Yakov to Metropolitan John[48] whether men were allowed to kiss women during feasts. Monomakh in the instructions to his children touched upon the question of marital relations saying, "Love your wives, but do not allow them to rule you." It is difficult to decide how far this rule, derived from the well-known epistle,[49] was borne out by custom. The way Christian ideas helped to elevate women is demonstrated by a question of the well-known Kirik and the answer of Bishop Nifont.[50] "If it so happens that a woman's scarf is sewn into a priest's vestments," asked Kirik, "is the priest allowed to conduct service in such a garment." "It is allowed," answered Nifont, "are women pagans?"

GENERAL STATE OF MORALITY

Regarding the general state of morality in Rus at this time, taking into account the nature of the period, the circumstances and state of morals in other contemporary European Christian nations, the historian cannot pass a very severe sentence on Rus society before the 1230s. During this time in the forefront were interprincely wars, but did many violent, bloody acts occur? The murder of Yaropolk Iziaslavich, the blinding of Vasilko, fratricide among the princes of Riazan, the murder of Igor Olgovich by the Kievans, the murder of Andrei Bogoliubsky by his trusted retainers, the hanging of Igor's sons by the Galich boyars, the blinding (most probably faked)[51] of Rostislav's sons in Vladimir-Zalessk, come to mind.

It is important to remember that the princes constantly repeated that they were brothers and therefore obliged to live in friendship and not enmity, to defend the Land of Rus from its enemies and not spill Christian blood in domestic quarrels. Some might say that the words did not match the deeds, yet answer may be made that words had their power when constantly repeated in the princes' own laws, as well as by the clergy and those who refused to take part in civil wars. If these words could not halt internecine strife, at least they could soften these wars. It is important that an oppressed prince might influence an oppressor by reminding him that his conduct was like that of Sviatopolk the Damned. It is significant that when the princes learned of the blinding of Vasilko they were terrified and cried out, saying there was no such wickedness in the Land of Rus during the times of their grandfathers or fathers. It is very important that when Iziaslav Mstislavich reproached the Kievans for the murder of Igor Olgovich he said that he could not himself escape censure. The relationships between the prince, the retinue and the townsmen were generally quite gentle, as far as was possible, given the contemporary lack of defined standards. "If we go [away] alone," said Igor of Seversk and his brothers, "and the rank-and-file are left behind, we will sin before God."

A thorough study of the chronicles shows that morals were more cruel to the east and northeast of the Dnieper river. Generally there was more cruelty in the princely branch of Sviatoslav of Chernigov's descendants, and even greater cruelty in those branches of the same family established far to the east, in the territories of Murom[52] and Riazan. We note that there is greater cruelty in the very forms and expressions of the Northeast.

VIII

LITERARY AND HISTORICAL WORKS

Simultaneously with Christianity literacy put down strong roots in Rus, the soil for such development being favorable. At that time there were no obstacles to the spread of literacy. Links with Byzantium continued, metropolitans and bishops came thence, Greek princesses married Rus princes, Rus princesses married Greek princes and travelled to Constantinople and Jerusalem, as for example Yanka Vsevolodovna and St. Evfrosinia of Polotsk. Not only did clergy travel to Jerusalem, laymen also made their way there. The passion for pilgrimages grew so intense that the clergy began to oppose it, even directly forbidding travel to Jerusalem. They admonished people to lead a Christian life in their homeland and imposed public penance on those who made oaths to go to Jerusalem. Such oaths, the clergy believed, were the ruination of the Land of Rus.

Frequent and close relations with Poland and Hungary gave access to the Latin tongue. It ought to be remembered that education was closely linked with religion. If somebody read a great deal, it meant that he was well versed in religion. This was the origin of a powerful religious trend which inevitably entailed a desire to spread literacy and to acquire books. The sons and grandsons of Yaroslav I inherited his passion for spreading learning. His son Sviatoslav collected books with which he filled his rooms. Two collections from his library are preserved to the present. The second son of Yaroslav I, Vsevolod, spoke five foreign languages which he learned at home. His son Monomakh suggested that Vsevolod learned them not out of necessity in the course of foreign travels, out of curiosity rather. Monomakh further said that knowledge of foreign languages earns respect from foreigners. The religious erudition of Monomakh is evident in his works. Sviatoslav (Sviatosha) Davydovich collected books which he then donated to the Kiev monastery of the Caves. Thanks to his encouragement the monk Feodosy[1] translated Pope Leo's epistle to Flavian, archbishop of Constantinople, from the Greek.

In the Tatishchev compilation,[2] the originality of which is undoubted, are numerous items about the princes' education. About Sviatoslav

Rostislavich it was said that he knew Greek and willingly read books, about Sviatoslav Yurievich that he was keen to read and kindly received scholars coming from Greece and Western countries, often speaking with them and holding disputations. About Roman Rostislavich of Smolensk it was written that he persuaded many to study, established schools where he maintained Greek and Latin teachers at his own expense, refusing to have uneducated priests. For this purpose he used his entire property, after his death leaving nothing in the treasury, causing the people of Smolensk to bury him at their own expense.

Mikhail Yurievich, according to the same chronicle compilation, was very well versed in the Holy Bible. He conversed with Greeks and Latins in their respective languages as fluently as in the Rus tongue, but disliked religious disputes. It was said about Yaroslav Vladimirovich of Galich that he knew foreign languages, read many books and could teach the true faith himself, compelled the clergy to teach laymen, appointed monks as teachers and gave grants to monasteries for the upkeep of schools. Chronicles preserved until the present day say about Konstantin Vsevolodovich that he enriched everyone through spiritual discussions because he often and diligently read books. The Tatishchev compilation says that he was very learned and kept scholars at his court, bought many old Greek books at high prices, and ordered their translation into the Rus language. He collected information about the deeds of famous ancient princes, wrote himself and others helped him. There were over one thousand Greek books alone, which he partly bought himself and partly were donated by various patriarchs.

During the times of Vladimir and Yaroslav children were sent to study with priests attached to churches. This custom continued and undoubtedly spread during this era. There is reliable information about the existence of schools attached to churches, bishops' courts and schools established by princes at their expense. Greek was taught there because religious books translated from Greek needed to circulate to strengthen the faith. These schools trained priests, as is confirmed in information about the aim of such a school established in Smolensk by Prince Roman Rostislavich. There is further information about schools in Volhynia. That the clergy of this period clearly understood the need to educate themselves is obvious from the words of one twelfth-century clergyman. "If the rulers of this world," he said, "and those preoccupied by their daily cares demonstrate a strong interest in reading, even more must we study and with our whole heart seek knowledge of God's words about the salvation of our souls." These words confirm the love of learning and the princes' learning in general.

LITERARY MONUMENTS

Which literary monuments of this period have been preserved to the present? As early as the times of Yaroslav I people of Rus began to compose their own religious works. The first such attempt was undertaken by Hilarion, the first metropolitan of Rus origin. Given the favorable conditions for the spread of literacy at this time, a larger number of similar monuments is to be expected. Indeed some religious works written by members of the clergy of that period have come down to the present. The majority are didactic works such as an address to a particular individual in connection with a certain event, to the nation, or to the whole flock.

ST. FEODOSY

Among the former deserving mention is the answer of St. Feodosy of the Kiev monastery of the Caves to Grand Prince Iziaslav about the problem of animal slaughter, and their consumption on Sunday. Feodosy answered that after the Lord came to earth everything Jewish grew silent. There is no sin in slaughtering animals on Sunday. Yet if meat to be consumed on Sunday is slaughtered on Saturday, this clearly is a Jewish custom.

Later Feodosy named the days people should fast. On the question of Grand Prince Iziaslav concerning the Latin or Varangian faith, Feodosy answered "Their faith is wicked and their law is not pure. They do not kiss icons, they eat meat during fast days, they conduct services with unleavened bread. Christians should not give their daughters in marriage to them or take their daughters for wives. They should not fraternize with them nor be godparents to their children or ask them to be godparents to their own children, nor eat from the same dish nor drink from the same cup. If they ask you for food, give it to them in their own vessels. If they have none, give them your own, and later wash them and say a prayer over them. The Latins have Holy Scripture and the Apostles as well as icons, they attend church, but their religion is not pure. They have defiled the earth with a multitude of heresies, because the Varangians live all over the world. People who live in the Latin, Armenian and Saracen faith will not have eternal life. You must not praise their faith, only your own, and work for it by doing good deeds. Be charitable not merely to your own family and domestics, but also to strangers. Heretics and Latins should be helped when in trouble and shown mercy, and you will be recompensed

by God. If you encounter people of another faith arguing with true believers, help the true believers against the false religion. Should someone
say that God gave people both this and that religion, answer 'Does God
uphold two religions? Don't you know that it is written, one Lord, one
faith, one baptism?'"[3]

METROPOLITAN NIKIFOR'S EPISTLE

The epistle of Metropolitan Nikifor[4] to Grand Prince Vladimir Monomakh is notable because of information on Monomakh's behavior, on the
relationship between spiritual and secular power, the metropolitan to the
prince. It was written during Lent when, according to the metropolitan,
there were both church laws and a rule to say something beneficial to the
princes. The metropolitan began by discussing various sins and found
none with which he could reproach Monomakh. This prince needed to
hear no sermons eulogizing fasting because he was brought up in piety
and reared in fasting. His abstinence during fast days was observed and
admired by all. "What may be said to a prince," Nikifor continues, "who
sleeps more often than not on bare ground, flees from his home, rejects
beautiful garments, who while walking in the forest wears orphan's
clothes[5] and only when there is need visits town and dons the clothes of
a ruler. What can be said to a prince who prepares for others abundant
meals and serves his guests himself, working with his own hands. His
charity reaches even to the remittance of taxes. Others indulge in gluttony
and drunkenness, whereas the prince only sits and watches others eat and
drink, satisfied with a little food and water. He makes his subjects happy,
watches his slaves get drunk, his hands are open, he never conceals his
treasure, never counts his gold and silver and instead gives everything
away, yet his treasury is never empty."

Finally the metropolitan seemed to find cause to reproach the prince,
having discovered a weakness in him. "It seems to me, my prince," he
says, "that, unable to see everything with your own eyes, you listen to
others and an arrow enters your open ears. Think about it my prince,
search diligently, spare a thought for those whom you banished, sentenced and despised. Remember all those who said something against
somebody else. Who slandered whom? Judge them yourself, remember
all and forgive them and you will be forgiven, give and you will be given
unto... Let not my words sadden you, O prince. Do not think that someone came to me to complain and I wrote to you! No, I am writing to you

simply as a reminder needed by rulers of this world, for they have much, but many temptations fall in their path."

Here already can be seen the custom of *grieving* used by the Russian clergy in early history. Attention should be paid to this address of the metropolitan to the prince. "This word is meant for you, the good head of our and all Christ-loving lands, hallowed from the womb and anointed by a mixture of imperial and princely blood."

Another epistle of Nikifor to Monomakh was written in response to the prince's question as to how the Latins were rejected by the holy ecumenical and Orthodox church. The metropolitan cited twenty reasons explaining the separation of the Western and Eastern churches.[6] In conclusion he said to Monomakh "Read this, prince, not once, but twice and more. Read it yourself and let your sons read it. Is it not right for princes elected by God and called to the true religion to understand Christ's words and the firm foundation of the church in order to teach and admonish the people entrusted to you by God?" The content of Metropolitan John's epistle to the Roman archbishop[7] concerning unleavened bread is identical in content to Nikifor's epistle.

EPISTLE OF BISHOP SIMON

The epistle from Simon, bishop of Vladimir and Suzdal, to Polikarp, a monk of the Kiev Caves monastery, is noteworthy for some items of historical information used elsewhere in this book.[8] The author of the epistle, Simon, was first a monk in the Caves monastery, later the abbot of the Nativity monastery in Vladimir-on-the-Kliazma, and in 1214 was appointed bishop to the Vladimir-Suzdal see. Polikarp was also a monk of the Kiev monastery of the Caves and was very ambitious. To tame him, Simon wrote this epistle. "Brother," begins Simon, "sit down in silence, concentrate your mind and say to yourself 'Man! Have you not left behind the world and your real parents? You have come here for salvation, but your conduct is in no way spiritual.' Why do you call yourself a monk? After all it is not the black habit which will spare you torment. Look how you are respected here by princes, boyars and all your friends. 'You fortunate man!' they say. 'You have come to hate this world and its glory. You care nothing for the things of this world, wishing only for things celestial.' Yet you do not live like a monk, and I am ashamed of you. Those who envy us here will receive the kingdom of heaven, while we will suffer.

"Arise my brother, arise and see to your soul. Do not be gentle one day and furious and spiteful the next. One day you are quiet, then again you start grumbling about the abbot and his servants. Be not false, do not use the excuse of bodily illness to absent yourself from the church gathering. As the rain makes the seed grow, so the church inclines the soul to good deeds. All that is done in solitude, in the cell, is worthless. Twelve psalms read in solitude are not worth one 'Lord have mercy' sung in church. You must think about why you wanted to leave the holy, blessed, honest Caves monastery, the abode of salvation? I think, brother, that God has moved you to do this, unwilling to suffer your pride, and has thrown you down as once he did Satan with his apostate forces, because you refused to serve the holy man, your lord and our brother Archimandrite Ankindin, abbot of the Caves monastery. The Caves monastery is like the sea in that it holds nothing decayed, but casts it up. Woe unto you that you have written to me about your vexation, your soul has perished. I ask you how you want to save yourself. Fast and be poor, do not sleep at night. If you cannot bear vexation, you will not achieve salvation.

"Rostislav's princess Verkhuslava has written to me saying that she wants to appoint you as bishop in Novgorod, Smolensk or in Yuriev. 'I will not spare,' she writes, 'even a thousand silver pieces for you and for Polikarp.' 'My daughter Anastasia!'[9] I answered her. 'You want to commit an ungodly act. Had he stayed in the monastery without leaving and with a clear conscience, obeying the abbot and all the brethren, being sober in all things, not only would he don priestly garments, he would deserve also to enter the heavenly kingdom.'

"You want to be a bishop? Well, but read the epistle of St. Paul to Timothy[10] and think whether you are the kind of man a bishop should be. If you deserved such an office, I would not have let you go, but with my own hands would have appointed you as bishop of the double see of Vladimir-Suzdal as Prince Yury wished, but I did not agree, seeing your faintheartedness. Perfection does not mean being praised by everyone, rather improving life and preserving your purity. This is why so many bishops were appointed from the monastery of the Caves in all the Land of Rus. Read the old Rostov chronicle and you will find more than thirty. If you count them all including my sinful self, there will be about fifty. Consider now the fame of this monastery! Having felt shame, repent and be satisfied with the quiet and serene life to which the Lord has brought you.

"I would gladly leave my bishopric to work for the abbot, but you yourself know well what keeps me here. Everyone knows that I, sinful

Bishop Simon, have a cathedral church here, the adornment of all the city of Vladimir, and a second church in Suzdal which I built myself. How many towns and villages these churches have, from which tithes are collected throughout this land! All of this is in the hands of my humble self, but in the presence of God I want to tell you that all this power and glory I would deem as nothing if only I could be a broom behind the gate, or be lying as dirt in the Caves monastery and be trampled upon by men."

METROPOLITAN JOHN'S EPISTLE

The epistle of Metropolitan John (most probably John II)[11] to a monk named Jacob is interesting for it points to some customs and mores. It is an answer to certain questions regarding church discipline. "It is not necessary," wrote the metropolitan, "to communicate and serve with those who eat meat and those who celebrate the Eucharist with unleavened bread, yet to eat with them for the love of Christ is not forbidden. If someone wants to avoid this for the sake of purity or because of illness, this is allowed, but pay attention that neither temptation arises from it, nor hatred. The lesser of the two evils shall be chosen. If, as you say, some in the Land of Rus do not take the sacrament during Lent, eat meat and all manner of unclean things, they must be turned away from this habit. When they persist, they shall be refused Holy Communion and regarded as outsiders and enemies of the faith. In the same way do we treat those who have two wives or practice sorcery. Those who disobey shall be punished severely, but neither killed nor maimed."

As it was not the custom at that time for Rus princesses who married foreign rulers to keep their Orthodox faith, the metropolitan opposed the custom of princes' daughters marrying in foreign lands where the eucharist was conducted using unleavened bread, namely Catholic countries. The metropolitan instructed everyone to do everything to turn to the right faith those who made offerings to devils, bogs and wells, people who married without church blessing, who divorced and took different wives. He called lawless those who sold Christian slaves to Jews and heretics, spoke against those who of their own free will, for gain, visited pagans and ate with them unclean food. He condemned all who often arranged feasts in monasteries, invited men and women to partake together and labored to surpass each other in arranging better feasts. Such zeal stemmed not from God but from the devil, said the metropolitan.[12]

KIRIK'S QUESTIONS

The questions of the monk Kirik[13] put to the Novgorod archbishop Nifont[14] and other spiritual men, and their answers, are of similar nature. This document tells about the custom of pilgrimages to holy places. Kirik discouraged people from doing so, and he asked whether this was right. The answer was that he did very well because people travelled in order to eat and drink and they did nothing. Another question was what if a woman is in labor and people take and cut bread and cheese and drink mead? The answer was "Woe to those drinking on account of a woman in labor." The custom is mentioned of announcing the baptism of a Bulgarian, a Polovetsian, a Chud for forty days and of a Slav for eight days. From this we learn that in Kirik's time some Slavs were still unconverted. The notions of that period are expressed in the rule that after sunset the dead were not to be buried. Better to bury them when the sun is high because the deceased sees sun for the last time before the general resurrection.

As far as morals are concerned, apparently some men openly lived with their mistresses. There is information about the custom of wives washing their bodies in water and giving this water to their husbands to drink if they noticed that they stopped loving them. Such people were subject to the same public penance as those who took their children to Latin priests to pray, or those who took sick children to magi.

POLITICAL AND GENERAL TEACHINGS

Now let us turn to religious instructions preached to the whole people. Here the teaching of St. Feodosy of the Caves monastery about godly princes is of primary importance. "God in His anger brings disasters or pagan attacks because we do not turn to God. Internecine wars are caused by the devil's temptation and bad men. God punishes a sinful land by death, famine, pagan attacks, drought and other scourges..." The following words are important for understanding of the morals and customs of the period. "Don't we act as pagans? If somebody meets a monk or a nun, a pig or a piebald horse, they turn back. They indulge in superstitions prompted by the devil. Others believe that sneezing is healthy for their head. Using sorcery, magic, lechery, drunkenness, usury, examples, thieving, lies, envy, false accusations, trumpets, mummers, psaltery, pipes, all sorts of games and ungodly things, the devil tempts people and distracts them from God.

"We can see as other evils the inclination to drink, lechery and devilish sports. When we are standing in church how dare we laugh or whisper? For holidays we need not have large feasts. It is better to avoid drinking. Woe to drunkards! By drinking excessively we repel our guardian angel and attract the devil. The Holy Spirit is remote from a drunkard, and hell is near...."

From a homily attributed to St. Feodosy it is learned how pagan customs mixed with Christian. "For dinner, two prayers, one at the beginning the other at the end. For the peace of someone's soul kutia,[15] but no dinners or suppers are needed for that purpose. Neither water nor eggs shall be added to kutia. Church hymns shall not be sung at a feast where drink is served apart from these three: at the beginning of the meal Jesus is praised, at the end the Virgin Mary, and afterwards the host." There are also several instructions given by St. Feodosy to the brethren of his monastery. In one place the saint says "If it were only possible I would plead every day and with tears in my eyes. I would beg and fall to your feet, that no one miss the time for prayers. When a man who works in the field or vineyard sees the fruit, he does not remember the toil. He who harvests the fruit joyfully prays to God. If he sees the field overgrown with thorns, what does he do? How many years have passed since I saw anyone coming to ask me how to save his soul?"

The homily of the Rus metropolitan Nikifor is remarkable for its beginning, which clearly shows that the Greek metropolitan did not know the Rus language. He did not speak his words to the people, writing them instead. "I have been denied the gift of tongues," he wrote, "which is why I stand among you voiceless and utterly silent. Because teaching is needed now as Lent approaches, I offer you my teachings in writing." The preacher likewise spoke against usury and drinking.

The homily of Bishop Luka Zhidiata of Novgorod,[16] who died in 1060, is remarkable for a simplicity fully matching the level of his flock. "Hear, O brethren," he exhorted, "this is the commandment we Christians should keep first of all, to believe in one God hailed in the Trinity, in the Father, the Son and the Holy Spirit, as the apostles taught and the holy Fathers confirmed. Believe in the resurrection, eternal life, and eternal suffering for sinners. Be not lazy in attending church for matins, midday prayer or vespers. In your room first bow to God, and only then sleep. When in church stand in the fear of God, do not converse, do not think about other things, instead pray to God with all your thoughts and He will forgive you your sins. Love every man, and your brethren in particular, have not one thing in your heart and another on your lips.

"Do not dig a pit for your brother lest God make you fall into worse. Suffer any offence, do not render evil for evil. Praise one another, and God will praise you. Do not cause quarrels, lest you be called a son of the devil. Make peace among men, and you will be the son of God. Do not condemn your brother even in your thoughts, rather remember your sins, and God will not condemn you. Remember and love strangers, the poor, those imprisoned in dungeons, and be merciful to your orphans (slaves). Brethren must not indulge in devilish games (masquerades) or speak indecent words and be angry every day. Hold not others in contempt, do not laugh at anyone, bear misfortunes and place your hope in God. Do not be violent or proud. Remember that perhaps tomorrow you will be stench, rot and worms. Be humble and meek. A proud man has the devil in his heart and God's word does not reach him. Honor old men and your parents, do not swear using God's name and do not ask others to swear, do not curse. Judge justly, take no bribes, engage not in usury, and fear God. Slaves, honor your prince and submit to God first, then to your lords. Honor in your heart God's clergy and servants of the church. Do not kill, do not steal, do not lie or bear false witness, nor quarrel, be not envious, do not slander, do not indulge in lechery with a female slave, nor with anyone else. Do not drink at the wrong time. Drink always with moderation, not to get drunk. Be not angry or insolent. Rejoice with those who are joyful and grieve with the sorrowing. Eat no unclean food, observe holy days and God will give you peace, Amen!"

This monument is very valuable for historians because it fully portrays the society to which it is addressed. At the same time it is noteworthy that the epistle of Luka Zhidiata reflects the general character of the Novgorod people as found also in the Novgorod sources. Both the Novgorod Chronicle and the homily are notable for their simplicity, brevity, succinctness and lack of ornamentation. Merely the style of Zhidiata's epistle is sufficient proof that it was written in Novgorod.

CYRIL OF TUROV'S SERMONS

The sermons of the Southern bishop Cyril of Turov[17] are different in character from the above work. Generally works written in the South differed from those of the North in that they are more ornate. This is due to the difference in the character of the people. The citizens of Novgorod required their bishop to speak in a style different from the Southern Rus. Zhidiata's teachings contain short expositions of the rules of Christian morality. Cyril of Turov's work is mainly an eloquent presentation of holy events celebrated by the church on the day a sermon is preached. His aim was to demonstrate to the people the importance and greatness of the event celebrated, to invite people to celebrate it to the glory of Christ or His saints. Hence the similarity between Cyril's sermons and the church hymns from which he borrowed the form and whole expressions. In both the composition is identical. The events are enlivened by a dialogue of the participants. In Cyril's works there is love of allegories and parables, and desire to transform events. He displays a particular skill in comparisons to bring events and phenomena closer to his listeners. Study of his works indicates that he was the precursor and fellow-countryman of later church orators from Southwestern Rus who for a very long period were almost the only church orators and models. Just as the style of Zhidiata shows that he is from Novgorod, the style of Cyril of Turov points to an author from Southern Rus.

Of the works of Cyril which have survived the ten sermons preached during the Sundays from Palm Sunday until Trinity are the most important. The first sermon (Palm Sunday) gives the reader a taste of the author's style. "Today Christ comes from Bethany to Jerusalem, riding on a donkey, and the prophecy of Zachariah is fulfilled. Having understood this prophesy, we rejoice. The souls of the saints are called the daughters of the celestial Jerusalem, while the colts are the pagans whom the apostles sent by Jesus forced to renounce the devil's flattery.... Today the apostles donned their vestments, those on which Jesus was seated. Herein is found the revelation of the blessed secret. Those vestments are the Christian virtues of the apostles who, by their teachings, brought pious people to God's throne and to the vessel of the Holy Spirit. Now nations take the path to God, some with vestments others with tree branches. Jesus showed the good and the true way to people of peace and to all great men of this world. Having sown along this way charity and gentleness, they may easily enter the kingdom of heaven. Those who break the branches are simple people and sinners who with a sorrowing heart and tender souls, through fasting and prayers, straighten their path and come to God..." and so on.

The end of the sermon is remarkable because it illustrates the main aim of Cyril's sermon. "After the sermons let us crown the holy church with songs as if with flowers, and beautify the holy days, and we will praise God and glorify our saviour Jesus." The lush Southern spring yielded Cyril many colors for his sermon on St. Thomas Sunday.[18] "Today spring appears fresh, and enlivens all earthly existence. The stormy winds blow gently and generate fruits, and the earth, giving nurture to the seed, brings forth verdant grass. For spring is the beautiful faith in Christ which, through baptism, produces a regeneration of man, and the stormy winds are the evil, sinful thoughts that, changed to virtue through repentance, generate soul-saving fruits. The earth of our being, having received the Word of God like a seed and, passing through an ecstatic labor, through the fear of him, brings forth a spirit of salvation.

"Today the newborn lambs and calves frisk and leap about joyfully and returning to their mothers gambol about inspired the shepherds, playing on their reeds, to praise Christ in joy. The lambs, I say, are the gentle people from among the pagans and the calves, the idolaters of the unbelieving countries. They, having accepted the Law through Christ's incarnation and the teachings of the Apostles and miracles, and having returned to the holy church, suck the milk of its teachings. And the teachers of Christ's flock, praying for all, praise Christ the Lord, who collected all the wolves and sheep into one herd.

"Today the trees send forth buds and fragrant flowers bloom, and behold the gardens emanate a sweet fragrance, and the workers laboring in hope acclaim Christ the giver of fruits. Before we were like trees of the forest that bear no fruit, but today the faith of Christ has been grafted on our unbelief, and those who already held to the roots of Jesse have burgeoned with the flowers of virtue and expect through Christ a regeneration in heaven, and the saints who labor for the Church expect a reward from Christ. Today the plowman of the Word leads the oxen of the Word to the spiritual yoke, sinks the plows of baptism into the furrows of thought and deepening them to the furrows of repentance plants in them the spiritual seed and rejoices in the hope of spiritual returns." And so on.[19]

The sermon for the Sunday of the Myrrh-bearing Women[20] brings to mind almost exactly the canticles and hymns sung and read during the last days of Passion week. In some passages there are almost identical expressions as, for example, at the beginning of the lament of the Mother of God.

"Son! Every living creature feels compassion for me, seeing how you were unjustly killed. Alas! My child, my light and the creator of creatures." Further on the words of Joseph [of Arimathea] to Pilate are nothing more than an extension of a church song "Come and let us gratify Joseph of eternal memory." The sermon ends with an eulogy to Joseph remarkable for its oratorical form, customary for that period. "To whom shall I compare this righteous man? Shall I call you heaven? Yet you were brighter than the skies in honoring God, because during Christ's passion the sky clouded over and hid its light, and you, rejoicing, carried God on your hands. Shall I call you flowering earth? Yet you are more honest than the earth, because while it was quaking with fear you, together with Nicodemus, gladly wrapped God's body in a shroud and placed it in the tomb,"[21] and so on.

The sermon preached during the Week of the Enfeebled[22] is the best example of Cyril's style. In the complaint of the enfeebled, crying out against his sufferings, the imagery characteristic of Cyril's fellow-countrymen comes to the fore. "Shall I call myself dead?" says the enfeebled one. "My belly craves food and my tongue is parched with thirst. Shall I consider myself alive? I cannot even move, let alone rise from my bed. My feet will not walk, my hands cannot do any work, I cannot even touch myself with them. I am a buried corpse, my bed is my coffin. I am a dead man among the living, and a living man among the dead, because I am fed like a living man but like a corpse I do nothing. I suffer hellish torment from those who shamelessly abuse me. Youths laugh at me, they insult each other using my name. For the old men I am like a parable of punishment. All mock and deride me and my suffering is twice as great because of this. Inside my illness torments me, outside I am insulted by those who humiliate me. The phlegm of those who spit on me covers my whole body, hunger overpowers me worse than my illness because even if I find some nourishment I cannot place it in my mouth with my hand. I beg all and sundry to feed me, and I share my poor victuals with those who feed me. I groan with tears in my eyes, tormented by painful illness, and no one comes to visit me."

Christ's answer is similar. "Why do you say that there is no man? For your sake I became a man, for your sake I left the scepter of the kingdom above and I wandered serving those in the kingdom below. I have not come in order that they serve me, I have come to serve others. For your sake, being incorporeal, I donned flesh and will heal diseases of the spirit and the flesh. For your sake, invisible to the angelic host, I appeared before all men because I do not want to despise you my image, lying in decay. I want to save him and to bring him to true reason, and you are saying there is no man? I became a man, and I will make man God, because I said 'There will be gods, and all are sons of the Almighty.' Who has served you more faithfully than I? I have created all creatures to labor for you. Heaven and earth serve you, heaven by giving moisture, earth by bringing forth fruit. The sun gives you light and warmth, the moon and stars illuminate the nights. For you clouds fill the earth with rain, and the earth brings forth all manner of grass and trees to serve you. For your sake the rivers are filled with fish and the desert feeds wild beasts, yet you say 'There is no man.'"

The sermon preached on the fifth Sunday after Easter contains a reproach to the people for not attending church to hear the bishop's words. "I had hoped, friends and brothers, that each week more and more people would flock to the church. Now I see that fewer and fewer people come. If I preached to you my own words, you would have done well not to come to church, but I announce to you as a pastor and read to you Christ's words."

The sermon on the state of the soul after it departs from the body also is attributed to Cyril of Turov. In this work enumerating the sufferings encountered he considers the seventh to be "the unruly word, indecent speech, shameless words and dancing, whether at feasts and at weddings, whether at nightly gatherings, during games and in the streets," and the fifteenth to be "any heresy and belief in evil meetings, sneezing, crowing of birds, fortune-telling and telling fairy tales, and playing of the psaltery."

OTHER SERMONS

Other interesting homilies of unknown geographical origin and authorship have come down from this period. They illustrate how the church fought against the consequences of interprincely clan relations and how, from the very beginning, it supported establishment of political relations. The author of one sermon addressed the princely retinue as follows. "If you support princes other than your own, you will be like adulterous wives." The sermon contains a call to be brave, consonant with the spirit of the time. "Son! When you go to war with your prince, ride forward with the brave. You will win honor for your family and good name for yourself. What can be better than to die before your prince!"

About the pagan priests it is enjoined "Watch out, my children, for pagan priests." About churchmen it is written "If you invite a monk into your home or any other deacon and you want be hospitable, pour no more than three goblets, then give him free choice. If he pours more wine, he is responsible. It is not permitted to shame God's servants by making them drunk. When they depart bow to them after receiving their blessing." About slaves, "Do not insult your household orphans,[23] love them more instead. Do not starve or keep them naked, because they are your household poor. The poor can ask for alms elsewhere, but slaves are solely in your hands. Love your slaves and teach them about salvation and repentance and free the old... If you do not feed or shoe your slave or handmaiden, and they are killed when stealing, you will answer for their blood. You are like an apostle in your home. Teach through awe and kindness. When slaves do not listen and do not fulfill your wishes, spare not the rod, up to six or twelve bruises, and if the fault is great, up to twenty, and when the fault is very serious, up to thirty bruises, but no more than thirty... Honor and love the slaves whom you have taken with you to war, for they will help you if there are difficulties and battles."

Information on the means used by preachers, reminiscent of Vladimir's conversion, and on the fate sometimes befalling zealous missionaries is found the *Life* of St. Avraamy of Smolensk. "This Avraamy consoled those who came to him with Christ's grace and so charmed their souls that the abbot himself could not bear it no longer, seeing so many people flocking to him. He wanted to forbid him to preach, saying 'I am responsible to God for you, so you must cease teaching,' and was very angry with him. Then he went to the town and stayed at the monastery of the Holy Cross and there even more people began to come to him and his teaching spread. He painted two icons, one depicting the Day of Judgement of the Second Coming, the other picturing the spiritual torments which nobody can avoid. To all who came he spoke of this terrible day and he honored the great and ecumenical teacher John Chrysostom and St. Ephraim and all the saints who proclaimed the Lord. Satan entered the hearts of the envious and stayed therein. Some began telling tales to the bishop, others reviled and vexed him, some others called him a heretic, and yet others said about him that he read forbidden books. Some said he misbehaved with women, while priests said that he corrupted all our children, who spoke as though nobody in town would hear a word against the blessed Avraamy. They all gathered, young and old, the whole city. Some said he must be put in prison, others that he be nailed to the wall and burned, yet others wanted to drown him, and they marched him through the town and all gathered at the bishop's court, the abbot, the priest, the monk, the prince and the boyars...."

VLADIMIR MONOMAKH'S INSTRUCTION

Apart from sermons by churchmen there is also the *Instruction* written by the most distinguished prince of the period, Vladimir Monomakh, for his children.[24] It deals with the obligations of a man in general and the duties of princes in particular. It is concerned with religious, family and social duties and constitutes a model for this type of didactic work found in later periods. "In your heart have the fear of God and give alms in abundance, because this is the beginning of all good." These are the opening lines of Monomakh's *Instruction*, and he goes on to explain his reason for writing it.

After the conflict with Davyd Igorevich at the Vitichi conference[25] he went north to the region of Rostov. When he was on the Volga he received an embassy from his cousins inviting him to join them on an expedition against Rostislav's sons, the princes of Galich, who refused to fulfill the general interprincely agreement. The cousins sent word to Monomakh, saying "Come quickly with us, we will chase away Rostislav's sons and take away their territory. If you fail to come, you are on your own and we are on our own." "Be as angry as you wish," Monomakh answered, "but I cannot come with you and violate my oath." The threat of the brothers to disunite greatly saddened Monomakh. Being thus distressed, he opened the Psalter and found the place "My soul is also sore troubled, but thou, O Lord, how long?"[26] Consoled by the psalm he decided there and then to compose the *Instruction* for his sons, the key idea of which is that man must never stray from the right path and rely always only on God, who will not let a man perish who is doing His will.

After copying from the psalter the passages expressing this idea, as well as the admonition of Basil the Great, Monomakh continues "Thus our Lord has promised us victory over our enemies through three means of conquering and overcoming them: repentance, tears, and almsgiving. My children, the commandment of God to conquer your sins through these three means is not severe. But I implore you, for God's sake, be not lazy, not forget these three means. For they are not difficult of attainment. Not through solitude nor an ascetic life, nor by such fasting as other good men endure, rather through easy efforts may you thus obtain the mercy of God... Give heed to me, and accept a half of my instruction if you are not disposed to adopt it all. Ask God to forgive your sins with tears in your eyes and not only in church, but also when you go to sleep. Do not forget one single evening to bow, because this and singing conquer the devil, and a man is forgiven his sins. When you are riding forth on your horse, if you have no special subject of conversation with a companion and cannot utter some other prayer, then say silently 'Lord have mercy!' This is the best prayer of all. Above all things, forget not the poor, but support them to the extent of your means. Give to the orphan, protect the widow and permit the mighty to destroy no man. Take not the life of the just or the unjust, nor order him killed....

"In conversation, whatever the nature of your speech, swear not by the name of God, for that is unnecessary. Whenever you kiss the cross to confirm an oath made to your brethren or any other man, first test your heart as to whether you can abide by your word, then kiss the cross. Once you have given your oath, abide by it, lest you destroy your soul by its violation.

"Receive with affection the blessing of bishops, priests, and abbots, and shun them not, but rather, according to your means, love and help them, that you may receive from them their intercession in the presence of God. Above all things, admit no pride in your hearts, but say 'We are but mortal. Today we live and tomorrow we shall be in the grave. All that you have given us is not ours, but yours, which you have lent us for a few days.' Hoard not treasures in the earth, for therein lies great sin. Honor the ancient as your father, and the youth as your brother... In your own household do not be idle, but supervise everything. Do not leave everything to your steward or young servant, lest guests speak slightingly of your home or your table.

"When you set out to war, be not inactive, depend not upon your captains, nor waste your time in drinking, eating, or sleeping. Set the sentries yourselves, and take your rest only after you have posted them at night at every important point around your troops. Then take your rest, but arise early. Do not put off your accoutrements without a quick glance about you, for a man may thus perish suddenly through his own carelessness.

"When journeying anywhere by road through your domain, do not permit your servitors to do violence to villages, whether your own or another's, or upon the dwellings or the fields, lest men revile you. Wherever you go, as often as you halt, give the beggar to eat and to drink. Furthermore, honor the stranger, if not with a gift, at least with food and drink, whencesoever he comes to you, be he simple, or noble, or an emissary. For travellers give a man a universal reputation as generous or niggardly.

"Visit the sick, and pay your respects to the dead, for we all are but mortal. Pass no man without a greeting, but give him a kindly word. Love your wives, but grant them no power over you.... Forget not what useful knowledge you possess, and acquire that with which you are not acquainted.... Do not be idle in doing good, especially do not neglect attending church. Let not the rising sun find you in bed...."[27] Finally

Monomakh tells his children about what he did. This story is important for the historian, and it has been used elsewhere in this history.

PILGRIMAGE LITERATURE

We have observed the passion for pilgrimages and for travel to the Holy Land which was popular at this time among the Rus. Description of one such pilgrimage made by Abbot Daniel has come down to our times.[28] This description is particularly interesting because it does not display the spirit of intolerance towards the Latin Christians who ruled at that time in Jerusalem.[29] King Baldwin[30] kindly received the Rus abbot, who in return spread his fame in the Land of Rus. "He summoned and received me kindly and liked me very much because he is a kind man, very humble and not proud. 'My prince and lord,' I said to him, 'I beseech you for God's sake and in the name of the Rus princes to allow me to place a candle in the Holy Sepulchre on behalf of all the Land of Rus.' He lovingly allowed me this and sent his man with me....

"God listened, and in the Holy Sepulchre, as in all the other holy places, the names of the Rus princes and princesses and bishops and abbots and boyars and my spiritual children I did not forget. Here I praise my God that I, a wretch, was worthy to write the names of the Rus princes in the monastery of St. Sabbas,[31] and today they are remembered in litanies for the rulers with their wives and children. Their names are Mikhail Sviatopolk, Vasily Vladimir, Davyd Sviatoslavich, Mikhail Oleg, Pankraty Sviatoslav, Gleb Menskoy and as many as I remembered.[32] A liturgy was sung for the Rus princes, and for all the Christians fifty liturgies, and for the dead also a liturgy was sung. To all who honor this with faith and love there is a blessing from God and from the Holy Sepulchre, and from all the holy places. My brothers and my lords! Do not scold my weak mind and my crudeness. This is not written to praise me, but for the sake of the Holy Sepulchre, for those who would with love honor and receive recompense from God our savior. The peace of God be with you all for ever and ever. Amen." Daniel met in Jerusalem many other Rus pilgrims from Kiev and Novgorod.

EPISTLE OF DANIEL THE EXILE

The work of another Daniel,[33] the so-called *Epistle of Daniel the Exile,* to Prince Yury Vladimirovich Dolgoruky,[34] likewise relates to this period. From this touching letter we learn merely that a relatively young man of unknown social origin and estate angered the prince and was imprisoned at the Lacha lake. In his letter Daniel says nothing of his guilt but from the strong remarks against men and women close to the prince it could be assumed that he ascribed his misfortune to their slander. It seems that this work was known among educated people and was appreciated for its stylistic ornaments, favored in the olden days. Daniel, as may be observed from his work, considered himself a wise man.

Here are several examples of his wisdom. "Let us proclaim as if through golden trumpets, brothers, the reason of our minds and let us play the silver organs and elaborate our wisdom... Do not look at me like a wolf looks at a lamb. Look at me instead the way a mother looks at her offspring. Look at the birds! They do not plant, they do not harvest, neither do they store their food in a granary. They rely on God's mercy.[35] So we, prince and lord, wish for your grace. For some Bogoliubovo is a wondrous place, for me it is bitter grief. For some Beloozero [White Lake] is a clear water lake, for me it is a lake of tar. For some Lake Lacha is a pleasant place, for me it is a place where I wept bitterly....

"My prince and my lord! Save me from this poverty, as a chamois from the snare, as bird from a trap, as a duckling from the talons of a hawk, as a sheep from the lion's mouth. For I, my prince, am as a tree by the roadside, which many cut up and use for fire. I have been insulted by all, for I am guarded by the fear of your storm.... As spring adorns the earth with flowers, so you my prince and lord revive a man with your grace, orphans and widows oppressed by the magnates... As a beast which is large but has no head, so good regiments perish without a good prince. The psaltery is tuned by fingers, the body is supported by veins, an oak tree is strong thanks to many roots, so is our city strong by your rule, because the prince is a generous father to all. Many servants who lose their mothers and fathers come to him. Those who serve a good master gain their freedom, those who serve a bad master are forced to labor long. For the prince is generous like a river without banks flowing through woods, giving water not only to men but to cattle and all the animals. When a prince is miserly like a river with a stony bank it is impossible to drink from that river, or give water to a horse. When a boyar is generous, he is like a sweet well, if he is miserly he is like a salty well.

"Do not have your homestead near the prince's court, do not have a village near the prince's village. For his steward is full of fire and his assistants are like sparks. If you can guard from the fire, you cannot guard from a spark. My prince and my lord! Do not deprive of bread a wise beggar, do not praise to the skies a rich man who is mad. The poor man is wise as gold in a poor vessel, the rich man is as stupid as a beautiful headdress filled with straw. My Lord! Do not judge me by my outward appearance. Look instead at my inner qualities. My clothes are poor, but my intellectual qualities are rich. I am young in years but old in wisdom Put clay vessels under my tongue and my words will pour forth the sweetest honey....

"It is not the sea that drowns ships, rather the winds, not the fire that melts the iron but the bellows. So it is not the prince himself who follows an evil path, but his counsellors lead him there. With good counsellors he will gain a high throne, with bad he will lose even a poor one... He is not a man among men who is governed by his wife. It is not true work to drive a cart reined by wives. What is an evil woman? A slatternly hostess, the devil's hireling, a rebellion, the blinding of reason, the beginning of all malice.... I have not been beyond the seas nor have I been tutored by philosophers. Like a honey bee I have been gathering diverse information and from it I have developed a thirst for knowledge in order to fathom the depth of the sea. All this is not directed by my own reason, rather by the will of God."

The following was added to the *Epistle*. "These words Daniel wrote while in prison by the White Lake,[36] sealed in wax and put into the lake. A fish ate them, was caught by a fisherman and brought to the prince, who opened it. The prince read the epistle and ordered Daniel freed from his bitter imprisonment."

POETRY

The earliest works of popular imagination date from the times of St. Vladimir. Their content is based on heroes' deeds in struggles with the steppe barbarians that interested contemporaries. During this era that struggle continued and, as earlier, was the main topic of songs and tales, now with princes replacing the heroes. The most famous and most popular name in this struggle was that of Monomakh. It would be unimaginable that the campaigns of the good sufferer for the Rus land against the pagans could fail to nourish poetic folk tales.[37]

Echoes of these tales may be detected at the beginning of the Volhynia Chronicle. "Grand Prince Roman, the unforgettable ruler of all Rus, died. It was he who conquered the heathen nations and with wisdom fulfilled all the divine commandments. He would strike against the infidels like a lion. He could be as full of wrath against them as a lynx. He annihilated them like a crocodile. Many were the times he crossed their lands like an eagle. He was as courageous as an aurochs. He continued the deeds of his grandfather, Prince Vladimir Monomakh, who destroyed the infidel sons of Ishmael, known as Polovetsians. He drove Khan Otrok from the steppes to Obezy beyond the Iron Gates. Only the horde of Khan Syrchan remained on the river Don, where he had only fish for food. It was at that time that Prince Vladimir Monomakh drank water from the Don with his golden helmet. He conquered the entire Polovetsian land and drove away those accursed sons of Hagar.

"After the death of Prince Vladimir Monomakh, Khan Syrchan sent his bard, Oria, to his brother, Khan Otrok then still in the land of Abkhazia. 'Brother!' he said, 'Vladimir is dead. Come back, brother, return to your native land.' And he added 'Tell these words I have spoken to my brother and sing him our Polovetsian songs. But, if he does not want to return, let him smell the fragrance of our prairie grass that is called wormwood.'

"When Khan Otrok inhaled the fragrance of the prairie wormwood he began to weep. 'It is still better,' he said, 'to die in one's native country than to win glory in a foreign land.' Thus Khan Otrok then decided to return to his native soil. From him was born Konchak who took from us the Sula. Otrok came barefoot, and on his shoulder he carried a cauldron."[38]

THE TALE OF IGOR'S CAMPAIGN

The poetic *Tale of Igor's Campaign*[39] about the ill-starred expedition of the princes of Severia, Igor Sviatoslavich and his brothers, against the Polovetsians has been preserved until our times in its entirety. The particular valor of these princes is described, as is their zeal to win fame in the struggle against the pagans, and their magnanimity, not wishing to abandon their men to the Polovetsians. Therefore they well deserved the love of the people. There are interesting details of the campaign, its unusual success at the beginning and unusual disaster at the end, which increased rather than diminished their fame. Finally there is Igor's miraculous escape from captivity. All this must have awakened strong interest in an event which later was the subject of a highly embellished poetic tale. The details of the expedition, as recorded in the chronicle, underline best the interest of Ancient Rus in this event, best explain the reason for, and the necessity of, the tale's existence. There is no need to suppose that its author was even from the Severian lands because at that time the descendants of Oleg dominated all of Southern Rus. The senior member of that branch, Sviatoslav Vsevolodovich, then ruled in Kiev. Therefore the disaster striking the Severian princes must have gained them wide sympathy also on western bank of the Dnieper.

The author of the tale did not wish to begin his story with the expedition of the princes of Severia against the Polovetsians. He wanted to use ancient tales as a kind of preamble. In fact he limited himself to later *poetic legends*,[40] beginning with the times of Vladimir Monomakh, whom he calls Vladimir the Old in contrast to the other, younger Vladimirs. These *poetic legends* of the times of Vladimir Monomakh he contrasted with songs based on the ideas of the prophetic Boian. Whoever Boian was, the composer of real or invented ancient Rus songs, or even Homer as some people think, it is obvious that the author of the *Tale of Igor's Campaign* contrasted the works of Boian with his own times. At the same time he did not want to return to remote times and events sung by Boian or, and this seems very probable, he contrasted the *invented poetic legend* with the *thought* contained in a tale. He presented the story of a true event without the smallest deviation from it, the content of a song, the author of which took greater liberties even when describing a true event or a real person. "Isn't it time, brothers, to tell a story of a war in the old words, the story of Igor's campaign, Igor Sviatoslavich! This lay must begin in the way of stories of our times, not according to Boian's way. The prophetic Boian, when he wished to sing a song for someone, let his thoughts spread wide, like a wolf running, like an eagle in the sky."

"Thus," continued the author of the *Tale*, "let's start, brothers, our tale from the times of old Vladimir and continue until the days of our own Igor, who fortified his mind, sharpened his heart with bravery, filled it with warlike spirit and led his warriors to the land of the Polovetsians to avenge the Land of Rus." After that passage he continues "Then Igor glanced at the bright sun and saw all his warriors covered with darkness."

Here an omission is immediately evident because the author promised to begin from Old Monomakh. A story about the struggle of Monomakh and the princes with the Polovetsians that followed must be assumed here, and as well as later a natural transition to Igor's expedition against the pagans. It is very likely that the poetic tale of Monomakh's expeditions and events in the steppe after his death quoted above was among the stories with which the author of the *Tale of Igor's Campaign* began his narrative.

True to his promise he relates the poetic legends that follow. His story is almost identical to the story of the chronicler, only poetic embellishments

are added. The story of the chronicle is much more detailed. It is interesting that the *Tale* praises Vsevolod Sviatoslavich more than Igor, his
older brother. In the battle Vsevolod is placed in the foreground. This is
the difference between the story in the *Tale* and the chronicle. The preference given to Vsevolod is explained by the chronicler who, when telling of the death of Vsevolod, adds that this son of Oleg exceeded
everyone in merit.

What is most interesting are the words of the author about interprincely quarrels. In strong terms he describes the disputes which took
place after Oleg Sviatoslavich was forced from his territory. "Then the
land was sown with quarrels and grew with them, the lives of Dazhbog's
grandsons[41] were lost in the princely sedition, a man's age was cut short.
Then in the Land of Rus the cry of those who then toiled on the land was
rarely heard, when crows screeched often, dividing the corpses among
themselves, and the jackdaws often croaked to each other as they perched
for their prey."

Elsewhere he says "Brother said to brother 'This is mine and this is
also mine.' About small things the princes spoke as of great things. They
started to assail each other, and the pagans from all sides came and won
victories in the Land of Rus." Describing the general grief in Rus on
hearing of the destruction of Igor's host, the author of the *Tale* again
mentions the internecine wars. "Kiev moaned for grief, Chernigov on
account of raids, and anguish spread in the Land of Rus. Yet the princes
created their own disasters and the pagans attacked the Land of Rus, taking tribute of one squirrel for each homestead." In this respect the complaint of old Sviatoslav of Kiev learning of the disaster which struck the
princes of Severia is of interest. "All evil comes from princely disorders.
The favorable moment is lost because of it... O Grand Prince Vsevolod
(III)! Will you not even in thought fly here from afar to guard your father's golden throne? For yours is to drain the Volga of water by splashing it with your oars, and empty the Don by drinking from your helmets.
Were you only here a slave girl would cost a nogata, and a male captive
a rezan."[42]

In the name of Sviatoslav the author addressed other princes as well,
demanding they help the Land of Rus take revenge on the pagans for
Igor's injury. Turning to the Vseslav branch, the princes of Polotsk, he
reprimanded them as the initiators of domestic conflicts enabling the
pagans to attack the Land of Rus. Here he means the first conflict following the death of Yaroslav, started by Vseslav of Polotsk. "O the Land of

Rus will groan," adds the author, "recalling the first period of history and the first princes. Old Vladimir (Monomakh) could not be confined[43] to the Kiev hills."

SONGS

Among the historic figures mentioned in ancient Rus songs and poems of this era, Vasily Buslaev of Novgorod was a real person.[44] Several features in the song about him accurately portray ancient times in Novgorod, others portray the common ancient period in Rus. "In the famous Great Novgorod there lived Buslay until he was ninety years of age. With Novgorod he lived in peace and did not quarrel, nor did he exchange angry words with the men of Novgorod. After Buslay's death his wife Amelfa Timofeevna was left with a young son, Vasily Buslaevich." This Vasily is presented in the song as a model, the leader of the wild and dissolute youth of Novgorod, famous for their exploits in the North, striking everywhere without the word of Novgorod, leaving in peace neither their own people nor foreigners. Vasily befriended drunkards, mindless people, boisterous gilded youth. While drunk he misbehaved in the streets, assailing and injuring passersby. People complained about the young rogue, but Novgorod tried neither to apprehend nor punish him.

He listened to a different authority, that of his old mother, to whom the city complained. The townsmen and the rich complained much about her son's bad behavior. She took him to task and scolded him. He was displeased by the reproaches and decided to gather a band of young men like himself who could do what they wanted and answer to no man. "Whoever wishes to drink and eat cooked food," he exclaimed, "come to Vaska, to the wide court, there you can drink and eat cooked food and wear gaudy clothes." There were many takers, twenty-nine men in all. They assembled at the fraternity of St. Nicholas. Vasily paid for each five rubles and for himself fifty rubles, and the church elder accepted them as brothers. In the evening merriment began, which the chronicler viewed as invented by the devil. They started wrestling and boxing in another place, then the boxing developed into a huge fray.

It is said that the German merchants, in agreement with Novgorod, made their residence secure against fighting, the usual Novgorod amusement. Not for nothing was there a legend in Novgorod that Perun,[45] when carried to the Volkhov river over a great bridge, let fall his club and said "Let the men of Novgorod remember me by this!" Brainless people kill each other with this club, giving pleasure to the devil, added the chronicler.

Vasily interfered in a fight and somebody rather clumsily struck him. He called to his mates that he was being beaten. His followers leaped to his aid and a brawl developed. "Soon the street was cleared, many were killed, two or three had arms and legs broken." When Buslaevich saw he had the upper hand he challenged the whole city to a battle and agreed with Novgorod that if he and his band won the citizens would pay him tribute until his death. If the men of Novgorod were victors, he would pay them tribute. "A great battle developed, and they fought all day until evening. Buslaevich and his men were winning. The men of Novgorod, seeing this, turned once more with gifts and requests to his mother."

Maternal authority is revealed here in all its might. The man who challenged the whole city of Novgorod to battle, and won, was taken by the hand by his mother's maid and led to his parental home. There his mother ordered him locked in a deep cellar, behind an iron door and Damascene steel locks.[46] Meantime, profiting from the absence of the leader, Novgorod gained the upper hand. The vanquished, catching sight of Vasily's mother's maid walking to fetch water from the Volkhov, begged her not to let them perish, that their leader be freed. The maid listened and opened the cellar where Vasily was locked up. He returned to his men and again brought them victory. "The wings of the bright falcons have grown again, the youths have more courage, the peasants (of Novgorod) must submit and make peace."

There is another song about how the same Buslaev went to pray. He visited his mother and hovered around her asking her blessing that he might travel to Jerusalem with his valiant band. His mother's reply is curious in that it clearly describes the period. "If you go to pursue good deeds, I will give you my blessing, but if you, my child, are going to rob, I will not give you my blessing, and the earth shall not carry Vasily's body." Buslaevich sailed with his men to Jerusalem and on the way met some seafaring merchants. In reply to their questions about his destination he gave a remarkable answer. "Seafaring merchants," he said, "my journey is not of my own will. In my youth I was in much fighting and many robberies, now in my old age I want to save my soul." When Vasily came to Jerusalem "he went to a cathedral church and had a mass said for the health of his mother and his own, and a requiem mass for his father and his entire family. The next day he had a mass said with prayers for his brave companions who in their youth fought often and committed many robberies." Buslaevich was not destined to return home from his travels. He neither believed in dreams nor in sneezing and trusted only his red elm tree.[47] He ignored warnings not to ride along a bewitched rock, and was killed under it. Thus the dissolute way of life of a Novgorod free spirit is reflected in the popular memory. The leader of Novgorod brigands has his place in the works of popular imagination together with the hero-warriors of Vladimir's period.

Among the historical figures of this period the Novgorod hundredman Stavr and his wife found their way into the ancient songs. In the chronicle for the year 1118 it is written that Vladimir Monomakh grew angry with the Novgorod hundredman Stavr, summoned him to Kiev and imprisoned him. From the chronicle we may deduce that Stavr was accused of the same crimes as other Novgorod boyars imprisoned with him, namely of robbing two citizens. In the song he is guilty of bragging about his wealth and denigrating the wealth and splendor of the grand prince. "What sort of a palace in Kiev has Grand Prince Vladimir? I, Stavr the boyar, have a large court, no worse than any in the city of Kiev. My residence covers seven versts and the rooms and chambers are built in white oak, the hall is hung with grey beaver, the ceiling is covered with black sables. The floor in the middle is made of silver. Hooks and clamps are made of gilded Damascene steel." The description of the interior of Stavr's house is interesting in that all ornaments are made of precious metals and furs. The imagination of the storyteller could yield nothing more fantastic.

The Novgorod chronicle for the year 1167 mentions Sadko Sytinich who built the stone church of St. Boris and St. Gleb. There is a song which mentions a rich Novgorod merchant Sadko, who brought from the Volga greetings to its brother Ilmen[48] and received a miraculous gift of countless treasures, with which he bought all the goods in Novgorod. This work, instead of a valiant leader of free spirits, portrays a rich merchant who, after getting drunk during a fraternity feast, bragged not about his power but about his wealth. Thus another aspect of Novgorod life left a trace in the creations of popular imagination. The similarity between Sadko in the song and in the chronicle lies in the fact that in both he is portrayed as a rich merchant interested in church construction. The piety of Sadko does not go without reward. Another song relates that when Sadko was in the power of the sea king he was saved by the sage words of St. Nicholas.[49]

From among *bookmen* whose works are unknown the chronicle mentions for 1205 (in Galich) one called Timofey, a wise bookman who came from Kiev. This Timofey spoke in parables against the torturer of the people of Galich, the Hungarian commander Benedict, "because in latest times Antichrist is called by three names."

CHRONICLES

The memory of important events and famous personalities remarkable among their contemporaries for one reason or another has been preserved among the people and transmitted from generation to generation in embellished narratives. Thanks to literacy there were those who in ornamental language attempted to record in writing information about some important event without deviation or poetic licence. Such licence would have been impossible for a recent well-known event. Yet they wanted to express the dominant view and need of the times, at this period the need halt the internecine wars and lack of cooperation between the princes.

This need is expressed most clearly in the *Tale of Igor's Campaign*. A people during its infancy has an inherent desire to know its past and to explain how the society in which it lived came about. A religious respect for the fathers requires that their memory be preserved. This inherent respect forces people to find in the legends of the past a teaching which is still alive. A whole people listens spellbound to stories of the deeds of their ancestors. In the absence of literacy those tales are transmitted orally and recorded when literacy begins to take root. This is a general law of the life of nations. There are no grounds to suppose that in the life of the Rus people things were any different, that the appearance of chronicles was delayed any later than the time Christianity appeared together with literacy. Moreover there were frequent and direct links with Byzantium which served as a guide in all aspects of civic spirit and offered a model of chronicles available even in Slavonic translation.

In saying that Byzantium was a model for everything relating to literacy the question of the form in which the first historical works appeared is answered. They appeared in the form of chronicles, annals, year-by-year recording of events lacking proper historical or scholarly link between them. The chronicles cannot be described generally as collections of dry expressions and short notes. Rather they are dry as well as ornamental, brief as well as abundant, according to local, personal, accidental or permanent factors, as will be shown later.

The question arises as to who in Rus at the beginning was noting events and composing a chronicle? It has been mentioned that among the princes, and probably in their retinues, were men keen to collect and read books, if only amateurs. Yet there was in Rus an estate for whom literacy was a duty, which was well aware of this duty. This estate was the clergy, which alone possessed at that period the time and means to occupy themselves with chronicle writing. The clergy, monks in particular, disposed of the means because they had opportunities to learn about events and their details, and obtain from reliable people information about faraway events. A prince came first to a monastery to announce planned enterprises and to seek blessing. It was to the monastery that he returned first with news that an enterprise was ended. Clergymen usually were employed as envoys and consequently knew better than others the course of negotiations.

It would be correct to assume that clergymen acted as envoys and participated in agreements, not so much out of respect for their dignity which could deflect danger from them, as because of their skills in written persuasion and large influence. They possessed literary skills, knowledge of writing an agreement, and awareness of customary forms. Why otherwise did the prince of Smolensk commission the priest Yeremey to conclude an agreement with Riga?

It may be assumed that clergymen as the first educated men were the initial secretaries of ancient Rus princes. Princes in difficult circumstances turned to clergymen for advice. It should be added that clergymen thoroughly noted details of military expeditions because they accompanied armies as observers. At the same time they stood close to the princes and obtained better information than warriors in battle. These considerations alone give grounds to assume that the first Rus chronicles were written by clergymen. The chronicles themselves also contain clear indications that they were written in monasteries. The original composition of short chronicles, and the first short notes, need not be sought elsewhere.

Knowing that the primary chronicle was compiled by the clergy raises the question of the form in which has it come down to us. The chronicle descended in multiple copies, the oldest not earlier than the fourteenth century. Among extant copies there is not one in which obvious interpolations are not immediately noticeable. Consequently all copies, both ancient and more recent, are compilations. Perusing these copies, it is obvious that the primary chronicle dealing with the beginning of the Land of Rus has preserved a common core unique not only in its language, which easily is explained by the time of compilation of this or that copy, but also in details of events. Some copies for certain years omit events found in others. Hence the first and most important question a historian must answer is how to evaluate these details, these additional pieces of information found in some, mainly late, compilations, and missing in others. Historical criticism of the previous century solved this problem by the principle that the only information to be used is that found in ancient copies. The additional information contained in the late compilations must be considered later compositions and inventions. In our time, when historical criticism has come of age, we cannot be satisfied with such a solution.

Simply because a chronicle is a late compilation the historian cannot dismiss it as unreliable. The author of a late compilation, for example in the seventeenth century, may have used older copies lost to us. Still, every new item found in more recent compilations must be appraised critically. The customary assertion that the compiler of a later version of, for example, the Nikon Chronicle,[50] *invented* this or that item absent in more ancient parchment copies, is of no significance.

A charter or some item might be suspect if intended to benefit some person or social estate close to the compiler, but only if it contained other suspicious indications. Furthermore, it is easy to notice information tinged with popular imagination and included by an artless compiler among a number of reliable items.

The historian actually should be grateful to the compiler and not reproach him for including inventions. No one is obliged to believe the conjectures of the ancient writer who tried to explain the names of famous places, to this effect inventing a series of people and events. Yet no one may say that an author of a more recent chronicle compilation invented an event which took place many centuries ago, which had no connection with him and which explains nothing. An example is that in the eleventh century in some year or other the Pechenegs[51] attacked the Land of Rus, that Askold and Dir[52] attacked the Bulgars, that in such and such a year a Pecheneg khan converted to Christianity, or that in another year a brigand was apprehended. Suspicion about such information is not useful to the critic. Discarding a biased attitude against information contained in recent compilations not found in the more ancient versions can change considerably the perception of how a chronicle is viewed. Looking at an original chronicle, both ancient and recent and more detailed copies, a distinction first of all needs to be drawn between information of Kiev and Novgorod origin. This is because simultaneously with the Southern or Kievan chronicle it must be assumed that there was also an original Northern or Novgorod chronicle, and the information from both is brought together in later compilations, the so-called Holy Wisdom,[53] Nikon and others.

An example is that the Kievan Primary Chronicle does not know what kind of tribute the Varangians took from the Northern tribes. The compiler of the Holy Wisdom Chronicle who used the primary Novgorod Chronicle does, stating "from each man one white squirrel." The chronology in the Nikon compilation ending with Vladimir Yaroslavich points also to Novgorod provenance, as does the information about Vadim. The original, Southern chronicle has no information where the two sons of Vladimir, Stanislav and Sudislav, ruled. The Novgorod chronicle states that Stanislav was placed in Smolensk, Sudislav in Pskov.

For the year 991 the legend of Perun seems a clear interpolation. "After Vladimir converted to Christianity, he took from Photius, patriarch of Constantinople, the first Kiev metropolitan Leon, and the Novgorod archbishop Yakim of Korsun... Archbishop Yakim came to Novgorod and ordered destruction of the pagan temple, that Perun be cut to pieces and thrown into the Volkhov river. After the idol was tied, it was dragged through the mud, struck with irons and pushed. At this time the devil entered the idol of Perun and screamed 'O woe is me! I have fallen into these cruel hands and was thrown into the Volkhov.' While he was floating under a large bridge he raised his cudgel and said 'With this let the children of Novgorod remember me, and with it the madmen who kill me shall make the devils joyful,' and said that no one should take him anywhere. A certain Pidblanin went early to the river, wanting to take pots to the city, when Perun swam up to the planks. The man pushed him aside with his pole saying 'You Perunishche[54] have eaten and drunk your fill. Now swim away, you evil spirit.'"

For the year 1034 in the Holy Wisdom and Nikon Chronicles there is information of undoubted Novgorod origin. "Grand Prince Yaroslav went to Novgorod and placed his son Vladimir on the throne and installed Bishop Zhidiata.[55] He wrote a charter for the people, saying 'You will give tribute according to this charter.' He was lame, but his mind was good and he was valiant in battle, a good Christian who could read books."

The information about the expedition of Uleb to the Iron Gate found in later compilations is also of Novgorod origin, and therefore is not in the Kievan chronicle, nor is the information on Bishop Luka Zhidiata and others. There is an indication as to when the primary Novgorod Chronicle was composed. In the Holy Wisdom compilation and others of the Novgorod Chronicle itself, for the year 1030 there is this information. "This year the Novgorod archbishop Akim died. Ephraim was his pupil, whom he taught." On this basis it can be assumed that the Novgorod primary chronicle was compiled in the eleventh century. This also explains how some of the additions, entered into the primary Kievan chronicle by compilers of later versions, were taken from the Novgorod chronicle.

In later compilations there are interpolations which could not have been borrowed from the Northern, Novgorod Chronicle, because they relate to events in the South, in Kiev. At the beginning of Igor's rule there is a passage "He had a commander called Sveneld and he tormented the Uglichians.[56] Igor imposed tribute on them and gave authority to Sveneld, who failed to take a town called Peresechen. He besieged it for three years and could hardly take it. The Uglichians fled down the Dnieper and came to the Dniester and stayed there. Also the Drevlianians paid a tribute to Sveneld of a black marten from each household, and Igor's retinue decided that to give this to one man was too much."

The knowledge about Pecheneg attacks found in the Nikon compilation for the years 990, 991 and 1001 could not have been taken from the Novgorod Chronicle. These entries are short and have no significance for the later chronicler. The same may be said about the information on the conversion of the Bulgar and Pecheneg princes, about the death of the Pecheneg prince Temir, killed by members of his family. The conclusion is that the Primary Chronicle as preserved in ancient copies is a shortened version in comparison to the later copies.

After these introductory remarks, discussion of the Primary Chronicle now follows. From its very first lines its source and model becomes obvious, namely the Byzantine chronicle. The Rus chronicler begins his story exactly as does his Byzantine colleague, by listing the countries which the descendants of Noah's three sons inherited. This list is taken from a Greek chronicle of George Hamartolos,[57] but the Rus chronicler inserted the passage "Near Illyria (Iliurik) *Slovenes,*" and later, at the end, a list of Northern rivers and nations, but where in the Carpathians are called the Caucasian or Ugorian mountains. Among the seventy-two nations of the Japhet tribe he included the Slavonic nation, mentioning as their original homeland the Danube lands. He describes the subsequent resettlement of these people in the North and Northeast, first voluntarily and later by force, under pressure from their enemies, the Vlachs.[58] To identify these Vlachs according to the notions of the chronicler, another passage in the chronicle may be used, the one where a Hungarian attack on countries along the Danube is described. "Coming from the East (the

Hungarians) crossed the large mountains and fought the Vlachs and the Slavs who were settled here. First the Slavs settled here, then later Vlachs came to the land of the Slovenes, later the Hungarians expelled the Vlachs and settled there together with the Slovenes, having subjected them to their rule." Thus the Hungarians encountered the Vlachs together with the Slavs.

From the story of the settlement of Slavonic tribes in present-day Russia and their life and destiny it becomes immediately clear that the chronicler was an inhabitant of Kiev, a member of the Polianian tribe.[59] This tribe was dominant, and the chronicle deals chiefly with it, for the compiler knew most about them. It elevates their ways over those of other tribes. The chronicler knew that in ancient times when the Polianians lived separately in family units on the Kievan hills the trade route from Scandinavia to Greece already was established along the Dnieper and the Northern rivers of the lake lands. From the first pages of the chronicle the geographical location of European Rus and the significance of its waterways can be understood. After information on the Pontic or Rus Sea there is an interpolated story of how St. Andrew journeyed north to Novgorod. It is clear that the tale must have appeared during Christian times, when it was learned that he had preached in Scythia. The interpolation starts "As it is said..."

After the interpolation concerning the apostle Andrew's journey follows the story of the foundation of the city of Kiev. During the times of the chronicler the usual explanation of place names was based on names of their alleged inhabitants. Thus the brothers Kiy, Shchek and Khoriv with their sister Lybed are cited to explain the names Kiev, the Shchekovitsy and Khorevitsy hills, and the Lybed stream. The chronicler relates two versions of the Kiy legend. One legend may be called the explanation proper. Secondly, during the times of the chronicler there were those who on the basis of the name "Kiy's ferry" explained that Kiy was a ferryman.

The chronicler rejected this dry interpretation and accepts a legend about Prince Kiy who went to Constantinople, received great honors from the emperor and on his return established a small town of Kievets on the Danube. Here the expression of the chronicler "as it is said" is very important. The source used by the chronicler becomes obvious, namely folk tales. Taking a legend about Prince Kiy and his family, the chronicler ascribes to his clan, his descendants and his brothers, rule over the Polianians. "Until this day from these brothers came the dynasty that ruled the Polianians."

Elsewhere, to illustrate the particular character of the other tribes, he adds "The Drevlianians had their own and Dregovichians had their own," and so on. This means that among the Drevlianians there was an independent princely ruler, and the Dregovichians had their own as well. It is known how the chronicler reasoned about the significance of Kiy and his family as rulers. His sources on the princes of the Dregovichians and the Drevlianians are even more scanty. The chronicle of Pereiaslavl-in-Suzdalia says "The Drevlianians lived on their own, and the Dregovichians began to live on their own and the Slovenians on their own, as the men of Novgorod and the people of Polotsk were without a prince," and so on.

After discussing the settlement of Slavonic tribes and other peoples who at that time paid the Rus tribute, the chronicler portrays the attacks of various steppe nations from the East against the Slavs in whose life these raids were unique. Here he used as sources partly Greek chronicles and partly local Slavonic legends and proverbs. He knew from the Byzantine chronicles that the White Hungarians[60] appeared during the reign of Emperor Heraclius and that they assailed Chosroes, the Persian emperor. From the Slavonic legends he knew about the oppression of the Duleb[61] women by the Avars. From the proverb "perished like the Avars," he explained the disappearance of this people without trace or descendants.

The chronicler then describes the customs and manners of the Slavonic tribes. Although this information could have been obtained from various legends and songs, he pointed to another, more exact source, the ancient morals and customs of the tribes preserved until his times. "This is still done by the Viatichians," he added, describing ancient pagan funeral rituals. It is noticeable that here as well the chronicler displays very scanty knowledge about the remote Northern tribes and writes in general, nonspecific terms. "These are the customs of the Krivichians and other pagans."

The description of Slavonic morals and customs is followed by an insertion on the customs and morals of various nations based on the Greek chronicle of George (Hamartolos).[62] The information on the life of East Slavonic tribes before Riurik ends with the story of the Polianians being oppressed by the Drevlianians and other neighboring tribes. Later there is information on the invasion of the Khazars, who forced the Polianians to pay tribute. An interpolation about the tribute of one sword from each hearth [household] also is included.

This story is clearly from a later period, written after the Khazars succumbed to the blows of the Rus princes. "The Khazars found the Polianians settled in these hills and woods, and they said 'Pay us tribute!' The Polianians, after giving it some thought, gave one sword from each hearth. The Khazars carried this tribute to their prince and the elders, and told them 'We have found new tribute.' The elders asked 'From whom did you take it?' 'From those dwelling in the woods,' they answered, 'in the hills above the Dnieper river.' The Khazar elders then said 'This tribute is not good, prince! We gained it by the sabre, with a weapon sharp on one side only. These people have a weapon sharp on both sides, the sword. They will take tribute from us and from other lands.' So it happened," added the chronicler, "the Rus have ruled the Khazars ever since."

The chronicle has no more to say about the period before Riurik. The picture seems very scant in detail, yet it cannot be assumed that the chronicler concealed anything from the reader, or that he knew more than he had written. Consequently the historian need look for nothing more. Indeed, what sort of details are required? A prince lived separately with his clan in his locality, ruling over it. When the conqueror was chased away, clan attacked clan and internecine wars began. The chronicler mentions towns and tells how they should be imagined, their relations with each other and with the rest of the population. Their inhabitants worked the land. Towns did not interfere with people who lived in the woods like animals, killing each other and kidnapping virgins. This was their way of life. What can be said apart from what the chronicler has written? His story is clear and complete.

The tribes fought each other, the stronger oppressed the weaker, but can we really hope to learn the details of those internecine struggles in the chronicle? The chronicler nevertheless recorded legends about movements of barbarian peoples from Asia, their sudden disappearance, one nation replacing another, and oppression of the settled tribes because they were weak and divided. These were the main facts of life among the tribes which since time immemorial settled on the great eastern plains of Europe. In this respect the Rus chronicler continued the work of the ancient historians. The lists of tribes were based on fresh traces as preserved until the time of the chronicler. He recorded the legend of the origins of his city, the capital city of all the Land of Rus, a legend formed according to the usual rules of this genre, which included local place names explained on the basis of personal names.

After the legend about the Khazar tribute the chronicle proper, the year-by-year recording of events, commences. In what year did the chronicler begin his own *chronicle?* He started it from 852 A.D. "From the reign of the emperor Michael the Greek the name of the Land of Rus appears for the first time." "We learned about it," continues the chronicler, "because during the reign of Emperor Michael the Rus attacked Constantinople, as is written in the Greek chronicle. For this reason we begin here and date it from here."

The Rus chronicler, taking as his model the Greek, also begins with enumeration. From Adam until the deluge so many years, from the deluge until Abraham so many years and so on, until he reaches the times of Emperor Michael and passes on to Rus history. "From the first year of Michael until the first year of Oleg the Rus prince, twenty-nine years, and from the first year of Oleg, when he ruled in Kiev, until the first year of Igor thirty-one years, and from the first year of Igor until the first year of Sviatoslav thirty-three years, and from the first year of Sviatoslav until the first year of Yaropolk twenty-eight years, and Yaropolk ruled eight years, Vladimir thirty-seven years, and Yaroslav forty years. Thus from the death of Sviatoslav until the death of Yaroslav was eighty-five years, and from the death of Yaroslav until the death of Sviatopolk sixty years." There is an interesting passage in the Nikon version where the time of the summoning of the princes is shown. "The Slavs came at the time of Emperors Michael and Basil and Patriarch Photius," and so on. Following this, the ending of the enumeration with the death of Sviatopolk Iziaslavich is important. It demonstrates that the chronicle was written between the death of Sviatopolk and that of his successor Vladimir Monomakh.

After this enumeration there follows for the year 858 information from either a Greek or a Bulgarian chronicle about the conversion of the Bulgarians. For the next year, 859, this entry is found. "The Varangians from overseas gathered tribute from the Chud, Slovenes, Merians and all the Krivichians, while the Khazars had tribute from the Polianians, Severians and Viatichians, one squirrel pelt from each household."

The interesting expression is "gathered" tribute instead of "when the Varangians arrived" and similar terms. After two years of much information regarding tribute paid to the Varangians there is a passage about the expulsion of the Varangians and the summoning of the princes. After two years the two brothers of Riurik died. Two years after the death of Riurik, Oleg left Novgorod. Of great interest here is the complete story narrated for one year, 862, of the calling of Riurik, the death of his two younger brothers, the distribution of towns, permission for Askold and Dir to go to the South.

Everywhere there are clear traces that what was known about the calling of the princes and their arrival was originally a separate story without years, which were introduced later. The break in the story forced by the introduction of dates is particularly obvious in the information on the expedition of Askold and Dir against the Greeks. "Riurik ruled in Novgorod in the year 6371 [863], in the year 6372 [864], in the year 6373 [865]. In the year 6374 [866] Askold and Dir went against the Greeks," and so on.

Only this original story, together with the introduction about pre-Riurik times, may have the title, *This is the Tale of Bygone Years Whence Came the Rus Land, Who First Started to Rule in Kiev and the Origins of the Land of Rus.*

The primary Kievan chronicler knew next to nothing about the circumstances surrounding the calling of the princes or the events of Riurik's reign. The legends about Gostomysl and Vadim were interpolated from the Novgorod Primary Chronicle into the later compilations. It is clear that the story of Oleg's expedition to the South and his establishment in Kiev was taken from oral tradition, Oleg having been the first to gather the tribes and impose order. All the ancient statutes were related to his times, for example the Novgorod tribute. Events were divided into years, where every year there was an expedition against one tribe, then the information on Oleg's activity stopped for seventeen years. For the year 903 Igor's marriage to Olga is recorded. This the chronicler had to place later, given Sviatoslav's minority at the time of his father's death. For 907 there is information on Oleg's expedition against the Greeks. The nature of this story points to its source in oral folk stories. It is impossible not to notice the obvious combination of two pieces of information made clear by the repetition of the same item on the tribute, first amounting to twelve grivnas a head, and then to twelve grivnas from each household.[63]

For 911 there is an item about a comet, taken probably from a Greek or Bulgarian chronicle. The agreement with the Greeks is found under 912. There is irrefutable evidence that Greek sources were used for agreements of the Byzantine empire with various barbarians, including the Rus. These agreements correspond to those concluded with other nations. It was necessary to come to terms with the Rus prince regarding clashes between Rus and imperial subjects in Constantinople, which must have been fairly frequent, and of which the Greek government was aware.

Complete correspondence of the agreements' content with contemporary circumstances and finally the language, which in many places is unclear, point to translation from the Greek. No doubt is left about the authenticity of Oleg's, Igor's and Sviatoslav's agreements. In all probability the chronicler had at his disposal a translation contemporary with the original, which must have been kept in Kiev by the princes, and kept very carefully. Trade relations with Byzantium were of primary importance for Rus and its princes. There is no doubt that in Constantinople the Rus were treated according to ancient agreements. It is strange to think that the *Normans* cared little about observing agreements. Perhaps Norman pirates showed little concern, but it has been noted that the Rus princes could not remain Norman pirates. Besides, where are the proofs that they cared but little about observing and complying with these agreements?

After Oleg's agreement, Igor attacked the Greeks. Where is the proof that his expedition was not forced by a breach of the agreement by the Greeks? When the Greeks told him they would pay him as much as they paid Oleg, he made peace with them. It might be assumed that the expedition was intended to restore previous relations. Sviatoslav conquered Bulgaria in accordance with the agreement with the Greeks, and later conducted a defensive war against them. Vladimir's expedition was linked closely in the chronicle with the intent to convert to Christianity. Yaroslav sent his son against the Greeks precisely because Rus merchants were oppressed in Constantinople, in violation of the treaty. It should be remarked that in general the expeditions of ancient Rus princes against Byzantium were continuous and customary, even though only six are mentioned specifically.

Following the legend about Oleg's death the chronicler included items about magi appearing among other peoples. This is understandable in view of the interest aroused by pagan priests among his contemporaries. The lengthy reign of Igor, from which very few traditions survived, is enriched by material from Greek and Bulgarian chronicles. The information about Igor's first expedition against the Greeks was taken from these sources. Information about the second expedition was taken from native legends, which also served to justify the failure of the first expedition. The same source can be detected in the story about Igor's death and Olga's revenge. Her orders and her conversion were described solely on the basis of local traditions without recourse to Greek sources. This point is proved by naming the emperor John Tzimisces,[64] during whose reign

Olga was converted, and the year of conversion. Still during Igor's reign, the year 943 marks the end of excerpts from Greek and Bulgarian chronicles relating to events in those parts. Thereafter apparently the compilers used only local oral traditions.

Mentioned earlier is the time when the legend about the missionaries of various religions in Vladimir's era finally took form. An interesting point should be noted here. At the time of the chronicler people who remembered the conversion of the Land of Rus were still alive. Even so, in his lifetime there existed various contradictory legends about that event, about the place where Vladimir was baptized. When the chronicler confirms that Vladimir was baptized in Korsun,[65] he adds "Those who allege that he was baptized in Kiev say it out of ignorance. Others say that it was in Vasiliev, still others say it was in another place." One of the surviving *Lives* of Vladimir says that this prince undertook an expedition to Korsun three years after his conversion to Christianity.

An obvious textual boundary is noticeable at the beginning of Sviatopolk's rule. Directly following the entry on Vladimir's death, after the title *On the Killing of Boris*, we read "Sviatopolk ruled Kiev after his father, and called the Kievans together and gave them property." After the material on the death of Sviatoslav, prince of the Drevlianians, we read "The accursed Sviatopolk took power in Kiev. He called the people together and distributed to some coats and to others martens and gave away large amounts." Clearly the chronicle contains a specially interpolated story about the murder of St. Boris and St. Gleb, indicated by the dedication. Thanks to strong development of church literature, in the later compilations of the chronicle there are numerous stories of the murder of St. Boris and St. Gleb as well as the suffering of the first Rus martyrs, the Varangians Fedor and John. In divers accounts of St. Boris and St. Gleb there are noticeable variations. In the story inserted into the chronicle it is written that St. Gleb travelled from Murom, supposing that his dying father summoned him. In other stories it is said that Gleb in the last days of St. Vladimir was in Kiev, not in Murom. When he learned that Sviatopolk sent killers to murder Boris he went up the Dnieper in secret and the killers caught up with him near Smolensk. To refute the first version it is necessary merely to note that in the forty-three days between the murder of Boris on the July 24 and the murder of Gleb on September 5 not all the events recounted in these passage could have happened. The envoy sent by Sviatopolk to Murom could not have returned to his prince with news that Gleb had set out on his journey before early September. If Sviatopolk, acting upon this information, sent the killers up the Dnieper, how could they have managed to sail six hundred and fifty versts in three or four days?

First of all, this story does not imply that Sviatopolk sent the killers only after he received news that Gleb was on his way. Expecting Gleb to take the obvious route, he could have dispatched the killers much earlier. Secondly, the story is devoid of any chronological indicators. It is noteworthy that the story found in the chronicle contains no contradictions. It does not contain Boris's words "I can recognize the face of my younger brother Gleb, like Joseph recognized the face of Benjamin."[66]

In any case it is clear that the events following Vladimir's death became sources of diverse legends, as were those accompanying the conversion of Rus to Christianity. On the other hand, it is worthwhile noting that in the material on the early events of Yaroslav's rule we can see a combination of information from the primary Kievan Chronicle with that from the Novgorod Primary Chronicle. Thus the passage which begins after the words "possessing them" and ending "and he attacked Sviatopolk. When Sviatopolk heard that Yaroslav was coming, mustering countless troops, Rus and Pechenegs, he marched to Liubech half way up the Dnieper and Yaroslav went along the other bank" may be considered an interpolation from the Novgorod Chronicle. First of all, the passage contains information on a Novgorod event, and secondly because in the story under the following year it is repeated once again "Yaroslav came and they *stood facing each other across the Dnieper.*"

Among the entries concerning Yaroslav's reign, for 1051, in the story relating to the beginnings of the Kiev monastery is found the first mention of its author and when he lived. "Feodosy lived in the monastery and led a virtuous life according to the monastic rule. He received anybody who would come to him, even if that person was a poor and lowly slave, and he accepted me when I was only seventeen years of age. I have written and recorded when the monastery was established, and why it is called the Caves monastery, and I will tell later about the life of Feodosy." For 1064 there is the new suggestion that, starting from the eleventh century, information was recorded by an eyewitness, whereas for the earlier period there are traces of oral traditions throughout. Telling among other absurd omens how fishermen caught a monster in the Setoml river, the chronicler added "and people looked upon him until evening." Thus in the second half of the eleventh century traces can be discovered of the

author of the famous primary Kievan Chronicle, just as somewhat earlier the traces of the primary Novgorod Chronicle have been discovered.

From the time when clear evidence appears of an eyewitness who
recorded events there is found dated information on events, for example
for the year 1060. "The Polovetsians came for the first time to attack the
Land of Rus, and Vsevolod came out against them on the second day of
February." No such record exists even for the most important [earlier]
events, apart from dates of princes' deaths, and even these only for the
post-conversion period. The fact that from this time the chronicler is an
eyewitness or a contemporary of the events is proved by details easy to
distinguish from the details of earlier folk legends. It is easy to understand
the sort of details that appear. Examples are in the story of Olga's vengeance and details found in the narrative of the Polovetsian victory in
1067 and its consequences. For the year 1051 the chronicler promised to
tell about the life of St. Feodosy. "Later," he says, "I will tell you about
the life of Feodosy." Then, for 1074, while telling the story of St. Feodosy's death, the chronicler provides information about his life. He writes
how Feodosy fasted and how he taught the brethren to fast, about the
flourishing state of the monastery in Feodosy's times and how the brethren loved each other, how juniors obeyed elders and dared not to speak
in their presence. This is meant to contrast such conduct with events after Feodosy's death in relation to Abbot Stefan. He writes about the great
hermits who lived during Feodosy's time and his treatment of these men,
about Damian the Miracle-Worker and others. The story about the life of
St. Isaac contains the following words. "Others told much about him, but
of other things I have been an eyewitness." For 1091 there is a story about
the discovery of St. Feodosy's relics, where the narrator presents himself
as the main actor and concludes by calling himself the disciple and slave
of Feodosy. Under the year 1093, in a pious meditation about God's chas-
tisements, it is written "Being a sinner I have angered God much and
often until today." For the year 1096, in the story about the Polovetsian
attack against the Caves monastery, it is written "They came into the
monastery to us, who were in our cells resting after matins… to us who
escaped to the rear of the monastery."

The same year, in one of the oldest compilations, the so-called Laurentian,[67] there is a later interpolation containing Monomakh's admonition
to his children intermixed with his letter to Oleg Sviatoslavich. It is a late
interpolation because the primary compiler of the chronicle, a contemporary of Monomakh, obviously could have had both these documents to

hand. He could have integrated them into his chronicle but he could not have put them precisely where they are found in Laurentian copy because they are placed between two inseparable entries. After the description of the Polovetsian attack the chronicler recounted the origins of various barbarian nations. "Ishmael fathered twelve sons and from them the Turkomans, Pechenegs, Turks and Cumans (whom we call Polovetsians) who came from the desert, and after them eight generations of unclean people whom Alexander of Macedonia locked in a mountain, and who will appear at the end of time." Directly after this passage should follow a chronicle story about people locked in a mountain, about whom he had heard from a man of Novgorod called Giuriata Rogovich. Yet between this story and the last quoted words "unclean people," Monomakh's admonition is interpolated, as is his letter to Oleg. An additional circumstance is also puzzling. Following the story about the war of Mstislav Vladimirovich of Novgorod against his uncle Oleg Sviatoslavich we find "Mstislav sent to Oleg and said 'Do not run away, but send to your brothers with a plea not to banish you from the Land of Rus, and I will ask my father to pray for you.' Oleg promised to do so." "Mstislav returned again to Suzdal," adds the chronicler, "and from there he went to Novgorod, his city, *thanks to the prayers of the reverend bishop Nikita.*" It is strange that a Kievan chronicler inserted this additional note when the Novgorod chronicler's custom of ascribing any success to the prayers of the bishop who happened to be contemporary of the event is well known. For example, under the year 1169, "Towards evening Prince Roman and the men of Novgorod were victorious, thanks to the power of the cross and the Holy Mother of God and the prayers of the pious Archbishop Elias."

One thing is doubtful. Archbishop Nikita was formerly a monk of the Caves monastery, famous for his holiness. This might have prompted the Kievan chronicler, also a monk of the same monastery, to ascribe Mstislav's victory to the prayers of St. Nikita. On the other hand it is difficult to suppose that this event was not described in detail in the Novgorod Chronicle. The story of the famous war of Mstislav and Novgorod with Oleg was transmitted in Novgorod from generation to generation. In 1216 the men of Novgorod recalled how their ancestors fought in the battle of Kolaksha. Karamzin[68] also noticed the difference between this story and other passages in Nestor's chronicle. The indiction[69] and year are noted at the end.

For the following year, 1097, there is an interpolated story about the blinding of Vasilko. It was noted that the style of this story is markedly different from the rest of the chronicle where there are no expressions such as "Boniak divided his forces into three parts and defeated the Hungarians by the sword, like the hawk defeats the jackdaw." It was noted that such expressions are akin to those in the *Tale of Igor's Campaign.* These expressions bear no similarity to the Primary Chronicle. They are more in line with the Volhynian Chronicle characterized by this kind of style, of which the first part describing events until the death of Roman the Great was lost, except for this passage about the blinding of Vasilko. This event is indeed connected with Volhynia and had a significant impact mainly on Volhynian history, and for that reason should be included in this chronicle. A Kievan chronicler could not have written "That night, leading to Belgorod, which is a small town about ten versts from Kiev... ." The author of the story is one of the protagonists, and made his name known by citing the words of Prince Davyd Igorevich, who called him the namesake of Prince Vasilko. The interpolation of this passage from the Volhynian Chronicle is obvious because following it previous events are repeated in the order of years from the chronicle into which the story of Vasilko was added.

Under the year 1106 we find "John, a good elder monk, died. He was ninety years old, a venerable old age. He lived according to God's laws and he was no less than the first holy man. I heard from him many words and I recorded in the chronicle what I had heard from him." Finally, after the year 1110 the following note is found. "Abbot Sylvester of St. Michael wrote this chronicle, hoping to receive God's grace, during the reign of Prince Vladimir in Kiev, and at that time I served as the abbot of St. Michael, in 6624 [1116], in the year of the ninth indiction, and those who read these books will be in my prayers."

Thus at the beginning of the twelfth century there is clear evidence concerning the famous Sylvester of Vydubets, who said of himself that he wrote a chronicle. The age of this Sylvester does not contradict the assumption that he was the first compiler of the primary Kievan chronicle. It is possible to connect with him the account recorded for 1064 when he, then aged seven, might have gone to look at the monster caught by the fishermen, and could have remembered this event vividly.

Even so there is a story which ascribes the compilation of the primary Kievan chronicle to a monk in the Caves monastery in Kiev, Brother Nestor. This version is supported by Sylvester's note even though on this basis it would be much more plausible that Sylvester was the chronicler rather than to assume the existence of somebody else, Nestor. The item for 1064 might be related to Nestor as much as to Sylvester, yet the passages in the story about the Caves monastery telling of the death of Feodosy and discovery of his relics, the Polovetsian assault on the monastery, all point to the chronicler as a monk of the Caves monastery. To match the version of Nestor as the chronicler with the evidence for Sylvester, who wrote the chronicle in 1116, it has been suggested that Sylvester was a copier or a continuator of Nestor's chronicle. In 1116 Sylvester could have copied the chronicle completed in 1110, and continued to record events for subsequent years.

Yet new objections appear regarding Nestor. These include striking disparities noted above in Nestor's story about the killing of Boris and Gleb and the information found in the chronicle, differences between Nestor's life of St. Feodosy and the chronicle account of him, as well as details about the author in his *Life*. As these contradictions cannot be reconciled without an extremely strained interpretation, certain scholars believe that either Nestor's chronicle was subjected to great changes and additions, or that it was not Nestor but someone else who was the author of the first chronicle that came down to us.

There are no decisive proofs to prefer the second assumption over the first. The important element is that from the second half of the eleventh century there are obvious signs of a chronicler in Kiev who was a contemporary witness, and that even earlier traces of a Novgorod chronicler are apparent. At the end of the eleventh century there is a source revealing the existence of a chronicler in Volhynia. Extant copies of the Primary Chronicle represent compilations from the Kievan, the Novgorod and the Volhynian chronicles. According to the evidence of Bishop Simon of Vladimir, contained in his letter to the monk Polikarp, there was also an ancient Rostov chronicle in which were recorded all names of bishops previously monks in the Kiev monastery of the Caves. It is also significant that ancient copies of the Primary Chronicle represent an abbreviated version of the chronicle and additional information must be sought in later compilations like the Nikon Chronicle and others. This information cannot be doubted, neither was it invented by later chronicle compilers. Opinions that an account taken from the Nikon copy is an invention because it is not found on Nestor's parchment have no place in scholarship. The same approach is applicable to the Tatishchev copy of chronicles because the same argument was used against their reliability, that anything absent from ancient copies must have been invented.

To follow Sylvester's note, ancient copies also differ more or less among themselves in details. All contain the all-Russian common chronicle, or to put it better, the *princely* chronicle, because it mainly tells of relations within the Riurik princely clan. In the chronicles of the twelfth and the beginning of the thirteenth century, as well as in the eleventh-century chronicle discussed here, some entries clearly belong either to the Kievan, the Chernigov, the Polotsk or the Suzdal chronicles. At the end of the twelfth century the activity of the Kievan chronicler clearly ceased. Only two chronicles remain, one undoubtedly written in Volhynia and the other, the Northern, compiled in the Land of Suzdal.

Even earlier, from the clear separation of Northern from Southern Rus starting in the reign of Vsevolod III, there is an obvious if not complete separation of the Northern and the Southern chronicles. Here are several passages from the chronicle relating to twelfth-century events where all hallmarks of the eyewitness chronicler, the contemporary of the events, as well as characteristics of local chronicles are clearly discernible. For the year 1114 in the Hypatian[70] copy is written "This year Mstislav re-founded [the citadel of] Novgorod, larger than the first. The same year the building of Ladoga in stone by Burgrave Pavel was completed during the reign of Mstislav. When I came to Ladoga I was told by the local people that there was a big cloud here and our children found glass beads big and small, with holes in them, and others could be found by the Volkhov river, washed out by the water. Over a hundred of these were collected. I was amazed by that, and they told me that it is not that strange, because old people went beyond Ugra and the Samoyeds,[71] and they themselves saw in the Northern lands that a cloud would appear and from this cloud young squirrels, as if newly born, would come down, grow and spread over the land. Also sometimes there is another cloud and from which small deer fell down, grew and spread over the land. This was told to me by Burgrave Pavel and all the people of Ladoga."

It is clear that the chronicler lived contemporaneously with the construction of the stone citadel in Ladoga. He spoke with Burgrave Pavel who ordered its construction. Yet where this chronicler was from, where he wrote his chronicle and from which chronicle this account was inserted into the Hypatian copy is impossible to decide. It is interesting that in the Novgorod Chronicle the construction of this citadel occurred two years later than in the Hypatian copy.

For 1151 in the Hypatian copy it is written "Iziaslav Mstislavich said what I *already heard earlier*, 'The place does not become the head, but the head the place'"[72] Here it is clear that the chronicler was a contemporary who spoke with the prince. For 1161 is this. "There was a great battle... and it was horrible to behold. Perhaps it is a sign of the second coming." For 1171 is written "On Saturday, in the morning we went with Vladimir from Vyshgorod." For 1187 it says "This autumn the cold was terrible. No one remembered such cold." For 1199, in the story about construction of the walls at the Vydubets monastery it says "At that time God by His grace... put a good thought into the God fearing-heart of Grand Prince Riurik... which he accepted with great joy as the good and faithful servant and immediately went to put it to work. So according to your blessed custom, accept this verbal gift concerning Christ Almighty, Who has mercy on all, and may my crude writing express praise to our benefactors."

It is clear that the author is a contemporary as well as a monk in the Vydubets monastery. Yet it is impossible to decide whether accounts of earlier events were in his work, or whether the story of the construction of the wall is a separate source and was included into the chronicle as an interesting work of rhetoric. There are details from which we can deduce that this chronicler did not belong to the brethren of the Kievan Caves monastery. The Laurentian copy for 1128 reads "The monks from the Caves monastery took over the church of St. Dmitry and called it St. Peter's church. It was a great sin and wrong."

The difference between the chroniclers, one from Chernigov and the other from Kiev, or at least from a place controlled by the sons of Monomakh, is obvious from the story about the expulsion of Oleg's sons from Kiev and the entry on Iziaslav Mstislavich found under 1146 in the Hypatian copy. In the earlier the intention to expel the sons of Oleg constantly is termed a bad idea inspired by the devil. In the later the exact opposite is said about the same event, namely the expulsion of Oleg's sons from Kiev and the arrival there of Iziaslav Mstislavich. "This was from God and through the power of the sacred cross, the plea of St. Michael and the prayers of the Mother of God." Later once again the voice of the previous chronicler is heard reproaching Davyd's sons because they refused to fight against Mstislav's son or seek freedom for Igor Olgovich, their cousin. "The sly and crafty devil did not want good to reign among brothers. He wished to add evil to evil and put in the minds (of Davyd's sons) the idea not to free their brother Igor, not to remember their fatherland, nor their solemn oath, nor divine love, that it would be good for the brothers to live in unity together and see to their fatherland."

All this suggests that the chronicler supported the sons of Oleg. A Kievan chronicler could not have entertained such lively concern for the affairs of Sviatoslav Olgovich nor could he, when discussing the arrival of Sviatoslav's allies, say that this happened through God's mercy. He could not have said that Sviatoslav expelled Iziaslav Davydovich and the *Kievan retinue* with him because of God's mercy.

The conjunction of two passages from different chronicles in this story is obvious. The chronicler supporting Oleg's descendants speaks about the unseemly words of Iziaslav Davydovich, about his expedition against Sviatoslav Olgovich and about Sviatoslav's decisiveness, his victory over his enemies. The incident was thus closed. Then the same event was retold, probably by the Kievan chronicler. "Iziaslav Mstislavich and Vladimir Davydovich sent their brother Iziaslav with Shvarn, and they followed him." It is likewise clear that the first mention of Moscow appears not in the Kiev Chronicle, but in Chernigov or Severian chronicles which so ardently supported Sviatoslav Olgovich, and contained such details about his movements. The Kievan Chronicle, clearly hostile to Oleg's family, could not be interested in, or even possess, details of feasts with which Yury of Suzdal entertained Sviatoslav, nor could it have been interested in the death of a boyar from Severia, the good old man Peter Ilich. The story for 1159 in the Hypatian copy on the Polotsk events despite all its details remains fragmentary because generally the chronicle is very scanty on relations with Polotsk. This particular passage thus constitutes an interpolation from the Polotsk Chronicle.

Characteristics of the Northern, or Suzdal, chronicle are clear. For example, the story of Rostislav Yurievich defecting to Iziaslav Mstislavich in the Laurentian copy differs from the story of the same event in the Hypatian copy. In the former copy Rostislav's deed is presented positively, nothing being said about his quarrel with his father. Evidently this version belongs to the Suzdal chronicler, the second to the Kievan. The stories in the Northern and Southern chronicles differ with regard to Iziaslav Mstislavich's expedition against the Rostov region, the peace between Yury and Iziaslav in 1149, Bishop Leon and Prince Andrei, and the relationship between Rostislav's sons and Andrei Bogoliubsky. In the description of Andrei's expedition against Novgorod the Laurentian copy reads "The men of Novgorod locked themselves up in the city with Prince Roman and defended themselves strongly and killed many of *our troops*." Here the hand of the Suzdal chronicler is obvious. In the Hypatian copy the same Suzdal story is interpolated and it also reads "This happened because of our sins."

In both copies the story of Andrei Bogoliubsky's murder is interpolated from the Suzdal chronicle with some variants, but in the Laurentian copy, among others, these words are addressed to Andrei. "Pray show mercy to our prince and lord Vsevolod, our own true brother." This directly points to the time of writing. The account of events following Andrei's death clearly belongs to the Northern, more precisely the Vladimir Chronicle. It mentions that the people of Rostov listened to evil men, "who did not wish *us* good, and were full of envy for *our* city."

For 1180 the Vladimir chronicler is clearly discernible because in the story of Vsevolod III's war with Riazan the expressions "*our* guards," "*our* people expelled" are used. For 1185, in the story of the consecration of Bishop Luka, the chronicler addresses these words to him. "Pray for the flock entrusted to you, for Christian people, for the people and the Land of Rostov." This passage clearly shows that it was written after Bishop Luka's death. For the same year in the Laurentian copy there is a curious account of the heroic deeds of Vladimir Glebovich, prince of Southern Pereiaslavl, a story clearly indicating a Northern chronicler, a supporter of Yury Dolgoruky's family. In the Suzdal Chronicle all honor for victory over the Polovetsians is attributed to Vladimir Glebovich. The Kievan chronicler describes it in different terms. The difference in the Suzdal (Laurentian copy) and the Kievan (Hypatian copy) chronicles concerning the description of the war of Vsevolod III and Riurik Rostislavich against the descendants of Oleg is also of interest. The Suzdal chronicle justifies Vsevolod in everything, whereas the Kievan justifies Riurik. For 1227 it reads "Bishop Mitrofan was appointed to the God-protected city of Vladimir, to the miraculous Mother of God church, to Suzdal, Vladimir and Pereiaslavl, attended by the noble prince Georgy [Yury] with his children, and his brothers Sviatoslav and Ivan, all the boyars and a multitude of people. I, a sinner, also happened to be there."

It was noted earlier that the composition known as *Nestor's Chronicle,* with continuations in the format in which it has been preserved, is the all-Russian chronicle.[73] The local chronicles, of *Volhynia* and Novgorod, contrast with it from the point of view of content. The story of Vasily about the blinding of Vasilko of Terebovl has been identified as a fragment from the first part of a lost Volhynian chronicle. The second part, beginning in 1201, is preserved under the title *Beginning of the Reign of Grand Prince Roman, Sole Ruler of all the Rus Land and Prince of Galich.* Yet immediately after the title we read "After *the death* of grand prince Roman," followed by his eulogy, a comparison with Monomakh.

Later, starting in 1202, the events following Roman's death are recounted. The hallmark of the contemporary chronicler-eyewitness is
found for 1226 in the story on the struggle of Mstislav of Toropets against
the Hungarians. "Mstislav went forth with the regiments, which humili-
ated and destroyed us, and the Hungarians went to their camps."

The Novgorod Primary Chronicle has not been preserved in its pure
form. In the copies known today information from this source contains
interpolations from the Kievan chronicle. In the oldest, the so-called
Synod copy, the first fifteen fascicles are missing. Another copy, called
the Tolstoy copy, begins at a curious point which probably belongs to a
later compiler who joined the Novgorod Primary Chronicle with the
Kievan. "Annals called the chronicle of the princes and Land of Rus, how
God has chosen our land to the end of times, and started cities, first the
Novgorod region, then the Kievan, and on the foundation of Kiev, which
was called thus after Kiy, as in ancient times King Romulus called his
city after himself Rome, as Antiochus called his city Antioch, and as Seleucus called a city after his name, and as Alexander named a city Alexandria after himself. Many places were named in this manner after their
kings and princes. So in our country the great city of Kiev was named
after Kiy. In ancient times he was a ferryman, who some say hunted near
his city. For great is God's providence as it is manifest of late. Where in
olden days pagans sacrificed to the devil on the hills there are now holy
churches built of stone with golden domes, and monasteries full of monks
who praise God constantly in their prayers, in their waking hours and in
their fasts, in tears. It is on account of their prayers that the world is still
standing. Because he who enters the holy church gains great things for
his soul and his body. We will return to our story, *On the beginning of
the Land of Rus and on the princes, how and whence they came.*"

This is followed by the passage we have cited several times earlier
about the ancient princes and their retinue, with the admonition that contemporaries follow their example. "I beg you, Christ's flock, lend your ears
with love. As were the ancient princes and their men...," and so on. It
should be noted here that the initial title, *Annals Called the Chronicle of
the Princes and the Land of Rus* and the following reflection on the origins
of towns belong to a later compiler, while the second title, *On the Beginning of the Land of Rus and on the Princes,* with a reflection on ancient
princes, was taken by him from an ancient chronicler about whom it is
difficult to decide whether he was from Novgorod or from Kiev. The passage about the ancient princes and boyars ends as follows. "My beloved

brethren, we will not be filled. Be satisfied with your lessons. As Paul writes, 'He who has gifts, let him use them. If teaching, let him teach.'[74] Do no violence to anyone, rather flower in kindness, loving strangers in the fear of God and faith in His salvation. Thus we will gain eternal life, so this we will do. From the beginning of the Land of Rus to this year, and all in order we will tell you, from Emperor Michael to Alexander and Isaac."[75] Earlier the hallmark of the first Novgorod chronicler, the student of Ephraim, was noted. The hallmark of the later compiler is found for the year 1144. "This year the archbishop, the saintly Nifont, ordained me a priest."[76]

Related to questions about Novgorod chronicle is the issue of the so-called *Joachim Chronicle* found in the first volume of Tatishchev's *History of Russia*.[77] There is no doubt that its compiler used the *Novgorod Primary Chronicle* which has not descended to us and which he attributes to the first bishop of Novgorod, Joachim. It is difficult to decide on what the compiler based this authorship. Perhaps it was this following passage regarding the conversion of Novgorod. "We were standing on the Market Side.[78] We walked around the markets and streets and taught people as best we could."

THE NATURE OF HISTORIOGRAPHY

Having studied the composition of Russian chronicles in the form in which they have come down to us, a few words must be said about their general character and several local characteristics. The chronicler was a cleric. This factor was strongest in determining the chronicle's character. The monastic chronicler sought a religious and moral meaning to the events he described. He offered his work to readers as a religious and moral homily. Hence the highly religious significance of this work in his own eyes and those of his contemporaries. Sylvester in his postscript said that he wrote his chronicle hoping to receive God's grace. It seems therefore that chronicle-writing was considered a religious activity desired by God.

In his initial discussion of ancient pagan history the chronicler abstained from pious admonitions and reflections. The activity of people who did not know the laws of God did not offer the right opportunity. The story of Olga the Christian marked the beginning of his pious admonitions and reflections. The disobedience of the pagan Sviatoslav towards his saintly mother offered the first opportunity. "He did not obey his mother, following the pagan customs, ignorant of the fact that people who do not obey their mothers come to grief. As has been said, 'Those who do not obey their father and mother will die.'"

Thus Sviatoslav's miserable death was presented as the result of his disobedience, whereas the death of St. Olga offered an opportunity for another reflection on the fame and beatitude of the righteous. There are no pious thoughts until he comes to the story of Blud's treason. "O wicked human flattery! Evil is that advice which counsels bloodshed. Violent are they who, having accepted honor or gifts from their prince or lord, yet think how to destroy their master. They are worse than devils." Beginning with the story of his conception Sviatopolk the Damned was subjected to censure, and a future villain predicted. "A sinful root bears a bad fruit."

The contrast between Vladimir the pagan and Vladimir the Christian also provided an opportunity for a sermon. The death of the two Varangian Christians could not remain without pious reflection on the premature joy of the devil who failed to foresee the speedy triumph of the true faith. In the story dealing with the beginnings of book learning the chronicler manifests great joy, praising the Lord for His infinite grace. "The books given for learning will fulfill in the Land of Rus a prophecy which says that in those days the words of book learning will be heard by the deaf, and the speech of those who stammer will be clear. This is because they have not heard bookish words before, yet God has been merciful to them. As the prophet says, 'and I will show mercy on whom I will show mercy....'"[79]

The information on Vladimir's death is followed by his eulogy, which related that during the time of the chronicler Vladimir was not as yet included among the saints. "This is truly wonderful, how much good he has done to the Land of Rus by converting it. We Christians do not give him the honor that is his due. Had he not converted us, today we would have been ensnared by the devil as were our forefathers who perished. Were we to pray to God for him on the anniversary of his death and were God to see our zeal towards him, He would glorify him, because we are worthy of praying to God for him, because we have known God."[80] Mention was made earlier of the praise of book learning included in the chronicle in connection with details about Prince Yaroslav's interest in such learning.

After Yaroslav's death we see the activity which became of primary importance in the chronicle, namely interprincely relationships, internecine warfare and later invasions by the steppe barbarians, the Polovetsians. It is understandable that the chronicler saw, as did his contemporaries, these internecine wars as the chief evil and took sharp issue with them. He regarded them as the result of the devil's inspiration, and foreign invasions and consequent defeats as punishment for the sin of internecine wars. "Because God in His anger brings foreigners to the land, princes when aggrieved should turn to God. Internecine struggle comes from the devil's temptation."

It has been observed how frequently princes violated oaths they swore to each other, the cause of internecine wars. The chronicler, for two reasons, religious and political, had to oppose violation of oaths which were also *crimes against the cross,* for oaths were sealed by kissing the cross. The sons of Yaroslav kissed the cross to Vseslav of Polotsk, then immediately broke their oath and imprisoned him. Vseslav was delivered from prison as a result of Iziaslav's expulsion. On this occasion the chronicler said "Here God has shown the power of the cross, for Iziaslav kissed the cross, and so did I and (Vseslav). God has brought the pagans, but the sacred cross has appeared and caused salvation, because on the day of the Exaltation of the Cross [September 14] Vseslav sighed and said 'O venerable cross! As I believe in you, save me from this dungeon.' God has shown the power of the cross to the Land of Rus. Let not those who have kissed the cross violate their oath. Should anyone violate his oath, may he be punished, and in the afterlife be doomed to eternal torment."

The beginning of family warfare among the sons of Yaroslav, the expulsion of Iziaslav by his younger brothers, and the violation of their father's commandment, provided the chronicler with an opportunity to pronounce these awe-inspiring words. "The devil was among Yaroslav's sons.... For it is a great sin to violate a father's commandment. The sons of Ham transgressed on Seth's land, and for four hundred years they were punished by God. From Seth's tribe came the Jews who killed the tribe of the Caananites, having received their lot and their land. Again Esau broke his father's commandment and killed, for it is not good to violate somebody else's bounds."[81]

The death of Iziaslav, who gave his life for his brother, provided the chronicler the opportunity to praise brotherly love. "Truly whatever sins he (Iziaslav) committed on this earth he will be forgiven, for he laid down his life for his brother, not wishing a larger principality, nor a larger property, but to avenge his brother's injury." When speaking about the vengeance of Vasilko of Terebovl, first wreaked upon the innocent inhabitants of the town of Vsevolozh and later on Davyd Igorevich's boyars, the chronicler added "The second act of revenge he committed he should not have done. He should have let God be the avenger, relying on His judgement." In the story about the struggles and reckonings among the princes the chronicler supported the senior against the junior, who are never defended but are reproached repeatedly. Thus in the South the chronicler opposed Yaroslav Sviatopolchich for stubbornness against his uncle and father-in-law. In the North, after relating the victory of Yury's sons over their nephews, the chronicler added "God ordered the princes not to act against the true cross, to respect their elder brother."

On the basis of the chronicler's attachment to this or that prince we may determine in which territory he was active. The Northern chronicler was particularly attached to his princes, the descendants of Yury Dolgoruky. He showed special respect for authority and attempted to inculcate this respect. The princes almost constantly are referred to by their name and patronymic, with the addition of the title *grand prince,* often accompanied by *pious, beloved by Christ.* Princely family festivities are mentioned, for example the haircutting ceremonies[82] which brought great joy to whole cities. Particularly interesting in this respect is the description of Konstantin Vsevolodovich's departure for Novgorod in 1206. The respect for authority which the Northern chronicler tried to instill is expressed further in the year 1175 on the occasion of Andrei Yurievich's death, and later in connection with the death of Vsevolod Yurievich in 1212.

The Northern chronicler was particularly attached to his prelates. It is clear from the very beginning that the Northern chronicler entertained very little sympathy for the men of Novgorod. He reproached them when he discussed Andrei's expedition in 1169, for frequent violations of oaths and for their pride. He agreed that the Novgorod way of life was ancient in origin, from the time of princely grandfathers, yet he denied the men of Novgorod the right to violate their oaths and expel their princes. Under 1186 the negative attitude of the chronicler towards the Novgorod way of life also is conveyed very clearly. "This year the citizens of Novgorod expelled Yaroslav Vladimirovich, and Mstislav Davydovich went to rule in Novgorod. *Such is their custom.*" For 1178, when describing the capture and the sacking Torzhok by Vsevolod III, the chronicler spoke out against violations of oaths. "Having captured the town, they took the men into captivity, and women and children they seized as their loot, and they took also the goods, burned the town on account of Novgorod's lies, because the citizens kissed the true cross and violated their oaths. We are told through the prophet...."

The chronicler wrote constantly of barbarian invasions as God's wrath for the people's sins. For 1093 "There was weeping in the town and not joy, because of our great sins and untruth for multiplying our lawless deeds. Because of this God sent the pagans, not because He favored them but because He wanted to punish us, that we might abandon our evil deeds. Thus we are punished by the pagans, because they are God's scourge, so that perhaps we would refrain from our evil ways." A similar view occurs later. The chronicler looked on other disasters similarly. "God punishes His servants by various disasters, by fire and water, enemy onslaughts and other punishments because to enter the kingdom of heaven a Christian must suffer many evils. As we sin, so are we punished. As we do, so is it done to us, but our Lord is good. Yet no one can say 'As God hates us, let us mend our ways.'"

Illnesses, every suffering and futile death purify man from sin. According to the chronicler, Prince Yaropolk Iziaslavich prayed "O lord my God! Accept my prayer, and when You send my death, as You did to my two brothers Boris and Gleb by a stranger's hand, let my sins be washed away by my blood." After the story of Prince Sviatoslav Yurievich's death the chronicler added "This prince was God's chosen man. For from the day he was born until he became a man he had a bad illness, such illness as the holy apostles and holy fathers besought from God. For those struck down by this illness, as the books say, the body is in torment, but the soul is saved. This was the lot of St. Sviatoslav, God's saint chosen among the other princes. God made him not a prince on this earth, but granted him the kingdom of Heaven." The same thought was expressed by the chronicler in the story of Andrei Bogoliubsky's death. Mstislav Rostislavich the Brave before a battle used to say to his retinue "Brothers! Think of nothing at all, only that today we are going to die for Christians and we will be cleansed of our sins and God will see in our blood that of martyrs." The chronicler held similar views even concerning warriors of other Christian denominations, for example the crusaders. Success, delivery from danger, usually were ascribed either to God's mercy and saints' prayers or to the prayers of ancestors, father, grandfather and great grandfather. After the description of the victory of Yury's sons over their nephews the chronicler added "God helped Mikhail and his brother Vsevolod [thanks to] the prayers of his father, grandfather and great-grandfather."

We noted the chronicler's negative attitude to folk entertainments, where remnants of pagan customs were still alive.

After this discussion of the religious, moral and political ideas of the chronicler, let us turn to some of his other notions. These were his ideas about the origins of the Polovetsians and examples of his ethnographic, historical and geographical observations. "They came from the Nithrib desert, between East and North. There are four of their tribes: Turkmen and Pechenegs, Torks and Polovetsians. Methodius writes about them 'Eight tribes came, whom Gideon cut down, and eight of them fled to the desert, and four were cut down. Others say the sons of Ammon, but it is not so, for the sons of Ammon are Bulgars, and the Saracens are sons of Ishmael and they call themselves *sarakyne*, and say we are *sarini*. The Bulgars boast that they are the descendants of Lot's daughter who conceived from her father. Therefore their tribe is unclean.[83] Ishmael had twelve sons and the Turkmen, Pechenegs, Turks and Cumans, who are also Polovetsians, are their descendants. They wander in the desert, and the eight generations were locked in the mountain by Alexander the Great, the unclean people, as Methodius of Pataria called them. They explored the eastern countries to a place called Soliche, and saw there unclean people from the tribe of Japhet and their uncleanliness for they eat all manner of filth, mosquitoes and flies, cats and snakes. Neither do they bury their dead, instead eat them as well as aborted foetuses and every unclean animal. Alexander feared they would multiply and make the earth unclean, so he drove them to Northern countries into the high mountains. At God's command the mountains moved and gates of brass were erected and covered with indestructible metal which cannot be destroyed by fire, for this metal is incombustible, nor can iron prevail against it. In the final days eight generations will walk the Yathrib desert, and these filthy nations in the Northern mountains at God's command will come to an end." Other historical, geographical and ethnographical information of the Primary Chronicle was discussed earlier.

Let us look now at the opinions of the chronicler regarding various physical phenomena. Each unusual physical event foretold something unusual in the world of man, usually something evil. In 1063 the Volkhov river in Novgorod flowed backwards for five days. This was not a good sign, said the chronicler. Four years later Prince Vseslav burned the city. The following year "there was a sign in the West, a large star, with bloody rays which appeared in the evening after sunset and stayed for seven days. This did not bode good. After that there were many princely

struggles and an invasion of pagans to the Land of Rus, for this bloody
star was a sign of bloodshed. In those same times a child was thrown into
the Setoml. This child was caught by the fishermen in their nets and they
looked at him until the evening and then threw him into the water because
they said on his face he had a shameful part which it was indecent to look
upon. Before that time the sun had changed and it was not yet light, as
if there were a moon, which the ignorant said was eaten. These signs do
not bode good, as we understand them."

Then follows a list of unusual portents observed in various countries
which foretold every disaster for the people. The chronicler ended this list
with these words. "These signs in heavens or the stars or the sun or by
birds bode good, but there are signs that bode ill, either war or hunger or
death." In 1091 we read "Vsevolod was hunting beyond Vyshgorod and
laid nets. The beaters were shouting, when an enormous snake fell from
the skies which frightened all the people. At the same time the earth made
a noise which many could hear." For 1102 "There was a sign in the sky
on January 29 for three days. A glow was in the sky from the east and a
rainbow from west to north, and this light was there all night as if it were
full moon. In the same summer there was a sign on the moon on the fifth
day of February. In the same month on the seventh day there was a sign
on the sun. The sun was surrounded by three rainbows and there were
other rainbows with their inner parts facing each other. Those who saw
this omen, pious people, prayed to God and cried beseeching Him to turn
this sign to good because omens are either for good or for evil." For 1104
"The sun was surrounded by a circle and in the middle of the circle there
was a cross, and before the cross a sun and outside the circle two suns
and above the sun except for the circle there was a rainbow with its horn
pointing north. The same sign was on the moon in the month of February on the fourth, fifth and sixth day, for three days and three nights." In
1110 "On the eleventh day of the month of February a fiery pillar appeared from the earth to the skies, and lightning lit the whole earth and
there was thunder in the skies at one in the morning." For 1141 "A
strange omen was in the sky and a terrible one. There were three suns
shining and three pillars from the earth to the sky, and above all the
hills there was something like a rainbow, and the moon stood apart."
Under 1203 "One evening at five the sky flowed down and everything
was scarlet. On the ground and on the buildings there was snow, and all
people could see it as if blood were spilled on the snow. They saw the

stars flowing in the skies, for stars were falling to the ground and those who saw it thought the end had come."

In 1186 there is a description of a solar eclipse. "In the month of May on the first day on Wednesday evening there was an omen on the sun, and it was very dark, and stars could be seen and the sun was like the moon, and from its horns heat was emanating, and it was very frightening for people to see God's omens." After the description of the solar eclipse in 1113, which according to the ideas of that time foretold the death of Grand Prince Sviatopolk, the chronicler added "These signs do not bode good. Not in all lands are there signs on the sun and the moon or the stars, only in some, and that land sees them." For 1143 there is a description of a storm. "There was a great storm near Kotelniche, such as has never happened before, and it destroyed buildings and goods and grain in the barns. It could be said that it was as if there was a fight and nothing was left in the stores. Some horses were drowned in a mudslide."

Under the following year we read "There was a sign beyond the Dnieper in the Kiev land. A fiery circle flew from the sky to the ground and left a sign in the shape of a big snake which stood in the sky for an hour and disappeared. The same summer there was much snow in the Kievan land, up to the horse's belly on Easter Sunday." In 1161 "There was a strange and frightening omen on the moon, which moved across the whole sky from east to west changing its shape. It diminished slowly until it disappeared completely and it became small, black and was bloody. Then it became like two faces, one green, another yellow, and in the middle two warriors fighting with their swords. One had blood pouring from his head and another had white liquid like milk flowing. Hence the old people said 'Not every omen is for good, for this foretells the prince's death.' (Iziaslav Davydovich was killed)." Under 1195 "The same winter, after St. Theodore's week [around November 9], on Tuesday at nine in the morning the earth in the Kievan land and the city of Kiev shook. Stone and wooden churches trembled, and all who saw this could not stand for fear. Some fainted, others trembled. The blessed abbots said 'This was God's sign. He displayed His power against our sins so that we might abandon our evil ways.' Others said 'These signs bode no good, for they foretell death for many, and bloodshed and a great rebellion in the Land of Rus, and this came true' (the internecine war between the descendants of Monomakh and Oleg)."

LOCAL CHARACTERISTICS OF CHRONICLES

After this survey of the general characteristics of our ancient chronicles, let us say a few words about the special features which distinguish various local chronicles. Two Northern chronicles have survived until our times, those of Novgorod and Suzdal, and two Southern, the Kievan with clear interpolations from Chernigov, Polotsk and probably other chronicles, and the Volhynian Chronicle. The Novgorod chronicle is distinguished by the brevity and asperity of its narrative. This is because of the paucity of its content. The Novgorod Chronicle relates events of one city and one territory. On the other hand it is difficult not to notice the influence of the local character. In the speeches of the men of Novgorod cited in the chronicle unusual brevity and power are notable. The men of Novgorod evidently did not like to talk at length, they did not like even to finish their speeches, yet they understood each other. It may be said that action for them is the end of a speech. Such is the famous speech of Tverdislav, who said "I am glad that there is no fault of mine and you, brother, hold the office of burgrave and prince."

The narrative of the Southern chronicles, in contrast, is characterized by a profusion of details, liveliness, figurative speech and even artistry. The Volhynian Chronicle in particular is distinguished by specific poetic language. It is difficult not to notice here the influence of the Southern nature, and the character of the Southern population. The relationship of the Novgorod to the Southern, the Kievan Chronicle is that of the sermon of Luka Zhidiata to the homily of Cyril of Turov. As for the narrative of the Suzdal chronicler, it is very dry, lacks the burst of the Novgorod language, yet is garrulous, although without the artistic flavor of Southern speech. It could be said that the Southern chronicles, the Kievan and Volhynian, relate to the Northern or Suzdal chronicle as *The Tale of Igor's Campaign*[84] does to *The Tale of Mamay's Battle.*[85]

Genealogy of Rus Rulers, 862-1125

Basil Dmytryshyn, *Medieval Russia.*
A Source Book, 850-1700.
The Academic International Press Edition, 2000.

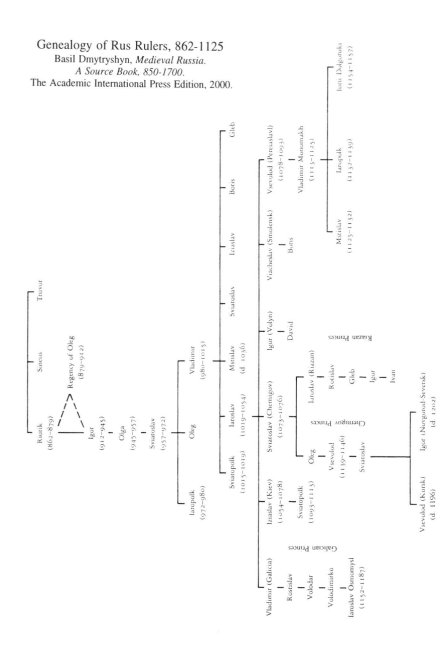

Russia in the Thirteenth Century

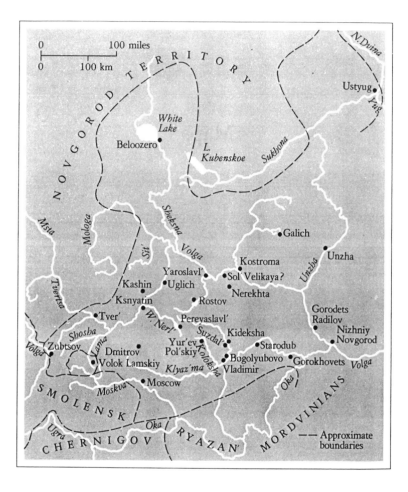

Suzdalia in the Thirteenth Century

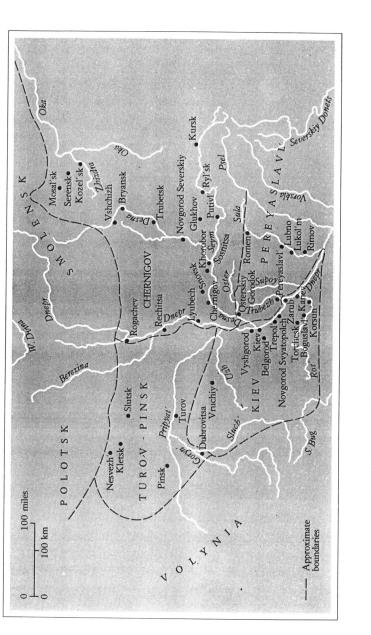

Kiev, Chernigov, Pereiaslavl, Turov-Pinsk in the Thirteenth Century

NOTES

Additional information on personalities and topics found in the text and notes is available in Edward J. Lazzerini, George N. Rhyne and Joseph L. Wieczynski, eds., *The Modern Encyclopedia of Russian, Soviet and Eurasian History* (MERSH, formerly *The Modern Encyclopedia of Russian and Soviet History*); Peter Rollberg, George Gutsche and Harry B. Weber, eds., *The Modern Encyclopedia of East Slavic, Baltic and Eurasian Literatures* (MEESBEL, formerly *The Modern Encyclopedia of Russian and Soviet Literatures, Including Non-Russian and Emigré Literatures*); Paul D. Steeves, ed., *The Modern Encyclopedia of Religions in Russia and Eurasia* (MERRE, formerly *The Modern Encyclopedia of Religions in Russia and the Soviet Union*); and David R. Jones, ed., *The Military Encyclopedia of Russia and Eurasia* (MERE, formerly *The Military-Naval Encyclopedia of Russia and the Soviet Union*), all published by Academic International Press.

INTRODUCTION

1. Mychaylo Hrushevsky, "The Traditional Scheme of 'Russian' History and the Problem of a Rational Organization of the History of the Eastern Slavs," *Annals of the Ukrainian Academy of Arts and Sciences in the United States*, Volume 2 (1952), pp. 357-358.

2. Paul Miliukov, *Ocherki po istorii russkoi kul'tury* (Notes on the History of Russian Culture), Volume 1, Part 2 (The Hague, 1964), pp. 113-120. This portion of the work was found among Miliukov's papers after his death in 1943, typed in the old orthography with numerous corrections and marginal notes. It was edited and put into publishable form in the new orthography by Nikolay Evfremovich Andreyev of Cambridge University.

3. M.P. Pogodin, "Zapiska o drevnem iazyke russkom (Note on the Ancient Rus Language)," *Izvestiia otdeleniia russkogo iazyka i slovesnosti Akademii Nauk* (Newsletter of the Section of Russian Language and Literature of the Academy of Sciences) 1856, No. 5, cols. 70-92. See also Addendum, Note 4, below.

4. See entry by Thomas S. Noonan, *Modern Encyclopedia of Russian and Soviet History* [hereafter MERSH] (Academic International Press, 1976-), Volume 21, pp. 233-235; also Miliukov, *Ocherki,* Volume 1, Part 2, pp. 172-173. Consult also Henryk Paszkiewicz, *The Rise of Moscow's Power*, translated by P.S. Falla (New York, 1983), Chapter 5, and map, p. 500.

5. V.O. Kluchevsky [sic], *A History of Russia*, translated by C.J. Hogarth, Volume 1 (London, 1911, reprinted New York, 1960), p. 204.

6. For a summary of the opposing argument, see Orest Subtelny, *Ukraine. A History*, 2nd edition (Toronto, 1994), p. 53.

7. Kluchevsky, *History*, Volume 1, Chapter XIII.

8. Robert F. Byrnes, *V.O. Kliuchevskii, Historian of Russia* (Bloomington, Ind., Indianapolis, 1995), p. 145.

9. Byrnes, *Kliuchevskii,* p. 144.

10. Nicholas V. Riasanovsky, *A History of Russia,* 4th edition (Oxford, 1984), p. 41.

11. Venedikt Myakotin, in *History of Russia,* edited by Paul Miliukov, Charles Seignebos and L. Eisenmann, Volume I (New York, 1968), pp. 93-94 (spelling modified). The original French edition was published in 1932.

12. Ellen S. Hurwitz, *Prince Andrej Bogoljubskij. The Man and the Myth* (Florence, 1980), pp. 21-22 (spelling modified).

13. Hurwitz, *Bogoljubskij,* pp. 85-86 (spelling modified).

14. Simon Franklin and Jonathan Shepard, *The Emergence of Rus, 750-1200* (London, 1996), p. 360. To confuse matters, there are two rivers called the Nerl, both within the same region, one a left-bank affluent of the middle Kliazma, the other a right-bank tributary of the upper Volga. Paszkiewicz, *Rise,* p. 86.

15. A.E. Presniakov, *Formation of the Great Russian State,* translated by A.E. Moorhouse, with an Introduction by Alfred J. Rieber (Chicago, 1970, reprinted by Academic International Press, 1993), p. 45.

16. "The idea of the translation of the special benevolence bestowed upon Byzantium by the Virgin foreshadows later Muscovite translation-of -the-empire themes such as the myths of the Third Rome and Monomakh's hat. But Andrei Bogoliubsky was not a tsar: the prerogatives of this office were still reserved for the Emperor and for Christ. The Byzantine Empire was still an important entity in Andrei's time, and his need to borrow Byzantine objects was more a result of recognition of his power and a need for its support than an attempt to challenge it." Hurwitz, *Bogoljubskij,* pp. 75-76 (spelling modified). The feast day arose in Byzantium in the tenth century to celebrate the apparition of the Theotokos to Andrew the Fool (Andreas Salos), who died in 936 at the Blachernae palace in Constantinople. There the relic of the Virgin's *maphorion* (veil) was enshrined, which acted as a talisman to repel the attack by the Rus in 860. The feast fell into oblivion until Andrei Bogoliubsky, for not very clear reasons, re-instituted it in Vladimir-Suzdal in the twelfth century. Another tradition commemorates one of the Blachernae icons which was kept in the right side of the monastery church, covered by a veil which miraculously lifted without human hands every Friday evening. This "habitual miracle" is not mentioned before the second half of the eleventh century or after 1204. Bogoliubsky's institution of the Russian obser-vance would fit into this time frame. See *Oxford Dictionary of Byzantium* (Oxford, 1991), p. 2170. Among the titles used for the Theotokos are *Paraklesis* (the Intercessor) and *Eleousa* (the Compassionate). The Intercession is therefore a Russian feast, although it seems also to have found its way into the calendars of other Orthodox Slavs. The Greek church celebrates the Intercession on October 28, which is the national holiday. October 1 is also the feast day of St. Romanos the Melodist, who is often depicted on Pokrov icons at an ambo. I am unaware

of any other instance of a secular ruler, even a Byzantine emperor, instituting a major feast day in the Orthodox church.

17. John Fennell, *A History of the Russian Church to 1448* (London, 1995), p. 58. Fennell cites an unpublished dissertation by C.L. Barrick, *Andrey Yur'evich Bogoljubsky, a Study of the Sources*, D.Phil thesis, Oxford, 1984.

18. Volume 5 of this series, p. 22. See also David Miller, "Legends of the Icon of Our Lady of Vladimir. A Study of the Development of Muscovite National Consciousness," *Speculum*, Volume 43 (1968), pp. 657-670.

19. Gail Lenhoff, "Canonization and Princely Power in Northeast Rus'. The Cult of Leontij Rostovskij," *Die Welt der Slaven*, N.F. 16 (1992), pp. 359-380. The rules governing canonization in the Orthodox church are somewhat less rigid than those obtaining in the West. "In its public worship… the Church usually prays only to those whom it officially has proclaimed as saints; but in exceptional circumstances a public cult may become established without any formal act of canonization." Timothy Ware, *The Orthodox Church* (Harmondsworth, 1963), p. 260.

20. Hurwitz, *Bogoljubskij*, pp. 58-59 (spelling modified).

21. Michael Cherniavsky, "Saintly Princes and Princely Saints" in *Tsar and People. Studies in Russian Myths,* second edition (New York, 1969), pp. 11-14.

22. Miliukov as quoted by Presniakov, *Formation*, p. 8.

23. Klaus-Detlev Grothusen, *Die historische Rechtschule Rußlands. Ein Beitrag zur rußischen Geistesgeschichte in der zweiten Hälfte des 19. Jahrhunderts* (The Historical-Juridical School of Russia. An Essay on Russian Intellectual History in the Second Half of the Nineteenth Century) (Gießen, 1962).

24. For treatment of Galich-Volhynia in the Ukrainian context, see Michael Hrushevsky, *A History of Ukraine* (Yale, 1941, reprinted Archon Books, 1970), Chapter VII, and Subtelny, *Ukraine*, Chapter 3.

25. Kluchevsky, *History*, Volume 1, Chapter XVII.

26. Paszkiewicz, *Rise*, pp. 199-202.

27. Presniakov, *Formation*, p. 35.

28. Dmitry was Vsevolod's baptismal name. The new town of Dmitrov also was named by Yury Dolgoruky in honor of his newly baptized son. Concerning the cathedral, Soloviev referred to S.G. Stroganov, *Dmitrievskii sobor vo Vladimire-na-Kliaz'me* (The St. Dmitry Cathedral in Vladimir-on-the-Kliazma) (Moscow, 1849).

29. Franklin and Shepard, *Emergence*, p. 351. For a biographical sketch of Vsevolod III, see entry by Martin Dimnik, MERSH, Volume 43, pp. 101-105.

30. "[Konstantin's] aim was to have the best of both worlds and to rule as grand prince not in Vladimir but in his northern city [Rostov] and yet to have Vladimir attached to Rostov as his own family possession. Twice Vsevolod sent for him, but each time he refused to budge." Fennell, *The Crisis of Medieval Russia 1200-1304* (London, 1983), p. 46.

31. See Chapter VIII, Note 67, below.

32. Eric Christiansen, *The Northern Crusades*, second edition (Harmondsworth, 1997), pp. 47-49.

33. Thus establishing a baneful apostolic succession of antipathy between generations of leading Russian historians. Soloviev hated Pogodin, Kliuchevsky hated Soloviev, Miliukov hated Kliuchevsky, Pokrovsky hated Miliukov (for personal as well as ideological reasons), and so on.

34. See Addendum, Note 1, below.

35. See Chapter VIII, Notes 33-34, below.

36. See Chapter VIII, Notes 39 and 83, below.

37. George Vernadsky, *Russian Historiography. A History* (Belmont, Mass., 1978), pp. 335-338.

38. PSRL, Volume 1 (St. Petersburg, 1846, second edition Leningrad, 1926-1927, reprinted Moscow, 1962); Volume 2 (St. Petersburg, 1843, second edition Leningrad, 1926).

39. *Russkaia letopis' po Nikonovu spisku* (Russian Chronicle According to the Nikonian Transcription), Volume 1 (St. Petersburg, 1767; PSRL, Volumes 9-10 (St. Petersburg 1862, 1885).

40. PSRL, Volume 3 (St. Petersburg, 1841); Volume 4 (St. Petersburg, 1848, second edition Petrograd, 1915); Volume 5 (St. Petersburg, 1851, second edition Leningrad, 1926). The textological history of the Novgorod chronicles, five in all, is too complicated to be unravelled here. A concise guide may be found in the entry by Dimnik, MERSH, Volume 25, pp. 82-89. Following publication of the Pskov chronicles in PSRL a number of hitherto unknown manuscripts were discovered, eventually giving rise to a new redaction by A.N. Nasonov, *Pskovskie letopisi*, vyp. 1 (Moscow and Leningrad, 1941, reprinted Düsseldorf and The Hague, 1967); vyp. 2 (Moscow, 1955). Soloviev also used an early printed version of the Holy Wisdom Chronicle, *Sofiiskii vremennik ili russkaia letopis' s 862 do 1534 god*, edited by P. Stroev (St. Petersburg, 1820).

41. *Russkaia letopis' s Voskresenskogo spiska* (The Russian Chronicle According to the Resurrection Transcription), Part 1 (Moscow, 1754), corresponds to PSRL, Volume 7 (St. Petersburg, 1856). The chronicle is named after the Resurrection monastery of New Jerusalem, founded in the seventeenth century by Patriarch Nikon, where the manuscript was preserved. See entry (unsigned) in MERSH, Volume 43, p. 75.

42. *Letopis' Pereiaslavlia-Suzdal'skogo*, edited by M. Obolensky (Moscow, 1851). See entry by A.G. Kuz'min, MERSH, Volume 47, p. 193.

43. *Letopisets, soderzhashchii v sebe rossiiskuiu istoriiu ot 852 do 1598 g.* (Moscow, 1819).

44. "Rodoslovnaia kniga velikogo rossiiskogo gosudarstva velikikh kniazei (Genealogical Book of the Great Russian Realm under the Grand Princes)," *Vremennik* MOIDR (Annals of the Moscow Society of Russian History and Antiquities), Volume 10 (1851); *Kniga stepennaia tsarskogo rodosloviia* (Book of Degrees of the Tsar's Genealogy), PSRL, Volume 21, Part 1, Section 1 (St. Petersburg, 1908, reprinted Düsseldorf and Vaduz, 1970).

45. V.N. Tatishchev, *Istoriia rossiiskaia*, Volume 3 (Russian History) (Moscow, 1774, reprinted Moscow and Leningrad, 1964); M.N. Karamzin, *Istoriia*

gosudarstva rossiiskogo, Volumes 1-2 (St. Petersburg, 1816) (see also Chapter VIII, Note 68, below); A.N. Artsybashev, *Povestvovanie o Rossii* (Narrative about Russia), Volume 1, Book 2 (Moscow, 1838).

46. I. Ewers, *Studien zur gründlichen Kenntnis der Vorzeit Rußlands* (Studies in the Basic Knowledge of Russia's Antiquity) (Dorpat, 1830).

47. "Iakov mnikh, russkii pisatel' XI veka i ego sochineniia (Yakov the Monk, Russian Writer of the Eleventh Century and His Works)," *Izvestiia II otdeleniia Akademii Nauk* (Newsletter of the Second Section of the Academy of Sciences) (Moscow, 1852); "Issledovaniia, zamechaniia i lektsii o russkoi istorii. Period udel'nyi (1050-1240) (Researches, Observations and Lectures on Russian History. The Appanage Period (1050-1240)," *Vremennik* MOIDR (Journal of the Moscow Society of Russian History and Antiquities) 1849, No. 2; "Kniaz' Andrei Iur'evich Bogoliubskii (Prince Andrei Yurievich Bogoliubsky)," *Zhurnal Ministerstva Narodnogo Prosveshcheniia* (Journal of the Ministry of National Enlightenment), Volume 14 (1849); "Mezhduosobnye voiny (Internecine Wars)," *Vremennik* MOIDR 1849, No. 2; "O nasledstvennost' drevnikh sanov v period vremeni ot 1054 do 1240 g. (On the Hereditability of Ancient Ranks in the Period of Time Between 1054 and 1240)," *Arkhiv istoriko-iuridicheskikh svedenii, otnosiashchiesia do Rossii* (Archive of Historico-Juridical Information Pertaining to Russia), edited by N. Kalachev, Volume 1 (Moscow, 1850).

48. A. Danilovich, "Istoricheskii vzgliad na drevnee obrazovanie slavianskikh i preimushchestvenno pol'skikh gorodov do XIII stoletiia (Historical Glance at the Formation of Ancient Slav and Principally Polish Towns up to the Thirteenth Century)," *Russkii Istoricheskii Sbornik* (Russian Historical Collection), 1844, Book 4.

49. I. Krasov, *O mestopolozhenii drevnego Novgoroda* (Concerning the Location of Ancient Novgorod) (Novgorod, 1851).

50. *Istoricheskoe opisanie odezhdy i vooruzheniia russkikh voisk* (Historical Description of the Clothing and Equipment of Russian Warriors), Part 1 (St. Petersburg, 1899). Soloviev obviously was citing from an earlier version of this publication.

51. "Soobshcheniia iz Kieva o naidennom v Nezhine klade starinnykh monet (Reports from Kiev Concerning a Cache of Ancient Coins Found in Nezhin)," *Moskvitianin* (The Muscovite) 1852, Volumes 4-5, Nos. 16-17; P.S. Kazanskii, "Issledovaniia o drevnei russkoi monetnoi sisteme v XI, XII i XIII vekakh (Studies on the Ancient Monetary System in the Eleventh, Twelfth and Thirteenth Centuries," *Zapiski Arkheologicheskogo Obshchestva* (Notes of the Archeological Society), Volume 3 (St. Petersburg, 1851).

52. E. Oskin, *Vnutrennie tamozhennye poshliny* (Internal Trade Duties) (Kazan, 1850).

53. K.A. Nevolin, *Istoriia rossiiskikh grazhdanskikh zakonov* (History of Russian Civil Laws), Volume 1 (St. Petersburg, 1851); Ewers, *Das älteste Recht der Rußen in seiner geschichtlichen Entwicklung* (The Oldest Russian Law Code

in its Historical Development) (Dorpat, 1826); E.S. Tobien, *Sammlung kritisch bearbeiteter Quellen der Geschichte des rußischen Rechts. Bd. II, t. II: Die Handelsverträge Rigas und Gothlands mit Smolensk vom Jahre 1228 und 1229 n. Chr.* (Collection of Critically Examined Sources for the History of Russian Law, Volume 2, Part 2: The Commercial Treaties of 1228 and 1229 A.D. Concluded with Smolensk by Riga and Gotland) (Dorpat, 1844). The texts of the treaties in question are found in *Pamiatniki russkogo prava* (Memorials of Russian Law), vyp. 2 (Moscow, 1953). See also Chapter VI, Notes 97 and 103, below.

54. The Latin text is best accessible in *Monumenta Germaniae Historica*, Volume 23 (Leipzig, 1925). Soloviev used the text contained in *Scriptores Rerum Livonicarum*, Volume 1, Part 1 (Riga and Leipzig, 1849). There is a version with Russian and Latin text, Genrikh Latviiskii, *Khronika Livonii*, edited with introduction and annotation by A.A. Anninskii (Moscow and Leningrad, 1938). A fresh German edition by A. Arbusow and A. Bauer, based on the discovery of new variants, is contained in *Henrici chronicon Livoniae, editio altera* (Chronicle of Henry of Livonia. An Alternative Edition) (Hannover, 1955). For the English reader the most convenient version is J.A. Brundage, *The Chronicle of Henry of Livonia* (Madison, Wisconsin, 1961).

55. The only original cited by Soloviev is "Johannis de Plano Carpini antivariensis archiepiscopi Historia Mongolorum quos nos Tartaros appellamus (History of the Mongols, whom we call Tartars, by Giovanni Piano di Carpini, Archbishop of Antivari)," *Réceuil de voyages et de mémoires, publié par la Société de Géographie* (Collection of Travel Accounts and Memoirs Published by the Geographical Society), Volume 4 (Paris, 1838), pp. 683-774. See also "Libellus historicus Ioannis de Plano Carpini, qui missus est Legatus ad Tartaros anno Domini 1246 ab Innocentio quarto Pontifice Maximo (The Historical Pamphlet of Giovanni Piano di Carpini, Who Was Sent as Legate to the Tartars in the Year 1246 by the Supreme Pontiff Innocent IV)," *The Principal Navigations, Voiages, Traffiques and Discoveries of the English Nation Made by Sea or Overland . . . at Any Time within the Compasse of these 1500 Yeeres, etc.,* collected by R. Hakluyt, Volume 1 (London, 1598). A modern English translation is available in Christopher Dawson (ed.) *The Mongol Mission* (London, 1955), more recently reprinted as *Mission to Asia* (New York, 1966). A Russian translation was made by A.I. Malein, Ioann de Plano Karpini, *Istoriia mongolov* (History of the Mongols) (St. Petersburg, 1911). For fuller information and bibliography, see entry by Hugh F. Graham, MERSH, Volume 28, pp. 62-64.

56. Soloviev relied on a French translation, *Voyages de Benjamin de Tudelle autour du monde* (Travels of Benjamin of Tudela Around the World) (Paris, 1930). For further information on this author, see Chapter VI, Note 98, below.

57. *Histoire de la Géorgie depuis l'antiquité jusqu'au XIX siècle, traduite du géorgien par M. Brosset* (History of Georgia Since Antiquity Until the Nineteenth Century, Translated from the Georgian by M. Brosset), Volume 1 (St. Petersburg, 1849).

58. P. Butkov, "O brakakh kniazei russkikh s gruzinkami i iasyniami v XII veke (Concerning the Marriage of Rus Princes to Georgian and Yas Princesses in the Twelfth Century)," *Severnyi Arkhiv* (Northern Archive), Volume 4 (1825).

59. G.F. Sartorius, *Geschichte des Hanseatischen Bundes* (History of the Hanseatic League) (Göttingen, 1802); by the same author, *Urkundliche Geschichte des Ursprunges des deutschen Hanse* (Basic History of the Provenance of the German Hansa) (Hamburg, 1830).

60. Maciej Stryjkowski, *Kronika Polska* (Warsaw, 1846).

61. Makarii, *Istoriia russkoi tserkvi,* Volumes 1-3 (St. Petersburg, 1857).

62. E.E. Golubinskii, *Istoriia russkoi tserkvi* (Moscow 1880-1881, second edition Moscow, 1903).

63. Filaret, "Bogosluzhenie russkoi tserkvy domongol'skogo vremeni (Liturgy of the Rus Church in the Pre-Mongol Period)," *Chteniia MOIDR* (Readings of the Moscow Society of Russian History and Antiquities) 1848, No. 7. Filaret (1782-1867) in secular life was Vasily Mikhailovich Drozdov. He became archbishop of Moscow in 1821 and was elevated to the rank of metropolitan in 1826. Vernadsky, *Russian Historiography*, pp. 387-388.

64. A. Zernin, *Ob otnosheniiakh konstantinopol'skogo patriarkha k russkoi ierarkhii* (Concerning the Relations of the Patriarch of Constantinople with the Rus Hierarchy (St. Petersburg, 1846).

65. *Paterik Kievo-Pecherskogo monastyria*, most readily accessible in the edition by the Archeographical Commission (St. Petersburg, 1911). Obviously Soloviev used an earlier version. A Ukrainian recension of this source is available, *Kyyevo-Pechers'kyy pateryk*, edited by D. Abramovich (Kiev, 1931).

66. Russian State Library, Manuscript Division, fond 310.

67. *Slovar' istoricheskii o sviatykh, proslavlennykh v rossiiskoi tserkvi, i o nekotorykh podvizhnikakh blagochestiia, mestno chtimykh* (Historical Dictionary of Saints Glorified in the Russian Church, and of a Few Other Heroes of Piety Locally Venerated) (St. Petersburg, 1836).

68. Kirsha Danilov, *Drevnie rossiiskie stikhotvoreniia* (Ancient Russian Poetry) (Moscow, 1818). See also *Drevnie rossiiskie stikhotvoreniia, sobrannye Kirsheiu Danilovym* (Ancient Russian Poetry Collected by Kirsha Danilov) (Moscow, 1958).

69. P.B., "Razbor trekh drevnikh pamiatnikov russkoi literatury (Analysis of Three Ancient Monuments of Russian Literature)," *Zapiski Arkheologicheskogo Obshchestva* (Notes of the Archeological Society), Volume 3 (St. Petersburg, 1851); *Pamiatniki russkoi slovesnosti* (Monuments of Russian Literature), edited by K. Kadailovich (Moscow, 1821); *Russkie dostopamiatnosti* (Russian Curiosities), edited by the Moscow Society of Russian History and Antiquities (Moscow, 1815); I.P. Sakharov, *Skazaniia russkogo naroda* (Russian Folk Tales), Volume 2, Book 8 (St. Petersburg, 1849); S.P. Shevyrev, *Istoriia russkoi slovesnosti* (History of Russian Literature), Volume 2, Part 2 (St. Petersburg, 1846, third edition St. Petersburg, 1887); A.Kh. Vostokov, *Opisanie russkikh i slovenskikh*

rukopisei Rumiantsevskogo Muzeuma (Description of Russian and Slavonic Books in the Rumiantsev Museum) (St. Petersburg, 1842). Other information may be found in Chapter VIII, below.

CHAPTER I

1. Rostislav Mstislavich (died 1167) was prince of Smolensk from 1127, grand prince of Kiev in 1154 and again from 1159 until his death. He was a grandson of Vladimir Monomakh and the founder of the Smolensk princely dynasty. During the third, fourth and fifth decades of the twelfth century he acted as subordinate to his father and brothers in their campaigns against the princes of Polotsk, the Chud, Lithuanians and Polovetsians. In 1144 and 1146 he participated in the wars of Grand Prince Vsevolod Olgovich against Prince Vladimir Volodarevich of Polotsk. In 1149 and 1150 he supported his brother Iziaslav against Yury Dolgoruky but they were defeated. Some time between 1133 and 1150 he established an independent bishopric at Smolensk, and endowed it richly.

2. Vsevolod Olgovich (died 1144), son of Oleg Sviatoslavich, was prince of Chernigov 1127-1139. He took advantage of the interprincely struggles to gain the Kievan throne, which he held from 1139 until his death. His reign was marked by increased exploitation of the citizens by his reeves Ratsha and Tudor. Vsevolod Olgovich regarded Kiev as his hereditary possession. This angered the citizens, whose disaffection was exploited by the princes' opponents. Following Vsevolod Olgovich's death on August 1, 1146 there was considerable social unrest. See Franklin and Shepard, *Emergence*, pp. 344-348.

3. Mstislav Iziaslavich (died 1170) was prince of Pereiaslav from 1151, Volhynia from 1154. He took part in the campaigns of his father Iziaslav Mstislavich against the Chernigov princes and Yury Dolgoruky. In 1152 he twice defeated the Polovetsians. Having become established in Volhynia, he began his efforts to conquer Kiev, which he occupied in 1160, placing upon the throne his uncle Rostislav Mstislavich (see Note 1, above), on whose death in 1167 he himself became grand prince. In 1169 he was expelled from Kiev by Andrei Bogoliubsky and retired to his principality of Volhynia, where he died shortly after.

4. Yury Vladimirovich Dolgoruky (1100-1157) was the sixth son of Vladimir Monomakh, during whose lifetime he was prince of Rostov-Suzdal. He is also renowned as the founder of Moscow, which is first mentioned in 1157. In 1125 he transferred the capital of his principality from Rostov to Suzdal. After the death of his brother Grand Prince Mstislav Vladimirovich, Yury intervened actively in the succession struggle which took place between 1132 and 1135, but at this stage he was unsuccessful. He was more fortunate in the second phase of the struggle, and in 1154 became grand prince of Kiev. He was a famous patron of the new architectural style, commissioning such churches as St. Boris and St. Gleb at his residence of Kideksha and the Transfiguration cathedral at Pereiaslavl-Zalessk. In 1156 the first kremlin in Moscow was completed. He established and fortified

the towns of Yuriev-Polsky (1150), Kostroma and Pereiaslavl-Zalessk (1152) and Dmitrov (1155). Under his rule the economic and political rise of Northern Rus began.

5. This younger brother was Gleb Yurievich, prince of Pereiaslav (died 1171), whom a recent historian justifiably has referred to as a "placeman." See Franklin and Shepard, *Emergence*, pp. 323-324 and Jaroslaw Pelenski, "The Sack of Kiev in 1169. Its Significance for the Succession of Kievan Rus," *Harvard Ukrainian Studies,* 11 (1987), pp. 303-316.

6. "Clan" is the term used to translate *rod,* the entire family descending from the legendary Riurik. Practically all the Rus princes of the period under discussion descended from Vladimir I.

7. A *rodich* (member of the princely clan) initially participated in the inheritance order of the entire Rus as a whole and later in particular lands, for example Chernigov, Smolensk and so on.

8. *Votchina* in the eleventh to fifteenth centuries was the predominant form of land holding. Frequently a votchina consisted of several holdings scattered over a vast territory, usually centered on a town or city where the ruling prince's seat was located and supplied the ruler and his retinue with revenue. For that reason the votchina acquired in Soloviev's work the meaning of a territory or district ruled by a prince.

9. Iziaslav Mstislavich (1097-1154) was the eldest son of the Novgorod prince Mstislav Vladimirovich. From 1134 he was prince of Vladimir-in-Volhynia, and from 1143 prince of Pereiaslav. Taking advantage of the 1146 uprising in Kiev against the sons of Oleg, Iziaslav became grand prince and carried on a long struggle against both Yury Dolgoruky and the dispossessed descendants of Oleg. As a result of these disorders the ecclesiastical link with Constantinople was interrupted, and in 1147 the learned Smolensk monk Klimenty was installed as metropolitan of Kiev. Iziaslav's reign is recorded in a special chronicle compiled by his boyar comrade in arms Peter Borislavich. See B. A. Rybakov, "Boiarin-leopisets XII v. (Boyar Chronicler of the Twelfth Century)," *Istoriia SSSR* (History of the USSR), 1959, No. 5. This chronicle later was incorporated into the Hypatian Chronicle. See following note, also Chapter VIII, Note 70.

10. Soloviev has the irritating habit of referring to "the chronicle" or "the chronicler" without indicating which source is being cited. The primary sources most quoted here are the Hypatian Chronicle in Volume 2 of the *Complete Collection of Russian Chronicles* (PSRL) originally published at St. Petersburg in 1843, and the relevant section of the *Nikon Chronicle,* PSRL, Volume 9 (St. Petersburg, 1862), though Soloviev himself used an older edition, *Russkaia letopis' po Nikonovu spisku,* Part II (St. Petersburg, 1768). For an English version, see *The Nikonian Chronicle,* translated and edited by Serge A. Zenkovsky and Betty Jean Zenkovsky, Volume II (Princeton, 1984).

11. *...vsledstvie izgoistva svoikh kniazei,* literally "because their princes had become izgoi," meaning princes excluded from the succession because none of their immediate kin had ruled in Kiev.

12. The word *plemia* means a branch or tribe, referring usually to a princely group descending from a more significant ruler like, for example, Vladimir Monomakh, the originator of the Monomashichi (sometimes known as Monomakhovichi) who established himself in a given territory or area. A princely branch (or tribe) form a more coherent grouping of rulers with common interests, as for example the Yurievichi, descendants of Yury Dolgoruky who controlled the Northeast of Rus. The Russian terms Monomashchichi and Yurievichi are plural forms of Monomakh and Yury denoting descendants of these princes.

13. *Posadnik* was a title originally given to a representative of the prince in charge of a town or a city. Usually appointed from among the boyars, the posadnik of Novgorod achieved first a semi-independent and later a fully independent status and was elected by the people of Novgorod in the city assembly. V.L. Yanin, *Novgorodskie Posadniki* (Posadniks of Novgorod) (Moscow, 1962) believes that as early as 1136 posadniks became the main agents of Novgorod independence, where princely power was severely restricted. The period under discussion may be considered transitional in that from being a princely appointee, the posadnik came to be elected by the citizens, and therefore a "mayor" in the true sense. In cases where the posadnik was an appointed princely official, the term "burgrave" is used.

14. The Karakalpaks, in Russian *chernye klobuki* (Black Hoods or Black Caps), were a group of semi-nomadic tribes settled in the South Rus plain, consisting of Berendey, Koui and other peoples, usually considered by the Russian sources as "our pagans," a permanent feature in the Rus military forces of the time.

15. See Volume 2 of this series.

16. See Note 4, above.

17. Very frequently secondary settlements separated from established towns, which continued with diminishing success to assert jurisdiction over the *prigorody* or bytowns. Thus Pskov was originally a bytown of Novgorod, Vladimir of Rostov, and so on.

18. *Tiun,* meaning "reeve" or "steward," was a prince's servitor of lesser standing.

19. The *veche* was a town (city) meeting or assembly (tenth to fifteenth centuries) called to discuss various questions of government or law, often chaotic and occasionally used by princes or boyars to create political pressure. This institution was best developed in Novgorod, but its authority varied widely in Rus. For this important institution see K. Zernack, *Die burgstädtischen Volkversammlungen bei Ost-und Westslaven. Studien zur verfassungsgeschichtlichen Bedeutung des Veče*, (The Civic Folk Assemblies among the East and West Slavs. Studies on the Constitutional and Historical Significance of the Veche) (Wiesbaden 1967).

20. Franklin and Shepard, *Emergence*, pp. 362-363.

21. See Note 5, above.

22. Dorogobuzh on the Goryn (Horyn) river, not the later town of the same name in the vicinity of Smolensk.

23. Polovtsy (Russian plural) or Polovetsians, a powerful Turkic-speaking tribal confederation inhabiting the southern Rus steppe from mid-eleventh century until the Mongol conquest of 1236-1241. They were known also as Cumans or Qipchaq (Kipchak).

24. The *tysiatskii* (thousand man) or chiliarch originally was an appointed military official responsible for a thousand troops. In time his responsibilities changed to suit the political situation in various lands. A chiliarch was mainly the commander of the local town (city) militia.

25. The Berendey were a nomadic Turkic tribe who together with Torks and Pechenegs settled in the steppes of Southern Rus near Kiev and Pereiaslav by the end of the eleventh century, and eventually formed with other tribes the Karakalpak group.

26. A *voevoda* was a military commander or governor, literally a leader of troops. It seems that voevoda performed military duties during wartime, leading the local regiment or regiments, and performed other administrative duties during peacetime.

27. See Chapter II, Note 1, below.

28. Franklin and Shepard, *Emergence*, pp. 350-351.

29. Vernadsky, *Kievan Russia* (Yale, 1948), pp. 210-211.

30. Concerning Bîrlad, see Chapter V, Note 29, below.

31. The dignity of the beard was protected in the Rus Justice by a fine of twelve grivnas. See Franklin and Shepard, *Emergence*, p. 219; also Vernadsky, *Medieval Russian Laws* (New York, 1947, reprinted 1969), pp. 27, 48. For a biblical parallel, see 2 Samuel 10:4-5.

32. The word *podruchnik,* a subject of a prince, a servant, here has a derogatory meaning.

33. Yas was the Old Rus name for the Alan tribes, Sarmatian nomads inhabiting areas between the Don and the Caucasus. Later they became known as Ossetians. See also Chapter VI, Notes 32 and 101, below.

34. The word used in the original is *koshchei*, a term of Turkic origin.

35. *Detskie,* literally "children." Probably originally the term meant children of boyars, but here it means lesser noblemen serving in the retinue.

36. *Mechnik,* "swordbearer," was a term used to designate a servitor in a retinue with various administrative duties at a princely court. See also Chapter VI, Note 46, below.

37. *Gde zakon tam obid mnogo*, "Where there is law, there is also much injury," is a well-known Russian proverb. In other words, disputes should if possible be settled without litigation. See also Addendum, Note 5, and Chapter VII, Note 38, below.

38. The chronicle account of Andrei Bogoliubsky's death is found in the *Nikonian Chronicle,* Volume II, pp. 157-160 and also Basil Dmytryshyn, *Medieval*

Russia. A Source Book, 850-1700, 4th edition (Gulf Breeze, Fla., Academic International Press, 2000), pp. 72-76.

39. The Bulgars were a Turkic-speaking, nomadic tribe which appeared in the northern Black Sea steppe during sixth or seventh century. During the period under discussion here they were settled in the area of the Volga-Kama confluence, forming the Volga Bulgar state which dominated that region until 1236.

40. The expression used here is *zhid,* obviously meant in this context to be pejorative, though apparently the term itself was not necessarily so in Kievan Rus. See Henrik Birnbaum, "On the Slav Word for Jew. Origin and Meaning," *Essays in Early Slavic Civilization* (Munich, 1981), pp. 26-35.

41. The term used in the original is *demestvennik,* at that time meaning the leading singer or precentor of a church choir. Later it came to mean an innovator or composer of church chants.

42. For an interesting study of this prince, see Introduction, Note 12, above.

43. See Chapter VI, Notes 72-73, below.

44. *Versta* (anglicized rendition "verst") equals 1,066.8 m., or approximately one kilometer.

45. Now the Ukrainian city of Khmelnitsky.

46. "Vsevolod, seeing that there was no convenient way of dissuading them from this purpose, promised he would blind [the two princes] and set them free…. That same day before evening he ordered that they have the skin above their eyes cut, and having shed enough blood declared to the people that their eyes had been put out. Then, immediately placing them in a sled, he had them conveyed out of the town until they were out of the reach of the populace, after which he sent them on to Smolensk." V.N. Tatishchev, *Istoriia Rossiiskaia* (Russian History), Volume 3 (Moscow-Leningrad, 1964), p. 119.

47. Roman was the baptismal name of the Rus martyr Prince Boris (died 1015).

48. "Livs" is an historical name for the Baltic tribal groups of today's Latvia.

CHAPTER II

1. For Konstantin Seroslavich's conduct during the war between Gleb and Mstislav Iziaslavich see Volume 2 of this series: "Finally Ksniatin or Konstantin Seroslavich was Yaroslav's envoy to Yury Dolgoruky in 1157." Probably Konstantin Seroslavich was identical with the "boyar Konstantin" mentioned in Chapter I of this volume. See pp. 14-15, above.

2. Adapted from the prose translation in the *The Penguin Book of Russian Verse,* introduced and edited by Dimitri Obolensky (Harmondsworth, 1965), pp. 13-14.

3. Anastasia, also called Nastasia, was the mistress of Yaroslav Vladimirovich of Galich. See preceding section.

4. Roman Mstislavich (died 1205) was prince of Novgorod 1168-1169, Vladimir-in-Volhynia from 1170 and briefly ruled in Galich (1199). He was the

son of the Kiev grand prince Mstislav Iziaslavich and a daughter of the Polish king Bolesław Krzywousty. He carried on a successful struggle against the boyars and clergy to strengthen princely power. His allies were the service boyars and the urban commercial stratum of the Volhynian towns. In 1188 he seized the Galich principality, giving Vladimir to his brother Vsevolod. Soon Roman was forced to abandon Galich, and with the help of his father-in-law Prince Riurik Rostislavich of Kiev Roman was restored to Vladimir. In 1195 he intervened in the interprincely disputes in Poland and was defeated at Mozgawa. In 1199, after the death of Prince Vladimir Yaroslavich of Galich, Roman once again seized the Galich principality and sought to extend his influence over the hinterland of Kiev. In foreign relations he had dealings with Byzantium, Hungary, Poland and even Rome, where Pope Innocent offered him a royal crown if would accept Catholicism. He was killed in an ambush laid for him by the Poles at Zawichost on the Vistula river. See Franklin and Shepard, *Emergence*, pp. 366-368.

5. King Géza II of Hungary (1141-1162) of the Árpád dynasty. After his death his son Stephen (István) III (1162-1172) competed for power with his brother Ladislas (Laslo) (1162-1163) and Stephen (István) IV (1163).

6. Manuel I Comnenos, Byzantine emperor, born 1120, reigned 1143-1180. For his role in Rus affairs see Andrew B. Urbansky, *Byzantium and the Danube Frontier* (New York, 1968), pp. 68-69.

7. The rumor, unconfirmed at the time, was indeed correct. Vladimir escaped in 1190.

8. Frederick Barbarossa (born 1123, king of the Romans from 1152, Holy Roman emperor from 1155) of the Hohenstaufen dynasty. He was renowned for his chivalry and political power. He died in Anatolia, on his way to the Holy Land during the Third Crusade in 1190.

9. Casimir the Just (Kazimierz Sprawiedliwy), prince of Cracow (1138-1194), was the youngest son of Bolesław III, left in his father's testament without land.

10. Sviatoslav Vsevolodovich (died 1194), a member of the Olgovich line of Chernigov, ruled also as prince of Kiev. See Chapter I, above.

11. For information concerning Metropolitan Nikifor, see Chapter VIII, Note 4, below.

12. The reference here is to the dispute between Yury Dolgoruky and Iziaslav Davydovich (died 1162) of the Chernigov line for the supremacy in Rus (Kiev). See Volume 2 of this series.

13. Bolesław Kędzierzawy (the Curly) (1120-1173) was one of the sons of Bolesław II of Poland. After his father's death he ruled in Mazovia.

14. Władysław Wygnaniec (the Exile) (1105-1159) was the oldest son of Bolesław III of Poland. After his father's death he ruled in Silesia from 1138 to 1146.

15. Mieszko III Stary (the Old) (1121-1202), third son of Bolesław III of Poland. After his father's death he ruled in Great Poland.

16. See Note 9, above.

17. Vladimir Yaroslavich's restoration in Galich with the help of Casimir of Poland and Nicholas took place in 1190. See above, p. 47.

18. The Viatichians were one of the Slavonic tribes of Rus. They lived in the basin of Oka river in the principalities of Suzdal and Chernigov.

19. See Chapter I, Note 45.

20. Władysław III Spindleshanks (Laskonogi, reigned 1228-1231), son of Mieszko III (1126-1173). His mother was the Kievan princess Evdokia. Spindleshanks granted the first real charter to the higher nobility of Poland, the Privilege of Genia, promising to observe just and noble rules drawn up by the council of barons and the bishop.

21. The Yatviags were one of the tribes in the Baltic group of peoples inhabiting present-day Northeastern Poland and Northwestern Belorussia (Belarus). They became extinct because of the military pressure of their neighbors.

22. This information is contained in [the Polish chronicler Maciej] Stryjkowski, who states that Roman yoked captive Lithuanians and Yatviags to the plough and forced them to cultivate clearings in the new settlements. We do not think we need take this literally, as in this instance Roman forced the Lithuanians and Yatviags to engage in cultivation, but contemporaries considered the venture unprofitable, hence this proverb, which later was taken literally. (Soloviev's note)

23. The *skhima* was a type of monastic vow leading to the strictest application of discipline.

CHAPTER III

1. The expression used here is *inoplemenniki*, which also could be translated "foreigners." It is true that the principality of Galich was subjected to Polish and Hungarian influence, but more likely Soloviev has in mind members of another *plemia*, or princely branch, who were not properly entitled to the rulership.

2. See Chapter I, Note 13.

3. Mstislav Mstislavovich Udaly (the Daring, died 1228) was the son of Mstislav Rostislavich Khrobroy (the Brave) of Smolensk (see Note 9, below). He was prince of Toropets from 1206, of Novgorod from 1210. He took part in campaigns against the Polovetsians in 1193 and 1203. Having become prince of Novgorod he struggled against Vsevolod III who continued the expansionist policies of Andrei Bogoliubsky. In 1212 and 1214 he conducted successful campaigns against the Chud and the Livonian knights. Later in 1214, having defeated Vsevolod Sviatoslavich "the Red" he placed Mstislav Romanovich on the Kievan throne. In 1216 he commanded the Novgorod army at the Lipitsa river, overcoming the princes of Vladimir-Suzdal. In 1218 he left Novgorod, defeated and expelled the Hungarians and occupied the throne of Galich. In the battle on the Kalka in 1223 he showed bravery but was incautious as a commander, causing the defeat of the Rus army. In his final years he fought against the Hungarians. Having quarrelled with Prince Daniel Romanovich and the Galich boyars, he

made peace with the Hungarian king and married his daughter Maria to the king's son Andrew, whom he named as his successor.

4. The *Chronicle of Pereiaslavl-Suzdal* covers the period 1138-1214 and is very close to the Laurentian chronicle. It contains information not found in other chronicles.

5. *...v Pronske sel kir Mikhail.* Instead of *kniaz'*, meaning "prince," Mikhail is referred to as *kir,* cognate with the Greek *kyrios*, meaning "lord."

6. For Prince Roman Mstislavich of Galich, see Chapter II, Note 4, above.

7. *Nogaty* (pl.) were small coins.

8. The expression used is *pokazali put' Romanu,* literally "showed Roman the way." This was a standard Novgorod euphemism to denote the rejection or expulsion of a prince.

9. Mstislav Rostislavich "the Brave" (died 1178) was prince of Smolensk from 1175 and became prince of Novgorod just before his death. His father was the Kievan grand prince Rostislav Mstislavich. In 1161 Mstislav was sent to Belgorod. In 1167 together with other princes he campaigned against the Polovetsians. He participated in Andrei Bogoliubsky's capture of Kiev in 1169, although in 1171 he helped his uncle Prince Vladimir Mstislavich of Dorogobuzh gain the Kievan throne. In 1174 he broke with Andrei Bogoliubsky, placed his brother Riurik in Kiev and withstood a nine-week siege of Vyshgorod by forces sent by Bogoliubsky. In 1178 as prince of Novgorod he conducted a vigorous campaign against the Ests. Later that year he died and was buried in that city. See Franklin and Shepard, *Emergence*, pp. 350-351.

10. Concerning Andrei Bogoliubsky (died 1173) see Introduction and Chapter I, above.

11. ... *khotia ispolniti otechestvie svoe*, probably meaning to remain faithful to the traditions of his princely branch.

12. The Chud were tribes inhabiting the shores of the Gulf of Finland, Riga and the Chud (Peipus) lake, including among others the ancestors of present day Estonians, and Finnish peoples further east, as far as the Urals and the White Sea.

13. The term used here is *pogost*. Originally it signified a rural habitation along the periphery of Kievan Rus, or the center of such a habitation where commercial activities took place. In time the term was applied to administrative and territorial units consisting of many settlements, as well as the central settlement of the district. At the head of the pogost were officials responsible for collecting the prince's tribute. When Christianity came to Rus the term also came to denote the center of a rural parish and the churchyard attached to it. See entry by S.O. Shmidt, MERSH, Volume 28, pp. 159-160.

14. Holy Wisdom or St. Sophia of Novgorod was the cathedral church of Novgorod which acquired the attributes of its ideological center and Novgorod's civic pride.

15. Mitrofan was elected archbishop of Novgorod in 1199 or 1201, probably the latter, since the chronicle entry gives a precise date, September 14, the feast of the Exaltation of the Holy Cross. Apparently he was deposed in 1218 then

restored in 1219, appointing his erstwhile rival Anton to the bishopric of Pereiaslavl. He died July 3, 1223.

16. *The Chronicle of Novgorod, 1016-1471*, translated by Robert Michell and Nevill Forbes (London, 1914, reprinted Academic International Press, 1970), pp. 41, 62.

17. The Court of Yaroslav was a section in Novgorod where the princely residence was located, and was identified with princely power in that city.

18. The *dikaia vira* or "wild bloodwite" was the murder fine paid by the members of a guild collectively, especially when the murderer was unknown.Vernadsky, *Medieval Russian Laws*, pp. 36-37.

19. *Chronicle of Novgorod,* p. 50.

20. *Chronicle of Novgorod,* p. 51.

21. John was consecrated bishop of Rostov in 1190. Formerly he was one of Vsevolod III's chaplains. In 1213 he resigned his bishopric and entered the monastery of St. Boris and St. Gleb.

22. See Note 1, above.

CHAPTER IV

1. Pereiaslavl in Rus proper, rather than Pereiaslavl-Zalessk, the new town in the Northeast. See also Chapter I, Note 45, above.

2. The term used in the original is *vziat' na shchit,* literally "to take upon the shield."

3. See Chapter III, Note 15, above. Mitrofan apparently was expelled in 1218 and restored the following year.

4. The transfer of the epicenter from Rostov to Vladimir was accomplished by Andrei Bogoliubsky in 1164. See Volume 2 of this series.

5. *Nizovye zemli* or *Ponizie,* meaning the "Lower Lands," rich agricultural lands downstream from Novgorod. Because the city was far from self-sufficient in foodstuffs, restricting grain supplies was a powerful weapon in the hands of the Vladimir-Suzdal rulers.

6. The measure mentioned here is the *kad',* equivalent to four chetverts, fourteen puds or just over five hundred pounds.

7. New Year according to the Old Russian calendar at that period fell on March 1. By the latter part of the sixteenth century it was moved to September 1.

8. For a concise account of the battle on the Lipitsa, see Fennell, *Crisis,* pp. 48-50.

9. The battle on the Koloksha river, near Vladimir, where Vsevolod III inflicted a decisive defeat on Riazan forces in February 1178. See Chapter I, above.

10. See Chapter VI, Note 67, below.

11. The Gorodishche was the princely fortified residence outside the wall of Novgorod.

12. See Chapter III, Note 8, above.

13. "They let (his) horses drink the water from the Volkhov" was a phrase used by the chroniclers to describe the attempts of various princes to subdue the independent stance of Novgorod. The Volkhov is the river which flows through Novgorod.

14. The text does not state the coinage. Probably grivnas, since at this time the ruble was only starting to emerge as a money of account.

15. The charters of Yaroslav were legendary privileges granted to Novgorod in 1014 by Yaroslav I Vladimirovich and considered by the citizens as cornerstones of their political independence.

16. *Chronicle of Novgorod*, p. 71. Presumably these events occurred the following summer, though there is no indication in the text.

17. Hair clipping was an old Slavonic custom of cutting a child's hair on his second, third or seventh birthday. It was connected also with name giving.

18. A hundred was a community unit in Novgorod as well as in other towns of Rus.

19. Prince Kálmán, son of King Andrew II of Hungary, was placed in Galich as a result of the Treaty of Spics (between the Poles and Hungarians) in 1214 and once again in 1219.

20. *Ponizie*, the "Lower Lands," consisted of the lower Dniester lands. See also Note 5, above.

CHAPTER V

1. Originally the archdiocese of Bremen had open boundaries, with a commission to evangelize the Scandinavian countries. When the church in these lands became autocephalous under the archbishop of Lund, the ambitious Bremen archbishop Hartwig II (1148-1168) was eager to expand his eparchy in new directions, chiefly the lands of the Eastern Baltic.

2. Alexander III (Orlando Bandinelli) was Pope from 1159 to 1181.

3. Concerning Meinhard, see Christiansen, *Northern Crusades*, pp. 97-98, 114, 132.

4. William Urban, *The Baltic Crusade* (De Kalb, Illinois, 1975), pp. 26-27.

5. Canute VI, king of Denmark (1182-1202), son of Valdemar I, conducted an active policy on the Baltic Sea, in particular in the Southwest.

6. Bertold of Livonia, bishop of Uexküll, the Cistercian abbot of Loccum, was appointed by Archbishop Hartwig to succeed Meinhard, killed in 1196. He in turn was martyred on July 24, 1198.

7. Bishop Albert of Uexküll or Albert von Buxhövden, was a nephew of Archbishop Hartwig II of Bremen and canon of Bremen cathedral. In 1199 he was appointed the third bishop of Uexküll. He was a statesman who set out to create an ecclesiastical empire in Livonia. See Gisela Gnegel Waitschies, *Bischof Albert von Riga. Ein Bremer Domherr als Kirchenfürst im Osten* (Bishop Albert of Riga.

A Bremen Canon as a Prince of the Church in the East) (Hamburg, 1958); Christiansen, *Northern Crusades*, pp. 79-80, 98-100.

8. The Military Orders in Palestine were modelled after monastic organization created in the Holy Land during the Crusades. The most powerful were the Templars. Two Orders of knights were active in the Baltic area, that described in this chapter, and the Order of the Teutonic Knights of St. Mary active in Prussia, which consisted of present Northeastern Poland and the present Kaliningrad (Königsberg) district of the Russian Federation.

9. Innocent III (Lotario de' Conti di Segni) was Pope from 1198 to 1216. At the Fourth Council of the Lateran (1215), Innocent advanced the most far-reaching claim to universal papal jurisdiction.

10. Friedrich Benninghoven, *Der Orden der Schwertbrüder* (The Order of the Sword Brothers) (Cologne and Graz, 1965).

11. Veno or Wenno von Rohrbach was master of the Militia of Christ, one of the crusader leaders in Wenden and subsequently the first master of the Order of the Sword Brothers in Livonia.

12. The Rogvolod branch refers to the princes of Polotsk who according to tradition did not belong to the Riurik's clan, but that of another Varangian (Viking) prince Ragnvald.

13. On Mstislav's campaigns see above, Chapter IV.

14. Odenpe, Otenpää or Odenpäh, in Russian Medvezhaia Golova (Bear's Head), is located 120 km west of Pskov, in present-day Estonia.

15. From Soloviev's own annotation it is apparent that the chronicler in question is Henry of Livonia. An English version is available, *The Chronicle of Henry of Livonia*, a Translation with Introduction and Notes by James A. Brundage (Madison, 1961). See Introduction, Note 54, above, also Christiansen, *Northern Crusades*, pp. 94-95. According to Henry of Livonia (p. 95), this expedition took place in 1210, not 1212.

16. ... *et acceperunt ab eis quadringentas marcas nogatarum.* The term is probably derived from the Estonian *nahk*, meaning "pelt." (Soloviev's note)

17. Soloviev uses the German term *Probst*, derived from the Latin *praepositus*, meaning the senior official of a cathedral or collegiate church.

18. The term *fokht* is used, cognate with the German *Vogt* or the Latin *advocatus*. In medieval Germany this denoted the lay administrator of the temporalities of a religious foundation. Clearly this is not the case here. The office in question was probably equivalent to a vicegerent. Brundage (p. 131) translates it as "magistrate."

19. Soloviev here and in the following passage uses the term *Rossiia* rather than *Rus'*, evidently following the Latin rendition of Henry of Livonia.

20. *Monumenta Livoniae Antiquae* (Monuments of Ancient Livonia), Volume III (Riga and Leipzig, 1842), p. 78. (Soloviev's note)

21. On the unrest in Novgorod, see Chapter IV, above.

22. Viachko is a diminutive of Viacheslav.

23. *Chronicon Livonicum vetus* (Ancient Livonian Chronicle), *Scriptores rerum Livonicarum* (Writers on Livonian Matters), Volume I, Part 1 (Riga and Leipzig, 1849), pp. 280, 284. (Soloviev's note)

24. *Chronicle of Novgorod*, pp. 63-64.

25. The Häme, in Russian *Iam* or *Em,* were a Baltic Finnish tribe attested since the middle of the first millennium A.D. on the coast in a region of forests and lakes. The *Tale of Bygone Years* mentions them as being tributaries of the Rus, and in the eleventh and twelfth centuries they paid tribute to Novgorod. At the end of the twelfth century they were conquered by the Swedes, to whom they were known as the Tavastians.

26. The Karelians were a Finnish tribe which inhabited an area north of the Neva river on the shores of the Ladoga and Onega lakes. Their present habitat straddles the Russo-Finnish border.

27. The term used is *yasak,* a tribute mainly in the form of furs, exacted from the native tribes.

28. The term used is *danniki* (pl.), which Soloviev explains in parentheses.

29. Bîrlad was a territory connected loosely with Rus in present-day Moldova, a center for runaway peasants and other marginal social groups. A similar place of refuge was Tmutorokan, a Rus principality on the Taman peninsula (eleventh century). See Volumes 1-2 of this series.

30. Concerning the Bulgars, see Chapter I, Note 39, above. The significance of the term "Silver Bulgars" is not clear.

31. ... *k Velikomu gorodu.* The Bulgar capital was frequently referred to as Velikie Bolgary (pl. of Great Bulgar).

32. Dregovichians, Severians and Viatichians were names of Eastern Slavonic tribes of Rus. See Volume 1 of this series.

33. Nightingale the Robber was a hero of a Russian folk tale. *Penguin Book of Russian Verse,* pp. 23-32.

34. The Letgolia was one of the tribes inhabiting present-day Latvia on the Eastern bank of the Daugava (Western Dvina).

35. The chronicle uses the term *gorod*, which Soloviev explains in parentheses.

36. Namely the encounter immortalized in the *Tale of Igor's Campaign.* See pp. 218-226, below.

37. The term Soloviev uses is *bisurman,* which was a general name given to non-Christians.

38. The device mentioned here probably refers to the "Greek fire."

39. The Koui were one of the service tribes, inhabiting the steppe near Chernigov.

40. Lukomoria was a legendary place by the sea, or the sea itself, probably referring to the Black Sea.

41. The term *verkhovnye zemli* (Upper Lands) refers to the lands in the upper reaches of the Dnieper.

42. Kumis is a light alcoholic beverage made of mares' milk, drunk by the steppe peoples.

43. The Torks were one of the tribes inhabiting the South Rus steppe.

44. Rostislav's Road was one of the military routes in the South Rus steppe.

45. The Lukomorians and Burchevichians were groups of Polovetsians. See Chapter I, Note 23, above.

46. Fennell, *Crisis*, pp. 66-68.

47. Dubrovitsk was a district of the Turov-Pinsk principality. Consequently these princes belonged to Sviatopolk's branch of the princely family. (Soloviev's note)

48. Brodniki ("Wanderers") were the warlike population of the Azov Sea and lower Don area in twelfth and thirteenth centuries. See Chapter VI, Note 85.

49. See Judges 6-8.

50. *Izgoi* were disinherited princes, omitted from the order of succession prevalent in Rus or expelled from their principalities. See also Chapter I, Note 11, above.

51. The Prus were a people of the Baltic group who inhabited present-day Northeastern Poland and the Kaliningrad region of the Russian Federation. They became extinct as a result of pressure from their neighbors. See Christiansen, *Northern Crusades*, pp. 208-212.

52. Cherkass was a name given in Russian to cossacks or various tribes of the Caucasus.

ADDENDUM

1. Soloviev's second volume first appeared in 1852, and subsequent publications during Soloviev's lifetime took place in 1856, 1862, 1866 and 1879. The text on which our translation is based (Moscow, 1960) follows the 1879 edition. On internal evidence this *Response to Critics* first appeared in the 1879 edition, since the Sergeevich publication with which Soloviev takes issue (see Note 6, below) was published subsequent to the 1866 reissue of this volume.

2. S.M. Soloviev, *Istoriia otnoshenii mezhdu russkimi kniaz'iami Riurikova doma* (Moscow, 1847). (Soviet editor's note) This publication was based upon Soloviev's magisterial thesis.

3. Konstantin Dmitrievich Kavelin (1818-1885) was a leading proponent of the Historico-Juridical school of Russian historians. See entry by J.L. Black, MERSH, Volume 16, pp. 75-78.

4. Pogodin, "Mezhduosobnye voiny i inoplemennye nashestviia (Civil Wars and Attacks by Foreigners," *Issledovaniia, zamechaniia i lektsii o russkoi istorii* (Researches, Notes and Lectures on Russian History), Volume 5 (Moscow, 1854) (Soviet editor's note). Pogodin (1800-1875) was a former teacher of Soloviev, but later the two developed a mutual antagonism. See entry by Edward C. Thaden, MERSH, Volume 28, pp. 153-156.

5. See Chapter I, Note 37, above, and Chapter VII, Note 38, below.

6. V.I. Sergeevich, *Veche i kniaz'. Russkoe gosudarstvennoe ustroistvo i upravlenie vo vremia kniazei Riurikovichei* (The Popular Assembly and the Prince. Rus Ruling Organization and Administration during the Age of the Riurikid Princes) (Moscow, 1867). (Soviet editor's note) Vasily Ivanovich Sergeevich (1832-1910) was a pioneer in the study of Russian legal history. See entry by Richard Hellie, MERSH, Volume 34, pp. 67-70.

7. Mark 13:12 (RSV).

CHAPTER VI

1. Oleg Sviatoslavovich (died 1204) was a prince of the Chernigov line of descendants of Sviatoslav.

2. The term translated here as "commoners" is *smerdy* (pl.).

3. The term *chernye liudi* ("black people") was used to denote free taxpaying people of non-noble origin. The collective noun *chern'* is used pejoratively to denote "the rabble."

4. In echoing the speech of the Severian princes, Soloviev here instead of "our men" uses the term "black people" to denote the foot soldiers of the urban levies.

5. Yaroslav I the Wise (died 1054) was a son of St. Vladimir. See Volume 1 of this series, Chapter VII, and Volume 2, Chapter I.

6. Mstislav Vladimirovich (died 1132), prince of Novgorod 1095-1117, prince of Pereiaslavl 1117-1125, grand prince of Kiev 1125-1132, eldest son of Vladimir Monomakh. He defeated Oleg Sviatoslavich, whom he compelled to attend the Liubech conference in 1097. He returned Murom to Oleg and reconciled him with the grand prince. In 1107 and 1111 he participated in the campaigns organized by his father against the Polovetsians. In 1113 and 1116 he conducted campaigns against the Finnic tribes bordering on Novgorod. After his father's death Mstislav continued to assert the overall authority of the grand prince of Kiev and to defend the Rus lands against external enemies. In 1129 he pacified the Polotsk princes and placed his own son Iziaslav in Polotsk. In 1130 and 1131 he successfully waged war against the Lithuanians. His name is connected with the oldest surviving original princely document, his charter issued around 1130 to the monastery of St. George in Novgorod. Vernadsky, *Kievan Russia*, pp. 96-98, emphasizes Mstislav's Nordic connections, since he was the son of Monomakh's first wife Gytha, daughter of Harold Godwinson, king of England, while Mstislav himself was married to Princess Kristina of Sweden. "In leaving Novgorod, Mstislav left behind there his son Vsevolod, whom the Novgorodians gladly recognized as their prince (1117). Thus he did not actually sever his connection with the northern metropolis and it is significant that after his first wife died he married a daughter of the mayor of that city (1122)."

7. Vsevolod Yaroslavich (1030-1093), grand prince of Kiev from 1078. Some time between 1046 and 1052 he married Maria, the daughter or niece of Constantine IX Monomachos (reigned 1042-1055), and their son Vladimir took

his maternal grandfather's surname. Vsevolod's daughter Evpraxia (in Latin Prax-edis, in German Adelheid) was married first to the margrave of Northern Saxony and then, on his death, to Emperor Henry IV. For a comprehensive sketch of Vse-volod, see entry by Sokol, MERSH, Volume 43, pp. 96-101; also Franklin and Shepard, *Emergence*, pp. 261-265.

8. Vladimir Monomakh (1053-1125), was prince of Novgorod and Kiev from 1113. See Volume 2 of this series, Chapter IV.

9. Riurik Rostislavich, prince of Smolensk and Kiev (died 1215).

10. Vsevolod III Yurievich, nicknamed "Big Nest" (1154-1212), was the young-est son of Yury Dolgoruky and brother of Andrei Bogoliubsky, on whose death he succeeded to the principality of Vladimir-Suzdal in 1174. For further details, see Chapters I-III, above, and entry by Martin Dimnik, MERSH, Volume 43, pp. 101-105.

11. Yury Dolgoruky (died 1157), prince of Suzdal and Kiev, father of Andrei Bogoliubsky and Vsevolod III. See Volume 2 of this series, Chapter VII, also entry by Richard Hellie, MERSH, Volume 45, pp. 73-76.

12. Vsevolod of Riazan, probably Mstislavich (died 1239).

13. Iziaslav Mstislavich, baptismal name Panteleimon (1097-1154), was the eldest son of Mstislav Vladimirovich, prince of Novgorod. From 1134 he was prince of Vladimir-in-Volhynia, from 1143 prince of Pereiaslavl. In 1146, taking advantage of the uprising in Kiev against the sons of Oleg, Iziaslav seized the Kievan throne and waged a lengthy struggle against Prince Yury Dolguruky of Rostov-Suzdal, who was allied to the descendants of Oleg (see Chapter VI). In the course of the struggle there occurred a breach in ecclesiastical relations with Constantinople with the installation of Klim Smoliatich as metropolitan. Iziaslav's reign was the subject of a special chronicle written by the boyar Pe-ter Borislavich, later incorporated into the Hypatian chronicle. See entry by Walter Hanak, MERSH, Volume 15, pp. 88-89.

14. Fedor, bishop of Suzdal, was connected with Andrei Bogoliubsky.

15. The battle of the Ruta river between Iziaslav Davydovich and Yury Msti-slavich in 1151 ended with Yury's defeat.

16. Daniel the Exile's *Epistle* is a literary work discussed in Chapter VIII. Soloviev assumes that the addressee is Yury Dolgoruky, but his claim is disputed. See Chapter VIII, Note 34, below.

17. *Kir*. See Chapter III, Note 5, above.

18. Rostislav Mstislavich (died 1167), from 1127 prince of Smolensk, grand prince of Kiev 1154 and 1159-1167, grandson of Monomakh, founder of the Smolensk princely dynasty. In his earlier years he fought under the command of his father and brothers against the princes of Polotsk, the Chud, the Lithuanians and Polovetsians. In 1144 and 1146 he participated in the war of the Kievan princes against Prince Vladimir Volodarevich of Vladimir-in-Volhynia. In 1149-1150 he supported his brother Iziaslav in his struggle for the Kievan throne against Yury Dolgoruky, in which the brothers were defeated. Some time between 1133 and 1150 he established an independent bishopric in Smolensk. For further details see entry by Dimnik, MERSH, Volume 31, pp. 162-165.

19. For the Berendey see Chapter I, Note 12.

20. The *poliud'e* was an expedition to collect tax or tribute from the rural population based on the principle of poll-tax.

21. The term used is *dym*, literally "smoke." Later on there was a regular impost known as the *podymnoe* or hearth tax.

22. The *shliag* was a coin mentioned in the earliest "strata" of the Rus sources, probably of Scandinavian origin (shilling).

23. The term used is *pogost,* for an explanation of which see Chapter III, Note 13.

24. *Istuzhniki,* literally sad, poor people.

25. *Poliud'e* and *pogorod'e* were tax-gathering expeditions, either by the princes or their representatives. See Note 18, above. *Pogorod'e* was the collection of taxes levied from urban population.

26. The measure used here for mead was the *berkovets*, equivalent to ten puds. The measure used for wine is the *korchaga* (meaning uncertain).

27. *Zhizhn'* (life), signifying means of upkeep.

28. See Chapter IV, Note 17, above.

29. According to custom, in addition to birthdays, the *imeniny,* the feast day of the saint for whom a person is named, also is commemorated. The person so celebrating is called, according to gender, an *imeninnik* or *imeninnitsa.*

30. Literally an emerald.

31. The Russian term is *svat* or *svakh.*

32. Concerning the Yas, see Chapter I, Note 33. Soloviev derived his information from P. Butkov, "O brakakh kniazei russkikh s gruzinkami i iasyniami v XII veke (Concerning the Marriage of Rus Princes to Georgian and Yas Princesses in the Twelfth Century)," *Severnyi Arkhiv* (Northern Archive), 4 (1825).

33. The aurochs (tur), was an animal, now extinct, of the *bos primigenius* species.

34. Lazarus Saturday was the Saturday before Holy Week, on which the raising of Lazarus from the dead was commemorated. See John 11:1-42.

35. *Perevar,* known as peasant ale or *braga* in Russian.

36. *Sviatoslav's Collection* (Izbornik Sviatoslava) was a collection of various texts compiled for Sviatoslav Yaroslavich, prince of Chernigov. There are two separate volumes, one dating from 1073 and the other from 1076.

37. *Otrok,* literally a "lad." This term was applied to young members of a retinue who participated in military and administrative tasks. In the twelfth century otrok was mentioned in the *Rus Justice* as a lower grade official of justice, customs and taxation administration. Cognate terms also used here are *detskie, pasynki* (stepsons).

38. *Molod', molodye, molodye liudi.*

39. *Grid', grid'ba,* a collective noun, *gridin* being the term used for an individual member, is a word of Scandinavian origin used to describe military men who formed the princely retinue. Generally it means ordinary warriors as opposed to senior warriors or boyars.

40. See Note 37, above.

41. *Dvorianin,* plural *dvoriane,* originally meant "courtier." The term is used for the first time in connection with Andrei Bogoliubsky's death in 1174, meaning a lower official dealing with fees, taxes and legal matters. Later this term acquired a different meaning of middle-ranking civil or military servant. After the Petrine reforms it became a general designation for landholding gentry. See entry by Richard Hellie, MERSH, Volume 10, pp. 77-79.

42. *Pomest'e* in the medieval period in Rus was a rare form of service tenure for warriors serving rulers. From the fifteenth century it developed as a major form of landholding as tenure on condition of service to the ruler. See entry by Hugh Graham, MERSH, Volume 29, pp. 29-33.

43. *Kliuchnik,* literally "keeper of the keys" designates a steward of an estate, or a manager of monastic lands.

44. A *pokladnik* was a servant in the bedchamber.

45. *spal'nik.*

46. The Russian term is *mechnik.* See also Chapter I, Note 36, above.

47. The term used is *koshchei,* a word of Turkic origin similar in meaning to *otrok.* See Note 37, above, also Chapter I, Note 34.

48. *kmetstvo,* meaning yeomanry, free men rendering military service. The word is cognate with the Polish *kmieć,* which came to signify "serf."

49. *Dobroimenitnye,* literally men of considerable means.

50. The *polk* at first was any military formation of substantial size or a tactical formation. On march or in battle formation it was possible to distinguish the left *polk* on the left wing, right on the right wing and the great *polk* in the center. From the sixteenth century it was a specific military unit based on an administrative-territorial district in Ukraine. In the seventeenth century new formation *polki* or regiments were established in Russia.

51. Concerning the battle of Kolakcha, see Chapter IV, Note 9, above.

52. The *Nikon Compilation* is a Russian chronicle collection, compiled between 1539 and 1542, presented to Patriarch Nikon in the seventeenth century. An English translation is available (see Chapter I, Note 10, above).

53. Soloviev uses the term *Chekhiia,* for which there is no exact equivalent in English. This sentence therefore loses something in translation.

54. Here we have an untranslatable nuance, the shift of meaning between the cognate words *vlast'* (power, authority) and *volost'* (territory or district).

55. For early East Slavonic tribes see Volume 1 of this series; also Vernadsky, *Ancient Russia* (Yale, 1948), pp. 308-370, and Pavel M. Dolukhanov, *The Early Slavs. Eastern Europe from the Initial Settlement to the Kievan Rus* (London, 1996), Chapters 7-9.

56. Truvor was one of the princes in the Varangian legend. Truvor, Riurik and Sineus were, according to this legend, the three brothers who founded Rus. See Volume 1 of this series, Chapter IV, also entry (unsigned) in MERSH, Volume 40, pp. 30-31.

57. On Andrei Bogoliubsky's death, see Chapter I.

58. Vasilko Rostislavich (died 1124), prince of Terebovl. For the episode of his blinding, see Volume 2 of this series, Chapter III. Franklin and Shepard, *Emergence*, pp. 269-270, Vernadsky, *Kievan Russia*, pp. 90-91, Serge A. Zenkovsky, *Medieval Russia's Epics, Chronicles and Tales* (New York, 1963), pp. 73-77 and entry (unsigned), MERSH, Volume 41, p. 226.

59. The term "Lower Towns" refers to the towns on the lower reaches of the Dnieper.

60. Ivan Danilovich Kalita (died 1340), grand prince of Moscow from 1325, and of Vladimir from 1328. He was one of the most important builders of Moscow as the leading power in Northeast Russia. See Volume 4 of this series, Chapter IV, and entry by Emily V. Leonard, MERSH, Volume 15, pp. 35-40.

61. The *Stepennaia kniga* (Book of Degrees) was a work of Russian historical literature from the sixteenth century (compiled in 1560-1563). It is an attempt to present a systematic account of the history of Russia. See entry by V.D. Nazarov, MERSH, Volume 37, pp. 135-136.

62. The *detinets* was a citadel or fortified area within a town or a city, for example in Novgorod.

63. An *ostrog* was a permanent or temporary fortified point enclosed by a wooden fence with pointed tips. In the eighteenth and nineteenth centuries it was also a prison surrounded by a wall.

64. A *predgorod* was a suburban settlement outside the gates of a town.

65. Not only Novgorod, but also Kiev was divided into "ends." The chronicler mentions [in Kiev] the Kopyrev "end." (Soloviev's note)

66. *Srublennye tserkvi* were wooden churches, a distinctive Russian architectural form, later used as the inspiration for construction of stone churches, replacing Byzantine models and creating unique architectural features.

67. Zarechie ("beyond the river") in Novgorod was the part of the city opposite the Holy Wisdom side on the right bank of the Volkhov river.

68. "Varangian churches" in Rus were the Latin as opposed to Orthodox churches.

69. All Saints Day is May 31 in the Orthodox calendar (November 1 in the Western).

70. The Dormition (in the West referred to as the Assumption) falls on August 15.

71. The question marks are in Soloviev's original text.

72. The *stareishina* were outstanding citizens heading urban communities.

73. *Plotskii konets* here is translated as Carpenters' "end." Administratively the city of Novgorod was divided into five wards or *kontsy,* literally "ends" (see above). Similarly *Goncharskii konets* is rendered as "Potters' 'end.'" Communities in Novgorod as well as in other cities often were named after the occupation of its members.

74. *Chern'* means common people or rabble, a general name for the lower orders of society.

75. A *desiatskii* was a squad leader, literally a leader of ten (warriors).

76. The *podvoiskii* was a court official involved in law enforcement duties. The *birich* was a herald or crier, a police official whose duties were to announce to the people the orders or statements of the authorities. *Iabednik* or *iabetnik* is rendered as "court herald."

77. The term used here is *pogost*. See Chapter III, Note 13.

78. The *stan* originally was a place where princes or their officials halted after a day's journey, often within a circle of wagons or a permanent wooden palisade. Later the diminutive *stanishche* denoted a military encampment. See entry by V.A. Kuchkin, MERSH, Volume 37, pp. 81-82.

79. See above, p. 265

80. A *sloboda*, less commonly *svoboda*, was an urban settlement enjoying specified immunities from taxes and other dues. See entry (unsigned), MERSH, Volume 35, pp. 238-239.

81. The *l'gota* was a tax exemption, generally granted to new settlers, for a specified number of years. See entry (unsigned), MERSH, Volume 19, p. 234.

82. *Cheliad* (collective noun) or *cheliadin* (individual member) were slaves or members of a lord's household, persons with specific legal status. *Raba* or *rab* was a general term describing any slave, not in particular persons of slave status in Rus. See entry (unsigned), MERSH, Volume 6, p. 221.

83. A *kholop* was a bondsman, or serf, someone with limited personal freedom, using land owned by a person of a higher status in return for rent paid in labor, product or money. See entry by Hellie, MERSH, Volume 16, pp. 162-169.

84. The more recent term is *oderen'*, replacing the earlier *obel'nyi* or *obel*. See entry (unsigned), MERSH, Volume 25, p. 155.

85. *Brodniki* (wanderers) was a name given to frontiersmen of the lower Don. Such communities began as fishermen and later developed military forms of organization. See also Chapter V, Note 48, above, also entry (unsigned), MERSH, Volume 5, pp. 191-192.

86. Soloviev refers here to an article by Pogodin, "Mezhdousobnye voiny (Internecine Wars)," *Vremennik Moskovskogo Obshchestva Istorii i Drevnostei Rossiiskikh* (Journal of the Moscow Society of Russian History and Antiquities), Volume 2, (Moscow, 1849), p. 55.

87. Little Russia was the official name of the Ukraine in Imperial Russia from the eighteenth to the twentieth century.

88. *Osmina* (eighth) was measure of weight equal to c. 63 lbs. or 0.4 bushels or 1.75 puds.

89. A rezan was small monetary unit. 50 rezan equals 1 grivna kun.

90. *malen'kaia kadka*. A *kad'* was a measure equivalent to four cherverts. See also Chapter IV, Note 6, above.

91. *Kuna*, literally a marten, was an old monetary unit or money in general, a local Rus name given to coins in parallel with Western denarii or Eastern dirhems. Their value differed regionally and there were also old and new kuna with different values. In the late fourteenth century it was replaced by the term *den'gi* or *serebro* (silver).

92. This is a reference to the *nav'*, a collective noun for the spirits of the unclean dead. Very often propitiatory meals, called *nav'e*, were prepared and the bath houses vacated so that the spirits could feed and bathe. G.P. Fedotov, *The Russian Religious Mind* (Harvard, 1946, reprinted 1966), Volume I, p. 350.

93. Russkaia Pravda was the oldest legal code of Rus comprising two parts, the Pravda of Yaroslav I the Wise, who ordered the collection of customary law and made his own additions, and the Pravda of the Sons of Yaroslav, who between 1054 and 1073 expanded and amended the previous code. See entry by A.A. Zimin, MERSH, Volume 32, pp. 218-221.

94. *Ukrop* in Russian means both "dill" and "boiling water."

95. Tmutorokan was a Russian principality which existed on the Taman peninsula during the tenth and eleventh centuries. Under Prince Mstislav (988-1036) it expanded its holding by annexing the lands of neighboring tribesmen. When Prince Oleg of Tmutorokan was captured by the Khazars and banished to Byzantium in 1079, the principality was governed by officials sent by the ruler of Kiev. Oleg was able to reassert his rule in the principality after his return from Byzantium in 1094, but Tmutorokan fell under the sway of the Byzantine empire shortly thereafter.

96. Yugra or Ugra was the territory beyond the Pechora and Yugra (Ugra) rivers and the Ural mountains under the control of Novgorod from the late twelfth century.

97. This treaty is reprinted in *Pamiatniki russkogo prava* (Monuments of Russian Law), vyp. 2 (Moscow, 1953), pp. 125-126 and in *Gramoty Velikogo Novgoroda i Pskova* (Documents of Great Novgorod and Pskov), ed. S.N. Valk (Moscow and Leningrad, 1949), No. 28.

98. Benjamin of Tudela (1116-1173) was a twelfth-century Jewish traveller from Spain, the first European to travel extensively in Asia. His work describing his journey to the East first was published in Constantinople in 1543. The most accessible version is the French translation, which Soloviev evidently consulted, *Voyages de Benjamin de Tudelle autour du monde* (Paris, 1830).

99. Giovanni Piano di Carpini or John of Plano Carpini (1182-1252) was a Franciscan friar and emissary to the Mongol Tatar khan. He was the author of an important work on the lands of the Mongols. He visited Rus in 1246 and described its situation following the Tatar invasion of 1237-1240. See Volume 4 of this series. A modern translation of Carpini's travel account is available in Christopher Dawson (ed.) *The Mongol Mission* (London, 1955), more recently reprinted as *Mission to Asia* (New York, 1966). For fuller information and bibliography, see entry by Hugh F. Graham, MERSH, Volume 28, pp. 62-64.

100. At this time Constantinople was under Latin domination following the Fourth Crusade (1204). It was recaptured by the Greeks in 1261. The Italians mentioned probably were Venetians, who were the chief backers of the Latin empire.

101. The Alans were numerous Iranian-language tribes of Sarmatian origin inhabiting the Northern Caucasus area, known also as Yas or Orsy. The Khazars

were a Turkic nomadic nation inhabiting the East European steppe in the second half of the first millennium. The Khazar khaganate dominated that area from the mid-seventh century and ceased to exist at the end of the tenth century.

102. William of Rubruck (died 1270) was a Flemish Franciscan monk who visited the Golden Horde between 1253 and 1255. He left a description of his journey, which took him also to parts of Rus. See Volume 4 of this series, Chapter I, Notes 83-84. A recent English translation of this travel account is *The Mission of Friar William of Rubruck. His Journey to the Court of Great Khan Möngke, 1253-1255,* translated by Peter Jackson (London, 1990). Halkuyt Society, Second Series, No. 173.

103. E.S. Tobien, *Sammlung kritisch bearbeiteter Quellen der Geschichte des russischen Rechts. Bd II, t. 2, Die Handelsverträge Rigas und Gothlands mit Smolensk vom Jahre 1228 und 1229 n. Chr.* (Collection of Critically Examined Sources for the History of Russian Law, Volume 2, Part 2: The Commercial Treaties of 1228 and 1229 A.D. concluded with Smolensk by Riga and Gotland) (Dorpat, 1844). The treaty is question is reprinted in *Pamiatniki russkogo prava,* vyp. 2, pp. 54-97.

104. *Volok* literally means a portage between two rivers. Sometimes it is used as a proper rather than a common noun. *Volotskii tiun* (portage reeve) was the title of the official appointed to control traffic, to whom the *volochane* (portage workers) were subordinate.

105. The *vesovshchik* (weighmaster) was responsible for maintaining proper weights and measures. Later the standard weigh scales were deposited in the vestry of the church of St. John the Baptist on the Opoki. See Chapter VII, Note 26, below.

106. A *veksha* was a coin of small denomination, equal in value to a *belka* or squirrel pelt.

107. *Skot* literally means "cattle." In the tenth to twelfth centuries this term was used to mean money. Compare the use of the Latin *pecunia*, originally meaning "cattle" but later meaning "money." See also Note 91, above.

108. *serebrennik.*

109. *T'ma* was a Russian word for the Mongol *tumen,* meaning a unit of ten thousand soldiers or a taxation district in the Mongol administration system. Here it means a number of ten thousand or a large number in general.

110. The Bulgars on the Volga. See Chapter I, Note 39, above.

111. On Frederick I, see Chapter II, Note 8, above.

112. The Vladimir Virgin was one of the oldest icons in Russia, of Byzantine origin. It was transferred by Andrei Bogoliubsky from Kiev to Vladimir, and in 1395 from Vladimir to Moscow. See David B. Miller, "Legends of the Icon of Our Lady of Vladimir. A Study of the Development of Muscovite National Consciousness," *Speculum,* 43 (1968).

113. See Chapter III, Note 21, above.

114. *stolets.*

CHAPTER VII

1. *Volkhvy* were magi or pagan priests. Possibly they were strongly influenced by or the same as Finnish shamans, and like the shamans achieved ecstatic, trance-like states while performing their functions. For a discussion of Rus paganism, see J.L.I. Fennell, *A History of the Russian Church to 1448* (London, 1995), pp. 77-90.

2. See Chapter I, Note 31, above.

3. Veles or Volos was possibly a great chthonic deity of the dead and a protector of flocks in ancient Slavonic religion. Franklin and Shepard, pp. 150-151; Fedotov, Volume I, p. 320.

4. See Chapter V, above.

5. On the Karelians, see Chapter V, Note 26, above.

6. This is a reference to the establishment of the Moscow patriarchate in 1589. Initially Patriarch Jeremiah of Constantinople proposed himself as the first patriarch of Moscow, but the successful candidate was Metropolitan Job of Moscow, a close friend of Tsar Fedor's all-powerful brother-in-law Boris Godunov. See Volume 13 of this series.

7. According to most sources John II became metropolitan of Kiev in 1077, not 1080 as Soloviev states. He is thought to have been a Greek from Constantinople. He received scant mention in the chronicles apart from his having conducted the funeral for Grand Prince Yaropolk Sviatoslavich, and dedicated churches at the Vydubits and Caves monasteries. He is best known for his writings (see below). See Fennell, *Russian Church*, pp. 48, 79-80, 96-98, 101.

8. Fennell (*Russian Church*, p. 101) gives the date of Nikifor's accession to the metropolitanate as 1104.

9. The metropolitans during this period were George, John II, John III, Ephraim, Nicholas, Nikifor I, Nikita, Michael II, Kliment Smoliatich, Constantine I, Theodore, John IV, Constantine II, Nikifor II, Matthias and Cyril I. (Soloviev's note)

10. Unrest in the Byzantine patriarchate in the 1140s was connected with the action against the monk Niphon and two monks, accused of heresy by Emperor Manuel Comnenus. The heretics apparently had the support of the patriarch Cosmas Atticus. See Michael Angold, *The Byzantine Empire, 1025-1204* (London, 1986), p. 228; *Cambridge Medieval History*, Volume IV, Part I (Cambridge, 1966), p. 242.

11. Concerning Metropolitan Michael, see Fennell, *Russian Church*, pp. 46-47, 115. Michael occupied the metropolitanate from 1130 to 1145.

12. These last words are curious. They demonstrate that Michael departed out of discontent and, fearing an attempt by the Rus authorities to depose him, extracted an oath from the clergy not to serve in the Holy Wisdom cathedral without presence of a metropolitan sent by Byzantium. (Soloviev's note) Concerning the Klim Smoliatich affair, see Fennell, *Russian Church*, pp. 46-48.

13. Nifont was archbishop of Novgorod from 1131 to 1156. He is perhaps best known as the addressee of Kirik's *Questions*, concerning which see Chapter VIII, below.

14. Theodore died in 1163. Rostislav Mstislavich attempted to have his brother's old protégé Klim reinstated. When this failed, Rostislav grudgingly agreed to accept the patriarchal nominee John IV (see following Note). Fennell, *Russian Church*, p. 48.

15. John IV (1164-1166). See Fennell, *Russian Church*, pp. 48-53.

16. According to Fennell (*Russian Church*, p. 48), "All in all, the evidence seems to show that in the pre-Mongol period the patriarchal throne exercised relatively little control over, and indeed barely interfered with, the Russian metropolitanate. And as a result the metropolitans themselves enjoyed a generous degree of independence from Constantinople which few of their numerous fellow-metropolitans in Byzantium could have dreamed of. The formal obligations of the Kievan metropolitans *vis-à-vis* the patriarchate were probably more honored in the breach than the observance. Unlike the metropolitans in Byzantium, they never seem to have paid any formal dues or taxes to the patriarch. Although they were members of a standing patriarchal synod, there is little to show that they attended regularly, indeed, probably most of them never attended at all; the trip from Kiev to Constantinople was a lengthy and onerous one, and they can have had little time left over from looking after their huge Russian province."

17. Theodore, also called by the diminutive Feodorets, was the central figure in a major power struggle by Andrei Bogoliubsky, rather lightly passed over by Soloviev. Theodore is thought to have been the nephew of one of Andrei's most powerful boyars, Peter Borislavich, and a former monk of the Kiev Caves monastery. "In 1156 Nestor, bishop of Rostov, was deposed in a purge by Klim Smoliatich's successor, Metropolitan [Constantine II]. His replacement, Leon, arrived in Rostov in 1158, but the reception was hostile. Some felt that Leon's appointment was invalid, other accused him of self-enrichment, Andrei apparently objected to his views on fasting. Twice he was forced to leave his eparchy, on the second occasion (according to the chronicler), to defend—without success— his dietary injunctions at a hearing in front of the emperor Manuel I. Andrei had had enough. Although Leon was not formally deposed, Andrei simply set up his own man, a certain Feodorets, as bishop, to reside not in the old see of Rostov but in Andrei's city of Vladimir-on-the-Kliazma. Eventually, c. 1165-8, he sent to the patriarch of Constantinople with a proposal for a reform of the ecclesiastical hierarchy which would take account of recent political changes; not only that his candidate should officially reside in Vladimir-on-the-Kliazma rather than in Rostov, but that the hierarchical dependence on Kiev should be ended and his bishop should be designated a metropolitan. In a sense the request for a separate metropolitanate was the logical culmination of Andrei's cultural programme on behalf of his own land. As we have seen, he abandoned his father's obsession

with the pre-eminence of Kiev. He wished neither to rule in Kiev, nor to be bothered with ecclesiastical appointments to Kiev; he took no political orders from Kiev, nor did he see why he should accept Kiev's whims when running his own Church. It was not a request for precedence over Kiev, but for separation, for equivalent dignity. Andrei's proposal was rejected. In his reply the Patriarch Loukas Chrysoberges elevated the *status quo* into a principle: that there should be one metropolitan for 'all *Rhosia*.' If Andrei could not change the rules, then at least he could turn them to his own advantage. Three options had been declined or blocked: to take charge *in* Kiev; to accept instructions *from* Kiev; to exert authority *without* Kiev. The fourth option, to which he now turned, was to exert authority *through* Kiev. His request for a metropolitanate happened to be rejected at roughly the same time as Andrei's branch of the family acquired a plausible claim to seniority. For the sake of decorum Andrei sacrificed his controversial man Feodorets, who was sent to Kiev and tortured. But the underlying problem was solved in practice, if not in theory, when Andrei's younger brother Gleb was installed as the Kievan prince. The ecclesiastical dispute, though by no means the sole cause, reveals some of the nuances of inter-regional tension which lay behind the campaign of 1169. The chronicle's comment—that Kiev was sacked because of its errors in the matter of fasts and feasts—is not so wildly wide of the mark as one might at first have imagined." Franklin and Shepard, *Emergence*, pp. 362-363. See also Hurwitz, *Bogoljubskij*, pp. 19, 27-29, 32-36, 45-46, 103-104.

18. *Pesii ostrov*. The location is uncertain.

19. Sataanill was one of the names for the Devil used in church literature.

20. PSRL, Volume 1, col. 356.

21. As suggested in Note 17, Theodore (Feodorets) took the fall for Andrei's thwarted ambitions. The seat of the metropolitanate eventually was transferred by Metropolitan Maxim to Vladimir-on-the Kliazma in 1299, though the incumbents continued also to be titular metropolitans of Kiev.

22. Novgorod, Rostov, Vladimir-in-Volhynia, Belgorod, Chernigov, Yuriev, Pereiaslavl, Kholm, Polotsk, Turov, Smolensk, Peremyshl, Galich, Riazan and Vladimir-on-the Kliazma. (Soloviev's note)

23. Paulicians or Bogomils were followers of a heretical sect in tenth-to-fourteenth-century Bulgaria and Serbia, strongly affected by dualistic beliefs.

24. Observance of the Feast of All Saints on May 13 was instituted by Pope Boniface IV in 609 or 610, and is still commemorated on that date in the Orthodox church. Pope Gregory III (731-741) dedicated an oratory in St. Peter's to All Saints, and fixed the anniversary for November 1. This observance was extended by Pope Gregory IV (827-844) and the Western church has commemorated it on that date ever since.

25. Hence this particular church, constructed from 989 to 996, was commonly known as the Tithe church. Fennell, *Russian Church*, pp. 42, 55.

26. See Vernadsky, *Kievan Russia*, p. 120. The full text of the charter is found in M.F. Vladimirskii-Budanov, *Khristomatiia po istorii russkogo prava* (Readings

in the History of Russian Law), 6th edition (St. Petersburg and Kiev, 1908), Volume I, pp. 212-215.

27. The ruble was originally an ingot (grivna) of silver notched at regular intervals to facilitate cutting. The noun "ruble" is derived from the verb *rubit'*, meaning "to cut off," and made its first appearance as a money of account about this time.

28. In canon law remarriage after widowhood or divorce was permissible. A third marriage was of dubious canonical validity and a fourth marriage was absolutely forbidden. Ware, *Orthodox Church*, pp. 301-302.

29. Concerning the *poliud'e* or circuit tax, see Chapter VI, Note 20, above.

30. On the *Kormchaia kniga* (Pilot Book) Soloviev consulted the following works: N. Kalachev, "O znachenii Kormchei Knigi v sisteme drevnogo russkogo prava (Concerning the Significance of the Pilot Book Within the System of Ancient Russian Law)," *Chteniia MOIDR* 1847, No. 3, and G.A. Rozenkampf, *Obozrenie Kormchei Knigi v istoricheskom vide* (Survey of the Pilot Book from a Historical Perspective) (Moscow, 1829, reprinted St. Petersburg, 1839). For further information and more recent bibliography see entry "Kormchaia kniga" by Martin Dimnik, MERSH, Volume 17, pp. 187-189.

31. A letter of Patriarch Germanos [II] to Metropolitan Cyril [I] in 1228 reads "Some in the Rus land buy people, educate them and present them to the bishop for ordination, without releasing them from their servile status." The patriarch demanded an end to this practice. (Soloviev's note)

32. No son named Georgy is mentioned anywhere else among Vseslav's progeny, but probably this was the baptismal name of Rostislav Vseslavich. (Soloviev's note)

33. The *Patericon* (in Russian Paterik) is a collection of legends and stories connected with the lives of saints. In this case it is the Patericon of the Caves monastery in Kiev, based on the correspondence of Simon, bishop of Vladimir (died 1226) and Polikarp, a monk of the Caves monastery and includes, among others, *The Story of the Establishment of the Monastery*, *Story of the First Monks of the Monastery* and *The Life of Feodosy of the Caves Monastery*. See Fennell, *Russian Church*, pp. 70, 101. See also Introduction, Note 65.

34. The œconomus, in Russian *ekonom*, was the steward or manager of the temporalities of the monastery. The *kelar'* (cellarer) was responsible for the monastery's supply of food and drink. Subordinate to them were the *dokhar'* (in charge of clothing and work tools) and the *ksenodokh* (guest master).

35. Lavra is a title of distinction accorded to the most important and esteemed monasteries in Russia. In addition to the Caves monastery in Kiev, the title was bestowed in later times on the Trinity monastery outside Moscow, the Alexander Nevsky monastery in St. Petersburg and the Pochaev monastery in Volhynia.

36. The tradition regarding conferral of stauropigia status is very plausible, but the acts assembled to prove this claim are of dubious authenticity. Those who argue against this attribution assert that the scribe who gathered these documents did not even know the order of succession among Yaroslav's descendants. In

reply it might be pointed out that after Iziaslav's expulsion it would have been
difficult to determine the normal order of succession, neither do we know all the
contemporary circumstances or all of the complex relations between Sviatoslav
and Vsevolod. (Soloviev's note). A stauropigia was a monastery independent of
local church organization and subordinate directly to the patriarch.

37. Concerning the Russkaia Pravda, see Chapter VI, Note 93.

38. The *dikaia vira* was the "dark" bloodwite paid by the guild collective in
particular when the murderer remained unknown. See Vernadsky, *Medieval
Russian Laws*, pp. 36-37.

39. Concerning the *Epistle of Daniel the Exile,* see pp. 276-278, below.

40. See Chapter VI, Note 76, above.

41. See Chapter I, Note 37, and Addendum, Note 5, above.

42. *krestnye gramoty.*

43. See Chapter I, Note 31, above.

44. *rusal'iami.* Despite their consonance and the fact that they occurred at
roughly the same time of year, the Roman feast of Rosalia and the Slavic commemoration of Rusalka are not cognate, even though ecclesiastical writers tried
to confuse them. "Besides the male and water kings, the Russian people believed
in female spirits dwelling in the rivers and forests, called *Rusalki.* They are very
dangerous and wanton; their pleasure is to lure young men and tickle them to
death. We can guess that Christianity has contributed much to the degredation of
those nature spirits, yet it is hardly credible that they once enjoyed a kind of fil-
ial affection from their worshippers. Forest and water were always objects of
apprehension and distrust for the Russian. The immense forests of the North are
indeed a very inhospitable and sometimes dangerous element for the agricultural
settler.... Modern anthropologists see in *Rusalki,* the female spirits of the waters
and woods, the souls of dead maidens or children who had committed suicide or
who had met a violent death. In the Spring festivities in honor of the *Rusalki...*
these unhappy female spirits are treated with kindness and pity. Some modest
gifts are brought to them, especially wreaths of flowers. The period from Easter
to Pentecost is the time of relief and release for all the spirits of the underworld.
They dare to appear on earth to share the communion and gifts of the living. The
Pentecost, which coincides, approximately, with the Roman Rosalia or the Greek
Anthesteria, brings this privilege to an end. When the spirits have been expelled
from earth, the *Rusalki* return to their water element." Fedotov, Volume I, pp. 12,
18; see also Linda J. Ivanits, *Russian Folk Beliefs* (New York 1989), pp. 75-82,
185-189.

45. Vasily Nikitich Tatishchev (1686-1750) was a Russian politician and historian. He was the author of a *Russian History* containing sources otherwise unknown and later claimed to be lost in the fire of Moscow in 1812. Some historians,
like N.M. Karamzin and recently Ya. S. Lurie, attacked this view, claiming that
Tatishchev simply falsified his sources.

46. Maria was an Ossetian princess. The date of her marriage to Vsevolod is
uncertain. Her first son, Yury, was born in 1189. She died March 19, 1205.

47. See Chapter III, Note 21, above.

48. See Note 7, above.

49. 1 Timothy 2:11-12.

50. On Kirik's *Questions,* see p. 266, below, and Fennell, *Russian Church,* pp. 74-76, 83, 91. Soloviev consulted Evgenii (Volkhovitinov), "Svedenie o Kirike, predlagavshem voprosy Nifontu episkopu novgorodskomu (Information Concerning Kirik, Who Posed the Questions to Bishop Nifont of Novgorod)," *Trudy i letopisi MOIDR* (Works and Chronicles of the Moscow Society of Russian History and Antiquities), Part 4, Book 1 (Moscow, 1828). The version of Kirik's *Questions* which Soloviev used was probably that which was incorporated wholesale into the travel account of the sixteenth-century Habsburg diplomat Sigismund von Herberstein.

51. See Chapter I, Note 46, above.

52. The town of Murom in the Riazan principality, at the time of Soloviev's writing in the Vladimir province. Once it was the center of the Finnish Muroma tribe which was absorbed into Rus in the twelfth century.

CHAPTER VIII

1. Feodosy (1036-1074) was abbot of the Caves monastery in Kiev, the founder of the coenobitic life in Rus and its first monastic saint. See John Fennell and Anthony Stokes, *Early Russian Literature* (London, 1974), pp. 32-40; also Fedotov, *Russian Religious Mind*, Volume I, pp. 110-131

2. See Chapter VII, Note 41, above.

3. Ephesians 4:5 (RSV).

4. Nikifor was metropolitan of Kiev from 1104 to 1121. He was of Greek origin, although some scholars, notably Tatishchev, are of the opinion that previously he was bishop of Polotsk. There is disagreement as well as to whether he was the nominee of the prince or of the assembled Rus bishops. See Fedotov, pp. 50, 204, 286, 292, 398, 402; Franklin and Shepard, *Emergence*, pp. 311-315; Fennell, *Russian Church*, p. 101.

5. "Orphan" means like a slave or a beggar. In the present-day Archangel government beggars are referred to as "orphans." This gives us an idea as to who were beggars and slave in primitive clan society. In subsequent documents the term is used continually in petitions, "the sovereign's orphans." (Soloviev's note)

6. In relation to present-day conceptions, the third and twelfth reasons are of special interest. Metropolitan Nikifor is accredited with yet another letter against the Latins, addressed to an unknown prince, which begins thus. "You have as your neighbor the Polish land, where the inhabitants celebrate communion with unleavened bread and accept the Latin teaching. I admonish you that for this reason they have strayed from the holy, ecumenical and apostolic church." Further on, the author reproaches the Latins for forbidding the worship of God in any language other than Hebrew, Greek or Latin. (Soloviev's note)

7. Apparently John avoided using the title "pope" when addressing the Roman pontiff. Either this stemmed from refusal to accept papal jurisdiction, or from the fact that the addressee was an antipope, Clement III (1084-1100), set up by Emperor Henry IV in opposition to Gregory VII (1073-1085) and his successors Victor III (1086-1087), Urban II (1088-1099) and Paschal II (1099-1118). This document also is transcribed into Herberstein's *Notes on Moscow* (see Chapter VII, Note 50, above).

8. Concerning Simon and Polikarp, see N.K. Gudzy, *The History of Early Russian Literature,* translated by Susan Wilbur Jones (New York, 1949, reprinted 1970), pp. 107-108. They are believed to have been the joint authors of the *Patericon* of the Caves monastery in Kiev (see Chapter VII, Note 33, above). Zenkovsky, *Epics,* pp. 102-103.

9. Simon apparently addresses Verkhuslava by her baptismal name, Anastasia.

10. 1 Timothy 3:1-7. "The saying is sure: If anyone aspires to the office of bishop, he desires a noble task. Now a bishop must be above reproach, the husband of one wife, temperate, sensible, dignified, hospitable, an apt teacher, no drunkard, not violent but gentle, not quarrelsome, and no lover of money. He must manage his own household well, keeping his children submissive and respectable in every way; for if a man does not know how to manage his own household, how can he care for God's church? He must not be a recent convert, or he may be puffed up with conceit and fall into the condemnation of the devil; moreover he must be well thought of by outsiders, or he may fall into reproach and the snare of the devil." (RSV)

11. See Chapter VII, Note 7, above. For further information on Metropolitan John II, see Fedotov, *Russian Religious Mind*, Volume I, pp. 187-197.

12. "One of Ioann's duties was to give practical guidance to his clergy on problems which they encountered in their pastoral work. To this end he wrote a series of *Canonical Responses*, with his views and rulings on miscellaneous issues on which his advice was sought. This is the earliest such work to survive, and it gives a rare glimpse of the everyday concerns of the clergy, of Christianity as it was lived, without a rhetorical or historiographical or hagiographical wrapping. Most of Ioann's responses are on matters of ritual or sexual purity: for example, is it acceptable to use for clothing the skins of animals which it is not permitted to eat? Should a woman who has been abducted in a pagan raid be treated as an adulteress? But John can be also socially revealing: 'You say that only boiars and princes get married with proper ceremony and blessing, while the common people do not; that the common people takes wives as if by abduction, with much leaping and dancing and hooting.'" Franklin and Shepard, *Emergence*, pp. 229-230.

13. Kirik was born in 1108 and died some time after 1136. He was a deacon and *domestik* (choir leader) in the St. Anthony monastery of Novgorod. He is generally thought to be the author of the *Voproshchanie Kirikovo* (Kirik's Questions) addressed to Archbishop Nifont. In 1134 Kirik wrote a widely distributed

treatise on astronomy with special reference to the church calendar. In 1136 Nifont commissioned him to put together a new version of the *Novgorod Chronicle Compilation* commonly known as the *Svod Nifonta* (Nifont Compilation). See also Chapter VII, Note 50, above.

14. Nifont was archbishop of Novgorod from 1130 to 1156. In 1135 he acted as mediator between the rulers of Kiev and Chernigov. In 1148 he went to Yury of Suzdal "for peace." The prince released the merchants from Torzhok but refused to grant peace terms. In 1149 he attended the synod convoked by Prince Yury. He denounced the prince's nominee Klim Smoliatich, and for his pains was detained in Kiev until the following year. In 1151 he completed the lead roofing of the Holy Wisdom cathedral, and in 1153 he dedicated the stone church of St. Clement at Ladoga. In 1154, after the expulsion of Davyd Rostislavich, Nifont headed the embassy requesting Yury to send his son Mstislav to be prince of Novgorod. He died April 21, 1156, having gone to Kiev "against the metropolitan." "Many others, too, said that having plundered St. Sophia, he went to Tsargrad; and they said many things against him, but with sin to themselves. About this each one of us should reflect: which bishop ornamented St. Sophia, painted the porches, made an ikon-case, and ornamented the whole outside; and in [Pskov] erected a Church of the Holy Saviour in stone, and another in Ladoga to St. Kliment? And I think God for our sins not wishing to give us his coffin for our consolation, led him away to Kiev, and there he died; and they placed him in the [Caves] monastery, in a vault in the [church of the] Holy Mother of God." *Chronicle of Novgorod,* pp. 12, 21.

15. Kutia is a meal prepared of cereals with honey, and eaten during funeral wake.

16. "Luka's address to unspecified 'brethren' forms the most striking contrast with Ilarion's oratorical sophistication. When or why it was written nobody knows. It is little more than a catalogue of the most elementary and basic tenets of Christianity…. So gaunt and artless is Luka's address that one can hardly envisage the recently converted Novgorodians making much, if anything, of the hotch-potch of doctrinal commands and ethical advice. Perhaps it was nothing more than a set of precepts written out by Luka for the edification of the clergy in Novgorod, short sermon notes on which their teaching might be based?" Fennell and Stokes, *Early Russian Literature*, p. 60.

17. See Gudzy, *Early Russian Literature*, pp. 94-98. Cyril's life and writings are discussed also in Fedotov, *Russian Religious Mind*, Volume I, pp. 69-83.

18. St. Thomas Sunday is the Sunday closest to April 12.

19. The foregoing passage is adapted from Zenkovsky, *Epics*, p. 85.

20. The first Sunday after Easter in the Russian Orthodox Church commemorates the *mironositsy zhena* (myrrh-bearing women), namely Mary Magdalene, Mary the mother of James and Salome, who came to the tomb to anoint Christ's body. Mark 16:1.

21. John 19:39.

22. The Week of the Enfeebled lasts from April 26 to May 3.

23. See Note 5, above.

24. Gudzy, *Early Russian Literature*, pp. 146-149; Fennell and Stokes, *Early Russian Literature*, pp. 64-79. For an English translation of this text, see Dmytryshyn, *Medieval Russia*, pp. 65-72.

25. The Vitichi conference following the interprincely conference in Liubech in 1097 was a meeting between Sviatopolk Iziaslavich, Vladimir Monomakh, Oleg Sviatoslavich, Davyd Sviatoslavich and Davyd Igorevich in 1100. It aimed to settle disputes about redistribution of territories between princes.

26. Psalm 6:3 (BCP).

27. The foregoing quotation is adapted from Dmytryshyn, *Medieval Russia*, pp. 66-68.

28. On Abbot Daniel's travel account, see A. Pronin, *History of Old Russian Literature* (Frankfurt, 1968), pp. 152-157. Daniel's journey was undertaken in 1106-1108 and his account was written some time before 1113.

29. The Latin kingdom of Jerusalem was the crusader state in Palestine which existed between 1099 and 1187.

30. Baldwin (1058-1118) joined the First Crusade in 1096, accompanying his brother Godfrey, who in 1099 after the capture of Jerusalem became the protector of the Holy Sepulchre, being unwilling to wear a crown of gold where Christ had worn a crown of thorns. Baldwin had no such scruples. Having ruled the county of Edessa from 1098 to 1100, after Godfrey died Baldwin engaged in a power struggle with the Latin patriarch Daimbert. Baldwin was crowned king on Christmas Day 1100, although his differences with Daimbert continued until 1102.

31. Sabbas (439-532) was an outstanding figure in early monasticism. In 478 he founded a monastic community in a wild gorge between Jerusalem and the Dead Sea. The foundation, now known as Mar Saba, is still an active Orthodox monastery. Soloviev calls this monastery a lavra. See Chapter VII, Note 35, above.

32. With the exception of Davyd Sviatoslavich, these are doubtless given names coupled with baptismal names of the princes in question.

33. See entry "Daniil Zatochnik" by N.N. Voronin, MERSH, Volume 8, pp. 174-175. There is a translation of this epistle, entitled "Daniel's Plea for Forgiveness" in Dmytryshyn, *Medieval Russia*, pp. 93-97. Soloviev seems to have thrown a number of passages together out of sequence. See also Pronin, *Old Russian Literature*, pp. 211-217.

34. According to most scholars the addressee was not Yury Dolgoruky, but Prince Yaroslav Vsevolodovich of Pereiaslavl (reigned 1238-1246). Soloviev cites V. Undol'skii, "Novaia redaktsiia (XIII veka) Slova Daniila Zatochnika (A New [Thirteenth Century] Redaction of the *Tale* of Daniel the Exile)," *Russkaia Beseda* (Russian Conversation), 1856, No. 2. A scholarly edition comparing the various redactions, is available in *Slovo Daniila Zatochnika po redaktsiiam XII i XIII vv. i ikh peredelkam* (The *Tale* of Daniel the Exile According to the Redactions of the Eleventh and Twelfth Centuries and Their Redactions), edited by N.N. Zarubin (Leningrad, 1932).

35. Compare with Matthew 6:26: "Look at the birds of the air: they neither sow nor reap nor gather into barns, and yet your heavenly Father feeds them. Are you not of more value than they?" (RSV)

36. The White Lake (Beloe Ozero) is in the west of the Vologda district.

37. Much of Soloviev's information about early Rus poetry is derived from the anthology by Kirsha Danilov, *Drevnie rossiiskie stikhotvoreniia* (Ancient Russian Poetry) (Moscow, 1818). A more modern edition is *Drevnie rossiiskie stikhotvoreniia, sobrannye Kirsheiu Danilovym* (Ancient Russian Poetry Collected by Kirsha Danilov) (Moscow and Leningrad, 1958).

38. Soloviev seems to have transcribed a rather garbled version of this chronicle passage. The foregoing has been adapted from Zenkovsky, *Epics*, p. 161.

39. A blank verse translation of this poem is found in Zenkovsky, *Epics*, pp. 137-160 and Dmytryshyn, *Medieval Russia*, pp. 77-92. For text and prose translation, see *Penguin Book of Russian Verse,* pp. 1-22. There was some controversy concerning the authenticity of this work. For a summary of the scholarly debate, see Fennell and Stokes, *Early Russian Literature*, pp. 191-206.

40. Poetic legends or *byliny* were Old Rus folk songs of the historical epic type. Transmitted from generation to generation, they were almost completely lost by the end of the nineteenth century. Remembered only in the remote regions of Northern Russia they were carefully collected and recorded. There are two basic cycles of *byliny*, the first connected with Kiev, St. Vladimir and the struggle with the nomads, the second with Novgorod and the life of the commercial city.

41. Dazhbog was the Slavonic God of sun and fire, mainly known to have been worshipped by Western Slavs. The title "Grandsons of Dazhbog" used here for the Rus princes might be a reference to the pre-Christian belief in the sacral character of princes, but in Slavonic lands it was a very rare phenomenon.

42. *Penguin Book of Russian Verse*, p. 13. The *nogata* and *rezan* were coins of small denomination.

43. ... *togo starogo Vladimira nel'ze be prigvozditi k goram kiev'skym*, literally "The Vladimir of old could not be nailed to the hills of Kiev."

44. "He personifies the bold Cossack of boundless youthful strength. Drunk, Vas'ka Buslaev wagers that he will defeat the Kievan and Muscovite retinues. In this skirmish, Vasilii Buslaev so loses his self-control that he cannot be assuaged: 'Let him wave a hand—a street collapses. He waves another, the alley collapses.' At the request of the prince, Vasilii's mother, approaching from behind, takes Vasilii by the shoulders and by this gesture stops him." Pronin, *Old Russian Literature*, p. 83.

45. Perun was the god of lightning and storm, of Indo-European origin and worshipped by all the Slavs. The cult of Perun was particularly connected with the Rus princely family and the stories of conversion contain various motifs linked with the struggle against this cult.

46. The city of Damascus at this time was renowned for its quality steel.

47. *veruia tol'ko v svoi chervelnnyi viaz.* The meaning is unclear.

48. Ilmen is a lake near Novgorod (here the reference is to its folklore personification).

49. *Penguin Book of Russian Verse,* pp. 32-42.

50. See Chapter I, Note 10 and Chapter VI, Note 52, above.

51. The Pechenegs were a Turkic people who appeared in 889 in the Black Sea steppe area. From mid-tenth until the end of eleventh century they warred against the Rus principalities. After a defeat inflicted by the Byzantine forces in 1091, gradually they were absorbed by the Polovetsians.

52. Askold and Dir, according to the *Tale of Bygone Years,* were Riurik's companions who went to Constantinople. On their way they won over the tribe of Polianians and together unsuccessfully attacked Constantinople in 866. In 882 they were murdered by Oleg.

53. The *Sofiiskii Vremennik* (Holy Wisdom Chronicle) is the title of an annalistic collection compiled by Matvey Mikhailov around 1432 at the Holy Wisdom cathedral in Novgorod. Fragments are incorporated in various later chronicles. It is of special interest since it contains information more ancient than that found in the *Russian Primary Chronicle.* See entry by V.A. Kuchkin, MERSH, Volume 36, pp. 125-126.

54. Pejorative use of the argumentative of Perun. See Note 43, above.

55. The text reads "Zhiriata" but this is obviously a misprint.

56. The Uglichians or Ulichians were an East Slavonic tribe inhabiting the lower Dnieper and later the Dniester region.

57. George Hamartolos ("the Sinner") was the Byzantine monastic author of a universal chronicle from Adam until the year 842.

58. The Vlachs (in Russian Volokhi) were a Romance-speaking semi-nomadic people who gave their name to the Rumanian province of Wallachia.

59. The Polianians were an East Slavonic tribe inhabiting the Kiev region.

60. The White Hungarians or Avars were nomadic people, probably originating in present-day Kazakhstan. They inhabited the steppe north of the Caucasus. Since 558 they were in contact with Byzantium. In 568 they occupied the Pannonian plain (present-day Hungary).

61. The Duleb were an East Slavonic tribe on the Bug river.

62. See Note 55, above.

63. *a potom po 12 griven na kliuch,* "then to twelve grivnas for every key." The meaning is uncertain. Probably the "key" is symbolic of the household.

64. John Tzimisces ruled from 969 to 976.

65. Korsun was a Byzantine city in the Crimea. According to the so-called "Korsun legend," St. Vladimir was baptized in that city, although see Andrzej Poppe, "The Political Background to the Baptism of Rus'. Byzantine relations between 986-989 [sic]" *Dumbarton Oaks Papers* 30 (1976), pp. 197-244.

66. Genesis 43:29-34. "And he lifted up his eyes, and saw his brother Benjamin, his mother's son, and said, 'Is this your youngest brother, of whom you spoke to me? God be gracious to you, my son!' Then Joseph made haste, for his heart yearned for his brother, and he sought a place to weep. And he entered his

chamber and wept there. Then he washed his face and came out; and controlling himself he said, 'Let food be served.' They served him by himself, and them by themselves, and the Egyptians who ate with him by themselves, because the Egyptians might not eat bread with the Hebrews, for that is an abomination to the Egyptians. And they sat before him, the first-born according to his birthright and the youngest according to his youth; and the men looked at one another in amazement. Portions were taken to them from Joseph's table, but Benjamin's portion was five times as much as any of theirs. So they drank and were merry with him." (RSV)

67. The Laurentian Chronicle is the intact parchment copied from an earlier manuscript by the monk Lavrenty, after whom the chronicle has become known. Lavrenty's work was commissioned around 1377 by Prince Dmitry Konstantinovich of Suzdal-Nizhny Novgorod (reigned 1356-1383), with a special blessing by the local bishop Dionisy. Lavrenty was chosen from one of the monasteries in Nizhny Novgorod and was sent to Vladimir to copy a major chronicle which was compiled early in the fourteenth century. This protograph, now lost, was commissioned in 1305 by the then grand prince of Vladimir, Mikhail Yaroslavich of Tver (reigned 1305-1317). The 1305 chronicle was a major compilation whose core consisted of an early thirteenth-century chronicle of Vladimir, together with later additions (and subsequent editing) of extracts from chronicles of Rostov and Tver. The thirteenth-century chronicle of Vladimir contained within the compilation of 1305 transcribed by Lavrenty apparently was composed as a commemoration of the rule of Grand Prince Yury Vsevolodovich (reigned 1212-1238), son of Vsevolod III. Yury's chronicle was based largely on an earlier chronicle of the grand principality of Vladimir (or possibly two interrelated ones) compiled in two stages between the 1170s and the 1190s. The chronicle clearly was begun during the reign of Andrei Bogoliubsky and was intended to provide a historical justification for his design to have Vladimir replace Kiev as the capital of Rus. Thus the passages in the Laurentian Chronicle concerning the history of Vladimir-on-the-Kliazma between the mid-twelfth and mid-thirteenth centuries derive directly from the chronicles of that period produced at the court of the grand princes of Vladimir during the times of their greatest power. The ideology and historical outlook which transfixed the chronicles of Vladimir strongly affected the principalities which subsequently were to strive for the grand-princely title. The chroniclers of the main aspirants, Moscow and Tver, were especially influenced by the writers of history in Vladimir, who in turn derived much of their information from the chronicles of Southern Pereiaslavl (Pereiaslavl-Russky), the southern city most aligned with Vladimir in the mid-twelfth century. The Southern Pereiaslavl chroniclers relied upon some major Kievan chronicle compilation, and also provided the northern chroniclers with the final (1118) redaction of the *Tale of Bygone Years* (Primary Chronicle) which has survived largely intact in the Laurentian Chronicle. The actual parchment was acquired in 1792 by the famous antiquarian and bibliophile Prince A.S. Musin-Pushkin, and is currently held in the Saltykov-Shchedrin Library, St. Petersburg. The text was the first to be printed

in the *Complete Collection of Russian Chronicles*, PSRL, Volume 1 (St. Petersburg, 1846, second edition Leningrad, 1926-1927, reprinted Moscow, 1962). For more details and extensive bibliography, consult Nikolai Dejevsky, MERSH, Volume 19, pp. 63-65.

68. Nikolay Mikhailovich Karamzin (1766-1826) was a Russian writer and historian. His *History of the Russian State,* published in eight volumes in 1816-1818 (unfinished) was the most important historical work preceding Soloviev's *History.* It is most readily accessible in the form of the 1842 edition (reprinted Moscow, 1988). See also Chapter VII, Note 45, above, and Chapter VIII, Note 70, below.

69. "From 287, indictions were numbered serially in cycles of five years, from 312 in cycles of fifteen years. The number of the indiction was regularly used for dating financial years (which began 1 Sept.) and sometimes for dating other documents." *Oxford Classical Dictionary*, 2nd edition (Oxford, 1970), p. 544.

70. The Hypatian copy or chronicle consists of three parts: (1) the so-called Primary Chronicle (up to 1117); (2) 1118-1199, the Southern Rus chronicle, the final redaction of which was carried out in the Vydubets monastery near Kiev in 1200. It is the family chronicle of Riurik Rostislavich. (3) From 1200 to 1292 it is the chronicle of Galich and Volhynia, including one or two items of Suzdal interest. The chronicle was so called because it was discovered by Karamzin at the Hypatian monastery near Kostroma. See entry by Dejevsky, MERSH, Volume 14, pp. 108-110.

71. Samoied or Samoiad, from *same-emne,* in the Saam language "the land of Saams," were a group of people speaking Ural-type languages inhabiting the northeastern part of the Novgorod territories.

72. See Volume 2, Chapter VI, Note 39.

73. Soloviev cites the work of his former mentor M.P. Pogodin, *Nestor. Istoriko-kriticheskoe rassuzhdenie o nachale russkikh letopisei* (Nestor. A Critical-Historical Discussion of the Beginnings of the Russian Chronicles) (Moscow, 1839); an unsigned rebuttal to an article by an author who simply identifies himself as P.B., "Razbor otveta g-na P.B. na vopros o Nestore (Discussion of the Reply by Mr. P.B. to the New Question Concerning Nestor), *Otechstvennye Zapiski* (Notes of the Fatherland), Volume 24 (1851); I.D. Beliaev, "O Nesterovoi Letopisi (Concerning the Nestor Chronicle), *Chteniia MOIDR,* 1846, No. 5; in the same issue P. S. Kazanskii, "Eshche vopros o Nestore (Yet Another Question Concerning Nestor)."

74. Romans 12:6-7. "Having gifts that differ according to the grace given us, let us use them; if serving, in our serving; he who teaches, in his teaching." (RSV)

75. "Emperor Michael" is Michael III (reigned 842-867) under whom initial contacts were made between Byzantium and Rus. "Isaac" is probably Isaac Angelos (reigned 1185-1195). "Alexander" presents a problem. There was an emperor of that name who ruled 912-913, but probably here the chronicler means Alexius II Comnenos (reigned 1180-1183).

76. *Chronicle of Novgorod,* p. 18.

77. See Chapter VII, Note 45, above. Tatishchev attributed the authorship of this chronicle to Joachim, archbishop of Novgorod in the eleventh century. In reality the chronicle was compiled in the seventeenth century. It contains a number of passages borrowed from ancient historical sources and a number of legends and conjectures by its authors, as was typical of the writing of chronicles in seventeenth-century Russia.

78. The Market Side (Torgovaia storona) was one of the major parts of Novgorod on the eastern side of the Volkhov, where the market and assemblies took place.

79. Exodus 33:19 (RSV).

80. Vladimir in fact was canonized in 1284. Fennell, *Russian Church*, p. 60.

81. The chronicler evidently confuses Seth, the third son of Adam, with Shem, the eldest son of Noah. Also does there not perhaps follow a confusion between Esau and Cain?

82. See Chapter IV, Note 17, above.

83. Genesis 19:30-38. "Now Lot went up out of Zoar, and dwelt in the hills with his two daughters, for he was afraid to dwell in Zoar; so he dwelt in a cave with his two daughters. And the first-born said to the younger 'Our father is old, and there is not a man on earth to come in to us in the manner of all the earth. Come, let us make our father drink wine, and we will lie with him, that we may preserve offspring through our father.' So they made their father drink wine that night; and the first-born went in, and lay with her father; he did not know when she lay down or when she arose. And on the next day, the first-born said to the younger 'Behold I lay last night with my father; let us make him drink wine tonight also; then you go in and lie with him, that we may preserve offspring through our father.' So they made their father drink wine that night also; and the younger arose, and lay with him; and he did not know when she lay down or when she arose. Thus both the daughters of Lot were with child by their father. The first-born bore a son, and called his name Moab; he is the father of the Moabites to this day. The younger also bore a son, and called his name Ben-ammi; he is the father of the Ammonites to this day." (RSV)

84. If indeed this is an authentic work of twelfth-century Southern provenance. See Note 39, above.

85. *Skazanie o mamaevom poboishche* (Tale of Mamay's Battle) was written in the first quarter of the fifteenth century to commemorate the victory of Dmitry Donskoy over the Tatars led by Mamay at Kulikovo Pole (Snipe Field) in 1380. Its fifteenth-century Northern provenance is contrasted here with the supposed twelfth-century Southern origin of the *Tale of Igor's Campaign*. See Pronin, *Old Russian Literature*, pp. 308-311.

INDEX

In view of the fact that, given the complex rules of succession prevailing, it is often difficult to determine which prince ruled which principality and when, this information is frequently omitted in the Index. Similar difficulties are encountered with ecclesiastics. To complicate matters further, there is frequent imprecision about the rank of the incumbent of the Novgorod see, who is frequently referred to as bishop or archbishop in identical contexts.

Abkhazia, 279
Abraham, Old Testament patriarch, 293
Adrian, abbot of Vydubets monastery, later bishop of Belgorod, 240
Adrian, Bulgarian bishop, 242
Adrian, heretic, 241
Advocate (fokht, Vogt, advocatus), 129, 337
Afanasy, monk, 250
Agapit, St., 221
Akim, archbishop of Novgorod, 288
Ako, counsellor to the prince of Polotsk, 122-123
Alans, 225, 330, 346
Albert von Buxhövden, bishop of Uexküll, 120-125, 127, 336
Alexander, prince of Dubrovitsk, 157
Alexander, steward of Shumavin, 67
Alexander (Alexius?), Byzantine emperor, 360
Alexander III, pope, 119, 336
Alexander of Macedon, 172, 299, 306, 312
Alexander Popovich, epic hero, 158
Alexander Vsevolodovich, prince of Bełz, 64-65, 67-69, 113
Alexander Yaroslavich, prince, 108, 111
Alexandria, 224, 306
Alexis, baptismal name of Prince Béla, 43
Alexis, bishop of Yuriev, 241
Alexis Mikhailovich, tsar (17th century), 178
Alexis Sbyslavich, Novgorod citizen, 85
Alexis Sviatoslavich, Kievan boyar, 117
Alexius II Comnenos, Byzantine emperor, 360
Alimpy, monk of the Caves monastery, painter, saint, 230
All Saints, feast of, 242, 344, 350
Amelfa Timofeevna, mother of Vasily Buslaev, 282
Ammon, 312
Ammonites, 361
Anastasia, baptismal name of Princess Verkhuslava, 264, 354
Anatolia, 332
Anbal, steward, conspirator, 20, 22
Ancient Livonian Chronicle 338
Ancient Rus, 165-166, 175, 179, 182, 231, 256, 279
Andrei, son-in-law of Prince Mstislav of Kiev, 157
Andrei Bogoliubsky, remains in North, 1-6; character and conduct in the North, 7-8; gives Kiev to Roman Rostislavich of Smolensk, 13-14; quarrel with sons of Rostislav, 14-15; fails against sons of Rostislav, 16-18; death, 19-22; aftermath, 22-23; also cited xv-xxi, xxiv, 9, 12, 24-26, 29, 31, 33, 39, 49, 76-79, 81, 83, 87-89, 116-118, 135, 139-140,

160-161, 168-169, 179, 181-182,
187, 194, 207, 224, 227, 229, 230,
238-239, 241-243, 251, 253, 256-
257, 304-305, 310-311, 321-322,
324, 330, 333-334, 341, 343, 349-
350, 359
Andrew, Hungarian king, 44, 62-69,
111, 113-114
Andrew, St., apostle, 290
Andrew the Fool (Andreas Salos),
321
Andreyev, Nikolay Evremovich,
historian, 320
Anglo-Saxons, 190
Ankindin, archimandrite of Caves
monastery, 264
Anna, daughter of Mstislav
Mstislavich, 111
Anthony (Anton), archbishop of
Novgorod, later bishop of
Peremyshl, 106-107, 109, 240-241
Anthony, bishop of Chernigov, 240,
242-243
Anthony (Anton), bishop Pereiaslavl,
242-243, 335
Anthony, founder of Caves
monastery, 248-249
Antichrist, 65, 68, 284
Antioch, 306
Antiochus, 306
Appanage period, xix, 324
Appeldern, Johann von, crusader, 132
Armenians, 226, 261
Árpád dynasty, 332
Arseny, abbot, 22
Arseny, archbishop of Novgorod, 109,
241
Arseny, bishop of Riazan, 75
Art, 229-230
Artsybashev, Nikolay Sergeevich,
historian, xxviii, 324
Asia, 155, 207, 292, 346
Asia Minor, xviii
Askold, early Varangian-Rus
chieftain, 287, 293, 294, 358
Assembly (veche), 224
Augustinian order, 119

Avars, 291, 358
Avdova hill, 98
Avraaamy of Smolensk, St., 273
Azov, Sea of, 224, 339

Baghdad, caliphate, xviii
Baldwin I, king of Jerusalem, 276,
356
Balkans, xvii
Baltic Sea, xxv, 38, 118, 221-222,
227, 331, 336, 338-339
Bashkirs 178,
Basil the Great, St., 274
Bear's Head (Odenpe), 133, 337, see
also Medvezhaia Gora
Béla III, Hungarian king, 44-46
Béla, Hungarian prince, younger
brother of Stephen III, 43
Belgorod, 12, 14, 16-18, 34, 37-38,
48, 71, 76, 117-118, 139, 177,
190-191, 196, 240, 247, 300, 334,
350
Beloozero, 16, 75, 136, 225, 233-234,
277
Belorussia (Belarus), 333
Bełsk, 64, 113
Bełz, 45, 51, 67, 69
Ben-Ammi (Old Testament,) 361
Benedict, monk, travelling companion
of Piano di Carpini, 225
Benedict Bora, Hungarian palatine,
"Antichrist", 65-66, 68, 284
Benjamin, brother of Joseph (OT),
297, 358
Benjamin of Tudela, travel writer,
xxviii, 224, 325, 346
Berendey, tribe, 11, 16, 33, 62, 141,
143-145, 187, 217, 329-330, 342
Berestovo, 240
Berthold of Livonia, bishop of
Uexküll, 120 336
Bîrlad, 135, 330, 338
Black people, 184, 340, see also
Chernye liudi
Black Sea, xix, 38, 164, 222, 224,
331, 338, 358
Blud, traitor, 308

Blue Forest, 150
Bobrok river, 69
Bogoliubovo, xxi, 20-21, 23, 138, 277
Bogomils, 241, 350
Boguslav, town, 48
Boguslav, brother of Novgorod chiliarch Viacheslav, 109
Bohemia, Bohemians, 190, 204, 343
Boian, prophetic bard, 280
Boleslav, Novgorod elder, 244
Bolesław II, Polish prince, 332
Bolesław III, Polish prince, 51, 332
Bolesław IV the Curly, Polish prince, 50, 332
Bolesław Krzywousty, Polish prince, 332
Bolesław, Polish prince, son of Władysław the Exile, 50
Boniak, Polovetsian khan, 148, 299
Boniface IV, pope, 350
Book of Degrees, xxviii, 212-213, 323, 344
Bookmen, 284
Boris, envoy from Riazan, 23
Boris, Polotsk prince, 37
Boris, Riazan boyar, 118
Boris, Rus prince, claimant to the Hungarian throne, 42
Boris, St., Rus protomartyr, xxiii, 16, 20, 23, 37, 213, 216, 229, 296-297, 301, 311
Boris Miroshkinich, brother of Burgrave Dmitry, 85
Boris Negochevich, Novgorod chiliarch, 109-111
Boris Romanovich, prince, 80
Boris Vseslavich, prince, 249
Boris Yurievich, prince of Gorodets, 191, 198
Boris Zakharievich, commander, 38, 80, 117-118
Boris Zhidislavich, commander, 16, 31, 116, 135
Boris Zhiroslavich, Novgorod burgrave, 77, 83
Borislav Nekurishinich, prominent

Novgorod citizen, 105, 196
Borivoy, town, 151
Bremen, 118-120, 336
Brest, 116, 140
Briachislav Vasilkovich, prince of Vitebsk, 22
Briagin, town, 190
Brodniki, 99, 158, 339, 345
Brody, town, 96
Bug river, 64, 143, 358
Bulgakov, Mikhail Petrovich, see Makary, metropolitan
Bulgaria, Bulgarians, 266, 293-295, 350
Bulgars, struggle of Suzdal princes against, 135-138; also mentioned, xvii, 22, 117, 135-139, 287, 289, 312, 331, 338, 347
Burchevichi, group of Polovetsians, 153, 339
Burgrave (posadnik), office of, 4, 21, 25-26, 329
Buslay, father of Vasily Buslaev, 282
Butkov, P., historian, 326, 342
Byliny (poetic folk legends), 357
Bytowns, 6, 329
Byzantium, Byzantine empire, Byzantines, xviii, xxvii, 22, 164, 224, 237, 259, 285, 289, 291, 294-295, 321-322, 358, 360

Caananites, 309
Cain (Old Testament), 361
Canonization, rules of, 322
Canute VI, Danish king, 120, 336
Carpathian mountains, 63, 66, 68, 113, 289
Carpenters' Quarter, Novgorod, 215, 344
Carthage, Carthaginians, 172
Casimir the Just, Polish prince, 47, 50-51, 59-60, 332
Caspian Sea, 155
Catholics, Catholicism, 45, 332
Caucasus, 289, 330, 339, 358
Central Europe, xxv, xviii
Charters of Yaroslav, 109-111

Chartoriysk, 116
Chartoryia river, 38
Chegirkan, Tatar commander, 157
Cherkass, 164, 339
Chernigov, descendants of Monomakh
    in, 71; also mentioned, xxiv, 2, 5,
    11, 15-19, 24, 26, 31-39, 50-57,
    62, 70, 74, 76, 82-83, 85, 92, 98,
    108-111, 115, 117-118, 144-148,
    150, 156, 158-160, 162, 164, 173-
    174, 187, 189, 198, 200-203, 205,
    209, 217, 219, 221, 223, 240, 242-
    243, 246-249, 253-254, 256, 258,
    281, 302-304, 314, 327-328, 332-
    333, 338, 340, 350, 355
Chernye liudi, 340; see also Black
    people
Cherven, 65, 140
Chicherin, Boris Nikolaevich,
    historian, xxiii
Chiliarch, office of, 187, 194, 197,
    251, 330
Chosroes, Persian emperor, 291
Christianity, xvii, 233, 235-236, 246,
    249, 254, 259, 285, 287-288, 295-
    297, 352
Chronicle Containing Russian History
    from 852 to 1598, xxviii
Chronicles, xxvii, 285-307; local
    characteristics of, 314-315
Chud, tribe, 80, 91, 121, 126-127,
    130-133, 200, 219, 222, 235, 266,
    293, 327, 333-334, 341
Chud (Peipus) lake, 334
Chud-Tormy, district, 126
Church history, xxviii, 326
Church organization, 236-243
Church Statute of St. Vladimir, 244,
    246
Churches and cathedrals:
    Annunciation (Novgorod), 230;
    Boris and Gleb (Kiev), 10;
    Dormition (Vladimir-on-the-
    Kliazma), xxi, xxiv; Forty Saints
    (Novgorod), 105; Holy Mother of
    God (Smolensk), 246; Holy Savior
    (Kiev), 249; Holy Savior (Pskov),
    355; Holy Savior (Vladimir-on-
    the-Kliazma), xxi; Holy Savior
    (Pereiaslavl), 90; Holy Savior
    (Torzhok), 244; Holy Wisdom
    (Kiev), 58, 207-208 237, 249,
    251; Holy Wisdom (Novgorod),
    80, 86, 94-95, 105, 107-109, 134
    240, 244, 245 334, 355, 358;
    Intercession on the Nerl river
    xxi-xxii; Mother of God
    (Vladimir-in-Volhynia) 64;
    Mother of God (Galich), 112;
    Mother of God (Kiev), 243;
    Mother of God (Suzdal), 230;
    Mother of God (Vladimir), 229-
    230, 232, 243, 305; Mother of
    God on the Hill (Novgorod), 226;
    Our Lady, German church
    (Novgorod), 226; St. Andrew
    (Vladimir), 31; St. Andrew
    (Pereiaslavl), 229; St. Basil
    (Kiev), 192; St. Basil (Red
    Square, Moscow), xxi; St. Boris
    and St. Gleb (Kideksha), 327; St.
    Boris and St. Gleb (Novgorod),
    107, 245, 284; St. Clement
    (Ladoga), 355; St. Cyril
    (Novgorod), 230; St. Dmitry
    (Kiev), 303; St. Dmitry (Suzdal),
    250; St. Dmitry (Vladimir-on-the-
    Kliazma), xxiv, 230, 322; St. Elias
    (Novgorod), 214; St. John the
    Forerunner on the Opoki
    (Novgorod), 244-245, 347; St.
    Michael by the Dnieper
    (Vydubichi), 230; St. Michael,
    Novgorod church (Kiev), 223; St.
    Nicholas (Novgorod), 105; St.
    Peter (Kiev), 303; St. Theodore
    (Pereiaslavl), 229; Three Holy
    Youths (Novgorod), 230; Tithe
    (Kiev), 10, 58, 243, 350;
    Transfiguration (Novgorod), 230;
    Transfiguration (Pereiaslavl), 327
    Transfiguration (Rusa), 230;
    Varangian (Latin) church
    (Novgorod), 214, 216

Churinia, wife of Slavin the chiliarch, 190
Churnaev, town, 151
Churnay, Tork prince, 151, 217
Churynia, boyar, 118
Cistercian Order, 119
Civil and commercial law, xxviii, 325
Clan (rod), 328
Clement III, antipope, 354
Clergy, activities of, 246-247
Complete Collection of Russian Chronicles, xxvii, xxviii, 328, 360
Constantine I, metropolitan, 237-238, 348
Constantine II, metropolitan, 238-239, 241, 348-349
Constantine IX Monomachos, Byzantine emperor, 340
Constantinople, xviii, xx, xxiv, xxvii, 43, 163, 224, 229, 236-239, 241-243, 259, 290, 294-295, 321, 326, 328, 341, 346, 348, 358
Convents, 249
Cosmas Atticus, patriarch of Constantinople, 348
"Court," "courtiers" (dvor, dvoriane), 197
Court of Yaroslav, Novgorod, 85, 207, 335
Cracow, 51, 59-60
Crimea, 358
Cross charters, 253, 352
Crusades, xviii, 337
Cumans, *see* Polovetsians
Customary law, 253-254
Cyril I, metropolitan, 348, 351
Cyril of Turov, author of sermons, 268-272, 355
Cyril, metropolitan, 115
Czechs, Czech land, 163, 204. *See also* Bohemia

Daily life, 231-232
Daimbert, Latin patriarch of Jerusalem, 356
Dalen, German castle, 119
Damascus, 357

Damian the Miracle-Worker, 298
Daniel, abbot, pilgrim, 276
Daniel Romanovich, prince of Galich; enthroned by boyars, 66-67; leaves Galich, 67-68; also mentioned, xxv, 62, 64, 66-69, 140, 156-157, 194, 229, 333
Daniel the Exile, author, xxvii, 185, 277-278, 356, 341
Danilov, Kirsha, folklorist, xxix, 326, 357
Danilovich, A., historian, xxviii, 324
Danislav Lazutinich, Novgorod boyar, 76-77
Danube river, 40, 152, 289-290
Dark bloodwite, 252, 352
Daugava river, *see* Western Dvina
David, biblical king, xxii
Davyd, prince of Chernigov, 160
Davyd, prince of Murom, 74, 76, 136
Davyd Igorevich, prince, 159, 274, 300, 309, 356
Davyd Mstislavich, prince of Toropets, 140
Davyd Rostislavich, prince of Smolensk, 10-11, 14-16, 18, 33, 35, 37-39, 45, 47-48, 75, 80, 82 51-54, 148-149, 176, 187, 196, 208, 257, 355
Davyd Sviatoslavich, prince, 356
Dazhbog, pagan deity, 281, 357
Dedilets, envoy from Riazan, 23
Demian Kudenevich, hero-warrior, 203-204
Denmark, 227
Derevsk, Land of, 204
Desna river, 147 201
Detskie, lesser servants, 330
Diatel, sorcerer, 139
Dionisy, bishop of Suzdal (14th century), 359
Dir, early Varangian-Rus chieftain, 287, 293-294, 358
Disinherited princes (izgoi), 158, 328, 339
Dmitrov, town, 91, 322, 328
Dmitry, baptismal name of Vsevolod

III, 322
Dmitry, heretic, 241
Dmitry Konstantinovich, prince of
  Suzdal-Nizhny Novgorod (14th
  century), 359
Dmitry Miroshkinich, Novgorod
  burgrave, 84-86
Dmitry Yakunich, Novgorod
  burgrave, 87, 93, 211
Dnieper river, xvii, xviii, xix, 11, 16-
  18, 33-35, 38-39, 47, 52, 56-57,
  62, 89, 92, 116, 127, 141, 143-
  145, 148, 150-160, 162, 183, 191,
  201, 213, 224-225, 227, 235, 258,
  280, 290, 292, 296-297, 314, 338,
  344
Dniester river, 336
Dobry Sot, village, 75
Dobrynia Dolgy, boyar, 30, 116
Dogs' Island, 239, 350
Dokhar', office of, 351
Don river, 146-148, 154, 339, 345
Donets river, town, 145, 150
Dormition, feast of, 344
Dorogobuzh, 9-10, 12, 117, 330, 334
Dorozhay, Novgorod commander, 136
Dorpat (Yuriev), 126
Dregovichians, protoslavic tribe, 139,
  205, 290-291, 338
Dreven, town, 153
Drevlanians, protoslavic tribe, 289-
  291, 296
Drozdov, Vasily Mikhailovich, see
  Filaret, metropolitan
Drucha river, 38
Drutsk, 37-38, 82, 221
Duality of faith, 255
Dubna river, 96
Dubrovitsk, 157, 339
Duleb, confederation of protoslavic
  tribes, 291, 358
Dushilets, elder of Lipitsa 109
Dvorianin, dvoriane, 343

East Slavonic tribes, 291, 338, 343
East Slavs, 320, 329
Eastern Rus, 233

Edessa, county, 356
Efrem, abbot, 32
Egyptians, 359
Ekbert, brother of Queen Gertrud of
  Hungary, 68
Elena, widow of Casimir the Just, 51
Elias, archbishop of Novgorod, 78
Emmanuel, bishop of Smolensk, 245
Ems, 224
English, xviii
Enthronement of princes, 185-186
Ephraim, archbishop of Novgorod,
  307
Ephraim, bishop of Suzdal, 250
Ephraim, metropolitan, 241, 348
Ephraim, pupil of Archbishop Akim
  of Novgorod, 288
Ephraim of Syria, St., 273
Epistle of Daniel the Exile, xxvii,
  185, 252, 276-278, 341, 352, 356
Esau (Old Testament), 309, 361
Estonia, Estonians, Ests, 119-120,
  126-127, 130, 133, 135, 334
Europe, xviii, 226
Evdokia, Rus princess, wife of
  Mieszko III, 333
Evfrosinia, daughter of Prince
  Rostislav Riurikovich, 189
Evfrosinia of Polotsk, St., 249, 259
Evfrosinia Mstislavovna, dowager-
  queen of Hungary, 44
Evpraksia (Praxedis, Adelheid),
  Kievan princess, wife of Emperor
  Henry IV, 341
Ewers, I., historian, xxviii, 324
Exaltation of the Holy Cross, feast
  of, 309, 334

Family morality, 256-257
Feast of the Intercession, xxii
Fedor, bishop of Belgorod, 247
Fedor, monk, 250
Fedor, St., 254
Fedor, Varangian, Rus protomartyr,
  296, 308
Fedor Danilovich, Novgorod boyar,
  108-109

Fedor Ivanovich, tsar (16th century), 348
Fedor Yaroslavich, prince, 108, 111
Feodorets (Theodore), prelate, xxvii, 185, 233, 238, 241, 341, 349-350, 353
Feodosy, founder of Caves monastery, writings of, 261-262; also mentioned, 247-249, 251, 259, 261, 266-267, 297-298, 301
Feodul, abbot, 23
Filaret, metropolitan (Vasily Mikhailovich Drozdov), xxix, 326
Filia "the Proud," Hungarian commander, 112
Filipp, Galich boyar, 66
Finland, 135
Finns, xvi, xvii, xviii, 134-135, 139, 233, 235-236, 334, 338, 340
Fires, 214-215
First Crusade, 356
Flavian, archbishop of Constantinople, 269
Fokht (Vogt, advocatus), office of, 129, 337
Foma, Novgorod hundredman, 83
Foma Lazkovich, boyar, 117
Foma Liaskovich, Novgorod commander, 136
Fourth Crusade, xxvii, 346
France, xv
Fredehelm, visiting crusader, 131
Frederick Barbarossa, Holy Roman emperor, 46-47, 229, 332, 347
Friedrich, visiting crusader, 131
Fulkon, bishop of Cracow, 60

Galich, xviii, xxiv, 3-4, 9-11, 13, 16-17, 40-42, 44-47. 49-50, 54, 56-69, 70-71, 89, 91-92, 98, 105, 111-114, 144, 155, 157, 159, 161-163, 190, 194, 203, 215, 217, 221, 229, 247, 249, 253-254, 257, 260, 274, 284, 305, 331-333, 336, 350, 360
Galich-Volhynia, xxiii, xxv, 322
Gaul, xv

Gavrila, archbishop of Novgorod, 240
Gavrilo Nerevinich, brother of Zavid, 82
Gemiabek, Tatar commander, 156
Genealogical Book, 323
Genghis Khan, 155
George, metropolitan, 348
George Hamartolos, Byzantine chronicler, 289, 291, 358
Georgia, xxviii, 32, 325
Georgy Vseslavich, prince of Polotsk, 249
Gerasim, monk, missionary, 236
Germany, Germans, in Livonia, 118-126; also mentioned, xviii, xxiv, 118-127, 129-133, 163, 203, 214, 216, 222-223, 225-227, 230, 232, 282, 326
German chronicles, 219
German colonists xxv
German knights, xxv
Germanos II, patriarch of Constantinople, 351
Gertrud, Hungarian queen, 63, 68
Gerzika, Rus principality, 121-122, 125, 127, 129-130
Géza II, Hungarian king, intervenes in Galich affairs, 42-44; also mentioned, 332
Gideon, biblical hero, 158, 312
Giuria, steward, 117
Giuriata Rogovich, native of Novgorod, 299
Gleb, prince of Minsk, 254
Gleb, St., Rus protomartyr, xxiii, 16, 21, 213, 216, 229, 297, 301, 311, 327
Gleb Rogvolodovich, prince of Drutsk, 37
Gleb Rostislavich, prince of Riazan, 23, 29-32, 72, 78, 116, 118
Gleb Sviatoslavich, prince, 35, 36, 39, 54, 152, 172-173, 192, 234-235
Gleb Vladimirovich, prince, 74, 104-105
Gleb Vseslavich, prince of Polotsk,

37, 250, 256
Gleb Yaroslavich, prince, 193
Gleb Yurievich, prince, rules in Kiev
    9-10, death 11-13; also cited 11-
    12 14-15, 116-117, 140, 143, 187,
    190, 203-204, 253, 328, 350
Gleb Zeremeevich, Galich boyar, 114
Glebov, town, 147, 254
Godfrey of Bouillon, protector of the
    Holy Sepulcher, 356
Golden gate, Kiev, 11, 23, 188
Golden gate, Vladimir, xxii, xxiii, 23,
    29, 232
Golden Horde, 347
Golubinsky, Evgeny Evstigneevich,
    church historian, xxviii, xxix, 326
Goriaser, murderer, 20
Goroden, 215
Gorodets, 3, 10, 16-17, 29, 96, 99,
    136, 138
Gorodets Ostersk, 9, 117, 188
Gorodishche, district of Novgorod,
    105, 335
Gorokhovets, town, 243
Goiryn (Horyn) river, 330
Gostomysl, 294
Gotland, Gotlanders, 119-120, 222,
    225, 347
Granada, 172
Grand-princely title, 184, 310
Great Court, Kiev, 192
Great Merla river, 96
Great Poland, 332
Great Russians, xv, xvi, xvii, xviii
Greece, Greeks, xviii, xxiv, 9, 163-
    164, 172, 224, 227, 229-231, 235-
    238, 240, 246, 259-260, 267, 290,
    293-295, 346, 348, 353
Greek fire, 338
Gregory, monk,
Gregory III, Pope, 350
Gregory IV, Pope, 350
Gregory VII, Pope, 354
Grid', grid'ba (bodyguard), 342
Grigory Khotovich, Kievan boyar,
    117
Grigory, chiliarch, 117

Gulf of Finland, 126, 133, 222, 334
Gytha, English princess, first wife of
    Vladimir Monomakh, 340

Hair clipping, custom, 110, 189, 310,
    336
Ham (Old Testament), 309
Häme, tribe 133-134, 338; see also
    Tavastians
Hanseatic League, xxviii, 326
Harold Godwinson, English king, 340
Hartwig II, archbishop of Bremen,
    336
Hebrews, 359
Henry IV, Holy Roman emperor, 341,
    354
Henry of Livonia, chronicler, xxviii,
    325, 337
Henryk, Bolesław's fourth son, 50
Heraclius, Byzantine emperor, 291
Herberstein, Sigismund von,
    Habsburg ambassador (16th
    century), 353
Hero-Warriors, 203-204
Hilarion, bishop of Rostov, 233
Hilarion, metropolitan, 261
Hill, the, district of Kiev, 58
Historical Dictionary of Saints, xxix
Historical-Juridical School, xix, xxiii,
    322, 339
Historiography, nature of, 307-314
History of Relations between the Rus
    Princes of the House of Riurik
    (Soloviev), 165, 175
Hohenstaufen dynasty, 332
Holm, German castle, 119, 121-123
Holy Land, 276, 332, 337
Holy orders, 246-251
Holy Roman empire, xxv
Holy Sepulchre 276
Holy Wisdom Chronicle, 287-288,
    358
Holy Wisdom Side, Novgorod, 344
Homer, 280
House of Riurik, 183-184
Hrushevsky, Mykhailo, historian, xvi,
    320

Hungary, Hungarians, occupy Galich 65-66; expelled by sons of Igor, 66; divide Galich with Poles, 69; also mentioned 13, 18, 40, 42-46, 52, 64, 67-68, 111-114, 161, 163, 190, 194, 221, 247, 259, 284, 289-290, 299, 305, 332-333, 358
Huns, 155
Hypatian Chronicle, xxvii, 228, 302-305, 323, 328, 341, 360
Igor, early Rus prince, 289, 293, 295
Igor, prince of Novgorod Seversk, 36, 38
Igor Glebovich, Riazan prince, 35, 72
Igor Olgovich, prince, 174, 186, 188, 196, 213, 257-258, 303
Igor Sviatoslavich, prince of Severia, 16, 34, 37-39, 143-146, 148-149, 153, 191, 254, 258, 279-281
Ilia Shchepanovich, Galich boyar, 65-66
Illyria, 289
Ilmen, lake, 284, 358
Indiction, 299, 360
Ingvar Igorevich, Riazan prince, 74, 105
Ingvar Yaroslavich, prince of Lutsk, 37, 57, 65, 67, 116
Innocent III, pope, 121, 332, 337
Instruction of Vladimir Monomakh, xxvii, 273-276
Intercession, feast of, 321
Inzhir ford, 144
Iron Gate, 279, 288
Isaac, St., 298
Isaac Angelos, Byzantine emperor, 307, 360
Isaiah, St., former monk of Caves monastery, 249
Ishmael, 299, 312
Ishnia river, 90-91
Italians, xviii, 346
Ivan, brother of Matey Dushilchevich, 105
Ivan Berladnik, 45-46, 215, 247
Ivan Danilovich Kalita, grand prince

(14th century), 212, 344
Ivan III, grand prince (15th-16th centuries), 165
Ivan (Ivanko) Dmitrievich, Novgorod burgrave, 107, 110
Ivan Miroslavich, Riazan boyar, 118
Ivan Mstislavich, prince, 116, 172
Ivan Rodislavich, boyar, 117
Ivan Vladimirovich, prince, 305
Ivan Vsevolodovich, prince, 87, 138
Ivan Zakharievich, Novgorod burgrave, 77-78
Ivanko Chudinovich, Chernigov boyar, 187
Ivanko Stepanovich, boyar, 116
Ivanko Timoshkinich, Novgorod citizen, 108, 110
Ivats, Novgorod citizen, 108
Ivor Mikhailovich, Smolensk commander, 99, 118
Izborsk, 206
Izgoi (disinherited princes), 158, 328, 339
Iziaslav Davydovich, prince, 19, 198, 201, 203, 219, 256, 303-304, 314, 332, 341
Iziaslav Glebovich, prince, 136
Iziaslav Mstislavich, prince, 1-2, 7, 12, 42, 56, 60, 65, 116. 160-161, 163, 185-187, 189, 195-196, 198, 201, 206-207, 213, 216-217, 219, 247, 258, 302-304, 327-328, 341
Iziaslav Sviatoslavich, prince, 309, 340
Iziaslav Vladimirovich, prince 66, 74, 76
Iziaslav Yaroslavich, prince, 49, 57, 84, 159, 187, 237-238, 246, 248, 251, 261
Izmoragd, nickname of Princess Evfrosinia Rostislavovna, 189, 342

Jacob, monk, 265
Japhet, biblical tribe, 289, 312
Jebe, Mongol commander, 155
Jeremiah II, patriarch of

Constantinople, (16th century) 236, 348

Jerusalem, 172, 249, 259, 269, 276, 283, 356

Jewry gate, Kiev, 198, 213

Jews, 22, 252, 261, 309, 331, 346

Joachim, bishop of Novgorod, 307, 361

Joachim Chronicle, 307, 361

Job, metropolitan of Moscow, later patriarch (16th-17th centuries), 348

Johann, provost of the Riga church, 127

John, bishop of Rostov, 88, 230, 256, 335

John, monk, 300

John, Varangian, Rus protomartyr, 296, 308

John Chrysostom, St., 273

John II, metropolitan: epistle, 265; also mentioned, 236, 257, 263, 265, 348, 354

John III, metropolitan, 348

John IV, metropolitan, 238, 348-349

John Tzimisces, Byzantine emperor, 295, 358

Joseph, Old Testament patriarch, 297, 358

Joseph of Arimathea, disciple, 270

Kalka, river, battle, 157-158, 204, 333

Kálmán, Hungarian prince, 69, 112, 336

Kama river, 135-136, 138, 222, 236, 331

Kamenets, 68-69

Kanev, 48, 153

Karakalpaks, tribe, 4, 10, 17-18, 34, 38, 48-49, 54, 57, 81, 150-154, 198, 203, 217, 329-330

Karamzin, Nikolay Mikhailovich, historian, xxv, xxviii, 299, 323-324, 352, 360

Karelians, 134, 236, 338, 348

Kavelin, Konstantin Dmitrievich,

historian, xxiii, xxvi, 165, 167-170, 175-176, 339

Kazan khanate, xxv

Kazanskii, P.S., historian, 324

Kelar' (cellarer), office of, 351

Kes (Wenden), 133

Khazars, 225, 291-293, 346-347

Kherson, 191

Kholm, 350

Kholokholna river, 95

Khorevitsy hill, 290

Khoriv, 290

Khorol river, 144

Khot Grigorievich, Yaroslav's vicegerent in Novgorod, 94

Khotovich, Grigory, chiliarch, 14

Khristofor, son of chiliarch Yakun Namnezich, 93

Kideksha, 327

Kiev, xv-xxii, 1-5, 7, 9-19, 23, 28, 32-39, 40, 45, 47-59, 62, 65, 70-71, 77, 81, 98, 105-106, 115-118, 136, 140-141, 143, 145, 150, 152, 156, 159-162, 164, 172-176, 182, 183-184, 186, 188-189, 191-192, 198, 202-205, 207-211, 215-217, 219, 221, 224, 227, 231, 233, 235-239, 241-243, 247-250, 256-258, 259, 261, 263, 280-282, 284, 287, 289-290, 293, 295-297, 301, 303-304, 306, 314, 327-328, 330, 332, 340-341, 349-351, 353, 355, 357, 359

Kievan government, xv

Kievan land, xvi

Kievan period, xvi

Kievan Primary Chronicle, 287-289, 294, 297, 300-302, 304, 306, 315

Kievan Rus, xviii, xviii, xix, xxv, 328

Kievan State, xv, xviii

Kievets, town on Danube, 290

Kirik, monk, questions posed to Bishop Nifont, 266, 349, 353-354; also mentioned, 257, 266, 354-355

Kiy, 290-291, 306

Kiy's ferry, 290

Kliazma river, 102, 321

Klim Smoliatich, prelate, xxvii, 236-
    238, 241, 328, 341, 348-349, 355
Kliuchevsky, Vasily Osipovich,
    historian, xvii, xxiii, 320-323
Kliuchnik (steward), office of, 343
Koban, Polovetsian khan, 152
Kobiak, Polovetsian khan, 143-144
Kochkar, Prince Sviatoslav's favorite,
    35, 117
Koloksha (Kolakcha, Kulaksha) river,
    battle, 31, 99, 200, 299, 335, 343
Kolomna, 31, 35, 73, 75, 85
Kolyvan (Reval), 133
Konchak, Polovetsian khan, 143-145,
    148, 279
Konduvdey, prince of the Torks, 151-
    153, 217
Königsberg (Kaliningrad), 337
Konrad, Polish prince, son of
    Władysław the Exile, 50, 60, 64
Konstantin, prince of Murom, 235
Konstantin Khotovich, Kievan boyar,
    117
Konstantin Prokopich, Novgorod
    citizen, 106
Konstantin Seroslavich, Galich boyar,
    11, 40-41, 331
Konstantin Vladimirovich, prince,
    104
Konstantin Vsevolodovich, prince,
    xxiv, strengthened by victory at
    Lipits river, 97-103; also
    mentioned, 74, 84-85, 87-88, 89-
    91, 95-96, 104, 115, 117, 154,
    256, 260, 310, 322
Konstantinov (Ksniatin), town, 96
Korachev, 147
Korsun, 48, 141, 296, 358
Kostroma, 91, 328, 360
Kotelniche, 314
Kotian, Polovetsian khan, 113, 155
Koui, tribe, 145-147, 217, 329, 338
Kozelsk, 115
Krasov, I., historian, xxviii, 324
Krivichians, protoslavic tribe, 205-
    206, 291, 293
Kristina, Swedish princess, wife of

Prince Mstislav Vladimirovich,
    340
Kromny, town, 214
Ksenodokh (guest master), office of,
    351
Kuchkovich, boyar, 19-20
Kukenoys (Kokenhausen) 121-126,
    129, 131
Kuksha, St., former monk of Caves
    monastery, 249
Kumis, fermented mare's milk, 338
Kursk, 105, 146, 217
Kuzma of Kiev, Andrei
    Bogoliubsky's servitor, 22, 224,
    226
Kuzma Raryshich, swordbearer, 117
Kza, Polovetsian khan, 148-149
Kza river, 30, 97

Lacha, lake, 277
Ladislas, Hungarian prince, 42-43,
    332
Ladoga, town, lake, 133-134, 205-
    206, 302, 338, 355
Larion, hundredman, 97
Latin Christians, 276
Latin empire of Constantinople, 346
Latin kingdom of Jerusalem, 356
Latin lands, 22
Latins, 125, 216, 224, 227, 260-261,
    263, 346, 353
Latvia, 331, 338
Laurentian Chronicle, xxv, xxvii,
    298, 303-305, 323, 334, 359-360
Lavor, Polovetsian, 149
Lavra, title of distinction awarded to
    a monastery, 351
Lavrenty, monk, 359
Lazar, bishop of Smolensk, 240
Lazar, boyar, chiliarch, 38, 85, 117,
    194
Lazarus Saturday, 342
Legislation, 251-253
Lenevarden, Daniel von, German
    knight, 124
Leo, pope, 259
Leon, bishop of Rostov-Suzdal, 181,

241-242, 304
Leon, metropolitan, 288
Leontinian heresy, 242
Leonty of Rostov, saint, xxii, 233,
   249, 322
Leszek, Polish prince, son of
   Władysław the Exile, 50, 60, 64,
   111-113
Letgolia, 140, 338
Letts, 122, 125, 127, 132
Life of St. Agapit of the Caves
   monastery, 221
Life of St. Avraamy of Rostov, xxix
Life of St. Avraamy of Smolensk, 273
Life of St. Feodosy, 195
Lipitsa, river, battle, xxiv, 97-98,
   104, 107, 109, 112, 114, 117-118,
   191, 200, 203, 254, 333, 335
Literacy, 259-261
Literary monuments, 261
Lithuania, Lithuanians, wars with,
   139-140; also mentioned, xxv, 38,
   61, 84, 118-119, 122-125, 127,
   132, 139-140, 153-154, 219-221,
   225, 327, 333, 340-341
Little Russia, Little Russians, xvii,
   220, 345
Liubachev, 69, 111
Liubech, 189, 297, 356
Liubech conference, 340
Liudin, district of Novgorod, 105-107
Livonia, 120-122, 124-125, 129-130,
   236, 337
Livonian knights, 333
Livs, 38, 118-120, 125, 127, 132, 331
Local government, 216
Loccum, Cistercian abbey,, 336
Lot (Old Testament), 312, 361
Loukas Chrysoberges, patriarch of
   Constantinople, 350
Lovat river, 140
Lower Lands, xxii, 93, 114, 335-336
Lower Towns, 211, 244, 344
Luka, bishop of Vladimir-Suzdal, 73,
   240, 305
Luka Zhidiata, bishop of Novgorod,
   241, 267-269, 288, 355

Luke, precentor, 23
Lukomoria, 146, 153, 338
Lukomorian Polovetsians, 153, 339
Lund, archbishopric, 336
Lurie, Ya.S., historian, 352
Lutsk, 12-13, 17, 19, 33, 37, 57, 65,
   67, 116
Lybed, 290

Magi, 233-236, 255, 266, 295, 348
Makary, metropolitan [Mikhail
   Petrovich Bulgakov], church
   historian, xxviii, xxix, 326
Manuel I Comnenos, Byzantine
   emperor, 42-43, 242, 332, 348-349
Manuil Yagolchevich, emissary from
   Novgorod, 94
Mari, tribe, xvi
Maria, Byzantine princess, wife of
   Prince Vsevolod Yaroslavich, 340
Maria, Ossetian princess, wife of
   Vsevolod III, 256, 352
Maria, Rus princess, wife of King
   Andrew of Hungary, 334
Market Side, Novgorod, 307, 361
Marriage alliances, 326
Martin, heretic, 241
Martiry, archbishop of Novgorod, 84,
   240
Matchmakers, 190
Mateiash Butovich, boyar, 30, 116
Matey Dushilchevich, 105-106
Matthias, metropolitan, 71, 348
Maxim, bishop of Belgorod, 240
Maxim, metropolitan, 350
Mayor (posadnik), office of, 329
Mazovia, 332
Mechnik (swordbearer), office of, 343
Mediterranean Sea, xviii
Medvezhaia Golova, see also Odenpe
   (Bear's Head), 337
Meinhard, German missionary bishop,
   119-120, 336
Merians, tribe, xvi, xxi, 235, 293
Merl river, 144
Methodius of Pataria, 312
Mezhibozh, town, 116

Michael, bishop of Smolensk, 76
Michael II, metropolitan, 237, 348
Michael III, Byzantine emperor, 293, 307, 360
Mieszko the Old, Polish prince, 51, 59, 60, 332
Mieszko III, Polish prince, 50
Mieszko, Polish prince, son of Władysław the Exile, 50
Mikhail, Novgorod burgrave, 85
Mikhail, prince of Chernigov, 26
Mikhail Borisovich, Murom boyar, 74, 116
Mikhail Stepanovich, Novgorod burgrave, 82-84, 86
Mikhail Vsevolodovich, prince of Riazan, later Chernigov, 74, 76, 108-111, 115, 156, 223
Mikhail Yaroslavich, grand prince of Tver and Vladimir (14th century), 332, 359
Mikhail Yurievich, prince, victory over sons of Rostislav, 27-29, death, 29; also mentioned, 9, 14-16, 23-25, 30, 34, 117, 141, 143, 260, 311
Mikhailov, town, 11
Mikhalko, Smolensk chiliarch, 52, 118
Mikhna, Andrei Bogoliubsky'e emissary, 116
Mikhno, swordbearer, 15-16
Mikulitsa, archpriest, 23
Military equipment, 198-200, 324; illustration, 199
Military forces, size of, 202-203
Military Orders, 337
Military organization, 193-204, 343
Military service, types of, 198, 200
Military tactics, 200-202
Militia of Christ, military order 337
Miliukov, Pavel Nikolaevich, historian and politician, xxiii, 320, 322-323
Miloneg Peter, builder, 230
Minsk, 254
Miroshka, town crier, 244

Miroshka Nezdinich, Novgorod burgrave, 83, 85-86
Miroshkins, prominent Novgorod family, 231
Missionary work, 236
Mitrofan, archbishop of Novgorod, 84, 86-87, 93, 106-107, 240, 334-335
Mitrofan, bishop of Vladimir, 305
Moab, Moabites (Old Testament), 361
Moiseich, Novgorod official, 105
Moizich (Moiseevich), Yefrem, conspirator, 20
Moldova, 338
Monasteries and Convents:
Alexander Nevsky (St. Petersburg), 351; Annunciation (Novgorod), 106; Caves (Kiev), 188, 191, 240, 242-243, 247, 249-251, 256, 259, 261, 263-266, 297-298, 300-301, 303, 348-349, 351, 353-354; Glushinsk (Kiev), 236; Holy Cross (Smolensk), 273; Holy Savior (Berestovo), 240; Holy Savior on the Nereda (Novgorod), 106; Hypatian (Kostroma), 360; Khutyn (near Novgorod), 109, 250; Mother of God, Rus monastery (Jerusalem), 249; Mother of God convent (Vladimir), 256; Nativity (Vladimir), 263; Otroch, 76; Pochaev (Volhynia), 351; Resurrection monastery of New Jerusalem, 323; St. Andrew (Kiev), 10; St. Anthony (Novgorod), 354; St. Arcadius (Novgorod), 107; St. Boris and St. Gleb (Rostov), 335; St. Cosmas and St. Damian, 22; St. George (Novgorod), 250, 340; St. Michael, (Vydubits) 240, 300, 303, 348, 360; Trinity-St. Sergius (near Moscow), 351
Monetary system, 228-229
Mongkul, nomad nation, 155
Mongols, xviii, xxv, 171, 224, 330

Morality, general state of, 257-258
Mordvinians, 135, 138-139, 222
Moscow, xxiv, 24, 27, 30, 74, 91, 115, 210, 327, 348, 351, 359
Msta river, 83
Mstislav, prince of Trepolie, 15
Mstislav Andreevich, prince, 77, 135
Mstislav Davydovich, prince, 82-83, 225, 310
Mstislav Iziaslavich, prince, war with Gleb Yurievich 10-12; death, 11-13; also cited, 1, 8-11, 14, 40, 76-77, 160-161, 195-196, 203, 217, 238, 242-243
Mstislav Mstislavich the Daring, prince, intervenes in war between Vsevolod's sons, 90-96; in Galich, 111-114; also mentioned, xxv-xxvi, 14, 70-71, 76, 79, 86-87, 89, 97, 99, 101, 103, 105-106, 115, 154-158, 189, 198, 200, 204, 219, 247, 302, 305, 327, 332-334
Mstislav Riurikovich, prince, 102
Mstislav Romanovich, prince of Smolensk, later Kiev, 52, 54, 56, 62, 92, 96, 105-106, 115. 145, 156, 333
Mstislav Rostislavich the Brave, prince, in the North, 79-70; death, 80-81; also mentioned xxv, 11, 14-18, 23, 25, 27, 29, 30-31, 34, 77-79, 81-82, 86-87, 126-127, 140, 162, 196, 253-254, 311, 333-334
Mstislav Sviatoslavich, prince of Chernigov, 39, 116, 156, 158
Mstislav Vladimirovich "the Great," prince, 12, 33, 38, 154, 159, 161, 174, 184-185, 210, 246-247, 250, 253, 299, 327-328, 340-341
Mstislav Vladimirovich, prince of Tmutorokan, 346
Mstislav Yaroslavich "the Mute," prince of Peresopnitsa, later Lutsk, 65, 67-69, 84, 116, 157
Mstislav Yarun, commander, 96
Mstislav Yurievich, prince, 9, 181, 355
Murom, 16, 23-24, 36, 73-75, 77, 91, 96, 99, 104, 135-138, 159, 162, 188, 203, 219, 235, 258, 296, 340, 353
Muroma, tribe, xvi, 353
Muscovite bookmen, xxii, 284
Muscovite land, xxiii
Muscovites, 27
Musin-Pushkin, Prince A.S., bibliophile (18th century), 359
Myakotin, Venedikt, historian, 321
Myrrh-Bearing Women, commemoration of, 270, 355

Namedays, 342
Naming of princes, 189
Napoleon I, 177
Nastasia, mistress of Yaroslav Osmomysl, 40-41, 331
Nav', spirits of the dead, 346
Nerekhta, 91
Nerev, district of Novgorod, 105-106, 214
Nerevin, Novgorod boyar, 78
Nerl river, xxi, 321
Nestor, bishop of Rostov-Suzdal, 241-242, 349
Nestor, chronicler, 299-301, 305, 360
Neva river, 134
Nevolin, Konstantin Alekseevich, historian, xxviii
Nezda, Novgorod citizen, 83
Nezdila Pekhchinich, commander of Velikie Luki, 140
Nezdiloy, son of Stanimir Dernovich, 105
Nezhin, 324
Nicaea, xxvii
Nicholas, bishop of Rostov, later Polotsk, 240-241
Nicholas, metropolitan, 247, 348
Nicholas, St., 284
Nicodemus, disciple, 271
Nifont, archbishop of Novgorod, 237, 257, 266, 307, 349, 354-355
Nightingale the Robber, 139, 338

Nikifor I, metropolitan, 348
Nikifor II, metropolitan, epistle of,
  262-263; also mentioned, 48-49,
  51, 236, 240, 247, 262-263, 267,
  332, 348, 353
Nikifor, Novgorod hundredman, 83
Nikifor Tudorovich, Novgorod
  citizen, 108
Nikita, archbishop of Novgorod, 299
Nikita, metropolitan, 348
Nikita Petrilovich, Novgorod
  chiliarch, 111
Nikolay Davydovich, prince, 249
Nikon, monk of Caves monastery,
  249
Nikonian Chronicle, xxvii, 191-192,
  203, 287-289, 301, 323, 328, 330,
  343
Niphon, monk, 348
Nithrib desert, 312
Nizhny Novgorod, foundation of,
  xxv, 138-139; also mentioned,
  222, 359
Nomads, 217
Nomocanon, 246
Norman-Slav kaganate, xvi
Normans, 295
North America, xviii
North German cities, 226
Northeastern Rus, xvii, xviii, xxi,
  xxii, xxv, 6, 79, 135, 161, 163,
  165, 208, 258, 322
Northeastern princes, xviii
Northern Caucasus, 346
Northern chronicle, 243, 289, 310,
  314
Northern Dvina, river, 76, 134, 222,
  236
Northern Rus, xxvii, 4, 8, 13-14, 81,
  88, 91, 103, 161-163, 203, 223,
  233-235, 239, 328, 357
Northwestern Europe, 163
Northwestern Rus, xxii, xxv
Novgorod, Great Novgorod, changes
  in, 80-86; delivered by Mstislav
  Mstislavich from Vsevolod, 86-87;
  wars against Chud, 126-132;

unrest in, 132-134; expeditions
  beyond the portage, 134-135;
  special character of Novgorod life,
  209-212; also mentioned, xviii,
  xxii, xxiv, xxvi, 2, 5, 16-17, 23,
  27-32, 36-38, 71, 74, 76-85, 87,
  91, 93-98, 101-103, 105-112, 114-
  116, 118, 126-127, 130, 132-135,
  162-163, 172-173, 183, 186, 188,
  190, 198, 200-208, 213, 215-223,
  225, 227-228, 230-231, 234-237,
  240-241, 244-245, 247, 249, 255,
  2564, 266-268, 282, 284, 287-288,
  290-291, 293-294, 297, 299, 301-
  302, 304-307, 310, 312, 315, 328-
  329, 331, 333-337, 341, 344, 349,
  350, 354
Novgorod Chronicles, xxviii, 197,
  205, 213, 221, 268, 284, 288-289,
  294, 297, 299, 306-307, 315, 323,
  335-336, 338, 355, 360
Novgorod Seversk, 2, 33-34, 66, 145,
  147-148, 150, 189, 201
Novgorod Sviatopolchsk, 158
Novy Torzhok, 79, 95-97, 244
Numismatic evidence, xxviii, 324

Obezy, Caucasian tribe, 155, 279
Odenpe (Bear's Head), 126, 130, 337
Oeconomus (ekonom), office of, 351
Oge, Peter, servant of Johann von
  Appeldern, 132
Oka estuary, 139
Oka river, xvii-xviii, xxv, 35, 73-75,
  135-137, 222
Old Riazan, 75
Old Rus, 86-87, 94, 108, 330
Old Russian saints, xvii
Oleg, early Rus prince, 293-295, 358
Oleg, prince of Kursk, 115
Oleg Sviatoslavich, prince, 3, 15, 17,
  19, 31-34, 52, 54, 147, 184, 188,
  210, 219, 256, 280-281, 298-299,
  314, 327, 340, 356
Oleg Vladimirovich, prince, 70, 74-
  76, 104
Oleksa Sviatoslavich, boyar, alleged

murderer of Prince Gleb Yurievich,
    14
Oleshie, 156
Olga, St., early Rus princess, 294,
    298, 295, 307
Olga Yurievna, wife of Yaroslav
    Osmomysl, 40
Olstin Oleksich, Chernigov boyar,
    117, 145
Olzhichi, 143
On the Beginning of the Land of Rus,
    306
Onega, lake, 338
Order of the Sword Brothers, 121,
    123-124, 126-127, 131
Onipolovtsy, inhabitants of Zarechie
    district of Novgorod, 105
Onufry, bishop of Chernigov, 237
Ornas, 225
Orsy, 346
Orthodox Christendom, xvii
Orthodox church, 322
Orthodox Slavs, 321
Oshel, Bulgar town, 137
Oskin, E., historian, 324
Oskol, 146
Ossetians, 330
Oster river, 56
Otrok, Polovetsian khan, 279
Our Lady of Vladimir, icon, 322, 347
Ovruch, 41, 44, 52, 57-58, 70-71, 152
Ovstrat, Novgorod boyar, 93

Pagan priests, 233-236, 255, 266,
    295, 348
Paganism, struggle with Christianity,
    233-236, 255, 267, 307, 352
Pakosław, Polish servitor, 69
Palestine, 121, 337, 356
Pannonian plain, 358
Panteleimon, baptismal name of
    Prince Iziaslav Mstislavich, 341
Paschal II, pope, 354
Paszkiewicz, Henryk, historian, 320-
    322
*Patericon of the Kiev Caves
    Monastery,* xxix, 250, 326, 351,

354
Patriarch of Constantinople, 236-239,
    243, 326
Pauk, governor of Shum, 117
Paul, St., apostle, 264
Paulicians, 241, 350
Pavel, burgrave of Ladoga, 302
Pechenegs, 177, 287, 289, 297, 299,
    302, 330, 358
Pechora river, 134, 346
Pereiaslavl (Southern or Rus), 9-10,
    15-16, 23-24, 26, 28-30, 56, 63,
    70, 75-76, 90-91, 93, 96, 99, 101-
    103, 108, 115, 117, 137, 140-141,
    143-144, 146-150, 154-155, 164,
    202-204, 206, 207, 217-219, 230,
    236, 242-243, 245-246, 249, 254,
    305. 327-330, 335, 340-341, 350,
    359
Pereiaslav-Suzdal Chronicle, xxviii,
    76, 323, 334
Pereiaslavl-Zalessk, xxiv, 28, 36,
    108, 132-133, 136, 174, 328
Peremyshl, 41, 66, 69, 111, 113-114,
    116, 350
Peresechen, town, 289
Peresopnitsa, 65, 67-69, 116
Persians, 172
Perun, pagan deity, 282, 288, 357-
    358
Peter, conspirator, 19-21
Peter, physician from Syria, 221
Peter Borislavich, boyar, chronicler,
    253, 328, 341, 349
Peter Ilich, boyar from Severia, 304
Petrila the taxgatherer, 192
Philip of Macedon, 172
Photius, patriarch of Constantinople,
    288
Piety, 154-255
Pilgrimage literature, xxvii, 276
Pilot Book, 246, 351
Pinsk, 16-17, 116, 139
Plano di Carpini, Giovanni, papal
    legate and travel writer, xxviii,
    224-225, 325, 346
Plesnesk, 44

Plotskinia, Brodnik commander, 158
Podol, district of Kiev, 57-58
Podruchnik (underling), xx, 330
Poetry, 278-279, 326
Pogodin, Mikhail Petrovich, historian,
    xvi, xxv, xxviii, 171-174, 180,
    320, 323-324, 339, 345, 360
Pogorod'e, town circuit tax, 342
Pogost (way station, trading center),
    188, 334, 342, 345
Pokrovsky, Mikhail Nikolaevich,
    historian, 323
Poland, Poles, divide Galich with
    Hungarians, 69; also mentioned
    xxv, 18, 41, 44, 47, 50-52, 59-60,
    63-66, 69, 69, 111-116, 161-163,
    190, 194, 204, 221, 259, 337, 353
Polianians, protoslavic tribe, xvi,
    xvii, 180-181, 290-293, 358
Polikarp, monk, later abbot of Caves
    monastery, 10, 240, 242-243, 249,
    251, 257, 263-264, 301, 351, 354
Polish gate, Kiev, 198, 213, 216
Political and general teachings, 266-
    268
Poliud'e, rural circuit tax, 342
Polonny, town in Volhynia, 10, 243
Polotsk, 3-4, 16-17, 28, 37-38, 52,
    80, 116, 118-119, 121-124, 126-
    127, 129, 159, 162, 172, 184, 201,
    205, 207, 210, 217-221, 225, 240,
    249-250, 252, 256, 291, 302, 304,
    314, 327, 337, 340-341, 350, 353
Polotsk Chronicle, 304
Polovetsians, struggle with, 140-145;
    illustration, 142; later campaigns
    against, 150-155; also mentioned,
    xxv, 10-11, 13, 31, 34, 36-38, 49,
    52-54, 58, 61-62, 67, 70-71, 104-
    105, 112-115, 117-118, 122, 136,
    146-151, 153-157, 164, 183, 191,
    198, 201-204, 217-221, 224, 227,
    229, 231, 254, 266, 279-280, 298-
    300, 305, 308, 311-312, 327, 330,
    333-334, 339-341, 358
Pontic (Black) Sea, 290
Pontius Pilate, 270

Popular Assembly, xix, 177-178, 207-
    208, 224, 340. See also veche
Popular Assembly and the Prince,
    The (Sergeevich), 176
Population, 215-216; obstacles to
    growth, 218-221
Porfiry, bishop of Chernigov, 32, 73
Posadnik (burgrave, mayor), office
    of, 329
Potters' Quarter, Novgorod, 215, 344
Predslava, aunt of Princess Evfrosinia
    Rostislavna (Izmoragd), 189, 249
Presniakov, Aleksandr Evgenevich,
    historian, 321-322
Primary Chronicle, 289, 300-301, 312
Prince, significance of, 183-184;
    titles, 184-185; enthronement,
    185-186; activities, 186-187;
    revenue, 187-198; way of life,
    189-193; retinue, 193, 196; senior
    and junior retinues, 196-197; the
    levy, 197-198
Privilege of Genia, 333
Prokhor, abbot of Caves monastery,
    250-251
Prokopy, Andrei Bogoliubsky's
    favorite, 20-21
Pronia river, 75
Pronsk, 72-76
Provost (Probst), office of, 337
Prus, tribe, 163, 339
Prus street, Novgorod, 93, 105-107
Prussia, 337
Pskov, wars against Chud, 116-132;
    unrest in, 132-134; also
    mentioned, xxii, xxvi, 80, 99,133,
    140, 201, 205-207, 288, 329
Pskov Chronicles, xxviii, 201, 206,
    323
Puresh, vassal Mordvinian princeling,
    139
Purgas, Mordvinian prince, 138
Putivl, 115, 145, 149, 188

Qipchak (Kipchak), 330; see also
    Polovetsians

Radek, Novgorod citizen, 108
Radilov Gorodets, 102
Radimichians, protoslavic tribe, 205
Ragnvals, Varangian prince, 337
Ratsha, reeve, 327
Ratzenburg, 129
Reeves, 21
Regensburg, 224
Resurrection Chronicle, xxviii, 323
Retinue, 116-118, 193, 196
Reval (Kolyvan), 130
Revenues of the Rus church, 243-246
Riasonovsky, Nicholas V., historian, 321
Riazan, events in, 104-111; also mentioned, 3-4, 13, 16, 23-24, 29, 31-32, 34-36, 39, 54, 71-75, 77-78, 85, 90, 98, 112-116, 118, 135, 162, 200-201, 203, 217-219, 258, 305, 335, 341, 350, 353
Riga, 121-125, 127, 130-131, 133, 225-226, 286, 334, 337
Riurik, early Rus prince, 204, 206, 291-294, 301, 328, 343, 358
Riurik Rostislavich, prince; rules in Kiev, 47-48; expelled from Kiev, 57; again occupies Kiev, 58; forced to take monastic vows, 58-59; also mentioned, 11, 14-18, 35, 37-39, 41, 44-45, 49-57, 59, 62, 65, 70-71, 77, 80, 116-118, 139, 145, 148, 150-155, 176, 182, 184, 201, 227, 230, 240, 247, 303, 332, 334, 341, 360
Riurikid princes, 5, 160
Rogachev, 38
Rogvolod, boyar, 118
Rogvolod, prince of Polotsk, 123
Roman, baptismal name of St. Boris, 37, 331
Roman church, 236
Roman Glebovich, prince of Riazan, 19, 31-32, 34-35, 72, 74
Roman Igorevich, prince, 65-66, 75
Roman Mstislavich, prince, invited to rule Galich, 42; participation in Polish civil wars, 50-51;

confirmed in Galich, 56-57; expels Riurik Rostislavich from Kiev, 57; sons expelled from Galich, 62-63; also mentioned 44, 48-49, 54-55, 58-60, 61, 63-65, 76-77, 80, 305, 331-332, 334, 337
Roman Nezdilovich, Chernigov boyar, 117, 145, 151
Roman Rostislavich, prince, given Kiev by Andrei Bogoliubsky, 13-14; sons quarrel with Andrei Bogoliubsky, 14-15; forces Riurik Rostislavich to take monastic vows, 58-59; dies fighting the Poles, 59-61; also cited 16, 33-34, 37, 40, 42, 44-45, 48-51, 54-57, 62-67, 69, 77, 79, 111, 139-140, 143, 155, 160-161, 185, 194, 198, 260, 278, 300
Roman Vseslavich, prince of Volhynia, 247, 249
Roman Yaroslavich, prince of Galich, 193-194, 218
Romanos the Melodist, St., 321
Romans, 172
Rome, 306, 332
Romulus, 306
Ros river, xxi, 11, 16, 24, 48, 143, 152-154
Rosatislav, prince of Pinsk, 116
Rostislav Ivanovich, prince, son of Berladnik, death, 45-46; also mentioned, 50
Rostislav Mikhailovich, prince, 110-111
Rostislav Mstislavich, prince, 1, 12-13, 24, 37, 39-40, 172, 176, 188, 191-192, 197, 227, 238, 241, 245-246, 254, 327, 334, 341, 349
Rostislav Riurikovich, prince, 48, 54, 59, 62, 65, 70, 118, 152-154, 189-190
Rostislav Vladimirovich, prince, 152-153, 173
Rostislav Vseslavich, prince, 351
Rostislav Yaroslavich, prince, 254
Rostislav Yurievich, prince, 304

Rostislav's Road, 152, 339
Rostov, Land of Rostov, rivalry with
    Vladimir, 23-27; final fall of, 30-
    33; also mentioned xix-xxi, 3, 5-9,
    16, 23, 77-78, 88, 90-91, 93, 99,
    103, 108, 117, 136-138, 158, 160,
    179, 188, 194, 196, 203, 205, 207,
    214-215, 219-220, 222, 233, 235-
    236, 238, 240-242, 249, 264, 274,
    301, 305, 322, 335, 349-350, 359
Rostov-Suzdal principality, 327
Rural population, 204-205
Rus church, xxvii, 236
Rus, Land of Rus; and its enemies,
    118-183; also mentioned xviii,
    xxi, xxiv, 1-3, 7-8, 14-15, 19, 23-
    26, 32-35, 37, 40, 45, 47-48, 50,
    55, 57, 71, 79, 81, 85, 91-92, 98,
    118, 123-125, 127, 129-130, 132,
    135, 137-141, 146-147, 149, 153-
    158, 162, 164, 166-167, 170, 182,
    183, 194-195, 218, 221-222, 224-
    225, 227, 229, 231-232, 233, 235-
    237, 243, 247, 251, 255, 257-258,
    259-261, 264-265, 267, 276, 278,
    280-281, 285-287, 289-290, 292,
    294-298, 305-306, 308, 314, 329,
    338, 353, 359-360
Rus Justice, 180, 221, 251, 330, 346,
    352
Rus (Black) Sea, 290
Rusa, 140, 230, 240
Rusalki, pagan spirits, 352
Russia, 6, 129, 290
Russian State, xiv
Russian Primary Chronicle, 358
Ruta, river, battle 185, 341
Rylsk, 115, 145
Rzhevka, 95

Sabbas, St., early monastic founder,
    276, 356
Sadko, Novgorod merchant, 284
Sadko Sytinich, Novgorod epic hero,
    284
Samovlastie (autocratic power), xx
Samoyeds, 302, 360

Sara river, 96
Saracens, 261, 312
Sarmatians, 346
Sartorius, G.F., historian, 326
Sataanill, 239, 350
Satan, 273
Scandinavia, Scandinavians, xvii,
    190, 227, 290
Scythia, Scythians, 155, 290
Sdeslav Zhiroslavich, commander, 38,
    117-118, 154
Sdil Savinich, Novgorod citizen, 108
Seim river, 147-148
Seine river, xvii
Seleucus, 306
Seliger, lake, 95
Semeon Borisovich, Novgorod
    burgrave, 106, 110
Semeon the Red, boyar, 114
Semiun Emin, Novgorod commander,
    later chiliarch, 106
Serbia, 42, 350
Serensk, 76
Sergeevich, Vasily Ivanovich, legal
    historian, xxvi, 176, 178-183, 340
Seth (Old Testament), 309, 361
Setoml river, 297
Severia, Severians, 16, 63, 139, 143-
    145, 147, 154, 162, 203, 205, 217,
    254, 258, 280-281, 293, 304, 338,
    340
Shakhmatov, Aleksei Aleksandrovich,
    historian, xxvii
Shchek, 290
Shchekovitsa, Shchekovitsy hill, 251,
    290
Sheksna river, 233-234
Shem, eldest son of Noah (Old
    Testament), 361
Shcherbatov, Mikhail Mikhailovich,
    historian, xxv
Shelon river, 140
Shosha river, 96
Silesia, 50, 332
Silver Bulgars, 136, 338
Silver gate, Vladimir, 23
Simon, abbot, confessor, 256

Simon, bishop of Vladimir, epistle to
Polikarp, 263-265; also
mentioned, 240, 243, 249, 257,
263, 265, 301, 351, 354
Sineus, Varangian-Rus chieftain, 206,
343
Sinope, 225
Sirmium, 43
Siuiurlia river, 146
Skvorets, friend of Nightingale the
Robber, 139
Slavic colonization, xvi-xvii
Slavin Borisovich, commander, later
chiliarch, 106, 190
Slavno, district of Novgorod 214
Slavonic legends, 291
Slavonic tribes, 291
Slavs, 180-181, 235, 266, 289-291
Slovenes (Slovenians), protoslavic
tribe, 205-206, 289-291, 293
Slovensk, 206
Smerdy (commoners) 340; see also
commoners
Smolensk, xviii, xxiv, 5, 12-17, 28,
32-34, 36-40, 45, 47-48, 51-56,
62, 76-77, 79-80, 82-83, 92, 95-
99, 101-102, 105, 107, 109-110,
118, 143, 148-149, 160, 162, 188,
203-205, 207, 209, 217-220, 225-
226, 237, 240-241, 245-246, 249,
260, 264, 286, 288, 296, 327-328,
333-334, 341, 347, 350
Snipe Field, battle (14th century), 361
Snoporod river, 150
Sol Galitskaia, 91
Soldaia (Sudak), 225
Soliche, 312
Soloviev, Sergei Mikhailovich,
historian, xv, xvi, xix, xxi, xxiii,
xxv-xxix, 165, 323, 325-326, 328,
339-342, 346, 348, 351, 353, 356-
357
Songs, 282-284
Southeastern Europe, 163
Southern chronicles, 315
Southern Rus, 3-4, 13-14, 39, 61, 72,
81, 91, 114, 117, 131, 162, 164,

203, 233, 235, 238, 269, 280, 289,
330, 339
Southern Rus Chronicle, 360
Southern steppe, xix
Southwestern Rus, xxiii, xxv, 61, 79,
88-89, 111, 161, 168, 269
Spain, Spaniards, 172, 346
Spartans, 172
Spics, treaty between Poles and
Hungarians, 336
St. Luke street, Novgorod, 214
St. Nicholas fraternity, Novgorod,
282
St. Thomas Sunday, 269, 355
Stanimir Dernovich, prominent
Novgorod citizen, 105
Starodub, 33, 115
Stauropigia, title of distinction
awarded to a monastery, 351
Stavr, Novgorod hundredman, 284
Stefan, abbot of Caves monastery,
251, 298
Stefan, deacon, 122
Stepan Tverdislavich, Novgorod
boyar, 94, 110-111
Stepan Zdilovich, Vsevolod III's
commander, 76
Stepanets, alleged murderer of Prince
Gleb Yurievich, 14
Stepanitsa, Kievan boyar, 117
Stephen III, Hungarian king, 42-43,
332
Stephen IV, Hungarian king, 332
Stephen the Elder, Hungarian prince,
brother of Géza II, 43
Stryjkowski, Maciej, Polish
chronicler, xxviii, 326, 333
Subtelny, Orest, historian, 320, 322
Subetey, Mongol commander, 155
Sudimir, native of Novgorod, 134
Sudislav, Galich boyar, 66, 112, 114
Sudislav Vladimirovich, prince, 288
Sula river, 144-145, 279
Sunday of the Myrrh-Bearing
Women, 270, 355
Suzdal, Land of Suzdal, struggle of
princes against the Bulgars, 135-

138; also mentioned xvi, xix-xx, xxiv, 3, 6-9, 16-17, 23, 25-28, 30-32, 36, 40, 46-48, 53, 58-59, 63, 70-72, 76-77, 81-82, 87-88, 90, 92-93, 97, 99, 103-107, 115-116, 127, 132, 135, 138, 160, 179, 181, 188, 190, 204-205, 207, 209, 211, 217-220, 222, 227-228, 230. 240-243, 250, 265, 299, 302, 304-305, 333, 359-360
Suzdal chronicler, 315
Sveneld, boyar, 289
Sviatopolk, prince of Turov, 71
Sviatopolk Iziaslavich, prince of Kiev, 45, 159, 174, 190, 193, 198, 212-213, 252, 256. 314, 356
Sviatopolk the Damned, 258, 293, 296-297, 308
Sviatopolk Vsevolodovich, 176, 332
Sviatopolk Yaroslavich, prince, 173, 247
Sviatopolk Yurievich, prince, 116
Sviatosha (Sviatoslav), religious name of Prince Nikolay Davydovich of Polotsk, 249
Sviatoslav, prince of Peremyshl, 66
Sviatoslav, prince of the Drevlianians, 296
Sviatoslav, Riazan prince, 35
Sviatoslav Igorevich, early Rus prince, 293-295, 307
Sviatoslav (Sviatosha) Davydovich, prince of Chernigov, 137, 221, 254, 259, 311
Sviatoslav Glebovich, prince, 72-74
Sviatoslav Igorevich, prince of Kiev, 45, 183, 187, 220
Sviatoslav Igorevich, prince of Vladimir-in-Volhynia, 64-66
Sviatoslav Iziaslavich, prince, 202
Sviatoslav Mstislavich, prince, 105-107
Sviatoslav Olgovich, prince, 5, 144-146, 186, 188-189, 196, 217, 219, 237, 242, 245, 303-304
Sviatoslav Rostislavich, prince, 77, 83, 259-260

Sviatoslav Vladimirovich, prince, 153, 305
Sviatoslav Vsevolodovich, prince of Chernigov, later Kiev, fights against Vsevolod, 34-37; gains foothold in Kiev, 37-39; also mentioned 15-19, 31,36, 40, 47, 81-82, 84-87, 89-90, 95-96, 98, 107, 115, 117-118, 136-138, 143-148, 150, 152, 154, 192, 195, 201, 242-243, 248, 256-257, 280
Sviatoslav Yaroslavich, prince, 159, 187, 192-193, 233-234, 240, 251, 259, 281
Sviatoslav Yurievich, prince, 260, 311
Sviatoslav's Collection, 192, 342
Sweden, Swedes, 163, 222, 227, 340
Sword Brothers, military order, 337
Swordbearer (mechnik), office of, 330
Sylvester, abbot of the St. Michael monastery, Vydubits, 300-301, 307
Synod copy, 306
Syrchan, Polovetsian khan, 279
Syria, 221

Tale of Bygone Years, 294, 338, 358-359
Tale of Igor's Campaign, 145-150, 279-282; also mentioned, xxvii, 40, 200, 219, 285, 299, 315, 338, 357, 361
Tale of Mamay's Battle, 315, 361
Taman peninsula, 338, 346
Taras, servant to Demian Kudenevich, 203
Tashukan, Tatar commander, 157
Tatars, invasion 155-158, 178; also mentioned, 225
Tatinets, 150
Tatishchev, Vasily Nikitich, historian, xxv, xxviii, 301, 307, 352-353, 361
Tatishchev Compilation, 256, 259-260
Taurida, 225

Tavastians, Swedish name for Häme, 338
Temir, Pecheneg prince, 289
Templars, 121, 337
Temuchin, Mongol khan, 155. See also Genghis Khan
Tepra, 117
Terebovl, 66
Teutonic Order, 226, 337
The Truth, heretical pamphlet, 241
Theodore, prelate, sometime metropolitan, see Feodorets
Theodorich, 122, 130
Theotokos, xxii, 321
Third Crusade, 332
Tiasmina, tributary of the Dnieper, 151, 191
Tikhoml, 69
Timofey, bookman, 284
Timothy, apostle, 264
Timofey, confessor to Mstislav of Toropets, 247
Timofey, priest, 113
Tithes, 243
Tmutorokan, 162, 172-173, 221, 249, 338, 346
Tobien, E.S., historian, xxviii, 324-325, 347
Toimokary, Finnish tribe, 106
Torchesk, 9, 14-15, 34, 44, 48-50, 71, 152, 154
Torks, 143, 151, 217, 231, 312, 330, 339
Toropets, 86-87, 95, 140, 158, 219, 247, 333
Torzhok, 78, 82-83, 86, 93-95, 102, 105, 107-108, 110-111, 140, 221, 228, 244, 310
Towns, size and number of, 217-218
Trade, 222-228
Tribute collectors, 135
Tripolie, 10, 15, 33, 38, 71, 148
Trubchevsk, 145
Trubech, 116
Truvor, early Varangian-Rus chieftain, 206, 343
Tudor, boyar, reeve, 37, 327

Turiisk, 140
Turkey, Turks, 225, 299
Turkomans, 299
Turov, 2-3, 10, 16-17, 71, 116, 143, 159, 188, 190, 203, 217, 219, 249, 350
Turov-Pinsk principality, 339
Turpei, nomadic tribe, 217
Tver, xxiv, 93, 95-96, 99, 210, 359
Tverdislav Mikhailovich, Novgorod burgrave, 86-87, 92-93, 105-107, 110, 130, 211, 315
Tvertsa river, 36, 94, 108

Uexküll, German castle, 119, 121, 336
Uglichians (Ulichians), protoslavic tribe, 289, 358
Ugorian mountains, 289
Ugra river, 302, 346
Ukraine, Ukrainians, xv-xvii, 345
Ukrainian nationhood, xxiii
Ukrainian-Rus, xv
Ukrainians, xvii
Uleb, 288
Underling (podruchik), 16, 330
Upper Lands, 147, 338
Ural mountains, 134, 155, 222-223, 334, 346
Urban II, pope, 354
Urban population, 204-205, 212-214
Ushitsa, 215
Ustiug, 136, 138, 222
Usviat, 140

Vadim, 294
Vlademar I, king of Denmark, 336
Varangian churches, 344
Varangian-Rus, 179
Varangians, xviii, 181, 206, 222-223, 261, 287, 293, 337, 343
Varlaam, monk, 250
Vasiata, elder from St. John's church, Novgorod, 244
Vasiliev, town, 10, 296
Vasilievo, 154
Vasilko Konstantinovich, prince, 90,

103, 108, 136, 138, 158
Vasilko Romanovich, prince of
Galich, 62, 65, 67-69, 112, 116
Vasilko Rostislavich, prince of
Terebovl, 196, 208, 247, 299-300,
305, 309, 344
Vasilko Yaropolchich, prince of
Mikhailov, 11
Vasilko Yurievich, prince, 9, 181
Vasily, abbot of Caves monastery,
251
Vasily, St., 254
Vasily Buslaev[ich], epic hero of
Novgorod, 282-284, 357
Vasily Mstislavich, prince, 105
Vazuza river, 95
Veche, 207-208, 329, 340; see also
Popular assembly
Veles (Volos), pagan deity, 235, 348
Velikie Bolgary, Bulgar capital, 338
Velikie Luki, 80, 84, 140
Velikii kniaz' (grand prince), xx
Venetians, 346
Veno (Wenno) von Rohrbach, grand
master of the Sword Brothers,
121, 337
Verkhuslava, daughter of Vsevolod
III, 190, 240, 256-257, 264, 354
Ves, Finnic tribe, xvi
Viacheslav, prince of Kukenoys, 123-
124
Viacheslav (Viachko), prince of
Yuriev, 131-132, 337
Viacheslav, Novgorod chiliarch, 109
Viacheslav Vladimirovich, prince,
174-176, 186, 192, 197-198, 247
Viachko, Novgorod citizen, 108
Viatichians, protoslavic tribe, 54,
139, 205, 217, 235, 291, 293, 333,
338
Viatka, town, river 135, 222
Victor III, pope, 354
Vienna, 224
Vistula river, 332
Vitebsk, 52-53, 225
Vitichi, 34, 274
Vitichi conference, 356

Vlachs, 289-290, 358
Vladimir Andreevich, prince of
Dorogobuzh, 9-10, 117
Vladimir Chronicle, 305
Vladimir Davydovich, prince, 304
Vladimir Glebovich, prince, 15-16,
31, 34-35, 56, 72, 141, 144-145,
148, 150, 219, 305
Vladimir Igorevich, prince of
Novgorod Seversk, 62-63, 71
Vladimir Igorevich, prince of Putivl,
145-146
Vladimir Monomakh, xx, xxvii, 3, 5,
13, 32, 39-40, 42, 48-51, 54, 57,
61, 70-71, 79, 84, 89, 154, 160-
161, 173-174, 176, 184-188, 191,
198, 201-203, 210-211, 213, 216,
228, 230, 236, 246-247, 252-254,
256-257, 259, 262-263, 274-275,
278-289, 282, 284, 293, 298-299,
303, 314, 327, 329, 340-341, 356
Vladimir Monomakh's Instruction,
273
Vladimir Mstislavich, prince of
Pskov, 26, 31, 34, 36-37, 54, 57,
64, 82, 95, 96, 99, 127, 129-130,
152, 195-196, 253, 334
Vladimir Riurikovich, prince, 59, 62,
70, 95, 99, 101-104, 106-107, 111
Vladimir Rostislavich, prince, 126
Vladimir Sviatoslavich, St., early Rus
prince, 81-82, 147, 243, 246, 260,
273, 278, 288, 295-297, 308, 328,
335, 340-341, 358, 361
Vladimir Volodarevich, prince of
Polotsk, 327, 341
Vladimir Vsevolodovich, prince of
Pereiaslavl, 155 75, 87, 90, 91,
96, 115
Vladimir Yaroslavich, Galich prince,
expelled from Vladimir;
consolidates his rule in Galich,
47; also mentioned 42, 44, 46, 48,
50, 56, 59, 66, 80, 221, 253, 333
Vladimir Yaroslavich, prince of
Novgorod, 173, 288, 332, 357
Vladimir-in-Volhynia, xxiv, 12, 42,

44-45, 51, 54, 57, 63-65, 69, 112,
116, 140, 161, 208, 249, 253, 328,
331-332, 341, 350
Vladimir-on-the-Kliazma (Vladimir
Zalessk), rivalry with Rostov, 23-
27: also xix, xx, xxi, xxii, xxiii,
1-3, 7-8, 8-9, 16, 21, 23-32, 34-
35, 37, 48, 57, 72-74, 76, 79, 83-
84, 86, 88, 90, 97-99, 101-104,
106-107, 111, 136, 138, 165, 179-
180, 182, 191, 205, 207, 214-215,
224, 226, 236, 238-239, 241, 243,
257, 263, 261, 301, 305, 329, 335,
349-350, 359
Vladimir-Suzdal, xxii, xxv, 264, 341
Vladimirko Volodarevich, prince of
Galich, 221, 253-254
Vladislav, burgrave of Ladoga, 133
Vladislav, Galich boyar, usurper,
takes power in Galich, 66-69, 183
Vladislav Vratislavich, expatriate
Pole, 117
Vladislav "Jan's brother," expatriate
Pole, 117
Vlena river, 36
Vnezd Vodovik, Novgorod burgrave,
110
Voevoda, office of, 330
Voislav Dobrynich, boyar, 117, 138
Volga river, xvi, xvii, xviii, xxv, 2,
10-12, 17-18, 29, 95-96, 102. 135-
137, 163, 233, 274, 284, 321, 331
Volga Bulgars, xxi, xxv, 22, 117
Volhynia, 111-112, 139-140, 143,
155-156, 161-163, 173, 188, 203-
204, 209, 217, 219, 243, 247, 260,
300-302, 305, 327, 332, 360
Volhynian Chronicle, 278, 300, 305,
315
Volkhov river, 108, 110, 213, 235,
282, 288, 302, 312, 336
Vologda, 236, 357
Volok, 91, 97, 102, 110, 225
Volokolamsk, 78-79
Voronezh, 31
Vorskla river, 143
Votchina, 328

Vseslav Briachislavich, prince of
Polotsk, 38, 80, 172, 201, 213,
248, 281, 309, 312
Vsevolod, prince of Gerzika, 125-
126, 129-130
Vsevolod, prince of Novgorod, 130
Vsevolod, prince of Riazan, 185
Vsevolod Glebovich, Riazan prince,
34-35, 39, 72-74
Vsevolod III Yurievich "Big Nest,"
embroils Riurik Rostislavich with
Roman of Volhynia, 48-59;
consolidates power in the North,
72-73; relations with Riazan,
Smolensk and Great Novgorod,
74-79; death, 87-89; war between
sons, 89-91; also mentioned, xxi,
xxiv, 5, 9, 14-16, 23, 26, 28-32,
34-35, 37, 40, 46-47, 52-56, 58,
70-73, 81-85, 90-91, 93, 103-104,
106, 114-118, 136, 143, 154, 160-
161, 176, 182-183, 185, 190, 196,
198, 200, 203, 208, 212, 216, 230,
240-241, 247, 253, 256, 281, 302,
304, 310, 311, 322-323, 335, 341,
352, 359
Vsevolod Konstantinovich, prince,
103, 115
Vsevolod Mstislavich, prince of Bełz,
44-45, 51, 96, 106, 109, 156, 185,
191, 203, 206, 210, 244, 340
Vsevolod Mstislavich, prince of
Riazan, 341
Vsevolod Olgovich, prince, 1, 5, 39,
51, 56, 160, 186, 192, 203, 247,
254, 327
Vsevolod Rostislavich, prince, 51
Vsevolod Riurikovich, prince, 190
Vsevolod Sviatoslavich, prince of
Trubchevsk, 145-147, 240, 281
Vsevolod Sviatoslavich the Red,
prince, 56-57, 62, 70-71, 91-92,
115, 333
Vsevolod Vladimirovich, prince, 66
Vsevolod Vsevolodovich, prince of
Cherven, 65
Vsevolod Yaroslavich, prince, 37,

159, 184, 187, 193, 249, 251-252,
    256, 259, 298, 313, 340-341
Vsevolod Yurievich, prince, 107-108,
    117, 310
Vsevolozh, town, 309
Vydubets, 303
Vydubichi, 230
Vyshata, 233
Vyshgorod, xxii, 7-8, 10-12, 14, 16-
    18, 24, 29, 35, 38, 47, 70, 92,
    117, 302, 313, 334

Week of the Enfeebled, 271, 355
Wenden (Kes), 130
Wenno, see Veno von Rohrback
West Slavs, 329
Western Dvina (Daugava), river, 118-
    127, 129, 162, 225-226
Western Europe, xviii, 163, 231, 260
Western Rus, 6
White Hungarians (Avars), 291, 358
White Lake, 206, 277, 357
White Sea, 334
Wild bloodwite, 86, 335
Wild Polovetsians, 53, 164, 203
William of Rubruck, 225, 347
Władysław Spindleshanks, Polish
    prince, 60, 333
Władysław the Exile, Polish prince,
    50, 332

Yadrey, Novgorod commander, 134-
    135, 222
Yakim, conspirator, brother of
    Kuchkovich, 19
Yakim, reeve, 109
Yakim Ivanovich, Novgorod citizen,
    108
Yakim of Korsun, archbishop of
    Novgorod, 288
Yakov, boyar, nephew of Vsevolod
    III, 117, 190
Yakov, monk, 257, 324
Yakov Prokopovich, Novgorod
    native, 134
Yakun Namnezich, Novgorod
    chiliarch, 93

Yakun Miroslavich, Novgorod
    burgrave, 77-78, 87, 95
Yakunich, Novgorod burgrave, 93
Yamiak river, 136
Yan Vyshatich, 233-234
Yanka, daughter of Prince Vsevolod
    Yaroslavich, nun, 249, 259
Yaropolk, brother of the Galich
    usurper Vladislav, 68
Yaropolk Iziaslavich, prince, 188,
    218, 243, 250, 257, 311
Yaropolk Rostislavich, prince, 15-16,
    23-27, 31, 36-37, 55, 78, 82
Yaropolk Sviatoslavich, early Rus
    prince, 293, 348
Yaropolk Yaroslavich, prince, 83
Yaroslav Ingvarevich, prince of
    Lutsk, 116
Yaroslav Iziaslavich, prince, rules in
    Kiev, 18; struggles against
    Sviatoslav of Chernigov, 18-19;
    also cited 9-13, 17, 19, 33, 39,
    116
Yaroslav Mstislavich, prince of
    Pereiaslavl, 29, 56, 109, 111
Yaroslav Sviatopolchich, prince, 159,
    310
Yaroslav Sviatoslavich, prince of
    Chernigov, 150, 192-193
Yaroslav Vladimirovich Osmomysl,
    prince of Galich-Volhynia,
    struggle with boyars, 40-41;
    death, 41-42; also mentioned, xxv,
    12, 36-37, 82-83, 190, 194, 215,
    222, 247, 254, 260, 310, 331
Yaroslav I the Wise, xxvi, 6-7, 52,
    158-159, 161, 184-185, 193, 209-
    212, 216, 221, 244, 246, 251, 259-
    261, 288, 295, 297, 308, 336, 340
Yaroslav Vsevolodovich, prince of
    Pereiaslavl, later Chernigov,
    xxvii, 33-34, 37-38, 50-56, 63, 70,
    75-76, 84, 87, 90-91, 93-99, 101-
    103, 106, 108, 112, 115, 131-133,
    136, 138, 140, 143, 145, 150-151,
    200-201, 212, 226, 236, 253, 356
Yaroslav's Court, Novgorod, 92-93,

95, 105, 107-110
Yaroslavl, 103, 233, 235
Yarun, 157
Yaryshev street, Novgorod, 214
Yas, tribe, 20, 155, 190, 330, 342, 346
Yasak, fur tribute, 338
Yatviags, tribe, wars with, 139-140; also mentioned 61, 229, 333
Yavold, brother of Galich usurper, Vladislav 67
Yavolod, Smolensk boyar, 96, 118
Yeremey, commander, 96
Yeremey, priest, 286
Yeremey Glebovich, boyar, 117, 136, 138
Yugra, 134, 222, 346
Yuriev, town, 30, 91, 97, 101, 132, 241, 264, 350
Yuriev (Dorpat), 131, see also Dorpat
Yuriev hill, 98
Yuriev-Polsky, 90, 136, 328
Yury, son of Konchak, Polovetsian khan, 155
Yury Andreevich, prince, 16, 27, 32, 78
Yury Dolgoruky, grand prince, xvi, xxi, xxvii, 40, 49, 84, 86-87, 116, 160, 163, 172, 174, 180, 185-186, 188, 191-192, 198, 201, 203, 210, 237-238, 247, 254, 264, 276, 304-305, 310, 327-328, 332, 341, 355-356

Yury Domamerich, Galich commander, 157
Yury Ivankovich, Novgorod burgrave, 105
Yury Ivanovich, Novgorod burgrave, 93-94
Yury Mstislavich, prince, 341
Yury Vitanovich, Galich boyar, 66
Yury Vsevolodovich, prince, recovers throne of Vladimir, 103-104; also mentioned, xxiv-xxv, 1, 5, 7-9, 12-14, 23-24, 27, 29, 39, 71, 75, 87-91, 96-97, 101-102, 106-108, 111, 114-115, 117, 136, 139, 230, 256, 352, 359
Yury Yaroslavich, prince, 116

Zachariah, Old Testament prophet, 269
Zagorie, village, 27
Zakharia, Novgorod boyar, 78
Zakhary, Novgorod burgrave, 77
Zarechie, district of Novgorod, 105, 214, 344
Zarub ford, 183
Zavid Nerevinich, Novgorod burgrave, 78, 82
Zawichost, battle, 332
Zernin, A., church historian, xxix, 326
Zhiroslav, Novgorod burgrave, 77-78, 113
Zubtsov, 95

FROM ACADEMIC INTERNATIONAL PRESS*

THE RUSSIAN SERIES

1 S.F. Platonov History of Russia **
2 The Nicky-Sunny Letters, Correspondence of Nicholas and Alexandra, 1914-1917
3 Ken Shen Weigh Russo-Chinese Diplomacy, 1689-1924
4 Gaston Cahen Relations of Russia with China...1689-1730
5 M.N. Pokrovsky Brief History of Russia
6 M.N. Pokrovsky History of Russia from Earliest Times
7 Robert J. Kerner Bohemia in the Eighteenth Century
8 Memoirs of Prince Adam Czartoryski and His Correspondence with Alexander I
9 S.F. Platonov Moscow and the West.
10 S.F. Platonov Boris Godunov
11 Boris Nikolajewsky Aseff the Spy
12 Francis Dvornik Les Legendes de Constantin et de Methode vues de Byzance
13 Francis Dvornik Les Slaves, Byzance et Rome au XIe Siecle
14 A. Leroy-Beaulieu Un Homme d'Etat Russe (Nicholas Miliutine)...
15 Nicolas Berdyaev Leontiev (In English)
16 V.O. Kliuchevskii Istoriia soslovii v Rossii
17 Tehran Yalta Potsdam. The Soviet Protocols
18 The Chronicle of Novgorod
19 Paul N. Miliukov Outlines of Russian Culture Vol. III Pt. 1. The Origins of Ideology
20 P.A. Zaionchkovskii The Abolition of Serfdom in Russia
21 V.V. Vinogradov Russkii iazyk. Grammaticheskoe uchenie o slove
22 P.A. Zaionchkovsky The Russian Autocracy under Alexander III
23 A.E. Presniakov Emperor Nicholas I of Russia. The Apogee of Autocracy
24 V.I. Semevskii Krestianskii vopros v Rossii v XVIII i pervoi polovine XIX veka
25 S.S. Oldenburg Last Tsar! Nicholas II, His Reign and His Russia
26 Carl von Clausewitz The Campaign of 1812 in Russia
27 M.K. Liubavskii Obrazovanie osnovnoi gosudarstvennoi territorii velikorusskoi narodnosti. Zaselenie i obedinenie tsentra
28 S.F. Platonov Ivan the Terrible Paper
29 Paul N. Miliukov Iz istorii russkoi intelligentsii. Sbornik statei i etiudov
30 A.E. Presniakov The Tsardom of Muscovy
31 M. Gorky, J. Stalin et al., History of the Civil War in Russia (Revolution)
32 R.G. Skrynnikov Ivan the Terrible
33 P.A. Zaionchkovsky The Russian Autocracy in Crisis, 1878-1882
34 Joseph T. Fuhrmann Tsar Alexis. His Reign and His Russia
35 R.G. Skrynnikov Boris Godunov
36 R.G. Skrynnikov The Time of Troubles. Russia in Crisis, 1604–1618
38 V.V. Shulgin Days of the Russian Revolutions. Memoirs From the Right, 1905– 1907. Cloth and Paper

39 A.E. Presniakov The Formation of the Great Russian State.
40 J.L. Black "Into the Dustbin of History"! The USSR From August Coup to Commonwealth, 1991. A Documentary Narrative
41 E.V. Anisimov Empress Elizabeth. Her Reign and Her Russia, 1741–1761
42 J.K. Libbey Russian-American Economic Relations, 1763–1999
43 Nicholas Zernov Three Russian Prophets. Khomiakov, Dostoevsky, Soloviev
44 Paul N. Miliukov The Russian Revolution 3 vols.
45 Anton I. Denikin The White Army
55 M.V. Rodzianko The Reign of Rasputin—An Empire's Collapse. Memoirs
56 The Memoirs of Alexander Iswolsky

THE CENTRAL AND EAST EUROPEAN SERIES

1 Louis Eisenmann Le Compromis Austro-Hongrois de 1867
3 Francis Dvornik The Making of Central and Eastern Europe 2nd edition
4 Feodor F. Zigel Lectures on Slavonic Law
10 Doros Alastos Venizelos—Patriot, Statesman, Revolutionary
20 Paul Teleki The Evolution of Hungary and its Place in European History

FORUM ASIATICA

1 M.I. Sladkovsky China and Japan—Past and Present

REFERENCE SERIES

The Modern Encyclopedia of Russian, Soviet and Eurasian History 60 vols.
The Modern Encyclopedia of East Slavic, Baltic and Eurasian Literatures 50 vols.
The Modern Encyclopedia of Religions in Russia and the Soviet Union 30 vols
Russia & Eurasia Military Review Annual
Russia & Eurasia Facts & Figures Annual
Russia & Eurasia Documents Annual
USSR Calendar of Events (1987- 1991) 5 vol. set
USSR Congress of Peoples's Deputies 1989. The Stenographic Record
Documents of Soviet History 12 vols.
Documents of Soviet-American Relations
Gorbachev's Reforms. An Annotated Bibliography of Soviet Writings. Part 1 1985–1987
Military Encyclopedia of Russia and Eurasia 50 vols.
China Facts & Figures Annual
China Documents Annual
Encyclopedia USA. The Encyclopedia of the United States of America Past & Present 50 vols.
Sports Encyclopedia North America 50 vols.
Sports in North America. A Documentary History
Religious Documents North America Annual
The International Military Encyclopedia 50 vols.
Nationalities and Ethnicity Terminologies. An Encyclopedic Dictionary and Research Guide

SPECIAL WORKS

S.M. Soloviev History of Russia 50 vols.
SAFRA Papers 1985-

*Request catalogs. Sample pages, tables of contents, more on line at www.ai-press.com